Applying Behavior-Analysis Procedures with Children and Youth

Beth Sulzer-Azaroff
University of Massachusetts, Amherst

G. Roy Mayer
California State University, Los Angeles

Holt, Rinehart and Winston
New York   Chicago   San Francisco   Atlanta
Dallas   Montreal   Toronto   London   Sydney

Dedicated to our students—past, present, and future.

Library of Congress Cataloging in Publication Data

Sulzer-Azaroff, Beth.
Applying behavior-analysis procedures with children and youth.
  Includes bibliographical references and index.
  1. Teaching.   2.   Behavior modification.
  I.   Mayer, G. Roy, 1940–   joint author.   II.   Title.
LB1025.2.S93   371.1'02   77-371
ISBN: 0–03–018236–0

cover photo credits (clockwise from top left): HRW Photo by Vivian Fenster; HRW Photo by
Russell Dian; Photo by Michael Weisbrot; HRW Photo by Russell Dian; Photo courtesy of
William Kincheloe; Photo courtesy of Elise Russack; HRW Photo by Russell Dian; Photo
courtesy of Frederick Kincheloe; HRW Photo by Vivian Fenster; center photo courtesy of
Elise Russack.

ACKNOWLEDGMENTS

pp. 20, 451–2   Excerpts reprinted from Baer, D. M., Wolf, M. M., & Risley, T. R. Some current dimensions of applied behavior analysis. *Journal of Applied Behavior Analysis,* 1968,
1, 91–97. Copyright 1968 by the Society for the Experimental Analysis of Behavior, Inc.
pp. 88, 290, 310   Excerpts reprinted from *The Journal of Psychiatry & Law,* vol. 4, no. 2
(1976). © 1976 by Federal Legal Publications, Inc., 95 Morton St., New York, N.Y. 10014.
Reprinted with permission of Federal Legal Publications, Inc. and the authors.
pp. 90–1   Contingency contract and excerpt, copyright 1974 American Personnel and Guidance Association. Reprinted with permission.
pp. 159, 292   Figures 11.2, 20.1. Copyright 1974; 1975 American Personnel and Guidance
Association. Reprinted with permission.
p. 239   Figure 17.2, from Gusatfson, C., Hotte, E., & Carsky, M. Paper presented at the 100th
annual meeting of the American Association on Mental Deficiency, Chicago, Illinois,
June 2, 1976.
pp. 296–7, 298   Excerpts reprinted from Foxx, R. M., & Azrin, N. H. The elimination of
autistic self-stimulatory behavior by overcorrection. *Journal of Applied Behavior Analysis,*
1973, **6**, 1–14. Copyright 1973 by the Society for the Experimental Analysis of Behavior,
Inc.
pp. 337, 455, 456   Excerpt and Figures 32.4, 32.5, reprinted from Cossairt, A., Hall, R. V., &
Hopkins, B. L. The effects of experimenter's instructions, feerback, and praise on teacher
praise and student attending behavior. *Journal of Applied Behavior Analysis,* 1973, **6**, 94,
95, 100. Copyright 1973 by the Society for the Experimental Analysis of Behavior, Inc.
p. 350   Figure 25.1, reprinted from Weisberg, P., & Waldrup, P. Fixed-interval work habits
of congress. *Journal of Applied Behavior Analysis,* 1972, **5**, 95. Copyright 1972 by the
Society for the Experimental Analysis of Behavior, Inc.
p. 351   Figure 25.2, reprinted from Mawhinney, V. T., Bostow, D. E., Laws, D. R., Blumen-

feld, G. J., & Hopkins, B. L. A comparison of students' studying behavior produced by daily, weekly, and three-week testing schedules. *Journal of Applied Behavior Analysis,* 1971, **4**, 262. Copyright 1971 by the Society for the Experimental Analysis of Behavior, Inc.

p. 453   Figure 32.3, reprinted from Moore, B. L., & Bailey, H. Social punishment in the modification of a preschool child's "autistic-like" behavior with a mother as therapist. *Journal of Applied Behavior Analysis,* 1973, **6**, 502. Copyright 1973 by the Society for the Experimental Analysis of Behavior, Inc.

pp. 460–1   Excerpt and Figure 33.1, from *Managing Behavior, Part I: The Measurement of Behavior,* by R. V. Hall. H & H Enterprises, Inc., P. O. Box 3342, Lawrence, Kansas 66044.

p. 472   Figure 33.3, reprinted from Renne, C. M., & Creer, T. L. Training children with asthma to use inhalation therapy equipment. *Journal of Applied Behavior Analysis,* 1976, **9**, 6. Copyright 1976 by the Society for the Experimental Analysis of Behavior, Inc.

p. 483   Table 34.1, from White, M. A., & Duker, J. Suggested standards for children's samples. *American Psychologist,* 1973, **28**, 703. Copyright 1973 by the American Psychological Association. Reprinted by permission.

pp. 495–6   Tables 35.2, 35.3, from Krumboltz, J. D. An accountability model for counselors. *The Personnel and Guidance Journal,* 1974. **52**, 642–644. Copyright 1974 American Personnel and Guidance Association. Reprinted with permission.

p. 503   Example from Educational Evaluation and Planning Package, Volumes 1 & 2, James E. McCormack *et. al.,* Massachusetts Center for Program Development and Evaluation. Reprinted with permission.

p. 504   Example from The Santa Cruz Characteristics Progression Observation Booklet, © 1973 Office of the Santa Cruz County Superintendent of Schools.

p. 506   Example from Trainer's Guide (Performance Inventory) reprinted from the trainer's guide for *Steps to Independence: Skills Training Series for Children with Special Needs.* For a revised version of this guide, write to Research Press Co., Box 3177, Champaign, IL. 61820.

p. 507   Example from Progress Assessment Chart courtesy of SEFA (Publications) Ltd.—The Globe—4 Great William St., Stratford-upon-Avon, England.

p. 508   Learning Accomplishment Profile; developed by Anne Sanford, Chapel Hill Training-Outreach Project; published by Kaplan Press.

Portions of units 4–6, 8–20, 22–26, 29–30 are adapted from *Behavior Modification Procedures for School Personnel* by Beth Sulzer and G. Roy Mayer. Copyright © 1972 by The Dryden Press. A Division of Holt, Rinehart and Winston. Reprinted by permission of Holt, Rinehart and Winston.

Foreword

Applied behavior analysis is the applied branch of the field known alternatively as operant conditioning or as the experimental analysis of behavior, which is a laboratory-based area of knowledge. To fully understand the procedures for educating children by means of the principles of applied behavior analysis, an understanding of the laboratory-derived principles is necessary. The authors of *Applying Behavior-Analysis Procedures with Children and Youth* have provided this background information. They describe schedules of reinforcement, stimulus control, DRO, DRL, multiple schedules, successive approximation, extinction, and many other concepts and procedures established in the laboratory studies. But they do not describe these concepts and procedures in isolation, as facts with only remote implications for education. Rather the description of these basic learning concepts is presented in terms of how they apply to typical problems of pupils and children, not to abstract subjects in an artificial laboratory situation. The authors have succeeded in describing laboratory-based findings so that readers can easily understand the basic principles of operant conditioning. Because explanations are given in terms of typical classroom and childhood situations, the reader is able to use these principles in solving immediate, practical problems.

Cookbooks are valuable. They tell us in step-by-step fashion what to do. In dealing with children, however, every child and every class and situation has distinctively different attributes which make any single and simple recipe inadequate. We need to know why a specific procedure is effective, when it should and should not be used, and with what type of problem. The field of applied behavior analysis has reached such an advanced degree of development that several such cookbooks are appearing. This book goes further and provides the rationale—the why, the when, and the when-not-to—for using certain procedures. Extinction is appropriate for some problems and reinforcement for alternative responses is better for others. The token economy is often effective when social reinforcers are insufficient.

Detailed tables provide guidelines for choosing which procedures to use for a given problem. All of this specificity makes the book invaluable as a "cookbook" source of specific, unambiguous advice as to how to solve particular problems. But, because it also tells us *why* certain procedures are effective and what their other effects are, we can select among alternative procedures with knowledge and the assurance that the choice will be suited to the distinctive situation.

The coverage of subject matter of this book is all that one could ask for in a college course designed to teach teachers, psychologists, and others who will work with children and youth about the new field of behavioral psychology applied to children. The content is self-contained and does not require any prior courses in conditioning and learning or in child development. Many technical terms are used and new concepts are introduced, but every such term is explained fully, illustrated, and used repeatedly without assuming prior familiarity.

Each unit of the book flows into the next unit in a logical and cumulative manner so that we have an integrated perspective of the subject matter. The initial units deal with the prerequisites for applying behavior analysis. The next section deals with methods of increasing behaviors, followed by units on methods of decreasing undesired behaviors which build upon and constantly refer back to the section on increasing behaviors. The next three units logically describe the methods for maintaining the benefits of the education—whether it was increasing or decreasing behaviors. The latter units describe how the readers can do their own studies to evaluate their own efforts. And lastly, the authors describe how the readers can communicate the results of their efforts through journal reports, or even reports to interested parties. This last section in particular, and the component treatment of research design, provide the graduate student with an excellent foundation for designing behavioral experiments which could fulfill thesis requirements. This wide range of coverage not only provides students with information about behavioral methods, but also supplies guidelines for them on how to design future studies and how to communicate the results.

A continuing controversy exists as to the role of the child in the family and in school. Are children to be treated as objects to be trained, educated, and disciplined? Is it the parent's and teacher's role to determine unilaterally what is right for the child and to focus attention on deviations with the objective of eliminating them? Recent attention to instances of child abuse has convinced us that parents do not have an absolute right over their children. And the emotional debate surrounding the use of physical punishment in schools reflects the growing conviction of many parents that the school also does not have absolute power over the students. The authors of this book reflect the behavioral position that we should influence children primarily by positive means and not by brute coercion. Further, the children's desires should be considered at every point in the decision-making process. They urge parents and child and youth service personnel to exhaust all of the positive methods before resorting to negative procedures. Recognizing that administrators, child and youth services personnel, parents, and children may have different desires, they repeatedly describe the need for and the means of communicating with all of these interest groups to assure that a new program will meet the objectives of each of their interests. Concern for the child as an individual is paramount. Responsible adults are shown how to achieve their objectives while treating the child in a positive manner as an individual entitled to individualistic expression.

The authors are uniquely qualified to write this book. Between them, they have had extensive experience as teachers of children in the public schools. They have been teaching teachers in colleges of education and have conducted research leading to the development of new and improved methods of educating and motivating children. They have worked directly with many different learning situations and many different populations in the course of their teaching and research activities. Their range of experience includes regular classroom instruction from the primary grades through high school, emotionally disturbed children, profoundly as well as mildly retarded children, special education classes, tutorials, autistic children, day-care programs as well as residential institutions, and parent-child interactions. This familiarity with the subject matter is evident on every page, where they continually illustrate and amplify general statements with findings from their own studies and typical teaching problems seen in their own experiences. Even the hypothetical children described to illustrate a point are ever so real in terms of the typical problems they have. The authors are immersed in their subject of how to educate children and we benefit from their expertise by virtue of reading this lively and real book.

The authors have given us a valuable and informative book.

Nathan H. Azrin

Preface

TO THE STUDENT

Both of us, when we completed our undergraduate training, took public school teaching positions. We, like you, were attracted towards working with children. Children are so guileless, so full of enthusiasm, so responsive. They're fun to be with, expressing and receiving warmth so freely, and yet they are continually challenging. We knew that an occupation involving children would be exciting and rewarding and that we'd never be bored.

Well, teaching younger children turned out to be pretty much like that. It was exciting and rewarding. But there were frustrations as well; challenges we were unable to meet to our satisfaction. Some children seemed unmotivated to learn. Others appeared motivated yet still unable, while others not only appeared unmotivated but their behavior actually interfered with their own and others' progress. (You'll see numerous illustrations drawn from our experiences throughout the book.)

Our way of coping was to seek further training. We studied about child behavior and participated in behavioral intervention programs with children and their families. We did learn to interact more effectively with children, and yet limitations remained. We felt the need for a systematic set of procedures that could be applied to new problems as they emerged, or to the prevention of problems in the first place. We also sought the means for gathering direct objective evidence of any apparent progress. It was in response to those needs that we studied about applied behavior analysis and eventually wrote *Behavior Modification Procedures for School Personnel* (Holt, Rinehart and Winston, 1972).

The feedback from that book suggested that we were on the right track for educators and many other child and youth change agents. Readers reported that the procedural guidelines helped them to function more effectively and accountably. Many, however, particularly those involved in settings that are not pedagogical in the strict academic sense—clinics, institutions, hospitals, the home—requested that their own particular problems be addressed as well. Since we ourselves have become increasingly involved in training, research, and consultation activities in such settings, we concurred. We also wanted to update the material by communicating some of the recently developed procedures and methodologies in the field; to further address several of the ethical and legal issues affecting the practice of applied behavior analysis. We decided to try to keep our offerings practical. Consequently, procedures requiring costly instrumentation, highly specialized professional training, such as medical treatment or intensive individual psycho-therapy, would be omitted. Above all, we wanted to emphasize our own personal values more heavily; that procedures should be effective but as minimally intrusive as possible and that clients should have as much control as possible over interventions that affect them.

The content and organization of this book is therefore directed towards greater client involvement—hence the phrase *with* children and youth rather than *for* children and youth in the title. In the initial section on considerations prior to implementing programs, mutual contracting for goal and procedural selection is emphasized. The order of presentation of the behavioral procedures, the main focus of the book, follows a particular pattern, beginning with strengthening procedures that are maximally intrusive, and concluding with those that are preferred, the minimally intrusive. Reductive procedures start with the least intrusive and progress towards those that are more intrusive. You are urged to consider these patterns as you become involved with program design—always attempting to strike a balance between minimizing intrusiveness while maximizing effectiveness. The last section is devoted to accountability, emphasizing our responsibility to demonstrate and communicate program outcomes to clients and consumers.

So, you can see that this book is aimed not at controlling children and young people but at engaging them as participants in and creators of their own behavior modification. Indeed, the procedures described here constitute an antidote to the arbitrary control that is often placed on children (as well as adults) by the necessary structure of society. These procedures teach children not only ways of operating within the system but also ways of effecting change in the system through productive countercontrol, of going about their work and play with minimum outside interference.

We know that, like us, you are fond of youngsters and want to serve them effectively. Actually, it is doubtful that someone who dislikes children could implement these procedures effectively, since they require spending a great deal of time observing, reinforcing, and generally interacting with children.

As you progress in the text, regardless of the objectives you have elected to achieve, you will find that you want to implement and evaluate the technology. However, as you do so, always consider the context within which you are operating: What are the goals of the individuals concerned, and the agencies, schools, or institutions? What is the purported and the actual chain of command? In other words, who has control of the reinforcing and aversive consequences and will it be possible to harness them for programming? Then consider how these factors mesh with your own value system. If there is not consonance among goals and procedures, negotiation may be necessary. In any case, your competence will be most convincingly demonstrated when, through a congruent working relation between you and the individual or agency that seeks your help, you are able to effectively apply behavior-analysis procedures in cooperation with children and youth.

TO THE INSTRUCTOR

In our attempt to develop as effective an instructional package as possible, we have designed both a book and an accompanying study guide. A set of general goals is provided in the book at the beginning of each unit. Full references, tables, flow-charts, and a glossary are also included. The study guide may be used within a traditional course format to guide learning or as a discussion, recitation, or laboratory manual. It can be used as study material to prepare for mastery quizzes or for interviews within a personalized system of instruction, PSI, format (Keller, 1968)[1] our preference. (See the introduction to the study guide and the instructor's manual for additional suggestions. Sets of quizzes and answer keys are available from the publisher.) You may wish to create accompanying laboratory materials, such as videotapes for observational recording, demonstrations of effective procedures, problem situations, and others. The study guide also includes *field activities* designed to provide your student with the opportunity to observe, design, implement, and evaluate programs and to become familiar with current research in the field.

Readers of this book will have varied professional goals. Some may wish to develop the competency to function as *professional applied behavior analysts,* in a role with that title or as an aspect of their functioning as psychologists, counselors, social workers, instructional programmers, or in other related professions. The book lends itself to adoption in courses in School Counseling, Education, Child Clinical Psychology, community or other behavioral-psychology-theory and practice courses, behavior therapy or modification courses, or courses covering group or case work strategies. If you wish to plan a program to enable students to develop a sizable repertoire of professional competencies, we recommend the following, over the span of one academic year, as about half of the students' overall assignment:

The full book should be read, all study guide questions completed, and mastery demonstrated through written or oral quizzes or certified simulated or actual field performance. Supplemental activities would include workshops on observation, recording, measurement, goal and procedural selection, discussions of legal and ethical issues, and the actual design, implementation, and evaluation of self and other behavior-change programs. A general and specific familiarity with recent research in the field is essential for effective, responsible practice. These basic competencies in the application of operant procedures with children and youth may then be expanded later through additional courses and field applications: respondent conditioning, research methodology, advanced learning theories, *practica,* internships, and others.

Some readers may wish to develop *technical* or *paraprofessional* competence in the field. Research staff, evaluation team members, and other technicians may function as observers, recorders, research assistants, or in related areas. We recommend approximately five hours per week of training for the length of a semester. Demonstrated mastery of technical and ethical concepts and selected procedures would be appropriate. Naturally, the exact content would depend upon specific instructional objectives. However, here is one suggested sequence:

The student should read Units 1–12, 15, 23, 24, 35, and the Epilogue. The study guide should be completed and mastery demonstrated for Units 1, 2, 3, 5, 6, 8, 11, 35, and the Epilogue. For the remaining units, broader objectives should be specified and mastered. Important application skills should be acquired by means of supervised, simulated, and actual field-based observation, recording, and other laboratory experiences.

[1] Keller, F. S. "Goodbye Teacher . . ." *Journal of Applied Behavior Analysis,* **1**, 79–89.

Professionals and paraprofessionals in other fields may wish to improve their current functioning through increased general knowledge and skill in applied behavior analysis. Among those frequently requesting such training have been psychologists, parents, teachers, guidance and rehabilitation counselors, health care professionals, social workers, administrators, supervisors, staff trainers, and the staffs of institutions, hospitals, schools, and clinics; also, correctional workers, learning specialists, special educators, and speech therapists. In essence, just about every field concerned with the behavior of youngsters has been represented. Methods, behavior modification or therapy, or applied behavior analysis courses and in-service workshops designed to train practitioner skills in those fields may be conducted over one semester. We would suggest that following an introduction to the field, relevant general and specific objectives be designed for Units 1–6, 8–12, 15–18, 23, 24, 27, 28, and the Epilogue. Mastery of the more specific objectives in Units 1–5, 8–12, 15–18, 23, and the Epilogue may be accomplished by passing quizzes on the study questions accompanying those units at a level of 90%. Research reports of current developments should be read and a self-modification program planned, conducted, evaluated, and presented.

Additional training during a second semester could emphasize complex behaviors and reducing, maintaining, and extending behaviors. To that purpose, consider assigning mastery of Units 13, 14, 19–22, 24, 27–30. Broad objectives may be specified for Units 7, 25, 26, 34, and 35. Supplemental activities might include simulated practice, discussions, and workshops. During this second semester, the student would profit substantially by planning, conducting, evaluating, and presenting the results of a simple behavior modification program with an actual client.

If you wish to use the book as a source for in-service training of specific topics, consider the following:

1. *Ethics and/or law*: portions of Units 1, 2, 3, 7, end of Units 8, 20, 22, and 28, beginning of Unit 34.
2. *Observation and measurement*: Units 4–6, material on graphing in Unit 35, plus a program such as Reese's *Observing, Defining, and Recording Behavior.*[2]
3. *Strengthening behaviors*: Units 8, 9, 10, 18, 24, 27, and 28.
4. *Teaching simple behaviors*: Units 8, 9, 10, 11, 12, 16, and 17.
5. *Teaching complex behaviors*: Same as #4 above plus Units 13, 14, and 15.
6. *Reducing mildly maladaptive, disturbing behaviors*: Units 8, 11, and 18, the *contingent observation* section of Unit 20, and the *Good Behavior Game* in Unit 27.
7. *Reducing seriously maladaptive behaviors*: Same as #6 above plus Units 19, 20, 21, and 22.
8. *Extending and maintaining behaviors*: Units 23, 24, 25, and 26.
9. *Accountability*: a. within-subject designs: Units 31, 32, and 33; b. communicating outcomes: Units 34 and 35.

We hope that these materials are sufficiently broad and flexible to meet your needs, and we invite comments to consider for future editions.

Beth Sulzer-Azaroff
G. Roy Mayer

January 1977

[2] Dept. of Psychology, Mount Holyoke College, South Hadley, Mass.

ACKNOWLEDGMENTS

First, we wish to thank our students, past, present, and future, whose interests, concerns, advice, feedback, and behavior in general have helped so much to shape the preparation of this book. It is to them that this book is dedicated.

We also would like to express our appreciation to our colleagues, on and off campus, who have been a source of so much of the material contained here. Our very special thanks are expressed to those individuals who have provided direct input: Ellie Reese—who collaborated directly in the preparation of the glossary by providing definitions, expressed with elegant simplicity—whose work serves as a model for excellence and whose friendship is treasured; Kent Johnson and Gregory Ramey, whose participation is frequently cited throughout the text, plus Christie Maass, Philip Chase, Roger McGookin, Catherine Todd, colleagues in field facilities, those involved in journal activities, and others too numerous to mention.

The various individuals who have provided technical assistance in the preparation of the manuscript deserve special thanks: Betty Dicklow, Sally Ives, Melissa Curran, Sally Reffner, Carol Shumate, Kinney Thiele, and Marylin Griffin.

To our families—Leonid, David, Richard, Lenore, Barbara, Kevin, and Debbie—we express our deepest love and gratitude for their understanding, support, and suggestions during the entire project. Finally, we express our appreciation to Edward Stanton Sulzer and to our parents, who arranged the fertile environment that has nourished our professional growth and productivity.

CONTENTS

		Foreword	iv
		Preface	vii
Unit	1	Introduction to Applied Behavior Analysis with Children and Youth	1
Unit	2	Goal Selection: Initial Considerations	11
Unit	3	Goal Selection: Ethical Considerations	26
Unit	4	From Goals to Objectives	40
Unit	5	Selecting Observational Systems	48
Unit	6	Interval Recording and Implementing Observational Systems	59
Unit	7	Considerations in Selecting and Implementing Procedural Strategies	78
Unit	8	Increasing Behavior: Reinforcement	98
Unit	9	Selecting Effective Positive Reinforcers	108
Unit	10	Implementing Effective Reinforcement Procedures	133
Unit	11	Reducing Behavior: Extinction	146
Unit	12	Stimulus Control: What is it?	162
Unit	13	Stimulus Control: Arranging Behavioral Antecedents, I	176
Unit	14	Stimulus Control: Arranging Behavioral Antecedents, II	188
Unit	15	Stimulus Control: Fading	203
Unit	16	Teaching New Behavior: Shaping	218
Unit	17	Teaching New Behavior: Chaining	236
Unit	18	Reducing Behavior: Positive Approaches	248
Unit	19	Reducing Behavior: Response Cost	268
Unit	20	Reducing Behavior: Timeout	280
Unit	21	Reducing Behavior: Overcorrection	295
Unit	22	Reducing Behavior: Punishment	304
Unit	23	Extending Behavior: Generalization Training	324
Unit	24	Maintaining Behavior: Intermittent Reinforcement	332
Unit	25	Maintaining Behavior: Interval and Limited-Hold Schedules	345

Unit 26 Maintaining Behavior: Ratio and Differential-
Reinforcement Schedules   356
Unit 27 Contingency Packages with Groups   369
Unit 28 Token Economies   383
Unit 29 Comparative Summary for Procedural Selection, I   407
Unit 30 Comparative Summary for Procedural Selection, II   421
Unit 31 Considerations in Evaluating Applied Behavior-Analysis
Programs   431
Unit 32 Single-Subject Designs: Reversal and Multiple Baselines   443
Unit 33 Single-Subject Designs: Changing-Criterion and Multielement
Designs and Further Issues in Accountability   459
Unit 34 Communicating the Outcomes of an Applied
Behavior-Analysis Program, I   477
Unit 35 Communicating the Outcomes of an Applied
Behavior-Analysis Program, II   487
Appendix: Behavior Assessment Systems   503
Glossary   511
Index   526

INTRODUCTION TO Applied Behavior Analysis with Children and Youth

After mastering the material in this unit, you should be able to

1. Define each of the following terms, and offer distinctive illustrations:
   a. Principles of behavior
   b. Behavioral procedures   *behavior/Response/condition*
   c. Variable _____
   d. Applied behavior-analysis program
   e. Applied behavior analysis (including the four essential components)
   f. Designs for experimental analysis

2. Discuss what can be done to prevent the misuse of the application of behavioral procedures.

3. Describe the purpose of the textbook.

Every day, many children and youth seem to be faced with serious, often apparently insurmountable problems. Those who are ill, despite their best intentions, fail to follow prescribed health practices. Students with educational deficits just can't seem to catch up. Youngsters who are in trouble with their peers and adults and those with various other problems in living and learning seem unable to muster sufficient effort to overcome their difficulties. A familiar example is the youth experiencing conflict with the law, who often seems to become enmeshed in an endless cycle of wrongdoing and conflict. Society's usual punishments seem ineffective in preventing recurrences of the troublesome behaviors.

Is there a way to break through the endless cycle? All of us who are concerned with the welfare of children and youth have given much thought to that question. The cycle comes as no surprise to many. After all, a youth who gets into trouble and is placed into detention still retains the behaviors that got him into his difficulties earlier. Upon return to the community his behavioral deficits and excesses return with him. He may lack appropriate academic, vocational, and social skills, so that, when he returns to his neighborhood, home, school, or job, he is no better off than before. The satisfactions that more skilled peers receive, in the form of approval for acceptable social behavior and academic or vocational accomplishments, are absent. Excesses also persist. Should he have well-established patterns of aggressiveness in conflict situations and no alternative means of handling conflict, is it surprising that he continues to behave aggressively?

There ought to be a better way to deal with this problem. Starting in the late 1960s, small homes for groups of "predelinquent" and "delinquent" youths around the United States began to adopt programs to enable residents to return to their homes and to function successfully there. What accounts for such successes? For one thing, the youths return home able to do many more socially acceptable things. They have developed skills that enable them to find satisfaction in school and in relations with peers and adults. They have learned their school subjects better and have increased their recreational and vocational skills. They can also converse with peers and adult authority figures effectively, follow instructions, assume responsible leadership, and manage their own behavior. Consequently they encounter fewer problems than they had previously encountered. At the same time, their families and community and school staffs have been taught better strategies for coping effectively with such youngsters.

The improvement of *behavior*[1] has not been limited to programs for youths in trouble with the law. In many community clinics youngsters and their parents are learning methods for controlling their own actions and for promoting more adaptive behavior. Children who had previously been out of control emotionally have gained self-control. Youngsters who formerly lacked skills have acquired them: self-care skills like dressing, eating, and health and safety practices; social skills like cooperating with siblings and parents or meeting family responsibilities; and constructive recreational skills. In some schools, children from all economic and cultural strata who have previously experienced academic deficiencies are catching up with and even surpassing their peers. They are learning with unusual effectiveness, how to solve problems, how to communicate orally and in writing, and how to create prose and objects of art. Teachers and children have learned how to achieve classroom environments that will support productive learning while minimizing disruption and destructive behavior. In many institutions for the retarded and the emotionally disturbed, youngsters are acquiring skills that will allow them to return to their communities as contributing members. They are learning to keep house, to shop, to cook, to travel on public transportation,

---

[1] When they first appear in the text glossary terms are indicated by boldface type; important nontechnical terms are indicated by italic type.

and to take advantage of community services and facilities. They are acquiring prevocational and vocational skills, so that they can contribute to their own and perhaps even to others' support. They are also learning social and recreational skills, how to dress and groom themselves in ways appropriate to the communities to which they will return, how to engage in group activities, and much more. So effective are these particular programs that youngsters are even learning to improve their physical environments by collecting litter and reducing vandalism.

APPLYING BEHAVIOR ANALYSIS

Many factors have contributed to the successes described. A generally improving standard of living alone has led to broader educational opportunities and improved social programs. There is, however, a growing body of evidence that one major determinant of success is the degree to which a specific program incorporates *effective behavioral procedures.* Such procedures, based on *principles of behavior* established over many years of systematic observation, can be implemented by caseworkers, counselors, community-agency personnel, parents, nurses, physicians, school principals, psychologists, teachers, and even youngsters themselves.

Principles of Behavior

A behavior principle is a rule describing the relation between what an individual does and specific conditions. Any kind of action may be involved: moving from place to place, saying words aloud or silently, crying, laughing, coughing, manipulating objects, secreting gastric juices. Conditions are equally numerous. Examples include the expression of approval or disapproval by other individuals, presentation or removal of food, the presence or absence or particular irritants or objects, even various weather conditions. An individual's actions may be observable, as saying words aloud, or *overtly* or not observable, as saying them silently or *covertly.* The conditions may be external, like expressions of approval, or internal like food introduced into the body. The conditions are also either modifiable (praise) or not (a thunder shower). The rules describing the relationships apply to all of these: The observable, the nonobservable, the internal, the external, the modifiable and the nonmodifiable.

One example of a behavior principle is that of immediate reinforcement. In simplified form, it can be stated that the rate of behavior will increase or maintain if the behavior is followed immediately by certain consequences. Flossie says, "Please, may I have a peach?" She is given the peach without delay. The next time Flossie wants something she says, "Please may I have _____?" Flossie's rate of saying "please" increases because requests prefaced by "please" are more frequently granted. (This principle will be presented formally in Units 8 through 10.) The behavior principle of immediate reinforcement describes the relation between the act (saying "please") and the condition (immediate granting of the request). Although many such principles of behavior have been discovered, others remain to be identified. Many currently known principles will be presented in this book.

Principles of behavior apply to both observable and unobservable acts and conditions. Our discussion will be limited to the study of those *variables* such as behaviors, responses, and conditions that can be observed. If a variable is not observable, it is impossible to describe its relation to another variable. If Flossie only thinks "please" but does not say it, how can we determine that granting her request is reinforcing? Furthermore, we have no way of knowing what effect immediate reinforcers have on the frequency with which she prefaces requests with "please."

Applying Principles of Behavior

An application of behavior principles to bring about behavior change is called a *behavioral procedure.* Parents, teachers, and youngsters who wish to change behavior deliberately arrange conditions that they hope will produce the desired results. Teachers may instruct, parents may issue directives, and youngsters may plan schedules for themselves. In fact, most of us complain about conditions over which we have no control, wishing that we could do something about changing or rearranging them: "You can talk about the weather, but you can't do anything about it"; "If only time would stand still." The more conditions we can manage for ourselves, the stronger our feelings of mastery over our environments will be. Our search for discovery and knowledge reflects this desire to identify conditions that can be modified in order to ensure particular outcomes.

When behavior change procedures incorporate principles of behavior, behavior is much more likely to be effectively influenced. When George deliberately arranges his schedule so that his favorite activity, watching baseball on television, *immediately* follows completion of his homework, he is incorporating the behavior principle of immediate reinforcement into his schedule. Once Polly has learned how to ride her bike, her father congratulates her less and less frequently; he is following a different principle, one that is especially suited to maintaining behavior. Neither George nor Polly's father may be aware that he is using appropriate behavior principles, but he is doing so nevertheless.

In fact, nearly everyone applies principles of behavior or uses behavioral procedures at some time or another. If conditions are modified in appropriate ways, even though the individual is unaware of behavioral principles as such, behavior change will be accomplished more effectively. Change agents who accomplish behavioral goals with their clients use behavioral procedures. Personnel working with "delinquent" youths in the group home program, Achievement Place (Phillips, Phillips, Fixsen & Wolf, 1971) also use effective behavioral procedures and teach the youths to use them too. But they are aware of those procedures and are consequently able to apply them both effectively and efficiently. Behavioral procedures have also accounted for improved academic performance among young children in several Follow Through programs (Becker, 1975; Bushell, 1973). Some improvement shown by retarded citizens (Thompson & Grabowski,

behavior procedure — delinquents, academic Performance, retardeds — mental patients

1972) and by mental patients (Allyon & Azrin, 1968) can be attributed to effective behavior procedures, as can increases in self-management (Bornstein & Quevillon, 1976), in creative art (Goetz & Baer, 1973), and environmental improvement (Clark, Burgess & Hendex, 1972).

Because change agents use behavioral procedures, either informally or in systematic **applied behavior-analysis programs**, it is to their advantage—and the advantage of those they serve—to learn how to use such procedures effectively. This book provides a comprehensive introduction to the field of applied behavior analysis, based on behavior principles and procedures, which are combined in a series of suggested approaches to effective and responsible behavior change.

Responsible Application of Behavior Analysis

Change agents who learn to use behavioral procedures effectively are well on their way to becoming **applied behavior analysts**. Applied behavior analysis is neither revolutionary nor underhanded. It is nothing more than good teaching within a more formal systematic framework designed to help people **learn** more effectively and to feel more confident and happier about themselves.

Like other human services, applied behavior analysis can be used with varying degrees of responsibility, depending upon both the analyst's knowledge and methods. Responsibility requires that the behavior analyst be thoroughly familiar with the principles and procedures of Behavior Analysis: how each principle is effectively implemented, what its strengths and weaknesses are, and its potential side effects. Responsibility also requires that ethical, legal, and humane factors be considered in designing programs. Some legal and ethical aspects of selecting goals and procedures will be described in Units 3 and 7, respectively. Humane concerns are emphasized throughout this book. The reader will note repeated stress upon client management and self-control, minimizing aversiveness, maximizing individual potential, constructiveness, and increasing the individual's repertoire of skills.

Certainly it is possible to use applied behavior analysis irresponsibly, either through lack of knowledge, lack of competence, questionable ethics, unfamiliarity with the law, or failure to consider humanistic aspects. The same is true of other intervention strategies, as of all kinds of human interaction and influence. A staff member who inadvertently increases self-destructive behavior by paying considerable attention to a child who is engaging in self-destructive behavior is an example. We see signs of irresponsible influence in many facets of society. Adults may frown at a young child's questions about human bodily functions, thus influencing the rate at which such questions are asked. Teachers may influence students by responding negatively or positively to certain types of conversation. Truax (1966) has shown us that even the relatively nondirective client-centered therapist can unwittingly influence the content of his clients' conversations.

Demagogues have always used behavioral procedures. Self-styled "behaviorists," convinced of their own superior wisdom, may also misapply behavioral procedures to the detriment of others. Such exploitation might be prevented in several ways. First, society could ban teaching of behavioral procedures, but that would be censorship, unacceptable in a democratic society. Besides, what is to prevent them from being discovered again? As we often apply such procedures unaware, they would continue anyway. Alternatively, all members of society could be educated in such procedures. Further, society could demand that program goals be jointly determined by all individuals involved and that behavioral practitioners design accountable programs that will objectively demonstrate the progress of the program and the effectiveness of the procedures. This alternative would provide many safeguards for individual freedom while encouraging the continual improvement of intervention strategies. Consequently, we shall adopt this approach in the following pages. After formal definition of applied behavior analysis, as conceptualized by its founders (Baer, Wolf & Risley, 1968, among others), we shall present some guidelines for **ethically responsible** practice. In particular, we shall examine identification of problems and selection of goals and procedures. Objective measurement, the basis of accountability, will be introduced, as will methods for demonstrating and communicating program effectiveness. We have concentrated on those behavioral procedures that seem to lend themselves most practically to application by change agents in institutions and community agencies serving children and youth, by family members, or by the youngsters themselves. Consequently we have included only those that are directly observable and that can be achieved with minimum apparatus. Procedures directed towards the modification of physiological events[2] through alterations in the internal or external environment are not included. The reader is referred to textbooks and journals on behavior therapy for information about such interventions.

Applied Behavior-Analysis Programs Defined

Formally defined, applied behavior analysis is a systematic, performance based, self-evaluative method of changing behavior. It is used in the prevention and amelioration of behavioral problems and in programs for learning. The unique contribution of this approach depends upon its main attributes.

First, we have already mentioned that behavior analysis is *performance based*. It is concerned with what people *do*: how they respond to aspects of their environments. Behavior analysis translates inner events into observable and measurable phenomena. Such terms as "laziness," "anger," and "depression" are **operationalized** so that they are represented by concrete behavior. The **rate** and duration of task completion, fighting, threats, self-demeaning statements, crying, and the like are observed and measured, so that a fairly precise and complete description results.

Second, behavior analysis utilizes principles of behavior that have been derived by behavioral scientists in both the laboratory and the field. Those prin-

[2] In *respondent conditioning* a neutral antecedent event comes to elicit a reflexive, or involuntary, behavior. In this book we discuss only those kinds of behavior that are often categorized as "voluntary," technically **operant**. Our presentation is limited to procedures for the modification of operant behaviors.

Cause-and-effect = relation
social importance

ciples are incorporated into *behavior change procedures* that are designed to *effectively* modify behavior in one of several directions: to *increase behaviors,* such as numbers of reading comprehension questions answered; to *teach behaviors,* such as tying a shoe or writing a poem; to *maintain behaviors,* such as continued uses of appropriate grammatical forms or attending to work tasks; to *extend* behaviors from one setting to another, such as extending high productivity in the resource room to high productivity in the sheltered workshop; to *restrict* behaviors to appropriate settings, for instance, restricting running and shouting to the playground; and to *reduce* behaviors, such as self-injurious responses, chronic complaining, or fighting.

Third, behavior analysis is *analytic.* It uses repeated direct behavior measurement (see Units 5 and 6) and particular systems, called **experimental analysis designs**, to evaluate the effectiveness of the procedure it applies. Those designs (see Units 31, 32, and 33) demonstrate **functional**, or cause-and-effect, **relations**. They are used to determine if a particular procedure is effective or if it is failing to accomplish its purpose. For example, teachers might decide to praise high school students for writing good themes. Through the utilization of the analytic system, the teachers will rapidly discover whether or not their procedure is responsible for producing objectively measurable improvement, thereby helping them decide whether to continue or to try something else.

Finally, and probably most importantly, applied behavior analysis is concerned with the improvement of socially important behaviors. Applied behavior analysis programs assist clients to improve behaviors that will promote their own personal and social development. Consequently, prior to its implementation, a program must clearly communicate and justify how it will assist the client to function more effectively in society, both in the near as well as in the distant future. It also must show how any changes that accompany the behavior change of focus will not interfere with the client's or the community's short- and long-range goals. Applied behavior analysis is thus available to clients who wish to improve their **repertoires** of skills, or to remove behaviors that interfere with adaptive functioning, and to agencies that serve those client goals. It does not deal with behaviors that have no social importance for individuals, such as bar pressing, as the experimentalist in the laboratory may justifiably do. Nor should it serve individuals or agencies whose goals are to the detriment of either clients or their immediate or broader societies.

Since applied behavior analysis treats observable behavior directly, the consumers of its services are aware of what is being done and can monitor changes. Nothing is secret, vague, or subtle. And because principles of behavior are used appropriately, the probability of success is high. Because it assumes responsibility for outcomes, with its task the improvement of individually and socially important behaviors, clients should be protected from exploitation. In sum, applied behavior analysis, practiced in an ethically responsible manner, should work towards the betterment of individuals and of society.

Though *behavioral procedures* constitute the core of formal *applied behavior analysis programs*, they are not one and the same. Behavior analysis implements behavioral procedures within a highly systematized intervention strategy. Only when behavioral procedures are combined with systematic measurement and evaluation do we call the activity an applied behavior analysis program, frequently abbreviated here as *behavior analysis, behavior analysis program,* or *behavioral program.* Anyone, including a behavioral analyst, may utilize behavioral procedures. However, only when the four major attributes cited in the formal definition above are included, can an intervention aptly be labled applied behavior analysis.

THE DECISION TO CHANGE BEHAVIOR

Behavioral change is implicit in all school and human service programs. Students come to school expecting to learn different behaviors. Clients approach therapists and counselors expecting to change their behavior. We view learning as involving varied motor, social, personal, and intellectual functions; not only cognitive functions such as being able to state facts and rules from memory but performance on many levels (see Guilford, 1959): using apt labels to describe concepts, such as "red" or "independence;" solving problems, like the answer to a question in geometry or how to respond to a social rebuff; evaluating, for example selecting a well-designed work of art from one that is poorly designed, or creating things, like short stories or papier-mâché puppets. In addition certain skills are prerequisite to academic and social learning: being able to attend to instructions and information, to follow directions, to imitate simple behaviors, and so on. Parents anticipate that their children's behavior will change as a function of therapeutic and school programs as do staff in community facilities, educators, and members of the community. It is expected that such learning experiences will generate behaviors that will enable youth eventually to earn their own livings and function as contributing members of society. Programing for behavioral change is, then, hardly a novel phenomenon. The decision is not *whether* behaviors should be changed, but *who* will participate in the programs as change agents and subjects, *what* the goals will be, and *which* specific methods will be used.

Selecting and Implementing Behavior Analysis

It should be apparent to the reader by now that applied behavior analysis programs require time, effort, patience, and occasionally extra resources. For reasons that will become clearer in later units of the book, formal applied behavior analysis programs are designed when informal procedures do not produce the desired outcome. No one attempts an applied behavior analysis program lightly, but rather studies the approach intensively and first uses it under proper supervision. Applied behavior analysis programs are designed then, when problem prevention or behavioral improvement is crucial, when problems persist despite the best efforts of those concerned, and when the clients or their surrogates want such services.[3] Applied behavior analysis may be appropriate if overall academic

---

[3] Ethical aspects of client involvement are discussed in Units 3 and 7.

progress in school shows signs of diminishing despite strong staff efforts; if individual children exhibit personal and social problems that have not been amenable to conventional guidance; if staff morale problems cannot be solved by meetings, unions, encounter groups, and special materials and resources; if the school system is the object of student hostility expressed by truancy and vandalism; if the community wishes to achieve broad social goals like increased literacy, reduced use of aversive control, better lives for retarded children, or reduced vandalism in schools; when informal procedures have failed; or if objective verification that selected procedures were effective is necessary. Applied behavior analysis is valuable to those who are fundamentally committed to social and personal betterment and to accountability in human services.

The decision to implement a behavior analysis program may arise from various sources. Clients or their parents may initiate a request for services. Communities, alert to problems emerging elsewhere, may wish to initiate preventive programs. For instance, vandalism and absenteeism in schools are increasing across the United States. A school board may wish to prevent the development of those problems in its own schools. A board member may read in the *Division of Program Evaluation, Research and Pupil Services Newsletter* published by the Los Angeles County Superintendent of Schools Office that schools in a particular district reported an average *increase* of 65 percent in vandalism costs. One school (which had actually been selected because it had the most serious behavior problems) reported an 18 percent *decrease* in the number of acts of vandalism and a 5 percent *decrease* in cost, even allowing for inflation (Mayer, 1976).

What was different about that one school? The staff received training in behavior analysis, and counselors with sophisticated training were available for frequent consultations. Behavioral procedures were implemented and monitored constantly so that the school program became much more consistent and reinforcing. On-task student behavior increased and off-task, disruptive and violent behaviors decreased (McGookin, Mayer, & Bibelheimer, 1974). Similarly, absenteeism was reported to have declined and grades improved in a barrio high-school class in Los Angeles after the introduction of a behavior analysis program (Farber & Mayer, 1972). The school-board member may be convinced that such programs are worth a try.

Sometimes an ongoing problem serves as the impetus for deciding to implement a program. Individuals may be dissatisfied with some of their deficits or problems and may design a program for themselves. Or they (or others close to them) may seek assistance from: a clinician or counselor, a teacher, peer, or pupil-personnel worker. When problems arise in the classroom, teachers usually attempt solutions on their own. But, when a problem persists, others are often consulted: the student, the parents, the principal, or perhaps a school psychologist, counselor, visiting teacher, resource teacher, social worker, or other pupil-personnel worker or consultant. Often such contacts result in a concerted effort toward a mutually determined solution. First, however, several preliminary steps should be taken. These steps will be discussed in Unit 2.

Summary

In this unit we have introduced the reader to the field of applied behavior analysis, and to the purposes of the book: to assist the reader in determining when, and how, to use specific behavioral procedures effectively in personal, social, and professional activities, and, in an ethically responsible manner, to incorporate those procedures into successful applied behavior-analysis programs. Such programs are appropriate to all forms of behavior change (eg., therapy, academic instruction, individual and group behavior management, self-management, counseling, supervision, and training). Applied behavior analysis treats all these forms as a system of effective teaching. Behavior change itself is an implicit goal of all school and human-service programs.

References

Ayllon, T. & Azrin, N. H. *The token economy.* New York: Appleton, 1968.

Baer, D. M., Wolf, M. M. & Risley, T. R. Some current dimensions of applied behavior analysis. *Journal of Applied Behavior Analysis,* 1968, **1**, 91–97.

Becker, W. C. Some effects of direct instruction methods in teaching disadvantaged children in project follow through. In T. Thompson & W. S. Dockens (Eds.), *Applications of behavior modification.* New York: Academic Press, 1975.

Bornstein, P. H. & Quevillon, R. P. The effects of a self-instructional package on overactive preschool boys. *Journal of Applied Behavioral Analysis,* 1976, **9**, 179–188.

Bushell, D., Jr. *Classroom behavior: A little book for teachers.* Englewood Cliffs, N.J.: Prentice-Hall, 1973.

Clark, R. N., Burgess, R. L. & Hendex, S. C. The development of anti-litter behavior in a forest campground. *Journal of Applied Behavior Analysis,* 1972, **5**, 1–5.

Farber, H. & Mayer, G. R. Behavior consultation in a barrio high school. *The Personnel and Guidance Journal,* 1972, **15**, 273–279.

Goetz, E. M. & Baer, D. M. Social control of form diversity and the emergence of new forms in children's block building. *Journal of Applied Behavior Analysis,* 1973, **6**, 209–217.

Guilford, J. P. Three faces of intellect. *American Psychologist,* 1959, **14**, 469–479.

Mayer, G. R. Do our schools procreate violence and vandalism? *Division of Program Evaluation, Research, and Pupil Services Newsletter* [Los Angeles County Superintendent of Schools], 1976, **14**, 1–2, 8.

McGookin, R., Mayer, G. R., & Bibelheimer, M. End of budget report, ESEA title III, Project 1005. In *Guidance objectives and learner success.* Fountain Valley, Calif.: School District, 1974.

Phillips, E. L., Phillips, E. A., Fixsen, D. L. & Wolf, M. M. Achievement Place: Modification of behaviors of pre-delinquent boys within a token economy. *Journal of Applied Behavior Analysis,* 1971, **4**, 45–59.

Thompson, T. & Grabowski, J. *Behavior modification of the mentally retarded.* New York: Oxford, 1972.

Truax, C. B. Reinforcement and nonreinforcement in Rogerian psychotherapy. *Journal of Abnormal Psychology,* 1966, **71**, 1–9.

Goal Selection: Initial Considerations

After mastering the material in this unit, you should be able to

1. Define each of the following terms, and offer distinctive illustrations:
   a. Clients
   b. Contingency managers
   c. Observers, recorders, behavioral technicians
   d. Applied behavior analysts
   e. Target behavior
   f. Goal
   g. Operational definition

2. Identify and describe three events that signal the probable presence of a behavior problem.

3. Give four illustrations of potential "simple" direct solutions, and discuss why each should be considered before implementing an applied behavior-analysis program.

4. Identify and discuss what is involved in setting goal priorities for applied behavior-analysis programs, mentioning the relevance of each factor.

5. Specify the behavior to be changed for yourself and for each of two clients who wish to change their behavior.

6. Describe the behavioral approach.

7. Describe the role of the behavior analyst in goal selection.

8. Discuss how test scores, records, and other materials are used and the purposes they serve in behavioral programing.

9. Describe and illustrate the purpose of narrative recordings and sequence analyses.

10. Observe the people identified in number 5, and use a sequence analysis to analyze the behaviors in question. Outline
the information obtained.

The mother of Lucretia seeks the advice of a psychologist: "I'm convinced my
child needs help. She is so difficult to manage." Is that information enough to
initiate design of a formal behavior-analysis program? Let us pause and consider
some of the factors that should go into such a decision, including realistic identification of the problem, designation of those to be involved and their respective
roles, and so on.

REALISTIC IDENTIFICATION OF PROBLEMS

Although we favor preventive behavior-analysis programs over problem intervention, when serious problems persist, something should be done about them. It is
important, however, to take a realistic view of what constitutes a problem. Occasionally, students, parents, teachers, or institutional staff members label a particular behavior a "problem" when in fact the problem exists only "in the eyes of
the beholder." At one time or another all of us have probably set unrealistic goals
for ourselves, aiming to become successful concert pianists, Olympic champions,
or writers of best-selling novels. When we recognized that the goals were unat-
tainable, we may have been tempted to identify our failures as behavioral problems. We may have claimed that we did not work hard enough, were not appreciated, and so on. In the same way, parents and teachers may set unreasonable
goals for their children and pupils, and failure to attain those goals may be
viewed as problem behaviors. Occasionally a person may appear to have a behavioral problem, when some other event has actually produced that perception.
A teacher may have been warned to watch out for Timmy by his previous teacher.
The mere fact that Timmy is now under closer scrutiny may produce heightened
reactions to what is normal misbehavior. Or Joyce may appear unusually boisterous
to the staff simply because she has a particularly loud voice.

What is a reasonable way to decide when a problem *is* a problem? There
is probably a real problem when one or more of these events occur.

Several Independent Requests for Assistance with
the Same Child

Lucretia has been sent home by neighbors several times for fighting with their
children. Her parents observe that other children avoid her. In discussion with a
counselor, they freely admit that they have no control over her. They report that
she bullies her younger siblings, as well as other children in the neighborhood.
It is safe to conclude that a problem exists.

Dexter knows that he has ability, for he always scores high on ability and
achievement tests, yet his school work is poor and his grades low. Dissatisfied, he

goes to the counselor for help. His humanities and science teachers also approach the counselor, convinced that Dexter is functioning below his level of ability. His mother visits the counselor too, unhappy with his poor progress. It is apparent that Dexter has a problem.

The principal has insisted that Pearl be excluded from school because her behavior is very odd. She does not talk as other children do; she neither responds to questions appropriately nor makes "normal" requests. She sings television commercials at unpredictable times and continually repeats a series of bizarre hand gestures. Her parents are distraught, and her family physician thinks that referral to a behavioral specialist is in order.

Functioning Different from that of Comparison Groups

Here is a good place to take advantage of standardized test scores and the results of other formal evaluations. The more evidence that can be gathered from various independent sources, the more valid will be the conclusion that a problem exists. Charlie scores three years below his grade level on a standardized achievement test, lower than 85 percent of his peers on a mental-maturity test, and several years below his chronological age level on a social-development inventory. Formal and informal observations provide useful data as well. The number of reading tasks completed in comparison with those of other members of his group; poor physical performance, as in throwing a ball; and erratic social behavior when interacting with other students are examples suggesting that all is not well with Charlie. Similarly, when the average reading score in a school is a few years below the national norm, a problem exists.

Dramatic Changes in an Individual's Behavior

Again, information from a number of sources helps to confirm existence of a problem. Henrietta has usually done well in school. Her grades have been above average, and she has had good relations with her classmates. Within the past month or two, she has stopped doing homework and has developed headaches and stomach aches just before she is to catch the school bus. By 10:00 A.M. her ailments tend to disappear. Henrietta also mopes around the house on weekends, complaining that she has no one to play with. Her behavior is out of keeping with her previous behavior, and it is apparent that something is wrong. If atypical behavior continues, something probably should be done. Let us see whose lives will be affected by the implementation of a behavior-analysis program.

PEOPLE INVOLVED IN BEHAVIORAL PROGRAMS AND THEIR ROLES

Many people are involved in a behavior-analysis program. In this book we shall mention various key people and the roles that they perform. First are the individuals whose behavior is the subject of the program, whom we shall call **clients**, "subjects," "students," or "patients." Second, change agents such as teachers, therapists, volunteers, high-school students (Gladstone & Sherman, 1975), clients themselves, parents, or others who systematically apply the behavioral strategies day to day are called **contingency managers**. Third, auxiliary workers, whose services are required occasionally for some technical aspects of the program, are called *observers, recorders*, or, in some job-classification schemes, *behavioral technicians*. Finally, the individuals with professional competence who design, implement, and experimentally analyze and evaluate the program, the *applied behavior analysts*. Frequently applied behavior analysts are trained psychologists, but they can also be psychiatrists, social workers, nurses, guidance and rehabilitation counselors, parents, teachers, speech therapists, and other human-services change agents who possess the requisite skills or *competencies*.

Behavior analysts attempt to describe to their clients what is likely to be involved in proposed programs: the probable roles to be played by each participant, the approximate amounts of time and effort that will be required, and the probability of success. Possible participants should be given time to consider their willingness to become involved. Once all participants have expressed their acquiescence and appear to be convinced that it is possible to conduct a cooperative program, there is a mutual commitment.

Besides these key people, others may also be affected: other staff members, relatives, administrators, community members, peers, and other people whose lives impinge upon those of the clients.

PRIOR CONSIDERATIONS

Considering all those who are directly or indirectly involved in a project that may involve a considerable investment of time and effort, it makes sense *first* to discover whether or not the problem can be treated in a faster, simpler manner. It must also be decided whether or not it has a high enough priority to justify a behavior-analysis program.

Direct, Informal Solutions

Is the problem behavior related to a physical malfunction? Is Henrietta ill? Perhaps she has a vision problem or something more serious. Whenever there are persistent physical symptoms, a physician should be consulted. More sleep, a better diet, or eyeglasses might solve Henrietta's problem.

Logistical changes can occasionally accomplish wonders. Sometimes a simple analysis of the sequence of interactions between the child and the physical environment (described later and in Unit 7) can help to identify the environmental changes that can produce desired results. Charlie may be easily distracted by activities in the classroom. Putting a partition between him and the rest of the class may be just what is needed to help him complete more assignments. Changes in lighting, furnishings, equipment, room arrangements, seating arrangements, or class placements can also provide simple solutions. The importance of having enough materials to occupy all children in a preschool class was demonstrated by Doke and Risley (1972), who showed that only when there were adequate materials did almost all their students participate in activities. Dexter's behavior might improve after a transfer to a different class, to a teacher with whom he has a good relationship. Or staff assignments might be altered. The manner in which staff responsibilities for students or clients are assigned may affect behavior. LeLaurin and Risley (1972) found that preschool children spent their time more productively when staff members were assigned to supervise children in areas or "zones" of the room, rather than supervising specific children.

Other obvious attempts hardly seem worthy of mention, but sometimes the obvious is overlooked. One tactic that falls under this heading is to *ask* the person to change his behavior. The teacher and counselor could meet with Dexter and simply ask him to try harder. Just knowing that others have an interest in him may be enough to encourage him. It is entirely possible that, in some situations, the offender does not know she is offending. Joyce may not be aware that her voice carries as far as it does. Perhaps taking her aside and quietly asking her to speak more softly, as well as modeling soft speech, will accomplish the purpose.

Effective behavior managers have known for a long time that it is a good idea to correct or reprimand individuals privately rather than publicly. O'Leary, Kaufman, Kass, and Drabman (1970) observed disruptive student behavior in five classes. They found that when reprimands were loud enough for other students to hear, the rate of disruption increased. When reprimands were audible only to the students to whom they were directed, the disruptive behavior declined. Although there is no supportive research in the literature, our guess is that public praise, usually an extremely effective method for encouraging certain behavior, may also produce paradoxical results from some students—for instance, adolescent youngsters who achieve status by "getting the teacher's goat."

Assuming, however, that simple solutions such as these do not produce the desired results, we may have to decide whether or not the problem merits a behavior-analysis program. Before starting, however, we should ask ourselves about priorities.

Priorities and Support

Although a given problem may seem to justify a behavior-analysis program, those who make such decisions should first review a few factors. Behavior analysts have many demands upon their time. How do they decide which of those demands take precedence? Unfortunately, there are no hard-and-fast rules, but certain factors may guide the decision-making process: likelihood of success, emergencies, the need for immediate assistance due to the occurrence of critical events, community and administrative support, the behavior analyst's competence, other services available, and practical considerations of money and personnel.

Predicting success.   Now that the literature on applied behavior analysis is burgeoning, it has become possible to make more educated guesses about the potential of a particular program for success. Journals, like the *Journal of Applied Behavior Analysis, Behavior Therapy,* and others cited in the reference lists at the end of each chapter in this book, contain reports of effective behavior-analysis programs in educational, clinical, institutional, work, community, home, and other settings. The behavior analyst who keeps informed[1] about procedures that have been repeatedly demonstrated to be effective, as well as new and promising ones, is more likely to make wise selections. It is usually a good idea for the beginning behavior analyst to try first to repeat (replicate) the procedures of demonstrated effectiveness designed by others before attempting to design new ones.

Emergencies and critical events.   A high priority should be given to critical events, or emergencies. Imminent danger to clients should be of prime concern. Problems like extreme aggressive or self-abusive behavior, serious addiction, and exposure to environmental catastrophe fall into this category. Major life decisions, like dropping out of school, transferring to different training programs, marrying, and so on, may also be placed here. Emergencies may arise among school or community-agency personnel as well: Impulsive decisions to resign and requests for transfers or different assignments resulting from frustrations in the setting should probably be placed at the top of the priority list. Clients and their parents are frequently responsible for drawing the attention of human-services staff or school personnel to emergency situations: sudden unwillingness to attend school, running away from home, pregnancy, threats of aggression by other students, and so on. If Pearl were excluded from school and refused admission to *any* school program, refusal would constitute an emergency.

Community and administrative support.   Parent groups, various boards and committees, and other organs of the community are often major determiners of priorities. Such groups may, for example, urge that primary emphasis be placed upon reading achievement, citizen responsibility, drug abuse, or some other issue. Because continued community support is so important to the success of any public-service program, particularly one that departs from traditional practices, this consideration is not a minor one. The public served by schools and other community agencies should be able to exert **countercontrol** by having a major say in how it is served. Establishing priorities that reflect community concerns and involving community representatives in program planning increase the likelihood of continuing support. An excellent model for such community involvement is the Achievement Place program (Risley & Twardosz, 1974). In that program, persons who represent the consumers in the community participate in planning and are consulted regularly by being asked to rate their satisfaction with the program.

Teachers, pupil-personnel workers, the staffs in community facilities, and even behavior analysts receive some of their more satisfying rewards from the administrators of their facilities: salaries, promotions, assignments, approval, and privileges. Conversely, withholding such rewards often reflects administrative disapproval of performance. The continued cooperation of those involved in a behavior-analysis program therefore requires the support of the administration.

---

[1] Readers who master this book will have the necessary knowledge and vocabulary to enable them to read and comprehend much of the professional literature.

Like the larger community, the administration is more apt to continue cooperating if it is involved in setting priorities.

The behavior analyst's competencies.   Along with other human-service practitioners—doctors, lawyers, teachers, social workers, counselors, and so on—applied behavior analysts do not institute programs that they are not competent to conduct. They should feel comfortable about programs that they have conducted adequately in the past under supervision and according to predetermined criteria. Sulzer-Azaroff, Thaw, and Thomas (1975) have spelled out approximately fifty behavior-modification competency responses and accompanying criteria. For example, a behavior analyst may have designed and tested an observational system. Competence may be judged to have been achieved when the trainee demonstrates that the system is both reliable and valid. Some behavioral procedures are quite complex and require fairly sophisticated skills. For instance, **graduated guidance** (see Unit 14) is designed to teach difficult motor skills. This procedure requires very precise physical and verbal skills. Special training is the best way to acquire those skills. Of course, it is recognized that, even after extensive supervised classroom and practical experience, not all behavior analysts will have received supervised training in every single procedure. Possible substitutes for such training include consultation, intensive study of materials like those to be presented in this book, observation, filmed instruction, and **program packages** that have been field tested for effectiveness and adequate procedural descriptions (Risley, 1975). As we shall emphasize later, however, any novel procedure should be approved by clients, agency administrators, and community representatives. It should reflect a balance between maximum effectiveness and minimum intrusiveness; that is, it should be as close as possible to natural or standard operating procedure. The determination of a behavior analyst's competence to continue applying procedures must be based on data resulting from the programs themselves: measured improvement in client responses and consumer satisfaction. But, above all, because applied behavior analysis requires accountability, the success of a particular procedure provides the ultimate evidence of the behavior analyst's competence to continue using it.

Relative availability of alternative programs.   If the behavior analyst is working in a school system in a community that has an effective drug-treatment program, drug-abuse cases are best referred to that program. If a problem seems to arise from family difficulties, local family clinics are appropriate referral agencies. Within the schools there may be services for various behavior categories: awareness groups, courses in psychology, guidance groups, and the like. Behavior analysts should acquaint themselves thoroughly with effective programs that the community and schools offer. Other considerations being equal, the primary function of behavior analysts is to fulfill the roles for which they are hired. For example, in a school setting, first priority should be accorded to behavioral programs related to education—even when other community services are lacking, except perhaps in emergencies. A behavior analyst assigned to any institution should place prevention or treatment of problems among the clients they serve, first.

Money and personnel. Money and the services, facilities, equipment, and materials that it can buy are certainly considerations in the establishment of priorities for behavior-analysis programs. If a particular program requires a special facility, for example, a playroom, additional observers and aides, individualized instructional materials, or some other costly item and if no money is available to fulfill the requirement, it makes little sense to attempt the program. This issue has been placed toward the bottom of the list for a reason, however: Lack of resources can often be circumvented. An imaginative and persistent behavior analyst can often find resources that are not immediately apparent. (Suggestions for free and inexpensive materials and support services are scattered throughout this book.)

To assist behavior analysts in setting priorities, we have provided the following check list.

Practical Considerations before Instituting an Applied Behavior-Analysis Program

1. Does a behavior problem exist?
   a. Have several people sought assistance for the problem? _____
   b. Does the person or group function very differently from the way that "typical" people or groups function? _____
   c. Have there been dramatic behavior changes? _____
2. Have direct or informal solutions been attempted?
   a. Physical examination? _____
   b. Changes in assignments and responsibilities? _____
   c. Changes in physical environment? _____
   d. Direct requests for behavior change? _____
(Negative responses to any of these questions suggest that informal methods should be considered before instituting a systematic applied behavior-analysis program, but if answers are affirmative or not applicable, one is justified in proceeding.)
3. Does the proposed behavior-analysis program have sufficiently high priority and level of support to justify proceeding?
   a. Is there adequate evidence that is it likely to succeed? _____
   b. Is the problem critical? _____
   c. Will the community support the program? _____
   d. Will the program receive administrative support? _____
   e. Does the behavior analyst have the competence to conduct the program successfully? _____
   f. Are there adequate funds, space, materials, and motivated personnel to conduct the program, or can reasonable substitutes be found? _____
   g. Are other community organizations unable to handle the problem adequately? _____

Affirmative responses to most of the items on this check list suggest that the most appropriate decision is to go ahead and begin selecting behavioral goals. We shall consider steps that should be followed in refining goals and planning the program later.

THE BEHAVIORAL APPROACH

Having determined that a problem actually does exist and that it has a high enough priority to merit intervention, the analyst must identify clearly the **target behavior** and the **goals** that are likely to ameliorate it. The target behavior is the behavior to be changed. The *goals* are behavior changes to be sought: increase, decrease, maintenance, development, or expansion of the target behavior.

Let us look at a few problem situations. Dexter is convinced that he needs help to function more in keeping with his capabilities. The parents of Lucretia, Charlie, Henrietta, and Pearl are all anxious for help in guiding their children more constructively. Teachers are also eager to plan effective programs for them. Both the problems and goals for such individuals are often stated in rather broad terms. Dexter is lazy; he should realize his potential and stop goofing off. Lucretia is hostile; she should learn better social skills. Charlie is retarded; he should be placed in a special-education program. Pearl is "autistic"; she needs help. Henrietta is a hypochondriac; she should be cured. Mr. Grump is a grouch; he should not be so sarcastic and pessimistic. Mrs. Kvetch should stop her chronic complaining. If only those goals could be reached, the problems would be solved.

The behavioral approach of this book is limited to what people do and say, what is directly[2] observable and measurable. We find that change can be more effectively programmed for such behavior. Communication is much less ambiguous when a goal is stated in precise terms. It is relatively easier to monitor changes in observable behavior. Does the term "Dexter's potential" communicate the same thing to everyone? How does one monitor changes in "laziness"? What appears to be "hostile," "complaining," "autistic," "hypochondriacal," or "sarcastic" behavior to one person may not appear the same to the next. "Social skills" is also a vague term. A "special education" does not necessarily imply improved performance. We do not mean that such terms are irrelevant; rather, we think that they do not lend themselves to program design and treatment strategies. Because of the confusion and inefficiency that they may generate, they must be redefined.

Operationalizing Problems and Tentative Goals

One aspect that distinguishes applied behavior analysis from many other forms of treatment is precision in goal specification. Goals are stated in behavioral language, and their selection is based upon analysis of the problem situation and upon ethical considerations. Let us look at some of the vague goals mentioned and see how they can be refined. A good way to approach the task is to ask "What would Dexter *do* (remember the "action orientation" of behavior analysis?) if he were to demonstrate greater 'realization of his potential'? Would he complete more assignments with greater accuracy, volunteer more correct answers, or ask to assist others in group activities? Would he read and report on more books, or would he obtain a work-study job and be given satisfactory performance ratings? What would Mrs. Kvetch do if she were no longer a chronic complainer? Would

[2] Private events may also be modified, but since precise, valid measurement of changes in private events remains to be perfected, we rarely consider them in this book.

she say 'I feel good' and make other positive statements more often, groan and sigh less, or what?"

Communication is facilitated by means of precision. At least, specification should convince those involved that they are all talking about the same thing. It is also easier to monitor changes in behavior that are defined so that they can be observed. A convincing argument that Dexter is lazy would probably require several observers to concur in evaluations based on subjective judgments. Subjectivity enters in far less frequently when completion of assignments, accuracy levels, or instances of volunteering are monitored.

When phenomena are broken down into measurable components, they are said to be **operationally defined.** An operation is something that someone does that has an effect upon the environment. Writing is an operation because it produces quantifiable changes on paper. Hitting is an operation because it results in measurable force delivered to a person or object. Screaming is an operation because it changes the measure of decibels of the acoustical environment. One of the first tasks of the behavior analyst is to clarify problems and goals by defining terms operationally.

A further caution: Although what people report that they do and what they actually do often agree, sometimes they do not. Baer, Wolf, and Risley (1968) noted that, in specifying goals, the issue is what individuals *do*, not what they *say* they do:

. . . [applied behavior analysis] usually studies what subjects can be brought to do rather than what they can be brought to say; *unless of course, a verbal response is the behavior of interest.* Accordingly a subject's description of his own nonverbal behavior usually would not be accepted as a measure of his actual behavior unless it were independently substantiated. Hence, there is little applied value in the demonstration that an impotent man can be made to say that he no longer is impotent. The relevant question is not what he can say but what he can do. (Baer, Wolf & Risley, 1968, p. 93; italics added)[3]

SITUATIONAL ANALYSIS

Once the problem and tentative goals have been operationally defined, test scores, records, and other materials should be reviewed, and the current situation should be analyzed. Here we shall consider the part played by such analysis in refining general goals into specific behavioral objectives.

Test Scores, Records, and Other Materials

Standardized test results, records in the teacher's grade book, assignment folders, library records, behavior-assessment systems (see Appendix I for sample behavior-assessment systems), and other records may also provide valuable information about the client's level of functioning. They may be relevant both to program

[3] Reprinted by permission from D. M. Baer, M. M. Wolf & T. R. Risley. Some current dimensions of applied behavior analysis. *Journal of Applied Behavior Analysis,* 1968, **1,** 91–97. Copyright 1968 by the Society for the Experimental Analysis of Behavior, Inc.

goals or *objectives* and to the selection of procedures. Dexter's school records may show that his scores in reading are above average, but that he completes very few reading assignments. His library card may show that he has taken out two books on fossils and that his scores on an interest inventory are high in the natural sciences. As he apparently has an interest in fossils, perhaps a goal related to reading about fossils and the energy crisis should be selected. Such records and tests furnish general indications of the client's level of functioning and suggest a reasonable starting place for determining the tasks that clients are most likely to attempt and the kinds of materials that are most appropriate.

Clients' records often contain useful "case materials." Data on physical condition, social and emotional development, and academic progress may contribute to decisions about goals and procedures. Dexter's records may indicate that he made reasonable progress until he reached ninth grade. Perhaps something about the class, the teacher, the materials, friends, or other events has affected his performance. The record may or may not provide such information. The fact that Dexter has progressed satisfactorily in the past, however, does say something about his capabilities: It would not be totally unreasonable to plan a program to assist him to the point at which he can progress at the rate of most of his classmates.

Narrative Recording and Sequence Analysis[4]

Narrative recordings are running descriptions of behavior in progress. The events described are then organized in a **sequence analysis** (Reese, Howard & Reese, 1977): (1) specific acts that relate to the goal, (2) antecedent events and conditions that seem to precipitate those acts, as well as (3) the events that follow as consequences of the act. It is important to note that environmental conditions—the time of day, day of week, ongoing activities, others present, weather, materials, and physical surroundings—may set the occasion for the behavior of concern. Sometimes it takes several full days of observation before the behavior analyst begins to focus on the various conditions most closely connected to the key behavior. Recording such conditions provides valuable information about where, when, and how to begin formal observation. Dexter may spend more time looking out the window on Monday mornings during math period. If so, then formal observations should be taken during Monday-morning math periods. Let us examine one way in which a narrative might be recorded. We shall assume that the following goals were selected for Dexter:

(1) To write more book reports
(2) To offer to assist others more frequently
(3) To answer correctly more questions during class discussion
(4) To study a topic more thoroughly by reading several pieces of source material and incorporate the information in oral or written reports.

[4] The observational systems used by Jean Piaget, Florence Goodenough, and various ethologists were forerunners of these systems.

Once a running narrative of Dexter's volunteering to assist others or to answer questions correctly, had been recorded, it could be reorganized into a *sequence analysis*: a list of the behavior(s) of concern and the events that precede and follow them. Figure 2.1 is an illustration of such a sequence analysis.

Client —————————————   Date —————————————

Observer ————————————   Time —————————————

Situational conditions ————————————————————

————————————————————————————————

Others present ——————————————————————

Ongoing activities —————————————————————

Antecedent Event	Dexter's Behavior	Consequent Event
Teacher asks, "Who will help the energy crisis committee to find information on fossil fuel?"	Looks out window	Teacher shrugs shoulders and says, "I'll help you myself as long as no one volunteered."
Teacher says, "Dexter, I know that you have a particular interest in fossils. You'd probably be particularly interested in the relation between fossils and the energy crisis. I'd like to count on your participation on the energy-crisis committee; may I?"	Replies, "Sure, I have some samples of coal I'd like to bring in to school tomorrow."	Teacher says, "Great." John smiles and nods approval.
John moans, scratches his head, and says, "I can't do this geometry problem."	Says, "You're dumb."	Teacher says, "You can hardly afford to call John anything when you don't complete your work either."
Sally moans, scratches her head, and says, "I can't do this geometry problem."	Says: "Here, let me help you. Remember the rule about right triangles?"	Teacher ignores Dexter. Sally smiles and gives Dexter a grateful "Thanks."

Figure 2.1 Sample sequence analysis.

A sequence analysis of this sort provides quite a bit of information about events related to goal behaviors. For example, not offering to participate, looking out the window, agreeing to help, and actually helping are all related to goal 2. Events that tend to precipitate such behavior include general requests for help, personal requests for help, needs expressed by some students, and needs expressed by different students. Analysis of consequent events indicates something about how various environmental reactions increase or decrease certain responses. With only the four illustrated episodes, we cannot do so. But, if 40 or 400 such events were recorded, a trend might become manifest: Dexter does things for people who smile and thank him; completes more tasks when his teacher mildly reprimands him for not doing his work; he completes fewer tasks when harshly reprimanded.

A sequence analysis also yields information about behavior that is present or absent from the individual's repertoire under various environmental conditions. In four days of observation, Mr. Grump has never once complimented his staff. Such behavior is probably not in his repertoire. He has, however, been observed nodding at a few staff members when they greeted him. Nodding is part of his repertoire. Watching Lucretia play, we have noticed that she does not ask for a toy but grabs it out of the hands of the other child. Politely requesting a toy is apparently not part of her repertoire. Charlie has trouble buttoning his coat. He does manage to button a few buttons, but he frequently fails to match buttons with their appropriate holes. Buttoning is part of his repertoire; correct buttoning is not. During two weeks observation at home and at school, Pearl has not once asked for anything or responded appropriately to an instruction. There is no evidence that functional language is part of her repertoire.

Sequence analyses permit estimates of the relative amounts of time that the client engages in certain behaviors. Dexter spends half his class time looking out the window. Lucretia chases other children in the park practically all the time. Mr. Grump makes many sarcastic remarks and goes for a smoke whenever he has a free moment. Pearl repeats a stereotyped sequence of hand movements more than 80 percent of the time. During her many trips to the coffeepot Mrs. Kvetch frequently tells her fellow employees how much better her former job was. All this information says something about the seriousness of the problem. Dexter literally is not orienting towards his work, Lucretia does threaten the other children, Mr. Grump uses a lot of sarcasm, Mrs. Kvetch does indeed complain, and Pearl's stereotyped hand movements occur alarmingly often. Observation may also help to identify potential incentives or reinforcers, as we shall see in later units. The opportunity to smoke is probably a reinforcer for Mr. Grump. Coffee or interacting with others around the coffeepot probably reinforces Mrs. Kvetch.

Both direct, anecdotal observations and records provide information of value to applied behavior analysts as they prepare to help design programs. Such information gives them a better picture of the clients' levels of functioning, the behaviors with which they enter the program, a general notion about reasonable goals, and some hints to potentially effective behavioral procedures.

Summary

In this unit we have provided guidelines for establishing priorities for behavior-analysis programs. A check list has been included to assist in this task. Rationales for operationalizing problems and goals and for analyzing the situation before final goal selection have also been presented. Each of these initial considerations is summarized in the flow chart in Figure 2.2; together, they form the first component of the model on which applied behavior-analysis programs should be conducted. (The broken line around *consider ethical implications*, indicates that it is the next component to be considered.)

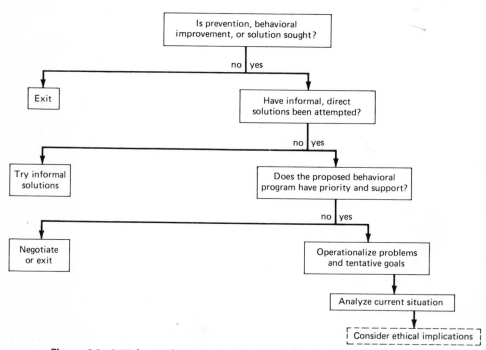

Figure 2.2 Initial considerations in changing behavior through behavior analysis.

References

Baer, D. M., Wolf, M. M. & Risley, T. R. Some current dimensions of applied behavior analysis. *Journal of Applied Behavior Analysis,* 1968, **1**, 91–97.

Doke, L. A. & Risley, T. R. The organization of day-care environments: Required versus optional activities. *Journal of Applied Behavior Analysis,* 1972, **5**, 405–420.

Gladstone, B. W. & Sherman, J. A. Developing generalized behavior modification skills in high school students working with retarded children. *Journal of Applied Behavior Analysis,* 1975, **8**, 169–180.

LeLaurin, K. & Risley, T. R. The organization of day-care environments: "Zone" versus "man-to-man" staff assignments. *Journal of Applied Behavior Analysis,* 1972, **5**, 225–232.

O'Leary, K. D., Kaufman, K. F., Kass, R. E. & Drabman, R. The effect of loud and soft reprimands on the behavior of disruptive students. *Exceptional Children,* 1970, **37,** 145–155.

Reese, E. P., Howard, J. S. & Reese, T. W. *Human behavior: An experimental analysis and its applications.* Dubuque: Brown, 1977.

Risley, T. R. Certify procedures not people. In S. Wood (Ed.), *Issues in evaluating behavior modification.* Champaign: Research Press, 1975.

Risley, T. R. & Twardosz, S. *Florida guidelines for the use of behavioral procedures in state programs for the retarded.* Tallahasee: State of Florida Department of Health and Rehabilitation Services, Division of Retardation, January 1974.

Sulzer-Azaroff, B., Thaw, J., & Thomas, C. Behavioral competencies for the evaluation of behavior modifiers. In S. Wood (Ed.), *Issues in evaluating behavior modification.* Champaign: Research Press, 1975. 47–98.

Goal Selection:
Ethical Considerations

After mastering the material in this unit, you should be able to
1. Define and discuss what the authors mean by the following terms:
   a. Advocate
   b. Voluntariness
   c. Coercion

2. Discuss each of the following general considerations in goal selection:
   a. Constructive or suppressive approach?
   b. Direct or indirect intervention?
   c. Who is to benefit?

3. Identify ways in which goal conflicts can occur.

4. Discuss how each of the following can reduce the likelihood of goal conflicts:
   a. Client participation
   b. Advocacy
   c. Parent involvement
   d. Staff and administrative involvement
   e. Behavioral contracting
   f. Institutional review

The various directions that a behavior-analysis program can take are suggested by analysis of the current situation and those aspects of the environment that operate to support or to interfere with a given behavior. Test scores, surveys, and formal and informal observations can contribute information that assists in selecting the target behavior. There are also humane, legal, and ethical considerations that are crucial to goal selection. They form the next major component of the applied behavior-analysis model.

CONSIDERING ALTERNATIVE GOALS

Some goals involve strengthening, acquisition, or **maintenance** of behaviors. Others involve reducing or "inhibiting" them. Some possible alternative goals for Dexter are increasing the amount of work he completes (strengthening), increasing the number of new academic skills he acquires (acquisition), extending the duration of higher work rates (maintenance), reducing the length of time that he stares out the window (reduction), eliminating refusals to perform academic tasks (inhibition). On the other hand, the chosen goal may not involve Dexter directly but may be focused instead upon his environment, such as rearranging furniture. The teacher may increase the rate of smiling approval when Dexter offers to assist another student or may limit the number of critical remarks made to Dexter. All these possible goals have the same general purpose: to improve Dexter's school performance. Which should be selected?

General Considerations

A number of ethical and legal considerations enter into selection of particular goals. In this section we shall discuss some of those considerations: constructive versus suppressive approach, direct versus indirect intervention, and benefits to client, staff, and society.

Constructive versus suppressive approach.   Let us consider a person whose problem behaviors make up most of his behavioral repertoire. If we eliminate them all, what do we have? An empty shell, a person with a few desirable behaviors and not much else. What have we and the client accomplished, other than keeping him or her out of trouble? Dexter could be taught to stop staring out the window, to stifle his yawns, and to remain silent instead of saying, "I don't care to do that." That would hardly be a major improvement. But suppose that he could be helped to accomplish more, volunteer more frequently, or come up with innovative problem solutions. Then we could conclude with greater confidence that his problems were being solved. Winett and Winkler (1972) have cautioned against behavioristic approaches that may produce docile and immobile children. Behavior analysts who operate in an ethically responsible manner can help to relieve such fears by helping their clients to develop constructive and useful behaviors.

Direct versus indirect intervention.   Earlier in the development of the applied behavior analysis field it was assumed that, if we could just persuade students to stop disrupting and misbehaving, they would learn more. Now, however, this assumption has been questioned. Ferritor and his colleagues (1972) were able to reduce disruption, yet school performance did not improve, though Sulzer and her associates (1971) and Ayllon and Roberts (1974) found that better school performance was accompanied by a reduction in disruptive behavior. Early studies in institutions and clinics were focused on indirect behavior, like self stimulatory behavior, rather than on deficits that clients displayed. Reducing aberrant behaviors, like self stimulation will not necessarily maximize on-the-job performance. It may help, but not enough. Teaching job skills provides the client with greater benefits. For Dexter, the most direct approach would be to select goals directly related to improved school performance.

Benefits to client, staff, and society.   Traditional behavior change strategies used in teaching, counseling, training, and therapy are based on implicit assumptions of benefits to clients. It has been commonly believed that what the behavior-change agent thought was best for the client was indeed best. In applied behavior analysis, assumptions based on mutual good faith are no longer permitted to guide selection of goals whose short- and long-term benefits to the client are dubious. When goals must be explicitly stated and acknowledged, they become public, and both change agents and consumers become accountable for them. It is no longer possible for change agents to convince themselves and others that whatever they do is automatically for the clients' benefit. They must explicitly state what the goal is and who is to benefit. We educators, clinicians, and staff members of community facilities must be able to defend a particular goal and to justify our actions related to it. The learning environment, for example, must be shown to support the attainment of behavioral goals.

A behavioral goal ought generally to be selected to provide both immediate and long-term benefits to the client. Academic goals that serve as stages in learning task hierarchies—holding a pencil, tracing, and writing; setting up, analyzing, and solving an equation—usually arouse little controversy. In our society learning academic skills is considered a good thing, and institutions have been established to further that purpose. But what of some of the subtler behaviors: attentional and attitudinal skills, social skills, interfering responses, and so on? How important is it for students or clients to work for long periods of time, to seek more political science information on their own, to volunteer often for extra projects, to follow both simple and complex directions, to work without disturbing others, to cooperate, to organize activities, and to refrain from aggression or inciting of others to engage in disruptive or destructive acts? Certainly we could easily defend such goals as essential to the development of other beneficial behaviors: If students do not pay attention, how can they learn? If there is pandemonium in a classroom, how can anyone learn? Yet there are times when the precision of behavior analysis causes the change agent to examine and then to retain or discard a set of goals.[1] The teacher asks: "Here I am insisting that students request permission to leave

[1] Budd and Baer (1976) point out that the decision in *Wyatt v. Stickney*, 325 F. Supp. 781 (M.D. Ala. 1971), 334 F. Supp. 1341 (M.D. Ala. 1971), 344 F. Supp. 373 (M.D. Ala. 1972), and 344 F. Supp. 387 (M.D. Ala. 1972), prohibits programs designed to extinguish socially appropriate behavior or to develop new behavior patterns which serve only institutional convenience.

Goal Conflict

1- client and behavior analyst
2- "   "   " others
3- Resolving goal conflict

Considering Alternative Goals   29

the room and punishing those who refuse to comply with the rule. Is the rule imposed because it makes sense or just because that's how my teachers did things when I was a student? How does such a rule benefit my students?" The counselor wonders: "Why do we spend most of our session discussing sports? Does the discussion serve any of our goals? Perhaps we are wasting time or possibly have neglected to identify an important goal, toward which we are 'intuitively' working: a smoother communication, enhancing our reinforcing properties for one another."

Long-term goals can often be reached through a succession of short-term goals. There may be occasions, however, on which short- and long-term goals come into conflict. To learn to conduct a chemistry experiment, the student must follow the instructions of the teacher to the letter; failure to do so may cause harm to him and to others. Nevertheless, when the long-term goal is to enable the student to do more creative work, emphasis on blind compliance with teachers' directions may impede progress. Teaching a child to follow a rigid daily routine may benefit him at home but may interfere with his adaptability in a less supportive environment later on. By asking, "Exactly what short- and long-term benefits will this goal achieve for the client in his present and future world?" behavior analysts can refine goals in ways that are more defensible ethically.

Goal Conflicts: Client and Behavior Analyst

Some goal behaviors are advantageous to clients; others, to behavior analysts or the agencies they represent. As agents for clients, behavior analysts must ensure that their clients benefit from their interventions. Lucretia's parents would probably find her easier to deal with if she were passive, rather than hostile and destructive. Producing such passivity would probably earn the behavior analyst the appreciation of the parents. Yet, as we have remarked, such goals would probably do little to benefit Lucretia. The behavior analyst should be guided above all by concern for the client. Although it probably requires more time and effort to teach adaptive and socially constructive modes of response, like nonaggressive kinds of assertive behavior, the benefit to Lucretia will be far greater.

It is conceivable that some goals that would benefit the client are unacceptable to the behavior analyst. For example, Lucretia might also benefit, in one sense, from lessons in karate, which would enable her to flatten more of her playmates. Here the behavior analyst has the right to demur and to enter instead into some form of negotiation with the client and other concerned individuals. (One convenient format for such negotiation is discussed under the heading "Behavioral Contracting" later in this unit.)

Goal Conflicts: Client and Others

Sometimes a goal that is beneficial to one person may be detrimental to others. If Shrinking Violet is taught to become very assertive, she may punch Sassy Sally in the nose or take her toys away. If Fern is to learn to brush her teeth and dress herself, her attendant will have to provide her with the necessary materials and take the time and effort to supervise her performance. Encouraging Dexter to complete more tasks may mean that his teacher must spend evenings and week-ends organizing additional assignments for him. If students learn to work quietly because their teacher is irritated by noise, they may never learn to work in a busy and active environment. If students are taught about family planning, so that when they do establish families their children will more likely be wanted and adequately provided for, the school administrator may be punished by legal actions from vocal groups of citizens. Conflict must be weighed against the needs of society as a whole.

Resolving Goal Conflicts

There are no pat answers when conflicts arise; there are, however, some vehicles for reducing the likelihood that they will develop into more serious problems. Client involvement; advocacy; participation by parents, as well as staff and community members, contracting; and institutional review are some of them. The important point is that consideration should be given to the client's social environment in order to predict whether or not the anticipated goal will be disadvantageous to any of the people in that environment. Only with foresight is it possible to avoid some of the social and legal confrontations that are becoming familiar in connection with controversial human services. As Martin has summarized the question, "In the final analysis, if the goal is not to produce a happy functioning person free from state interference, then it will, and should, run into constant legal problems" (1974, p. 11).

Client participation.   Goal conflicts can be avoided and cooperation facilitated when the client is directly involved in selecting goals. Dexter may, for example, select goals like writing more and longer book reports because he enjoys reading and writing. But he may be unwilling to do more physics assignments because he is not fond of the subject. Mr. Grump may be more willing to try to reduce his sarcasm than to increase his use of praise because he feels "phony" praising his staff.

Sometimes the client selects a goal that is unrealistic or inappropriate to the setting. Judy might decide to become the most popular girl in school, a goal that is probably not reasonable for her. The behavior analyst may offer instead to help her learn some social skills that will enable her to get along with some of her classmates more effectively. The behavior analyst is responsible for assisting the client to select goals that are reasonable and attainable, but the client should be the one to make the ultimate selection from among those goals.

Advocacy.   We have entered an era in which more and more people are demanding that their views be represented in decisions that affect them. Groups of individuals who have traditionally been underdogs in our society are now insisting upon equal status in many areas. The rights of young clients are no less important. When clients are mature adults, they can often act on their own to protect their rights. Until recently, children, retarded people, and men and women with serious emotional disturbances and behavioral deficits were considered incapable of participating in decisions affecting them. Parents or guardians have traditionally acted on their behalf. Certainly parents and guardians, whose lives are intimately involved with those of the clients, should also be consulted about behavioral goals. But it is possible, and ethically and legally advisable as well, to involve clients directly in the process of specifying goals.

Questions are now arising about how young the consenter might be—the Federal Health, Education and Welfare Department proposed guidelines on experiments with children require consent to be obtained from children nine years old and above. Additional questions are whether an institution can act in the place of a parent and give consent, meaning that a child would have no protection against what the institution had decided to do; and whether there are substantive rights belonging to a child that cannot be waived even with parental consent. (Martin, 1974, p. 8)

When a client clearly does not have the capacity to participate in such a decision—for example, when a child lacks speech or an adult totally fails to communicate—an **advocate** should be appointed to represent his or her interests. The advocate, who may be a community representative, like a clergyman, a law student, or even a panel of interested citizens, considers the goal from the point of view of the client (Reynolds, 1973). The advocate is clearly the client's agent, not the agent of an organization or institution. Advocates put themselves in the place of their clients and argue on their behalf. This arrangement makes it more likely that the best interests of the clients will be served.

Parent involvement in goal selection. Parents have legal responsibilities toward their minor offspring, as well as the "moral obligation," in our society, to bring their children up "properly." Perhaps more important, they also control many contingencies in their youngsters' lives. A parent should have the right to participate in selection of goals for minor children, particularly when the goals are related directly to the parents' responsibilities. Additionally, when they participate, they are less likely to function at cross purposes with the program.

Some goals that may be selected by youngsters, particularly by adolescents, may be unacceptable to their parents. One of Judy's goals may be to spend more time in extracurricular activities, yet her parents may feel that she spends entirely too much time in such activities already and should concentrate more on her lessons. Here the behavior analyst might act as an arbitrator, helping Judy and her parents to arrive at a mutually acceptable goal.

Occasionally, legal minors have problems that they are unwilling to share with their parents. They wish to work with the behavior analyst in confidence. For example, a teenager may approach the behavior analyst asking for help to cut down her smoking, and the parents may not even know that their child *does* smoke. Involving parents in selection of goals in such situations may do more harm than good. The behavior analyst must use some subjective standards: Is the client sufficiently mature to know what he or she wants? Would the goal be acceptable to the parents if they knew the whole story? Will the client permit the behavior analyst to discuss the problem with others who are responsible for him or her—perhaps a teacher, the principal, or a doctor? Obviously, there are no simple solutions to such problems. The behavior analyst should, however, be encouraged to consider the ethics of each situation from as many vantage points as possible.

Staff and administrative involvement in goal selection. Aside from parents, educators and clinicians also have legitimate interests in the selection of goals for their charges. When a particular problem manifests itself, the staff involved in the setting should participate in goal selection. Frequently one of the staff members has brought the problem to the attention of the behavior analyst in the first place. Naturally that person has some commitment to seeking a solution. Dexter's poor academic performance has been noted by his teacher, as well as by himself. It would be reasonable for the teacher to express feelings about the appropriateness of goals under consideration. Again active participation in goal specification would probably increase the likelihood of the teacher's taking an active role in the program.

Staff members who are not directly involved with a client may also have some interest in goals that may affect them indirectly. Goals should not, for example, violate the philosophical orientations of the staff or institutional policy. A reasonable way to avoid potential conflict of this kind is to present the goals under consideration to the staff and administration before instituting the program. Staff and administration can also contribute by identifying potential difficulties with proposed goals or may suggest alternative goals that would serve the same purposes more effectively. When confidentiality is an issue, considerations should be similar to those discussed in connection with parental involvement.

Behavioral contracting. Conflicts in goal selection may arise when benefits and costs differ for different members of the group affected. One way to balance negative and positive attributes is to negotiate a contract (Sulzer, 1962; Keirsey, 1965; Krumboltz, 1966; Brooks, 1974; Homme, Csany, Gonzales, & Rechs, 1970). Contracts may be used to stipulate both program goals and procedural details. The latter type of contract will be discussed in Unit 7. The former type involves consideration of potential goals by the client first and by others involved next. The negotiation should consist of a discussion of the various ways in which each participant might be positively and negatively affected. Only when all possible short- and long-term benefits and costs to the client and others involved have been considered should the final contract be negotiated. Benefits may include enhanced personal, social, and academic repertoires or reductions in responses that are personally aversive or interfere with desired outcomes. Costs may include increased time and effort; loss of reinforcement like material goods, power, control; loss of other social rewards; or increases in aversive stimulation (more noise in the classroom, having to listen to unpleasant conversations). It is to be hoped that a complete airing of those costs and benefits beforehand will permit specification of a mutually acceptable goal.

A contract that aims at a goal toward which the client agrees to work in the absence of coercion will incorporate the properties of **voluntariness** and **informed consent**. That is, all parties voluntarily entering into the contract indicate their consent to adoption of the goal. By incorporating those properties, behavior analysis contracts meet both ethical and legal demands. Voluntariness and consent play key roles in various formal codes of conduct (for example, the American Psychological Association's general code of ethics, 1963; its ethical code for research with human participants, 1973; and the U.S. Department of Health, Education, and Welfare's guide for protection of human subjects, 1971). The problem of coercion has been the subject of many recent court cases (Wexler, 1973; Schwitzgebel, 1971; Martin, 1974; *Connecticut Civil Liberties Newsletter*, 1974). A **behavioral contract** freely negotiated by concerned parties, though it may not necessarily be legally binding, provides evidence that care has been taken to incorporate voluntary consent into the program.

The option to withdraw from a behavioral contract. Protection from coercion is important to the client's freedom to select a given goal. Another aspect of voluntariness is the client's freedom to withdraw from the program at any time. Dexter may decide to change his vocational choice and performing well in the subjects for which behavior-analysis programs have been designed is no longer important to him. The option to withdraw should be incorporated in the behavioral contract. The terms or conditions under which withdrawal may take place should also be stipulated. Because usually a number of people are involved in the program, they, too, have a right to be informed and consulted about a decision to terminate. Of course, the specific terms will depend upon individual factors. Yet when everything is spelled out in advance misunderstandings should be minimized. Let us consider Lucretia, with her tendency to fly off the handle. It is conceivable that she might, in a moment of fury, decide that she wants out of the program immediately. For her, perhaps a clause requiring a forty-eight-hour cooling-off period before a final decision to terminate should be stipulated. It is also possible that the advocate for a young retarded child might become disturbed by some aspect of the program. The contract could stipulate that any decision to terminate the program should be preceded by a meeting in which questions or misconceptions can be clarified.

Institutional review. The U.S. Department of Health, Education and Welfare (1971) requires that all institutions have permanent human-rights committees to review program proposals before submission for H.E.W. funding. Each committee is to be composed of people from varying backgrounds who are not directly involved professionally in the activity under review (in a school system perhaps the school board or committee; in an institution perhaps the board of directors). Although the guidelines were developed to protect experimental "subjects" in grant and contract programs supported by H.E.W. and although the client in a behavior-analysis program is not necessarily a "subject" in the same sense, the dividing line is a fine one. Some behavior-analysis programs have minimal "experimental" overtones, because they apply frequently replicated "standard" procedures (for example, contingent teacher attention or the "good-behavior game"). Others really are "experimental," as when a procedure based on laboratory studies is first applied. Technically there should be little need for scrutiny by a human-rights committee of behavior-analysis programs designed to attain standard goals of a school or institution by means of procedures that involve little experimentation and no external funding. We argue, however, that discretion is the better part of valor. Both the goals and the procedures of all behavior-analysis programs that are likely to be questioned by the public or that obviously deviate from standard practice should be subject to such approval before being adopted. The review process may be expedited if program-proposal forms and consent forms are prepared for clients, parents, and advocates. Approval then consists of simple written permission for programs not involving deprivation, negative procedures, or coercion. Any of the latter categories should be subject to more elaborate scrutiny.

Our main reason for this position is pragmatic. A board can be selected to represent the various points of view of the community; it can then serve as a "minicommunity." If it expresses hearty approval of a goal or procedure, it is likely that the larger community will share that enthusiasm. The likelihood of enduring community support is enhanced because committee members participate in the design. On the other hand, when board members are reluctant to approve a program, the behavior analyst should rethink it. Perhaps the goals or procedures have not been adequately explained or justified. Possibly they are not appropriate in view of policy, legality, or prevailing community standards.

Let us examine some actual episodes. It was common practice for residents of state institutions for the retarded in one state to be deprived of meals at the whim of their caretakers. A behavior-change program in which only certain destructive acts would result in delayed access to food was devised. The program, because it was clearly set forth, produced a wave of professional and public outrage. Reliance on food deprivation as an instrument of behavior change was then prohibited altogether. Had a board of community representatives scrutinized the behavior-change program ahead of time two things would probably have happened: The board would have been alerted to the prevailing and far more unethical practice of unsystematic food deprivation and could have voiced opposition to the proposed program; and the behavior-change agents would then have had to devise some other, generally acceptable intervention procedure. The public furor could have been avoided, and the clients would have been more effectively and ethically served.

A second example illustrates how caution helps to avoid problems. A large city school system had a very high proportion of low-achieving students. A behavior-analysis program was discussed with the school committee. The committee, recognizing the need for effective intervention, supported the proposed program, but, reflecting the feelings of the community it represented, it stipulated that neither food nor material rewards be used in the program. The behavior analyst, after some effort, was able to marshal an array of powerful reinforcers that were acceptable to board members. Community support thus endured throughout the program.

Clearly, taking the extra step of seeking institutional review can serve a number of distinct purposes. It can provide a sounding board for community opinions. It can identify areas that require clarification and highlight situations in which stronger justification is needed. It can provide the impetus to revise or refine goals and procedures in order to enhance the likelihood of committee and community support. Finally, but perhaps most important from a humanitarian point of view, the public nature of applied behavior analysis may bring prevailing practices to the attention of the community. Those that are unacceptable may be prohibited, thus ensuring protection of clients' rights even when other methods and approaches are adopted.

PROVIDING ETHICAL SAFEGUARDS

The measures discussed—client involvement in goal selection; advocacy; participation by parent, staff, and community representatives; contracting; and institutional review—all provide safeguards for the client's rights. Behavior analysts who have relied on those measures can feel confident that their goal-selection procedures are ethically responsible. One additional factor, voluntariness, should also be considered before final goal selection, however.

Voluntariness, Incentives, and Threats in Goal Selection

When a behavior analyst speaks of "voluntariness," a conceptual problem may arise. *Webster's New Collegiate Dictionary* defines "voluntary" as "1. Proceeding from the will or from one's own choice or full consent. 2. Unconstrained by interference; self-impelled; freely given, done etc." (1949, p. 957). Other definitions include nonoperational words like "intent" and "will." As the procedural sections of this book will demonstrate repeatedly, the individual is continually subject to environmental rewards and constraints. Some of the rewards are obvious: salaries, material gifts, awards, bonuses. There are also subtle rewards: eye contact, nods of approval, agreement from some, disagreement from others, privileges, certain activities, observing other people being rewarded, and an endless array of others. The behaviorist argues that a response persists when it has previously yielded at least some reward (been **reinforced**,[2] in technical language) and continues to do so occasionally. Similarly, threatened or experienced negative consequences, including simple elimination of rewards, also constantly operate upon behavior. Some constraints are obvious: Speeding over 90 miles an hour may lead to arrest or death on the highway; failure to fulfill job responsibilities may lead to dismissal; failure to complete assignments results in poor grades. Others are far more subtle: uninteresting conversation greeted by inattention, subtle expressions of disapproval in response to particular expressions of particular opinions; omission of approval in response to others. How long would any of us continue studying if we were not rewarded with grades, salary increments, approval from important people in our lives, self-satisfaction, or at least potentially useful or provocative mate-

---

[2] Reinforcement will be discussed in Units 8–10.

rial? Do we avoid negative consequences—poverty, loss of prestige, social derision —by remaining in a job, attending school, maintaining a household, and so on? It is apparent that in all our lives some rewards and constraints have been or still are in operation. Total voluntariness, from the behavioristic point of view, is a myth; positive and negative constraints are never absent from the individual's life.

In *Beyond Freedom and Dignity* (1971) B. F. Skinner suggests that it is far more appropriate to recognize that both obvious and subtle positive and aversive environmental events do affect behavior. Society and its members can then plan lives in which alternative positive outcomes can be maximized through positive means. This conception of voluntariness is the one that is appropriate for the behavior analyst concerned with ethical goal selection. The term must be defined to acknowledge the role of past and present events, along with the expressed feeling that it is "voluntary" by members of the community. It can be more clearly conceptualized as the client's voicing agreement with the goals of the behavior-change program in the absence of coercion.

What is coercion? Its two forms are oppressive force and disproportionately powerful incentives. If a behavior results in either of those two consequences, we cannot speak of voluntariness. Let us consider a couple of examples.

Willie comes to class, takes out his material rapidly, and promptly begins to work. His performance is qualitatively excellent. When the teacher requests assistance with an exhibit, Willie offers to participate.

Most of Ms. Hydra Carbon's students are busily at work on their chemistry assignments. Two are off in the corner, laughing and distracting the others. Ms. Carbon moves about the room commenting positively on the work being done by the attentive students and ignoring the laughing students.

First, some aspects of Willie's reinforcement history: Willie has received A's for working well in the past. His girlfriend admires his seriousness. His teacher smiles and nods at him from time to time as he works on his assignment and gestures appreciatively when he offers to participate. Willie looks at his work and sees that he has learned to solve a challenging problem: "That was a tough one, but I did it." Is Willie's performance voluntary? Let us suppose that his dad had promised him a motorcycle, car, or trip to Europe if he did well in his studies? Would Willie's behavior still be voluntary?

Ms. Carbon's classroom-management procedure may also have been rewarded in the past by desired student reactions—the laughing students' settling down to work, positive evaluation from a supervisor, approval from a peer, and self-approval ("I'm a patient teacher, and that pays off!"). Is her behavior voluntary? Perhaps she has been promised that if she does not shout at her students so much she will be promoted to department head. Would her behavior still be labeled voluntary?

On the other hand, Willie may have experienced frowns, poor grades, and ridicule from his friends for poor performance in the past. Maybe his dad denied him the use of the car for the remainder of the year if his grades did not improve. Would any of those threatened negative consequences mean that Willie's classroom performance is not voluntary? Would disapproval by the supervisor, negative student reactions, or threat of dismissal or reassignment to a less desired position serve as evidence that Ms. Carbon's management procedures were not being voluntarily applied?

We hope that it is apparent that voluntariness is not an absolute; rather it is a condition that falls within a range on each of several continua. In Figure 3.1, just how voluntary is Linus's choice not to pelt Lucy with a snowball? In order to meet the ethical requirements for voluntary goal selection, it is suggested that any incentives and threats be clearly identified and that unduly strong threats or incentives be minimized. Figure 3.2 shows graphically the network of factors related

Figure 3.1 Voluntary behavior change?

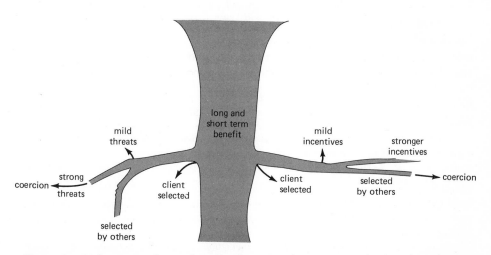

Figure 3.2 Voluntary goal specification. The more clients are involved in the selection of goals that yield short- and long-term benefits, the greater the voluntariness. The further out on the limb of threats and incentives, the greater the coercion. Voluntariness almost breaks off completely as goals are selected by others and powerful threats prevail.

to voluntariness. Note that coercion occurs as incentives and threats become stronger and as the client becomes less involved with goal selection.

Summary

The emphasis in this unit has been on ethics in goal selection. Ethical safeguards are necessary whenever human services are provided. Client involvement; advocacy; parent, staff, and community participation; contracting; and institutional review all help to provide such safeguards. Assuming provision for short- and long-term client benefit as Figure 3.2 shows, the more powerful the threats and incentives, the closer to coercion one comes. Voluntariness disappears completely when goals are selected by others and potential consequences are aversive. Consequently, we should attempt to strive for a balance between effectiveness and incentives or threats. Voluntariness increases as the consequences become less intrusive or more natural.

References

American Psychological Association. *Ethical principles in the conduct of research with human participants.* Washington, D.C.: Author, 1973.

American Psychological Association. *Ethical standards of psychologists.* Washington, D.C.: Author, 1963.

Ayllon, T. & Roberts, M. Eliminating discipline problems by strengthening academic performance. *Journal of Applied Behavior Analysis,* 1974, **7**, 71–76.

Brooks, B. D. Contingency contracts with truants. *The Personnel and Guidance Journal,* 1974, **52**, 316–320.

Budd, K. & Baer, D. M. Behavior modification and the law: Implications of recent judicial decisions. *The Journal of Psychiatry and Law: a special reprint,* Summer 1976, 171–244.

Connecticut Civil Liberties Newsletter, 1974.

Ferritor, D. E., Buckhold, D., Hamblin, R. L. & Smith, L. The noneffects of contingent reinforcement for attending behavior on work accomplished. *Journal of Applied Behavior Analysis,* 1972, **5**, 7–17.

Homme, L., Csanyi, A. P., Gonzales, M. A. & Rechs, J. R. *How to use contingency contracting in the classroom.* Champaign: Research Press, 1970.

Keirsey, D. W. Transactional casework: A technology for inducing behavior change. Paper presented at the meeting of the California Association of School Psychologists and Psychometrists, San Francisco, 1965.

Krumboltz, J. D. *Revolution in counseling: Implications of behavioral science.* Boston: Houghton Mifflin, 1966.

Martin, R. *Legal challenges to behavior modification.* Champaign: Research Press, 1974.

Reynolds, J. Aspects of child advocacy practice. Paper presented for workshop symposium, Counseling and Advocacy, at the annual meeting of the American Psychological Association, Montreal, August 1973.

Schwitzgebel, R. K. *Development and legal regulation of coercive behavior modification techniques with offenders.* (Rockville, Md.: DHEW Publication, No. (HSM) 73–9015, 1971.

Skinner, B. F. *Beyond freedom and dignity.* New York: Knopf, 1971.

Sulzer, B., Hunt, S., Ashby, E., Koniarski, C. & Krams, M. Increasing rate and percentage correct in reading and spelling in a fifth grade public school class of slow readers by means of a token system. In E. A. Ramp and B. L. Hopkins (Eds.), *A new direction for education: Behavior analysis*. Lawrence: University of Kansas, 1971.

Sulzer, E. Reinforcement and the therapeutic contract. *Journal of Counseling Psychology*, **9**, 271–276.

U.S. Dept. of Health, Education and Welfare. *Institutional guide to DHEW policy on protection of human subjects*. Bethesda: Author, 1971. (DHEW Publication No. [NIH] 72–102).

Webster's new collegiate dictionary. Springfield, Mass.: Merriam, 1949.

Wexler, D. B. Token and taboo: Behavior modification, token economies and the law. *California Law Review*, 1973, **61**, 81–109.

Winett, R. A. & Winkler, R. C. Current behavior modification in the classroom: Be still, be docile. *Journal of Applied Behavior Analysis*, 1972, **5**, 499–504.

From Goals to Objectives

After mastering the material in this unit, you should be able to

1. Define each of the following terms and offer distinctive illustrations:
   a. Criterion level
   b. Topography
   c. Behavioral dimensions
   d. Behavioral objective
   e. Task analysis

2. Develop and specify a single behavioral objective for a client or yourself, following the format provided in this unit: List the problem, goal, and objective. Justify the selection of the objective by explaining how it may be readily accomplished and how it meets the criteria for acceptability summarized in Figure 4.1.

SELECTING THE GOAL

It should be apparent from the discussion in Unit 3 that goal selection is a judgmental process. What we have attempted to do is to provide the reader with some guidelines for selecting mutually acceptable goals that are meaningful, relevant to clients and others in their lives, and ethically responsible. Once the process has begun and behavioral contracts or other decision-making arrangements have been initiated, various possible goals are considered. If there are more than one, it is advisable to give high priority to a goal that both meets the criteria for acceptability already discussed and is likely to be readily accomplished. The rationale

40

for the latter advice will become clearer in the units on reinforcement. For the moment, we note simply that success in reaching a goal that is readily attainable encourages participants to continue with other goals that may require more effort or time. In Figure 4.1 we summarize several issues involved in setting priorities for goal selection. Answers to the questions raised in the figure should assist behavior analysts and their clients to select goals cooperatively.

Behavioral objective { 1 – Desired Response / 2 – Situation / 3 – Criteria

SPECIFYING THE BEHAVIORAL OBJECTIVE

Once a goal has been selected, the next major step is to refine it into a behavioral objective. A **behavioral objective** is a precisely specified goal, stated so that three essential elements are made clear: the desired **response**, with all its essential properties, or behavioral dimensions; the *situation* in which the response is to occur, including setting, materials, personnel, and so on; and the **criteria** for determining when the objective has been accomplished (based on Mager, 1962).

Imp.

Specifying Response Properties

Several years ago one of the authors was working with a child who had essentially no functional speech. Almost all her language consisted of "echolelic" repetitions of sounds that she had just heard. One parent would say, for example, "Come here," and, rather than complying, she would say, "Come here." The instructor would say, "What's your name?" and she would respond, "What's your name?" The task was to teach the child to use language in meaningful ways—ways appropriate to situations in the real world—so that she could obtain what she needed, describe events appropriately, supply information to others, and so forth. A behavioral procedure was selected. It was decided that echolelic responses would not be *reinforced*, or rewarded. When they occurred, such reinforcers as food, attention, praise, and so on would be withheld. Conversely, any verbal response that was not echolelic would be immediately reinforced every time that it occurred. Within a few sessions the child had begun to use many new words and phrases. But a very important tactical error in the program became quickly apparent. Because the exact nature of the desired response had not been carefully defined, something odd happened: The child began to say strange, often very inappropriate things. She would repeat phrases from television commercials or talk about plumbing equipment, saying "Fix the faucet" when there was no faucet in the room. In effect, she was being taught to use inappropriate language. After reanalysis, the goal was defined as noncholelic responses with some real relevance to the world about her; they had to be related to objects or events in her present or recently past environment. When only such responses were reinforced, the child's language began to approximate "normal" language.

The point of this experience is that we must be very precise about the nature of the response desired and the situations in which it is to occur. Only then will behavioral procedures be effective. Consideration must be given to the

General

1. Is the goal
   a. Constructive?
   b. Likely to be supported in various settings?
   c. Likely to be maintained in the natural environment?
2. What is the likelihood of success in achieving the goal?
3. Does the behavior analyst have sufficient
   a. Knowledge of procedures?
   b. Competence to implement procedures?
   c. Interest to achieve the goal?
4. Can existing programs achieve the goal more efficiently?
5. Does the goal permit placing more and more responsibility on the client?
6. Is the goal accessible to direct measurement?
7. Does the goal fit appropriately into the task-analysis sequence?

Client's Perspective

1. How important is the goal for the
   a. Client?
   b. Significant others?
2. How much time and effort will be required by the client?
3. Is the goal acceptable to the client?
4. What short-term benefits and costs are likely to accrue to the
   a. Client?
   b. Significant others?
5. What long-term benefits and costs are likely to accrue to the
   a. Client?
   b. Significant others?

Behavior Analyst's Perspective

1. How important is the goal for the
   a. Client?
   b. Significant others?
2. How much time and effort will be required by the behavior analyst?
3. Is the goal acceptable to the behavior analyst in terms of
   a. Personal ethical values?
   b. Professional ethical values?
   c. Legal guidelines?
4. What short-term benefits and costs are likely to accrue to the
   a. Client?
   b. Significant others?
   c. Behavior analyst?
5. What long-term benefits and costs are likely to accrue to the
   a. Client?
   b. Significant others?
   c. Behavior analyst?

Significant Others' Perspectives

1. How important is the goal for the
   a. Client?
   b. Significant others?
2. How much time and effort will be required by others?
3. Is the goal acceptable to others in terms of
   a. Personal ethical values?
   b. Legal guidelines?
4. What short-term benefits and costs are likely to accrue to the
   a. Client?
   b. Significant others?
5. What long-term benefits and costs are likely to accrue to the
   a. Client?
   b. Significant others?

Figure 4.1   Goal selection: Setting priorities (Sulzer-Azaroff and Ramey, 1976)

The goals must be precisely specified
1 – Topography   4 – Duration
2 – Intensity   5 – accuracy
3 – Frequency   6 – acceptable

Specifying the Behavioral Objective   43

various **behavioral dimensions** of the response. If appropriate, its **topography,** its form or shape, should be specified. The dancer's arm should extend from the body at such and such an angle. The letter "b" should be written with a straight line, varying no more than 10 degrees from the perpendicular, and a partial circle touching the perpendicular line in two places; the bottom point of contact should be exactly at the bottom of the perpendicular line and the top point of contact no higher than halfway up and no lower than one third of the way up the line.

Sometimes the dimension of **intensity** has to be specified. A teacher is instructed to praise and reprimand *softly*, so that other students do not overhear. The student learning to form letters must write with sufficient intensity so that the letter can be read from 18 inches away. The ball must be thrown with sufficient intensity so that it reaches another person five feet away.

The **frequency** of a response within a given period—solving ten physics problems a day or tying shoes three times in a row per session—may be important. *Duration*—the length of time that a dancer exercises or a telephone conversation lasts—may also be important. The *accuracy* of a response must often be defined: Exactly what constitutes a correct response? A full sentence? Phrases identical to those in the book or phrases that incorporate key words? Is an abbreviation acceptable? Are responses considered correct if they meet a set of prespecified criteria? For writing a theme, the criteria may include a minimum of five paragraphs, containing a thesis sentence and several examples or other related material; each paragraph following the previous one in a logical sequence; and all sentences complete. For a musical composition they may include so many bars and harmony conforming to rules indicated in the textbook. For a sculpture criteria may be that it not fall over and that its parts be securely attached. For making a telephone call correct dialing and perhaps an even distribution of talking and listening may be specified. In our examples, there is a progression from objective to subjective criteria. When works of art and social behaviors are identified as *accurate* or *acceptable,* much subjectivity intrudes, and specification of response properties is difficult. In his clever book *Goal Analysis* (1972) Mager suggests one approach to identifying crucial details by which to judge the acceptability of a response. Knowledgeable judges are asked to sort a great many response samples into two piles, acceptable and not acceptable, along one dimension related to goals; the dimension may be organization, craftsmanship, politeness, cooperativeness, and so on. Then the sorter looks at the two piles and describes how they differ. Well-organized themes may have clearly specified central topics mentioned in the opening sentences. A well-crafted object may have smooth surfaces and symmetrical components. Perhaps a taped conversation includes few interruptions. Once a series of such sorting processes has taken place, the dimensions agreed upon by the judges can be listed as the standard of acceptability.

Specifying the Situation

The next essential in selecting the behavioral objective is to specify the situation, the conditions under which the desired response is to occur. If Dexter is to write more reports, is he to do all his preparation during social-studies class, or can he work during other periods or any time at all? To what materials can he have access? If Lucretia is to play cooperatively with other children, sharing materials and not hitting, pushing, or grabbing, how many children is she to play with, where, and with what toys? Obviously, it would not be appropriate for her to share toys during her nap or at mealtimes. The *conditions* delineate the realistic limits within which the response is to occur.

Specifying Criteria

The criterion is the standard for determining whether or not the behavioral goal has been reached. For example, preliminary data show that a youngster who is seriously asthmatic consistently fails to follow his physician's instructions. The doctor knows that her patient is capable of complying, for he has occasionally done so in the past. The goal for the child is that he comply with instructions to use his inhalation equipment. Must he use the equipment a certain number of times every single day? If the physician considers that 90 percent compliance for three weeks in a row would demonstrate success, the criterion is stated as 90 percent of the prescribed number of uses each day for three weeks. Because *correct* use of the equipment is essential, the doctor might add the criterion that an 80 percent correct level is required for achievement of the terminal goal.

A behavioral criterion usually includes a statement of the anticipated *frequency* of the response over time (rate) and the *duration* of the response—how long it should persist. That is, Lucretia must offer toys upon request at least once in each of three out of four half-hour blocks of time every day for two weeks.

Above all, the essential standard for determining whether or not a significant behavioral change has occurred is, according to Baer, Wolf, and Risley (1968), its *practical importance*. If behavior has been altered enough to satisfy significant individuals like teachers, parents, and students, the criterion can be said to have been met. Such a criterion, *which is mutually agreeable to all*, should be established before administration of the behavior-change program in order to avoid subsequent indecision, disagreement, or bias in determining whether or not the goal has been reached. The **criterion level** selected should not be the *ideal* level but the minimum that is *acceptable* to all. This choice does not, of course, prevent higher levels of performance; it simply serves as a guide to evaluating the effectiveness of the behavior-change program.

Sample Objectives

The following illustration is presented in a format that we have found useful in teaching the writing of objectives.

Illustration 1:
Problem: Lucretia does not play cooperatively with other children.
Goal: Lucretia will offer toys on request.
Situation or Conditions: Two other children, array of toys.

Criterion Level: At least once in each of three out of four half-hour blocks of time each day.
Behavioral Dimensions (FITA):
    Frequency (duration): two weeks.
    Intensity: not applicable.
    Topography: toy handed to (not thrown to) playmate.
    Accuracy: not applicable.
Behavioral Objective: Playing with two other children and an array of toys, Lucretia will hand a toy to a playmate upon request at least once in each of three out of four half-hour blocks each day for two weeks.

Many different objectives could have been developed in connection with the problem of uncooperative play. For example, topography could have been Lucretia's giving permission for another child to use her toys. But the concerned parties agreed that the dimensions and criterion level chosen were satisfactory.

Illustration 2:
Problem: Violet does not converse with her peers.
Goal: Violet will answer and ask questions.
Situation or Conditions: Recreation room, free play with small group of other children.
Criterion Level: At least one answer and one question.
Behavioral Dimensions (FITA):
    Frequency (duration): at least once a day for five consecutive days.
    Intensity: loudly enough to be clearly heard by the counselor.
    Topography: answering and asking questions verbally.
    Accuracy: speaking in complete sentences.
Behavioral Objective: Violet will ask and verbally answer questions with complete sentences loudly enough to be heard across the room by the counselor at least once daily for five consecutive days during free play.

Additional Resources

Many resources are available to assist designers of behavioral programs to achieve meaningful personal, social, academic, and vocational objectives. A sample listing is provided at the end of this unit.

Task Analysis = *To brake down the component of behavior into some simpler components.*

. . . A **task analysis** describes the subskills and subconcepts a student must acquire in order to master a complex skill or an interrelated set of concepts and principles. Such an analysis should be complete, presented in the proper amount of detail, with relationships among component skills and concepts clearly specified. It should indentify when and under what circumstances each component skill is to be performed. In short, the task analysis provides a blueprint of the things a student must master if he is to reach the objectives that have been set. (Anderson & Faust, 1973, p. 82) [emphasis added]

Behavioral objectives may be simple or complex, depending upon their components and the repertoires and abilities of those who are to achieve them. For Dexter, "Handing in his completed assignment each day before 3:00 P.M. for two weeks in a row" is a fairly simple response. The behavioral requirement probably does not have to be broken down into component tasks. The objective for

Lucretia, however, is far more complex. "Offering toys on request" should be broken down further:

Hands toy to another child on request = selects appropriate toy +
places toy gently in hand of another child.

Sometimes these behaviors need to be broken down into even finer components. Cutting cake with a fork appears to be very simple behavior, but not for Fern. For her the task must be broken down into very tiny components: the position of the cake plate before her, the correct grasp, the proper motion, and so on. Skidgell and Bryant (1975) have performed a complete task analysis of dining skills for individuals severely deficient in them. Similar analyses are being undertaken for various skills by behavioral programmers in many settings for the severely and profoundly retarded, as well as for much more sophisticated clients like college students, guidance counselors, and even applied behavior analysts (Bernal et al., 1976).

   Before attempting to instruct someone else in a task, we must describe the components precisely for ourselves. Before conducting a full-fledged task analysis, if it seems warranted by complex objectives, we recommend extensive reading (for example, Anderson & Faust, 1973) and practice (see Sulzer-Azaroff, McKinley & Ford, 1977).

Summary

In this unit we have focused on one major aspect of designing a behavior-analysis program: the selection of an objective and its components in a way that will satisfactorily resolve the issues raised in Figure 4.1. We have presented two illustrations in a format that should help the reader to write behavioral objectives. Figure 4.2 provides a summary of the components of the applied behavior analysis model developed so far. Next we shall turn to measurement, which provides clear evidence whether progress toward objectives has or has not been made.

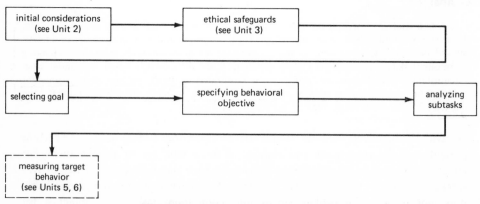

Figure 4.2 Selecting goals and objectives.

Some Recommended Sources for Preparing Objectives

Bloom, B. S. (Ed.) *Taxonomy of educational objectives: Handbook I: Cognitive domain*. New York: McKay, 1956.

Gronlund, E. *Stating behavioral objectives for classroom instruction*. New York: The Macmillan Company, 1970.

Instructional Objectives Exchange (IOX), Distribution Center, P.O. Box 24095, Los Angeles, Calif. 90024.

Krathwohl, D. R., Bloom, B. S. & Mosin, B. B. *Taxonomy of educational objectives: Handbook II: Affective domain*. New York: McKay, 1956.

Mager, R. F. *Developing attitudes toward learning*. Palo Alto: Fearon, 1968.

Mager, R. F. *Goal analysis*. Palo Alto: Fearon, 1972.

Mager, R. F. *Preparing instructional objectives*. Palo Alto: Fearon, 1962.

Popham, W. J. & Baker, E. I. *Classroom instructional tactics*. Englewood Cliffs, N.J.: Prentice-Hall, 1973.

Vargas, J. S. *Writing worthwhile behavioral objectives*. New York: Harper & Row, 1972.

Wheeler, A. H. & Fox, W. L. *Managing behavior, Part 5: A teacher's guide to writing instructional objectives*. Lawrence, Kans.: H and H Enterprises, 1972.

References

Anderson, R. C. & Faust, G. W. *Educational psychology*. New York: Dodd, Mead, 1973.

Baer, D. M., Wolf, M. M. & Risley, T. R. Some current dimensions of applied behavior analysis. *Journal of Applied Behavior Analysis*, 1968, **1**, 91–97.

Bernal, G. Hilpert, P., Johnson, K., Peters, J., Ramey, G., Siedentop, D., Souweine, J. & Sulzer-Azaroff, B. Behavior analysis–task analysis: Optimizing reviewer skills. Paper presented at the meeting of the Association for the Advancement of Behavior Therapy, New York, December 1976.

Mager, R. F. *Goal analysis*. Palo Alto: Fearon, 1972.

Mager, R. F. *Preparing instructional objectives*. Palo Alto: Fearon, 1962.

Skidgell, A. & Bryant, R. *The Mansfield training program in dining skills—Training manual*. Mansfield Depot, Conn.: Mansfield Training School, Psychology Department, 1975.

Sulzer-Azaroff, B., McKinley, J. & Ford, L. *Field activities for educational psychology: Carrying concepts into action*. Santa Monica, Ca.: Goodyear Publishing Co. Inc., 1977.

Sulzer-Azaroff, B. & Ramey, G. Priority setting in applied behavior analysis. Talk presented at the meeting of the Midwest Association of Behavior Analysis Association, Chicago, May 1976.

Selecting Observational Systems

After mastering the material in this unit, you should be able to
1. Define the following terms and offer distinctive illustrations:
   a. Precise behavioral measurement
   b. Objective measurement
   c. Valid measurement
   d. Reliable measurement
   e. Dependent variable
   f. Enduring behavioral products
   g. Reactivity
   h. Transitory behaviors
   i. Discrete behaviors
   j. Coefficient of agreement

2. Discuss two factors to consider in selection of dependent variables.

3. Briefly describe how to ensure that observations can be reliably recorded and how to determine whether or not the behavioral measures are reliable.

4. List the advantages of being able to measure permanent products.

5. Define, illustrate, and describe a situation in which each of the following would be the most appropriate observational method. Justify your answers.
   a. Event recording
   b. Duration recording

6. Describe two ways of calculating reliability of event recording. Discuss which is best and why. Construct an illustration for each, and calculate the reliability.

7. Describe how to calculate reliability for duration-recording systems. Construct an illustration, and calculate the reliability.

Lucretia's grandmother came to visit. After spending a day with her only grand-child, she chided her daughter, "How can you say that she is overly aggressive with other children? To me she seems to have improved so much since the last time. I think you're just expecting too much. All youngsters have occasional squabbles." How accurate is Lucretia's grandmother's assessment? Does Lucretia become involved only in occasional little arguments, or is she just as aggressive as she has been?

Some might attempt to answer such questions by talking further with Lucretia's parents and other adults. In an attempt to be more objective, they might prepare a *case study*, citing past and present episodes and conditions in Lucretia's life. A further step toward objectivity would be to obtain information through narrative recording and sequential analyses. Still more precise, however, would be repeated direct measurement of aggressive behavior components, along with measurements of cooperative play. That is the approach in applied behavior analysis.

Precise behavioral measurement is used to determine clearly and objectively the effectiveness of applied behavior-analysis programs and to generate scientific predictions for the future.

. . . underlying every science is observation and measurement, providing a description of events and a way of quantifying them so that experimental manipulation may be ordered. The ultimate goal in science is, of course, an ordering of facts into general, consistent laws from which predictions may be made, but it inevitably starts with observation. (Bachrach, 1962, pp. 30–31)

The subject toward which we now turn is precise behavioral measurement—the selection and implementation of techniques for quantifying behavior so that eventually it can be analyzed experimentally.

Precise behavioral measurement requires selection and implementation of **objective, valid,** and **reliable** measures. By *objective* we mean that the observers who record behavioral data do not allow their own feelings or interpretations to affect their recordings; obviously, the component responses of target behaviors must be very carefully specified. *Valid* measures are those that actually do measure directly the behavior that they are supposed to measure, rather than representing that behavior indirectly in ways subject to distortion through individual interpretation. To be valid, measures must be objective, though objective measures are not necessarily valid. For example, an observer may record instances of parental attention following positive child behavior; if, however, he or she objectively records *all* instances of parental attention, regardless of how the child has behaved, the recording is objective but not valid. A reliable measuring device remains standard, regardless of who uses it on what occasions. Objective, valid, and reliable measures provide the data, or evidence, of any changes that occur throughout a behavior-analysis program; it is upon these data that the accountability of behavior analysis rests. The public may inspect the behavior analyst's data to judge the effectiveness of a particular program. In these days of demand for accountability in human services, the objective measurement required by applied behavior analysis permits satisfaction of such demand.

In previous units we have focused on behavioral goals and objectives. Because the behavioral objective includes the target behavior (the behavior to be altered), the conditions under which the change is to occur, and the standards by which to assess accomplishment of the objective, we are already well on our way to developing an effective measurement system. In the careful designation of response properties that constitute the target behavior, objectivity is maximized: "Lucretia is not to hit other children," rather than "Lucretia is not to be aggressive or hostile." We have seen that the former, directly observable description is much more objective than the latter in that it does not require individuals to determine what is "hostile" and what is not. Specifying the criteria by which attainment of objectives is to be judged provides an indication of the appropriate measure. "Lucretia is to share her toys at least once in each three out of four half-hour blocks of time." This statement indicates that it is "sharing" that must be measured.

SELECTING DEPENDENT VARIABLES

When a target behavior like sharing is translated into quantifiable terms—like "hands toys to others on request within ten seconds"—the measure of the event (here the frequency) is called the **dependent variable**. Naturally the measure of the target behavior is the key dependent variable. But it may also be important to measure other variables (or *parameters*), the values of which may be altered as a function of the program. For instance, we may wish to determine whether or not increased sharing is accompanied by a change in hitting behavior. We would then measure hitting behavior also. Or the counselor interested in seeing how many tasks Dexter completes may also wish to examine the teacher's behavior toward Dexter. Dexter's completion of tasks and the teacher's attention might be the dependent variables selected for measurement. In deciding which dependent variables to select, we must check the sequence analysis and identify the target behaviors and the most frequent contingencies, those that are most apt to suppress, interfere with, or facilitate target behaviors.

Once the dependent variables have been selected, an appropriate measurement system must be chosen. In this unit we focus on selecting valid measures and methods for constructing measurement systems. In the next unit we shall focus on implementing them. These discussions will carry the reader through the next several steps in the behavior-analysis model: selecting a valid and reliable observational recording system to assess baseline performance.

SELECTING VALID MEASURES

We would not use a bathroom scale to measure shoe size or a ruler to determine the weight of a bar bell. A valid measurement system must be appropriate to the variable that it is to measure. In applied behavior analysis there is often general agreement upon what is a valid measure. A clearly stated memory objective is relatively easy to assess by means of tests or interviews. Productivity is determined by counting assembled products. But sometimes it is difficult to discover valid measures for particular behavior. How do we measure responses characterizing an "outgoing child" "creative writer," a "socialized youth"? If we were to stand on a street corner and ask fifty people at random, we would hear many different answers. Let us consider "socialization." For one person a valid measure of socialization is type of clothing. For another it may be the frequency of certain language categories. Another may emphasize posture or nonverbal communication. Still others may mention types of jobs, attendance or punctuality, or rates of overt or subtle aggression.

In applied behavior analysis it is important that all those involved agree that the selected measures are appropriate. Parents may think that a valid measure of socialization is their child's rate of compliance with instructions. The group leader may measure socialization by degrees of neatness of dress. Some behavior analysts might prefer duration of remaining on tasks. Clearly without prior agreement, all these people would be working toward different goals, and very likely they would not agree in the end that the program was successful. Fortunately, when participants share in identifying the problem and selecting the goal, it is easier to obtain agreement on the measures.

If the program is designed so that its results can be generalized to predictions about other clients with similar characteristics, a broader determination of validity may be appropriate. Representative judges may be requested to indicate the extent to which they agree that a given measure is valid. For example, if the goal is to increase creativity in writing, several possible measures may be listed: use of metaphors, number of words, descriptions of sensory impressions, and so on. Several acknowledged experts may then be asked to select those measures that they believe most valid in assessing creativity in writing.

Writing samples from before, during, and after a behavioral intervention can be gathered to demonstrate effectiveness. The panel of judges can be presented with these samples in random order and asked to sort them along the dimension that was to have been measured, in this instance creativity. If the writing samples judged most creative are those that scored high on the behavioral measures and if those rated least creative by the judges are those that scored low, then there is confirmation that the measures are valid. Furthermore, when demonstrated changes in measured responses are coupled with *consumer satisfaction* data (Braukmann et al., 1975), measured by positive ratings from the public served by a particular program, reported changes can be said to have been validly measured.

SELECTING RELIABLE MEASURES

Aunt Minerva has a bathroom scale that varies as much as five pounds from one weighing to the next. If she weighs herself once and the scale reads 150 pounds, she steps off and immediately steps on again. She repeats this process until the scale reads 145 pounds. At that point she walks away smiling: "The diet is working." Of course, her conclusion may be erroneous. The scale is not reliable, and she really has no way of knowing whether the diet is working or not. A reliable scale, one that measures consistently, would provide her with more appropriate evidence. Behavioral measurement requires the same sort of consistency. Before formal data can be collected, it is necessary to ensure that observations can be reliably recorded. This goal is best accomplished through *operationalizing* target behavior precisely and training and supervising those who record the behaviors.

Behavior analysts must demonstrate that their recording systems are reliable. One way is to try simultaneous recording by two independent observers.[1] There must be close agreement between the two, demonstrating that the behavior under observation is being measured in the same way. If a high percentage of agreement is not obtained, any recorded change in observed behavior by a single observer may reflect a change in observing and recording responses, rather than in the observed behavior itself (Baer, Wolf & Risley, 1968). One source of error, for instance, might be an observer's expectations: He or she might err without awareness, recording results in an anticipated direction. For example, if the observer is aware that a reinforcer has been presented, he or she may be more likely to record an increase in behavior. If the reinforcer has been withdrawn, the observer may record a decrease in behavior. Reliable observers should not be informed of the experimental manipulation; they should be informed only of what behavior is to be observed.

To ensure themselves of consistency, observers may record their measures directly while the behavior is being video- or audio-taped. Later, they can then record the same behavior independently from the tape. The level of agreement can be assessed for **reliability** if a second or third independent observer scores the same behavioral sample. Such procedures have been used to ensure that quiz papers are being scored reliably. Students in a **personalized system of instruction** (**PSI**) course (Keller, 1968) took quizzes and brought their answer sheets to a proctor for scoring. To approximately every tenth quiz a sheet of carbon paper and a second blank quiz paper were attached. The carbon copies could be scored independently to determine how closely the scorers agreed (Sulzer-Azaroff et al., 1976). For a grade-school project, quiz papers were scored on a sheet, rather than directly on the quiz papers (Sulzer et al., 1971). Two independent ratings could then be compared. In one project in which housekeeping skills were taught to young retarded women being prepared for community placement (Thomas et al., 1976), reliability on evaluation of neatness in folding clothes, rated according to preselected criteria, was assessed by a second judge, who rated the folded clothing independently. A similar method was used to evaluate reliability in recording of floor sweeping and table wiping. Later, in the section on recording techniques and their implementation, specific methods for calculating reliability coefficients will be discussed. A reasonable rule of thumb is that the percentage of agreement between the two sets of observations should reach 80 and preferably higher. For a relatively simple and clear behavior, like accurate spelling, addition or buttoning, however, a much higher coefficient should be demanded.

[1] **Inter-observer agreement assessment.**

BEHAVIOR-RECORDING TECHNIQUES

Once valid and reliable measures have been identified, a method of recording those measures must be selected. Several methods can be adopted by behavior analysts. When a behavior produces an *enduring product*, one sort of recording is appropriate; when the results are *transitory*, others are preferred.

Measures of Permanent Product

Some behavior leaves physical evidence in the form of an enduring product. Correctly completed arithmetic problems are written on paper and can be preserved. Assuming that the complexity and difficulty of the problems are kept constant, we can simply count the numbers of correctly completed arithmetic problems and compare differences in rate under different conditions. The number of paragraphs written, of reports turned in, of beds made, of dresses sewn, of woodworking projects completed, of windows broken, and of graphs drawn can all be directly measured, either as soon as they occur or later. There are several advantages to measuring permanent products. The validity of quantitative or qualitative measures can be demonstrated easily if independent judges are asked to evaluate the products by their own criteria: "Which arithmetic paper is better?" or "Rate these papers on a seven-point scale from 1 = terrible to 7 = great." Strong agreement between the behavioral and judgmental ratings helps to validate the measures.

Reactivity, the effects produced by experimental procedures themselves, may distort the validity of the data. For example, when the environment is altered by the presence of live observers or elaborate recording equipment, it may be difficult to separate the effects of these changes from those produced by the behavior-change program itself. Professor Fogg has brought his multimedia training program to impress working personnel with the importance of making frequent contacts with clients. The next day the professor visits the workshop and records the number of contacts between supervisors and clients. He returns on two other occasions, a month apart. Will the data collected be valid? Probably not. Supervisors may simply be reacting to Professor Fogg's presence—recalling his message that contacts should be increased. Because permanent products may be measured after a passage of time, such reactivity can be minimized.

Permanent products are also easier to assess for reliability of measurement. A workshop supervisor and a group of clients are involved in a program designed to increase productivity. The supervisor is to increase her number of contacts with clients. Both supervisor and clients keep logs of such contacts, specifying dates and times. With records of this kind it is relatively simple to obtain a reliability score from comparison of the logs, following the formula

$$\frac{\text{number of agreements (A)}}{\text{number of agreements (A)} + \text{number of disagreements (D)}} = \frac{A}{A + D}$$

Measuring Transitory Events

Many kinds of behavior with which behavior analysts are concerned do not yield permanent products. Their measurement is more difficult. Sitting quietly and attending to a task, contributing to group discussions, smiling, placing toothpaste on a brush, praising staff members, fighting, tardiness, and the like are transitory, in that they cannot be assessed accurately after the fact. In order to measure such behavior, it is necessary to record observations while it is going on or to find some method of preserving it. To record behavior as it occurs usually requires the presence of a live observer, some instrument like an audio or video tape recorder to preserve the event, or closed-circuit television to transmit an image of the event to another area for observation.

Event recording. **Event recording** is the counting of the times that a specific behavior occurs in a specific interval: ten minutes, a session, a class period, a day, the duration of a meal or a television program. Recording may be accomplished by trained observers employed for that purpose, contingency managers, or even clients themselves (Fixsen, Phillips & Wolf, 1972).

Event recording is particularly appropriate for measuring responses that are discrete, those that have clearly definable beginnings and ends. The numbers of pages completed, days present, answers correct, paper airplanes thrown, bites by sibling, and experiments or tasks successfully completed, as well as the minutes late in arrival, are all discrete events. These events can be recorded in various ways: on a check list, with pencil and paper, with some sort of reliable wrist counter (Lindsley, 1968), with a hand counter (like those used to count the number of people who enter museums, or a shopping center) or with electromechanical counters. Another way to record events is to transfer toothpicks, beans, pennies, or some other type of small object from one pocket to another.

Task analyses lend themselves nicely to event recording. The operationalized sub-components are simply listed with spaces in which presence or absence can be checked off. In Figure 17.2 (Unit 17), the task of shampooing hair (Gustafson, Hotte & Carsky, 1976) is easily measured by recording each sub-task as a separate event. In finer analyses, the component tasks can be rated on a scale, for example, 1= none, 2=some, 3=all. Figure 5.1 shows a portion of Flossie's dining-skills chart. Breakfast, lunch, and dinner (B, L, and D) are scored for each day: 1 if the target behavior does not occur, 2 if it occurs sometimes but not throughout, and 3 if it persists throughout the entire meal.

A counting instrument popular with behavior analysts is the abacus wrist or watch band (Mahoney, 1974). It consists of four or more rows of nine beads attached tautly (to prevent sliding) to a wide, usually leather band. Each row represents a different place value: ones, tens, hundreds, thousands, and so on. Each time that an event occurs a bead is moved on the ones column of the abacus. When the tenth event occurs, all beads in the ones column are returned to their original position, and one bead in the tens column is shifted. When the 100th

	Monday			Tuesday			Wednes-day			Thursday			Friday			Saturday			Sunday		
	B	L	D	B	L	D	B	L	D	B	L	D	B	L	D	B	L	D	B	L	D
Eats bite-sized pieces (less than 1 inch square)																					
Uses correct utensils																					
Napkin is folded in half on lap																					
Closes mouth while chewing																					
Talks while mouth is free of food																					

Figure 5.1   Task analysis check list: Dining skills.

event occurs, the beads in the tens column are reset, a bead is shifted in the hundreds column, and so on (see Figure 5.2).

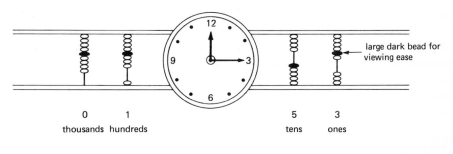

= 153

Figure 5.2   Wrist abacus.

Reliability of event recording.   An observer recorded that Lucretia hit Violet over the head with her plastic sand spade fifteen times. How could we be certain that the events were recorded reliably? We could position a second observer some distance from the first and ask both to record hitting behavior simultaneously. Then we could compare the two totals. The formula for estimating reliability is

$$\frac{\text{smaller total}}{\text{larger total}}.$$

If the second observer recorded 12 hits, the formula would read $\frac{12}{15}$ or .80. This estimate of reliability may be inexact, however. It is possible that observer 1 has counted fifteen episodes and missed another ten. Observer 2 may have missed several episodes recorded by observer 1 and scored several missed by observer 1. When informal observation suggests that some target responses are being missed by observers, then, to ensure the reliability of event recording, observational periods should be broken down into intervals, as in Table 5.1.

TABLE 5.1.   EVENT RECORDING WITHIN INTERVALS

Observer 1		Observer 2		Agreement
Time	Number of Events	Time	Number of Events	
10:00	1111	10:00	111	.75
10:15	111	10:15	111	1.00
10:30	11111 111	10:30	11111 1	.75

At least with this sort of comparison, we can be more confident that both observers are more likely to have recorded the same events.

Flossie and her mother wanted to record the number of times that Flossie screamed at her older brother. Because the independent recorders were often in different parts of the house, they wanted to be sure that each recorded the same screaming episodes. So they divided their recording sheet into a series of time blocks and marked each screaming event in its time segment (Figure 5.3). Narrowing the field some increased the likelihood that the same events would be recorded. Reliability could then be estimated by the formula

$$\frac{\text{agreements}}{\text{agreements} + \text{disagreements}} \times 100 = \% \text{ agreement}$$

A dual watch-counter combination described by Katz (1973) is useful for recording such data.

The reliability of task-analysis scoring is checked by calculating a coefficient of agreement between two individuals' independent scoring of the event, using the same formula

$$\frac{\text{number of agreements}}{\text{number of agreements} + \text{disagreements}}$$

item by item. If Flossie and her dad were independently scoring her dining skills and both scored "eats bite-sized pieces" as 2 during breakfast on Monday, that would be an agreement. If Flossie scored 1 and Dad scored 2, that would be a disagreement. A low agreement score for a week's meals would mean that either the definitions needed further refinements, that both Flossie and her dad needed more practice or training, or that accurate scoring would have to be rewarded. To help decide which course to follow perhaps Flossie's mother could be asked to serve as a reliability observer for a period of time, during which a cue suggest-

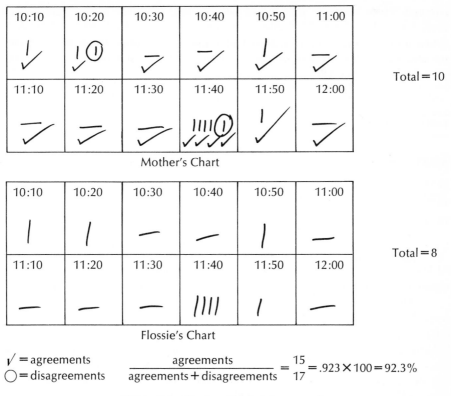

Figure 5.3   Charts of Flossie's screaming.

ing the appropriate refinement might emerge (for example, Flossie may be too rigid, scoring more 1s than she deserves).

Duration Recording

If the duration of an event is of particular concern, then a wall clock, a stop watch, or a time clock can be used. Suppose that Mike's mother is interested in reducing the time that it takes him to begin his yard work. She can start a stop watch at the moment that "work time" is announced and stop it when Mike starts the lawn mower, recording the elapsed time, in this case his **latency** of responding. In one study (Campbell & Sulzer, 1971), it was important to measure how long students had their workbooks available, so that their work rates on specific assignments could be calculated. The students punched cards in a time clock when they were about to start an assignment and punched out when they stopped. As with event recording, the reliability of a **duration-recording** system is estimated by the formula

$$\frac{\text{shorter duration}}{\text{longer duration}} = \text{index of agreement.}$$

Durations within intervals may be compared for greater precision.

Summary

A system of objective, reliable, and valid measurement is basic to all applied behavior-analysis programs. It is only through the use of such a system that change agents can make their clients and the consumers of their services aware of progress. In this unit we have presented the concepts of validity and reliability of measurement and have introduced the reader to two systems for recording behavioral events. Next we shall turn to some more complex methods of measuring behavior.

References

Bachrach, A. J. (Ed.) *Experimental foundations of clinical psychology*. New York: Basic Books, 1962.

Baer, D. M., Wolf, M. M. & Risley, T. R. Some current dimensions of applied behavior analysis, *Journal of Applied Behavior Analysis*, 1968, **1**, 91–97.

Braukman, C., Fixsen, D. L., Kirgin, K., Phillips, E., Phillips E. & Wolf, M. M. Achievement Place: The training and certification of teaching parents. In W. S. Wood (Ed.), *Issues in evaluating behavior modification*. Champaign: Research Press, 1975. Pp. 131–152.

Campbell, A. & Sulzer, B. Motivating educable mentally handicapped students toward reading and spelling achievement using naturally available reinforcers in the classroom setting. Paper presented at the meeting of the American Educational Research Association, New York, February 1971.

Fixsen, D. L., Phillips, E. L. & Wolf, M. M. Achievement Place: The reliability of self-reporting and peer-reporting and their effects on behavior. *Journal of Applied Behavior Analysis*, 1972, **5**, 19–30.

Gustafson, C., Hotte, E. & Carsky, M. Everyday living skills. Unpublished manuscript, Mansfield Training School, Mansfield Depot, Conn., 1976.

Katz, R. C. A procedure for currently measuring elapsed time and response frequency. *Journal of Applied Behavior Analysis*, 1973, **6**, 710–720.

Keller, F. S. Good-bye, teacher. *Journal of Applied Behavior Analysis*, 1968, **1**, 79–89.

Lindsley, O. R. A reliable wrist counter for recording behavior rates. *Journal of Applied Behavior Analysis*, 1968, **1**, 77–78.

Mahoney, K. Count on it: A simple self-monitoring device. *Behavior Therapy*, 1974, **5**, 701–703.

Sulzer, B., Hunt, S., Ashby, E., Koniarski, C. & Krams, M. Increasing rate and percentage correct in reading and spelling in a fifth grade public school class of slow readers by means of a token system. In E. A. Ramp and B. L. Hopkins (Eds.), *A new direction for education: Behavior analysis*. Lawrence: University of Kansas, Follow Through, Department of Human Development, 1971.

Sulzer-Azaroff, B., Johnson, K., Dean, M. & Freyman, D. Experimental analysis of proctor quiz scoring accuracy in personalized instruction. Paper presented at the meeting of the American Psychological Association, Washington, D.C., 1976.

Thomas, C., Sulzer-Azaroff, B., Lukeris, S. & Palmer, M. Teaching daily self-help skills for long term maintenance. In B. Etzel, J. LeBlanc & D. Baer (Eds.), *New developments in behavioral research: Theory, method and application*. Hillsdale, N.J.: Erlbaum Associates, 1976.

Interval Recording and Implementing Observational Systems

After mastering the material in this unit, you should be able to
1. Define the following terms and offer distinctive illustrations:
   a. Whole-interval time sampling
   b. Partial-interval time sampling
   c. Momentary time sampling
   d. Coded interval-recording sheet
   e. Ordinate
   f. Abscissa
   g. Adaptation
   h. Baseline

2. Define, illustrate, and describe a situation in which interval time-sampling recording would be the most appropriate observational method. Justify your answer.

3. Describe a situation in which each of the following would be the most appropriate observational system:
   a. Whole-interval time sampling
   b. Partial-interval time sampling
   c. Momentary time sampling.

4. Discuss how to select and obtain valid and reliable interval-recording data. Construct an illustration, and calculate the reliability.

5. Describe a second method for calculating the reliability coefficient for interval data. Discuss when that method is preferable.

6. Select an observational system for your own or your client's behavior.

7. List various people who can be trained to collect observational data.

8. Discuss the advantages and disadvantages of having observational data collected by a client and by a contingency manager.

9. List at least four different methods of cuing an observer.

10. Discuss the advantages and disadvantages of using automated recording systems.

11. Describe how reliable data could be obtained for a situation of your choice, and how you would train the observers and maintain their observational reliability.

12. List some factors that can reduce a reliability score. Specify how we could control for, or minimize, each factor listed.

13. Describe how we can tell when a representative baseline has been obtained.

14. Describe the major advantages of a baseline.

15. Collect reliable baseline data on your own or your client's target behavior. Also begin to collect data on at least one possible collateral behavior. Graph the data.

Lucretia's parents have decided that they will observe her closely to see how long she plays cooperatively with other children. They want to measure the frequency of cooperative play episodes. It soon becomes obvious, however, that cooperative play does not lend itself to counting. The behavior analyst informs them that their problem is not unique and that systems of measurement have been devised to solve it. Such systems are called "interval time-sample systems."

INTERVAL TIME-SAMPLE RECORDING

Many kinds of behavior are not clearly discrete. It is difficult to tell when some responses begin and end. In such instances interval **time-sampling** recording provides the clearest data. For instance, let us suppose that a client makes many loud and disruptive noises, screeching, shouting, hitting furniture, and rattling his chair. It would be difficult either to count the number of times that each response occurred or to measure their duration. When does one episode of chair rattling end and another begin? As with a stop-action camera, it is possible to assess the presence or absence of such responses within brief time frames. Those data may then be used as samples of the client's behavior. That is what is involved in an interval time-sample recording system. The simple presence or absence of given responses in an interval is scored. If the system requires that the response be emitted throughout the entire interval for its presence to be scored, it is a **whole-interval time-sampling system**. It is used when it is important to know that the behavior is not interrupted. If the system requires only a single instance of the response within the interval to be scored, it is a **partial-interval time-sampling system**.[1] Partial intervals are used to record fleeting behaviors like uttering swear words or making bizarre gestures. If the system requires that the response be occurring at the moment when the interval ends, it is called a **momentary time-sampling system** (Powell, Martindale & Kulp, 1975). Momentary time samples are appropriate to behaviors such as Pearl's stereotyped hand movements and Kevin's thumb-sucking, that are apt to persist for a while. It is reasonable to expect that the sample will represent their occurrence proportionately. For example, a timer sounds at the end of a ten-minute interval. The observer notes whether or not Kevin has his thumb in his mouth.

Lucretia was observed with the same two children for five half-hour play periods each week. An observer watched for ten seconds to determine whether or not she grabbed toys from the other children. If she did, the entire interval was scored minus. If not, the interval was scored plus. The five seconds following each ten-second observation period, the observer spent recording the score. A similar partial-interval time-sample system was used to score parents' attention to Lucretia; then the observer scored the interval with a check. Figure 6.1 is an illustration of the recording sheet that could have been used.

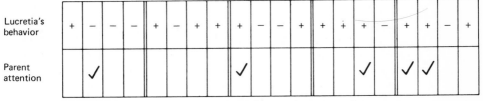

Figure 6.1   Score sheet for partial-interval time-sample system.

A similar example could be used to illustrate the whole-interval time-sampling system. A response would be scored only if it occurred throughout the interval. Grabbing toys, a fairly brief response, would not be an appropriate variable to measure with the whole-interval system. Playing with toys belonging to other children, however, would be appropriate for such a recording method, for that behavior would be likely to persist for some time. In Figure 6.1, any interval throughout which Lucretia held another child's toy would be scored +. (The whole-interval time-sampling system may also be used to estimate the duration of a response, for several scored intervals strung together show that the behavior has persisted. If four fifteen-second blocks were scored + in this example, they would indicate that Lucretia had another child's toy for at least one minute.) Sometimes it is necessary to sample several behaviors simultaneously. A

---

[1] Sometimes called *interval spoilage*.

coded interval-recording sheet can be used for this purpose. A letter is designated
for each behavior. The occurrence of a behavior is scored by making a slash mark
through its letter during the interval. Such a system can be used to take whole-
interval, partial-interval, or momentary time-sample measurements of the behaviors of one subject. It can also be used to measure performance by different individuals in a group. A coded interval sheet would be appropriate for Dexter, who
is concerned about keeping to his tasks. He wants an estimate of the proportion of
time during which he engages in activities that interfere with his school work—
handling other materials or daydreaming, for example. As his counselor has suggested, he will record his teacher's behavior—whether the teacher has attended
to him positively, negatively, or not at all. An excerpt from Dexter's coded sheet
is shown in Figure 6.2.

Dexter	$\not{T}$ M D^{10}	$\not{T}$ M D^{20}	T M $\not{D}^{30}$	T M D^{40}	T M D^{50}
Teacher	$\not{+}$ − 0	+ − $\not{0}$	+ − $\not{0}$	+ − 0	+ − 0
Dexter	T M D^{10}	T M D^{20}	T M D^{30}	T M D^{40}	T M D^{50}
Teacher	+ − 0	+ − 0	+ − 0	+ − 0	+ − 0

Figure 6.2 Coded interval-recording sheet.

The rows of symbols are repeated five more times, so that the entire school day
can be monitored. A very soft click sounds every ten minutes on a prerecorded
audio tape. Dexter then marks the appropriate interval by slashing the code
letter: T for on-task, M for handling other materials, D for daydreaming. The
teacher's behavior is also scored for positive (+), negative (−), or no (0) attention.
Naturally, each of these behaviors has been precisely operationalized. A partial
interval time-sample system is used: If either M and/or D behavior occurs at *any
time during the interval*, the respective code letter is slashed. Otherwise T is
slashed. Note that Dexter has scored himself as on task during the first two intervals but as daydreaming in the third. During those same intervals his record shows
one interval with positive teacher attention and two with no teacher attention.

A coded scoring sheet can also be used just as effectively for whole-interval
and momentary time sampling. Its major advantage is that it simplifies the recorder's job, requiring a simple slash mark, rather than several symbols to be written
within a brief time.

One limitation of interval time-sampling recording is that it is not practical
for studying important, but infrequent behavior. Fights between two particular
students, for example, may occur no more than once a week. Because observations are not continuous, it is possible that such infrequent events will not be
recorded. If such behavior occurs in class as often as once a week, however, it is
probably necessary to do something about it. Arrington (1943) suggests as a general rule that, if the dependent variable occurs on an average of less than once in
fifteen minutes, some other observational procedure should be selected. Usually
event sampling is a good alternative.

VALIDITY AND RELIABILITY OF INTERVAL RECORDING

A valid measure of a behavior permits quantification without distortion. In-seat behavior was measured by Powell, Martindale & Kulp (1975), who filmed the subject for thirty twenty-minute sessions. Time in-seat was measured continuously with a stop watch. Those presumably valid data were used as a standard against which the interval-recording data were compared. The researchers found that whole-interval time sampling consistently underestimated the continuous measure, which is understandable, for the subject had to remain in-seat through the full observational interval to be scored. Partial-interval time sampling consistently overestimated the continuous measure, and momentary time sampling was off both ways. When intervals were short, however, eighty seconds or less, distortion was minimized. Estimation of a behavior that occurs fairly often but is not amenable to event recording should be possible with brief time-sampling intervals. If an interval is reserved for writing down data, it too should be kept brief, for behavior occurring during the observation interval will not be scored. The longer the recording interval, the more will be missed.

Selecting a Valid Interval Time-Sampling System

The purpose of the measurement should determine which of the three interval systems to use in a given situation. It is generally preferable to select a measure that is "conservative" in relation to an intended outcome. For example, because whole-interval time sampling slightly underestimates the duration of the response, it may best be used when striving for an *increase* in the dependent variable. This would tend to bias the outcome by underestimating changes. Suppose the behavioral goal were to increase on-task behavior. A whole 10-second interval time sample would record only those intervals in which on-task responding occurred throughout. Any increases in duration of on-task behavior lasting less than 10 seconds would not be recorded since the full interval was not spanned. The result would be an underestimate of improvement in on-task behavior. If many intervals were scored positively, however, then there was indeed a substantial change, a slightly greater one even than the scores reflect.

Because whole-interval time sampling yields an underestimate, it is not appropriate when we are seeking behavior reduction, of disruptive noise, for example. As it is not likely that noise will persist unabated throughout an interval, many intervals would remain unscored. A partial-interval system is thus more appropriate, for it is biased toward overestimation. A convincing presentation of data would show entire intervals free of the undesirable behavior, especially as the inflationary aspect of the recording system is known. An interval scored for no emission of disruptive noises would thus indicate that not even a brief disruptive noise occurred during that interval.

Provided that it is truly random and that measures are taken frequently enough, the momentary time sample should yield a valid behavioral sample. Because only brief episodes are recorded, response and recording must occur simultaneously, and short intervals are therefore desirable. Let us consider the examples that we have already cited. At any one moment either task performance or disruptive noise could be missed; many more observations are thus required than with the two other time-sample systems, either by an observer doing short-interval recording or by the contingency manager taking data at less frequent intervals but over a longer period. Behaviors that have longer durations, like on-task behavior, are more likely to be sampled by the momentary system than are brief responses, like sneezes or hitting other children. Longer-lasting behaviors thus require fewer observations to represent the "true" value. Regardless of the interval system used, consistency through all baseline and treatment phases is necessary.

The *reliability* of measurement in interval recording rests on the same foundations as in other recording systems. Behavior must be precisely operationalized and recorders carefully trained and supervised. It is easy, however, for recorders to lose track of given intervals, particularly when they are very brief. In our experience, reliability is sacrificed when observational intervals are briefer than ten seconds.

We have described the method for estimating reliability by means of *coefficients of agreements*:

$$\frac{\text{number of agreements}}{\text{number of agreements} + \text{number of disagreements}}$$

When either a very large or a very small proportion of intervals is scored, however, this formula should be altered so that only intervals in which the response is present are included in the calculations (Hawkins & Dotson, 1975). When behavior is infrequent—like acts of aggression that occur once or twice a day—the unaltered formula yields a spuriously inflated coefficient. In Figure 6.3, observers

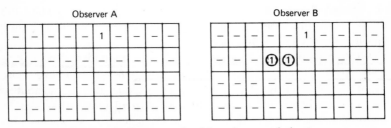

Figure 6.3 Two records of less frequent behavior.

A and B agreed on the sixth interval, but observer B recorded additional episodes in the fourteenth and fifteenth intervals. Overall agreement was not good. Yet the unaltered formula would yield

$$\frac{A}{A+D} \qquad \frac{38A}{38A+2D} = .95$$

The altered version, which takes into account only the three scored intervals (6, 14, and 15) yields a more realistic figure:

$$\frac{1A}{1A + 2D} = \frac{1}{3} = .33.$$

Reliability checks should be made before collection of baseline data, as well as during each phase of the program. An effort must be made to ensure that the observers do not cue one another, that they are indeed observing only the client's responses. A high percentage of agreement (for example, 90 percent) suggests that scoring techniques are reliable (Wright, 1960). If the reliability coefficient falls far below 80 percent, changes should be made before proceeding.

Poor agreement among observers generally results from failure to provide adequate operational definitions. For instance, "aggressive behavior" may be too imprecise a term. Defining "aggression" as hitting that produces an expression of pain (crying, saying "ouch" with a pained expression, and so on) may solve the problem. Subsequent reliability scores will likely be higher and the investigators justified in proceeding.

Obviously, technical skills are necessary to select and implement valid and reliable recording systems. Such skills may be developed under supervision on the job or through intensive reading and practice or participation in "packaged" training workshops like Ellen P. Reese's multimedia workshop "Observing, Defining, and Recording."[2] Table 6.1 offers a guide to the selection of behavior recording techniques, for those who are trying to increase their technical competence.

IMPLEMENTING OBSERVATIONAL SYSTEMS

Having selected appropriate measures, Lucretia's parents and other adults are preparing to record her behavior in group settings. Dexter has selected his plan, and observers have been identified to measure Pearl's behavior in various settings. It is time to proceed with behavioral measurement. Observers must be trained, and an observation schedule planned. Recording and graphing can begin, through an adaptation period followed by a **baseline** phase. Then behavioral procedures and experimental designs can be selected and implemented.

Behavioral-Recording Staff

Human-services agencies for children and youth should employ *behavioral technicians*. Their primary function is to design and implement observational recording systems, to supervise data collection, and to design and execute graphing schemes for continual monitoring (see Sulzer-Azaroff, Thaw & Thomas, 1975). Increasingly, state civil-service departments, for example Minnesota, are building

[2] Department of Psychology, Mount Holyoke College, South Hadley, Mass.

TABLE 6.1.   A GUIDE TO SELECTING BEHAVIORAL RECORDING TECHNIQUES[a]

Type of Measure	Definition	Example	Advantages and Disadvantages
1. Permanent Product Recording	Records the enduring outcome of the behavior	Number of completed math problems, windows broken, dresses sewn	Readily assessed for reliability of measurement
2. Event Recording	Records the number of times a specific behavior occurs over a specific interval	Number of books read, paper airplanes thrown, meals eaten	1. Appropriate for behaviors that have clearly definable beginnings and ends 2. May be recorded on a checklist, wrist counter, hand counter, or transfer of objects (e.g., pennies) from one pocket to another
3. Duration Recording	Records the length of time a behavior occurs	Length of time to complete homework	May be recorded with the aid of a wall clock, stopwatch
4. Interval Time Sampling Recording	Records the presence or absence of a given response within a time interval		1. Records behaviors that are not clearly discrete 2. Useful for behaviors that occur at least once every 15 minutes
a. Whole Interval Time Sampling	Records the response when it is emitted throughout the entire interval	On-task behavior	1. Tends to underestimate the occurrences of the behavior 2. Useful when it is important to know that the behavior is not interrupted
b. Partial Interval Time Sampling	Records the response when a single instance of the response occurs in the interval	Swearing, bizarre gestures	1. Used to record behaviors that may occur in fleeting moments

TABLE 6.1.   A GUIDE TO SELECTING BEHAVIORAL RECORDING TECHNIQUES[a]
(continued)

Type of Measure	Definition	Example	Advantages and Disadvantages
			2. Tends to overestimate the occurrence of the behavior
c. Momentary Time Sampling	Records the response if emitted at the moment the interval terminates	In-seat behavior, frequent stereotypic behaviors	Useful to record behaviors that are apt to persist for a while

[a] Prepared by Gregory Ramey.

that function into their human-services career ladders. At the present writing, however, such staff positions are more the exception than the rule.

When behavioral technicians are not available, other possibilities must be explored. For example, parents, senior citizens, mentally retarded people (Craighead, Mercatoris & Bellack, 1974), college students on practicum or internship assignments, older children (McLaughlin & Malaby, 1975), peers, or even clients themselves may serve as observers. Some programs designed to alter daily living skills require monitoring in many settings around the clock, which is often particularly difficult. Then either the contingency managers or the clients themselves may have to serve as behavioral recorders.

Engaging clients in observing and recording their own behavior is increasingly popular. Self-observation and recording often lead to subsequent behavior change (Kazdin, 1974), as well as to decreased work loads for behavioral technicians or contingency managers. Furthermore, self-recording is an integral part of self-management or **self-control** programs. Thoresen and Mahoney (1974), for example, consider it "the life blood of effective self-control methods" (p. 41).

A variety of self-recording systems have been used. Many of those previously discussed can be used by clients for recording their own behavior. For example, they can transfer objects from one pocket to another, score the frequency of a particular behavior on a piece of paper, use a counter, and so on. Automated recording systems, like video tapes, have also been used to provide observational feedback to students, teachers, counselors, and others (Hosford, Moss & Morrell, 1976; Kagan, 1972; Thomas, 1971; Walz & Johnson, 1963).

Self-recording has been used with youthful clients, some as young as six years of age (Ballard & Glynn, 1975; Broden, Hall & Mitts, 1971; McCoy et al., 1975; Fixsen, Phillips & Wolf, 1972; Glynn, Thomas & Shee, 1973, Kazdin, 1974; Thoresen & Mahoney, 1974). Self-recording is not, however, as simple to implement as it may at first appear. Thomas (1976) found that second-grade students varied in accuracy of recording from 56 to 95 percent. Accurate and reliable self-recording, though problematic, is much more likely to occur if reinforced (Broden, Hall & Mitts, 1971; Fixsen, Phillips & Wolf, 1972; Kazdin, 1974). Similarly, Thoresen and Mahoney have noted:

> Training in the discrimination and recording of a behavior is essential. Such training may be enhanced by modeling, immediate accuracy feedback, systematic reinforcement, and graduated transfer of recording responsibilities (external to self). . . . Discrete behaviors and simple recording systems appear to enhance self-monitoring accuracy. (1974, p. 63)

As a treatment technique, self-observation and self-recording also entail some problems. The effects are often temporary: "Unless supplemented by additional behavior change influences (e.g., social reinforcement), self-monitoring does not offer promise in the long-term maintenance of effortful behavior" (Thoresen & Mahoney, 1974, p. 63). Furthermore, self-monitoring may not result in any behavioral change at all unless it is accompanied by reinforcement of the target behavior. For example, Ballard and Glynn found that self-recording of writing by third-grade students "did not increase the number of sentences, number of different action words, or number of different describing words, or improve the quality of the stories" (1975, p. 387). Only after self-selected and self-administered reinforcement were added did rates of response increase substantially and stories receive higher ratings for quality. A similar effect was shown with three female adolescent offenders (Seymour & Stokes, 1976). Presenting tokens following recording of work and cues increased particular behaviors, which in turn evoked more staff praise. It is thus helpful for self-recorders to have a vested interest in the progress of the program. Rigorous training and supervision plus frequent reliability assessments are particularly important. When such factors as training and reinforcing contingencies are taken into consideration and implemented, self-recording systems can help to maximize client involvement, save time, and assist the client toward greater self-management or self-control (see Unit 7).

When the contingency manager, who conducts the day-to-day operation of the program, must also record behavioral data, special adjustments are necessary. In a study by Farber and Mayer (1972) the classroom teacher recorded assignments completed. Kubany and Sloggett (1973) have noted, however, that classroom teachers are usually so involved with instructional activities that they occasionally forget data recording and may thus be unreliable. The same would be true of institutional attendants, supervisors in sheltered workshops, and others who are recording their own and clients' behavior: Other activities may demand their attention so that they fail to record data regularly. It is impossible to ask such individuals to record time-sample data in short intervals like ten-second time blocks. In this predicament some solutions are possible.

One alternative is to observe and record intermittently at predetermined random times throughout the time period. Either a momentary sample may be taken, or a whole or partial measure may be taken during a brief interval (like ten seconds). Then the observer returns to the regular task until the next predetermined time. In a prevocational sheltered-workshop training program, the supervisor wished to measure the percentage of on-task behavior by several clients. Because she was usually occupied directly in activities with the clients, it was impossible to record their behavior continuously. A series of random observational times was therefore prearranged. Numbers ranging from one to ten were placed in a bowl. A number was drawn, recorded, then replaced in the bowl. The procedure was repeated many times until a long series of numbers had been noted. Each number indicated the number of minutes that would elapse before the next observation. At all other times the supervisor could go about her usual activities. When each alotted interval had elapsed, she stopped momentarily and recorded the behavior for each client. She tended, of course, to become engrossed in her activities and feared that she would miss the indicated times and even more that she would be reminded to record the behavior only by cues from the clients— that is, when behavior was disrupting—thus biasing the data and causing it to be nonrepresentative. A cuing system was therefore devised to prevent such bias. The numeral series was given to a client whose behavior was not to be recorded. His task was to set a kitchen timer, as recommended by Kubany and Sloggett (1973), for the number of minutes indicated. At the sound of the timer, the supervisor would stop what she was doing and record whether on-task behavior was occurring at that moment or not. In this way a fairly representative and valid sample of data was collected.

With some client populations a kitchen timer may not be appropriate or convenient. Other methods for cuing recording intervals are available: an inexpensive pocket parking-meter reminder, a timer that can be set for intervals up to an hour and then emits a soft buzzing sound (Foxx & Martin, 1971), a click, a chime, or some other pleasant sound prerecorded on a cassette tape. If the chime is distracting to clients, observers may use ear buttons so that they alone hear the signals. A prerecorded cassette tape with an ear button is ideal for cuing unbiased observation. It may remind the observer to locate a client ("Find Pearl"), to "observe hand gestures," to record a "score in box 10," and so on. It can also be programmed to facilitate recording of group behavior ("Scan the group from left to right, and count the number of children who are on-task"). Reliability assessments can be greatly simplified with cassette recorders adapted for dual listening. Other possible devices include a portable pocket-sized timer that operates on battery power and emits an audible tone for a predetermined fixed interval (Worthy, 1968) and one that is fitted into a soap case and signals on a schedule that varies about a predetermined average.[3]

As an alternative to audible cuing systems, a light cue can be arranged. An electrical timer—the type of timer that turns on the morning coffee—is attached to a lamp. Such a timer can also be used to activate the audible cuing system (Bernal et al., 1971). For some clients such a system might prove less obtrusive. Such systems may also be used to cue contingency managers to implement their procedures. Regardless of the system used, because the contingency manager has a vested interest in the outcome of the program, reliability must be assessed regu-

[3] A wiring diagram for this variable "intervalometer" may be obtained from Louis Bowly, Director of Training, Mansfield Training School, Mansfield Depot, Conn.

larly throughout to ensure that there is no drift in the observations. An arrangement should be made for another observer to come in unobtrusively for unscheduled recording sessions. Close agreement between the two observers would assure the contingency manager that the measures had not been severely affected by anticipated outcomes.

Automated Recording Systems

There are times when it is neither practical nor convenient to have an observer present to record behavior. Transitory behavioral events may then be preserved on tapes at various intervals throughout the day. For example, Bernal and colleagues (1971) developed a device for automatically activating a recorder at various points in the daily routine of a family.

Reactivity may be a problem when automated recording is used. Johnson and Bolstad (1975) compared audio tape recording in the home under two conditions: when an observer was present and when he was absent. They found that the observer's presence apparently had no more effect on family behavior than that of a tape recorder. Not that neither has an influence. Roberts and Renzaglia (1965) found that clients who were receiving counseling and were aware that their words were being recorded behaved differently from those who were unaware of being recorded. Other investigators have shown that observers' presence had effects (Mercatoris & Craighead, 1974; White, 1973). Others (Hagen, Craighead & Paul, 1975; Johnson & Bolstad, 1973; Wiggins, 1973) have reported no reactivity after extensive habituation to observation on unpredictable schedules with delayed feedback, which protected the anonymity of the data source for evaluative or nonevaluative purposes. As we shall demonstrate in our section on the collection of baseline data, a sufficient adaptation period must be provided for.

Other automated recording systems include films and video tapes recorded through one-way mirrors, through aluminum shadescreens like the inexpensive aluminum shadescreen box (Brechner et al., 1974), by cameras mounted on walls, and even by nonprofessional operators in the setting. Films and video tapes have the advantage of preserving both motor and verbal behavior, and they can be replayed when the scoring of a behavioral event is questionable. It is not always necessary for live observers to score behavior continuously in order to achieve reliable data. Tape recorders and cameras can be used to sample behavior at preselected times. In one study (Sanders, Hopkins & Walker, 1969) a time-lapse still camera was mounted in a classroom to obtain permanent photographic records of behavioral samples by automatically exposing the film according to a predetermined schedule. The researchers found that their system had several advantages: It saved observer time, the equipment was easily obtained, and records could be stored easily. The method was inexpensive, and the percentage of agreement among scorers was very high. The continued development of instruments designed to preserve transitory behavioral events should result in ever more efficient and reliable recording systems.

Training and Supervising Behavioral Recording Staff

Many target behaviors are simple and precise, and assessment of reliability can be done almost *pro forma*. Multiple-choice quiz answers, single correct answers (like "The square root of 16 is ___✓___"), number of buttons buttoned, number of objects sorted or assembled, as well as clear responses like presence or absence in a setting and location in a room are generally scored reliably, and little training is required. But much socially relevant behavior, with which applied behavior analysis is particularly concerned, is not so clear-cut. Subjectivity can easily confound the measurement of "social isolation," "cooperative behavior," "neatness," and other behavior evaluated judgmentally. In Units 2 and 4 we have discussed the importance of operationalizing such terms by refining them into component responses. Even a response as deceptively simple as "sitting" may, however, be rated differently by different observers. One observer may define a response in which a child has his knees on a chair as sitting, whereas a second may not. To be certain that a given recording system is sufficiently reliable, independent measurements should be taken by at least two observers several times under the conditions that will prevail throughout the program. If the independent measures do not yield high coefficients of reliability, a reliability training program is essential.

Training for reliability may involve more precise identification and communication of component responses or clearer directions for recording data. During training, observers can communicate with one another to clarify definitions and recording methods. One effective method for training observers is to use a video-tape sample of the behavior to be measured. This sample allows repeated presentation of the same material until all observers agree. Resolution of confusing observational problems can be clarified and embodied in a scoring manual. An outstanding example of this process was a scoring manual for dining skills prepared by Skidgell & Bryant.[4] The ultimate test of the reliability of a scoring system is that it can be handed to untrained observers, who then study the scoring system, independently rate a sample of behavior simultaneously with a trained observer, yielding a high reliability coefficient. Eventually observers should demonstrate that they measure behavior under the conditions that will prevail throughout the program as reliably as presumably the *criterion observer*, the observer whose recording serves as a standard against which others are judged. After several sessions of such practice, it can be comfortably assumed that observers are adequately trained.

Maintaining Observational Reliability

Having demonstrated consistently high accuracy in recording over several sessions is no guarantee that reliability will persist. In two reported studies (Fixsen, Phillips & Wolf, 1972; Romanczyk et al., 1973) it was demonstrated that reliability of

[4] A. Skidgell & R. Bryant. *The Mansfield Training Program in Dining Skills.* Mansfield Training School, Department of Psychology, Mansfield Depot, Conn.

measurement fluctuated over time. Romanczyk and colleagues (1973) assessed reliability among observers throughout the course of a classroom study. Two assessors recorded data along with the regular observers. One assessor was identified as a reliability assessor; the second was not. The data recorded by the observers more closely matched those of the identified assessor than those of the other. What is more, the data were inflated in the anticipated direction according to the goal of the program. Biasing of measurement arose from two sources: Knowledge that reliability was being assessed and perhaps cues from the identified assessor and expectations of the changes that were supposed to occur. Knowing that their measures will be assessed for reliability apparently ensures that observers will be scrupulous in their recording (Craighead, Mercatoris & Bellack, 1974). _Frequent reliability checks should therefore be made throughout the course of a program, and observers should be informed that they are being made._ Ideally, observers should not be aware exactly when such assessments are being made, though in some situations this ideal is impractical. As expectations about results may also bias outcomes, it is best not to inform observers of the expected outcomes of a study. But this course, too, may be impractical, for treatment programs are often very obvious. Sometimes though, video recordings of behavior samples may be mixed so that observers can score them without knowing whether the treatment is in progress or not.

Knowing that reliability is going to be assessed regularly may help observers to maintain high levels of accuracy. A second method is to reinforce accuracy. Johnson and colleagues (1976) found that accuracy in scoring quizzes increased substantially following administration of a training package. One of the package components was a grade contingency—a grade of "A" reserved for those who improved or maintained high accuracy levels. Only when accurate reporting was rewarded did it remain high and stable. It seems that, along with all other categories of behavior, reliable observation is best maintained when observers are reinforced from time to time. (In Units 24–26 we shall describe how to maintain behavior.)

Recording Behavioral Data

Once a recording system has been planned and observers trained to implement it, the time has come to begin data collection in earnest. The data-recording system allows the behavior analyst to estimate the current functioning of clients with respect to their target behaviors. Data are recorded and then graphed at the end of each session. The shapes of the curves provide information about the quantitative values of the target behaviors: how many times Lucretia hits, during how many intervals Dexter remains on-task, the percentage of times that Pearl follows instructions, how many times the workshop supervisor approaches clients. The vertical line, or **ordinate**, is usually labeled with the behavioral measurement scale: rate, percentage, and so on; units of time: sessions, days, or the like, are arrayed on the horizontal line, the **abscissa** (see Figure 6.4).

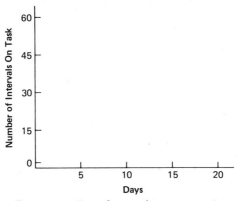

Figure 6.4 Form for graphic presentation.

Adaptation

How do people behave when they enter a room filled with unfamiliar faces? What does a child do when he first enters a new class in the middle of a school year? When an unfamiliar observer visits a ward, is the initial behavior of staff and clients typical of their later behavior? Probably not. Ward staff may interact with clients more pleasantly than usual. When people enter an unfamiliar group, they often remain quiet for a while and only gradually begin to approach others. After a time they begin to settle into the situation and behave in a manner more typical of their usual behavior. The child entering the class in midyear responds in a similar manner. Is it appropriate to begin collecting the baseline data that will provide a standard against which future change is to be measured as soon as an observer or client enters a new environment? Obviously not, for the initial behavior is not typical. The *period of adaptation* to the new environment should pass before the baseline phase is formally initiated.

Applied behavior-analysis programs are often carried out in the natural settings. When a stranger goes in to observe and record data, the major requirement is that students or clients become accustomed to his or her presence. This familiarization process can usually be accomplished within a few days. Adaptation is facilitated by placing the observer in an inconspicuous spot, and when he or she makes every attempt not to interact with the clients. The reasons should become clear in our discussion of **social reinforcement** in Unit 9.

Let us take a look at Dexter's on-task behavior as recorded in Figure 6.5. It is very high during the first three days of observation. Perhaps reactivity is raising its head again. Possibly the novelty of recording his behavior has had an unusual facilitating effect on his performance. Such atypical functioning cannot serve as an adequate standard against which to measure change. Consequently, the first few days should be considered an adaptation phase.

If the presence of an observer seems consistently to affect the performance of the clients, to the extent that observational data are seriously biased, alterna-

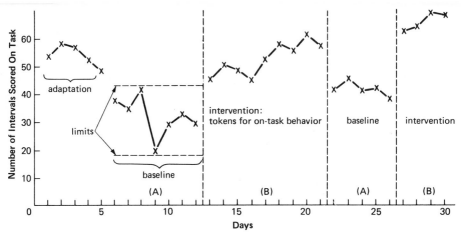

Figure 6.5   Graph of Dexter's on-task behavior.

tives must be sought. One-way observational facilities may minimize distractions caused by the presence of an observer. Several inexpensive portable models have been described by Porter, Herson, and Payne (1972). Automatic recording instruments can also be used.

Baseline Measurement *Baseline = Operant level* اب‍ لیه‌ ی ی‌ل‍ ری‌ ی‍ست‍
                                                        و ع ج ع ف ی‍.

When behavior is presumed to have returned to its typical state, adaptation has occurred. The graphic representation of behavior lends further support to the notion that adaptation has occurred when unusual fluctuations begin to diminish. A reasonable baseline[5] assessment can then be made. The baseline phase consists of repeated measurements of the dependent variables over several days or even weeks. It continues until the outer limits within which it fluctuates have presumably been identified (see Figure 6.5). We note that the range within which the number of intervals are scored on-task varies from 20 to 42. The baseline will then serve as a standard, against which the treatment procedure may be compared. To be fairly confident that the baseline is a valid representation of typical performance, the phase should be maintained for several days, preferably for a week or two. Then the effect of any unusual events will be minimized.

Once the intervention phase begins, baseline (nontreatment) conditions can be reintroduced periodically for a few days or sessions to see if any changes in the behavioral measure persist once the intervention ceases. This design, labeled "ABAB" (A = baseline, B = treatment), is often used to evaluate the effectiveness of an intervention (see Figure 6.5). Intervention effects may, on the other hand, be tested by collecting baseline data on several independent kinds of behavior of one client, on a single behavior among a few clients, or on the same behavior of one client in different settings. Baselines are maintained for different lengths of time

[5] Often labeled **operant level.**

to show that when, and only when the intervention occurs, behavior changes substantially. This evaluation system, called a **multiple-baseline design**, the ABAB design, and other baseline-intervention combinations will be treated extensively in Units 31–33.

There is an additional advantage to the collection of baseline data. It allows the observer to measure objectively the occurrence of a behavior that may have seemed worse than it actually was. For example, it may be that a large student was seated near the teacher. And, though she does not leave her seat more often than other students, it is more obvious to the teacher when she does. The collection of baseline data, then, serves as a check on the validity of the selected objective. If the objective in this illustration included more in-seat behavior, it would probably have to be changed. Assuming that baseline data do validate the need for intervention, the next step is to select an appropriate procedure.

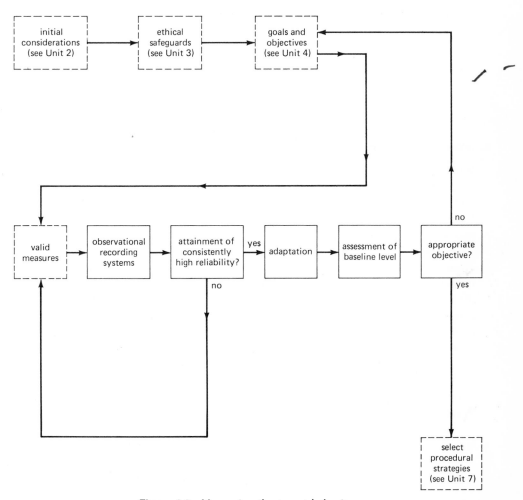

Figure 6.6 Measuring the target behavior.

Summary

In this unit we have discussed the selection of observational systems appropriate to measuring continuous behavior. We have also considered how various measurement systems may be implemented. Figure 6.6 summarizes the applied behavior-analysis model developed so far and highlights major steps in both selecting and implementing observational systems. The baseline data are assessed once a measure has been demonstrated to be reliable and valid. The collection of reliable baseline data can also serve as a check on the appropriateness of the selected objective. If the data indicate that the selected objective is inappropriate, then it should be dropped, and perhaps another, more appropriate objective can be selected. If appropriate, procedural strategies can be selected during baseline data collection.

References

Arrington, R. E. Time-sampling in studies of social behavior: A critical review of techniques and results with research suggestions. *Psychological Bulletin,* 1943, **40**, 81–124.

Ballard, K. D. & Glynn, T. Behavioral self-management in story writing with elementary school children. *Journal of Applied Behavior Analysis,* 1975, **8**, 387–398.

Bernal, M. E., Gibson, D. M., Williams, D. E. & Pesses, D. I. A device for automatic audio tape recording. *Journal of Applied Behavior Analysis,* 1971, **4**, 151–156.

Brechner, K. C., Linder, D. E., Meyerson, L. & Hays, V. L. A brief report on a device for unobtrusive visual recording. *Journal of Applied Behavior Analysis,* 1974, **7**, 499–500.

Broden, M., Hall, R. V. & Mitts, B. The effect of self-recording on the classroom behavior of two eighth-grade students. *Journal of Applied Behavior Analysis,* 1971, **4**, 191–199.

Craighead, W. E., Mercatoris, M. & Bellack, B. A brief report on mentally retarded residents as behavioral observers. *Journal of Applied Behavior Analysis,* 1974, **7**, 333–340.

Farber, H. & Mayer, G. R. Behavior consultation in a barrio high school. *The Personnel and Guidance Journal,* 1972, **51**, 273–279.

Fixsen, D. L., Phillips, E. L. & Wolf, M. M. Achievement Place: The reliability of self-reporting and peer-reporting and their effects on behavior. *Journal of Applied Behavior Analysis,* 1972, **5**, 19–30.

Foxx, R. M. & Martin, P. L. A useful portable timer. *Journal of Applied Behavior Analysis,* 1971, **4**, 60.

Glynn, E. L., Thomas, J. D. & Shee, S. M. Behavioral self-control of on-task behavior in an elementary classroom. *Journal of Applied Behavior Analysis,* 1973, **6**, 105–113.

Hagen, R. L., Craighead, W. E. & Paul, G. L. Staff reactivity to evaluative behavioral observations. *Behavior Therapy,* 1975, **6**, 201–205.

Hawkins, R. P. & Dotson, V. A. Reliability scores that delude: An Alice in Wonderland trip through the misleading characteristics of inter-observer agreement scores in interval recording. In E. Ramp & G. Semp (Eds.), Behavior analysis: Areas of research and application. Englewood Cliffs, N.J.: Prentice-Hall, 1975. Pp. 359–376.

Hosford, R. E., Moss, R. E., Morrell, G. Developing law abiding behavior. The-self-as-a-model technique: Helping prison inmates change. In J. D. Krumboltz and C. E. Thoresen (Eds.) *Counseling methods.* New York: Holt, Rinehart & Winston, 1976, 487–495.

Johnson, K. R., Sulzer-Azaroff, B., Dean, M., & Freyman, D. An experimental analysis of proctor quiz scoring accuracy in personalized instruction courses. Paper presented at the meeting of the American Psychological Association, Washington, D.C., August, 1976.

Johnson, S. M. & Bolstad, O. D. Methodological issues in naturalistic observation: Some problems and solutions for field research. In L. A. Hamerlynck, J. Handy & D. A.

Mash (Eds.), *Behavior change: Methodology, concepts, and practice.* Champaign: Research Press, 1973. Pp. 7–67.

Johnson, S. M. & Bolstad, O. D. Reactivity to home observation: A comparison of audio recorded behavior with observers present or absent. *Journal of Applied Behavior Analysis,* 1975, **8**, 181–185.

Kagan, N. *Influencing human interaction.* East Lansing: Michigan State University, Instructional Media Center, 1972.

Kazdin, A. E. Self-monitoring and behavior change. In M. J. Mahoney & C. E. Thoresen (Eds.), *Self-control: Power to the person.* Monterey: Brooks/Cole, 1974.

Kubany, E. S. & Sloggett, B. B. Coding procedure for teachers. *Journal of Applied Behavior Analysis,* 1973, **6**, 339–344.

McCoy, J. F., Epstein, L. H., Parker, F. C., Brush, M. E. & Stephens, R. M. *Effects of self-monitoring, contingencies, and contracts on the academic behaviors of college students.* Paper presented at the meeting of the Association for Advancement of Behavior Therapy, San Francisco, December, 1975.

McLaughlin, T. F. & Malaby, J. E. Elementary school children as behavioral engineers. In E. Ramp and G. Semp (Eds.), *Behavior analysis: Areas of research and application.* Englewood Cliffs, N.J.: Prentice-Hall, 1975, 319–328.

Mercatoris, M. & Craighead, W. E. The effects of non-participant observation on teacher-pupil classroom behavior. *Journal of Educational Psychology,* 1974, **66**, 512–519.

Porter, J., Herson, J. L. & Payne, J. S. A portable observation-experimental booth. *Journal of Applied Behavior Analysis,* 1972, **5**, 379–380.

Powell, J., Martindale, A. & Kulp, S. An evaluation of time-sample measures of behavior. *Journal of Applied Behavior Analysis,* 1975, **8**, 463–469.

Roberts, R. R. & Renzaglia, G. A. The influence of tape recording on counseling. *Journal of Counseling Psychology,* 1965, **12**, 10–16.

Romanczyk, R. G., Kent, R. N., Diament, C. & O'Leary, D. O. Measuring the reliability of observational data. A reactive process. *Journal of Applied Behavior Analysis,* 1973, **6**, 175–184.

Sanders, R. M., Hopkins, B. W. & Walker, M. B. An inexpensive method for making data records of complex behaviors. *Journal of Applied Behavior Analysis,* 1969, **2**, 221.

Seymour, F. W. & Stokes, T. F. Self-recording in training girls to increase work and evoke staff praise in an institution for offenders. *Journal of Applied Behavior Analysis,* 1976, **9**, 41–54.

Sulzer-Azaroff, B., Thaw, J., & Thomas, C. Behavioral competencies for the evaluation of behavior modifiers. In Scott Wood (Ed.), *Issues in evaluating behavior modification.* Champaign, Ill.: Research Press, 1975, 47–98.

Thomas, D. R. Preliminary findings on self-monitoring for modifying teaching behaviors. In E. Ramp and B. H. Hopkins (Eds.), *A new direction for education: Behavior analysis 1971* (Vol. 1) Dept. of Human Development, University of Kansas, 1971, 102–114.

Thomas, J. D. Accuracy of self-assessment of on-task behavior by elementary school children. *Journal of Applied Behavior Analysis,* 1976, **9**, 209–210.

Thoresen, C. E., & Mahoney, M. J. *Behavioral self-control.* New York: Holt, Rinehart & Winston, Inc., 1974.

Walz, G. R., & Johnson, J. A. Counselors look at themselves on videotape. *Journal of Counseling Psychology,* 1963, **10**, 232–236.

White, G. D. Effects of observer presence on mother child behavior. Paper presented at the meeting of the Western Psychological Association, Anaheim, Ca., 1973.

Wiggins, J. S. *Personality and prediction: principles of personality assessment.* Reading, MA: Addison-Wesly, 1973.

Worthy, R. C. A miniature, portable timer and audible signal-generating device. *Journal of Applied Behavior Analysis,* 1968, **1**, 159–160.

Wright, H. F. Observational child study. In P. H. Mussen (Ed.), *Handbook of research methods in child development.* New York: Wiley, 1960, 71–139.

Considerations in Selecting and Implementing Procedural Strategies

After mastering the material in this unit, you should be able to
1. Define and illustrate the following terms:
   a. Behavior-analysis procedure
   b. Dependent variable or behavior
   c. Independent variable
   d. Treatment or intervention
   e. Stimulus
   f. Contingencies
   g. Contingency analysis
   h. Behavioral contract
   i. Self-management
   j. Countercontrol

2. Describe how each of the following relates to selection and implementation of procedures:
   a. The law
   b. Procedural effectiveness
   c. Competence of behavior analysts and contingency managers
   d. Conditions and properties of the procedure
   e. Support for the procedural application
   f. Accountability
   g. Flexibility
   h. Informed consent and behavioral contracting
   i. Countercontrol

3. Describe the importance of monitoring and graphing procedural effects and reliability data.

4. Outline and discuss the importance of the steps included in the model for behavior change.

5. Identify several reasons why a program might not achieve its stated objective.

6. Do a sequence analysis (using observation and interviews) of problem behavior and goal behavior for yourself or a client.

7. From the sequence-analysis data gathered in number 6, sketch a tentative program strategy.

8. Set up your graph, and include baseline and reliability data on it. (Do not attempt procedural implementation until you have studied the appropriate procedures in Units 8–31.)

Violet wants to be more outgoing. She and her counselor have agreed on a set of goals for her. She is to engage in conversation with other children by asking and answering questions. How this goal is to be accomplished depends very much upon the procedures for behavior change that are selected and how effectively they are implemented. In this unit we shall consider how such procedures can be selected, implemented, and monitored in an ethically responsible manner. Emphasis will be given to such factors as the selection of events that function as antecedents and consequences of the target behavior, as well as to some of the legal, ethical, and practical aspects of cooperative procedural selection and implementation.

BEHAVIOR-ANALYSIS PROCEDURES

We have mentioned that a **behavior-analysis procedure** is an intervention designed to modify behavior according to certain principles. We shall speak of these procedures as **independent variables** because manipulating them is what should cause changes in measured responses—the **dependent variables**. For example, the application of a given reinforcement system (perhaps Violet's awarding herself a check mark each time that she asks or answers a question) is the independent variable. It changes behavior in some measurable fashion (for Violet, initiating a number of questions and answers). The period of time during which the behavioral procedure is in effect is labeled the **treatment** or **intervention phase**. If a sequence of procedures is followed, there are several treatments or interventions.

In Units 8–29 many procedures will be discussed at length. The operations or activities that constitute each procedure, the principles of effective application, and the advantages and disadvantages of each will be considered. In Units 30 and 31 we shall summarize procedures for increasing, occasioning, extending, reducing, and maintaining behaviors and for teaching new behaviors. Those summaries should serve as the basis for informed procedural selection.

A behavioral procedure consists of presenting, withholding, or removing stimuli. A **stimulus** is an object or event that may affect an individual's behavior by operating upon the visual, auditory, tactile, olfactory, or other modality. Stimuli may operate from outside the individual (the ringing of a bell or a flash of light), or they may be internal (pressure from a full stomach, a pounding heart, or thoughts—cognitions or images). The types of stimuli that will be emphasized in this book are those that can be observed concurrently by more than one person. Internal stimuli will not be included, though oral descriptions of thoughts, which can be concurrently observed, will be considered.

In applied behavior analysis the temporal arrangement of the stimulus in relation to behavior is especially relevant, as we shall see especially when we discuss the antecedent and consequential stimuli of procedures for increasing and decreasing response rates.

Stimuli that affect behavior may be delivered, withheld, or eliminated by clients themselves, by contingency managers, or by others. They may also occur naturally (for example, sunlight, rain, and heat). Physical features like furniture, room arrangements, and colored walls can function as stimuli. The science of ecology includes the study of the interrelationship of organisms and such natural and physical environmental stimuli.

CONTINGENCIES

Contingencies are relations between responses and consequential or **antecedent stimuli**. In a sense, the stimuli depend upon the responses, in an *if . . . then* formula. If a person goes out (the response) into the bright sunshine, *then* he will feel warmth (the stimulus)—an example of a *natural* contingency. Natural contingencies teach organisms a great deal. If we go out in the rain, we get wet. If we feel a draft, we learn that closing the window will eliminate it. If we run on the ice, we often fall. If we tease an animal, it may growl or bite.

Educational, clinical, and human-services personnel manipulate contingencies by presenting, withdrawing, and withholding stimuli, depending upon responses. If a child sees the word "cat" and says it aloud, she will be praised. "If you do 100 push-ups, you'll receive an "A" in physical education." If students smoke in the halls, they will be expelled. "If you follow certain rules, you will feel better." "If I practice the piano, the music will sound better." "If I stop nagging my children to clean up and praise them for being neat, they'll keep a neater room."

You can see that contingencies may be arranged by people to affect their own behavior or to affect the behavior of others. In applied behavior analysis, contingencies are identified and systematically rearranged in keeping with **principles of behavior**, so that behavioral objectives may be achieved.

Although principles of behavior apply to people in general, specific contingency arrangements must be appropriate to individuals, for each person has a unique combination of genetically and environmentally determined characteristics. Learning histories teach each person to respond to contingency arrangements in a unique way. For instance, Sonia's physical structure, combined with the fact that she grew up in a northern climate and was given skating lessons, makes access to an ice-skating rink a strong reinforcer. For Juan, who grew up in the Everglades and broke his arm the first time that he skated with his teenage buddies, ice skating has little appeal. Some people are generally reinforced by attention from people with given characteristics; others are reinforced only by attention from specific people.

Identification of Contingencies

Beside their usefulness in goal selection (Unit 2) sequence analyses, or contingency analyses (Goodwin, 1969), are helpful in identifying the contingencies operating on a client's target responses. Such analyses provide hints about contingencies that are increasing, maintaining, expanding, restricting, cuing (occasioning), interfering with, or reducing specific responses. They also provide information about contingencies that may be incorporated into an individually tailored behavioral procedure.

Table 7.1 illustrates a more elaborate form of sequence analysis than that presented in Unit 2. It is adapted from a format developed by Goodwin (1969). The top half of Table 7.1 is used to specify the problem behavior and to approximate its frequency (the second column), the incidents immediately preceding it (antecedents, first column), and its consequences (third column). The lower half of Table 7.1 is used in the same way to specify goal behavior. If the goal behavior has not occurred at all, only items 6–7 in the third column can be answered. Usually, though, the goal behavior has been observed, and information about its antecedents and consequences can be most useful in planning a subsequent treatment strategy. Such information has been collected in Table 7.1. The differences in the antecedents of the problem and of goal behaviors in numbers 2, 3, and 5 and the differences in consequences in number 1 are noteworthy. Items 5–7 under the heading "General Consequences" are designed to identify consequences (reinforcers, punishers, and the like) that will affect the probability of future behavior.

Such forms have not only been found helpful by educators and clinicians but are also valuable tools for consultation with parents. Johnson and Katz (1973) have noted that training parents to define and record their children's behavior objectively, including correlated antecedent and consequent events, may be clinically useful because it develops observational skills that can be used in continuing assessment after professional intervention. In addition, observations conducted by parents may facilitate positive contacts between parents and their children.

Information for sequence analyses may be gathered through both direct observation and interviews. Tharp and Wetzel discuss how interviews are frequently used to supplement observation: "Direct observation of target behaviors, while highly desirable, cannot be accomplished for all behaviors. Interview and questionnaire data are valuable elements in the assessment structure" (1969, p. 74). The consulting behavior analyst must, however, always remember that

TABLE 7.1.   SEQUENCE-ANALYSIS CHART: (The ABC's of Behavior Analysis)

Present Antecedents of Problem Behavior: A	Problem Behavior: B Observable Problem Behavior and Approximate Frequency or Duration of Occurrence	Consequences of Problem Behavior: C
1. Activity (All subject matter)		1. How do you respond? (Teacher goes to child and talks with him "to calm him down")
2. Location of client (Rear of classroom)		
3. Activity of parent or teacher (Working at desk or with other students)	Waving hands in front of face and over head while grunting audibly to entire class and teacher.	2. How do others respond? (Students stop work temporarily, then go back to work; generally they ignore it)
4. Activity of others (Students and children working on assignments)	On the average, eight times a day.	
5. At what time of day does the behavior occur most frequently: math class, meal time, ten minutes into lesson, or the like. (Ten minutes into assignments)		3. What progress is made on the activity or assigned task? (Completion once student is calmed down)
6. Previous experience of the client with activities (Successful completion)		4. Other
7. Other		

interview data are more subject to error than are direct observations. It is always better to have objective observational data on which to base decisions.

It is helpful, when attempting to select a procedure for behavior change, to inquire into the history of the problem and to obtain answers to such questions as: What are the antecedents and consequences of the target behavior? Under what conditions does the behavior seem most frequently to occur? How does the client spend most of his or her time? What will be rewarding to the client? What does the client avoid? What other events, privileges, and objects appear to function as reinforcers? How does the client obtain access to such reinforcers? What stops occurrence of the client's behaviors? With what frequency or on what schedule have such negative and positive consequences occurred in the past? These questions might be arranged in a check list. The answers could serve to identify a hierarchy of reinforcers, punishers, and other consequences occurring naturally in

TABLE 7.1.   SEQUENCE-ANALYSIS CHART: (The ABC's of Behavior Analysis) (continued)

Present Antecedents of Goal Behavior: A	Goal Behavior: B Goal Behavior in Operational Terms, Giving Approximate Frequency or Duration of Occurrence	Consequences of Goal Behavior: C
1. Activity (All)		1. How do you respond? (Teacher does not)
2. Location of client (Near teacher's desk)		2. How do others respond? (No response)
3. Activity of parent or teacher (At desk or working with student)	Complete assignment without waving of hands and grunts.	3. What happens to the activity or assigned task? (Completed)
4. Activity of others (Working on assignments)	On the average, two full days a week.	4. Other
		General Consequences
5. At what time of day does the behavior occur most frequently: math class, meal time, ten minutes into lesson, and so on. (Any time)		5. What does client do when given a free choice (companions, location, activity)? (Reads adventure books alone at table)
6. Previous experience of the client with activity (Success)		6. What has worked or is working to motivate or reinforce client's behavior? (Praise, pats on shoulder)
7. Other		7. What has worked to stop behavior? (A firm "Stop that!")

the client's environment, as well as influential factors that might help to bring about the desired behavioral change. Such information can be obtained at the same time that baseline data are being collected. The questions may be asked of teachers and parents (Cantrell et al., 1969). Valuable information is often obtained in conference with the client. In the absence of such an analysis, the likelihood that appropriate behavioral strategies will be identified is reduced.

SELECTING PROCEDURAL STRATEGIES

Sequence analyses and interviews help us to identify contingencies that may be used with specific clients. Other sources of information are charts, records, and similar case material. After information has been gathered, the most appropriate procedures must be selected. Our purpose in this section is to guide the behavior analyst to making an ethically responsible, as well as a legally and functionally sound, selection. We shall consider such factors as laws, evidence of effectiveness with specific populations, the competence of the behavior analyst and contingency manager, restrictive conditions, environmental support, accountability, flexibility, informed consent, and countercontrol.

Behavior Analysts, Procedural Selection, and the Law

As the systematic application of procedures for behavior change becomes more widespread, legal activity is keeping pace. That is a healthy sign because it represents increasing public awareness that clients' rights can be violated. Authority to determine the fate of individuals arbitrarily should not be delegated to any elite group: psychiatrists, correctional officers, teachers, school and institutional administrators, or behavior analysts. Recent court decisions ensure that people with severe disabilities and deficiencies will receive constitutional protection along with all others. For example, in a landmark case, *Wyatt* v. *Stickney* (1972), it was decided that institutionalized individuals should have private space, should not be segregated from the opposite sex, should be able to wear their own clothing, should not be unnecessarily restricted in their movements, should not be deprived in specific ways, and should enjoy other "constitutionally guaranteed" rights. Both at the Federal and the state levels, legal decisions regulating the conduct of human services are continually being made. It is the responsibility of the behavior analyst, as of all other human-services personnel, to know the law as it applies to his or her practice (see Schwitzgebel, 1971; Budd & Baer, 1976; Martin, 1974; Wexler, 1973).

The popular press has frequently reported instances in which "behavior modification" has been the target of a series of legal actions. Although the visibility of systematic behavior-change programs makes them clearer targets than other less obtrusive intervention strategies, behavior analysis has also not been immune from errors of omission and commission. Sometimes intrusive procedures have been selected arbitrarily when nonintrusive ones might have accomplished the same purpose. At times, clients have not been sufficiently involved in program design, and occasionally people's rights have been violated. "[T]he most important reason 'behavior modification' is so much under attack is that the broad label encompasses many techniques that are potentially dangerous, unwarranted and which probably should be inhibited" (Martin, 1974, p. 3).

Included in Martin's list of "behavior modification" techniques are psychosurgery, chemotherapy, neuropharmacology, electroconvulsive treatments, techniques labeled "brainwashing" by laymen, such behavioral instrumentation as implanted electrodes, and genetic screening and manipulation. Arguments about whether they are or are not "behavior-modification" procedures (we think not) and whether they are or are not effective, aside, physical treatment requires supervision by medical practitioners. Our concern here is with ethically responsible behavioral procedures that are based upon the laws of *learning* and that can help clients to learn constructive, adaptive, and personally enhancing behaviors.

Evidence of Procedural Effectiveness

A fundamental guideline for the selection of specific behavior-analysis procedures is their demonstrated effectiveness with populations similar to the client. The best way to identify such procedures is to keep abreast of the research literature. The publications cited in the reference section at the end of each unit contain reports of new and refined behavior-change methods. This book, beside describing many effective procedural alternatives, should provide the reader with the basic language and knowledge to comprehend the literature. In identifying given procedures, particular care should be given to fundamental aspects of method, especially descriptions of subject and staffing, as well as procedural operations.

Competence of the Behavior Analyst and Contingency Manager

A procedure with which the behavior analyst has already demonstrated competence must be selected. For instance, a token economy has many subtle intricacies (see Ayllon & Azrin, 1968); a decision to enhance Dexter's academic performance by means of a token economy should be undertaken only if the behavior analyst knows from experience what is involved. If not, the analyst must make every effort to obtain adequate supervision or consultation. This point is also extremely important for the contingency managers, who conduct the daily operation of the program. It is crucial that procedures be implemented with precision. These change agents *must be adequately trained to reach a predetermined criterion level of performance, and they must be regularly supervised.* Studies repeatedly demonstrate that training alone is not enough to guarantee that a procedure will be implemented properly (Cossairt, Hall & Hopkins, 1973; Panyan, Boozer & Morris, 1970; Quilitch, 1975; and others). Consistent feedback, praise, and perhaps other contingency arrangements, like rewards for compliance with procedural instructions, must be programmed. The same principles of behavior apply to increasing, teaching, and maintaining staff behavior as to the comparable changes in behavior of children and youth. If adequate supervision or some form of monitoring is not feasible, an alternative procedure should be selected.

Conditions and Properties of the Procedure

Wyatt v. *Stickney* (1972) and other recent state and federal legislation stipulate that treatment and education should be conducted under the least restrictive conditions possible. Even though it may be much simpler to monitor behavior or to implement contingency arrangements in a closed environment, such an environment is probably not ethically defensible. Similarly, confining school children to isolated or segregated areas is not defensible unless no other alternatives exist. Given the choice between a procedure that can work only in a closed area and one that can work in an open environment, the behavior analyst should choose the latter.

Lucretia could be confined to a room by herself with her own personal change agent; her behavior might then come rapidly under control. But a procedure incorporated into her daily routine is more ethically defensible, and, though it may work more slowly, its results will be more readily transferable and more easily maintained.

Some procedures involve application of positive reinforcement, whereas others incorporate aversive stimuli. Some involve withholding of positive stimuli, others removal of positive or negative stimuli. Each operation defines a different procedure, and each will be described subsequently. From a functional point of view, each has advantages and disadvantages. Other factors being equal, positive approaches are ethically preferable to negative ones. To increase Dexter's academic productivity, his teacher could scold him or ask him to leave the room whenever he daydreamed; or she could reward him with access to a favorite activity when his academic output improved. Both procedures would likely serve the goal, but the latter is more defensible ethically and, in the long run, functionally as well.

Unfortunately, certain kinds of behavior are extremely resistant to modification by exclusively positive means. If a behavioral goal is considered of serious importance to the client and those in his or her immediate environment, it may be necessary to resort to aversive procedures temporarily. The reader should also be aware that recent judicial decisions have restricted the use of aversive procedures like timeout (*Morales* v. *Turman*, 1973), restraint (*Wyatt* v. *Stickney*, 1972), and electric shock (*Wyatt* v. *Stickney*, 1972). Roos has argued, however:

Aversive conditioning has been used primarily to eliminate (or decelerate) behavior which is highly debilitating to the individual and/or his environment. There is now considerable evidence that judicious application of aversive conditioning can be dramatically successful in suppressing long-standing highly incapacitating behaviors (Wolf, Risley, and Mees, 1964; Lovaas, Freitag, Gold, and Kassorla, 1965; Tate and Baroff, 1966; Bucher and Lovaas, 1968). It can be argued, therefore, that selective application of aversive conditioning can be a highly humanitarian procedure. It can free individuals from crippling behavior, enabling them to interact more meaningfully with their environment and thereby enhancing their opportunities to develop their human qualities. (1972, p. 146)

Were Lucretia to continue her aggression against others, despite efforts to reward not aggressing, there would be a reasonable argument for supplementing reinforcement with an aversive contingency, on the grounds that the safety of other children was being endangered.

Once the rate of aggression had been substantially reduced it would be possible to switch back to reinforcement alone to maintain nonaggression. We should like to propound a rule that, when an aversive procedure is under consideration, informed consent be obtained, the human-rights committee be consulted, the procedure be supervised by a professional who has demonstrated competence in the safe and responsible application of the procedure, and that *the program include positive reinforcement of desirable behaviors, as well as a mechanism for discontinuing the aversive procedure as soon as feasible.*

Support for Application of Procedures

Environmental and historical factors may facilitate or impede implementation of procedures. Some procedures require less effort than others, and some require materials or special facilities. A token system for Dexter might involve tokens, charts, material rewards, special activities, the cooperation of other people, additional effort by the teacher, and the like. A reasonable way to assess those requirements and the possibility of meeting them in the environment is to spend time observing normal behavior in the natural setting. For Dexter, it might be necessary to visit the classroom for several hours on each of several days. Then more reasonable decisions about the appropriateness and feasibility of procedures could be made.

There are occasions, however, on which it is not feasible to work directly within the environment in which the goal behavior is ultimately to occur. Sometimes the environment is simply not capable of supporting the behavior analysis program: Insufficient space, materials, or trained personnel and possibly the interference or apathy of staff or peers may rule out the program in that setting. Then it may be justified to select alternative environments on a temporary basis, provided that long-range plans are ultimately to reintegrate clients into the mainstream of society. Current educational philosophy in the United States emphasizes the importance of integrating students with special deficits and problem behaviors into regular classrooms with their peers (mainstreaming), on grounds that the segregated "learning deficient" student suffers from the absence of stimulation furnished by more capable peers (Mann, 1975).

When behavioral deficits and problems are serious, however, everyone suffers. If a client continually disrupts activities or monopolizes the instructor's time, then no one can learn effectively. One youngster behaved in a variety of very disruptive ways. Big for his age, with little functional language and very few academic skills, he could not readily be contained in a class of his peers. He would grab other children's materials, grunt and make other loud noises, climb on the furniture, and in general drive everyone up the wall. He was placed in a preacademic group with just two other children. The goal was to prepare him for eventual reinstatement in a group of his age mates. He was to learn to remain seated and to attend to tasks for reasonable lengths of time, to follow simple directions, to reduce his noise, and to stop taking other children's materials. He was also to learn a few functional verbal phrases. When those goals had been accomplished, the child was gradually reintegrated into his own age group—at first, for only a few minutes a day during periods when his presence would be minimally disruptive and little by little for increasingly longer periods. Although the teacher of the regular class could not conduct the required intensive training, she was able to support the maintenance of behaviors that had been established in the temporary artificial setting.

Accountability

Applied behavior analysis is eminently **accountable**. The continual collection of data and demonstrations of functional relations provide measures for evaluating the effectiveness of a procedure.

Suppose that future courts should decide to employ outcome measures as a means of evaluating treatment adequacy. This approach would imply that initial behavioral assessments would be made of individual treatment needs, the outcomes of different types of treatment programs with various patient populations would be compared over time, and those programs that produce the most favorable results would be implemented on a wide scale. Presumably, the programs would also be subjected to certain basic input criteria, such as those proposed by *Wyatt*, to protect the basic rights of the residents. What would be the implications of outcome-oriented treatment measures for the field of behavior modification? Experimental analyses of behavior modification techniques have demonstrated repeatedly that environmental contingencies can be arranged to modify deviant behavior patterns and to develop and maintain new skills in persons with behavioral or developmental problems (e.g., *Journal of Applied Behavior Analysis,* 1968–present). Many of these studies involved classes of persons for whom a right to treatment has been judicially recognized. To the extent that the target behaviors selected for treatment in these studies are considered the relevant outcome variables, behavior modification has demonstrated its effectiveness as a treatment approach. (Budd & Baer, 1976, p. 180–181)

In selecting procedures, we prefer those that lend themselves to evaluation, because they permit ready identification of failures or breakdowns in effectiveness and offer the comfort of knowing that such danger signs will be spotted rapidly. In fact, the ethical responsibility of applied behavior analysts is enhanced by their willingness to subject their methods to such thorough and continuing scrutiny. It is to be hoped that this aspect of applied behavior analysis will serve as a model for other human-service disciplines so that their procedures may also be more regularly and precisely evaluated.

Flexibility

Hand in hand with accountability is flexibility in selecting procedures. Procedures should be readily modifiable, so that, if evidence suggests that they are not functioning as anticipated, they can be discontinued. An array of alternative procedures may be proposed, on the assumption that all will be tried, either in sequence or in combination, until the appropriate one is identified. The behavior analyst should beware of becoming so intrigued with a particular procedure that he or she uses it in preference to others, regardless of its effectiveness in a particular instance. **The Good Behavior Game** (see Unit 28) may work for some but not for others. A **token** program (Unit 29) may work for Dexter but not for Lucretia. Graduated guidance (Unit 14) may be the only effective method of teaching motor skills to youngsters like Charlie, who learns at a much slower rate than his age mates, and Pearl, whose behavior often interferes with effective functioning. But it may not be too effective with some high-school physical-education students. A responsible behavior analyst will be ready to discontinue a procedure should it not "pan out" and to substitute another.

Informed Consent and Behavioral Contracting

It is fortunate that the large array of available behavioral procedures often permits the client to select one that is to his or her liking. The function of the behavior analyst is to gather together the procedures appropriate for accomplishing mutually determined goals and to discuss with the client (or when appropriate the advocate, parents, or caretakers) the pros and cons of each: implementation methods, speed and durability of effectiveness, risks, positive side effects, and other qualities that we shall discuss later. As a trained professional, the behavior analyst should be able to provide guidance in selection of a procedure, but clients (or their agents) should make the final selection. In fact, the Wyatt decision (1972) expressly states that patients have the right not to be submitted to aversive conditioning without "their express and informed consent after consultation with counsel or interested party of the patient's choice" (*Wyatt v. Stickney*, 1972, at 380).

Several investigators concur about the need to *confer with the client about the contingencies to be used in the program.* Lovitt (1969) and Lovitt and Curtiss (1969) found that children exhibited higher rates of academic behavior (studying, problem solving, and so on) when they were allowed to choose their own reinforcers than when the teacher chose them—even when the reinforcers were identical. In the same way, Fixsen, Phillips & Wolf (1973) reported that, when predelinquents were given complete responsibility for determining the consequences of rule violations, they participated more in the discussion of consequences and reported more of the rule violations than when teachers or parents determined the consequences.

Unless the client is conducting a self-management program (and self-management procedures are being used more and more), the contingency manager must also participate in selecting procedures. It is then more likely to be consistently applied. Contingency managers—teachers, counselors, parents, or institutional staff members—are aware of the limitations on their time and resources and are therefore better able to predict whether or not they will have the time and resources to implement the program.

Involvement of the client and contingency manager is obviously important for enhancing the effectiveness of most behavioral programs. When clients and contingency managers participate cooperatively in goal selection, as well as in the selection of objectives, *the behavior analyst should be prepared to change any previously defined objective or procedural strategy at this point.* As with goal selection, and for reasons similar to those presented in Unit 3, selection of procedures should include consultation with and the informed consent of those indirectly involved. For example, even when parents are not themselves involved as contingency managers, their informed consent is usually necessary, as is that of the administrative staff and the human-rights committee. The behavioral contract is probably the best vehicle for recording such consent. If the goal and procedure, anticipated outcomes, and possible benefits and risks are spelled out in detail ahead of time *and approved*, both client and behavior analyst have maximum protection.

Contracting for Selection of Procedures

The behavioral contract, as we have noted previously, explicitly states the goal, or **terminal behavior**. In addition, the contingencies to be applied can be stipulated in the contract in a manner *mutually* acceptable to the client, contingency manager, staff, parents, and behavior analyst. For example, it has been mutually agreed that Harry must stop harassing his brothers. A contract is drawn up. The consequences of specific acts are stipulated: His brothers will ignore him for five minutes if he does harass them, his parents will lend him the car if the brothers report no harassing for two days in a row, and so on.

Brooks has reported a successful use of contingency contracts with junior high-school truants. An example of one of the contracts that he used follows, accompanied by several of his comments,

NAME: Bill C.

PROBLEM: Excessive period and full-day truancy.

BACKGROUND: Bill has consistently missed part or all of his school day for the past year and one quarter. He has been counseled regarding his truancy, his mother has been contacted, and he has been somewhat restricted at home. His mother seemed to be unable to help him because of her working hours.

BEHAVIORAL IMPLEMENTATION: (1) Bill will attend all classes he is scheduled into every day. (2) Bill will have each of his teachers initial an attendance card at the end of each class period. (3) Bill will have his counselor initial his attendance card at the end of each school day. (4) Bill will exchange the completed attendance card with his mother in accordance with the reward schedule stated below. (5) Bill will chart the cumulative frequency of period attendance on a graph in the counselor's office at the end of each school day. (6) Bill will attend a group rap session once each week.

REWARD SCHEDULE: Successful completion of the above implementation will be rewarded in the following manner:

1. Bill will exchange the signed attendance card with his mother and will receive ten cents (10¢) for each class attended. This money will be saved for a trip to Disneyland on December 31st. (Note: Bill can hold the money himself or have his mother hold it for him.)

2. Bill will be allowed to go to Disneyland on December 31st for the New Year's Eve party.

When school resumes in January, a conference will be held to determine the need for a new contract.

SIGNATURE AND AGREEMENT STATEMENTS:

I agree to follow the provisions of the contract and to dispense the rewards only if the provisions of the contract are met.

_____
Mrs. C.

I agree to follow the provisions of this contract.

_____
Bill C.

I agree to monitor this contract and to make a verbal progress report to Bill and his mother at the end of each week.

_____
Counselor

Bill did not miss one class for three full weeks, and Mrs. C. followed through on her part of the contract. At the end of the three-week period a conference was held, and Bill decided that he thought he could handle full-time attendance. It was mutually decided by Bill and the counselor that for a three-week period the attendance card previously filled out daily need be filled out only on Friday to cover the entire school week. Bill felt that his presenting the completed card to his mother was sufficient reward. After three weeks Bill was maintaining full attendance, so his behavior modification program was discontinued. (1974, pp. 318–319)

Another, simpler contract that requires that the teacher initial it is illustrated in Table 7.2 (McGookin and colleagues, 1974). The contract is spelled out on the front of a card. The back is used to keep a running record of the goal behavior and reinforcers obtained.

Self-Management

One way of maximizing participation is to choose a self-management procedure. Glynn, Thomas, and Shee have noted that "a practical means of attaining this goal lies in the development of procedures of behavioral self-control. . . ." (1973, p. 105). Self-control procedures not only embody ethical and humanistic values, but they can also be very effective. Individuals take responsibility for changing some aspects of their own behavior. Their responsibility generally involves some or all of five basic components: selection of their own goals, monitoring their own behavior, selection of procedures for behavior change, implementation of the procedures, and evaluation of the effectiveness of the procedures.

The behavior analyst may function as a consultant or resource person or may take responsibility for some aspects of the program should the client request it or be unable to manage some aspects alone. For instance, Dexter, with his advanced capabilities, may be able to take full responsibility for managing his own program, whereas Charlie may be able to mark his self-care accomplishments on a chart but may have a difficult time evaluating the effectiveness of a tooth-brushing program. Pearl, who has no functional language, will probably be unable, during the initial stages of the program, to participate in any self-control procedures.

A self-management procedure used by Glynn, Thomas, and Shee (1973) combined self-monitoring and participation in selection of procedures. Second-grade children were instructed that whenever a "beep" occurred they were to check their cards only if they were working at their assigned tasks. Each check mark was worth a minute that could be spent with classroom reinforcers of their choice. Accuracy was socially reinforced by teachers and peers. This aspect was important, for self-reporting by youngsters is more likely to be accurate when accuracy is reinforced (see Broden, Hall & Mitts, 1971; Fixsen, Phillips & Wolf 1973; and Kazdin, 1974, for examples of accurate self-recording). In the study by Glynn, Thomas, and Shee (1973), on-task behavior was as high during the self-management phase as when others recorded behavior and delivered reinforcers. The program was both effective and time saving. Similar procedures should be applicable to various groups, assisting clients one step closer to developing self-control.

TABLE 7.2. SAMPLE CONTRACT AND RECORD FORM

Goal-Completion Card

Name: Michael   **Card:** 1   **Date:** 3/27/77

Student Goal: Michael is working on getting along with others.
For each recess without fighting he will receive 10 points to be traded in for 10 minutes of free reading in class.

Teacher	Subject or Behavior	Points	Mon. Yes	No	Tue. Yes	No	Wed. Yes	No	Thurs. Yes	No	Fri. Yes	No
1. 10:00	recess	10	MJB		MJB							
2. 11:30	recess	10	MJB									
3. 1:15	recess	10			MJB							
4.												
5.												
6.												
7.												
8.												
9.												
10.												

Front

Assign-ment	Date	Teacher Initial	Time Earned	Time Left	Time Ret.	Permission to Go/Teach. Initial	Time Spent	Balance of Time
getting along	3/27	MJB	20				20	0
	3/28	MJB	10					10

Back

Countercontrol

Related to informed consent and involvement in selection of goals and procedures is the possibility of providing people with skills for countercontrol: control or influence exerted by the client over the behavior of the contingency manager, with or without the client's awareness. Information about behavior analysis is being disseminated more and more through textbooks, workshops, articles, courses, the press, television "talk shows," and other sources. Provided clients **control** sufficient contingencies for the contingency manager (e.g., their improved behavior, approval, etc. is reinforcing) such information should provide individuals with the techniques for resisting unwanted controls. As new behavior-control methods are developed, knowledge of behavioral procedures allows pople to counter exploitation.

Just as a professional in behavior modification may use his understanding of behavioral principles in an attempt to alter other persons' behavior, so those other persons can make use of their own understanding and control of themselves and their environment to resist, or indeed to counter-influence the behavior of the professional. The behavior influence process is always a reciprocal one: The behavior manager attempts to shape the behavior of some other person through changing the consequences of that person's behavior, but, at the same time, the manager's behavior is in turn shaped by the other's response. Control always results in countercontrol. (Brown, Wienckowski & Stolz, 1975, pp. 14–15)

One major purpose of this book is to disseminate information about behavior analysis. As people learn more about behavioral procedures, we believe they will better understand social factors that influence behavior in general. Such understanding will serve as a buffer or safeguard against exploitation by others.

IMPLEMENTING AND MONITORING PROCEDURES

Once a procedure has been selected in an ethically responsible manner, following an adequate baseline period, the intervention procedures are implemented. Various behavioral procedures are discussed in Units 8 through 28, and their advantages are compared in Units 29 and 30. In fact, procedures form the core of this textbook. Actual implementation should await thorough study of the procedures.

The effects of procedures should be consistently monitored to determine whether or not they are achieving stated objectives. The data should be graphed during treatment, as well as during the baseline period, in order to provide constant feedback on the effectiveness of each selected behavioral change procedure. When parents, teachers, and other agents can see from a graph that a procedure *is* bringing about the desired change, they are, it is to be hoped, reinforced. Such reinforcement helps to *maintain* their own participation in the treatment program, which is extremely important if behavior change is to be achieved. Often, during the early phases of a behavior-change program, a small change may be overlooked unless data are collected and graphed, especially when the problem behavior is serious. If vandalism in a school system had decreased, so that the percentage of unbroken windows had increased by only 5 percent, the improvement might not be instantly apparent. Unless data were collected during the first few days after the behavior-change program had been implemented, it might have gone unnoticed, and the procedure might have been dropped prematurely.

Graphing methods will be discussed in more detail in Unit 35. Here we shall briefly describe a working graph on which Dexter's task completion is charted (see Figure 7.1). The ordinate **y-axis** is labeled with the behavior to be changed, the dependent variable. The abscissa **x-axis** is labeled for appropriate time intervals. Dotted vertical lines indicate changes in procedures. To be confident that the measures are consistent throughout, regular agreement between observers should be independently measured. The data from these checks can then be plotted directly on the graph, as in Figure 7.1. If there is a great disparity between the two points representing measurements of the same dependent variable, the measures must be refined.

Graphing the data also reduces other kinds of misunderstanding. For example, people may be convinced that the client is improving simply because treatment is being provided. Fortunately, at least for the client's progress, the data can correct such misconceptions. Graphs, then, function in ways similar to "fever charts" (Patterson & Gullian, 1968). Plotting data helps to avoid misunderstanding by showing how much progress has actually been made and how much remains to be accomplished. It provides constant and immediate feedback on the effectiveness of particular procedures. If, after a sufficient period of time, an anticipated behavior change has not occurred, the data tell us to stop! We must reevaluate the program and make necessary changes. If change is occurring too slowly, al-

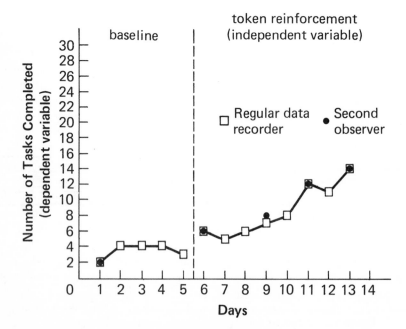

Figure 7.1 Dexter's math progress.

terations in the program may also be indicated. But, if data show that change is occurring at a satisfactory rate, then procedures should be continued. Regular collection and graphing of observational data are essential to the efficiency and effectiveness of the treatment program.

There can be several reasons why a program does not achieve its stated objective: The objective, contingencies, or selected procedures may be inappropriate and ought to be revised. Often procedures are not being implemented as originally agreed. In addition to collecting data on the dependent variable (the behavior to be changed), it is therefore also helpful to collect data on the independent variable (the treatment program). For example, if the independent variable is to praise Dexter verbally at least once for every ten minutes of consistent "on-task" behavior (like doing math homework), an event sample should be taken from time to time while he is doing his homework to be sure that praise is being delivered as agreed. As we have mentioned previously, consistent monitoring, feedback, and reinforcement are important to contingency managers (see Herbert and Baer, 1972), as well as to instructors. As with cuing for behavioral measurement, it is also helpful—and necessary in many instances—to cue contingency managers when to deliver independent variables. A variety of cues will be discussed in Units 12–15. Other suggestions have already been provided in the section "Behavioral Recording Staff" in Unit 6. For example, a timer can be set at varying intervals of five to ten minutes whenever Dexter starts his homework. Its going off then serves to cue the parent to praise him for being at work, provided that he has been continuously working.

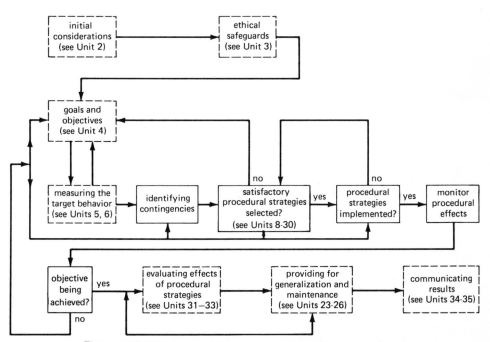

Figure 7.2 Selecting and implementing procedural strategies.

Summary

In this unit we have provided the reader with guidelines for structuring a behavioral-analysis program that should be both responsible and effective. Figure 7.2 summarizes the model in a flow-chart format.

Once an objective has been selected and a measurement system implemented, potential contingencies are identified, to serve as components of procedural strategies. But a variety of factors must be considered if ethical, legal, and functionally sound procedures are to be selected. They include the law, procedural effectiveness, competence of the behavior analyst and contingency manager, conditions and properties of the procedure, support for application of the procedure, accountability, flexibility, informed consent and behavioral contracting, and countercontrol. After mutually satisfactory procedures are selected, they are implemented and their effects monitored. Monitoring helps to determine whether or not the objective is being achieved. If so, the program continues. If not, either the objective, contingencies, or selected procedures may be inappropriate and in need of revision. Or perhaps behavioral strategies are not being implemented as agreed. Each possibility should be checked out until the reason is discovered and appropriate program modifications made. The next three steps in the model will be discussed in subsequent units, but they are included in Figure 7.2 to provide the reader with an overview of the complete model.

Throughout these first seven units, we have suggested methods for resolving some of the major philosophical and ethical issues that are of current concern in our society. As behavior analysis continues to develop, additional issues will arise. We agree with Brown, Wienckowski, and Stolz (1975) that public debate about behavior-analysis procedures is bound to continue. Constant professional evaluation and public discussion, however, can help to prevent abuses, as well as to foster greater public understanding and acceptance of the benefits.

London (1974) contends that ". . . a decent society regulates all technology that is powerful enough to affect the general welfare, at once restricting the technicians as little as possible and as much as necessary." In that context, both continued monitoring of behavior modification by the public and further research on this important technology are needed to serve society and the individuals who make it up. (Brown *et al.*, 1975, p. 24)

References

Ayllon, T. & Azrin, N. H. *The token economy.* New York: Appleton, 1968.

Broden, M., Hall, R. V. & Mitts, B. The effect of self-recording on the classroom behavior of two eighth grade students. *Journal of Applied Behavior Analysis,* 1971, **4**, 191–199.

Brooks, B. D. Contingency contracts with truants. *The Personnel and Guidance Journal,* 1974, **52**, 316–320.

Brown, B. S., Wienckowski, L. A. Stolz, S. B. *Behavior modification: Prespective on a current issue.* Rockville, Md: DHEW (ADM), 75–202, 1975.

Bucher, B. & Lovaas, O. I. Use of aversive stimulation in behavior modification. In M. R. Jones (Ed.), *Miami symposium on the prediction of behavior: Aversive stimulation.* Coral Gables: University of Miami Press, 1968.

Budd, K. & Baer, D. M. Behavior modification and the law: Implications of recent judicial decisions. *The Journal of Psychiatry & Law;* a special reprint, Summer 1976, 171–274.

Cantrell, R. P., Cantrell, M. L., Huddleston, C. M. & Wooldridge, R. L. Contingency contracting with school problems. *Journal of Applied Behavior Analysis,* 1969, **2**, 215–220.

Cossairt, A., Hall, R. V. & Hopkins, B. L. The effects of experimenter's instructions, feedback, and praise on teacher praise and student attending behavior. *Journal of Applied Behavior Analysis,* 1973, **6**, 89–100.

Fixsen, D. L., Phillips, E. L. & Wolf, M. M. Achievement Place: Experiments in self-government with pre-delinquents. *Journal of Applied Behavior Analysis,* 1973, **6**, 31–47.

Glynn, E. L., Thomas, J. D. & Shee, S. M. Behavior self-control of on-task behavior in an elementary classroom. *Journal of Applied Behavior Analysis,* 1973, **6**, 105–113.

Goodwin, D. L. Consulting with the classroom teacher. In J. D. Krumboltz & C. E. Thoresen (Eds.), *Behavioral counseling cases and techniques.* New York: Holt, Rinehart & Winston, 1969.

Herbert, E. W. & Baer, D. M. Training parents as behavior modifiers: Self-recording of contingent attention. *Journal of Applied Behavior Analysis,* 1972, **5**, 139–149.

Johnson, C. A. & Katz, R. C. Using parents as change agents for their children: A review. *Journal of Child Psychology and Psychiatry and Allied Disciplines,* 1973, **14**, 181–200.

Kazdin, A. E. Self-monitoring and behavior change. In M. J. Mahoney & C. E. Thoresen (Eds.), *Self-control: Power to the person.* Monterey: Brooks/Cole, 1974. Pp. 218–246.

London, P. Behavior technology and social control—Turning the tables. *APA Monitor,* April 1974, p. 2.

Lovaas, O. I., Freitag, G., Gold, V. J. & Kassorla, I. C. Experimental studies in childhood schizophrenia: Analysis of self-destructive behavior. *Journal of Experimental Child Psychology,* 1965, **2**, 67–84.

Lovitt, T. C. Self-management projects with children. Unpublished manuscript, University of Washington, 1969.

Lovitt, T. C. & Curtiss, K. Academic response rate as a function of teacher- and self-imposed contingencies. *Journal of Applied Behavior Analysis,* 1969, **2**, 49–53.

Mann, P. H. (Ed.) *Mainstream special education: Issues and perspectives in urban centers.* (USOE Project No. OEG-0-72-3999 [609]) Reston, Va., Council for Exceptional Children, 1975.

Martin, R. *Legal challenges to behavior modification.* Champaign: Research Press, 1974.

McGookin, R., Mayer, G. R., Bibelheimer, M., Byrne, M. J., Thompson, L., Jackson, G. M., *Guidance objectives and learner success.* Fountain Valley School District, California, 1974.

Morales v. Turman, 364 F. Supp. 166 (E.D. Texas 1973).

Panyan, M., Boozer, H. & Morris, N. Feedback to attendants as a reinforcer for applying operant techniques. *Journal of Applied Behavior Analysis,* 1970, **3**, 1–4.

Patterson, G. R. & Gullian, M. E. *A guide for the professional for use with living with children: New methods for parents and teachers* (Rev. ed.) Champaign: Research Press, 1968.

Quilitch, H. R. A comparison of three staff-management procedures. *Journal of Applied Behavior Analysis,* 1975, **8**, 59–66.

Roos, P. Reconciling behavior modification procedures with the normalization principle. In W. Wolfensberger (Ed.), *The principle of normalization in human services.* Toronto: National Institute on Mental Retardation, 1972.

Schwitzgebel, R. K. *Development and legal regulation of coercive behavior modification techniques with offenders.* (Rockville, Md.: DHEW Publication (HSM) 73–9015, 1971.

Tate, B. G. & Baroff, G. S. Aversive conditioning of self-injurious behavior in a psychotic boy. *Behavior Research and Therapy,* 1966, **4**, 281–287.

Tharp, R. G. & Wetzel, R. J. *Behavior modification in the natural environment.* New York: Academic Press, 1969.

Wexler, D. B. Token and taboo: Behavior modification, token economies and the law. *California Law Review,* 1973, **61**, 81–109.

Wolf, M. M., Risley, T. R. & Mees, H. Application of operant conditioning procedures to the behavior problems of an autistic child. *Behavior Research and Therapy,* 1964, **1**, 305–332.

Wyatt v. Stickney, 344 F. Supp. 387 (M.D. Ala. 1972).

unit 8

Increasing Behavior: Reinforcement

After mastering the material in this unit, using examples[1] not described here, you should be able to

1. Define and illustrate each of the following terms:
   a. Positive reinforcement
   b. Positive reinforcer
   c. Unconditioned reinforcer
   d. Conditioned reinforcer

2. Describe and illustrate how to develop conditioned reinforcers.

3. Describe two methods that can be used to identify reinforcing stimuli.

4. Describe what the authors mean when they say, "Select reinforcers appropriate to the level of individual functioning." Discuss how this point relates to the use of edible and tangible reinforcers.

Several children, ranging in age from seven to twelve years, were patients in a residential treatment center for asthmatics. The staff had tried repeatedly to teach them how to use inhalation equipment in order to avoid more intensive forms of treatment—intravenous-fluid therapy, hospitalization, and drugs that have undesirable side effects. These attempts were to little avail; the patients seldom used the equipment appropriately. After measuring inappropriate use for several days, the staff chose one subtask, eye fixation, as the target behavior. Criteria for appro-

---

[1] An excellent source for everyday illustrations of behavior principles is Miller (1975).

priate eye fixation were set. When a child met the criteria, he received a ticket. Twenty-five tickets could be exchanged for a surprise gift. The rate of appropriate eye fixations took an immediate leap upward and stayed there. Several days later, the same strategy was initiated in connection with a second subtask: facial posturing. When success with that component was demonstrated, the third and last subtask, diaphramatic breathing, was targeted. Children could also earn tickets for meeting the criteria for that response. All the youngsters remained at the treatment center for at least six months, which made it possible to determine whether or not correct use of the equipment could be maintained. It was, which meant that drug treatment could be reduced for some of the children. Presumably, they became healthier and less dependent upon intensive medical care (Renne & Creer, 1976).

A class of second-grade youngsters, described as below grade level academically and disruptive, were observed for seven days. Then a procedure was adopted in which the students could earn tickets with no redeemable value if disruption was reduced by 30 percent. Disruptive behavior stayed pretty much the same. Next the tickets could be turned in for sessions of tutoring in reading by either older peers or college students. The children then became much less disruptive. Curiously, they also gained significantly in word-analysis skills, as measured by the Metropolitan Achievement Test (Robertson, DeReus & Drabman, 1976).

A group of adolescents working in a Neighborhood Youth Corps program were being paid by the hour. Their performance was generally inadequate, even after thorough job descriptions had been prepared. The system of payment was then changed, so that it was based on ratings on a check list of job performance. Job performance improved to nearly perfect levels (Pierce & Risley, 1974).

Similar dramatic results are being reported in all sorts of programs serving children and youth. Young people are learning more in school (Ayllon, Layman & Kandel, 1975), developing more effective social skills (Minkin et al., 1976), performing better in sports (McKenzie & Rushall, 1974), learning to manage their own behavior (Bornstein & Quevillon, 1976), eating more nourishing meals (Madsen, Madsen & Thompson, 1974), ceasing to suck their thumbs at home (Knight & McKenzie, 1974), and learning many other personal, social, academic, and vocational skills. Their teachers, supervisors, parents, and advisers are also becoming far more effective in developing and supporting those skills (Harris, Bushell, Sherman & Kane, 1975; Jones & Eimers, 1975; and many others).

How are these impressive results being accomplished? One major aspect of all these programs is effective **reinforcement**. Reinforcement is used in a vast majority of applied behavior-analysis programs, particularly those in which some responses are targeted for rate increases. Because **reinforcement procedures** are so integral to practice in the field and because they form the nuclei of so many varieties of behavior-change programs, they are the first category of procedures that we shall consider in detail. After presenting this foundation, we shall move on to procedures that are directed toward more complex goals: **extinction,** designed to reduce response rates; **stimulus control** procedures for refining the conditions in which target responses are to occur; **shaping** and **chaining** to help clients learn new behaviors and strengthen existing ones; and other procedures for *reducing, maintaining,* or encouraging the **generalization** of newly strengthened or acquired behaviors in other settings.

We shall define and illustrate each procedure and discuss the advantages and disadvantages of each. The major emphasis in each section will be upon the effective use of the procedure for both short-term and long-term benefits to clients. As our discussion progresses, the reader will notice that many procedures can be effectively used in combination. In the field they often *are* used in combination. The units on contingency packages for use with groups offer numerous illustrations of such combinations. After the presentation of these various procedures and combinations we shall summarize them in Units 29 and 30, so that change agents can select those best suited to specific behavioral objectives.

Let us begin with **positive reinforcement**. What is it? How does it work? And how can it be used effectively to increase rates of behaviors that are *already part of individuals' repertoires of responses,* behaviors that they have been observed **emitting**[2] in the past. Then **negative reinforcement**, which also promotes increases in rates of behavior, will be discussed.

POSITIVE REINFORCEMENT

Definition and Discussion

When a stimulus—an object or event—is presented or occurs as a consequence of or contingent upon a **response** and when the rate of that response increases or maintains, we speak of "positive reinforcement." When the children in Renne and Creer's study (1976) used their inhalation equipment properly, tickets were given to them as a consequence. The rate of equipment use increased to a very high level and remained there. We can say that the children's use of the equipment was positively reinforced by the presentation of tickets. Because rates of nondisruptive behavior increased in Robertson, DeReus, and Drabman's program (1976) when tickets for tutoring time were presented, the tickets were reinforcing.

Positive reinforcement occurs in everyone's life. A child does something that pleases his parents, and the parents smile and respond affectionately. The child then repeats that action more frequently. An adult does a good job and is praised by her superior and given a promotion or a raise. If she continues to perform well, the praise and promotion have been positively reinforcing. When we ask for something politely, the request is frequently granted, and we continue to make polite requests. A bird poking around leaves finds food from time to time; when we are thirsty and drink from a fountain our thirst is quenched. Just as the

---

[2] **"Emission"** is a technical term used in behavioral analysis. The verb "to emit" is used in connection with a certain category of behavior called "operant behavior," behavior that's modified by its consequences. Operant behavior corresponds closely to behavior colloquially called "voluntary" (Catania, 1968). The term "emit" will be used throughout this book, for only operant behaviors are discussed here.

bird's rate of poking among leaves remains high, so does our rate of turning on faucets when thirsty.

In each of the positively reinforcing episodes described, an object was presented or an event occurred as a consequence of a particular behavior, and the rate of that behavior increased or remained high. That object or event, the *stimulus,* which followed as a consequence of the behavior, is called a **positive reinforcer**. Tickets exchangeable for surprises, tutoring time, food, smiles, affection, raises, promotions, and the like were the positive reinforcers in the illustrations.

As there is a relation between behavior and the consequent stimulus event, we can say that the positive reinforcer is *contingent upon* the behavior. One purpose of the contingency analysis previously described is to identify under what conditions such relations occur.

Many of the positively reinforcing events in a person's life occur **naturally**; no one deliberately arranges for their occurrence. Putting one's nose to a rose is reinforced by sweet fragrance. Very frequently, however, we or others do arrange to provide positive reinforcement in order to increase or maintain rates of certain behavior. A student may deliberately schedule her study times so that they are followed by an activity that is fun, in order to maintain her study rate at a high level. An employer probably deliberately arranges to pay salaries contingent upon employees' performing at acceptable levels. Teachers arrange consequences, like grades, gold stars, or special privileges, contingent upon performance, so that students will continue performing well. Sometimes, as we have discussed earlier, very powerful positive reinforcers follow responses that individuals are either unlikely or say they are unwilling to make. High salaries may encourage workers to continue to perform boring tasks well. Power, wealth, and peer approval have maintained rates of bullying, stealing, and even committing murder.

In applied behavior analysis, positive reinforcers are arranged to follow a targeted behavior, in order to increase it to or maintain it at criterion level. Assuming that guidelines for ethical selection of procedures are followed, **positive reinforcement procedures** should result in an outcome to the client's advantage.

Using Positive Reinforcement Procedures Effectively

Substantial research on positive reinforcement has yielded a set of very valuable principles, which can be applied to increase effectively behaviors that do not occur at a sufficiently high rate. We now know that not just any reinforcer will be effective in every situation; rather, the selected reinforcer should have properties that are demonstrably reinforcing to the specific individual under specific conditions. We also know that *immediacy* of reinforcement is crucial and that any delay must be bridged by presentation of a signal that reinforcement will be delivered later. We have learned how important it is that reinforcement be scheduled as often as possible, preferably every time the desired response occurs, and that situational and social factors may affect the rate at which the behavior increases. Each of these factors will be discussed extensively in the following pages. At this point, let us turn to the *quality* of reinforcement, considering first how stimuli develop their reinforcing properties and next various categories of reinforcers. Suggestions will be offered, in order that the reader will be able to select an array of reinforcers appropriate to particular individuals and to specific conditions under which behavior is to increase.

Selecting Appropriate Reinforcers

"One man's meat is another man's poison." You may love licorice; I hate it. You may go out of your way to say "Good morning" to a secretary who has a dish of licorice candies on her desk. I would go out of my way to say "Good morning" to her only if she smiled and gave me an enthusiastic greeting, and I would refuse any proffered licorice. Some individuals may work to earn participation in specific activities, like soccer games, whereas others would be turned off by the prospect of such a "reward." Some teachers are rewarded by a class of physically active, busy students engaged in a certain degree of excited conversation; others may feel gratified only when all students are quietly working at their desks. The question is "How does one go about selecting the appropriate reinforcer?" To do so in a rational manner, it is necessary to consider how objects and events develop reinforcing properties for given individuals under specific conditions.

How stimuli become reinforcers.   Some stimuli are effective reinforcers even without any identifiable history of experiences. We shall use the term **unconditioned reinforcers** to describe them: food for an individual who has not eaten for a while, liquids for one deprived of fluid, warmth to one who is cold, and so on. Other stimuli acquire their reinforcing properties only as a function of a series of events in the individual's life. They are called **conditioned reinforcers**.

A conditioned reinforcer is a stimulus, an object, or an event that, though initially **neutral** has, *through frequent pairings with strong unconditioned or conditioned reinforcers, assumed reinforcing properties.* By itself it serves to increase or maintain the behavior of a specific individual. Conditioned reinforcers develop as individuals interact with their environments. The strength of conditioned reinforcers therefore varies from individual to individual, depending upon the reinforcement history of each. Tiny Tina, recently born, is fed, held, and cuddled. Her parents use certain gestures. When they are pleased with her actions they praise her: "Good Baby." Over a long time, the gestures, the praise, and other events that have been frequently paired with food and comfort begin to signal that food or comfort is apt to be forthcoming. Eventually, the once "neutral" events begin to strengthen behavior, even in the absence of unconditioned reinforcers. They have become conditioned reinforcers.

A conditioned reinforcer may also be an object. It is easy to understand how pennies, trading stamps, or box tops become conditioned reinforcers. But what happens if the objects or events that become conditioned reinforcers for most of us fail to be paired with unconditioned reinforcers or other effective conditioned reinforcers? Trading stamps would have no effect on the behavior of someone who had no way to redeem them. Some children grow up without experiencing typical combinations of unconditioned and conditioned reinforcers, like the coupling of food with verbal praise. This fact may explain why some students and clients do not appear to respond to such typical conditioned reinforcers as approval and good grades.

In the event that typical conditioned reinforcers are not effective with a particular individual, it may be necessary to turn first to unconditioned reinforcement or unusual conditioned reinforcers. They can then be paired with the more usual reinforcers, so that over time the latter should take on reinforcing properties of their own. For example, when little Elroy enters first grade, the teacher finds that he fails to follow many routine class directions. Praising him when he occasionally engages in desired behavior appears to have little or no effect. The teacher notices, however, that hugs and pats seem to be very effective. Hugs and pats are therefore paired with praise for quite a while. Most contingency managers will agree that it is fine to hug and pat a six-year-old, but such treatment is not appropriate for a student who is, say, eleven or twelve years old. What should be done about the older student? If this illustration seems familiar, it is because situations like it are often handled in a most appropriate manner. Praise is linked with known reinforcing activities: "Fine job, Elroy. Now we'll play catch." Praise begins to develop its own reinforcing properties, so that it will not be necessary to provide a recreational activity every time Elroy does his job. Little by little the frequency with which hugs and pats are paired with praise is reduced. Praise begins to have an effect, even when hugs and pats are not presented.

Another example from one of the authors' clinical cases may serve to clarify how a child may be taught to respond to conditioned reinforcers in the natural environment. A five-year-old girl was brought into the clinic. She hardly spoke a word that made sense in the context of a given situation, and she would only rarely look at or respond to gestures or verbal directions from the clinician. On the rare occasions when she did something that approximated a desirable behavior, the behavior analyst would say "Good" or smile. This approach appeared to have little effect. It was then decided that a more effective reinforcer, food, would be adopted to teach the child how to use appropriate language and to follow directions. Lunch was brought to the clinic, and the child was given small bites of food for any approximations to functional speech or to following directions. This method was very effective. Before long the youngster was saying many words and responding appropriately to a wide variety of directions. At the time the child was not attending school, but her parents and the behavior analyst agreed that she should be prepared to go to school as soon as possible. Because all concerned knew that it would be impractical for the child's teacher to follow her around with lunch and a spoon, a program for developing reinforcers was carried out. From then on, each time that food was given it was linked either with a phrase like "good," "fine," "yes," and "you're doing so well" or with an action like smiling, hugging, or nodding. As time progressed and the child learned some behaviors well, it was possible to omit food reinforcement for them. She was soon engaging in the desired behavior even when she was reinforced only with a word like "yes." At the end of a year of this type of treatment, the little girl entered a special-education class. After completing her third year in that class, she was continuing to progress with only the conditioned reinforcers used by the teacher.

It should now be possible to explain how conditioned reinforcers acquire their reinforcing properties as a function of each individual's learning history. The encouraging aspect of the process is that functionally neutral stimuli can become reinforcing. Even though a conditioned reinforcer that is natural for most youngsters in a particular setting lacks reinforcing properties for some, it can be paired with a reinforcer that is known to be functional for those individuals. Over time it will begin to assume reinforcing value for them too.

Matching reinforcers with individuals.   Because an individual's learning history plays such an important part in the search for conditioned reinforcers, it is essential that reinforcers be matched to individuals. Before any potential reinforcer is adopted for a behavioral program, its effectiveness with the individual must be demonstrated. Little Elroy's teacher found that hugs and pats were effective with him. She demonstrated this effectiveness by first counting the proportion of directions followed for several days when no hugs and pats were administered; then she began to hug or pat Elroy each time that he followed a direction. To test whether or not following directions was dependent upon the hugs and pats, all were discontinued for a few days. The teacher noted that Elroy had followed directions much more frequently when hugs and pats were delivered, so they were again introduced, and his following of directions again increased. The teacher had demonstrated the reinforcing properties of hugs and pats for Elroy. They could now be used to promote other behaviors and eventually to develop other conditioned reinforcers. Although it may not always be necessary to follow such an elaborate routine to demonstrate the effectiveness of reinforcers, successful programing demands that individuals and reinforcers be matched on the basis of objective observation. If the rate of a behavior already in the client's repertoire does not increase as a result of an immediate consequential stimulus, one possible explanation is that the stimulus is not sufficiently reinforcing for the client in that situation. Other stimuli should be tried until one is demonstrated to be effective.

A method for selecting appropriate tangible reinforcers (objects) is to offer a pair of choices to individuals and to observe which alternative each selects. Various pairs can be offered in sequence, so that each object is eventually matched with every other; it is then possible to determine which is selected most often. This procedure is particularly useful with nonverbal children. Sometimes people can be asked to select their own reinforcers, but they must know themselves very well. It is usually a good idea to check out each reinforcer to see whether or not it is really effective: For example, if it is withheld contingently, does the behavior decrease? Does the behavior increase when it is delivered contingently? A student may say that he would love a volume of Shakespeare's plays, as a reward for turning in his English assignments, because he wants to please his teacher, not because he really likes Shakespeare. One way to check the validity of his statement is to look at his library card to see what books he has taken out lately. It may be that a good collection of science-fiction stories will be a far more powerful reinforcer. (Later we shall discuss how to identify effective activity reinforcers.)

Consumable reinforcers vary in effectiveness according to how much has recently been consumed by the individual. In selecting a reinforcer, it is a good idea to keep this point in mind. There are ethical concerns involved in depriving a client of food, and there may be practical problems in planning interventions before meals. In such instances, it is better to select strong conditioned reinforcers that are not so vulnerable to such fluctuations.

A very important point, not to be overlooked when selecting reinforcers, is that the selected reinforcer must be appropriate to the level of individual functioning. For example, in an arithmetic class, one student may appear to work only for consumable reinforcement, another for social reinforcement, and still another for **intrinsic motivation**, that is, for no apparent extrinsic rewards or reinforcers. Even though all three enthusiastically eat chocolate candy whenever given the opportunity, should chocolate candy be used to reinforce each one to do his daily math assignment? *No!* Chocolate would be appropriate only for the first student. Green and Lepper's research suggests that perhaps "the use of extrinsic rewards . . . can undermine the intrinsic interest of a child in the activities for which he received a reward" (1974, p. 54). Students who were told that they would receive *and* who did receive tangible rewards or activities for engaging in classroom activities that were already intrinsically reinforcing—like playing with markers and solving puzzles—*decreased* the amount of time they spent on the activities once the extrinsic rewards were terminated. Although other researchers have questioned the permanence of such effects (Feingold & Mahoney, 1975; Ramey, 1976), it is still reasonable to be conservative in applying extrinsic reinforcement. We do not wish to imply, however, that individuals who engage in certain tasks or activities at an "intrinsic" level should never be extrinsically reinforced for that behavior. Rather, infrequent extrinsic reinforcement *that comes as a surprise*, instead of as a promised reward, is an excellent way to support well-established, apparently intrinsically reinforcing behavior. Furthermore, "to prevent the undermining of intrinsic motivation, extrinsic rewards should be phased out as soon as possble" (Green & Lepper, 1974, p. 54). In subsequent units on maintaining behavior we shall describe ways in which extrinsic reinforcers can be phased out.

The search for reinforcers that will be effective with a particular client should be conducted systematically, starting with those that are most natural to a situation and moving gradually toward more artificial ones. If the reinforcers usually occurring in a situation include praise or attention, those should be tried first. If gold stars, happy faces, or grades are natural to the setting, it is good to begin with them. Then, assuming that *all the other techniques for effective reinforcement are followed consistently for a reasonable period of time (perhaps a week or two)* and the anticipated rate increase has not occurred, it is time to search for different reinforcers. The progression should be from the *natural* toward stimuli that would be *artificial* or *intrusive* in the situation. If attention, praise, smiles, favorite school activities, pats, and hugs had not worked with Elroy, then the teacher could have progressed to presentation of objects (like tokens or chips) that would be exchangeable for activities: music, special games, picnics, and so on. If they also did not work, toys, trinkets, nutritionable edibles, or sweets could be tried. Then, once a strong reinforcer had been discovered, it would be possible to use it to increase the rate of the target behavior, while gradually shifting back to more natural reinforcers. We shall discuss this procedure in detail in Unit 24.

The reason for attempting to use the most natural reinforcers is because it is then much easier to shift back to normal routines. In addition, natural reinforcers are not intrusive and are less likely to arouse the concern of staff, parents, and the public; nor do they set the client apart from others. If Elroy were the only student in his class receiving candy for following directions, the other students would surely notice, and Elroy might react negatively to being treated differently from the others. Although such problems are not insurmountable (and, in fact, we shall discuss ways of handling them later on), it is preferable to avoid them in the first place. In the next unit we shall present several categories of reinforcers, ranging from those that are artificial in the daily routines of most homes, schools, institutions, and community agencies to those that are most natural in those settings: tangible and edible items, exchangeable items, activities, and social events.

Summary

Positive reinforcement is the first behavioral procedure that we have introduced. It is a positive, constructive procedure that forms the basis of many of the more complex procedures to be discussed in subsequent units. In this unit positive reinforcement has been defined and illustrated, conditioned and unconditioned reinforcers have been differentiated, and the reader has also been introduced to methods of identifying and effectively using reinforcers. In the next unit we present an array of different types of potential reinforcers to assist the reader further in selecting effective reinforcers for children and youth.

References

Ayllon, T., Layman, D. & Kandel, H. J. A behavioral-educational alternative to drug control of hyperactive children. *Journal of Applied Behavior Analysis,* 1975, **8**, 421–433.

Bornstein, P. H. & Quevillon, R. P. The effect of a self-instructional package on overactive preschool boys. *Journal of Applied Behavior Analysis,* 1976, **9**, 179–188.

Cantania, A. C. *Contemporary research in operant behavior.* Glenview, Ill.: Scott, Foresman, 1968.

Feingold, B. D. & Mahoney, M. J. Reinforcement effects on intrinsic interest: Undermining the overjustification hypothesis. *Behavior Therapy,* 1975, **6**, 367–377.

Green, D. & Lepper, M. R. Intrinsic motivation: How to turn play into work. *Psychology Today,* 1974, **8**, 49–54.

Harris, V. W., Bushell, D., Sherman, J. A. & Kane, J. F. Instructions, feedback, praise, bonus payments, and teacher behavior. *Journal of Applied Behavior Analysis,* 1975, **8**, 462.

Jones, F. H. & Eimers, R. C. Role playing to train elementary teachers to use classroom management "skill package." *Journal of Applied Behavior Analysis*, 1975, **8**, 421–433.

Knight, M. F. & McKenzie, H. S. Elimination of bedtime thumbsucking in home setting through contingent reading. *Journal of Applied Behavior Analysis*, 1974, **7**, 33–38.

Madsen, C. H., Madsen, C. K. & Thompson, F. Increasing rural Head Start children's consumption of middle-class meals. *Journal of Applied Behavior Analysis*, 1974, **7**, 257–262.

McKenzie, T. L. & Rushall, B. S. Effects of self-recording on attendance and performance in a competitive swimming training environment. *Journal of Applied Behavior Analysis*, 1974, **7**, 199–206.

Miller, L. K., *Principles of Everyday Behavior Analysis*, Monterey: Brooks/Cole, 1975.

Minkin, N., Braukman, C. J., Minkin, B.L., Timbers, G. D., Timbers, B. J., Fixsen, D. L., Phillips, E. L. & Wolf, M. M. The social validation and training of conversational skills. *Journal of Applied Behavior Analysis*, 1976, **9**, 127–139.

Pierce, C. H. & Risley, T. R. Recreation as a reinforcer: Increasing membership and decreasing disruptions in an urban recreation centre. *Journal of Applied Behavior Analysis*, 1974, **7**, 403–411.

Ramey, G. The effects of extrinsic rewards on the subsequent choice behavior of developmentally delayed children. Unpublished Masters thesis, University of Massachusetts, 1976.

Renne, C. M. & Creer, T. L. Training children with asthma to use inhalation therapy equipment. *Journal of Applied Analysis*, 1976, **9**, 1–11.

Robertson, S. J., DeReus, D. M. & Drabman, R. S. Peer and college-student tutoring as reinforcement in a token economy. *Journal of Applied Behavior Analysis*, 1976, **9**, 169–177.

unit 9

SELECTING EFFECTIVE POSITIVE REINFORCERS

After mastering the material in this unit, you should be able to
1. Define and offer Illustrations of each of the following terms:
   a. Edible reinforcer
   b. Satiation
   c. Tangible reinforcer
   d. Tokens
   e. Extrinsic reinforcer
   f. Exchangeable reinforcer
   g. Activity reinforcer
   h. Premack principle
   i. Social reinforcer
   j. Specific, or labeled, praise
   k. Group contingency
   l. Countercontrol

2. Offer a rationale for the use of edible or tangible reinforcers.

3. Discuss some of the problems that may be encountered when using edible and tangible reinforcers in a behavior-analysis program. Offer some solutions to these problems.

4. Comment on the issue of "treating all children equally."

5. Describe how edible, tangible, exchangeable, activity, and social reinforcers are used informally in everyday life.

6. Outline a method of identifying effective reinforcers for a particular individual.

7. Discuss the advantages and disadvantages of selecting and using effectively each of the varieties of reinforcers discussed in this unit.

8. Select an array of reinforcers that would be effective for your-self or a client.

"I use behavior-analysis procedures," says Ms. Charming. "All the clients in our workshop are given M&Ms every day. But," she adds, "sometimes it works, and sometimes it doesn't." Ms. Charming is reflecting one of the common oversimplifications of applied behavior analysis. Certainly behavior analysts have been known to present candy to clients from time to time, but the practice is not universal in the field, nor should it be. In fact, one area in which skilled behavior analysts can make a major contribution is in guiding the selection of minimally intrusive reinforcers that will provide for continued effectiveness. In this unit we shall present a very broad array of reinforcers, categorized according to variety: edible, tangible, exchangeable, activity, and social. From this array it should be possible to select those that represent the best balance between effectiveness and intrusiveness for a given situation.

EDIBLE REINFORCERS

Human infants turn their mouths to the side on which their cheeks are touched when food is the consequence. On the other hand, if food is delivered when their heads are turned away from the touch, they rapidly learn to turn their mouths away (Siqueland & Lipsett, 1966). Edible reinforcement can be extremely potent, especially when the individual has been deprived of food (or fluids) for a long time. (Table 9.1 lists a number of edible reinforcers for children and youth.) Given a person who has not eaten for quite a while, the presentation of edibles will, with rare exceptions, strengthen or maintain the behavior that it follows. If Flossie receives a peach when, and only when, she says "please" in asking for it, the frequency with which she says "please" will increase.

    Edible reinforcers have been used by practitioners to teach language, physical, and social skills to children with severe behavioral deficits. Wolf, Risley, and Mees (1964) gave a severely disturbed (autistic) boy small bits of food while training him in speech acquisition and wearing glasses. Meyerson, Kerr, and Michael (1967) were able to teach a nine-year-old retarded girl to walk by reinforcing her attempts with edible items. Risley (1968) used candy to teach preschoolers to imitate the behavior of their teachers, and Azrin and Lindsley (1956) reinforced children's cooperative responses with candy. Even more complex social behaviors, like the use of syntactical sentence structures (Wheeler & Sulzer, 1970), have been facilitated by means of edible reinforcers. Similarly, providing refreshments at parent or staff meetings tends to encourage higher attendance.

    Among the various reinforcers used to increase academic productivity in a special class for educable retarded children were extra milk and cookies (Campbell & Sulzer, 1971). Reese (1973) delivered edible items to a seriously retarded student who was learning number labeling and arithmetic skills. In a "normal" public-

TABLE 9.1.   FREQUENTLY USED LOW-COST EDIBLE AND TANGIBLE REINFORCERS FOR CHILDREN AND YOUTH*

Children	Youth
Edibles: small bites or amounts of	Edibles: small quantities of
extra milk	potato chips
baby food	fruit juice
canned or fresh fruit	peanuts
pudding	candy bars
cheese	soft drinks
raisins	other favorite foods
luncheon meat	Teen magazines
fruit juice (in plastic cups)	Car and sports magazines
cupcakes	Grooming aids
small quickly consumed candies	makeup
like M&Ms and mints	combs
pretzels, chips, crackers	hair cream, aftershave lotion,
cookies	and so on
"mini-sandwiches"	Other tangibles
soft drinks	pens
dry cereals	felt pens
second portions of lunch or dessert	money
nuts[a]	pictures of movie stars
popcorn[a]	psychedelic posters
minimarshmallows	records
peanuts[a]	cassette tapes
pickles	paperback books
ice cream, sherbet	free meal ticket or certificate
Tangibles	key chain
dolls	calendar
toy soldiers, Indians, cowboys[b]	stationary
clay[b] or nontoxic molding	notebook
materials	small toys for siblings
marbles[b]	playing cards
jacks[b]	school pennant
kites	school decals
crayons[b]	school shirt
magic marker[b]	paperweight
coloring book	address book
puzzles[b]	positive notes home
pencil	ticket to sports event
eraser	ticket to concert
note pads	ticket to stage or screen event
colored pencils[b]	certificate of accomplishment
colored paper	"rental equipment"
comic books	tools
books	items from mail-order catalogue
whistles or other noise makers[b]	phonographs, television
jump rope	cassette players
balls	bicycle

* See Unit 28 for additional suggestions on obtaining free and inexpensive items for token programs.

   [a] Avoid using with very young or severely retarded children as they may choke.

   [b] Avoid using with children apt to place objects in mouth.

TABLE 9.1.   FREQUENTLY USED LOW-COST EDIBLE AND TANGIBLE REINFORCERS FOR CHILDREN AND YOUTH* (continued)

Children	Youth
jewelry[b]	art supplies
toy cars (hot wheels and the like)[b]	musical instrument
toy rings[b]	games
paper dolls	
gliders	
baseball or football cards	
yo-yo	
models[b]	
monster books or magazines	
play money	
badges[b]	
certificates	
gold stars	
positive notes home	
special award sheets	
balloons	
frisbees	
magnets	
checkers[b]	
scout equipment	
"tattoo" transfers	

school classroom, Coleman (1970) allowed four students to earn candy for "working" behavior. The earned candy was shared with all members of the class. Working behavior increased, and disruptive behavior decreased. Students in three classes for deaf children were signaled with a light flash contingent upon ten seconds of visual attending (Craig & Holland, 1970). The light indicated that M&Ms and cereal bits had been earned. Visual attending increased 50 percent or more.

Ludwig consistently turns in very sloppy papers to the instructional staff. Because he usually eats his cookies with enthusiasm, the staff decides to allow him to earn an extra cookie or two as reinforcement for improvement in neatness. They first require that Ludwig write one line neatly before he receives an extra cookie. It is essential that the initial response requirement be easy for the youngster to achieve. Otherwise the reinforcer may not be forthcoming. It is possible that staff members will make a poor prediction and that one neat line is too much for Ludwig. They will then have to alter the requirement to a level that he can achieve. It is usually a good rule to start a response requirement near the average baseline level or the level at which the client is currently functioning. The requirement can then be gradually increased, and the contingency manager runs little risk of having to withhold the reinforcer (which would be disturbing to many contingency managers like parents and teachers, not to speak of Ludwig himself).

Practical Concerns Connected with Edible Reinforcers

There are a few important factors to consider when using edible reinforcers. It is necessary to make previous arrangements with parents, caretakers, or hospital

Figure 9.1   One man's poison is another man's reinforcer.

staff. Some children have allergies or other health problems associated with food. For instance, too many sweets are hazardous to diabetics. Too much nonnutritious food eaten before meals may interfere with children's appetites and their total diet may become unbalanced. It is best to try nutritious foods—fruits, vegetables, milk, fruit juices, and such protein items as meats and cheeses, raisins, and nuts—first. Sweetened pieces of cereal, candy, soda, and so on should be used only if the others do not work. **Satiation**, the reduction in performance or effectiveness of a reinforcer that occurs after a considerable amount of the reinforcer has been consumed is a problem with food. To postpone that effect, only very small bits of food (perhaps a teaspoonful) or quantities of fluid (about a half-ounce) should be administered each time. Food reinforcement may consist of several mini-meals, rather than three large ones (Azrin & Armstrong, 1973).

Very young children and those with severe deficits are apt to grab for food, and it should therefore be kept out of reach. Aprons with pockets are particularly useful for dry foods. Since food delivery interrupts the flow of a training program, as soon as possible, other, less intrusive reinforcers should be substituted for immediate delivery of food. For that reason, it is particularly important to pair positive social events, like **praise** and smiles, with the delivery of food.

TANGIBLE REINFORCERS

Just as adults will work for sports cars, yachts, lakeside cabins, scuba gear, jewelry, antiques, and fine china, many youngsters will make an effort to earn *tangible reinforcers*. Let us recall how hard the asthmatic patients described in Unit 8 worked to earn their surprise gifts. When other techniques fail, youngsters will often work for trinkets, small toys, school supplies, and other items. (Many tangible reinforcers for children and youth are listed in Table 9.1; in Unit 28 sources of free or inexpensive tangible rewards are suggested.)

Some problems may be encountered when tangibles are used in a behavior-analysis program. If the item is large or expensive, it may be impractical to deliver it immediately each time that the target behavior occurs. Also the client may become sated very quickly and may cease to make an effort. It is better, therefore, to use small, inexpensive objects, like charms or gum-ball trinkets.[1] One alternative is to select objects that have many parts: paper shapes, paste-on mosaic patterns, pegs for peg boards, parts of models, and the like. There are also objects that youngsters collect, for example, bottle caps, marbles, doll clothes, baseball cards, foreign stamps or coins, "tattoos" or small transfers, gummed labels, stars, insignia, and so on. One way to *prime* or encourage clients to begin to respond for such items is to start out by allowing the client to earn a few of them very easily or by giving them "free." The child could be given an album or collection case, with the beginning of the collection already supplied. A second alternative is to provide an item or mark immediately following the behavior; this token is to be saved and exchanged at a later time. Marks (checks and numbers) and objects (chips, gift certificates, washers, and so on) are *tokens*. Tokens will be discussed in the section on exchangeable items and more extensively in the section on token systems in Unit 28.

Issues Connected with Tangible Reinforcers

Sometimes people object to the notion of "paying" or "bribing" children and youth to behave properly. But let us look at the behavior of most adults. No

---

[1] Be certain that clients will not put small, tangible items into their mouths.

matter how much people are dedicated to their professions, how long would they continue to work in the absence of a contingent paycheck, which could later be exchanged for many tangible reinforcers? Probably not indefinitely. "Then," we might ask, "why not limit reinforcement to the traditional reinforcers, like grades and praise, which educators and change agents have always used with relatively good effects?" The answer to this question is simple: Traditional reinforcers do not work well with some youngsters; with others, they fail completely. The readers of this textbook are probably particularly interested in seeking alternative solutions for clients who are not responding appropriately to traditional reinforcers.

Some parents and change agents seem to resist the idea of treating some of their children or clients differently from others, to giving different reinforcers to different children or "different strokes for different folks." Accepting the fact of individual differences, however, these authors believe that "nothing is more unequal than the equal treatment of unequals." It is standard for teachers to provide students with different learning materials reflecting their current levels of functioning. Similarly, appropriate reinforcers must be provided for academic and social behaviors if learning is to occur.

The question, "Won't the other youngsters become upset and behave negatively if others are receiving special reinforcers?" concerns many. But, because each group is different, there is no single answer or solution to this question. Surprisingly, more often than not, once a special reinforcement program has been designed for a single individual, the whole group improves. This outcome is similar to Christy's findings. In working with two classes of children, aged 3.5 to 6 years, she found that

The use of verbal contingencies and food rewards with individual children was an effective management procedure that did not decrease performance in the observing children. On the contrary, as compared to initial baseline rates, all eleven children displayed either increases in the target behavior or decreased variability by the final phase of the study, and for the children with relatively low base rates of sitting, the increases were marked. Further, witnessing peer contingencies and reward resulted in increases in neither aggression nor disruptive behavior. Verbal complaints consisted almost entirely of requests for rewards, and they decreased in frequency with successive contract conditions and declined to zero within each condition. Apparently, these children were not acting "negatively in response to perceived reward discrepancies." (1975, pp. 194–195)

Peers appear relieved at times and even cheer the success of their fellows. It may be that a client's behavior has been punished so often or reinforced so infrequently that his peers are pleased that he is now receiving some rewards and that the group is becoming more pleasant. As much as we wish it were so, however, this is not always true.

Sometimes clients ask, "How come Ludwig has special privileges?" There are several ways of dealing with this situation. Sometimes such questions can be effectively ignored (Christy, 1975). Or, it can be pointed out that Ludwig is receiving the reinforcers (special privileges, objects, or activities) for making *progress*. It is also possible to invite others to design programs for themselves in areas in which they need to *improve*. If considered appropriate, such programs may be

implemented. Again, the emphasis is upon improvement over previous performance. It is *not* on what one individual is doing in comparison with what another
is doing. Alternatively, Ludwig's program may be changed, so that he earns reinforcement not only for himself but also for the whole group. This alternative will
be elaborated upon in the section on group contingencies.

Conversely, what about depriving a client of unearned edibles, while
others around him are enthusiastically consuming their goodies? Such incidents
do cause concern among personnel and observers (not to speak of the deprived
youngster) and perhaps rightly so. Our way of handling this issue is to give all
children a minimal portion—milk and one cookie. Additional portions must be
earned. Although one does trade off some effectiveness (see the section "Amount
of Reinforcement" in Unit 10), enhancing consumer satisfaction more than com-
pensates for the concession. Actually recent legal precedents support this approach
(*Wyatt* v. *Stickney*, 1972), again underscoring the advisability of providing for all
minimum basic needs noncontingently, while programing extras as contingent
reinforcers.

Tangible reinforcers are *extrinsic*; it is, however, surely preferably from the
point of view of children's-service personnel, that their clients continue to
increase their rates of performance of target behaviors in the absence of externally
managed reinforcing contingencies. If they are already doing so, it certainly makes
little sense to introduce extrinsic reinforcers into the system. As Green and Lepper
have stated, however: "Many important and potentially interesting activities,
including, for example, reading, may seem like drudgery rather than fun until one
has acquired a few rudimentary skills. There is no question, therefore, that extrinsic
motivation is often needed to get people to do things they wouldn't do without it"
(1974, p. 50). Krumboltz and Krumboltz have made a similar point: "For many
types of behavior which ultimately bring their own reward, the initial reinforcer is
merely a temporary expedient to get the behavior started. Sometimes a shift from
a concrete reward to a less tangible one is a step toward gradually helping the
child become independent of external rewards" (1972, p. 111–112). Tharp and
Wetzel have noted:

The ultimate aim of all intervention plans is to so correct the deviant behavior as to make
the target eligible for incorporation into the social control (reinforcement) network which
shapes us all into Civilization. The aim, then, is to *humanize*. For some disordered children,
it is necessary to begin with candy or money, after all, we all begin with milk. (1969, 87–88);
(italics added).

Reinforcement programs are designed to help individuals become less and less
dependent upon material reinforcers. The reinforcement program must start where
an individual is and gradually move toward the place at which she should be.

EXCHANGEABLE REINFORCERS

Tokens are reinforcers that are exchangeable for objects or events that possess
reinforcing properties for an individual. They have some properties of tangible
reinforcers and some attributes of other, more natural reinforcers. They can be

delivered immediately following a target behavior and also signal that other, probably more powerful tangible or activity reinforcers are forthcoming.

Informal **token reinforcement systems** are used in many programs for children and youth. For example, a teacher uses a token system when she gives points for school achievement, which will raise the students' final grades. The tickets exchangeable for prizes delivered to the asthmatic children for proper use of inhalation equipment in Renne and Creer's study (1976) and those delivered to the children to use in purchasing tutoring in the work of Robertson, DeReus, and Drabman (1976) were tokens. A parent is also using a token system when she gives check marks or gold stars that can be turned in later for money or special privileges. But such token systems have often been used in haphazard fashion. Through the use of appropriate behavioral methodology, formal token systems can accomplish effective and efficient behavioral change (see Ayllon & Azrin, 1968). The value of token systems and their effective use are discussed extensively in Unit 28.

ACTIVITY REINFORCERS

An activity that is "fun" may well serve as a reinforcer. When we plan a schedule that provides for a pleasant activity to follow a behavior that we are trying to increase, we are using the activity as a reinforcer. "First I'll mow the lawn, then go for a swim"; "After I work overtime for a month, I'll go on a trip." A student may allow herself to listen to music after finishing her studying. If her rate of studying increases as a function of that arrangement, listening to music is a reinforcer. Parents make use of *activity reinforcers* in teaching their children to assume responsibilities or to increase other kinds of behaviors.

Dexter's parents let him borrow the car when he has completed all the yard work. His mom teaches him to make homemade pizza after he has completed his homework. Flossie is allowed to watch television after she has picked up her toys. Judy's dad takes her for a hike one day when she is especially cheerful and cooperative. Assuming that these activities are reinforcing for the youngsters, their rates of responding will increase.

In the Achievement Place program (Phillips, Fixsen & Wolf, 1971) such privileges as shopping trips, outings, special assignments, and recreational activities are made available to youths who complete their assigned tasks and meet their responsibilities. Table 9.2 presents a list of activities that have been found to be reinforcing for children in various behavior-analysis programs. Note that some are very natural to the situations in which they are used, whereas others are less often a part of the usual routine. Free play, recess, and playground games are normally part of a school program, whereas private study booths would be unusual in many school situations. In general, however, activities seem to be regarded by many as less intrusive than edible or tangible reinforcers. They are usually less costly and more transferable. Satiation is less a problem, for an activity reinforcer is available only for a specific time and the target behavior must occur again before its next presentation. Charlie could store up closetfuls of trinkets and car models but not of activities. He would be sated with the former much sooner.

Matching individuals with reinforcing activities is just as important as matching them with tangible reinforcers. To determine what activities are potentially reinforcing for youngsters, we must watch what they do with enthusiasm, give them chances to select activities, or simply ask them. To verify the effectiveness of an activity as a reinforcer, we must test it, as with the tangibles, determining whether rates of a behavior increase systematically when the activity is presented following it and decrease when the activity consequence is withheld.

Thanks to Premack's work (1959), we know that another method for discovering an effective reinforcing activity is to identify an individual's high-frequency behaviors. On the basis of a series of laboratory studies with both animals and humans, Premack was able to demonstrate that those behaviors in which a person voluntarily engages may actually be used to reinforce low-frequency behaviors. This phenomenon, subsequently labeled the **Premack principle**, is used to make access to high-frequency behavior contingent upon performance of a low-frequency behavior. If a child frequently plays with a doll but does not do spelling exercises, access to the doll can be made contingent upon completion of an exercise. This principle has been used with impressive effectiveness by Ayllon and Azrin (1965) with a population of hospitalized, long-term psychiatric patients. In order to engage in high-frequency behaviors—like leaving the ward, interacting socially with the staff, playing games, and making commissary purchases—the patients had to have begun to perform socially useful work. Similarly, a group of nursery-school children had been observed spending considerable time running and screaming, as reported in a study by Homme and his colleagues (1963). By making running and screaming contingent upon sitting quietly, the investigators were able to increase the frequency of sitting quietly.

For youth-services practitioners, the most appealing aspect of a reinforcement procedure in which the Premack principle is employed is probably the fact that potential reinforcers are already present in their programs. There are always some behaviors in which youngsters engage (even if they are sitting and "doing nothing") with greater frequency than others. All that remains is to reorganize the program in such a way that access to those high-frequency behaviors is made available directly following the performance of the low-frequency behavior that is to be strengthened. For example, first- and second-grade students increased the rates at which they completed daily copying assignments when they were allowed access to a playroom after completion and scoring of their papers (Hopkins, Schutte & Garton, 1971).

At this point the reader may argue that this procedure is not new—which is certainly true. Parents, teachers, and behavior analysts do make frequent use of the Premack principle. When a mother says, "You must clean up your room" (low-frequency behavior), "then you may go out and play" (high-frequency behavior); when a teacher schedules a ball game (high-frequency behavior) contingent upon the class's completion of an assignment (low-frequency

TABLE 9.2.   REINFORCING ACTIVITIES

Characteristics, Settings	Suggested Consequences	Reference
Elementary school, "Follow Through" program	Minutes of free play, story time, recess, special playground games, trip to zoo	Bushell, Jr.
Young children	Running errands, room monitor, cleaning the board, grading papers, tutoring[a]	Drabman & Tucker, 1974
Grades K, 3, 5, 6, elementary school	Private study booth, use of class typewriter, time in gym, use of piano[a]	Packard, 1970
Grades 1–4, to improve reading	From parents: praise, opportunity to stay up late	Ferri, 1972
Ages 8–12, underachievers, minorities, low socioeconomic, special classes, regular school	Field trips (fishing, boating, swimming, parties), trips to farm, bank, hospital, pet shop[a]	Chadwick & Day, 1971
Grades 3–6, academic and behavior problems, elementary school	Field trips, cartoon films, class parties, trips to special school events (basketball games, and so on)[a]	Walker & Buckley, 1972
Grade 4, middle school, small, rural, economically deprived	Released time, recreation program[a]	Jacobs, 1970
Grade 4, excessively noisy during free-study period, low-middle and middle class	Extra time added to gym period; two-minute break to talk, sharpen pencils, and so on[a]	Schmidt, 1969
Age 9, low achiever; classroom	Time to read or build puppets.[a]	Brook & Snow, 1972
Grade 5, disruptive; urban, public school	Access to game room; extra recess time; opportunity to buy ditto master, have ditto copies run off, review grades, reduce detention, change cafeteria table, remove lowest test grade, assist the teacher, see movie, have "good-work letter" sent to parents, become classroom helper, become ball captain, do bulletin board[a]	Ayllon & Roberts, 1974
Grade 5, male, academic and behavior problems	Access to arts-and-crafts program[a]	Brigham, Graubard & Stans, 1972
Grades 5, 6, low socioeconomic; public school	Sharpening pencils, seeing animals, taking out balls, participating in sports, special writing on black board, being on committees, special jobs, games,	McLaughlin & Malaby, 1972

[a] Data were provided in the studies to demonstrate successful use of these activities.

TABLE 9.2. REINFORCING ACTIVITIES (continued)

Characteristics, Settings	Suggested Consequences	Reference
	records, coming in early, seeing grade book, special projects[a]	Broden et al., 1970
Grades 7, 8, several years behind in at least one area, severe reading and speech difficulties, delinquency; public junior high school	Choice from a list of activities made up by students themselves	
Grades 7, 8, home-economics classroom, rural, public school	Radio tuned to favorite station (voice-operated relay turning radio off when noise reached certain level)[a]	Wilson & Hopkins, 1973
Ages 12–16, serious behavior problems; community group home	Use of tools, telephone, radio, recreation room; going outdoors; television time; work avoidance; home time	Phillips & Phillips, 1971
Junior-high and high-school students	For individual: talking to a friend, time in class to do homework, looking at teen magazine, not having to take a test, helping a younger child learn, playing Scrabble, grading papers, reading a book, doing a puzzle (1,000 pieces), leaving class early, working on crafts or models, looking at a car or sports magazine, playing chess, checkers, or monopoly	Blackham & Silberman, 1975
	For class: listening to the radio, bringing in television to watch special programs, class party, sitting with friend listening to records, field trips, class debate, watching a movie	
Older children	Playing records, dancing, pool, ping-pong, time to make cards or presents (at Christmas and the like)	Drabman & Tucker, 1974
Ages 9–12, IQ 68–103, behavior problems; classroom	Time in "reinforcement room" (games, toys, arts and crafts, personally owned toys)[a]	Greenwood, Sloane & Baskin, 1974
Retardates, CA 6–8, IQ 73–81; lab-demonstration school at Pennsylvania State University	Free time, painting, sandbox, records, recess, several toys[a]	Jones & Kazdin, 1975

119

TABLE 9.2. REINFORCING ACTIVITIES (continued)

Characteristics, Settings	Suggested Consequences	Reference
Mentally handicapped (intermediate level, educable)	Extra swim period, ten minutes for a game at milk break, fifteen minutes in library, film on Friday, field trip (once every two weeks), feeding fish for a week, choosing story, riding elevator, turning filmstrip projector, turning off lights, five minutes' writing on chalk board, crafts activity, putting blinds up or down, being leader in line, fetching milk at break, passing out milk at break, passing out straws at break, distributing milk at noon, carrying library books upstairs, carrying library books downstairs, running errands by the day, pulling down screen, erasing and washing chalk board, cleaning erasers, captain of team at recess, first up to bat at recess, leading the pledge, taking care of calendar by the week, sitting at teacher's desk for reading, sitting at teacher's desk for spelling, filing Peabody cards, passing out paper, passing out scissors, buying extra straws, first in line for drink at recess, helping collect displays, time in science laboratory, helping custodian, answering telephone by day, making telephone call, extra cookie at break, helping secretary fetch milk for other classrooms[a]	Campbell & Sulzer, 1971
Ages 3–12	Blowing up a balloon and letting it go; jumping down from high place into arms of adult; playing with typewriter; watching train go around track; running other equipment like string toys and light switches; listening to own voice on tape recorder; building up and knocking down blocks; pushing adult around in swivel chair; pulling other person in wagon; looking out window; playing short game	Sulzer & Mayer, 1972

120

TABLE 9.2. REINFORCING ACTIVITIES (continued)

Characteristics, Settings	Suggested Consequences	Reference
	(tick-tack-toe, easy puzzles, connecting dots); blowing bubbles (soap, gum); reading one comic book; painting with water on blackboard; pouring water through funnel from one container to another; cutting with scissors; modeling with clay or putty; throwing ball or bean-bag; climbing ladder; turning on flashlight; sitting on adult's lap; looking at projected slide; listening to short recording, watching short film (view master, film-strip); walking around in high heels; wearing funny hats; carrying purse or briefcase; rolling wheeled toy down incline; popping balloon, paper bag, or milk carton; stringing beads; playing with magnet; operating jack-in-the-box; playing with squirt gun; solving codes and other puzzles; singing a song, listening to a song; performing before a group (singing a song, reciting a poem or riddle, doing a dance, stunt, or trick); blowing out match; combing and brushing own or adult's hair; looking into mirror; playing instrument (drum, whistle, triangle, piano, and the like); using playground equipment; drawing and coloring pictures; being hugged, tickled, kissed, patted, swung around, turned around in swivel chair, pushed on swing or merry-go-round, pulled in wagon.	

behavior); when a client plans to practice an exercise (low-frequency behavior) before listening to a favorite record (high-frequency behavior); when a school principal says, "After we resolve this particular difficulty, the plans you have for attending school regularly, we can discuss your other concerns about changing your schedule," they are employing the Premack principle. Premack's contribution was to study this phenomenon systematically among many species, using careful empirical measurement and quantification. He found that the principle applies to all types of subjects, giving an objective basis to a common procedure. This point is important because it emphasizes the need for **objective verification** that certain behaviors are indeed high- or low-frequency behaviors for a specific individual. The reinforcing activity must be selected on the basis of formal observation (that is, of how often and for how long the client engages in the activity on his own), rather than of judgments of what he "seems" to enjoy doing, what others think *all* children like to do, or even what the client reports liking to do. Although the three latter criteria for selecting a reinforcing activity may well yield the same activities as high-frequency behavior, often enough they do not. Try the following exercise, and see what happens.

1. List in descending order the five things that you spend the most time doing other than eating, sleeping, and working the number of hours that your job requires.
2. Keep a daily record for at least a week of how much time you actually engage in the activities listed in 1. Note the time spent with each, in descending order.
3. Compare 1 and 2.

If you have performed this exercise, you should now have an array of effective reinforcing activities for yourself. Let us suppose that you spend your largest block of time watching television. You can then make television watching contingent upon the performance of some lower-frequency behavior, like writing letters.

Similarly, a parent, nurse, educator, or community worker can use a child's high-frequency behavior to reinforce some desired behavior that does not occur as often as it should. If, for instance, the child spends a great deal of time playing with a particular toy but fails to take his diabetes medication, the parent or nurse may provide the toy only after the child has taken the medication.

It is often difficult to dispense high-frequency activities immediately to children in a group setting. Circumstances make certain activities inappropriate at particular times and places. Shooting a ball into a basket is clearly inappropriate when the rest of the class is engaged in a quiet activity, like a spelling test. One solution is to use tokens that can later be exchanged for access to the high-frequency behavior.

SOCIAL REINFORCERS

Social reinforcers are presented by other individuals within a social context. Examples of common social reinforcers include "attention" (that is, looking at, answering, nodding, and so on), smiling, and verbal statements. Table 9.3 presents a list

TABLE 9.3.   SOCIAL REINFORCERS FOR CHILDREN AND YOUTH

Children	Youth
Nod	Nod
Smile	Smile
Tickle	Laugh (with, not at)
Pat on shoulder, head, knee, back	Wink
Hug	Signal or gesture of approval
Wink	Orienting glance directly toward face
Kiss	Assistance when requested
Signal or gesture to signify approval	Positive comment on appearance
Swing around	Pat on the back
Touch on cheek	Handshake
Holding on lap	Asking client to discuss something
Fulfillment of requests	before group
Tickle	Asking client about items of interest to
Eating with children	individual
Assistance	Asking client to demonstrate something
Joining class during recess	Saying[a]
Saying[a]	very good
yes	okay
nice	beautiful
good	good for you
great	exactly
fine	thank you
very good	that's interesting
fantastic	_____ is excellent
very fine	that's great
excellent	yeah
unbelievable	great
marvelous	right
atta-girl, atta-boy	I agree
far out	good job
I like that	good idea
right on	fantastic
right	fine
that's right	fine answer
correct	what a clever idea!
_____ is really paying attention	unbelievable
wonderful	you really are creative, innovative,
you really pay attention well	and so on
you do that well	see how you're improving
I'm pleased with (proud of) you	that looks better than last time
that was very nice of you	keep up the good work
that's good	you've apparently got the idea
that's great	little by little we're getting there
wow	see how _____ has improved
oh boy	mmmm
very nice	you're really becoming an expert at
good work	this
good job	do you see what an effective job
great going	_____ has done?
good for you	you are very patient

[a] With specific reason added.

TABLE 9.3.   SOCIAL REINFORCERS FOR CHILDREN AND YOUTH (Continued)

Children	Youth
_____ is a hard worker today; good for you	that shows a lot of work
that's the way	you look great today
that's interesting	it really makes me feel good when I see so many of you hard at work
much better	that's the best job I've seen today
okay	you're paying attention so nicely
you should show this to your parents	the interest you're showing is great
you're doing better	it makes me happy to see you working so well
that's perfect	that's a thoughtful (courteous) thing to do for _____
that's another one you got right	_____ has gotten his materials and has started to work already; good going!
you're doing very well	_____ is ready to start
see how well _____ is doing?	you're really very considerate of one another
look how well he (she) did	
_____ is really working	
watch what he did; do it again	
show the class your _____	
_____ is really working hard; he is going to be able to _____	
wow, look at _____ work	
you look nice today	
_____ is working nicely; keep up the good work	
I can really tell _____ is thinking by what she just said	
_____ is sitting quietly and doing his work; good for you	
_____ is listening with such concentration; that's very polite, _____, thank you	
you should be proud of the way you're sitting quietly and listening to me while I'm giving a lesson	
_____ just earned another point by sitting quietly and listening while I was reading; good job, _____	
_____ walked quietly to her seat; thank you	
good, you sharpened your pencil before class; now you're ready to go	
_____ has all of her supplies on her desk and is ready to go, good!	
_____ has gotten his materials and has started to work already, good going!	
it's nice to see the way_____ raises his hand when he wants to share something with the class	
the whole class is really being polite in listening to one another	
this whole row is sitting quietly with their chairs on the floor; great!	

of social reinforcers that are frequently used with children and youth. The literature abounds in studies demonstrating that various social reinforcers can be used to increase the rates of children's behaviors. For example, Johnston, Kelley, Harris & Wolf (1966) tried social reinforcement to modify a preschool boy's use of playground equipment. Not only did the boy start to use the equipment more; so did other children on the playground. Allen and her colleagues (1964) have reported a study of a child whose play activity was characterized by withdrawal from her peers, accompanied by a demand for teacher attention. The teacher helped her to develop more appropriate behavior by giving her attention only in response to interaction with another child. No attention was given when she played by herself or when she attempted interaction with an adult.

Several investigators (Allen et al., 1967; Broden et al., 1970; Kazdin, 1973; Kazdin & Klock, 1973; Kennedy & Thompson, 1967) have increased rates of paying attention through social reinforcement. In one study (Broden et al., 1970) two very disruptive second-grade students were seated next to each other. When the teacher systematically increased the amount of attention for appropriate attending by one of the pair, his rate of attending increased. The attending of the other boy also increased, to a lesser degree, even though his own attending behavior was not being treated directly at that time. When the latter boy's attending behavior was treated by the teacher later on, it improved even further. In another study (Kazdin, 1973) social reinforcement increased attending by target students, as well as by adjacent peers who were not being treated. Kazdin and Klock (1973) showed that contingent smiles, patting, and touching increased the attentive behavior of eleven of twelve mentally retarded school children. Kennedy and Thompson (1967) used reinforcement during counseling. The child was given candy, accompanied by verbal praise and smiles, when he maintained eye contact with the counselor for at least a minute. His attending behavior was reported to have increased during counseling and also in the classroom. Similarly, in group counseling, socially reinforcing comments like "good," "that's wonderful," and "great," as well as smiles, were found to increase the verbal behavior of low-verbalizing sixth- and seventh-grade students (Tosi et al., 1971).

Recent evidence (Bernhardt & Forehand, 1975) suggests that **specific**, or **labeled, praise** is particularly effective. Specific praise is focused upon the aspect of the behavior that particularly deserves it: "How wonderful that you remembered to take your medicine without being reminded!" "Congratulations! You were able to remember to integrate the material with examples that are relevant for you." Specific praise places the emphasis on the behavior, rather than on the child, which is important. For, when praise is withheld from inappropriate behavior, it helps clients to recognize (or **discriminate**) that it is not they but their behavior that is inadequate. Specific praise increases the likelihood that specific aspects of behavior will be repeated in the future.

Surely we all realize how much the behavior of adults is affected by social reinforcement. Reminding ourselves of this fact, however, can be quite useful for purposes of staff development and self-improvement. Praise from peers and supervisors, feedback in the form of knowledge of client improvement or other information about teaching or therapeutic effectiveness, and even feedback from self-recordings have been shown to function as effective staff reinforcers. In one instance, nonprofessional institutional personnel increased their daily use of operant training methods when a feedback system, consisting of information about sessions conducted, was publicly disseminated among the staff (Panyan, Boozer & Morris, 1970). Similarly, Cooper, Thomson, and Baer (1970) found that feedback about definitions of appropriate child responses and percentage of attending to appropriate child responses produced increases in such attending. Cossairt, Hall, and Hopkins (1973) investigated whether or not feedback to teachers alone would improve teacher performance. By itself feedback produced inconclusive results, but when it was paired with praise, performance did improve. For those concerned with staff training, probably a combination of feedback about trainees' progress and about consequent student improvement with praise for increases in targeted trainee behaviors will be very productive.

Reinforcement, in the form of praise or approval from others, has also been shown to enhance individual's self-esteem or self-reference statements, assessed by means of paper-and-pencil tests. For instance, Ludwig and Maehr (1967) found that, when approval statements about students' performances in a physical-education class were made, the students' self-reference statements changed in a positive direction. People have also been taught to praise themselves (Wisocki, 1973). Self-praise too appears to have a reinforcing effect upon the behavior to be increased, as well as upon self-esteem.

Social reinforcers offer several distinct *advantages* over other reinforcers. They can readily be delivered immediately each time a behavior occurs in individual and small-group situations and, very frequently, even in large groups. People do not tend to become very quickly sated with social reinforcers. These factors, as we shall see in the next section, are crucial to strengthening behavior effectively. Change agents can usually take the time to praise, nod, smile, or make eye contact, even when surrounded by many youngsters. Social reinforcers are therefore practical. The only cost is the effort involved in remembering to deliver them or in devising signaling systems, like taped prompts (for example, periodic chimes) or visual prompts (periodic light flashes or cue cards), to cue their delivery. Most important, social reinforcers are natural in social settings. They do not usually intrude excessively into the ongoing program. Because they can be used over long time spans, they are particularly suited to supporting recently modified behavior. There need not be a complete cessation of contingencies when social reinforcers are employed in a program. That fact is crucial to response maintenance, as we shall see later.

Because social reinforcers have so much to commend them, they should play a role in every reinforcement program. Even when tangibles, edibles, activities, or exchangeable reinforcers are necessary because social reinforcers are not effective enough in a given situation, the delivery of other types of reinforcers should be paired as often as possible with positive social stimuli. In that way the social stimuli should begin to assume conditioned-reinforcement properties, as described in Unit 8. Then it should be possible gradually to substitute social reinforcers for the others. (See Unit 28 for a more complete discussion of this point.) Social events should be paired with other reinforcers for sensorily impaired young-sters also. Oral praise and tactile stimuli, like pats, gentle back rubs, and scratch-ing, can communicate social approval to the visually impaired child. Visual stimuli, like smiles, nods, and gestures of approval, and tactile stimuli are particularly ap-propriate for those with impaired hearing.

Group and peer reinforcing contingencies.   Sometimes social reinforcement results indirectly from the management procedures that are used. Group reinforcement and peer reinforcement are examples. In group reinforcement, a whole group of individuals, perhaps a class or all the students sitting in one section, are treated as a unit, as a single behaving individual. Taylor and Sulzer (1971) conducted a study with a preschool group. Under one condition, extra recess time was made available to the whole class if all the children had rested quietly during naptime. In another study (Elam & Sulzer, 1972) a special-education class earned privileges if the whole class met the behavioral requirements during academic work time. Ulman and Sulzer-Azaroff (1973) studied the differential effects of individualized tangible reinforcement, in which pennies were awarded to each individual for arithmetic items correctly completed, and "collective" reinforcement, in which all pennies earned were divided equally among all members of a group of re-tarded young adults. Both tangible reinforcement conditions were effective. The group-contingent condition was found to be as effective as the individual-contingent condition but a lot less time-consuming. Schmidt and Ulrich (1969) used a decibel meter to monitor noise in a regular public-school classroom. Rein-forcing ten minutes of "quiet time" in the classroom with extra gym time re-sulted in effective reduction of sound intensities.

Group contingencies often produce social responses among group mem-bers; students encourage one another to meet the requirements, or they reinforce one another for working (occasionally generating threats from some class mem-bers; Axelrod, 1973). One of the more encouraging side effects of group con-tingencies that has been observed is facilitation of peer tutoring and a consequent increase in student academic accomplishment (Hamblin, Hathaway & Wodarski, 1974). Students working for individual reinforcement tend to be concerned only with their own performance. When reinforcement depends upon the performances of others in the class, students begin to teach one another. In Hamblin, Hathaway, and Wodarski's program (1974), reinforcement for the group was based upon the bottom three scores in the class. This arrangement generated tutoring of the poorer students by more able students and resulted in superior achievement by the group as a whole. Similarly, in a study by Frankowsky and Sulzer-Azaroff (1975), group contingencies generated collateral positive verbal and nonverbal social behaviors. Although group contingencies do tend, under some conditions, to produce social reinforcement from peers, other indirect responses may also be generated: desir-able ones like encouragement and tutoring or undesirable ones like threats and possibly peer punishment. For this reason, behavior analysts who use group contingencies should be careful to *monitor* these side effects in order to determine whether they facilitate or impede progress.

Peer-reinforcing contingencies directly involve the subject's peers in the conduct of the program. Peers may be asked to direct their attention to fellow students who are working appropriately, rather than disrupting (Solomon & Wahler, 1973), or they may be trained to record behavior and dispense points exchangeable for reinforcing activities (Greenwood, Sloane & Baskin, 1974). Sometimes individual students earn reinforcers that are shared among the whole group (Walker & Buckley, 1972). Each of these procedures represents an attempt to harness the powerful reinforcing properties that peers tend to have for one another. Procedures for incorporating group and peer contingencies into applied behavioral programs will be discussed further in Units 27 and 28.

Countercontrol.   Children and youth also control powerful social reinforcing contingencies for contingency managers, in addition to those for one another. (Remember the comment by Brown, Wienkowski, and Stolz, 1975, quoted in Unit 7: "Control always results in countercontrol.") Recognizing the influence that students have on teachers' behavior, several investigators (Graubard, Rosenberg & Miller, 1971; Sherman & Cormier, 1974) purposely trained students in the contingent use of specific behavioral procedures (like reinforcement and extinction). Graubard and his colleagues astutely noted that, first, children spend more time with classroom teachers than do professional consultants or administrators; second, students have the greatest personal interest in changing their teachers; and, finally, "the positive use of power leads to self-enhancement and positive feelings about the self" (1971, p. 83). Each student was given the responsibility for accelerating praise rates and decelerating negative comments by the teachers. The behavioral program proved effective within a short period of time. Furthermore, as the investigators noted, "the children's labor contributing to effective change was free; and it is certainly less costly to employ pupils using reinforcement readily available in the classroom, than it is to pay clinical personnel within the traditional medical model, to change behavior" (p. 89). Perhaps one day children and youth will be formally taught to use effective reinforcement procedures with their parents, teachers, and other contingency managers when they engage in behaviors that facilitate learning and social-emotional development. All would seem to benefit by such an approach.

Summary

In this unit we have presented a very broad array of potential reinforcers for programs serving children and youth. It should be apparent that effective reinforcers can be found for everyone. The search for an effective reinforcer may, however, require some imagination, flexibility in programming, creativity, and time. Sometimes it may be necessary initially to select reinforcers that are somewhat intrusive, in order to overcome inertia. As a behavior begins to be emitted at a fairly acceptable rate, however, it should be possible gradually to introduce less and less intrusive reinforcers into the situation. Remember, though, that, if the behavior fails to continue, it is not behavior analysis that is at fault. Rather, we must explore the conditions that are known to influence reinforcer effectiveness. These will be the subject of the next unit.

References

Allen, K. E., Hart, B. M., Buell, J. S., Harris, F. R. & Wolf, M. M. Effects of social reinforcement on isolate behavior of a nursery school child. *Child Development,* 1964, **35**, 511–518.

Allen, K. E., Henke, L. B., Harris, F. R., Baer, D. M. & Reynolds, N. J. Control of hyperactivity by social reinforcement of attending behavior. *Journal of Educational Psychology,* 1967, **58**, 231–237.

Axelrod, S. Comparison of individual and group contingencies in two special classes. *Behavior Therapy,* 1973, **4**, 83–90.

Ayllon, T. & Azrin, N. H. The measurement and reinforcement of behavior of psychotics. *Journal of the Experimental Analysis of Behavior,* 1965, **8**, 357–383.

Ayllon, T. & Azrin, N. H. *The token economy.* New York: Appleton, 1968.

Ayllon, T. and Roberts, M. D. Eliminating discipline problems by strengthening academic performance. *Journal of Applied Behavior Analysis,* 1974, **7**, 73–81.

Azrin, N. H. & Armstrong, P. M. The "mini-meal": A method for teaching eating skills to the profoundly retarded. *Mental Retardation,* 1973, **2**, 9–13.

Azrin, N. H. & Lindsley, O. R. The reinforcement of cooperation between children. *Journal of Abnormal and Social Psychology,* 1956, **52**, 100–102.

Bernhardt, A. J. & Forehand, R. The effects of labeled and unlabeled praise upon lower and middle class children. *Journal of Experimental Child Psychology,* 1975, **19**, 536–543.

Brigham, T. A., Graubard, P. S., and Stans, A. Analysis of the effects of sequential reinforcement contingencies on aspects of composition. *Journal of Applied Behavior Analysis,* 1972, **5**, 421–429.

Broden, M., Bruce, C., Mitchell, M. A., Carter, V. & Hall, R. V. Effects of teacher attention on attending behavior of two boys in adjacent desks. *Journal of Applied Behavior Analysis,* 1970, **3**, 199–203.

Broden, M., Hall, R. V., Dunlap, A., Clark, R. Effects of teacher attention and a token reinforcement system in a junior high school special education class. *Exceptional Children,* 1970, 341–349.

Brook, F. S. and Snow, D. L. Two case illustrations of the use of behavior modification techniques in the school setting. *Behavior Therapy,* 1972, **3**, 100–103.

Brown, B. S., Wienkowski, L. A. & Stolz, S. B. *Behavior modification: Perspective on a current issue.* Washington, D.C.: U.S. Department of Health, Education and Welfare, National Institute of Mental Health, 1975.

Bushell, D. Jr. *A token manual for behavior analysis classrooms.* Department of Human Development, University of Kansas, Lawrence, Kansas, n.d.

Campbell, A. & Sulzer, B. Naturally available reinforcers as motivators towards reading and spelling achievement by educable mentally handicapped students. Paper presented at the meeting of the American Educational Research Association meeting, New York, February 1971.

Chadwick, B. A. and Day, R. C. Systematic reinforcement: Academic performance of undergraduate students. *Journal of Applied Behavior Analysis,* 1971, **4**, 311–319.

Christy, P. R. Does use of tangible rewards with individual children affect peer observers? *Journal of Applied Behavior Analysis,* 1975, **8**, 187–196.

Coleman, R. A conditioning technique applicable to elementary school classrooms. *Journal of Applied Behavior Analysis,* 1970, **3**, 293–297.

Cooper, M. L., Thomson, C. L. & Baer, D. M. The experimental modification of teacher attending behavior. *Journal of Applied Behavior Analysis,* 1970, **3**, 153–157.

Cossairt, A., Hall, R. V. & Hopkins, B. L. The effects of experimenter's instructions, feedback, and praise on teacher praise and student attending behavior. *Journal of Applied Behavior Analysis,* 1973, **6**, 89–100.

Craig, H. B. & Holland, A. L. Reinforcement of visual attending in classrooms for deaf children. *Journal of Applied Behavior Analysis,* 1970, **3**, 97–109.

Drabman, R. S., Tucker, R. D. Why classroom token economies fail. *Journal of School Psychology,* 1974, **3**, 178–188.

Elam, D., & Sulzer, B. Group versus individual reinforcement in modifying problem behaviors in a trainable mentally handicapped classroom. Unpublished paper, Southern Illinois University, 1972.

Ferri, H. J. Wethersfield School Department interim report on evaluation of the use of various types of incentives in education programs, 1972.

Frankowsky, R. J. & Sulzer-Azaroff, B. Individual and group contingencies and collateral social behaviors. Paper presented at the meeting of the Association for the Advancement of Behavior Therapy, San Francisco, December 1975.

Graubard, P. S., Rosenberg, H. & Miller, M. B. Student applications of behavior modification to teachers and environments or ecological approaches to social deviancy. In E. A. Ramp & B. L. Hopkins (Eds.), *A new direction for education: Behavior analysis, 1971.* Lawrence: University of Kansas, 1971. 80–101.

Green, D. & Lepper, M. R. Intrinsic motivation: How to turn play into work. *Psychology Today,* 1974, **8**, 49–54.

Greenwood, C. R., Sloane, H. N. & Baskin, A. Training elementary aged peer behavior managers to control small group programmed mathematics. *Journal of Applied Behavior Analysis,* 1974, **7**, 103–114.

Hamblin, R. L., Hathaway, C. & Wodarski, J. Group contingencies, peer tutoring, and accelerating academic achievement. In R. Ulrich, T. Stanchnik & J. Mabry (Eds.), *Control of human behavior modification in education.* Vol. 3. Glenview, Ill.: Scott, Foresman, 1974, 333–340.

Homme, L. E., DeBaca, P. C., Devine, J. V., Steinhorst, R. & Rickert, E. J. Use of the Premack principle in controlling the behavior of nursery school children. *Journal of the Experimental Analysis of Behavior,* 1963, **6**, 544.

Hopkins, B. L., Schutte, R. C. & Garton, K. L. The effects of access to a playroom on the rate and quality of printing and writing of first and second grade students. *Journal of Applied Behavior Analysis,* 1971, **4**, 77–87.

Jacobs, J. Project No. 9–0257, Grant No. OEG–4–9–109257–0045–010. A comparison of group and individual rewards in teaching reading to slow learners. Southern Illinois University, Carbondale, Illinois 62901. June, 1970, U. S. Department of Health, Education, and Welfare, Office of Education, Bureau of Research.

Johnston, M. K., Kelley, C. S., Harris, F. R. & Wolf, M. M. An application of reinforcement principles to development of motor skills of a young child. *Child Development,* 1966, **37**, 379–387.

Jones, R. T., Kazdin, A. E. Programming response maintenance after withdrawing token reinforcement. *Behavior Therapy,* 1975, **6**, 153–164.

Karraker, R. J. Increasing academic performance through home managed contingency programs. *Journal of School Psychology,* 1972, **10**, 173–179.

Kazdin, A. E. The effect of vicarious reinforcement on attentive behavior in the classroom. *Journal of Applied Behavior Analysis,* 1973, **6**, 71–78.

Kazdin, A. E. & Klock, J. The effect of nonverbal teacher approval on student attentive behavior. *Journal of Applied Behavior Analysis,* 1973, **6**, 643–654.

Kennedy, D. A. & Thompson, I. Use of reinforcement technique with a first grade boy. *The Personnel and Guidance Journal,* 1967, **46**, 366–370.

Krumboltz, J. D. & Krumboltz, H. B. *Changing children's behavior.* Englewood Cliffs, N.J.: Prentice-Hall, 1972.

Ludwig, P. J. & Maehr, M. L. Changes in self concepts in stated behavioral preferences. *Child Development,* 1967, **38**, 453–469.

McLaughlin, T. F. and Malaby, J. Intrinsic reinforcers in a classroom token economy. *Journal of Applied Behavior Analysis,* 1972, **5**, 263–270.

Meyerson, L., Kerr, N. & Michael, J. L. Behavior modification in rehabilitation. In S. W. Bijou & D. M. Baer (Eds.), *Child development readings in experimental analysis.* New York: Appleton, 1967, 214–239.

Packard, R. G. The control of "classroom attention:" A group contingency for complex behavior. *Journal of Applied Behavior Analysis,* 1970, **3**, 13–28.

Panyan, M., Boozer, H. & Morris, N. Feedback to attendants as a reinforcer for applying operant techniques. *Journal of Applied Behavior Analysis,* 1970, **3**, 1–4.

Phillips, E. L., Phillips, E. A., Fixsen, D. & Wolf, M. Achievement Place: Modification of behavior of pre-delinquent boys within a token economy. *Journal of Applied Behavior Analysis,* 1971, **4**, 45–61.

Premack, D. Toward empirical behavior laws: I. Positive reinforcement. *Psychological Review,* 1959, **66**, 219–233.

Reese, E. P. A general procedure for applied behavior analysis. Unpublished paper, Mt. Holyoke College, 1973.

Renne, C. M. & Creer, T. L. Training children with asthma to use inhalation therapy equipment. *Journal of Applied Behavior Analysis,* 1976, **9**, 1–11.

Risley, T. Learning and lollipops. *Psychology Today,* 1968, **1**, 28–31, 62–65.

Robertson, S. J., DeReus, D. M. & Drabman, R. S. Peer and college-student tutoring as reinforcement in a token economy. *Journal of Applied Behavior Analysis,* 1976, **9**, 167–177.

Schmidt, G. W. & Ulrich, K. E. Effects of group contingent events upon classroom noise. *Journal of Applied Behavior Analysis,* 1969, **2**, 171–179.

Sherman, T. M. & Cormier, W. H. An investigation of the influence of student behavior on teacher behavior. *Journal of Applied Behavior Analysis,* 1974, **7**, 11–21.

Siqueland, E. R. & Lipsitt, L. P. Conditioned head-turning in human newborns. *Journal of Experimental Child Psychology,* 1966, **3**, 356–376.

Solomon, R. W. & Wahler, R. G. Peer reinforcement control of classroom problem behavior. *Journal of Applied Behavior Analysis,* 1973, **6**, 49–56.

Sulzer, B. and Mayer, G. R. *Behavior modification procedures for school personnel.* Hinsdale, Dryden Press, 1972.

Taylor, L. K. & Sulzer, B. The effects of group and individual contingencies on testing behavior. Unpublished paper, Southern Illinois University, 1971.

Tharp, R. G. & Wetzel, R. J. *Behavior modification in the natural environment.* New York: Academic Press, 1969.

Tosi, D. J., Upshaw, K., Lande, A. & Waldron, M. A. Group counseling with nonverbalizing elementary students: Differential effects of Premack and social reinforcement techniques. *Journal of Counseling Psychology,* 1971, **18**, 437–440.

Ulman, J. D. & Sulzer-Azaroff, B. Multielement baseline design in educational research. In E. Ramp & G. Semb (Eds.), *Behavior analysis: Areas of research and application.* Englewood Cliffs, N.J.: Prentice-Hall, 1975, 377–391.

Walker, H. M. & Buckley, N. K. Programming generalization and maintenance of treatment effects across time and across settings. *Journal of Applied Behavior Analysis,* 1972, **5**, 209–224.

Wheeler, A. & Sulzer, B. Operant training and generalization of a verbal response form in a speech deficient child. *Journal of Applied Behavior Analysis,* 1970, **3**, 139–147.

Wilson, C. W. and Hopkins, B. L. The effects of contingent music on the intensity of noise in junior high home economics classes. *Journal of Applied Behavior Analysis*, 1973, **6**, 269–275.

Wisocki, P. A. A. covert reinforcement program for the treatment of test anxiety: Brief report. *Behavior Therapy*, 1973, **4**, 264–266.

Wolf, M. M., Risley, T. R. & Mees, H. L. Application of operant conditioning procedures to the behavior problems of an autistic child. *Behavior Research and Therapy*, 1964, **1**, 305–312.

Wyatt v. *Stickney*. 344 F. Supp. 373 (M.D. Ala. 1972, North. Div.)

Implementing Effective Reinforcement Procedures

1. After mastering the material in this unit, using examples not described here, you should be able to describe and illustrate the following:
   a. Immediacy of reinforcement
   b. Situational conditions
   c. Deprivation
   d. Reinforcer novelty
   e. Reinforcer sampling
   f. Competing contingencies
   g. Reinforcement schedules
   h. Negative reinforcement

2. List five factors, besides selecting appropriate reinforcers, that influence effectiveness of reinforcement.

3. Explain why immediacy is so important during the initial stages of a reinforcement procedure and how it is incorporated during the various stages of programs with individuals and groups of youngsters.

4. Discuss how situational conditions may influence the effectiveness of a reinforcement procedure.

5. Describe how the quantity of reinforcer delivered may influence effectiveness and how to find out how much is enough.

6. Discuss how novelty influences effectiveness of reinforcers and how it might be used in a specific program of relevance to the reader.

7. Design a plan for using reinforcer sampling in a behavioral program.

8. Discuss the role of competing contingencies in a reinforcement program.

9. Distinguish negative reinforcement from positive reinforcement and punishment, and describe how it operates.

10. Discuss the pros and cons of using negative reinforcement and how to use it effectively.

"Aha," says Ms. Charming. "Now I have some ideas about new reinforcers to try in the workshop. I can attempt to use social, activity, exchangeable, tangible, or edible reinforcers beside M & Ms." The selection of appropriate reinforcers, however, is only part of the process. Once those consequences have been selected, several other factors must be considered so that their effectiveness can be maximized. Among them are immediacy of presentation, conditions, amount of reinforcement, novelty, reinforcer sampling, and scheduling. Then, on the small chance that all those factors fail to combine effectively to increase behavior, negative reinforcement may serve temporarily to help clear the hurdle. In this unit each of these aspects is explained and discussed.

OTHER FACTORS TO CONSIDER IN MAXIMIZING EFFECTIVENESS OF REINFORCEMENT

Immediacy of Reinforcement

One basic principle of behavior is that *immediate* reinforcement is more effective than delayed reinforcement(Skinner, 1938). One of the main reasons why is discussed by Reynolds:

. . . Delayed reinforcement is not as effective as immediate reinforcement, partially because it allows the organism to emit additional behavior between the response we wish to reinforce and the actual occurrence of the reinforcer; thus, the intervening behavior is also reinforced, with the result that what is reinforced is the response followed by some other behavior rather than just the response alone. (1968, p. 29)

Charlie's supervisor may decide to give him a positive rating because he has improved in his vocational-training skills. The supervisor may fail to use any other reinforcers for this improvement, deciding that the positive rating alone will be sufficiently rewarding. Now let us suppose that Charlie is engaged in distracting the other trainees at the time that the rating forms are delivered. The rating may well reinforce *that* behavior. The supervisor, then, will have to backtrack and indicate which behaviors are supposed to be reinforced. Some form of immediate reinforcement would help Charlie to distinguish acceptable from unacceptable behaviors.

The desirability of immediate reinforcement presents a problem to many contingency managers who are interested in more effective group-management procedures. When a strong reinforcer is used in a large group setting, it is often difficult to reinforce the behavior of individual members. A teacher may decide to take students on a field trip, as a reinforcer for their having completed all their assignments for a week. Naturally, it would be impossible to deliver the trip to each student immediately, contingent upon the completion of an assignment. Fortunately, there is an alternative, and that alternative again lies in the use of conditioned reinforcement. The contingency manager can use a signal to indicate that a stronger reinforcer will be presented: "Good, I see you are getting your work finished. This way you'll be able to go on the trip Friday." If a verbal statement is not effective, a token system may be tried. A token can be given immediately to the students as each one completes a subsection of work; a specific number of tokens can be required for each to go on the trip. That is essentially how the delay was bridged for students who earned tickets exchangeable for later tutoring (Robertson, DeReus & Drabman, 1975).

Another factor may serve to encourage those who find it impossible to reinforce immediately the many members in their groups or classes. The fact is that people can gradually learn to tolerate longer and longer reinforcement delays. Probably every reader has experienced long delays in the receipt of a paycheck or a grade, yet the behavior of working or studying does not disintegrate. How do adults learn to tolerate long delays in reinforcement? Through experiencing *gradually* longer and longer delays.

Most children, too, learn to accept delays in reinforcement. If a particular child has not done so, he can be taught tolerance for delays if they are programmed into the routine gradually. When Charlie persists in pestering his supervisor to look at his work or constantly asks to have his accomplishments praised, it is probably because he has not learned this type of tolerance. The supervisor may then set up a program with Charlie to help him bridge the time gap. For a while, he may try to check the work upon request. Little by little he can begin to delay for a moment or two, simultaneously using verbal prompts: "I'll be over to check your work in a couple of minutes." After many instances of brief delay, he can gradually lengthen the interval.

Situational Conditions

As previously described, immediacy facilitates discrimination. When reinforcement is delivered immediately, individuals can more easily identify which of their behaviors lead to reinforcement and which do not. Another factor that can facilitate discrimination, and thus rapid learning, is clear specification of the environmental conditions, or stimuli, under which reinforcement will be delivered. If Kevin must complete all his chores before 9:00 A.M. in order to receive reinforcement, these conditions should be stipulated. If hand raising is to be reinforced during study time but not during recess or discussion time, when only spontaneous participation is reinforced, that should also be so specified. Clear specification of the stimuli that must be present if behavior is to be reinforced enhances the likelihood that the behavior will occur at the appropriate time and place. And, if consistently presented these stimuli will soon come to cue, or **occasion**, occurrence of the behavior: The hands on the clock approaching the hour of nine will become a signal to complete chores. Study time will become a signal to raise one's hand before speaking. How such cues, or **discriminative stimuli**, are developed will be considered later.

Amount of Reinforcement

The decision about the quantity—*how much* reinforcement to deliver—depends upon a number of factors: the type of reinforcer used, the deprivation conditions, and the effort required to make the response. We recall that edibles lead to satiation more rapidly than activity and social reinforcers. An empirical approach is the best way to find out how much is enough: Try it out, and see. Count the number of hours since the client has eaten. See if the target behaviors continue to be emitted when reinforced with small amounts of food.

With social reinforcers, **deprivation** (how long it has been since the reinforcer was last delivered) and satiation play a smaller role. A smile or saying "good boy" may be effective, even though the child has received several such reinforcers in the recent past. Contingency managers should be aware, however, that one can also become sated by conditioned reinforcers. Sulzer, Mayer, and Cody have illustrated the possibility of such an occurrence:

... [S]uppose praise from the teacher has been found to be reinforcing to Jim. Jim does not successfully complete his math assignments but does well on all of his other subjects. The counselor observes that Jim's teacher gives him lavish praise for the well done subject matter. The counselor might conclude that Jim is satiated. He would then suggest to the teacher that she stop, or reduce,[1] the amount of praise she gives Jim for his performance on subject matter other than math, and that the praise given to math assignments be contingent on their successful completion. Hopefully, Jim would do better in math in order to receive the teacher's praise. (1968, p. 45)

Social reinforcers can also be insufficient (for example, a slight nod or a weak smile) or too strong (vigorous nodding or an ear-to-ear grin). People who socially overreinforce are called "gushy" or "saccharine," and the social reinforcers that they deliver often lose much of their reinforcing value to the individual.

All other factors being equal, it takes more reinforcers to sustain hard work than to sustain easy work. Ask yourself whether or not you would take a course requiring twice as much work for the same number of credits as another interesting course teaching you an equivalent amount. Given the choice of working on math, which is easy for Jenny, or chemistry, which is hard for her, she would probably select math. Offering more reinforcement for working in chemistry—increasing the credits, providing more teacher approval, giving her a high-status job like lab assistant, or the like—would shift the balance. It is often diffi-

---

[1] Such a switch to an intermittent schedule of reinforcement appears to facilitate behaviors that occur in more than one setting (generalization). This point will be elaborated upon later in the text.

cult for parents, teachers, and others to alter their social-interactional habits and to present reinforcers for good performance, rather than criticism and sarcasm for poor performance. In order effectively to teach themselves or one another to increase the rate of the former, more effortful kinds of social interaction with children and youth, they may need additional reinforcement (for example, feedback about client success, praise from peers or supervisors, release from duties, extra free time, easier assignments).

Reinforcers that can be exchanged for various consumable or activity reinforcers, like tokens, are only minimally affected by satiation. Even the individual with a large bank account will usually be reinforced by receiving more money. The same is true of events that signal delayed delivery of items or activities that reinforce the individual: a smile, a promise, or the like. By now it should be apparent that there is no simple formula for determining what quantity of reinforcement to deliver. The final judgment must be made on the basis of empirical data.

Novelty

"Other things being equal, organisms will often prefer to put themselves in novel situations" (Millenson, 1967, p. 397). This conclusion was based on the results of a number of studies indicating that an organism would work for the opportunity to experience novel stimuli. Teachers often learn to make use of this phenomenon.

One very clever idea was used in a classroom program recently. A surprise box was prepared, with slips of paper containing all sorts of different directions: Draw a picture of a cow; wash the blackboard; get a drink of water; write a paragraph describing your pet; five minutes of free time; tutor a friend in reading; and so on. The students could draw slips from the box when they had completed their assignments. Not knowing what the slip might contain added lots of excitement to the game. (Similar programs are described in Units 27 and 28.) Shrewd spouses use a related idea when they set up "job jars," and Chinese restaurants help to reinforce their customers by providing cookies containing novel fortunes. Elementary-school teachers often program their class activities so that there is variation from one to the next: first reading, then gym, math problems, art, and so on. In doing so, they are using the reinforcing effects of novelty.

More and more schools and community facilities are setting up special activity centers. Such a center provides novel learning experiences for children and youth. For example, the activity center in a local school provides instruction in woodworking, baking, construction, macramé, and other crafts. Each day a number of novel learning activities is scheduled. As students complete their assigned work, they may go to the activity center for a fixed period of time. Another high school recently reported how parents and students participated in conducting such programs. Those who had particular hobbies scheduled special classes. The classes included tie dyeing, guitar playing, calligraphy, auto-engine repair, model building, sculpture, kite building, social dancing, ceramics, identi-fication of edible wild plants and natural-foods cookery, and other workshops of particular interest to teenagers. The students could earn instruction in those skills by completing their regular assignments. Although some of these relatively novel activities occasionally appear as part of a high-school curriculum, rarely is access to them made readily available contingent upon students' completion of specific requirements.

Reinforcer Sampling

Although novelty may enhance the potential reinforcing properties of an object or event, sometimes emotional reactions interfere with the individual's experi-encing the reinforcer in the first place. Frightened or unsure, he may fail to find out what a good thing he is missing. People may be "scared stiff" the first time they stand up on water skiis, ride a roller coaster, or perform before an audience. Yet we are all acquainted with people for whom these events have become very reinforcing. Those individuals have undoubtedly adapted to the situations; events are no longer so frightening because they have had opportunities to experience them sufficiently often.

Sometimes the individual has not had experience with an object or an event, and therefore its potential reinforcing properties are unknown to him. Holz, Azrin, and Ayllon (1963) found that, when mental-hospital patients were persuaded to try reinforcers, like certain foods, they would subsequently work to acquire those reinforcers. For these reasons, Ayllon and Azrin, in their book *The Token Economy*, suggest a **reinforcer-sampling** rule: "Before using an event or stimulus as a reinforcer, require sampling of the reinforcer in the situation in which it is to be used" (1968, p. 91).

Many teachers, parents, and other contingency managers make it a prac-tice first to display a new book, start a fascinating story, teach a new game, organ-ize a new project, and otherwise expose children to novel events or objects. Once the children begin to enjoy an experience, it becomes a reinforcer and can be made contingent upon the performance of a targeted task: "As soon as we finish our reading, we will use the remainder of the period to play the new game we played yesterday."

In a **token-economy** program (Sulzer, Loving & Hunt, 1973) some excellent children's films had been borrowed from the local university's film library. The idea was to have the students in the program pay points that they had earned for completed academic work to gain admission to the films. Not knowing anything about the films, the students would not spend their points for such an activity. It was then decided to start showing the films anyway, running each without cost until an exciting spot had been reached. At that point the projector was turned off, and the students were asked if they would like to purchase with points the opportunity to see the remainder of the film. Without exception, all the students did so. This reinforcer-sampling procedure may appear slightly insidious, but the students enjoyed and learned from the film, and a powerfully effective reinforcing contingency with which to motivate the students to perform academically had been identified.

Competing Contingencies

Human beings live in complex societies, with a multiplicity of contingencies impinging upon them simultaneously. Think about the reinforcing and punishing contingencies operating on you at any one time. Your performance of assigned tasks at school or work may be rewarded; nonperformance may be punished. Your social interactions yield you the attention of friends—or perhaps their neglect. The chores you do at home are greeted by consequences from parents, spouse, or roommates: some good, some bad, some nonexistent. Similarly, activities outside the home, like shopping, recreation, traveling, and just about all of your other actions produce reactions from the environment. Some environmental reactions are stronger and exert greater influence than others, and sometimes these contingencies are in direct competition with one another. In all likelihood, responses that yield you life-support items like food, clothing, and shelter are stronger than those that yield weaker reinforcers, like approval from someone you do not know very well or do not particularly care for.

So it is with children and youth. Various contingencies may be operating in competition with one another. Were he in isolation, attention from the teacher when a task was completed might sustain Elmer's productivity. But he is not usually in isolation. Other real and potential reinforcers (and punishers) are present in the room. Elmer may find Jane's giggling at his grimaces far more reinforcing than the teacher's attention to his on-task behavior. Or he may find avoiding the potential ridicule of his buddies for his conformity to school rules more reinforcing. Again, his teacher might, in isolation, find a slight improvement in Elmer's performance reinforcing. Far more reinforcing might be the result of ejecting Elmer from the room and no longer having to contend with his antics.

Effective reinforcement therefore requires that contingencies currently in operation in the client's life be assessed. When strong contingencies operate to sustain behaviors that compete with target behaviors, stronger contingencies must be substituted, or the entire effort will be of no avail. For example, it could be arranged to reinforce Elmer heavily for remaining on task and to reinforce the other students in the class for ignoring his disruptive behavior and for encouraging or tutoring him. The teacher might arrange things so that when Elmer earned his reinforcement, he would earn it not only for himself but also for the whole class. For instance, he could earn extra minutes of recess or time for the class to read comic books. In the event that such contingencies resulted in the other students' putting too much pressure on him, the program could be revised to allow the class to earn its reinforcers even when Elmer did not, the group could be reinforced for ignoring Elmer's misbehaviors.

For the teacher who is more reinforced by removing Elmer from the room, **supplementary reinforcers** might be brought to bear for keeping him in class and working with the problem. Approval from supervisors and consultants for improvements in Elmer's behavior, changes in responsibilities more to the teacher's liking, and encouragement from peers might combine to shift the balance of reinforcement.

Scheduling

Scheduling of reinforcement involves the "rule followed by the environment . . . in determining which among the many occurrences of a response will be reinforced" (Reynolds, 1968, p. 60). If Mike is called on *every* time that he raises his hand, his hand raising is being continually reinforced. Hand raising for Mike is on a **continuous reinforcement schedule** (CRF). More than likely, however, students are only occasionally called upon when they raise their hands. Then hand raising is on an **intermittent reinforcement schedule**.

There are many different **schedules of reinforcement**, and each has different properties or effects. Different schedules may be geared to procedures designed to shape, increase, maintain, or decrease behavior. It is primarily with the issue of increasing behavior that the present discussion is concerned. The effects of scheduling on other behavioral aspects will be considered in detail later.

When the goal of a program is to increase behavior, a very rich or continuous schedule of reinforcement will most effectively serve the purpose. For example, if parents are trying to teach their children a new routine, the more often they reinforce them, the better. The parents may want to teach their children to pick up after themselves. As part of the procedure, they may want them to put their dirty dishes in the sink. Each time that the children do so, the parents may praise them. When the behavior is pretty well established through continuous reinforcement, the frequency of reinforcement can be reduced. The fact that reinforcement frequency can be reduced once a behavior has been fairly well learned is fortunate. It is physically impossible for a parent, teacher, or anyone else to reinforce every occurrence of every desired behavior. Indeed, as we shall find later on, continuous reinforcement is not a desirable method for maintaining well-learned behaviors. It serves the purposes of behavior management best when, and only when, a behavior is to be increased.

NEGATIVE REINFORCEMENT

Positive reinforcement, one basic procedure for increasing the occurrence of a behavior that already exists in an individual's repertoire, has been discussed. We shall now look at an alternative basic procedure that will accomplish the same end: negative reinforcement (or *escape conditioning*).

Negative Reinforcement Defined

Reinforcement is a procedure that serves to *maintain or increase a behavior*, whether the process is labeled "positive" or "negative." Positive reinforcement is the *presentation* of a stimulus as a consequence of a response and has the function of increasing or maintaining that response. When a child says, "Milk, please" and receives milk, the milk is a *positive reinforcer* if the child's rate of saying "please" subsequently increases. In negative reinforcement, the increase is a function of escape from, or *removal* of, an **aversive stimulus** as the consequence of a response. Therefore, a *behavior or response has been negatively reinforced if it increases or maintains because of the contingent removal or reduction of a stimulus.* If the removal of a stimulus has the effect of increasing or maintaining a behavior, that stimulus is called an "aversive stimulus."[2] Like positive reinforcement, negative reinforcement is defined solely by its effect upon behavior. To repeat, negative reinforcement *increases* or *maintains* behavior.

Negative reinforcement is a universal phenomenon. There are many everyday situations in which it occurs. We are reinforced when we escape from the heat of the noonday sun, close a window to shut off a draft, respond to a child to escape her crying, take off our shoes when they pinch our feet, and kindle a fire to escape the cold. In each of these examples, a behavior effectively eliminates an aversive stimulus: Closing the window eliminates the draft, and responding to a crying child stops the crying. Each behavior *works*: It produces a positive outcome. It is thus likely to occur again. Individuals learn behaviors that *help them to experience relief from aversive stimuli.*

Negative reinforcement is often used by parents and child-care workers. Mike is nagged until he does his homework or takes out the trash. Flossie has to stay in her room until she apologizes for what she has said. Clyde says that he does not want to jump off the diving board. His Dad teases him: "What's the matter, are you chicken?" Clyde takes the dive to terminate the teasing. Mike's behavior (taking out the trash) has been negatively reinforced by the removal of the nagging. Flossie's apologizing works to release her from her room. Clyde's behavior, jumping off the diving board, also removes an aversive stimulus: his father's teasing. In each instance, these behaviors have been strengthened because they have turned off something painful or aversive: They have been negatively reinforced.

The behavior of children often negatively reinforces the behavior of adults. This observation should not come as a surprise. Everyone is familiar with the child who cries or throws a temper tantrum to "get his way." Why? Because it gets him what he wants—and that is positive reinforcement. The parent or teacher, by giving in to the child's demands, is negatively reinforced: Letting the child have his way stops or removes the tantrum or aversive stimulus. Older youths may not throw tantrums, but they too use negative reinforcement. Clyde stops scowling or sulking, without awareness, when his mom stops making demands upon him. An attendant yells at a child who is causing a disturbance (screaming, hitting, and the like). Yelling works to remove the aversive disturbance. Under similar circumstances the adult is thus likely to yell again. Another adult might send the child out of the room or beat him because of aversive behavior. This behavior too can

---

[2] The term "negative reinforcer" is also used as a synonym for the term "aversive stimulus," the removal of which results in an increase in behavior. We shall avoid this term because of the confusion it frequently occasions.

be reinforcing to the adult because aversive behavior has been terminated. Sending the child out of the room or beating him has been negatively reinforced and is likely henceforth to occur more frequently under similar circumstances.

Sometimes young people manage to avoid, through negative reinforcement, having to perform tasks or school assignments. When an assignment that may involve considerable time is given, youngsters complain. To stop the complaining (the aversive stimulus), the adult reduces the chore or school assignment. Subsequently, to avoid aversive consequences, lighter tasks are assigned.

Negative Reinforcement Compared with Other Procedures

In the language of the layman, the term "negative reinforcement" is often confused with other procedures. But behavior analysis gives to each procedure its own specific operational definition. It would probably be helpful for the reader to be alerted to the differences in those various operations (see Table 10.1). For instance, **negative reinforcement** involves the *removal* of an aversive stimulus; **punishment** (see Unit 22) involves the *presentation* of an aversive stimulus. The **timeout** and **response-cost** procedures (see Units 20, 19) lead to *removal* of positive stimuli contingent upon a response. **Extinction** (see Unit 11) is the label given to the *discontinuation* of reinforcement, and recovery (Reese, Howard & Reese, 1977) is the term used to describe the condition in *effect* when aversive consequences are no longer delivered contingent upon a response. For the time being, however, we should concentrate upon clarifying the negative-reinforcement operation and distinguishing it from all other operations.

Negative Reinforcement in Home, School, and Community

If negative reinforcement is an effective method for increasing a behavior, should it be used with children and youth? Let us look again at the procedure. If negative reinforcement is to be used, an *aversive* stimulus must be present. Then it is possible to reinforce a behavior by removing the aversive stimulus contingent upon the emission of the behavior. As we shall see in more detail in Unit 22, however, undesirable side effects like escape, avoidance, and aggression are likely to occur when aversive stimuli are used (Azrin & Holz, 1966). In addition to their

TABLE 10.1. OPERATIONAL DEFINITIONS OF REINFORCEMENT PROCEDURES

	Positive Stimulus	Aversive Stimulus
Contingent Presentation	positive reinforcement	punishment
Contingent Removal	time out and response cost	negative reinforcement
Contingency Discontinued	extinction	recovery

role in the reinforcement process, aversive stimuli often promote collateral escape responses. The individual tends to leave, or escape, the aversive environment; Jim stays away from school, and Fred "tunes out" his nagging parent by thinking about other things. Aversive stimuli may also promote aggression. It is not unusual for a child to respond *aggressively* after she has been nagged, kept after school, isolated in a room at home, teased, or ridiculed. Furthermore, all too frequently, aggressive behaviors are learned because they themselves frequently work to remove an aversive stimulus. For example, Lucretia is likely to stop teasing Elmer if she is slapped for doing so. Similarly, Nurse Barton is likely to stop nagging Helen if Helen disrupts the ward by screaming at the nurse when she nags. Elmer's and Helen's aggressive behaviors have been negatively reinforced, because they have terminated the aversive teasing and nagging. Aggression, as well as escape and avoidance, often disrupts social relations and may also produce competing responses that interfere with continuing programs. A youngster who is clenching his fists, experiencing physiological responses (like perspiration and increased pulse rate), or actually fighting will not be in the best shape to profit from instruction at that moment.

Some circumstances may, however, justify the use of negative reinforcement. For example, there are many people who will refuse to do something, even though the attempt may result in financial gain, increased prestige, or other forms of strong positive reinforcement. Yet they may make the effort if it will stop ridicule by their friends. A fifty-cent piece may not entice a youth to plunge into a cold ocean, stand up on a pair of skis, ride a horse, stand on the rim of a cliff, or walk into the depths of a cave, but the ridicule of his friends may be sufficiently aversive to make him want to terminate it and therefore to take the "plunge." There are times when some very strong reinforcing contingencies are necessary to assist an individual over a hurdle, to persuade him to try something new or to make an extra effort to continue his progress. Occasionally, available positive reinforcers may not be sufficient to motivate individuals to do things that are very difficult for them, and negative reinforcement may be the only answer.

Teachers, parents, and child-care personnel often use negative reinforcement to increase the behaviors of children and youth. For example a junior-high-school teacher was having difficulties with student tardiness. His class was the first of the day, and many students would wander around the halls to see if there was any "action" before coming to class. The school rule was such that, if a student received five tardy marks, he would be expelled. These marks were also reflected on report cards. Many of the students already had three or four marks early in the first quarter of school. The teacher decided to set up a program of negative reinforcement: A tardy mark was removed from the teacher's roll book for each week that a student had perfect on-time attendance. To maximize the effectiveness of the program, the teacher also positively reinforced coming to class on time with comments like "I sure am glad to see you make it here on time today"; "You are becoming a responsible class"; "Joe, you have really improved. Let's cross off another of these checks. Soon you won't have any"; "You are doing so well; let's have ten minutes of free time." The program worked successfully. After all the checks had been removed, the students continued to come to class on time. On-time behavior, which seemed to be strengthened initially by the combination of negative and positive reinforcement, appeared to be maintained by social and natural environmental reinforcers.

Here are other examples in which negative reinforcement may seem justifiable, at least during initial program phases: The group-home manager says, "If your room passes inspection five days in a row, you'll be excused from kitchen duties on the weekend"; the nurse informs Helen, "If you remember to take your medication regularly on your own for a week, you won't need to come back to the clinic next week. Also, you won't be hospitalized so frequently"; a classroom teacher says, "Jim, you may leave class when your work is completed" or "Class, if you complete this page of work with 90 percent or more correct you won't have to do the next two." If these programs are to be really effective, however, they must also be combined with positive reinforcement, as in the example of the teacher who sought to eliminate tardiness. (The assumption in the latter examples is that assigned school work and the classroom are aversive to most students. It is a sad comment on our educational procedures that this assumption is so often justified. The classroom and assignments become aversive because they are paired with other aversives—threats, low grades, and the like, or with nonreinforcement—"This is what they are expected to do; they should want to do this. I shouldn't have to reinforce them for doing so." Once educators and the public come to realize the tremendous importance of reinforcing the effortful responses involved in learning new and difficult material, academic assignments will no longer be aversive to many students.)

Negative Reinforcement Used Effectively

In the event that negative reinforcement is selected as the procedure of choice, it should be used in a manner similar to that of positive reinforcement. For example, the aversive stimulus should be removed *immediately* following *each* occurrence of the behavior. Also care must be taken to make sure that the stimulus is really aversive. For, as noted in the discussion of positive reinforcement, what may be aversive to one individual may be a positive reinforcer to another.

Summary

Many of the problems that face contingency managers in changing the behaviors of children and youth can be handled by means of positive or negative reinforcement: procedures designed to increase the occurrence of already existing behaviors. Positive reinforcement is a very useful strengthening procedure. In the three reinforcement units (Units 8–10) several types of positive reinforcers have been described, including tangible, exchangeable, consumable, activity, and social reinforcers, and illustrations of associated procedures have been presented. The specific reinforcing stimulus, immediacy, amount, antecedent stimulus arrangements, and reinforcement schedules influence reinforcer effectiveness. Occasionally, interfering conditions arise—like more powerful reinforcers for behaviors that interfere with the target behavior under other stimulus conditions. When that sort of a situation occurs, one possible solution is to shift temporarily back to stronger contingencies. Or the interfering conditions may be treated directly. In later sections of the book we shall offer various suggestions for accomplishing the latter alternatives.

Negative reinforcement is commonly used in the physical, social, and educational environment to teach and change the behaviors of all of us. Although negative reinforcement is basically an aversive procedure, like positive reinforcement, it is one of the basic ways in which we all learn. At times we do work, invent, create, or learn not for incentives or positive reinforcement but only to remove aversives. We may wish to consider negative reinforcement, then, when positive reinforcement fails or is insufficient. Because of its aversiveness and possible undesirable side effects (aggression, escape), negative reinforcement is not the procedure of choice. When selected, the aversive stimulus must be carefully identified and removed immediately after each occurrence of the behavior.

References

Ayllon, T. & Azrin, N. H. *The token economy*. New York: Appleton, 1968.

Azrin, N. H. & Holz, W. C. Punishment. In W. K. Honig (Ed.), *Operant behavior: Areas of research and application*. New York: Appleton, 1966. Pp. 380–447.

Holz, W. C., Azrin, N. H. & Allyon, T. Elimination of behavior of mental patients by response produce extinction. *Journal of the Experimental Analysis of Behavior*, 1963, **6**, 407–412.

Millenson, J. R. *Principles of behavior analysis*. New York: Macmillan, 1967.

Reese, E. P., Howard, J. S. & Reese, T. W. *Human behavior: Analysis and application*. Dubuque, Ia.: Brown, 1977.

Reynolds, G. S. *A primer of operant conditioning*. Glenview, Ill.: Scott, Foresman, 1968.

Robertson, S. J., DeReus, D. M. & Drabman, R. S. Peer and college-student tutoring as reinforcement in a token economy. *Journal of Applied Behavior Analysis*, 1976, **9**, 169–177.

Skinner, B. F. *The behavior of organisms*. New York: Appleton, 1938.

Sulzer, B., Loving, A. & Hunt, S. The contingent use of reinforcers usually available in the classroom. Paper presented at the meeting of the American Educational Research Association, Chicago, 1973.

Sulzer, B., Mayer, G. R. & Cody, J. J. Assisting teachers with managing classroom behavioral problems. *Elementary School Guidance and Counseling*, 1968, **3**, 40–48.

Reducing Behavior: Extinction

After mastering the material in this unit, you should be able to

1. Define and offer illustrations of extinction.

2. List and explain, in two sentences or less, each of the advantages of using extinction.

3. List and give illustrations of the properties of a behavior undergoing extinction.

4. List and offer illustrations of factors known to influence the rapidity with which a behavior is eliminated through extinction.

5. List and offer illustrations of the variables that serve to facilitate or maximize the effectiveness of extinction.

6. List and explain, in two sentences or less, each of the disadvantages of using extinction.

7. Describe specific situations in which extinction would and would not be the behavioral procedure of choice; justify each position that you take.

Little Bonnie, swinging her feet from the supermarket shopping cart, points to the cookies, "Want that"; the maraschino cherries, "Want that"; and to six or seven candy bars, pleading "Daddy—want that." Daddy does not appear to hear her, until they reach the fruit stand. "Want that," says Bonnie, reaching for an orange. "All right—but hold it, and you can eat it when we get home." Technically, Bonnie's requests for the foods that her dad considers to be nonnutritious are being exposed to **extinction** conditions; only the request for the orange is reinforced.

In this unit we discuss extinction, a procedure by which responding is *reduced*. The response may be any such undesirable response as incorrect answers and annoying, functionless, or maladaptive behavior. Before proceeding, the reader should review the material on priorities, goals, and objectives in Units 1–4, in order to decide whether or not such a procedure can be ethically defended under certain circumstances.

GENERAL CHARACTERISTICS

Extinction Defined

Viewed as an operation, extinction is fairly simple and straightforward, although it is not the easiest procedure to carry out in practice. It is a procedure in which *behavior that has been reinforced previously is no longer reinforced*. Ultimately, the consistent nonreinforcement of a behavior tends to result in reduction of that behavior to its prereinforcement level. For instance, if Bonnie is never given candy, she will eventually stop asking for it.

Extinction is used by most people at various times in their lives, but especially by individuals who are responsible for, and concerned with, other people's behavior. Parents, teachers, behavior analysts, employers, and even partners in marriage often use extinction, though perhaps without awareness, to attempt to reduce particular behaviors. A mother ignores her whining child in order to reduce whining. Teachers withhold good grades, praise, privileges, and other reinforcers when their students perform inappropriately. Counselors may ignore certain undesirable statements from their clients, and employers often withhold raises from employees whose performance fails to meet the job requirements. When husbands or wives stop giving attention to particular comments from their spouses, that behavior is on extinction.[1]

There has been a great deal of research on extinction, both in the laboratory and in applied settings. Quite a bit has been learned about its properties. Therefore, after the procedure has been illustrated and its advantages discussed here, emphasis will be given to those properties. The variables that are known to influence the effectiveness of extinction and the disadvantages involved in using it will be considered as well. Recognition of those factors should help the practitioner to use extinction effectively and should provide a basis for deciding when extinction is and when it is not a method of choice.

---

[1] Although the operations performed in the extinction procedure are often labeled "punishment" in everyday use, we make a clear distinction between *extinction* (withholding reinforcement contingent upon behavior) and *punishment* (presenting an aversive stimulus contingent upon behavior, to be discussed in Unit 22). The term "extinction" is also used to describe the loss of conditioned attributes of an originally neutral stimulus in **respondent** conditioning. That process is not considered in this book.

Extinction Illustrated

A teacher asks her class the question "What holiday do we celebrate on the Fourth of July?" Jimmy stands up, waves his hand frantically, and shouts, "I know, I know." The teacher ignores Jimmy and calls on George, who has raised his hand and remains silent and in his seat. Jimmy's hand waving, calling, and out-of-seat behavior are undergoing extinction. Archibald also volunteers an answer and is recognized by the teacher. "We celebrate the adoption of the Constitution on July Fourth." The teacher ignores Archibald's incorrect response and calls on Jennifer. "We celebrate Independence Day on July Fourth." "That's right, Jennifer. Good for you." Archibald's incorrect response is placed under extinction conditions while Jennifer's response is reinforced.

In a counseling session, Henrietta tells the counselor about all her current aches and pains. Her foot hurts; she has a headache. And last night she really felt dizzy just when it was time to clear the table. Assured by the doctor that Henrietta's complaints have no organic basis, the counselor averts his gaze and makes no response while Henrietta is on that particular subject. When she mentions that she has received an "A" on a spelling paper, the counselor responds enthusiastically. The somatic complaints are placed on extinction by the counselor. Other specific categories of verbal behavior are not.

When Mom is working at her desk, she prefers not to be .disturbed. She tells the children not to talk to her whenever she is at her desk. The children agree that at those times they will ask Dad their questions or wait, except in an emergency. When Joey and Sally ask her to read them a story while she is seated at her desk, she does not answer; she just simply continues her work. Eventually, Joey and Sally learn not to ask Mom questions when she is at her desk.

ADVANTAGES OF EXTINCTION

Effectively Reducing Behavior

Extinction, often used in combination with other procedures, has been found to be effective in reducing a wide variety of undesirable child behaviors. Crying (Hart et al., 1964) and throwing glasses (Wolf, Risley & Mees, 1964) were reduced substantially when the reinforcing consequences for those responses were removed. Within recent years there have been many reports of programs that have used extinction as a means of effectively reducing undesirable classroom behaviors. Disruptive classroom behavior (Thomas et al., 1969; Zimmerman & Zimmerman, 1962; O'Leary & Becker, 1967), aggressive behavior (Scott, Burton & Yarrow, 1967; Brown & Elliot, 1965), tantrums in the classroom (Carlson et al., Madsen, 1968), nonstudy behavior (Thomas, Becker & Armstrong, 1968; Hall, Lund & Jackson, 1968), and excessive classroom noise (Wilson & Hopkins, 1973) were all successfully handled in this manner. In many of these instances, a more rapid decrement in the undesirable behavior was accomplished with the simultaneous reinforcement of the desired behaviors. For instance, in the Wilson & Hopkins study (1973), popular radio music was automatically presented when noise in a junior high-school class fell below a level of 70 decibels and withheld when noise increased above that level; an acceptable noise level was rapidly attained.

The effectiveness of extinction has also been recognized in counseling activities. The authors of one study have noted that "extinction procedures . . . have been shown to be effective counseling techniques for weakening or eliminating deviant behaviors" (Krumboltz & Hosford, 1967, p. 33). Extinction is used in counseling much as it is used in the classroom. Reinforcement is withheld for undesired verbalizations or other behaviors. For example, a goal of increased verbal participation was specified for five students participating in group counseling. The attention of the counselor was discontinued whenever a student left the counseling table or failed to participate in other ways. Verbal participation was immediately reinforced with attention, interest, and positive verbal responses.

Parents have also used extinction effectively. For example, in one study (Hall *et al.*, 1972), it was reported how parents effectively decreased their four-year-old child's whining and shouting behaviors by consistently ignoring them.

Extinction can be used, as in the study just described (Hall *et al.*, 1972), to help distraught and demoralized parents regain some degree of self-respect. Parents of disturbed children can discover that the children have been controlling their behavior by means of obnoxious tantrums, and one of the best ways for the parents to reestablish some degree of control is to assert their own self-control through extinction. They can withhold their attention for obnoxious behavior.

Long-Lasting Effect

If extinction is used with maximum effectiveness, its results can be enduring (Skinner, 1938). Many of the studies cited in this unit have demonstrated the long-term effectiveness of extinction. The undesirable behaviors were rarely emitted following the extinction program.

Aversive Stimuli Not Required

Because extinction involves simply the nondelivery of reinforcement, rather than presentation of aversive consequences, it avoids the negative effects that often result from the use of aversive control. (Such effects will be discussed at greater length in Units 19–22.)

PROPERTIES OF EXTINCTION

When all reinforcement is permanently withheld following the emission of a specific behavior, that behavior should gradually diminish to its prereinforcement level and perhaps ultimately cease altogether. There are, however, some general and predictable properties that characterize a behavior as it is undergoing extinction. They include temporal aspects, temporary increase in response rate and intensity, extinction-induced aggression, and spontaneous recovery.

Gradual Behavioral Reduction

Extinction usually does not have an immediate effect. Once the reinforcing consequences are removed, the behavior continues to be emitted for some indeterminate amount of time before it finally ceases (Skinner, 1953). The whining child or nagging spouse whines or nags for a while, even when such behaviors yield no reinforcement. Jimmy will probably continue to call out many times before stopping. Archibald may continue to give the same incorrect answer several times before emitting the correct one.

Several factors are known to influence the rate at which a behavior is reduced through extinction. They include the *number of reinforced trials,* the *schedule* on which the response has been reinforced in the past, the *deprivation level* of the individual, the *effort* needed to make the response, and the use of *procedural combinations* (Millenson, 1967). In general, a behavior that has been frequently emitted and reinforced in the past—an established behavior—is much more resistant to extinction conditions than one that has been only rarely emitted and reinforced. Also a response that has been reinforced on an intermittent reinforcement schedule is more resistant to extinction than one that has been continuously reinforced. Had the teacher recognized Jimmy every time that he jumped out of his seat and said "I know, I know," the behavior would probably have disappeared sooner when she withheld such recognition than it would had she reinforced such behavior frequently but inconsistently.

The more deprived an individual or the longer the period of time since she has received a given reinforcer, the longer a behavior will continue to be emitted under extinction conditions. This factor is especially important when the behavior has been maintained by edible reinforcement (Holland & Skinner, 1961). A hungry child whining for a cookie will emit many more responses in the absence of reinforcement than the same child would after having completed a big meal.

A response that requires considerable effort will be extinguished more rapidly than one that is emitted with ease. A two-year-old would probably persist in the response "Cookie, cookie" much longer than in the response "Mommy, may I please have a cookie," for the latter undoubtedly requires much more effort than the former.

When extinction is used in combination with reinforcement of an alternative or incompatible behavior, the response will diminish more rapidly. Reese, Howard, and Rosenberger (1974) found that institutionalized retarded males produced far fewer errors when an alternative, reinforceable response was available to them than when errors were placed under extinction alone. Were Jimmy frequently recognized by the teacher when he sat and raised his hand quietly, his less desirable form of responding would diminish more rapidly than if he had no such reinforceable behavioral alternative available. The same is true of extinction in combination with other procedures for reducing undesirable behaviors: response cost, time out, punishment, and overcorrection. These procedures are described in Units 18–22. Were Archibald to have points removed for his incorrect response, in addition to not receiving praise, he might tend to emit the incorrect answer less frequently in the future than if his wrong answer were simply ignored (unless, of course, removing points were the only form of attention Archibald received). Such combined procedures will be discussed in later sections.

Increases in Rate and Intensity of Responding

Brief increases in the rate and intensity of responding immediately after the cessation of reinforcement have been observed in both animals (Millenson, 1967) and human beings (Kelly, 1969). They are especially likely to occur when a large proportion of the responses have been reinforced. What happens when a candy machine fails to deliver? The individual pulls the plunger more and more frequently and with greater vigor before giving up and going away. The infant whose crying is ignored for the first time will continue to scream with increasing intensity before the crying begins to subside and ultimately ceases.

Inducing Aggression

A brief period of aggressive behavior may also accompany extinction in its early phases (Skinner, 1953, p. 69). The discontinuation of positive reinforcement has been found to produce aggression in pigeons (Azrin, Hutchinson & Hake, 1966) and in squirrel monkeys (Hutchinson, Azrin & Hunt, 1968). Kelly (1969) has demonstrated a similar response in human males. In the last study, subjects were reinforced with money for pulling a knob. The discontinuation of delivery of the money resulted in several subjects' engaging in a forcible hitting response. This result is similar to the "vending-machine phenomenon." After the frustrated customer yanks at the lever with an increasing rate and intensity, he not uncommonly kicks or bangs the machine. Examples of this kind of response are also found in applied settings. The good student who cries in exasperation when he does not receive a good grade and the youth who, accustomed to being selected for special privileges, pokes the fellow next to him when another youth is offered privileges are probably exhibiting **extinction-induced aggression.**

Spontaneous Recovery

Another phenomenon that has been observed in connection with extinction is the reappearance of the "extinguished" response following a time interval but without any intervening reinforcement of the response. This phenomenon is called **spontaneous recovery** (Skinner, 1953). Although this particular property is a transitory one and the frequency of the "recovered" response is very limited, recognition of its existence can save contingency managers from making wrong moves. Let us consider a school example. Reggi, thanks to his older brother, came to school with a vocabulary of off-color words that would tend to make a turnip blush. The behavior analyst, to whom the problem was referred, observed that Reggi's use of such words seemed to be strongly maintained by various sources in the environment. The teacher frowned and scolded him, thus attending heavily to the response. Classmates giggled and gasped; the principal lectured. Perhaps because Reggi had received little attention in the past, all the attention from teacher, peers, and principal served to reinforce his language strongly. A full-scale extinction program was put into effect. The teacher began to turn away when Reggi swore. The students were reinforced for ignoring such language, and they ultimately stopped attending to it. The principal no longer discussed the topic with Reggi. His swearing gradually subsided and ultimately appeared to have been eliminated. Then, several days later, although the response had not been reinforced, Reggi uttered a choice four-letter word. It was a crucial moment. The teacher could have decided that the whole procedure had been a failure and begun to scold Reggi again. The other reinforcers could also have been presented again, and the behavior might then have assumed its former, even greater strength. But the teacher was prepared for the predictable minimal recovery of the behavior, and she was able to continue the extinction procedure until such recovery no longer manifested itself.

USING EXTINCTION EFFECTIVELY

Identifying and Withholding Sources of Reinforcement

Does Sam respond rudely to his parents because his peers approve, because his parents become angry, because his siblings smile at such responses at home, or because of all these reinforcers? Does Jack take money from the teacher's purse because it will buy him food or items that he cannot afford? Or does he increase his prestige with his pals by bragging about his "accomplishment"? Does Kevin frequently leave his seat because the assigned material is aversive (Is his leaving the seat being negatively reinforced) or because his teacher attends to him for leaving his seat? Extinction requires that *all* major sources of reinforcement contingent upon the response be withheld. Again, the method for determining which reinforcers are maintaining the behavior is based upon formal observation. Once the response has been operationally defined, the probable reinforcing object or event is withheld for a period of time. If the behavior subsequently declines, one reinforcing contingency has probably been identified. In order to be certain that the reinforcer is indeed functionally related to the emission of the behavior, it can again be temporarily reintroduced. If the behavior then increases and drops again when the reinforcer is withheld again, a source of reinforcement has been determined. This procedure can be repeated for each of the suspected reinforcers. Once the major sources of reinforcement maintaining a particular undesirable behavior have been identified, they should, if possible, be permanently removed. Let us suppose in Sam's case that all the suspected reinforcers were demonstrated to have reinforcing effects upon his rude behavior at home. When the parents withheld their anger, the behavior began to diminish. When the siblings, praised for ignoring Sam's response, no longer smiled at it, it diminished further. When Sam's peers were told of his difficulties at home, they agreed to ignore, rather than to approve, such responses. The task of the parent and, perhaps, the behavior analyst would be to ensure the elimination of those sources of reinforcement until the behavior ultimately disappeared. The behavior analyst could have periodic meetings with Sam's parents in order to show them a record of the declining frequency of rude responses and to encourage their continued cooperation in contributing to the reduction of the responses. Ultimately the reinforcement represented by a better-behaved child would probably be sufficient to maintain the parents' behavior.

The importance of determining empirically the functional properties of a presumed reinforcer is underscored by an example from classroom literature. O'Leary and his colleagues (1969) attempted to reduce the disruptive behaviors of seven second-graders by ignoring disruptive and praising desirable behaviors. As we have seen earlier, such an approach had demonstrated its success with other populations. In this instance, however, the combination of praise and ignoring was not effective, whereas a new procedure, a token economy, did achieve the desired improvement.

A point worthy of repetition here is the importance of guarding against allowing occasional reinforcers to slip in unnoticed during an extinction procedure, because they would provide an intermittent schedule of reinforcement. The more often such uncontrolled reinforcement occurs, the longer the behavior tends to persist. Were Sam's best friend to give Sam a signal of approbation for a rude response, unknown to their parents, the behavior would take longer to extinguish. The same would be true if the parents happened to be tired or upset one day and became angry before they were able to control their outburst. This kind of thing does happen and understandably so. But by structuring the environment— for instance, by praising those who ignore rudeness and guarding against such events—we can increase the efficiency of the extinction procedure.

Specifying Clearly the Conditions for Extinction

Mom told Joey and Sally that, when she was working at her desk, she would not respond to them, except for emergencies. The children quickly learned that Mom at the desk meant that pestering would not bring attention from her; pestering Mom was reduced rapidly. Had no information been exchanged about the conditions under which extinction would occur, talking to Mom at the desk would still diminish eventually, but it might take much longer. "Remember, if you ask for candy, you won't get it," Dad reminds Bonnie, "but, if you wait patiently, you may pick a piece of fruit." Bonnie's "I wanna"s for candy will quickly subside. In the next unit, the importance of specifying conditions under which extinction and reinforcement occur will be elaborated. Here the important point to note is that the conditions should be communicated simply before the situation. If a lengthy explanation is given—for example, "I told you not to bother me at my desk"—

it may constitute attention and can serve as a reinforcer. Naturally, however, at the appropriate time, the nonemission of the targeted undesirable behavior should be reinforced. When Mom leaves her desk she tells Sally and Joey how she has appreciated their not interrupting her and promises to play a game with them as a reward.

Maintaining Extinction Conditions for a Sufficient Time

The short burst of high-rate responding, which often occurs when extinction is first implemented, can often be very discouraging. When the teacher decided to ignore Reggi's colorful language, he responded by bursting forth with a stream of epithets, the meaning of which the teacher had not even known himself until he had reached adulthood. The teacher might well have branded the technique of ignoring undesirable behavior a failure. But was it? The only way the teacher could find out was to ride the crest of the wave for a while (and hope the other students were no more sophisticated than the teacher himself had been at their age) and to see if it would begin to subside. Assuming that the teacher's frowning and scolding were the reinforcing events, the behavior would ultimately diminish. At such times, data collection can be a tremendous asset. The frequency of Reggi's emission of off-color words per day could be tallied, perhaps with the help of a golf counter. If the data showed a small but steady decrease in the response rate, there would then be room for optimism, which would reinforce the teacher. Sometimes the decrease is so gradual that it would escape notice in the absence of recorded data. The basic point of this discussion, however, is that the temporary increase in the response can be anticipated. Anticipating the increase as a predictable phenomenon should help the practitioner not to abandon the extinction program.

Combining Extinction with Other Procedures

Although extinction by itself can be a very effective method for reducing an undesirable behavior, we recommend that it be combined with other procedures. In Units 18–22, we shall discuss combining extinction with other reductive procedures. Here, and in other units, our emphasis is on providing reinforcing consequences for alternative responses while a particular undesirable response is undergoing extinction. There are two reasons for providing reinforcement for alternative responses, which are probably apparent to the reader by now. One reason concerns the tendency of individuals to emit behavior until some reinforcing consequence occurs. The other has to do with "killing two birds with one stone."

Because extinction implies discontinuation, or withholding, of reinforcement for a particular response, it is important to determine whether or not individuals have "sufficient" reinforcement available from other sources. When Sam's rude responses were no longer yielding him parental attention, the parents would have to make sure that Sam did not lose out on receiving their attention altogether. For, if Sam could find no constructive way to make his parents notice him, he would probably continue trying different (even destructive) behaviors until one succeeded. And that other alternative might be worse than rudeness. He could, for instance, begin slamming doors, kicking furniture, or hitting his siblings. The point, then, is that the individual whose specific behavior is undergoing extinction should receive lots of reinforcement for desirable behaviors. Sam could be praised or smiled at for doing his chores. He could be given extra privileges for responding politely and so on.

If we were to visit a large institution for the mentally retarded, we might observe various bizarre behaviors being emitted by some of the residents: stereotypic responses, like head weaving, repetitive hand movements, rocking, and ritualistic pacing of a given area. What explains the development and maintenance of such seemingly functionless behaviors? Perhaps extinction is the answer. When a large number of people gathered in an understaffed facility lack adaptive behaviors likely to be naturally reinforced by their environment, they may emit functionless or even maladaptive behaviors until reinforcement is eventually obtained. The reinforcement may be in the form of sensory stimulation—changing visual, tactile, or auditory patterns—or in the form of social attention from peers or staff members, who may inadvertently reinforce through attention.

This phenomenon does not occur when the environment is structured to maximize reinforcement for adaptive behaviors. A description of a visit to a facility for the retarded illustrates this conclusion. Women ranging from profoundly to moderately retarded were busily engaged in adaptive activities: rhythm band, exercise class, language groups, crafts projects. Staff and peers praised their participation, and accomplishments were given lots of attention. Bizarre stereotypic behavior, observed very frequently among people at similar functional levels living in such settings, was entirely absent.

People like to be reinforced and tend to feel better about themselves when they receive positive attention. By planning the reinforcement of desirable behaviors simultaneously with the extinction of undesirable behaviors, the behavior analyst can achieve a constructive outcome. The desired behavior should increase, along with positive feelings and attitudes about oneself. When the desired behavior *interferes* or is *incompatible*[2] with the undesirable behavior, reinforcement of that desired behavior should speed up the process even more. Putting Sam "on extinction" for rude language should ultimately lead to the diminution of that response, but reinforcement of polite language will simultaneously increase it *and* reduce rudeness. Polite and rude responses cannot be emitted at the same time. Two things, then, are being accomplished at once.

DISADVANTAGES OF EXTINCTION

Many of the disadvantages of the extinction procedure have been implied in our discussion of the properties of extinction. We shall now consider them more fully.

---

[2] This point will be elaborated further in Unit 18.

Delayed Effects

The elimination of a response through extinction takes time, which can present problems under some circumstances. A child's responding with rude behavior may be tolerable for a longer time than his responding with running out into a street full of traffic. The child himself may be extinguished before the response is eliminated. A response suggesting imminent danger to the child or to others must be stopped immediately. Unless some additional fast-acting procedure, like punishment or response cost, is combined with it, extinction is not the method of choice in such circumstances.

Temporary Increase in Rate, Intensity, and Aggression

Because the increase in rate and intensity and the display of aggression often emitted during the early stages of the extinction program are temporary, they should present no serious disadvantage to the practitioner. There are times, however, when such displays are less than desirable. It would not be a good idea for a teacher to start an extinction program on a day when the school board is making its annual visit to the school or for a mother to start on the morning after she has hosted a big party. The early stages of the extinction program require lots of patience, and personal pressures can make it difficult for the teacher or mother to remain patient. Later, as the temporary behaviors begin to diminish substantially and the practitioner is reinforced for continued efforts, things become much easier, and less patience is required.

Imitation of Inappropriate Behavior

Some behaviors, particularly those commonly labeled "aggressive," are likely to be **imitated** by peers when they are followed by specific extinction conditions. Some studies have shown that boys are particularly likely to imitate aggressive behaviors when they are ignored by adult superiors (Bandura & Walters, 1963; Bandura, 1965). If a teacher ignores destructive behaviors like hitting and throwing objects, these behaviors may be imitated by classmates. Probably total extinction conditions cannot be achieved for such behaviors in a group setting, because peers are apt to attend to them. In any event, we would not recommend the use of extinction for aggressive behavior in a group setting, for the teacher or group leader may lose control, with pandemonium the result. An alternate reductive procedure would be more appropriate.

Identifying and Controlling Reinforcing Consequences

Sometimes reinforcing consequences are fairly obvious to the observer. At other times, they are not. Sometimes it takes considerable painstaking investigation to discover what reinforcers are maintaining the behaviors. Identification of the reinforcing consequences is particularly difficult when responses are being maintained on very thin reinforcement schedules. The reinforcer may be presented so seldom that the observer may fail to notice it. The mother of fifteen-year-old

Henrietta came to the behavior analyst at a community clinic quite distraught. Her daughter's personality had changed drastically. From a happy, outgoing girl who was always busily engaged in all kinds of activities with her friends, she had turned into a social isolate. She sat around the house and refused to go out with her friends. Even telephone conversations were generally short. When her mother asked for an explanation, Henrietta would say only, "I don't feel like going out" or "Those kids bore me." Sufficiently concerned, the behavior analyst helped to search for the cause of the problem. Was the girl sick? Was she undergoing a depressive neurosis? He asked the mother to observe her daughter more closely. One day Henrietta's classmate Jim called for help with an algebra problem. The mother noticed that her daughter's face lit up and that the spark of enthusiasm returned. On thinking back, the mother remembered that Jim had occasionally called for help with algebra in the past. Suddenly, the potential reinforcer was apparent. Had the mother not been nearby when her daughter answered the telephone, the episode might have gone unnoticed. Let us assume for the moment that the call from Jim was the event that intermittently reinforced Henrietta's remaining at home. This assumption could possibly be substantiated by the more formal observation that she went out with her friends on days when no algebra homework was assigned to Jim and when he was absent from class. The next problem then would be to determine whether either the behavior analyst or the mother controlled the reinforcing consequences. They did not, as things stood. It would, of course, be possible to ask Jim not to call, to ask him to call at specific times, to set up regular tutoring sessions, or to remove the telephone. The behavior analyst and mother wisely decided that they should not interfere in the situation, assuming that it would pass in time. Henrietta was left to wait at home by the telephone. Extinction was not programmed. On those occasions when she did go out, her mother gave her some extra snack money, hoping thus to reinforce her going out with friends.

Frequently it is difficult to control reinforcing consequences delivered by peers. Boisterous and hyperactive behaviors often receive reinforcement in the form of peers' smiles, giggles, and imitation. Such behaviors may be fine outdoors or on the playground, but they often interfere with instructional activities. There are several ways in which a contingency manager may achieve extinction conditions when the behavior is being reinforced by peers. One of the most obvious is to reinforce the peers for not attending to disruptive behavior. For example, whenever a peer withholds his attention from disruptive antics, the contingency manager can reinforce him with praise or with some social or tangible event or object known to be reinforcing to him. This peer's behavior—ignoring the disruptive antics—would then serve as a positively reinforced **model** for the rest of the group. (In Unit 14 we shall discuss model selection further.) Other peers may imitate the model's behavior and thus provide the contingency manager with an opportunity to reinforce their behaviors of withholding attention to disruptive behavior. As their ignoring behavior continues to be reinforced, some optimal extinction conditions will gradually be achieved.

Patterson (1965) used an extinction procedure with a peer-support system successfully to reduce the hyperactive behavior of a nine-year-old boy. Earl's behavior consisted of excessive movements in and out of his seat, excessive talking, and hitting. Patterson's approach was to set up a situation in which Earl and his classmates could obtain candy or pennies from a "magic teaching machine" whenever Earl displayed ten seconds of attending behavior. His classmates were also rewarded for withholding their attention during his antics. By reinforcing students for not attending to disruptive behavior, the teacher rapidly obtained extinction conditions and was himself reinforced by the more favorable classroom environment (see Figure 11.1).

Solomon and Wahler (1973) discovered that peers continually attended to disruptive behavior (talking, being out of seat, and classroom play) of five sixth-grade boys. Their approach for dealing with this situation was to select five high-status peers (from a class of thirty) who were identified by their teacher as willing to cooperate with adults. These students were trained in extinction and reinforcement techniques, and they were able to apply the behavioral procedures with remarkable success. The "problem" children produced less deviant behavior and more prosocial behaviors. If more children were trained in behavioral approaches, they too could help their peers and at the same time become more aware of themselves and their relationships with others. They would thus acquire skills that would assist them with their own personal and social development. Such students might become better equipped to deal with their immediate and future responsibilities. Peers can provide a free, ready, and willing source of assistance.

Sometimes it is impossible to remove reinforcing consequences. Some behaviors have their own built-in reinforcers. As long as thieves are not caught, they are reinforced for stealing by the attainment of material goods. It would be pretty difficult to *remove* the reinforcing consequences of speeding in a car (it takes one places faster), cheating on examinations (it may yield higher grades),

Figure 11.1 What's happening? What should the teacher do?

drinking lots of alcohol, eating lots of sweets, engaging in sexual activities, or engaging in self-stimulating behaviors like masturbation, nose picking, rocking, and perhaps head banging. When either the identification or the control of the reinforcing contingencies is very difficult or impossible, therefore, it is preferable to turn to other methods of reducing the undesirable behavior.

Summary

Extinction can be a very effective procedure for reducing undesirable behaviors. Used by itself or in combination with other procedures, it has demonstrated its effectiveness in a wide variety of situations. To assist the practitioner in deciding whether or not extinction is an appropriate procedure in a given situation, we present Figure 11.2. Appropriate responses to the encircled questions should be obtained before an extinction procedure is selected.

Extinction takes time. In fact, the behavior may get worse before it gets better. One must be able to tolerate this temporary worsening of the behavior. As a general rule, extinction alone should not be used with destructive or aggressive behaviors.

Efficient use of extinction requires identification and withholding of *all* reinforcing consequences for the undesirable behavior. If it is not possible to remove the reinforcing contingencies for a specific response, an alternative reductive technique should be used.

In situations in which the behavior to be reduced is not an aggressive one, a temporary initial worsening of the behavior can be tolerated, and all the reinforcers for the behavior can be withheld over an extended period of time, including during spontaneous recov-

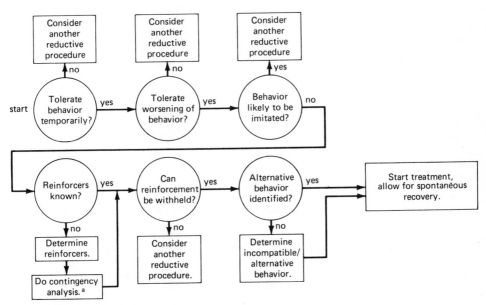

ᵃ Sequence analysis.

Figure 11.2 Deciding to use extinction. Reprinted from R. B. Benoit & G. R. Mayer. Extinction: Guidelines for its selection and use. *The Personnel & Guidance Journal*, 1974, **52**, 290–295.

ery, extinction is a reasonable choice. Its effectiveness will be further facilitated, when desirable behaviors are reinforced simultaneously with the extinction of undesirable behaviors. Generally, any reductive procedure is more effective when desirable behaviors are simultaneously reinforced.

References

Azrin, N. H., Hutchinson, R. R. & Hake, D. J. Extinction-induced aggression. *Journal of the Experimental Analysis of Behavior*, 1966, **9**, 191–204.

Bandura, A. Influence of models' reinforcement contingencies on the acquisition of imitative responses. *Journal of Personality and Social Psychology*, 1965, **1**, 589–595.

Bandura, A. & Walters, R. H. *Social learning and personality development*. New York: Holt, 1963.

Benoit, R. B. & Mayer, G. R. Extinction: Guidelines for its selection and use. *The Personnel and Guidance Journal*, 1974, **52**, 290–295.

Bijou, S. W., Birnbrauer, T. S., Kidder, J. D. & Tague, C. Programmed instruction as an approach to teaching reading, writing, and arithmetic to retarded children. In S. W. Bijou & D. M. Baer (Eds.), *Child development: Readings in experimental analysis*. New York: Appleton, 1967.

Brown, P. & Elliott, R. Control of aggression in a nursery school class. *Journal of Experimental Child Psychology*, 1965, **2**, 103–107.

Carlson, C. S., Arnold, C. R., Becker, W. C. & Madsen, G. H. The elimination of tantrum behavior of a child in an elementary classroom. *Behavior Research and Therapy*, 1968, **6**, 117–120.

Hall, R. V., Axelrod, S., Tyler, L., Grief, E., Jones, F. C. & Robertson, R. Modification of behavior problems in the home with a parent as observer and experimenter. *Journal of Applied Behavior Analysis*, 1972, **5**, 53–64.

Hall, R. V., Lund, D. & Jackson, D. Effects of teacher attention on study behaviors. *Journal of Applied Behavior Analysis*, 1968, **1**, 1–12.

Hall, R. V., Panyan, M., Rabon, D. & Broden, M. Instructing beginning teachers in reinforcement procedures which improve classroom control. *Journal of Applied Behavior Analysis*, 1968, **1**, 315–322.

Hart, B. M., Allen, K. E., Buell, J. S. Harris, F. R. & Wolf, M. M. Effects of social reinforcement on operant crying. *Journal of Experimental Child Psychology*, 1964, **1**, 145–153.

Holland, J. G. & Skinner, B. F. *The analysis of behavior*. New York: McGraw-Hill, 1961.

Hutchinson, R. R., Azrin, N. H. & Hunt, G. M. Attack produced by intermittent reinforcement of a concurrent operant response. *Journal of the Experimental Analysis of Behavior*, 1968, **11**, 489–495.

Kelly, J. F. Extinction induced aggression in humans. Unpublished master's thesis, Southern Illinois University, 1969.

Krumboltz, J. D. & Hosford, R. Behavioral counseling in the elementary school. *Elementary School Guidance and Counseling*, 1967, **1**, 27–40.

Millenson, J. R. *Principles of behavior analysis*. New York: Macmillan, 1967.

O'Leary, K. D. & Becker, W. C. Behavior modification of an adjustment class: A token reinforcement program. *Exceptional Children*, 1967, **33**, 637–642.

O'Leary, K. D., Becker, W. C., Evans, M. B. & Saudargas, R. A. A token reinforcement program in a public school: A replication and systematic analysis. *Journal of Applied Behavior Analysis*, 1969, **2**, 3–13.

Patterson, G. R. An application of conditioning techniques to the control of a hyperactive child. In L. P. Ullman & L. Krasner (Eds.), *Case studies in behavior modification*. New York: Holt, 1965. 370–375.

Reese, E. P., Howard, J. & Rosenberger, P. A comparison of three reinforcement procedures in assessing visual capacities of profoundly retarded individuals. Paper presented at the meeting of the American Psychological Association, New Orleans, August 1974.

Scott, P. M., Burton, R. V. & Yarrow, M. R. Social reinforcement under natural conditions. *Child Development*, 1967, **38**, 53–63.

Skinner, B. F. *The behavior of organisms.* New York: Appleton, 1938.

Skinner, B. F. *Science and human behavior.* New York: Free Press, 1953.

Solomon, R. W. & Wahler, R. G. Peer reinforcement control of classroom problem behavior. *Journal of Applied Behavior Analysis*, 1973, **6**, 49–56.

Thomas, D. R., Becker, W. C. & Armstrong, M. Production and elimination of disruptive classroom behavior by systematically varying teacher's behavior. *Journal of Applied Behavior Analysis*, 1968, **1**, 35–45.

Thomas, D. R., Nielsen, L. J., Kuypers, D. S. & Becker, W. C. Contributions of social reinforcement and remedial instruction in the elimination of a classroom behavior problem. Unpublished manuscript, University of Illinois, 1969.

Wilson, C. W. & Hopkins, B. L. The effects of contingent music on the intensity of noise in junior high home economics classes. *Journal of Applied Behavior Analysis*, 1973, **6**, 269–275.

Wolf, M. M., Risley, T. R. & Mees, H. L. Application of operant conditioning procedures to the behavior problems of an autistic child. *Behavior Research and Therapy*, 1964, **1**, 303–312.

Zimmerman, E. H. & Zimmerman, J. The alteration of behavior in a classroom situation. *Journal of the Experimental Analysis of Behavior*, 1962, **5**, 59–60.

STIMULUS CONTROL: WHAT IS IT?

After mastering the materials in this unit, you should be able to

1. Define and illustrate each of the following terms:
    a. Stimulus control
    b. Occasion
    c. Control
    d. Generalization
    e. Discrimination
    f. Discriminative stimulus (S^D)
    g. Complete stimulus control
    h. S^D-presentation procedure (stimulus change)
    i. Elicit
    j. Differential reinforcement
    k. S-delta (S^Δ)

2. Differentiate between complete and incomplete stimulus control by means of description and illustration.

3. Identify and discuss five reasons why an S^D might fail to occasion the appropriate response.

4. Discuss and illustrate with an example how stimulus control is developed.

5. Give an illustration of when two S^Ds that differ slightly from each other control different responses.

6. Describe and illustrate with an example the importance of stimulus control in concept formation.

It is densely overcast, and an aircraft filled with vacationing families is approaching its destination. The pilot, guided only by instruments, makes a perfect landing. Ms. Ophelia, Shakespearean scholar, selects a passage from *Twelfth Night* and renders an extraordinarily perceptive interpretation. In the small hours of the morning, an ambulance siren wails as a stricken patient is rushed to City Hospital; Dr. Daring, responding to the call, makes an expert diagnosis, and a miraculous cure is achieved. How are all these and many other marvels of modern human accomplishment achieved? Through **stimulus control**.

STIMULUS CONTROL DEFINED AND ILLUSTRATED

Stimulus control is said to exist when there is a high probability that a particular response will occur in the presence of a particular antecedent stimulus. When it is observed that an antecedent stimulus, like the position of the dials on an aircraft flight panel, affects the probability that a given response—landing—will occur, we say that the response is "under the control" of that antecedent stimulus. In this unit we shall discuss how responses that have already been acquired may be brought under stimulus control. In essence, we shall consider behaviors that are already in the individual's repertoire *but*—and this "but" is very important—have still to be brought under the control of the specific conditions under which they should occur. We shall also describe methods for developing stimulus control in order to accomplish the task.

The principal advantage of "self-managers," teachers, trainers, consultants or other contingency managers being able to bring behavior under stimulus control is to increase the likelihood that given behaviors are emitted under given circumstances. We shall discuss and illustrate the events that operate to produce stimulus control: reinforcing, or other consequences that follow the response in the presence of the antecedent stimuli. Then we shall explore in detail some effective procedures[1] for developing stimulus control. Initially we shall consider situations in which responses are to be emitted only in the presence of specific **antecedent stimuli** or groups of stimuli: ". . . [S]timuli are environmental events that do, or can be made to influence behavior" (Becker, Engelmann & Thomas, 1971, p. 4). Later we shall consider more complex forms of stimulus control, in which different antecedent stimuli are to signal the occasion for different responses.

The gauges on the pilot's panel signal that it is okay to come in for a landing. Landing the plane, which is a behavior in the pilot's repertoire, is emitted only in response to appropriate antecedent signals. Similarly, when the telephone rings, Penny's mother picks it up and says, "Hello." At the sound of the fire alarm, the students scramble from their seats, line up, and evacuate the building. When the

---

[1] Negative (aversive) procedures, like the punishment of a response emitted in the presence of a given stimulus will not be discussed here. When the material on punishment (see Unit 22) has been mastered, it should be possible for the reader to design such a procedure. At that point, however, the reader will also be aware of the problems inherent in using punishment to develop stimulus control.

teacher writes "5×4" on the chalk board, the students answer "20." A study guide contains a set of study questions with instructions to the student to complete each: "Define stimulus control, and provide an example from your own daily life." The student provides an acceptable definition and illustration. Clyde's father listens to his child describe how a friend ate his candy bar without permission. He asks, "Was that an *honest* thing to do?"; the child answers, "No." In music class, students correctly identify a musical passage by its harmonic and rhythmic properties. A consultant suggests that a teacher use qualitative praise when students earn it. The teacher tells Jan that her theme is excellent, pointing out original but appropriate analogies. A modern-dance instructor says, "Watch me, and reach out like this"; the students closely match his performance. "Here is the Russian letter **л** . Find it on your page"; the students correctly locate the matching letter.

All these examples illustrate behavior under *stimulus control.* In each instance, an antecedent stimulus event like a signal, cue, prompt, instruction, or sample was presented. Technically, that event *set the occasion for,* or *occasioned,* the specific response. As given responses were reliably occasioned by specific stimuli, stimulus control was demonstrated. (The word *control* has many meanings. In this instance it simply describes a predictable relation between a response and an event. There is no implication that one individual is using control in a self-serving way or that there are no other possible behaviors in which the individual may engage.) Note that the relation between the stimulus and response differs here from that described for simple reinforcement. In reinforcement, a stimulus event occurs *following* a response and increases or maintains the probable rate at which that response occurs. In stimulus control, because of the history of particular consequences that have followed a response in the presence of an *antecedent* event, the antecedent stimulus enhances the probability that a response will occur.

STIMULUS GENERALIZATION AND DISCRIMINATION

If we are to concern ourselves with antecedent stimuli and the roles that they play in controlling behavior, a distinction must be made between two behavioral processes: **generalization** and **discrimination.**[2] "When an individual responds in the presence of a new stimulus in the same way as to a previously taught stimulus having some of the same characteristics, the event is called **stimulus generalization**" (Becker, Engelman & Thomas, 1975, p. 145). Dr. Daring has observed her supervising physician, the great Doctor Sir John D. Agnosis, drawing conclusions based on a particular set of symptoms. When she has imitated his behavior under similar conditions, positive feedback has been given. Now, when Dr. Daring responds to the similar symptoms in her own patient, she offers an "expert" diagnosis. Her behavior is controlled by current stimuli similar to those for which reinforcement has occurred in the past. An appropriate generalization is made.

---

[2] Behavioral processes are the results of (or the *effects* of) specific operations or procedures.

A loud ring sounds; Penny runs to the telephone and says, "Hi." No one responds. The ring sounds again, and Penny observes Daddy opening the door and greeting visitors. Penny has responded to the similar characteristics of the ring of the telephone and that of the doorbell. She is generalizing. In this instance, however, in contrast to the medical illustration, the generalization is inappropriate.

A new patient is brought before Dr. Daring, who notes some similarities between this patient and the last. Rather than jumping to a conclusive diagnosis on the basis of those similarities, however, she examines the results of some lab tests and offers a different, but again a correct, diagnosis. Fortunately, in this instance, she has not generalized inappropriately from similar but not identical characteristics. The differences are apparent to her, and she has responded differently to them. She has **discriminated** between different stimuli.

We can see that sometimes it is desirable to teach students or clients to generalize—to respond in the same way to similar but not identical stimuli. If a student is taught that the symbol R is pronounced "rrr," it would be appropriate for him to respond with that sound to variations of the printed R: R, r, $\mathcal{R}$, r . If a shy client is taught to look at the counselor while conversing, it is hoped that this response will generalize to her conversations with other people. Later we shall see how both generalization and discrimination combine during concept formation and, in Unit 23, we shall discuss more extensively how generalization is taught for purposes of facilitating the control of newly acquired or strengthened behaviors in *other* settings. The emphasis in this section, however, will be upon teaching people to make appropriate discriminations, so that a given antecedent stimulus, called a **discriminative stimulus** (abbreviated S^D), operates to occasion a particular response, whereas other S^Ds occasion different responses.

PRESENTING DISCRIMINATIVE STIMULI

When a particular response is under stimulus control, it is possible to increase the probability that it will occur simply by presenting the discriminative stimulus.[3] This procedure, sometimes called a *stimulus-change procedure*, is tremendously useful in teaching, training, and consulting activities. It is the procedure used when instructions or suggestions are given or when prompts or hints are used to encourage a behavior. This textbook is a collection of S^Ds. Discriminative stimuli may also be presented in conjunction with other procedures designed to teach new behaviors, to reduce responding, and to extend and maintain responding. In fact, henceforth the concept of stimulus control will be incorporated into many of our discussions, for it plays a crucial role in human behavior.

When stimulus control is well developed, it may appear to the observer that the S^D is actually producing the behavior: The telephone ring appears to produce an answer; the instructions "Come here" appear to occasion an approach to the individual giving the instructions. Remember, however, that we are describing

---

[3] Discriminative stimuli that occasion low rates of response or none at all will be discussed later.

a probabilistic relation between the future presentation of a stimulus and a response that follows it: There is not a one-to-one relation between the stimulus and the response, as there is in respondent or reflexive behavior, in which a light shown into the eye in a darkened room, for example, **elicits** a pupillary reflex. An S^D simply increases the likelihood that a response will occur because in the past certain responses emitted in the presence of that stimulus have been reinforced. Sometimes the telephone does not occasion answering behavior. Timid Tillie may remain in her seat while the rest of the group lines up for the fire drill. Herbie may define stimulus control mistakenly as respondent conditioning. Clyde could defend his friend: "He was hungry; it wasn't dishonest." The music passage could be identified incorrectly, and the teacher could forget to tell what aspects of the theme contribute to its excellent quality. Twinkle Toes Smith could lurch and trip as he reached, and Vladimir might incorrectly indicate the letter *d* as matching the ♪. It is apparent that **complete stimulus control** has not developed in these instances. We shall use the term complete stimulus control to describe the presence of a very high proportion of appropriate responses in the presence of the designated S^D but not in the presence of irrelevant stimuli. It is clear that the **stimulus-presentation procedure** (stimulus change) requires that stimulus control be completely developed; otherwise, an S^D like a sign, signal, or instruction would be presented, and the appropriate response would not necessarily occur.

A dual problem, however, is encountered when a particular S^D fails to occasion a designated response. The fire bell rings, and Violet fails to line up with the others. We do not know whether the failure results from weak or absent stimulus control or whether the response of getting in line is absent from her repertoire. If a designated response is absent, it must be developed. Violet would have to learn how to line up. If a designated response is part of the individual's repertoire, the task becomes one of bringing it under control of the appropriate antecedent stimuli. Lining up in the presence of the bell would be reinforced immediately each time it occurred by a reinforcer effective for Violet. Then, once control was complete, simple presentation of the S^D would probably be enough to occasion the response. When the fire bell rang, Violet would line up.

ASSESSING FOR STIMULUS CONTROL

When it is observed that a particular S^D fails to occasion a designated response, it is important to try to determine the reasons for this failure. Is the response absent or is stimulus control lacking? What do instructors do when they wish to determine whether or not a student has already acquired some knowledge? If the learning involves appropriate verbal responses to verbal stimuli, oral or written tests are given. The psychologist wishing to assess the self-care repertoire of a client tests it by presenting a series of tasks and noting the responses. The language therapist asks the client to emit sounds or identify objects. A supervisor asks a staff member to carry out a given task and observes how effectively it is accomplished. A parent says, "Now, can you button your shirt for me?" and waits to see whether or not the child complies. Informal tests and probes of this sort as well as more formal behavioral inventories (see Appendix 1), are often used to determine whether or not specific responses are within the responder's repertoire and are reliably emitted in the presence of a given stimulus.

Should the selected S^D fail to occasion the appropriate response, further probes should be attempted before concluding that the response is absent from the repertoire. Other instructions, prompts, or demonstrations should be tried. When Violet fails to respond to the fire bell, the teacher can try different verbal instructions or point to the other children lining up. Perhaps that will occasion Violet's taking her place in line. The teacher will then realize that the task is one of teaching Violet to respond to the appropriate antecedent stimulus, the bell, rather than one of teaching her to line up. (Systematic methods for priming a response in the presence of the appropriate antecedent stimulus will be discussed later in this unit.)

OTHER EXPLANATIONS

It is important not to be too hasty, however, in jumping to a conclusion that stimulus control is absent. The response may be under the control of appropriate S^Ds but may not occur because it is under the control of other S^Ds that are occasioning *interfering responses* in that particular situation. For example, a child is brought to a speech clinic for an articulation assessment. The speech therapist instructs the child to say "Susie." The child fails to respond. Rather, she looks about the room, at the pictures, toys, and faces of the strange adults present. Those S^Ds are occasioning responses that interfere with the sought-after response. Recall that earlier we recommended that an adaptation phase be provided in all programs and that the setting be carefully selected. To eliminate the hypothesis that interfering conditions are responsible for response failure, the speech therapist would provide for an adaptation phase, allowing the child to become acquainted with her and the new surroundings and removing conditions that might cause interference.

A given S^D may fail to occasion the appropriate response because of sensory or motor problems. Problems like deafness, blindness, and severe motor limitations, as in people with cerebral palsy, can make it impossible for an individual to respond to a particular S^D. The S^D may be inappropriate for a person with a sensory handicap, as an oral instruction is inappropriate for a deaf person. Or the appropriate response may not be part of the client's repertoire, as a fine motor skill is not likely to be possessed by a client with cerebral palsy. It is often possible to substitute a different S^D for the usual one. Rather than oral instructions, gestures, demonstrations, written instructions, or physical guidance might be appropriate for the deaf student. For the blind client, auditory or tactile stimuli can be substituted for visual ones. When responding is impaired because of motor difficulties, often some apparatus can be substituted: a hand-operated wheelchair for a paraplegic or specially designed eating utensils for the person with cerebral palsy.

It is also possible that the response is in the repertoire and under appropriate stimulus control at other times or places but that, because *consequences delivered in the current situation are not reinforcing,* the discriminative stimulus fails to occasion the response here and now. A houseparent in a halfway home for youthful offenders has been asked to keep records of the youths' school attendance and completion of household chores. He fails to comply, complaining that he is too busy with other, more important matters. Does failure to comply necessarily mean that following instructions is missing from his repertoire (that record keeping is not under control of the stimulus of the supervisor's instructions)? To eliminate the hypothesis that the problem is one of inadequate reinforcement conditions, rather than of a lack of stimulus control, we must assess the recent reinforcement history. Better still, a powerful reinforcement system should be provided: A very simple set of requests for record keeping should be made, and, if the staff member complies, heavy reinforcement should be immediately and consistently presented. If the rate of responding increases considerably, it can be inferred that initial failure to comply was related to reinforcement conditions.

Presuming that the response is part of the individual's repertoire, the failure to respond to the S^D could be a function of insufficient reinforcement in the past or some other **learning-history** factor, like punishment. During the first day of school, Violet left her seat to examine the toys on the shelf. Her teacher scolded her and told her firmly that she was to remain seated in school. So, when the fire bell sounds, Violet fails to respond appropriately. One could check out the possibility that something in the learning history may account for failure to respond by introducing powerful reinforcing consequences. Violet could be gently guided to the line and praised lavishly for lining up when the fire bell sounds. A few trials with those consequences should indicate whether it is necessary to teach Violet a *new* response (to line up) to be added to her repertoire or simply to reinforce lining up effectively in order to increase her rate of the response.

At this point the behavior analyst makes a decision. Suppose the appropriate response does not result from increasing reinforcement, removing stimuli that might interfere with the emission of the response, or presenting other S^Ds like **prompts**, instructions, or demonstrations to occasion the response. If assisting the response with physical support apparatus fails too, then it must be taught as a new behavior. Conversely, if the behavior has been emitted but under irrelevant stimulus conditions, the task is to develop stimulus control. Before we discuss teaching *new* behavior (see Units 16, 17), let us see how to bring already acquired behavior under stimulus control.

DEVELOPING STIMULUS CONTROL

Unlike the essentially automatic effectiveness of powerful reinforcers such as nourishment and warmth with newborn infants, the antecedent stimuli illustrated here are not automatically effective. Nor is the responding of the same kind as that which occurs when *unconditioned stimuli,* which you may have read about in textbook passages on classical or respondent conditioning, are presented. (Let us remember Pavlov's dog, which salivated when meat powder was placed in its mouth, and the human subjects who blink when air puffs are directed at their eyes.)[4] Only as the individual begins to experience certain events is stimulus control established. Here is how behavior analysts (Terrace, 1966; Keller & Schoenfeld, 1950; and others) have described the development of stimulus control and discriminative behavior: In the simplest instance of stimulus-control development, a selected response is emitted. When that response is emitted under specific stimulus conditions, it is reinforced. If those stimulus conditions are not in effect, the response is not reinforced (see Table 12.1).

As it is only in the presence of a ringing telephone that a voice responds, the child soon learns that no one will talk to him if the telephone has not first rung. It is this difference in reinforcement conditions, the **differential-reinforcement operation**, that teaches an individual to emit a given response in the presence of some stimuli and not others. The operation is the same in simple as in com-

TABLE 12.1.   DEVELOPMENT OF STIMULUS CONTROL

Antecedent Stimulus Conditions	Response	Consequence
Telephone rings	Picks up telephone, says "Hello"	"Hello"
In the absence of a ring	Picks up telephone, says "Hello"	No "Hello"

plex learning, as we shall see. For the sake of clarity, however, we shall proceed with the discussion of procedures for developing stimulus control by using relatively simple situations. Then, at a later point, we shall show that more complex learning, like learning higher-level cognitive skills (problem solving, moral concepts, and so on), is developed in similar ways.

DIFFERENTIAL REINFORCEMENT DEFINED AND ILLUSTRATED

Differential reinforcement consists of two basic operations. First, a given response, emitted in the presence of or upon presentation of one or more particular stimuli, is reinforced. Second, the same response is not reinforced (is placed on extinction) if it is emitted in the absence of the stimulus or group of stimuli. As the response is repeatedly reinforced in the presence of these particular stimuli, the antecedent stimuli begin to assume control. Eventually the response will tend to persist in the presence of the stimuli, even if it is no longer reinforced every time.

Let us consider an illustration from a study by Kazdin and Erickson (1975). A group of severely retarded children failed to follow instructions like "Sit down";

[4] The application of respondent-conditioning principles to alter physiological responding, not covered in this book, is a major topic in many books on behavior therapy.

"Catch the ball"; "Roll it to me." During training, each time a child followed an instruction correctly, food and praise were delivered. If the instructions were not correctly followed, the child was physically guided to complete the response correctly and initially given food and praise. Later food and praise were given only for unguided correct responses; incorrect responses were placed on extinction. Eventually the children learned to follow instructions without any guidance. Their behavior came under the control of the instructional stimuli.

Although the differential-reinforcement operation for developing stimulus control described earlier appears to be simple, sometimes this apparent simplicity is deceptive. For anyone who has attempted to teach a beginning language, dance, science, or for that matter any academic skill; for the individual who has attempted to teach various behaviors to clients with serious learning deficits; for the clinician who has attempted to assist a teacher or parent to use effective but unfamiliar behavior-management techniques; for the parent who struggles to teach an off-spring the subtleties of appropriate moral and social behavior; for individuals who attempt to alter their own habitual patterns of reacting to certain situations—for all these individuals, achieving complete stimulus control may prove quite a challenge. There is much more involved than initially meets the eye. The appropriate response must occur. The prerequisite stimuli must control some attending behavior of the individual, and the two events must occur simultaneously if reinforcement is to be delivered. This may be more easily said than done. For instance, the severely retarded children in Kazdin and Erickson's study (1975), though they could probably emit all the requisite responses, failed to emit them at the appropriate times—when instructed to do so. The task of the instructor, then, was to see to it that the responses did occur under proper circumstances and that they were effectively reinforced.

If we are to be convinced that a given response is under proper stimulus control, the response must be emitted under appropriate stimulus conditions. It must also *not* be emitted in the presence of irrelevant stimulus conditions. "This is the numeral 'two,' boys and girls. Say 'two.' " The children chorus, "Two." "Very good," says the primary teacher. In the presence of the numeral 2, saying "two" is reinforced. At this point, however, one could hardly claim that the young students are discriminating the 2 from any other numeral. Only when a series of different numerals were presented simultaneously, and the 2 correctly labeled by the children, would we be convinced that the verbal response "two" was under the control of the numeral 2. We have already implied that the way to control correct responding to a particular antecedent is to reinforce responses in the presence of the stimulus but not in the presence of other inappropriate antecedent stimuli. Then the appropriate antecedent stimuli will develop discriminative properties, occasioning high rates of responding, whereas the inappropriate antecedent stimuli will develop discriminative properties that occasion low rates of responding. Antecedent stimuli that have been present when particular responses have not been reinforced are called **S-deltas**, $(S^\Delta s)$[5] (see Table 12.2).

[5] The designations S^D and S^Δ are defined differently by different authors (for example, Reynolds, 1968; White, 1971).

TABLE 12.2.   DISCRIMINATION OF ANTECEDENT STIMULI

Antecedent	Behavior	Consequence
S_2^D $\longrightarrow$	"two" $\longrightarrow$	S^{r+} "good"
S_7^Δ $\longrightarrow$	"two" $\longrightarrow\!/\!\longrightarrow$	

Two or More Stimuli, One Appropriate Response

The environments in which the differential-reinforcement operation would be used most often are those in which more than one stimulus is present. A number of examples of such stimulus-control situations have already been offered. We described one situation in which the ring of the telephone was confused with that of the doorbell (see Table 12.3).

TABLE 12.3.   DIFFERENTIAL REINFORCEMENT WITH SEVERAL STIMULI

Antecedents	Behavior	Consequences
$S_{\text{telephone ring}}$ $\longrightarrow$	$R_{\text{"Hello" into telephone}}$ $\longrightarrow$	$S_{\text{"Hello"}}$
$S_{\text{doorbell ring}}$ $\longrightarrow$	$R_{\text{"Hello" into telephone}}$ $\longrightarrow\!/\!\longrightarrow$	No answer

Only picking up the telephone when it rings will be reinforced by hearing some-one speaking. Consequently, over many trials of reinforced responding in the presence of the telephone ring, that ring will become discriminative for answering the phone. With the passage of time, this ring will occasion answering, even though occasionally no one answers the "hello" (see Table 12.4).

TABLE 12.4.   OCCASIONING A BEHAVIOR

Antecedent	Behavior	Consequences
$S^D_{\text{telephone ring}}$ $\longrightarrow$	$R_{\text{"Hello" into telephone}}$ $\longrightarrow$	$S^{r+}S$ Voice usually responds
$S^\Delta_{\text{doorbell ring}}$ $\longrightarrow\!/\!\longrightarrow$		

How do pictorial signs develop controlling properties?

For a male, entrance in the presence of (☖) is allowed, but in the presence of (☖) it is not.

We encounter this sort of discrimination-learning situation in all areas of human services. The child who is developing social skills must learn that it is okay to run up and hug relatives but not strangers. It is all right to be in the house unclothed or dressed in underwear but not outside. It is acceptable to run and scream on the gymnasium floor or the playground but not in the library or during a concert.

Various academic and social target behaviors illustrate aspects of discrimination learning. Given a set of words, Marjorie is to identify the one that means "horse." From an array of flasks, Elmer is to select the one that contains ammonia. After noting the price tags on two blouses, Fern is to select the one that she has enough money to afford. From the set of drawings that he has produced, Pablo is to select the one that he thinks is best to submit to the art fair. Of a variety of social events, Clyde is to learn those under which an aggressive response will be condoned.

We have seen that the procedure for teaching students to emit a given response in the presence of a single stimulus but not in that of another is to use effective differential reinforcement strategies: reinforcing the response emitted in the presence of the appropriate stimuli and withholding reinforcement in the presence of inappropriate stimuli (for example, when an *error* has been committed). In addition, even more rapid discrimination may be acquired if aversive stimuli are also presented as consequences of the inappropriate response. If Little Leroy walks into the ladies' room and his peers tease him, he will probably learn the difference between the symbol for the men's room and ladies' room more quickly than if there were no teasing. As we shall see in the units on aversive contingencies (punishment, response cost, time out, and so on), such contingencies also tend to generate undesirable collateral effects, like aggression and escape behaviors. One must then balance the potential advantage (more rapid acquisition of the discrimination) against the potential disadvantage of collateral effects that may interfere with either the learning itself or the social situation in which instruction is taking place. Following the presentation of the varied instances in which multiple discriminative stimuli may be involved, we shall discuss some methods for maximizing the positive aspects of reinforcing correct responding while minimizing the interfering effects of aversive consequences.

Two or More Stimuli, Two or More Distinct Responses

Somewhere along the way, as we have considered stimulus control, you have probably realized that an S^Δ for one response is probably an S^D for another. Learning to read is an example of this sort of stimulus-control situation. When seeing the *p*, the student must use the label "p"; when seeing *q* the student is to say "q." A 2 is "two," and a 7 is "seven." Subtle cues like turned-down lips and knitted eyebrows are discriminative for extinction, whereas turned-up lips and eyes crinkled at the corners suggest that reinforcement conditions are in effect. What events account for the acquisition of those discriminations? (See Table 12.5.)

TABLE 12.5. DEVELOPING MULTIPLE STIMULUS CONTROL

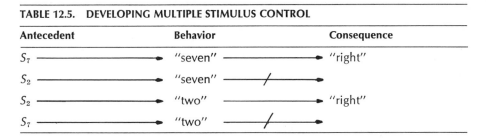

Antecedent	Behavior	Consequence
S_7	"seven"	"right"
S_2	"seven"	
S_2	"two"	"right"
S_7	"two"	

After a while 7 becomes discriminative for saying "seven" and 2 for saying "two" (see Table 12.6).

TABLE 12.6. HOW FACIAL EXPRESSIONS DEVELOP DISCRIMINATIVE PROPERTIES

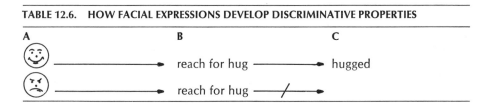

A	B	C
	reach for hug	hugged
	reach for hug	

After a while only smiles occasion approaching for hugs. You'll note that in each of these instances differential reinforcement occurs: A particular response in the presence of a particular stimulus is reinforced. Other responses are not reinforced. Different responses in the presence of different stimuli are reinforced differently.

Many cognitive skills are developed in this manner. Let us consider the ability to sort, or *classify*. Items with a particular property are placed in one group, those with another into another group and so on: "The perfect products go in this box; imperfects in another"; "Identify the poems that illustrate epic and those that illustrate lyric genre." *Comprehension* may be demonstrated by giving several different instructions and evaluating the responses. Translating a series of phrases written in a foreign language is an obvious example. Each question has a response that is correct. Different responses are incorrect. When someone can take a set of instructions, like a recipe or a list of steps to follow in assembling a tool or implementing behavioral procedures, and emit the appropriate response, this sort of discrimination has been acquired, by means of differential reinforcement.

Many Varied Antecedent Stimuli, One Appropriate Response

In this section we are reaching a much more complex level of responding. Responses that fit this category are generally called *concepts*: redness, elegance, honesty, and many more. A concept is actually an abstract critical property common to a number of antecedent stimuli. That critical property, technically labeled an *abstraction*, exerts stimulus control over a particular response. Let us consider traffic signs to illustrate this situation.

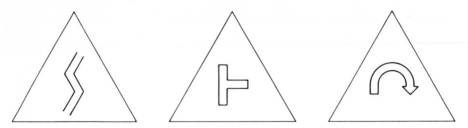

Even though each differs from the other, they have one property in common: that they encourage cautious driving behavior. A student in a drivers' education course is said to have formed the concept of a "caution sign"; he drives cautiously in the presence of all signs possessing single abstract properties, like a triangular shape. Furthermore, he must not emit that response in the presence of irrelevant stimuli, those that do not possess that common abstract property.

Again, the procedure for training this form of stimulus control remains the same: differential reinforcement. In this instance, however, reinforcement of the response is delivered contingent upon the occurrence of that response in the presence of any of a variety of antecedent stimuli possessing that *abstract property*; reinforcement is not delivered if the response is emitted in the presence of stimuli that do not contain that property (see Table 12.7).

TABLE 12.7.   DEVELOPING CONCEPTS

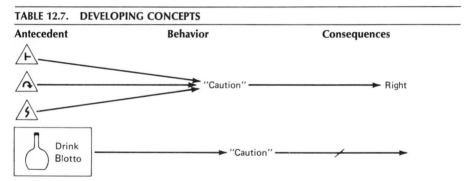

Clyde's father is attempting to instruct him in the concept of "honesty." When his friend asks for permission to have a candy bar before consuming it, his father says the act is "honest." When the candy bar is taken without asking, his attempt to label the behavior "honest" is not reinforced. When Clyde reports that little Bonnie, next door, has gone to her friend's house without permission, Clyde learns that the word "honest" does not apply. Numerous instances of reporting behaviors accurately are labeled "honest" whereas instances of inaccurate reporting are not. The abstract properties (having permission, accuracy of reporting, and others) are the aspects of the stimulus events that are common to all instances of behavior called "honest," whereas stimulus events not containing those properties are not.

Ms. Charming is a highly skilled supervisor. She seems to know exactly when to offer advice, when to provide support, when to listen, and when to compliment. Apparently, she is responding differently to cues that are common to each of those separate situations. She has learned to identify as "real" requests for help, questions posed in a particular way and accompanied by specific verbal and nonverbal cues. She has learned to identify those situations in which compliments will effectively increase particular responses. She has learned that her staff members will respond positively if she is quietly attentive when they are excited. Ms. Charming can be described as responsive to subtle social cues. The cues occasion appropriate supervisory behaviors because in the past, when she emitted each category of behavior in the presence of a group of stimuli possessing a particular abstract property, it was differentially reinforced.

Let us think of categories of behavior that society labels "intelligent," "responsible," "sophisticated," "civilized," or "expert." We can recognize the role played by stimulus control in the development of these complex behaviors. Surely, then, we must see how essential it is for behavior analysts serving children and youth to know how stimulus control is developed effectively.

Summary

In this unit, we have introduced stimulus control. The concept has been defined and illustrated, and its development has been discussed. Unlike the procedures discussed in the previous units, stimulus control focuses on antecedent stimuli. It is said to exist when specific antecedent stimuli influence the occurrence of the response. These contingent antecedent stimuli are called S^Ds, stimuli that signal reinforcement, and $S\Delta$s, stimuli that signal nonreinforcement. Individuals must learn to discriminate between such stimuli if stimulus control is to occur. They are taught to discriminate between S^Ds and $S\Delta$s through differential reinforcement.

The basic stimulus-control procedure involves simply presenting the controlling S^D. At times a single S^D occasions a single response. Other forms of the S^D-presentation procedure include two antecedent stimuli and a single correct response, two S^Ds that differ only slightly from each other but are to control different responses; many S^Ds that are different in some respects and similar in others and are to control single, as well as multiple, responses; and others. When stimulus control is incomplete, however, it must be developed further. In the next two units we describe methods for enhancing both antecedent stimulus properties and reinforcement conditions in order for the controlling properties of a given antecedent stimuli to become more complete.

References

Becker, W. C., Engelmann, S. & Thomas, D. R. *Teaching: A course in applied psychology.* Chicago: SRA, 1971.

Becker, W. C., Engelmann, S. & Thomas, D. R. *Teaching 2: Cognitive learning and instruction.* Chicago: SRA, 1975.

Kazdin, A. E. & Erickson, L. M. Developing repsonsiveness to instructions in severely and profoundly retarded residents. *Journal of Behavior Therapy and Experimental Psychiatry*, 1975, **6**, 17–21.

Keller, F. S. & Schoenfeld, W. N. *Principles of psychology.* New York: Appleton, 1950.

Reynolds, G. S. *A primer of operant conditioning.* Glenview, Ill.: Scott, Foresman, 1968.

Terrace, H. S. Stimulus control. In W. K. Honig (Ed.), *Operant behavior: Areas of research and application.* New York: Appleton, 1966.

White, O. R. *A glossary of behavioral terminology.* Champaign: Research Press, 1971.

Stimulus Control: Arranging Behavioral Antecedents, I

After mastering the material in this unit, you should be able to
1. Define and illustrate each of the following terms:
   a. Stimulus properties
   b. Prompts
   c. The verbal instruction or "tell" procedure
   d. Critical stimuli

2. Describe, illustrate, and discuss the importance of each of the rules for developing stimulus control effectively.

3. Illustrate and discuss the importance of the variables that should be considered before selecting a specific set of verbal instructions for the "tell" procedure.

4. Describe and illustrate how to develop verbal instructions into discriminative stimuli.

Discouraged by the sterility of material written by the students in a creative-writing course, the teacher sought the assistance of a behavior analyst. The task was analyzed, and effective strategies were implemented. The students' writing became more creative. A client requested help in controlling his temper. Stimulus-control procedures were chosen, and self-control was improved. In each instance, the system was fairly straightforward. The relevant stimulus properties were identified, and the targeted behaviors were differentially reinforced in their presence.

Developing stimulus control can be much more of a problem, however, when the appropriate behavior is not readily emitted under selected stimulus conditions. Such situations are often encountered in educational and training programs. Teaching difficult motor, cognitive, and vocational skills may involve that sort of a problem. The task then becomes a little more complex, requiring a strategy for "priming" the behavior under selected conditions. In this unit and the next we discuss procedures for arranging behavioral antecedents for effectively developing stimulus control.

DEVELOPING STIMULUS CONTROL EFFECTIVELY: STIMULUS ASPECTS

A number of factors should be considered in planning a differential-reinforcement procedure for effectively developing stimulus control. Some of those factors are related to the discriminative and reinforcing aspects of the stimulus: clearly identifying the antecedent stimulus properties, using effective reinforcement procedures when the response is emitted in their presence, and focusing the responder's attention upon the relevant antecedent stimuli. These aspects will be discussed first. Next, we shall examine response aspects, particularly methods of "priming" a response so that it will be more likely to be emitted in the presence of the relevant antecedent stimulus.

Clear Identification of Relevant Stimulus Properties

The manner in which stimulus control develops is frequently illustrated with simple letters (b, d), numerals, (2, 7), or signals. One reason is that then the distinctions are very clear, and the methods can be easily communicated. But most people who wish to acquire behavior-analysis skills are concerned with much more complex stimuli. A parent may wish to teach his child how to classify behavior as honest or dishonest. A teacher may wish to teach a class how to interpret "feelings" expressed in art. A youth counselor may wish to teach adolescent boys to control their anger, a speech therapist to show a client how to discriminate correct from incorrect articulation. As the procedure for developing stimulus control requires that reinforcement be either delivered or withheld contingent upon the emission of a specific behavior when certain stimulus conditions are in effect, it is crucial that the contingency manager be clear about the exact properties of these stimulus conditions.

Depending upon the types of stimuli concerned, one should specify such properties as the **topography** of the S^Ds (their form, position, size, and so on) and other relevant stimulus properties. As with the response specifications discussed in Unit 4 (size, shape, color, texture, pitch, volume, and so on), the program designer must ask, "Under what very specific circumstances will the target response be reinforced? Under what specific circumstances will reinforcement be withheld?"

Clyde's father clearly classifies *all* instances of taking property belonging to others without permission as "dishonest." Consequently, he delivers reinforcement for Clyde's labeling behavior according to a consistent set of rules.

In an attempt to bring components of creative behavior under stimulus control, Glover and Gary (1976) focused upon four properties: fluency, flexibility, elaboration, and originality. Defining each behaviorally, they were able to demonstrate increases in appropriate responses through instructions that reinforcement would be contingent upon increases in those response categories and through delivering reinforcement contingent upon those increases. When students were informed that they would earn points for increasing numbers (fluency) of responses, the numbers of responses increased; when they were instructed that novel responses would be reinforced, more novel (original) responses were produced.

Probably the most challenging aspect of teaching such **complex behaviors** as creativity, concept formation, problem solving, and analytic evaluation is the specification of relevant stimulus properties. Before instructing an individual in a concept like "redness," "geometric form," or "ethnicity," one must identify the relevant stimulus properties—those that are common among the various instances of the concept. To teach problem-solving skills or evaluation techniques, strategies and criteria must first be identified, so that stimulus properties may then be clearly identified. As we continue in our discussion of stimulus control, we shall refer from time to time to examples of this kind. It is important to remember that, regardless of the complexity of the relevant stimulus property, the differential-reinforcement procedure is basic to the development of stimulus control. The problem is usually not with this basic operation. More frequently there is difficulty in selecting the stimulus properties that should occasion reinforced responding and those that should not. Program designers must either become quite adept at discriminating antecedent stimuli that are to be developed into S^Ds from those that are to become S^Δs, or they must seek consultation.

Think about it for a moment, and you will realize that it is at this point that the subject-matter expert or specialist comes into the picture. The expert wine taster is distinguished by his ability to discriminate between examples of excellent wine and examples of not-so-excellent wine. The expert coach discriminates between acceptable and unacceptable movements or team plays. The respected critic distinguishes among poor, average, and great productions. The master teacher is able to judge exactly when a student is improving. It is not the responsibility of applied behavior analysts to become expert in such sophisticated content areas. They should, however, recognize their own limited repertoires and refer to experts when necessary. What they *should* be able to do, then, is to translate information obtained from those sources into behavioral terms, so that contingency managers will know whether to reinforce a response or not, depending upon the antecedent stimulus conditions. This is pretty much what Glover and Gary (1976) did. They read about creativity, found that it is composed of the qualities identified, and asked "What is a person doing when acting creatively?" The answer was translated into a set of response definitions, and instructional stimuli were prepared.

At that point, it became possible to teach each of the "creative" responses by delivering instructions and differentially reinforcing appropriate responses.

Sometimes troublesome distinctions between antecedent stimuli may be clarified through observations or audio or video tapes. For instance, a client and speech therapist could listen to brief speech samples and decide which should be reinforced and which should not. The youth counselor and client could view a tape of a modeled situation in which an episode that might provoke anger is displayed. While viewing, decisions could be made about the indicators that should demand attention. "See, when George hassles Charlie, Charlie begins to lose his cool. Does that sort of hassling bother you too? How can you be more sensitive to the cues that tell you you are beginning to feel bugged? Let's play that sequence again and think how you'd feel. When you think you're about to become angry, let's stop and consider alternative ways of handling the situation." Refer to the earlier material on behavioral objectives (Unit 4), and note how a clearly stated behavioral objective serves this purpose. It is this sort of clarification of stimulus properties that enables us to take the next step, using effective reinforcement procedures.

Using Effective Reinforcement Procedures

Effective differential reinforcement for stimulus control requires that the same rules noted in Units 8–10 be followed. To increase responding in the presence of potential discriminative stimuli (S^Ds), we must reinforce the response immediately and as often as possible with an appropriate amount and type of reinforcer. Then, once responding in the presence of the S^Ds has reached a high consistent rate, it should be possible gradually to build in delay and intermittent reinforcement and to shift to less powerful reinforcers. (A more extensive discussion of how to accomplish this changeover will be found in Units 24–26.) In the initial stages of teaching a student to discriminate a 7 from a 2, each time that a numeral is correctly labeled reinforcement should be delivered immediately. When Clyde correctly labels a behavior "honest," optimal reinforcement procedures should be used until the concept appears to be firmly established. Only later would it be advisable to reduce the frequency and immediacy of reinforcement or to use a less powerful reinforcer. When Granny's rule of child rearing "Be consistent" is implemented, behavior will more readily come under strong stimulus control.

Focusing Responder's Attention upon Relevant Antecedent Stimulus Properties

The operation for developing stimulus control is fairly straightforward: Reinforce the selected response in the presence of or immediately following a particular stimulus. The procedure may or may not be relatively simple to carry out. Although the contingency manager may have selected a particular S^D, the relevant aspects of the discriminative stimulus conditions may not be so apparent to the responder. For example, the S^D selected may be a *small, informal grouping of peers sitting in a semicircle*. It is supposed to occasion the response *contributing to the discussion*. This S^D may, however, be unclear to the student, for there is usually a multitude of stimuli present in the environment. Objects are placed around the room. Sights, odors, tactile sensations, and sounds abound. Various individuals are responding in various ways: with different postures, facial expressions, vocal tones, and so on. Many of these stimuli are also present when the target response is reinforced, and those stimuli may therefore also come to occasion the response. Although sometimes this multiplicity is not a problem, it often is. When a discussion is planned, students should respond to the informal arrangement of furniture and to instructions to hold a discussion. Stimuli from the room itself, the presence of other students, and other irrelevant stimuli should not cue discussion, for there are other times when entering into discussion interferes with the work of other students. The task, then, becomes one of orienting the student *toward the relevant* **stimulus properties**.

Let us consider a couple of other examples to emphasize the importance of this point. An art teacher is attempting to teach her students how paintings can communicate moods. She illustrates by showing a reproduction of Monet's *Water Lilies,* asking the class to indicate the mood expressed. One student mentions "peace," another "serenity." Then Picasso's *Guernica* is displayed, and a student says that it communicates "agitation." The teacher and some of the other students agree with the interpretations of the moods of these two pictures. It is apparent, however, that the majority of the students are reticent about offering their impressions and appear to be at a loss. At this point, the teacher decides to assist them to focus on the relevant aspects of the stimuli: line, color, medium, subject, arrangement, and so on. "Let's look at *Water Lilies*. The edges are blurred. The pastel colors, especially the blues and soft purples, convey a feeling of. . . ."; "In the Picasso painting, the sharp black lines contrast with the white, the angles. . . ." The relevant aspects are emphasized. Now, when another example is displayed, the students focus their attention on the relevant properties and are able to express themselves more knowledgeably and confidently. Naturally, reinforcement in the form of peer and teacher approval is likely.

A parent complains that his teenage son is driving him up the wall so that he suffers a series of splitting headaches. The youth is rude and leaves a mess in his wake wherever he goes. The consulting psychologist observes his behavior several times, at the invitation of the parents. The psychologist notes that indeed the young man does speak rudely and that he does create and leave lots of litter about. She also notes the fact that he does speak politely and pick up things from time to time. The parents appear to be focusing most of their attention on the disruptive behavior, ignoring the acceptable behavior. In discussing the problem afterward, it is decided that a shift in focus is desirable. A scheme is designed to enhance the parents' attending to the stimulus property now identified as most relevant: the desirable behaviors.

Returning to the art-appreciation example, we see that instructional sequences can be designed to assist students to focus their attention on each of the relevant properties noted: line, color, medium, subject, arrangement, and so on. Brief instructional sequences can be arranged to focus attention, say, on color. Pairs of the same pictures can be colored differently and responses reinforced when color differences are detected and discussed. Another exercise may involve showing a series of picture pairs, each pair differing only in the sharpness of the lines. Responses made on the basis of differences in line are then reinforced. The same procedure could be followed with other relevant properties; eventually combinations of two properties, then of three, and so on could be presented until two very different pictures—like *Water Lilies* and *Guernica* could be compared.

For parents wishing to learn to respond appropriately to acceptable behavior, perhaps the task seems overwhelming. To assist them, practice exercises can also be designed: It is possible to tape-record segments of family interactions (with the consent of all involved, of course) and to listen for instances of politeness or cooperation. At another time, the psychologist can listen for parental attention following acceptable behavior, rude behavior, and so on. Later the psychologist may sit in the room, signaling when attention should be given. As a next step, an audio tape programmed with a series of intermittent chimes can be used to remind the parents to stop and "catch their son being good" and to reinforce the behavior with attention and approval.

There are many other methods for focusing the responder's attention upon the relevant properties of an antecedent stimulus. When learning form-discrimination: numbers, letters, shapes, and the like, students may be asked to trace distinctive parts of each stimulus with their fingers; or yarn, clay, and other textures may be added to the critical parts as temporary prompts (see Fauke et al., 1973). We discuss this system for magnifying critical features of stimuli and other prompting strategies in greater detail later (see Unit 14).

DEVELOPING STIMULUS CONTROL EFFECTIVELY: RESPONSE ASPECTS

Often, although appropriate stimuli have been clearly identified and presented, effective reinforcement procedures implemented, and attention focused upon the appropriate stimuli, the response nevertheless fails to be emitted at the specified time. Waiting for the response to be emitted under those circumstances is a luxury that most cannot afford. In this unit and the next we address ourselves to various methods for facilitating the emission of the response in the presence of the S^D in hierarchical order, from the most natural and efficient to the most artificial or intrusive: the "tell," "show," and "guide" procedures and then other artificial or intrusive prompting procedures.

Using Instructional Prompts: The Tell Procedures

Except in the specific instance of teaching receptive or expressive language, like following instructions, the ultimate objective of most procedures for establishing stimulus control is that the response be emitted only in the presence of specific critical stimuli. If the critical stimuli must be supplemented by additional stimuli, like instructions or hints, then the response is not under appropriate stimulus control. We call such supplementary stimuli prompts. The expert tennis player's responding should depend upon the angle and speed of the approaching ball, wind conditions, and the position of the opponent. It should not have to depend upon a coach's instructions: "Aim to the left rear of the court; keep the ball low. . . ." The student of Spanish should be able to form a full question without the teacher's prompting, "Remember the sign for the interrogative that preceded a question in Spanish?" Teachers who are students of effective behavior-management techniques should be able to "catch the students being good" without a consultant's coaching them on the spot. They should be able to observe unaided that Dreadful Desmond has actually been working for thirty seconds and should be given attention. Tiny Tina, learning to button her coat, should eventually be able to accomplish the feat without her Mama standing beside her and saying: "Take the button. Turn it to the side. Find the button hole. Push part of the button through. Grab the other side. Pull it through all the way. Good, you've done it."

Yet instructional prompts are freely used by coaches, consultants, clinicians, teachers, and parents for good reason. It is appropriate to use them *temporarily* to facilitate the emission of the response when stimulus control is not complete: when the environmental conditions are set and the response is not being emitted. If the tennis player's stance suggests that a proper return will not be made, he must be reminded; if the Spanish student's initial written work indicates that he has failed to remember to preface the question with an inverted question mark, he must be instructed. The essence of the procedure is to occasion the appropriate response under the appropriate conditions, so that reinforcement may be delivered. When the teacher has been coached to respond to Dreadful Desmond, the consultant can nod approval to her. Perhaps next time the prompt will not be needed.

Using the Tell Procedure Effectively

So what is new about the **"tell" procedure**? Teachers and consultants have been giving instructions since the beginning of time (not to speak of animals: Watch a bird chirping "instructions" to its young). Well, some variables have been identified that can influence our use or choice of verbal instructions. They include careful analysis of response components, determining whether or not the response is in the individual's repertoire, and determining whether or not it is under instructional control.

Analyzing response components. Recall that it is essential to describe precisely the response to be reinforced in the presence of a specific antecedent stimulus. If instructional prompts are to be used effectively, they too should be delivered with great care and precision. If the response consists of a sequence of parts (a response **chain**; see Unit 17), the instructor must make the series of events very clear to the learner. Have you ever been instructed in a response like shifting the gears of a car, doing a fancy embroidery stitch, taking a statistical test, sorting out a bridge hand, operating a potter's wheel, or folding egg whites into batter? Were you confused? The confusion may have resulted from instructions delivered out of sequence. The conscientious student, then, responding appropriately to each separate instruction, performs a series of acts in the wrong order.

If you plan to prompt a response by means of instructions, then be sure that you have analyzed all the components of the response, and practice the instructions ahead of time, to ensure that they have been delivered correctly. Now *that* instruction is deceptively simple. Think about something that you can do with great ease but with which one of your students or clients is experiencing difficulty: hitting a soft ball with a bat or maneuvering a soccer ball, using a fork and knife to cut a tough piece of steak, tying a shoe lace, filling out a job application, adjusting the mirror in a microscope, asking for a date, or solving a problem with a slide rule. How readily would you be able to reel off, in logical sequence, each of the components involved?

When the response to be brought under stimulus control is a complex skill or concept composed of various subtasks, as are many of the examples in the preceding paragraph, a more formal **task analysis** (Anderson & Faust, 1974) should be conducted (see Unit 4).

It is indeed fortunate that verbal instructions alone are often sufficient to prime the selected response so that it is emitted at the designated time. Because of the inadequacies of language, however, instructions, however precise, may sometimes result in incomplete stimulus control. What kinds of words would you use to prompt someone to play a violin with the proper sort of feeling or to relax while parachuting? Even if the words were found, without demonstrations or other prompts, stimulus control would probably still remain incomplete. In such instances stimulus control may be enhanced by other prompting strategies (like those to be discussed here) or by direct contact with the differential consequences operating in the natural environment.

Determining that the appropriate response is in the repertoire.   Earlier we discussed the importance of assessing for stimulus control in the respondent's repertoire. Here we are concerned about whether or not the response alone, regardless of antecedent stimuli, is in the repertoire.

No matter how logically and precisely we give Claude instructions in balancing a soccer ball on his foot while running, it is a lost cause. That behavior is not part of his response repertoire. It is not possible to use instructions to facilitate the emission of a complex response if the response or its critical components are not in the individual's repertoire. Instruct yourself to paint a masterpiece, write a Pulitzer Prize-winning book, or win at the Olympics. It is likely that the response will not occur, for you probably do not have the requisite component responses in your repertoire. Similarly, all the instructions in the world will not be effective if a student or client does not possess the requisite response. An infant cannot respond to a request to tie a shoe because holding the string, looping it, pushing it, pulling it, and holding onto looped strings are not part of his repertoire. An advanced chemistry student may not be able to conduct an experiment according to instructions because she may have failed to learn one of the component tasks involved—perhaps how to use a piece of apparatus. Instructions work only when the response and its components are part of the person's repertoire. (Do not despair: You may still paint your masterpiece, write your prize-winning book, or win the Olympics. Just turn to Units 16 and 17 and learn how to add to your response repertoire!) For your students or clients, determine first whether or not the response is in their repertoires by observing whether or not it has ever occurred. If not, teach the response (Units 16 and 17), and *then* use instructions to facilitate its emission.

Determining whether or not the response is under instructional control. As people develop, more and more of their actions come under the control of instructional stimuli. Words take on more and more "meaning" in terms of the guidance that they provide. The teacher instructs, "Now play an A-minor chord," and the advanced music student responds accordingly. When chemistry students are told to "take a flask of HCl and fill a burette to the 15-milliliter mark. Then add two drops of phenolphthalein . . .," they perform the procedure correctly. Yet for many students the appropriate responses are not under the stimulus control of oral instructions. Similarly, the "poor reader" is at a disadvantage because the printed word does not adequately control his behavior. The "meaning" of the oral or written words has not been learned. So much of the frustration in teaching, as well as in other human relationships, arises from the inadequate stimulus control exerted by spoken or printed words. It is agreed that "We'll meet at 1:00 P.M."; one member is there at 1:00 P.M., but the other arrives forty-five minutes later. The instruction did not exert tight enough control over the latter person's response. "Remember to write your name on your examination paper," instructs the professor, and three papers are turned in without names. "You may leave your seat to sharpen your pencil, to seek help with your work, or to assist another student with his. Leaving your seat to bother other students with irrelevant conversation is not allowed." A student does the latter and irritates the teacher. The job application instructs, "Write a brief résumé of your job experience in the space below." The nonreader fails to do what is asked and is not hired. A mother says, "Raise your arms, so I can help you on with your sweater." The child for whom those instructions lack control, for instance a child whose development is delayed, fails to comply. If stimulus control by instructions is limited or absent, it is not possible to use them to facilitate emission of the response. *Effective teaching*, then, requires that *before using instructions* to prompt responding, it must *first be determined whether or not such control exists*. This is done by repeating oral or written instructions several times in a variety of sample situations. If the client responds correctly, instructional control is demonstrated. Fine; go ahead. If not, either instructional control must be taught as described in the next section, or other prompting strategies must be used.

Developing Instructions as Discriminative Stimuli to
Prompt a Response

Instructions become discriminative for specific responses in exactly the same man-ner as do other stimuli. In fact, one example that we used in Unit 12 (Kazdin & Erickson, 1975) was a perfect illustration of this situation. When children failed to follow instructions, the response was guided directly after the delivery of the instructions, and reinforcement was delivered. In another situation, Fjellstedt and Sulzer-Azaroff (1973) taught a student to follow instructions. In this instance the youngster actually did follow instructions—but later, rather than sooner. Stimulus control was incomplete. When asked to take out his work and start, he dawdled and took many minutes to respond. A requirement was added to the procedure: For the response to be consequated with reinforcement, it had to follow the instruction within a predetermined period of time.

Using Instructional Prompts to Develop Control by
Verbal Stimuli

Verbal stimuli are not limited to the category of supplementary stimuli or prompts. They may also be the *critical stimuli*—those that ultimately are to assume discrim-inative control over the behavior. Questions used in evaluation of college courses or in conversations among friends are examples. In the presence of the stimulus "Name the sixteenth president of the United States," the response "Abraham Lincoln" is reinforced. This sequence involves a simple *memorization* response, with the critical S^D being the question. Verbal or "tell" prompts may also be used to supplement such critical verbal antecedent stimuli: "Remember, we have been studying about the president who was born in a log cabin?" (the supplementary verbal prompt); "Who was the 16th president?" (the critical S^D). The appropriate response is reinforced: "Right." Although it is not our intention to develop a tech-nology of *cognitive* ("knowledge") instruction in this textbook (see Becker, Engel-mann & Thomas, 1975, for example), let us look briefly at some other simple and more complex antecedent stimulus-response combinations of the type that are often called "cognitive behaviors." We shall see that those behaviors develop in the same basic manner as do other forms of stimulus control and that instructional prompts may be used to support that development.

Prompting for memorization through the "tell" procedure has been illus-trated. Verbal prompts may be used temporarily to supplement *comprehension* responses as well. The critical stimulus "up" on an elevator button is to occasion a response demonstrating that the person comprehends which button to push. As Little Leroy hesitates, Mama prompts him, "Where do we want to go?" or "Sound out the words on the buttons." Leroy responds "up" and points to the "up" button. Mama praises him as he pushes the "up" button, and his behavior is further reinforced by the arrival of the elevator.

For *concept development,* the critical stimuli are a group of antecedent stimuli all having at least one critical feature in common. Sandpaper, tree bark, and Dad's unshaven face all have a critical feature in common: roughness. "Feel this. Feel this. How do they feel?" Mama can prompt Tiny Tina's response by means of a supplementary hint: "What do we call something that feels bumpy?" If she presents and points out what feature the critical stimuli have in common, Tina is more likely to respond appropriately.

Problem-solving strategies consist of series of responses. For example, a student is told that, in a problematical situation, one does the following: analyzing the situation, considering the alternatives, weighing the pros and cons of the alternatives, selecting and implementing a strategy, and checking the solution with the reinforcer, which is, of course, the correct solution. The auto-mechanics teacher presents a problem: "I turn on the ignition, and the engine fails to start." He reviews the five-step strategy with the group. The students follow those steps and are reinforced by the motor's turning over.

In teaching creativity, verbal prompts may be used temporarily to occasion some of the response components. The critical instruction may be to "design a gift that is both functional and creative. Here is a shoe box, some pieces of cloth, some metal foil, and some rubber cement." A verbal statement like "Remember, foil can be folded and retain its shape," may enhance the likelihood that a functional gift worthy of reinforcement will be created; perhaps the reinforcer will be the accomplishment itself or the admiration of others.

Evaluation or judgmental responses may be temporarily occasioned by verbal prompts. In the presence of a complex object or event, a series of matching responses is to be performed and an evaluative statement made. If the judgment is acceptable to others, it is called "fair" or "just." Grungy George gazes at Prudence's precise stitchery. Her display of sunbursts and assorted geometric forms is exquisite. He prompts himself to judge on the basis of criteria that he has memorized. He matches each characteristic: neat stitches, secure seams, novel forms, unusual colors, uncharacteristic uses of materials. Then he delivers the blue-denim ribbon to Prudence. His judgment is reinforced when his peers cheer his decision.

In each of these instances of simple and complex responding, when the designated response is no longer dependent upon the supplementary verbal prompt but is reliably occasioned by the critical S^D, then stimulus control is complete. It is necessary to discontinue supplementary prompts with care, however. Strategies for accomplishing a smooth transition from prompted to complete stimulus control will be discussed later (see Unit 15).

Summary

We have now seen how stimulus control is developed effectively for clients with varied repertoires. Procedures for the development of simple and complex motor, cognitive, social, personal, and vocational skills were presented. When the goal is to develop stimulus control of sufficient strength so that S^D presentations reliably occasion the appropriate response, the following procedures can be implemented: (1) Clearly identify relevant stimulus properties; (2) Focus attention on relevant stimulus properties; and (3) Use effective reinforcement procedures.

A procedure for "priming" the occurrence of a behavior under specific antecedent conditions was discussed and illustrated: the "tell" procedure or use of instructional prompts. It is a procedure that we all use. Several variables that have been identified as influencing its effective use were presented. A careful consideration of these variables will maximize its effectiveness. Additional prompting strategies are discussed in the next unit.

References

Anderson, R. C. and Faust, G. W. *Educational psychology*. New York: Dodd, Mead and Co., 1974.

Becker, W. C., Engelmann, S., and Thomas, D. R. *Teaching 2: Cognitive learning and instruction*. Chicago: Science Research Associates, 1975.

Fauke, J., Burnett, J., Powers, M. A., and Sulzer, B. Improvement of handwriting and letter recognition skills: A behavior modification procedure. *Journal of Learning Disabilities*, 1973, **6**, 296–300.

Fjellstedt, N. & Sulzer-Azaroff, B. Reducing latency of responding to adult instruction by means of a token system. *Journal of Applied Behavior Analysis*, 1973, **6**, 125–130.

Glover, J. and Gary, A. L. Procedures to increase some aspects of creativity. *Journal of Applied Behavior Analysis*, 1976, **9**, 79–84.

Kazdin, A. E. and Erickson, L. M. Developing responsiveness to instruction in severely and profoundly retarded residents. *Journal of Behavior Therapy and Experimental Psychiatry*, 1975, **6**, 17–21.

Stimulus Control: Arranging Behavioral Antecedents, II

After mastering the material in this unit, you should be able to
1. Define and illustrate each of the following terms:
   a. The modeling, or "show," procedure
   b. Matching-to-sample
   c. The physical-guidance procedure
   d. Graduated guidance

2. Describe and illustrate how to develop imitative prompts as discriminative stimuli.

3. Describe the way to strengthen imitative responding.

4. Identify the factors that can enhance the likelihood that imitation will occur; give an illustration of each.

5. Describe and illustrate how to use physical guidance effectively.

6. Distinguish between a natural S^D and an artificial S^D. Describe how artificial S^Ds are selected and used to facilitate learning.

7. Describe how the S^D-R combination can be maintained by means of reinforcement.

We have examined the "tell" procedure in detail in Unit 13. We have shown that prompting a response by means of verbal instructions often successfully occasions the response, so that it is emitted in the presence of the critical stimuli that are eventually to control it. Sometimes, however, despite the best efforts of the contingency manager, verbal instructions fail to function as effective prompts.

The responder may not be able to translate a particular set of instructions into action. "Now follow through," the golf pro instructs, as the duffer continues to muff his drives. People whose receptive language abilities are severely *delayed* also frequently fail to profit from instructional prompts. Sometimes, as we mentioned earlier, language itself is inadequate to prompt the response targeted for stimulus control. When such situations occur, one can use the "show" or "guide" procedure or some other intrusive prompting strategy to occasion the response.

PROVIDING A MODEL: THE "SHOW" PROCEDURE

Obviously, bringing a behavior under stimulus control through verbal instructions is often expedient. It can be quite effective, simply to direct, "When you wish to compare and contrast two literary figures, look at the following characteristics. . . ." Because the method is generally so effective, books, lectures, seminars, discussions, and workshops have been developed as primary instructional strategies. There are, however, many instances in teaching, training, self-management, and consulting in which no adequate response is occasioned by the presentation of a series of verbal instructions. "Clean up your room, Joey, before you go out to play." On inspection after Joey has left, his room looks as if Hurricane Hannah has hit the place. The sign says, "Speed limit, 55 MPH," and Eager Edgar moves along at a steady 70 MPH. "I shall not eat any desserts for the rest of the year," says Diligent Dottie, and Mr. Novice vows that he will scold irritating behavior less and praise good behavior more. Both fail to follow through on their resolutions. The teacher announces, "Look, more new books for you to read!" and only two of eight children respond by reading (Haskett & Lenfestey, 1974). When such incomplete or inadequate instructional stimulus control is demonstrated and attempts to bring the behavior under instructional control either have been unsuccessful or are apparently too time consuming or require too much effort, it is time to try the "**show**" technique, to prime the response by modeling the behavior oneself or having someone else demonstrate it.

When the students in a study by Haskett and Lenfestey (1974) failed to respond to encouragement and the presentation of new books, tutors began to pick up books and to read aloud. The students soon began to follow suit, and reading and reading-related responses began to increase substantially. Stereotyped motor behaviors, like rocking and repetitive hand movements, are frequently encountered among institutionalized retarded persons. Such individuals rarely learn to gesture appropriately in response to verbal instructions but may, given stimulus-control training, learn by first imitating, then eventually responding to the instructions alone.

For the client with less aberrant behavior, modeling may also facilitate the acquisition of a complex response. Sometimes the instructor has difficulty in finding adequate verbal instructions to prompt the response, or perhaps demonstration is simply much more efficient. Occasionally, clients do not comprehend the words that could be used to describe the response. The demonstrations that physical-education instructors, art teachers, music teachers, and others frequently use are illustrative of such situations: for example, "Serve the ball like this." Eventually it is possible to dispense with the demonstration and simply to say, "Show how you serve the ball." As with verbal instructions, it is important for the instructor to have the demonstration sequence carefully worked out ahead of time and eventually to apply fading techniques (discussed in the next unit).

Developing Imitative Prompts as Discriminative Stimuli

From the earliest months of an infant's life, imitative behavior is taught through reinforcement. "Peek-a-boo" says Mama, covering her eyes, smiling, and laughing. Baby makes the initial moves toward matching Mama's behavior by bringing his hands to his eyes, or Mama assists by guiding his hands. When Baby responds to "peek-a-boo" with an approximation of his own, bells ring, fireworks explode, and trumpets blare: "Look! He's playing peek-a-boo!" In other words, Baby is heavily reinforced for imitating Mama. Junior stands beside Daddy and rubs shaving cream over his face, pretending to shave as Daddy shaves. Daddy says, "You're a big man, just like Dad!" Imitative responses are similarly prompted and reinforced throughout childhood: "See how Penny picks up her toys. You try to do that too." Through the frequent reinforcement of many instances of imitative responding, the general response class of imitation is learned effectively.

Imitation is often too well learned, and probably every developing individual has experienced occasions when imitating other people's behavior has led to trouble. Junior learns to imitate not only Daddy's shaving techniques but also his vocabulary. Junior picks up Dad's briefcase, pretends to head out the door, and says, " 'Bye, Honey, see you tonight," in a deep voice just like Daddy's voice. The adoring parents beam at his cleverness. But when Junior angrily responds to Mama just as Daddy does—"Shut up, you #!*#!"—his inappropriate responding is not reinforced and may be punished. Junior must learn to discriminate when imitating is and when it is not appropriate.

Imitation is the act of matching the behavior of another individual. **Matching-to-sample behavior** resembles imitative behavior in some respects. It consists of selecting from a number of alternatives an object that corresponds to, or matches, a particular sample. Perhaps the sample is the numeral 7. There are cards with the numerals 2, 7, and 9. A correct matching-to-sample response is the selection of the 7 card. In imitation, the response of another individual functions in a sense as a sample S^D; the behavior occasioned is the imitative act.

Increasing Imitative Responding

Although most people in our society do learn to imitate effectively in their early years, some imitate only infrequently. If well-established imitative responding is essential to the acquisition of certain behaviors, as it often is, then generalized imitative responding must first be strengthened. Imagine trying to teach someone who cannot imitate to knit, solder, slam a Ping-Pong ball, or shuffle cards. Actually, the individual whose imitative abilities are underdeveloped is in serious jeopardy. Learning to speak, to engage in social behaviors, or to acquire complex physical or preacademic skills—like orienting toward instructional materials—is impeded, for all these behaviors require strong imitative skills. To remove such an impediment to development, it is necessary first to strengthen the individual's skills, by heavily reinforcing imitation under many circumstances. For example, Lovaas and colleagues (1966) and Baer, Peterson, and Sherman (1967) reinforced imitation of demonstrated responses by initially nonresponsive, autistic, and severely retarded individuals. The procedure, a standard stimulus-control training procedure, was to present instructions (for example, "Touch your head") together with a demonstration of the behavior. If the response was part of the individual's repertoire, imitation occasionally occurred and was then reinforced by means of praise, small bits of food, and so on. Ultimately it became possible gradually to remove, or fade out, the demonstrations and to present verbal instructions alone (see Unit 15 on fading of prompts). These same techniques are currently being used to teach gestural language to persons with delayed or absent speech, not only those whose hearing is impaired, but also the severely and profoundly retarded and the severely emotionally disturbed, enabling them at last to enter into communication with others in their world.

Using the "Show" Procedure Effectively

In addition to developing **imitative prompts** as S^Ds through the reinforcement of imitation, there are a few other factors that can influence the probability that a particular imitative response will occur: the selection of the models, the people whose actions are to be imitated; similarity between the model and the observing clients; combining instructions with modeling; the simplicity of the behavior to be modeled; reinforcement of the model's behavior; the observer's previous experience; and the competence of the model.

Model selection. Two basic factors are worthy of consideration when selecting models. The first is *similarity*: the common characteristics or elements shared by the models and individuals who observe them (for example, age, grade, interests, physical appearance, and experiences). Imitation is more likely to occur when children and youths observe, or are told, that they and their respective models have similar attributes (Bandura, 1968; Byrne, 1969; Byrne & Griffitt, 1969; Rosekrans, 1967; Stotland & Hillmer, 1962).

Other children and youths are obviously more similar to the observing client than are adults. Many clients are more likely to imitate a behavior demonstrated by peers, particularly friends (friends are usually similar to one another in a variety of characteristics), than one demonstrated by adults. This emphasis on similarity does not, however, imply that individual differences should not exist between models and observers. We should not confuse "similar" with "identical." Differences are unavoidable and actually helpful. In fact, too much behavioral similarity appears to handicap a group's ability to promote change. For example, in discussing group counseling in the schools, Mayer and Kahn caution against forming a group containing very similar clients: "It limits generalization because the group becomes more dissimilar to the classroom. Further, if the group members all engage in the same problem behavior (stealing, classroom disruption, drugs, etc.) they will tend to reinforce one another's problem behavior . . ." (1976, pp. 2–3). Similar arguments form one of the bases for the current emphasis on *mainstreaming* (Mann, 1975), integrating youngsters with special educational needs within "regular" classes of their age mates. Some diversity must exist if appropriate behaviors are to be modeled. Group members, then, should not all have the same behavioral problems (deficits or excesses) but should be *similar* in a variety of other characteristics in order to facilitate imitation.

Imitation is more likely to occur when observing clients are told that they have certain qualities or attributes in common with the model. Clients may not readily observe the similarities until they are called to their attention. Contingency managers can thus bolster imitative prompting by informing their clients of existing similarities.

The second factor to be considered when selecting models is *prestige*. Groups usually contain some individuals whose behavior is more likely to be imitated than that of others. These individuals are often referred to as "prestigious," as "leaders." They are usually persons whose behavior has in the past received considerable reinforcement from many sources, particularly the peer group. For instance, Ernie may be friendly, a good athlete, pleasant in appearance, and inclined to smile a lot. These factors may have led to his behavior's receiving more than the usual amount of reinforcement. Observing this fact, other youths would be more likely to imitate him, rather than an individual who has received little reinforcement (Bandura, Ross & Ross, 1963a; Mayer, Rohen & Whitley, 1969). The selection of prestigious models introduces some diversity and helps to promote appropriate behaviors. Care must be taken, however, as already indicated, to ensure that the models are similar enough to the observers to enhance further the likelihood of imitation. If little or no similarity exists between the prestigious model and the observer, imitation is less likely.

Because age frequently adds to the prestige factor, it is sometimes helpful to select older peers as models. Many tutoring programs capitalize on this technique. When older peers are selected as models, similarity can be enhanced by selecting those who have "experienced the same type of problems. Their growth in this area allows them to demonstrate approximations to the desired behaviors that are not too complex or unrealistic for the other clients to imitate" (Mayer & Kahn, 1976, p. 3). For example, Warner and Swisher used audio-taped models of youths who were former drug users. The goal of such groups was to teach "alternative ways of experiencing life without the use of artificial aids like drugs" (1976, p. 511). The taped models served as a component of their group-counseling program with adolescent drug abusers.

Combining modeling with instructions. To enhance further the likelihood that modeling will be effective, we can combine it with verbal instructions. Novel and relatively stable abstract performances, like Piagetian conservation (for example, pointing out that the total amount of water has not changed in being transferred from one large vessel to several smaller ones), can be taught by combining modeling with verbal instructions and the presentation of rules guiding the model's behavior (Zimmerman & Rosenthal, 1974). The provision of verbal instructions and rules governing or explaining the model's behavior appears to facilitate not only imitative behavior but also the generalization and retention of the acquired concepts (Zimmerman & Rosenthal, 1974).

Behavioral simplicity.   Sometimes a modeled behavior is too complex for the client to imitate. According to Bandura (1965), an imitative behavior is more likely to be rapidly acquired if it includes some components that the individual has previously learned and if the complexity of the stimulus is neither too great nor presented too rapidly. We alluded to this point previously when we suggested using as models older peers who have had similar experiences and have overcome similar difficulties in the recent past. When a model does demonstrate a behavior too complex to be imitated by the client, however, it must be broken down into its components. These components should then be explained, modeled, and role-played. For example, the vocational-training supervisor is orienting Fern to her new workshop assignment. She selects a client who she thinks will provide an appropriate model to demonstrate the task for Fern. This procedure will work well if Fern has had prior experience with similar tasks. But suppose that this is her first workshop experience. The complex behavioral sequence may be too much for her. Simply requesting the behavior and providing a good model will probably be insufficient preparation. Fern may first have to practice imitating each component behavior separately before attempting the complete task. Afterward she may be more likely to imitate the more complex behavior of the model.

Reinforcement of the model's behavior.   In addition to reinforcing the client's imitative behavior, reinforcing the model's own behavior also increases imitative behavior (Bandura & Kupers, 1964; Bandura, Ross & Ross, 1963a; 1963b). As we have mentioned previously, this technique offers one way to develop model "prestige." For example, children who saw a model reinforced after selecting a particular picture from a pair were more likely to imitate that choice than they were to imitate a choice that had been punished or presented with neutral consequences (Levy et al., 1974). Similarly, high-school juniors learned information-seeking behaviors like talking, reading, listening, writing, visiting, and observing, by listening to the audio tapes of other high-school juniors. The tapes revealed how other students had handled their career decisions. Verbal information-seeking responses were modeled and reinforced by peers and a counselor (Stewart, 1969). This combined use of modeling and reinforcement has been shown to be very effective in increasing the information-seeking behaviors of youth (Krumboltz & Thoresen, 1964; Lafleur & Johnson, 1972).

The following episode illustrates alternative ways in which imitative S^Ds may be used in the classroom. Suppose that Dexter seems to understand how to square numbers. He correctly says one day that 5² equals 25. Yet the next day he says that 5² equals 10. There are several ways that the teacher can handle such a situation. She can provide the appropriate response, thus acting as the model and prompting Dexter to give the correct response. Or she can call upon another child, Tim. Assuming that Tim gives the appropriate response, it can be reinforced, and Dexter can then be asked to solve the problem again. Hearing Tim praised for the correct response, Dexter is more likely to give the correct solution. His behavior, too, can then be reinforced, thus strengthening his correct response. Dexter's reinforced response will then be more likely to be imitated by the rest of the class. In the future Dexter and his classmates will probably continue to respond correctly to that question. Similar procedures can be used to increase other client behaviors, like hanging up coats, paying attention, bringing berries (see Figure 14.1), and so on. Imitative behavior, therefore, can be facilitated by providing a situation in which the model's behavior is reinforced.

Previous observer experience and model competence. Individuals are more likely to imitate the behavior of another if they have experienced failure in a prior task (Mausner, 1954; Gelfand, 1962), have previously participated in a cooperative experience with the model (Mausner & Block, 1957), and have observed that the model is competent or answers questions correctly most of the time (Kanareff & Lanzetta, 1960; Rosenbaum, Chalmers & Horne, 1962). However, the model must demonstrate competence in the target behavior in order for imitation to be likely (Croner & Willis, 1961).

These factors—past failure, previous cooperative experiences with the model, and model competence—frequently serve to foster imitative behavior. Consider the following illustration. Ursula's soufflés fell, but Penny's were always flawless. One day while the two girls were instructing each other in the latest

Figure 14.1 Reinforcing the model to promote imitation.

dance steps, Ursula asked Penny to help her with cooking. As a result of Penny's help, Ursula's soufflés rose higher and higher. Had Penny not been doing well at cooking or had she not previously worked cooperatively with Ursula, Ursula would probably not have asked her to help.

WHEN TELLING OR SHOWING FAILS:
PROMPTING WITH PHYSICAL GUIDANCE

Generally it is possible to prompt a response in the presence of a stimulus by means of either instructions, modeling, or often a combination of the two. There are occasions, however, in which neither suffices, and the specific response fails to be emitted even with such assistance. "When you hit the ball, you must follow through," instructs the golf pro, and then he gives a demonstration. The duffer, regardless of having seen experts perform many times and having heard and perhaps even read the instructions, fails to execute the appropriate follow-through. The pro then may provide physical prompts by actually moving the duffer's arms through the proper swing. After two or three times, the duffer begins to "get the feel of the motion." Verbal instructions, paired with the movement, begin to take control, and eventually physical prompting is no longer necessary.

When a client's development is seriously delayed or when a response that is not fully accurate has been well practiced and occasionally reinforced, **physical guidance** may be a particularly useful method for accomplishing an instructional goal. Striefel and Wetherby (1973) taught a profoundly retarded boy who had no vocal behavior to follow instructions by using a "putting through" or physical-guidance procedure. Verbal instructions were presented in combination with guided responding in a series of steps that eventually terminated in the reduction of guidance, until appropriate responses occurred following instructions alone. Similar forms of physical guidance are used by parents, as when, for example, they guide a youngster's arms to help him put a sweater over his head. Conscientious teachers correct inappropriate pencil holding by guiding the correct grasp, and the driver trainer guides the beginning driver's handling of the steering wheel, gradually lessening his assistance as imitative and instructional prompts attain stimulus-control properties. (The gradual reduction of physical prompts will be discussed later.)

Using Physical Guidance Effectively

If physical guidance is to be used as a means for prompting a response, several factors should be considered. First, conditions must be arranged to enhance the likelihood that the learner will attend to the appropriate *kinesthetic cues*, the way that his body feels to him while engaging in the response. Second, stimulus control must gradually be transferred from the physical prompt to another discriminative stimulus. The retarded child must eventually learn to follow instructions, the driver to respond to the visual stimuli before her, and the writer to respond to the visual and kinesthetic cues provided by the positioning of the pencil.

Securing the client's cooperation and guiding minimally.   A relaxed client who is being put through certain motions can concentrate all his attention on the way his actions look and feel. A tense or resisting client will feel only tension and may learn to resist even more if the motions are forced by someone else. (Forcing anything is not advisable on most grounds, for it generates interfering emotional behavior and is ethically questionable.) Although this rule applies to all instructional procedures, it is especially important here, where the ultimate objective is for individuals to take over responding on their own, as trainers gradually reduce their assistance. The setting should be relaxed and comfortable, the surroundings pleasant, and the contingency manager relaxed, with a calm voice and expression. It does not hurt to provide a few reinforcers noncontingently at the beginning of a training session or to intersperse easier tasks throughout the session. The client must be adapted to being touched by the contingency manager, for a flinching client produces responses that interfere with his learning. With a "normal," rational adult learner, such adaptation should occur rapidly, and training can proceed easily. With a very anxious or fearful person, it is better to proceed very slowly, obtaining the client's confidence before taking each step. If the anxious client is verbal and can imitate and follow directions, it may be appropriate to provide some relaxation training first (see Paul, 1966; Bernstein & Borkovec, 1973; and other sources on relaxation therapy). For persons with serious disabilities, it is better to wait out resistance patiently, proceeding with physical guidance only when relaxation eventually does occur. If necessary, the instructor can maintain physical contact and move passively with the resisting client until the resisting movements cease and the instructor is able to guide the movements gently. The amount of pressure exerted should be the *minimum* amount required to guide the movement.

OTHER PROMPTING STRATEGIES

Sometimes an irrelevant intrusive stimulus may control a response. We have already cited many instances in which instructions, demonstrations, and guidance possess controlling properties and have shown how they can be used to prompt a response in the presence of the appropriate S^D. Here we emphasize the instance in which a response is controlled by a property of a stimulus configuration that is really not a critical property of the stimulus. Consider the following example (Figure 14.2):

Underline the Hebrew letter aleph:

Figure 14.2

The reader probably selected the אֵ and correctly so. But the basis for selection was most likely an irrelevant cue: the size or darkness of the letter. Here is another example of prompting by magnifying critical features, in order to focus the learner's attention on the relevant properties of the numerals 2 and 7 (Figure 14.3):

Figure 14.3 Magnifying critical features.

Note that the stimulus properties that are different are highlighted. Now consider this example:

> Roses are red, violets are blue,
> Twenty-one and one are twenty-_____?

The reader has probably supplied the correct word "two," but the response has been occasioned by a property other than the appropriate one. The rhyming properties of blue and two are what probably has acted as a control, rather than the appropriate S^D: "Twenty-one and one equal what?"

The fact that irrelevant or **artificial** intrusive stimuli function to **prompt** responses should not be a major cause for concern. The important thing is that the response be emitted in the presence of the relevant stimuli, even through artificial means, so that it can be reinforced. Later the prompt can be gradually eliminated, or *faded*, so that only the relevant properties remain. Prompting procedures of this type are used frequently by teachers, parents, and other behavior-change agents. Teachers hint by supplying parts of the word or by describing other cues: "Remember, that was going on at the same time as the Spanish Inquisition." "Where do your shoes belong?" says the parent as she looks toward the closet. The speech therapist points to the roof of her mouth to prompt proper tongue placement, and the counselor helping a youth to make career plans reminds his client that he has already listed a series of criteria for making his choice. In each instance, prompting occasions the correct response. Realizing the value of using artificial intrusive S^Ds as temporary expedients for prompting the initial emission of a response, the developers of **programmed instruction** techniques (Skinner, 1958; Taber, Glaser & Schaefer, 1965; and others) have made heavy use of this strategy. We, too, recommend the use of these temporary expedients if they seem necessary to occasion a response initially, as long as the selection of intrusive S^Ds is judicious and control is shifted back to the appropriate S^D as soon as possible.

Selecting Intrusive (Artificial) Prompts

Some prompts are so artificial as to appear oversimple. Groucho Marx's famous question "Who is buried in Grant's Tomb" is a "dead giveaway" (Oops!). Other

prompts are "gimmicky"; that is, too many hints are given, or they are too contrived:

"When did Columbus discover America?"

How do we know when to avoid certain prompting strategies and when to select
others? To answer this question, it is first essential to assess the behavioral repertoire of the student or client and then to consider the array of controlling stimuli
that have been identified.

When it has been determined by means of the informal testing we described
previously, that a given response is not under the control of the relevant S^D, the
whole array of prompts potentially available to the instructor should be considered. This array should then be ordered in a *hierarchy* from the most natural (the
one most closely resembling the relevant S^D) to the most artificial (the one that
bears the least resemblance to the S^D). Let us take an academic example. To teach
the student to respond appropriately to the S^D "Which letter is the aleph?" various
alternative prompting strategies are available: The size of the aleph can be enlarged or its hue intensified, or it can be embellished with a pattern, a light can
be focused on it, it can be cut out of sandpaper to have its own unique texture,
and so on. Of all the possible alternatives, probably a prompt that draws the
learner's attention to the configuration of the letter by magnifying its critical features is most natural, whereas some technique that occasions the response while
distracting attention from the letter's configuration is most artificial or intrusive.
Assessment to select an appropriate prompting strategy involves sequential presentation of prompts, from the most to the least natural until the response is appropriately emitted. For skills, the hierarchy progresses from instructional to imitative to
physical prompts. For verbal behavior the hierarchy progresses from instructional
prompts that are least informative through the array of artificial or intrusive prompts
that culminates in the "giveaway" prompt. Instruction then begins with the most
natural prompt that occasions the target behavior. Teaching can progress from
there with the preparation of a program that gradually replaces the prompt with
the appropriate S^D.

Avoiding Overuse of Prompts

Avoid overusing artificial prompts. Too many presentations of the large, dark aleph
may make the students overdependent upon that stimulus. They may then attend
only to the size, rather than to the verbal prompt "Find the aleph." Sometimes
children learn to "read" passages in preprimers by using the pictures to prompt
their responses. This behavior is not true reading, for in reading the response must
be under the control of the written word stimulus and not that of the picture.
Primary-school teachers often avoid overdependence on irrelevant cues by repro-
ducing the text with simplified instructions, then ultimately without pictures at all.

Behavior analysts must also be careful not to use prompts that appear to be
aversive to clients. As Krumboltz and Krumboltz have noted:

. . . [M]ost people do not like to depend on others to give them cues. They want to be independent and will readily interpret someone else's deliberate cue as an effort to control. Adolescents in their strenuous efforts to achieve an independent identity, are particularly sensitive to cues which they may perceive as a challenge to their own good judgment. (1972, p. 76)

We must be very sensitive to any verbal or nonverbal behavior that the client emits in response to a cue. A frown, a change of topic, or a move toward leaving may tell us that the cue is aversive, rather than functioning as an S^D. Under such circumstances, the selected cue should be terminated and an alternative, non-aversive one selected.

REINFORCING THE ANTECEDENT-RESPONSE COMBINATION

By now we have progressed quite far in our discussion of stimulus control and its development. We have described some examples of stimulus control, both in simple and in complex situations, and we have described a series of procedures designed to avoid extinction while enhancing the controlling properties of a stimulus. We have gone ahead to describe ways in which one can prompt a response in order to increase the likelihood that it will occur in the presence of the appropriate discriminative stimulus. Once this response begins to be emitted reliably in the presence of the stimulus, it is still necessary to ensure that it has been firmly established. The way to do so, of course, is to use the principles of reinforcement, which have been described repeatedly. Again one has to provide for immediate, consistent reinforcement, effective for the individual and administered in a reasonable quantity. This kind of optimal reinforcement program should be continued until some predetermined criterion for demonstrating that the stimulus control has been established is met. Usually it is a good idea to also set criteria in advance that are to demonstrate that the S^D-response combination is actually persisting over time. Therefore, the usual criterion is that behavior occur over several days and many trials.

Let us consider a few examples of this rule. The students have learned to select the 7 when presented with the numbers 2 and 7 and have been correctly labeling both numerals for several days in a row. The correct selection is still being reinforced. The teacher probably praises the students, perhaps gives them stars, draws happy faces on their papers, or some equivalent. Effective positive reinforcement is delivered immediately and consistently for several days. In our art-appreciation example (see Unit 13) many samples containing the abstract properties that are to bring the response of labeling-moods under stimulus control are presented, and again, the instructor reinforces correct responses each time they occur and with an effective reinforcer like praise or approval. In such a complex discrimination-learning situation, a particularly effective form of reinforcement is *labeled*, or *behavior specific*, *praise*. The teacher does not only offer approval but also focuses the student's attention on the reason for the approval: "Yes, George, you identified this painting as conveying a mood of peace and serenity, since you apparently observed the softness of the lines and the colors that tend to be associated with such a mood." Let us recall the youth counselor who assisted his adolescent client to learn sensitivity to cues indicating that an angry response was imminent. The counselor should arrange for the program to continue for a period of time. Situations that have previously provoked overt angry responses by the client and apparently are no longer doing so should continue to occasion the presentation of plenty of effective reinforcement. (For some people, public praise is probably not a terribly effective reinforcer. Some much more subtle feedback mechanism, perhaps eye contact, a nod, a pat on the back, or the like will probably work more effectively.)

Summary

Several specific procedures for "priming" the emission of a behavior under selected antecedent conditions have been presented in Units 13 & 14: the tell, show, guide, and artificial prompting procedures. In deciding which to use, it is often helpful to start by presenting the appropriate S^D just before the response. If the response is not emitted, some prompting method, like instructions, modeling, or physical guidance should be used. If prompting is not effective, perhaps the client must first be trained to follow instructions, to imitate, or to move under guidance. Or, as with imitation, perhaps a more appropriate model, whose behavior is observed to be reinforced, can be selected. Whichever procedure is selected, the factors that influence its effectiveness should always be considered. Once the response does occur reliably, then it is possible to begin to transfer or fade control from one of the auxiliary, or artificial, S^Ds, the guidance, show, or tell prompts—to the appropriate S^D, as described in Unit 15. Heavy reinforcement of the S^D-response combination should continue until the behavior is established. Once it has been established, reinforcement is delivered less and less frequently but always contingent upon the specific S^D-response combination.

References

Baer, D. M., Peterson, R. F. & Sherman, J. A. The development of imitation by reinforcing behavioral similarity to a model. *Journal of the Experimental Analysis of Behavior,* 1967, **10**, 405–417.

Bandura, A. Vicarious processes: A case of no-trial learning. In L. Berkowitz (Ed.), *Advances in experimental social psychology.* Vol. 2. New York: Academic Press, 1965. Pp. 1–55.

Bandura, A. Social-learning theory of identificatory processes. In D. A. Goslin & D. C. Glass (Eds.), *Handbook of socialization theory and research.* Chicago: Rand McNally, 1968.

Bandura, A. & Kupers, C. J. Transmission of patterns of self-reinforcement through modeling. *Journal of Abnormal and Social Psychology,* 1964, **69**, 1–9.

Bandura, A., Ross, D. & Ross, S. A. Imitation of film-mediated aggressive models. *Journal of Abnormal and Social Psychology,* 1963a, **66**, 3–11.

Bandura, A., Ross, D. & Ross, S. A. A comparative test of the status envy, social power, and secondary reinforcement theories of identificatory learning. *Journal of Abnormal and Social Psychology,* 1963b, **67**, 601–607.

Bernstein, D. A. & Borkovec, T. D. *Progressive relaxation training: A manual for the helping professions.* Champaign: Research Press, 1973.

Byrne, B. Attitudes and attraction. In L. Berkowitz (Ed.), *Advances in experimental social psychology.* Vol. 4. New York: Academic Press, 1969.

Byrne, B. & Griffitt, W. Similarity and awareness of similarity of personality characteristics as determinants of attraction. *Journal of Experimental Research in Personality,* 1969, **3**, 179–186.

Croner, M. D. & Willis, R. H. Perceived differences in task competency and asymmetry of dyadic influence. *Journal of Abnormal Psychology,* 1961, **31**, 68–95.

Gelfand, D. M. The influence of self-esteem on rate of verbal conditioning and social matching behavior. *Journal of Abnormal and Social Psychology,* 1962, **65**, 259–265.

Haskett, G. J. & Lenfestey, W. Reading-related behavior in an open classroom: Effects of novelty and modelling on preschoolers. *Journal of Applied Behavior Analysis,* 1974, **7**, 233–241.

Kanareff, V. & Lanzetta, J. T. Effects of success-failure experiences, and probability of reinforcement upon acquisition and extinction of an imitative response. *Psychological Reports,* 1960, **7**, 151–166.

Krumboltz, J. D. & Krumboltz, H. B. *Changing children's behavior.* Englewood Cliffs, N.J.: Prentice-Hall, 1972.

Krumboltz, J. D. & Thoresen, C. E. The effects of behavioral counseling in groups and individual settings on information seeking behavior. *Journal of Counseling Psychology,* 1964, **11**, 324–333.

Lafleur, N. K. & Johnson, R. G. Separate effects of social modeling and reinforcement in counseling adolescents. *Journal of Counseling Psychology,* 1972, **19**, 291–295.

Levy, E. A., McClinton, B. S., Rabinowitz, F. M. & Wolkin, J. R. Effects of vicarious consequences on imitation and recall: some developmental findings. *Journal of Experimental Child Psychology,* 1974, **17**, 115–132.

Lovaas, O. I., Berberich, J. P., Perloff, B. F. & Schaeffer, B. Acquisition of imitative speech in schizophrenic children. *Science,* 1966, **151**, 705–707.

Mann, P. H. (Ed.) *Mainstream special education: Issues and perspectives in urban centers.* (USOE Project No. CEG-0-72-3999 [609]). Reston, Va: Council for Exceptional Children, 1975.

Mausner, B. The effect of prior reinforcement in the interaction of observer pairs. *Journal of Abnormal and Social Psychology,* 1954, **49**, 65–68.

Mausner, B. & Block, B. L. A study of the additivity of variables affecting social interaction. *Journal of Abnormal and Social Psychology,* 1957, **54**, 250–256.

Mayer, G. R. & Kahn, J. A behavioral framework for group counseling with school children. Unpublished manuscript. California State University at Los Angeles.

Mayer, G. R., Rohen, T. H. & Whitley, A. D. Group counseling with children: A cognitive-behavioral approach. *Journal of Counseling Psychology,* 1969, **16**, 142–149.

Paul, G. L. *Insight vs. desensitization in psychotherapy.* Stanford: Stanford University Press, 1966.

Rosekrans, M. A. Imitation in children as a function of perceived similarity to a social model and vicarious reinforcers. *Journal of Personality and Social Psychology,* 1967, **7**, 307–315.

Rosenbaum, M. E., Chalmers, D. K. & Horne, W. C. Effects of success and failure and the competence of the model on the acquisition and rehearsal of matching behavior. *Journal of Psychology,* 1962, **54**, 251–258.

Skinner, B. F. Teaching machines. *Science,* 1958, **128**, 969–977.

Stewart, N. R. Exploring and processing information about educational and vocational opportunities in groups. In J. D. Krumboltz & C. E. Thoresen (Ed.), *Behavioral counseling: Cases and techniques.* New York: Holt, Rinehart and Winston, 1969. Pp. 213–234.

Stotland, E. & Hillmer, M. L., Jr. Identification, authoritarian defensiveness, and self-esteem. *Journal of Abnormal and Social Psychology,* 1962, **64**, 334–342.

Striefel, S. & Wetherby, B. Instruction-following behavior of a retarded child and its controlling stimuli. *Journal of Applied Behavior Analysis,* 1973, **6**, 663–670.

Taber, J. K., Glaser, R. & Schaefer, H. *Learning and programmed instruction.* Reading, Mass.: Addison-Wesley, 1965.

Warner, R. W. & Swisher, J. D. Drug-abuse prevention: Reinforcement of alternatives. In J. D. Krumboltz & C. E. Thoresen (Eds.), *Counseling Methods.* New York: Holt, Rinehart and Winston, 1976. Pp. 510–517.

Zimmerman, B. J. & Rosenthal, T. L. Observational learning of rule-governed behavior by children. *Psychological Bulletin,* 1974, **81**, 29–42.

Stimulus Control: Fading

After mastering the material in this unit, you should be able to

1. Define and offer illustrations for each of the following terms:
   a. Fading
   b. Fading for errorless learning
   c. Correction procedure

2. List and give illustrations of the major variables that facilitate fading.

3. Discuss how fading can be used to minimize errors.

4. Describe what can be done to correct clients' errors.

5. List the advantages and possible disadvantages of fading.

Helen now takes her medication on time without being reminded. When Tiny Tina is served her dinner, she picks up a utensil, rather than digging in with her hands. Proctors use effective prompting strategies in their interactions with the students—with no coaching from their supervisor. These accomplishments have resulted from the implementation of a fading procedure.

Fading involves shifting stimulus control from supplementary antecedent stimuli to natural ones. Many such newly acquired behaviors should ultimately be emitted "spontaneously" (in the presence of the S^Ds of the natural environment), rather than always in response to prompts or supplementary stimuli. When individuals are described as showing "expertise," "intrinsic motivation," "initiative" or "self-control," they are usually behaving in the absence of *obvious* external cues or S^Ds. A youth is considered an expert photographer because he can take, develop, and print pictures without external guidance. When he spends lots of time on that pursuit, he is called "motivated." When a child goes to the dictionary to look up a word without an adult's suggesting that she do so, she is "showing initiative." When a youth does not aggress in the face of provocation, without external "support," he is demonstrating "self-control." **Fading** is one technique by means of which behaviors can be *maintained* in the absence of such external support, cues, or supplementary prompts.

FADING DEFINED AND ILLUSTRATED

Fading is the gradual removal of an S^D or a prompt (Becker, Engelmann & Thomas, 1975). Effective fading procedures transfer stimulus control to more natural or appropriate S^Ds. In fading, although goal behaviors or approximations to goal behaviors are regularly reinforced, the S^Ds that have temporarily served to occasion these behaviors are slowly and progressively removed. The procedure is designed to produce a terminal behavior that occurs in the absence of prompts and in the presence of natural S^Ds.

Suppose that a teacher is trying to instruct a student to translate the Spanish word *gato* into the English word "cat." Many prompts could serve to occasion the English word: a picture of a cat, the sound "meow," a purring sound, the initial "ka" sound, and so on. Such prompts may help the student to give the right answer, thus making the response eligible for reinforcement. Continued use of such prompts, however, would probably tend to make the student dependent upon them. The ultimate goal of replying "cat" when the word *gato* is presented alone might never be achieved unless the supplementary prompts were removed.

Motor skills can also be taught more effectively by means of fading techniques. For example, verbal prompts can be used initially to assist clients in learning how to assemble and disassemble a piece of equipment in the laboratory or workshop. The instructor can specify each step as the clients progress through the task. After they have performed the task several times, the instructor can then gradually fade out the supplementary verbal prompts, and the trainees can perform without them.

Parallels to these examples can also be found in physical-education, language, and music training (Carlson & Mayer, 1971). In each situation, the instructor gradually fades out the prompts or instructions connected with specific verbal, motor, or physical tasks. A good physical-education example is teaching a client how to catch a baseball. The instructor begins by showing the client how to hold it in a glove, and so on, while praising correct or improved responses. During subsequent sessions, the instructor gradually reduces the instructions. In music, when the clients are introduced to a song, they first receive the music and the words. Once they have acquired the tune, they need only a copy of the words. Finally they need no prompts whatever, not even musical accompaniment. In language instruction, oral and written prompts are faded out in a similar manner.

As Millenson has noted, "in the world outside the classroom, spoken and written prompts are rarely present. Thus in formal teaching it is important that prompts used at the start be dropped out before the student is regarded as trained" (1967, p. 273). If prompts are not faded, they may tend to become crutches. Fading helps to remove the necessity for such crutches. Also, because fading is gradual, a situation in which the client may fail to emit behavior that would be reinforced is avoided.

Fading is commonly used by parents in the home. To teach a youngster to use a toy or new tool, the parent may first use modeling and instructions. As the individual learns how to use the object, such supplementary discriminative stimuli are gradually withdrawn. Similarly, when a parent teaches a child how to eat, many prompts or supplementary S^Ds are first used. He guides the child's hand, in which the spoon is held, first to scoop up the food and then to put it into the mouth. As the child becomes more proficient in using the spoon, such prompting is gradually withheld. Eventually the child is able to eat without any prompting. Many self-help skills, like dressing and undressing, are taught in a similar fashion. McReynolds (1972) used fading as a method of weaning a child from a pacifier. Every two days one eighth of an inch was cut off the open end of a three-piece pacifier. After approximately two weeks, the child threw it away. It became too much trouble trying to hold it in his mouth. The pacifier had lost all its controlling properties. No thumb sucking or other excessive oral activity was noted over a one-year follow-up period.

Fading often plays an important part in counseling and therapy. In the initial stages of role playing, the role is often clearly delineated and the setting carefully arranged. This specification is necessary because usually many of the role-playing responses are not within the client's behavioral repertoire. Such prompts are gradually withdrawn as the client's sophistication in role playing increases. Similarly, in directing counseling interviews school counselors find that they must initially assume much more responsibility with elementary-school children than with high-school children (Carlson & Mayer, 1971). We have also used verbally directed role playing, gradually fading the verbal instructions, to teach proctors in a course on personalized systems of instruction (PSI) to use appropriate prompting and correction procedures (Johnson & Sulzer-Azaroff, 1976). To teach Helen to take her medication on time, the nurse or her parents would fade out their verbal reminders, shifting control to the relevant S^D, the clock.

Using Fading Effectively

Fading out supplementary prompts, as control shifts to natural stimuli, can be accomplished smoothly and effectively, with minimal disruption. This end is best accomplished by removing prompts gradually—not too abruptly—and by moving toward more natural prompts. Subtle skills are involved in transferring stimulus control from physically guided to self-guided motor behaviors, from demonstrations to instructions, and from irrelevant to relevant S^Ds. Some of those skills are described in the following sections, along with several methods for avoiding or minimizing errors.

Gradually removing prompts.   Once the desired response has been reliably occasioned by prompts, they should be gradually removed until all are gone. The teacher training students to respond "cat" to the stimulus *gato* may initially have had to say the whole word or to show a picture of a cat (or even a real one) to prompt the correct response. The verbal prompt could then be slowly diminished little by little: to "ca," then to "c," then just to the initial mouth movements. The picture might gradually be altered first to a line drawing, then to a pair of whiskers, and so on until nothing was needed. Figure 15.1 illustrates such a series of diminishing prompts. An important guideline to follow is to *prompt just barely enough to occasion the response, while avoiding abrupt reductions in the prompting.* If the client begins to make many mistakes, one can reasonably assume that reduction has been too abrupt. If there are signs of boredom, fading may be too gradual. Careful observation is essential here.

Corey and Shamow (1972) used a fading procedure to teach reading to nursery-school children aged 4 to 5.8 years. Words were first illustrated with pictures. Gradually, the pictures became progressively darker while the words remained at full strength. This method appeared to reduce early reading errors and to result in high retention of oral reading behavior. Similarly Haupt, Van Kirk, and Terraciano (1975) taught nine- and ten-year-old children number facts (addition, subtraction, multiplication facts) by gradually covering the answer to a number fact with layers of cellophane or tracing paper. This fading procedure produced fewer errors and better retention than regular drill for these children who had had long histories of unsuccessful experience with typical number-fact drill procedures. When the removal of prompts is carefully engineered to reduce errors to almost zero level, the system is called *fading for errorless learning.*

Proceeding toward least intrusive prompts.   Various strategies, like verbal, imitative, physical, and other intrusive prompting, were discussed in Units 13 and 14, where we began with the least intrusive prompts, those that do the least to alter prevailing environmental conditions, and proceeded to those that are more and more intrusive. For example, presenting artificial gimmicks or physically guiding an individual's movements is far more intrusive than modeling the behavior, which

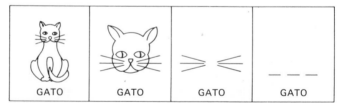

Figure 15.1   Example of a series of diminishing prompts.

may be more intrusive in some circumstances than telling how it. is to be done. In fading, the process is reversed. We initiate fading with the strategy that is currently controlling the appropriate response and gradually proceed through those that are less and less intrusive. Fern has been making her bed. She makes it successfully when her movements are physically guided. If Fern is to move into a community home and care for herself, she should make her bed without any prompting at all. To achieve that objective, the first step is to pair instructions with physical guidance. The contingency manager then fades out physical guidance, substituting imitative prompts while continuing the instructions. Then the demonstrations are faded until only the instructions remain. Instructions may then be faded and replaced by some unspoken language—perhaps pointing to the bed. Even that prompt is ultimately faded until the critical S^D, the unmade bed alone, comes to occasion bed-making behavior. In the following sections we shall discuss how control is transferred to the next less intrusive strategy.

Transferring control from physically guided prompts. A physical prompt should be faded as soon as possible, in order to prevent overdependence upon it. If Violet's Dad hangs onto the bicycle each time that she tries to ride and does not gradually begin to withdraw his assistance, Violet may refuse to ride by herself. If Flossie's apprehensive mother is afraid to remove her hand from beneath Flossie as she practices her back float, Flossie may never learn to float unsupported. Such physical prompts should be presented with either demonstrations, instructions, or both. Physical guidance can then be gradually removed while the demonstration or instructions remain. Little by little, instructions alone should come to suffice. Ultimately, instructions are also faded, and the critical stimuli, the kinesthetic cues (how the clients' bodies feel to them), should assume discriminative control.

Sometimes simply reinforcing a few guided trials is sufficient, and individuals take over movements on their own. For others, the abrupt transfer from physical guidance to no physical guidance is too large a step, and a few intervening ones must be added. The *graduated-guidance procedure* (formally described by Foxx & Azrin, 1972) is particularly appropriate for those who are agreeable to its use. Graduated guidance begins with as much assistance as necessary; the teacher uses the minimum amount of pressure necessary for the motion to be completed. Guidance is first focused on the body part that is the locus of action, for example, the hand in spoon feeding. Little by little, the pressure is reduced, and the locus of guidance moves away. Here is an example: A driving student has been oversteering; instructions, modeling, and even some guidance have been insufficient to prompt the appropriate motions. The instructor places his hand directly on the driver's hand and exerts enough pressure to promote smooth steering. As the instructor begins to feel the hand of the student responding appropriately, he gradually diminishes his pressure on the hand. As more and more of the responsibility for handling the wheel is taken over by the student, the instructor continues to reduce the pressure, moves the locus of the contact to the driver's wrist, lower arm, and elbow—and ultimately away from the arm altogether. Control has shifted to the driver gradually and slowly enough so that errors have not been allowed to emerge. The graduated-guidance procedure has been used to teach many complex responses, like self-care and vocational skills (Thomas et al., 1976).

We advise against using graduated guidance as a fading procedure for achieving stimulus control with violently resistant or uncooperative clients. To do so may be ethically questionable, as well as counterproductive, a point elaborated in Unit 14.

Striefel, Bryan, and Aikens (1974) have demonstrated the transfer of stimulus control from guidance to verbal stimuli. First, clients were physically guided to imitate a series of movements. During the transfer phase a verbal instruction was presented immediately before a behavior was modeled. Correct responses were followed by increasing the delay between the verbal instruction and the modeled behavior. Eventually, the clients "anticipated" the modeled behavior, responding before the response was modeled. The fact that the delay was introduced gradually and that the method provided maximum opportunities for reinforcement surely facilitated the transfer.

Transferring control from demonstrations and instructions. The basic system for transferring control from physical prompts is the same for imitative demonstration and instructional prompts. Unless the client responds or begins to respond before a prompt has been fully presented, the prompt should be faded gradually. Demonstrations consist first of the fully modeled target behavior and little by little become less complete, fading into more and more subtle gestures and eventually vanishing altogether. Skilled coaches can do an excellent job with this sort of fading, as can effective parents, teachers, and counselors. Tiny Tina's mom prompts her to wave bye-bye by modeling the response herself. As Tina becomes progressively more adept at waving bye-bye, her mom will not fully model the behavior. Eventually, Tina will wave bye-bye when verbally prompted. Ultimately, the words "Bye-bye Tina," the stimulus that should naturally cue her response, will assume control.

One of the self-care skills taught in the study by Thomas and colleagues (1976) was folding clothing after it was removed from the dryer. First, the response was fully guided with an accompanying instructional narrative. Next, the guidance was faded, and demonstrations were substituted. Demonstrations were then gradually faded; gestures, like pantomimes of holding the corners, were supplied when necessary. Eventually, the gestures became superfluous, and little by little instructional prompts were also withdrawn. By the end of the training, the clients needed only to be presented with bundles of their clothes in order to fold them appropriately. Helen's mom could fade her reminder to take medication by pointing to the clock for a few days until the behavior was well established.

Shifting control from irrelevant to relevant S^Ds. In each of the situations just considered, fading was used to shift control from the most intrusive to the most natural antecedent stimuli. The S^Ds that occasioned the response were relevant to the response but simply provided more support than the environment could be expected to continue to provide. Fading was directed toward shifting control to those S^Ds that were present in the natural environment. Earlier we have discussed intrusive prompts, many of which are not at all relevant to the responses that they occasion. Those too must be faded and replaced by S^Ds present in the natural environment.

Cheryl sits on a cushion holding *Winnie the Pooh* upside down and "reading" the story aloud: " 'What I want is some honey,' said Pooh." Indeed those words are on the page, but is Cheryl reading? No—because the correct response is under the control of a stimulus that is irrelevant to reading. The stimulus to which Cheryl is responding is the book itself—the cover and probably the pictures. Her responding must be occasioned by the relevant property, the group of printed words, before it can be considered reading.

The way to accomplish that shift is to introduce both stimuli; the irrelevant S^D (to occasion the response) and the relevant potential S^D, toward which attention is supposed to be focused. Then eventually the irrelevant stimulus can be faded, gradually enough so that there is adequate opportunity for frequent reinforcement to continue. Watch a primary-reading teacher, or recall your own experiences. A picture of a car is shown with its written label below. At first the student responds to the pictorial S^D. The teacher approves and indicates that the word written below also says the same thing, "car." Then the picture may be covered and only the letters exposed. The students may begin to respond correctly to the letters, the relevant stimuli. Some students do learn to read just that rapidly. But for many the shift must be accomplished much more gradually, with attention focused first on the stimulus properties. The letters may be traced with fingers, pencils, or string. The word may be matched with another identical word. The individual letters may be labeled aloud in sequence. The word may be traced in writing or copied. Eventually the word "car" will be said in the presence of the printed word alone.

In the matching-to-sample technique fading is systematically programmed to accomplish shifts of stimulus control from irrelevant to relevant stimuli in much the same way as we have described. An S^D is presented, and the task is for the student to respond by selecting a matching stimulus from among several stimuli. The situation can be arranged so that initial responding allows for matching to the initially controlling but irrelevant stimulus and gradually shifts to the relevant stimulus.

A program demonstrated by Ellen Reese and her students in the film *Born to Succeed* (1971) provides an elegant illustration of matching-to-sample. Reese and Werden (1970) designed the program used in the film to teach number concepts to severely retarded children; size fading was used to help the children discriminate one numeral from another. In one part of the program, for example, each child was shown five sets of objects that differed in number and was asked to select the set that corresponded to a particular numeral (see Figure 15.2). Before the program most of the children could recognize some numerals, and some of them could recite the words "one, two, three" in order. But they could not match or pair either numerals or names with actual numbers of objects, nor could they match two sets of objects on the basis of number. If they were shown a set containing three objects, they could not select from five alternatives another set

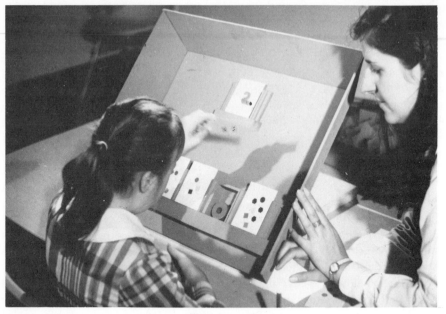

Figure 15.2

that contained three objects. The first training program was therefore designed to teach them to match sets of objects on the basis of number. As the children had no difficulty discriminating differences in size, the objects in the sample set and in the correct alternative were very large, (see Figure 15.3) whereas the objects in

Figure 15.3

all the incorrect alternatives were very small. Initially, the children could select the correct set on the basis of size alone. As the program progressed, the size of the objects in the incorrect alternatives was gradually increased. By the end of the program, all the objects were the same size, and the correct choice had to be based upon number. The size difference was gradually faded out as stimulus control was transferred from size to number.

In approximately 3.5 hours (spread over several weeks) all the children learned to match as many as four objects; then they were taught to match numbers of objects to numerals. This second fading program took even less time (approximately two hours) than the first. Training was transferred from these two matching tasks to seven other tasks, including two that did not involve matching: counting a given number of objects when they were handed to the child and counting out a requested number of objects from a set of thirty and handing them over to the experimenter. Reese has since reported that these gains were maintained a year later and that most of the children had acquired further skills with numbers. Most could tell time [on the hour,] and some could exchange five pennies for a nickle (Reese, Howard & Reese, 1977).

Matching-to-sample and other stimulus-control procedures can be designed so precisely that almost no errors are allowed to occur. This design allows for **errorless** learning. An alternative to the size prompt would be to start with an irrelevant stimulus. The revelant stimulus would be gradually introduced while the irrelevant one would be faded. The following is an illustration of this alternative.

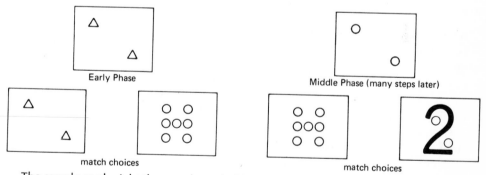

The sample card might then go through this sequence:

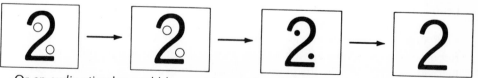

Or an *audio* stimulus could be superimposed, activated as the student presses the choice button:

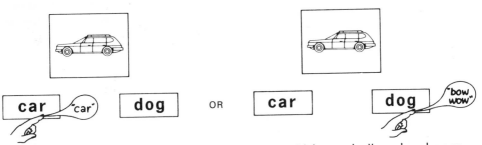

In this instance, the volume of the audio cue would be gradually reduced once the response had been established (McDowell, 1968; McDowell, Nunn & McCutcheon, 1969).

Procedures for shifting control from irrelevant to relevant properties must be used with caution, however. Unless the individual's attention is under the control of the critical or relevant property of the stimulus during training, transfer of control will not occur. It is important that the irrelevant stimulus not prevent the individual from orienting toward the relevant stimulus. Such a result could occur if the audio mechanism were operated in some manner other than by the student's pushing the word panel. The student might attend to that manipulandum (mechanism) or to the speaker, rather than to the critical property, the word. Then the rate of responding in the presence of the relevant stimulus would decrease rapidly when the irrelevant stimulus was no longer present (Anderson, 1967; Terrace, 1966).

Minimizing Errors

An error or inappropriate response is a response that fails to conform to the specifications of a behavioral objective. Let us suppose that the objective is for the client to indicate awareness of five specific body parts by pointing to the appropriate parts when instructed to do so three consecutive times. Failing to respond by pointing to his head when so instructed would constitute an error of omission. Pointing to his foot when instructed to point to his head would constitute an error of commission. Shaking his head, rather than pointing to it, would also constitute an error of commission. The primary problem with errors is that, once they have occured, they are much more likely to occur again (McCandless, 1967; Terrace, 1963). Each time that the client points to his foot, rather than to his head, when instructed to do the latter, the probability that he will repeat the error increases. In the previous sections on fading we have presented methods for minimizing errors. Prompts supporting correct responding are maintained for a sufficient period so that errors of commission are not likely to be emitted. Regardless of how carefully instruction is programmed, however, errors are bound to occur from time to time. Sometimes an inappropriate stimulus occasions the desired response; sometimes the appropriate stimulus occasions an inappropriate response. Behavior analysts should therefore be aware of procedures that will, first, assist them in avoiding situations that promote errors and, second, reduce the probabil-

ity that an error once committed will recur. If errors are apt to be committed because the differences between appropriate (S^D) and inappropriate (S^Δ or S delta) antecedent stimuli are very subtle, steps can be taken to avoid the likelihood that the wrong stimulus will occasion the response—primarily by being careful about introducing S^Δs into the situation.

Initial introduction of potential S^Δs very different from potential S^Ds. I was quite familiar with the word "hyperbola," having become initially acquainted with the term in a geometry course. One day a friend used the word "hyperbole," and I corrected his use and pronunciation of the term. He told me that I should look up the term in the dictionary, which I did. Sure enough, there was "hyperbole." I had committed an error. With all your knowledge of stimulus control, you will recognize this example as one of incomplete stimulus control. My response was under the control of only the first eight of nine letters. Had I never seen or heard the word "hyperbole" I might never have acquired the discrimination between the two. Hyperbole was bound to come along, however. When a stimulus that is very similar to the appropriate S^D is likely to make its appearance in the natural environment, but should occasion a different response, errors can be minimized if the client is properly prepared—taught not to emit the particular response in the presence of the inappropriate antecedent stimulus. Preparation is optimized if very different stimuli are first introduced and then stimuli that more closely resemble the S^D are progressively introduced.

A clever primary teacher, when introducing the numeral 2 will point to a numeral with a very different topography, like 8, 4, or some other numeral that has few or no properties in common with 2. The teacher realizes that the students are then more likely to answer "no" correctly to the question "Is this a 2?" Similarly, a parent attempting to teach concepts of honesty will indicate very flagrant instances of dishonesty, so that the child does not become confused. Clyde's mother asks, "When Bonnie took your tricycle and said she didn't, was that an honest thing to do?" Clyde responds, "No." "You bet not!" retorts Mom. Later she will be able to teach much subtler distinctions, like the differences in degrees of accuracy of reporting—or the difference between telling an untruth to protect another's feelings and telling an untruth to protect oneself from possible negative consequences.

The major advantage of initially presenting S^Δs that are quite different from the S^Ds is that the learner is much more likely to be correct. Consequently, the ratio of reinforced responses to nonreinforced responses is going to be much greater. Although later it will be possible to introduce S^Δs that are more and more similar to the S^Ds, during initial instruction this sort of procedure minimizes the negative side effects that frequently accompany extinction.

Initially introducing S^Δs briefly and at weak intensity. Again we must thank the laboratory investigator for discovering methods of improving correctness in responding to differential stimuli. A pigeon's responding, fortunately for our purposes, does not easily come under the control of verbal instructions, and so other techniques have had be devised to help it learn to discriminate. But then those methods can be easily adapted to teaching human beings who experience difficulty in making verbal discriminations. Terrace (1966) and his colleagues are among those investigators who have developed the method of initially presenting S^Δs only briefly and at weak intensities. By doing so, they have been able to teach their pigeon subjects to make some extremely fine visual discriminations. In one sequence with human subjects, these techniques were used to teach the discrimination of 2 from 7 by means of flash cards: In each instance the student was asked to select the 2, and at first only one card with a 2 was presented. After several correct responses, a second card was paired briefly with the card showing the 2. On the second card a 7 was very lightly traced. Because the 2 card was presented for a longer period of time and was much more clearly visible, students were much more apt to select it. As long as few or no errors occurred, the sequence continued, with the sevens presented for longer and longer time periods and more and more clearly drawn until both numerals were of the same intensity and were presented for equal periods. As we have discussed earlier, in the event that many errors began to be emitted, it would be advisable to drop back a step or two, allowing the student several correct choices before proceeding.

The technique described here may be used with a wide variety of stimuli: visual, audio, tactile, and so on. It may also be used in combination with the technique of starting first with topographically different S^Δs; for example, rather than introducing a 7 as the potential S^Δ, a very dissimilar visual stimulus could have been used. Such "errorless learning" procedures have been successfully used with students who have failed to learn under more traditional trial-and-error procedures: persons with delayed development and those who appear to have perceptual handicaps (Sidman & Stoddard, 1967). The amount of effort involved in programming stimuli is more than compensated for when students with long histories of failure finally succeed.

Correcting Errors

When an individual is required to keep trying to answer a question, solve a problem, or emit any other behavior until it is correct, a *correction procedure* is being used. A wealth of research has shown that providing an individual with information about the appropriateness of his or her responses, plus requiring active correction of the error will facilitate the development of stimulus control, especially when the goal is to develop complex forms of stimulus control (Suppes & Ginsburg, 1962; Holland & Porter, 1961; Moore & Goldiamond, 1964). Correction procedures have also included regressing to earlier steps in the instructional procedure (Sidman & Stoddard, 1967) and branching out to supplementary steps (Markle, 1969) when the individual makes repeated errors or makes additional errors during attempted correction.

Some individuals do not comprehend language easily; words like "right" and "wrong" simply do not have strong controlling properties. The absence of the comment "right" does not therefore function as an extinction procedure, and the presentation of "wrong" does not function as punishment. Such individuals may have delayed or impaired language development or hearing impairments, or they may simply be very young. With such individuals, any response from others may constitute "attention"—not only the comment "wrong" but also the representation of the trial. To prevent the inadvertent reinforcement of incorrect responses in such instances, each wrong response should be indicated by a word or gesture, but then a *pause* should follow before a correction procedure is introduced. Then, not only will inadvertent reinforcement be avoided, but also the word or gesture will eventually begin to signal a period of nonreinforcement, and that stimulus will thus begin to develop discriminative properties. (Such stimuli, called "conditioned aversive stimuli," will be discussed at greater length in Unit 19). With such individuals, it is probably a good idea to repeat earlier steps or *branch* to supplementary steps following pauses.

Providing correct practice trials after incorrect responses.   When an incorrect response is emitted, it is usually advisable for the client to practice the correct response several times before a new trial is presented. If a student is learning to shift a car and the gears grind, he should practice shifting several times before proceeding. If a client responds to an incorrect stimulus—when asked to say "sss" she says "th"; when shown a 2, she says "seven"; when asked to walk, she runs—she should be asked to practice the correct response a few times, in order to provide several more reinforced trials and to experience success before proceeding. (In addition, requiring effort and time may render the practice slightly aversive, thus reducing the likelihood that the error will be repeated.)

Disadvantages of Fading

Although minimizing errors has obvious advantages in the acquisition of a specific complex behavior, the question of whether or not consistent, error-free responding is desirable for a client has yet to be resolved experimentally. Considering errorless performance in another area, discrimination learning, Terrace has stated: "It should be noted . . . that numerous factors would detract from the wisdom of trying to train all discrimination without errors. Perhaps the most important of these is the lack of frustration tolerance that would result from a steady diet of errorless discrimination learning" (1966, p. 335). Krumboltz and Krumboltz (1972) have elaborated upon this concern, pointing out that, if individuals are to persist after failure, it is better not to provide a mistake-free environment. To train them to persist after failures, one arranges for them to succeed after one failure, then after perhaps two failures, and gradually but irregularly increases the number of failure experiences followed by success. Usually those who have learned to persevere have been lucky enough to encounter the particular combinations of success and failure that have taught them that "creative persistence," defined here as systematically trying different approaches to solve a problem, does eventually produce success.

When fading is programmed to avoid errors, other problems may also arise. Aside from the time required to do such programming, it may not be necessary. The client or student may be able to learn without errors with little or no fading. The frequency of mistakes is one way to tell whether or not a strategy for achieving the terminal objective has been programmed well enough. On the other hand, if the client shows signs of boredom, reinforcement has been too frequent, or fading steps have been too small. On such occasions, fading should proceed at a more rapid pace.

MAINTAINING STIMULUS CONTROL

The original intent of differential reinforcement for stimulus control was to enable behavior analysts or contingency managers, whether managing their own behavior or that of someone else, eventually to control behavior through the presentation of antecedent stimuli. At this point, such stimulus control should be firmly established. Regular reinforcement is still required in the procedure, however, and so it would not be possible to say that stimulus control has been sufficiently firmly established to permit the use of an S^D-presentation procedure alone. This comes to pass through gradual reduction in the quantity of reinforcers, a shift in their quality to more natural ones, and the gradual introduction of a delay period before delivery of the reinforcement. In Units 25 and 26 guidelines for maintenance of behavioral change will be discussed at length. Here let it suffice that the reinforcer following a response emitted in the presence of an S^D will be delivered less and less frequently until a point is reached at which the behavior is emitted reliably in the presence of the S^D, with only an occasional presentation of reinforcement. By now the primary-school child labeling 2 and 7 correctly is reinforced only occasionally and probably with weaker reinforcers like "Uh huh" and a nod. The youth counselor can arrange meetings with his client, during which he can give the client feedback about the apparent control that he has demonstrated earlier, rather than giving him some sort of immediate reinforcement. The crucial point to remember in initiating such a change in quantity or density, immediacy, and quality of reinforcement is that, if stimulus control appears to be disintegrating, the shift has been too abrupt. At that point, it is necessary to back up to a much earlier stage—again, the more optimal reinforcement situation—to reestablish the response-antecedent stimulus combination, and then to begin once again to thin out the reinforcement but at a slower pace.

Summary

Fading is an integral part of effective stimulus control; it involves the gradual removal of S^Ds. It is a procedure that helps to bring behavior dependent upon external, intrusive, or irrelevant prompts under the control of natural S^Ds, those managed by the client or derived from the natural environment. Fading promotes behavioral maintenance, reducing dependence upon supplementary prompts supplied by others. In this manner it maximizes success and feelings of competence for clients and serves to minimize frustration and failure.

References

Anderson, R. C. Educational psychology. *Annual Review of Psychology,* 1967, **18**, 129–164.

Becker, W. C., Engelmann, S. & Thomas, D. R. *Teaching 2: Cognitive learning and instruction.* Chicago: Science Research Associates, 1975.

Carlson, J. D. & Mayer, G. R. Fading: A behavioral procedure to increase independent behaviors. *The School Counselor,* 1971, **18**, 193–197.

Corey, J. R. & Shamow, J. The effects of fading on the acquisition and retention of oral reading. *Journal of Applied Behavior Analysis,* 1972, **5**, 311–315.

Foxx, R. M. & Azrin, N. H. Restitution: A method of eliminating aggressive-disruptive behavior of retarded and brain damaged patients. *Behavior Research and Therapy,* 1972, **10**, 15–27.

Haupt, E. J., Van Kirk, M. J. & Terraciano, T. An inexpensive fading procedure to decrease errors and increase retention of number facts. In E. Ramp & G. Semb (Eds.), *Behavior analysis: Areas of research and application.* Englewood Cliffs, N.J.: Prentice-Hall, 1975. Pp. 225–232.

Holland, J. G. & Porter, D. The influence of repetition of incorrectly answered items in a teaching machine program. *Journal of the Experimental Analysis of Behavior,* 1961, **4**, 305–307.

Johnson, K. & Sulzer-Azaroff, B. *An experimental analysis of proctor prompting behavior in a personalized instruction course.* Paper presented at the meeting of the American Educational Research Association, New York, April, 1977.

Krumboltz, J. D. & Krumboltz, H. B. *Changing children's behavior.* Englewood Cliffs, N.J.: Prentice-Hall, 1972.

Markle, S. M. *Good frames and bad.* New York: Wiley, 1969.

McCandless, B. R. *Children: Behavior and development.* Hinsdale, Ill.: Dryden, 1967.

McDowell, E. E. A programmed method of reading instruction for use with kindergarten children. *Psychological Record,* 1968, **18**, 233–239.

McDowell, E. E., Nunn, L. K. & McCutcheon, B. A. Comparison of a programmed method of beginning reading instruction with the look-and-say method. *Psychological Record,* 1969, **19**, 319–327.

McReynolds, W. T. A procedure for the withdrawal of an infant oral pacifier. *Journal of Applied Behavior Analysis,* 1972, **5**, 65–66.

Millenson, J. R. *Principles of behavioral analysis.* New York: Macmillan, 1967.

Moore, R. & Goldiamond, I. Errorless establishment of visual discrimination using fading procedures. *Journal of the Experimental Analysis of Behavior,* 1964, **7**, 269–272.

Reese, E. P. *Born to succeed: Behavioral procedures for education.* (Film) Hanom Communications, Box 625, Northampton, Mass., 1971.

Reese, E. P., Howard, J. S. & Reese, T. W.: *Human behavior: An experimental analysis and its applications,* Dubuque: Brown, 1977.

Reese, E. P. & Werden, D. A fading technique for teaching number concepts to severely retarded children. Paper presented at the meeting of the Eastern Psychological Association, Atlantic City, April 1970.

Sidman, M. & Stoddard, L. T. The effectiveness of fading in programming a simultaneous form discrimination for retarded children. *Journal of the Experimental Analysis of Behavior,* 1967, **10**, 3–16.

Striefel, S., Bryan, K. S. & Aikins, D. A. Transfer of stimulus control from motor to verbal stimuli. *Journal of Applied Behavior Analysis,* 1974, **7**, 123–135.

Suppes, P. & Ginsburg, R. Application of a stimulus sampling model to children's concept formation with and without overt correction responses. *Journal of Experimental Psychology*, 1962, **63**, 330–336.

Terrace, H. S. Discriminative learning with and without errors. *Journal of Experimental Analysis of Behavior*, 1963, **6**, 1–27.

Terrace, H. S. Stimulus control. In W. K. Honig (Ed.), *Operant behavior: Areas of research and application*. New York: Appleton, 1966. Pp. 271–344.

Thomas, C. Sulzer-Azaroff, B., Lukeris, S. & Palmer, M. Teaching daily self-help skills for long term maintenance. In B. Etzel, J. LeBlanc & D. Baer (Eds.) *New developments in behavioral research: Theory, method, and application*. Hillsdale, N.J.: Erlbaum, 1976.

TEACHING NEW BEHAVIOR: SHAPING

After mastering the material in this unit, you should be able to
1. Define and illustrate each of the following terms:
    a. Behavioral dimensions
    b. Shaping (illustrate the use of shaping with an individual and with a group)
    c. Successive approximations
    d. Programmed instruction

2. List and illustrate the major variables that facilitate shaping.

3. Give an example of combining S^Ds with shaping.

4. Discuss how shaping is related to programmed instruction. Discuss how shaping is related to personalized instruction.

5. List the advantages of teaching by means of programmed instruction.

6. List the criteria you would set for evaluating the effectiveness of an instructional program.

7. Describe how to carry out an effective shaping program for a specific client's behavior and for a group's behavior.

8. Give an example of combining fading with shaping.

Penny, a four-and-one-half-year-old preschool student, was medically diagnosed as having cerebral palsy. She had been walking only since she was three years old. Hardiman and colleagues (1975) reported how Penny learned to participate in six large motor activities: step walking, sliding, rolling, and others. In contrast to our earlier examples, in which behaviors were increased through simple or differential reinforcement, contingent attention was insufficient here. Although it did successfully increase Penny's participation in motor activities, her skills in these activities did not improve. Apparently, *skilled* participation in the activities was not part of her behavioral repertoire. The skills had first to be acquired. Next they had to be strengthened through reinforcement. In this unit we focus upon **shaping**, a procedure that may be used for teaching new motor, cognitive, social, and personal behaviors. Here and in Unit 17 we shall learn about several procedures and their variations that could be used to teach Charlie how to write and how to climb, as well as adequate self-care skills; to teach Violet to speak more loudly and clearly; to help Dexter to complete his tasks; and to help Igor to acquire computational and reading skills.

SPECIFYING BEHAVIORAL DIMENSIONS

Teaching new behaviors by means of shaping and chaining involves reinforcement procedures applied in a more sophisticated manner than has been described so far. That is the major emphasis of this unit. Before proceeding with this discussion, however, we must emphasize one major point again: It is very important first to specify the dimensions of the goal behavior. Previously, the specification of goal behaviors has been relatively simple. A behavior already observed in the individual's repertoire has been precisely defined and selectively strengthened until it has reached an acceptable level. When the major concern is to build a new behavior, however, as it is in shaping and chaining (Unit 17), it becomes even more important to decide exactly what characteristics that behavior must have. It is not enough to say that the client should be able to write the number 1. The dimensions (see Unit 7) of that behavior must be specified. For example, Charlie should be able to write the number 1 each time that he is instructed to do so for n trials (frequency), with a firm enough stroke that it can be seen (intensity). The number should be a straight line varying no more than, say, 10 degrees from the vertical. Its height should not be greater than or less than the distance between two of the horizontal ruling lines on the paper (topography). Without this kind of specification, some aspects of the behavior may be neglected, and adequate performance may never be reached. For instance, without the frequency dimension specified, a single correct production of the number 1 could be construed as proof that the new behavior had been learned. But it could be possible that the line had been drawn only by happenstance and would not be repeated under the same conditions.

SHAPING

Shaping is a procedure used to form a behavior that does not already exist in the individual's repertoire. It is not possible to form a new behavior simply by reinforcing it or to occasion its occurrence by means of a stimulus-control procedure, for the behavior has never been emitted. It is not possible to reinforce an infant's language if the infant has never said something that resembles a comprehensible word. No amount of instruction or prompting will occasion the complete response. Neither will a young child write numbers or letters or a youth solve a complex algebra problem if such a behavior or its components are not in his repertoire. First, the behavior or its components must be emitted; then, and only then, can it be strengthened. Shaping is one procedure designed to teach new behaviors, so they can then be selectively strengthened.

Shaping Defined and Illustrated

The procedure for shaping a new behavior begins with a response as it exists in the repertoire and involves reinforcing slight changes in the behavior as it gradually approaches the target behavior. Elements, or subsets, of a behavior that *resemble* the desired behavior are thus selectively reinforced. For example, Charlie has never made a mark that approaches a straight line, but the teacher wants to teach him to write the number 1. On occasion, Charlie has drawn something that looked like a curvy line. If the teacher selectively reinforces the production of such a line, its production will increase. But something else will probably also happen: Some of the lines will be curvy, but others will be a little straighter. Reinforced responses often vary, or **generalize**, in this manner (Reynolds, 1968). The teacher will then be in a position to reinforce selectively that subset of responses (drawing straighter lines) and can continue in this manner until an acceptable line is consistently produced. At the same time, old responses or inappropriately directed changes (curvier lines) will not be reinforced. The series of slight changes, or subsets, that are reinforced because they are more similar to the target behavior are technically called **successive approximations**. Shaping, then, *is a procedure in which successive approximations to a target behavior are reinforced.*

As another illustration of the shaping procedure, let us consider how Pearl could be taught to attend to the therapist when requested to do so. At first, any direction of attention to the therapist, on request to "look at me," would be accepted (reinforced). Once such orienting (body angle no more than 45 degrees away from the therapist) was well established (in more than 90 percent of trials over three days), the next step could be to make reinforcement contingent upon closing the angle to no more than 25 degrees. After that, the criterion for acceptance could gradually be raised until Pearl consistently turned her body toward the therapist when asked to look at her. Then the focus could shift to Pearl's orienting her head so that she was apt to see the therapist's face, an essential requirement if Pearl were to learn functional language and many other skills. If approximations of orienting toward the therapist did not occur, they could be guided by means of graduated guidance. Shaping has been used in this way to teach many youngsters deficient in attending to a teacher or therapist to acquire this essential prerequisite behavior.

The organization of most textbooks, workbooks, teachers' guides, and training manuals is based on the assumption that, in order to acquire new skills, one must gradually move from previously acquired skills toward more sophisticated instructional goals. When a set of responses is acceptable at one level but a different set is required at later levels, the behavior of the student is submitted to a procedure that is very much like shaping. A handwriting workbook, for instance, can be designed along such lines. At first, letters that can be easily discriminated from other letters are presented. Then the student is guided through a series of steps in which more and more precision is required.[1] In this instance, reinforcement might take the form of teacher approval or perhaps the ever-increasing similarity of the letters to the model or sample letters printed in the book. Usually it is a combination of both.

Shaping is frequently used in developing nonacademic behaviors as well: motor responding (Hardiman et al., 1975; O'Brien, Azrin & Bugle, 1972) and social behaviors like assertiveness (Bloomfield, 1973), conversational skills (Minkin et al., 1976), sharing, and smiling (Cooke & Apolloni, 1976). In a study by Harris, Wolf, and Baer (1967), a little boy was observed to spend almost no time on the climbing frame in the school playground. It was decided that climbing on the frame was the sort of vigorous activity that would further his physical development. Teacher attention was selected as the contingent reinforcer: "The teachers attended at first to the child's proximity to the frame. As he came closer, they progressed to attending only to his touching it, climbing up a little, and finally to extensive climbing. Technically, this was reinforcement of successive approximations to climbing behavior" (1967, p. 154). By means of this procedure, the boy ultimately came to spend more than half of each recess on the climbing frame.

Shaping procedures have also been found effective in the indirect reduction of social and personal problem behaviors. Such reduction is accomplished by substituting more adaptive behaviors acquired through the reinforcement of successive approximations. College students who were rated high in performance anxiety successfully overcame their "stage fright" by proceeding through a series of graded tasks (Kirsch, Wolpin & Knutson, 1975). These tasks ranged from reading lists of unrelated words, reading another student's speech, writing an original speech, delivering the speech from notes, and delivering the speech from note cards. (Requiring the fifth step only for a group of students in a "different" condition yielded even better results. The shaping procedure yielded higher self-report scores, however.)

A similar procedure was used to reduce avoidance responses among snake-phobic students (Barlow et al., 1970). In this study, closer approaches to the snake were socially reinforced. When a therapist modeled the successive approximations himself, the rate of approaching increased even more rapidly.

We have also heard of instances in which shaping procedures have been used to teach young people how to behave during job interviews, on dates, while proctoring peers and to develop dining skills and many other functional personal and social behaviors. The steps are specified, and approximations are reinforced.

Language development is another area in which shaping plays an important

---

[1] B. F. Skinner and S. A. Krakower (1968) have designed a series of writing workbooks that rely on a shaping procedure.

role. Although for the most part language is acquired by means of imitative, chained (complex combinations of simple responses), differentiated, and generalized responses, there are some circumstances in which it must be shaped. If, for instance, the client has not learned to imitate verbal samples adequately or has some well-practiced but inappropriate speech patterns, proper speech may have to be shaped. An illustration is the early verbal learning of the infant. When the infant babbles, the parents reinforce any similarities between the baby's speech and acceptable words. At first, they reinforce sounds that are distant approximations to real words, like "ook" or "kuk" for "cookie." Later, closer approximations are required for reinforcement. As the child grows older, other individuals also reinforce improved speech patterns and help to extinguish the poor ones. Others are more likely to respond to statements and requests that communicate successfully than to poorly and inappropriately enunciated words.

Occasionally, school-age clients have inappropriate speech patterns. Speech therapists or, in their absence, regular teachers can use shaping procedures to correct the deficiencies. For instance, if a client pronounces the word "tree" as "fee," an approximation in the form of "tee" or "ree" can be reinforced. The "tr" sound used by itself may also occasion reinforcement. Ultimately, reinforcement can depend on the proper and consistent pronounciation of the word "tree."

Procedures similar to those that we have just discussed can be used to teach a wide variety of behaviors: social cooperation, attending to classwork, assertiveness, and completing tasks. We shall return to some of these terminal behaviors as illustrations in the following discussion.

Shaping with Groups

There is no reason why shaping cannot be used with groups of youngsters. Approximations can be set for a group, just as for an individual, with reinforcement delivered as described in the section on group-reinforcement contingencies. A large activity center is set aside in a high school, where group activities like photography, guitar, and dance workshops are conducted by student experts in those areas. These workshops are very popular among students. But completion of assignments in some academic subject areas is a problem, so a shaping program is designed. To shape the behavior of assignment completion, the baseline (average percentage of assignments completed by the whole group) is calculated. It is found to be approximately 52 percent. Then, during each week of intervention, the requirement is raised little by little. When the criterion percentage of assignments is completed, the whole class is excused to attend the activity center.

Approximations can be set similarly for group performances in community homes, workshops, and recreational groups. Such a system would probably function well for patients in hospital wards, who are supposed to complete assigned exercises or other health routines individually. When all achieve approximations of their respective assignments, a group-reinforcing activity can be delivered. One must be cautious, however, in assigning tasks to individuals, for, if one patient is given too difficult an assignment, all the others will be penalized. This situation can be avoided through the use of a collective contingency of the kind discussed in Unit 9.

Shaping and Programmed Instruction

Programmed instruction epitomizes educational application of the shaping procedure. It is derived directly from behavioral principles discovered in the laboratory. In his pioneering articles on the topic, Skinner (1958) discusses methods of using behavioral procedures to teach academic skills. He emphasizes the importance of reinforcement, primarily confirmation of correct responses, as the student progresses in steps from one academic level to the next. Usually, an instructional program starts with questions that can be easily answered by the student and proceeds gradually, in order to ensure that the student will be reinforced with correct responses. Because the steps in an instructional program may be arranged to maximize success by a variety of methods—for example, hints or prompts and very gradual increases in difficulty—and because being correct is itself reinforcing, the student is usually reinforced at a fairly constant rate.

The programmed-instruction procedure generally follows the same course. First, very simple responses are asked of the student. Correct responses are immediately confirmed. These responses are rough approximations to the desired terminal responses. On successive trials, the textbook or teaching machine reinforces successively closer approximations to the criterion behavior. An instructional program may take many forms—books, tapes, strips of paper, or microfilmed slides—and it usually follows a series of finely graded steps, often called *frames*. The frames proceed from simple to more complex levels. This gradual, cumulative progression helps the student to be correct and reinforced as often as possible.

Figure 16.1 is a page from a programmed reading text for elementary-school children (Sullivan, 1965). The student uses a strip of cardboard to cover the answer column, completing an item only after he has moved the strip down to check his answer. Seeing a correct answer is assumed to be reinforcing. The advantages of shaping learning through programmed instruction, with or without the aid of a teaching machine, are numerous: The material is organized and presented in a logical sequence; frequent and active responding is required from the student, which, in turn, expedites learning; the student receives immediate feedback; and students can start at their own levels, move at their own rates, and not be held up or forced ahead by classmates.

The approach to developing an effective program is empirical. Students work on a tentative program, and their performances are evaluated. If a student fails to learn, it is the fault of the program, not of the student. Items or frames may be revised, reorganized, expanded, or reduced until most students do manage to learn the material.[2] Or, if it is suspected that the problem is motivational, supplementary reinforcers may be added temporarily. In a classroom program

[2] Instructional programming is a sophisticated skill outside the scope of this book. The topic is treated at length in Taber, Glaser, and Schaefer (1965).

supermarket

cart
push

section
finally
cookies

cart

cream

refilling

vegetables

dee**d**

boxes
help

When they reached the superm __rket, Walter insisted on pushing the cart. Ann would rather have pushed her own c_____, but she wanted to make Walter feel better, so she let him __ush it.

While Ann was in the frozen food section, Walter and her cart were off in the s __ction marked cookies, cakes, and candies. When she f __nally did catch up with Walter, Ann had to take back all the boxes of c____kies that he had dumped into the cart.

Before Ann could turn around, Walter and the __art had disappeared again. At last she discovered him in the ice __ream section, r __filling the cart. "Take it all out, Walter," Ann said. "I have to put these vegetables in there."

Just as Ann was about to lower her __egetables into the cart, Walter saw a chance to do another good dee __. A lady in the cereal section was balancing several large b __xes in her arms. Away Walter raced to h_____lp her, cart and all.

Ann's vegetables landed

     __ 1. in the cart.
     __ 2. on the floor.
     __ 3. on the shelf.

Figure 16.1 A sample page from Sullivan Associates Programmed Reading Series, *Programmed Reading, Book 7,* p. 131. (Reprinted by permission from *Programmed Reading, Book 7,* by Sullivan Associates. Copyright © 1965 by Sullivan Press. Published by Webster Division, McGraw-Hill Book Company.)

conducted by Sulzer and her colleagues (1971), points exchangeable for tangible and activity reinforcers were delivered contingent on correct answers in the Sullivan workbook (1965). The students' performances improved markedly.

The programmed-instruction movement initially generated a flurry of published instructional programs. Many were carefully and appropriately prepared and empirically tested. Some, however, failed to meet the requirements of effective programming. Instructional programs must be based on the rules for effective shaping if they are to function adequately. A well-developed program is usually accompanied by data on its effectiveness with the students for whom it was developed. If the student population is adequately described, a teacher can feel safe using the program with a population that has similar characteristics. It is a good idea, however, to be sensitive to both group and individual performance on any particular instructional program. If too many errors are made or if the students become bored and distracted, the program is not performing its intended function. Its presentation should either be limited to a subpopulation of students for whom it is doing an effective job, be further revised, or be replaced. In fact, seldom does a program work for all students in a class. Careful monitoring and supervision are thus necessary to identify the particular subpopulation for which it is appropriate.

Using Shaping Effectively

Keeping an eye on the goal.   As in the use of other behavior-analysis procedures, the first step in shaping is clear specification of the terminal behavior, along with the criteria for success. Other requirements for the use of behavioral-analysis procedures should also be met (see Units 2–7). A precise statement of the goal reduces the likelihood of strengthening irrelevant responses and increases the likelihood of reinforcing appropriate approximations. Let us suppose that Violet has almost never responded to a question in an audible voice in the presence of adults. If the terminal goal is vaguely stated, as "improving the responding of the client," there is likely to be a failure to observe and reinforce some approximations to the desired behavior. Violet, for instance, may speak loudly and shout when playing with friends. In the absence of such a specific goal as "speaking sufficiently loudly in the presence of an adult to be easily heard at least once a day for five days," the approximations with peers may well be overlooked or possibly even punished. With the specific goal in mind, however, the adult is more likely to reinforce loud vocalizations, no matter where emitted, as the first step toward the terminal goal.

It is also helpful to increase the client's awareness of the goal. Krumboltz and Krumboltz have clearly emphasized this point:

Merely reinforcing a child for improvements is not always sufficient. If we wish to help a child judge progress, we usually need to give him a good idea of the goal to which his improvements will lead—that is, the ultimate standard of performance toward which he may strive. He also needs to understand the reasons why the standard of performance has been established. In this way he can make judgments and become increasingly independent.

Standards of performance can be taught for simple, physical and academic skills as well as for complicated moral decisions. (1972, p. 42)

Helping clients to set appropriate standards of performance can thus be a step toward helping them to become *their own judges and reinforcing agents.*

Finding a starting point. As a ceramic vase must be shaped from a lump of clay, so a new behavior must be shaped from an existing behavior through reinforcement of successive approximations. A starting point has to be found, even though the initial behavior may bear little or no apparent resemblance to the final performance. Observing the client in the natural setting becomes very important. Through observation, one or more behaviors in which the client engages at a fairly frequent rate and that may bear at least some resemblance to the final goal behavior can be identified. Let us consider shaping a student's completion of assigned arithmetic papers. Observation over a period of a few days indicates that the client, Igor, usually attempts the first problem, then gives up and either scribbles on his paper or crumples it. Further observation, however, demonstrates that, on one occasion, when a review sheet of simple problems was handed out, Igor completed about half the assignment before crumpling up his paper. Two alternative starting points are suggested in this situation: The teacher can start with the regular arithmetic assignment and can shape from the partial completion of one problem, or the teacher can start with problems similar to those found on the review sheet. This decision can be based on a number of factors: practical considerations, like the availability of prepared materials; the time available for preparation of new individualized assignments; or the similarity between the starting behaviors and the terminal behavior. If the review sheet contains simple multiplication problems and the terminal goal is the solution of ten multiplication problems involving two decimal places, the terminal and starting behaviors bear a substantial resemblance to each other. It may then be preferable to drop back to the simpler review items. On the other hand, the review sheet may contain verbal problems requiring simple computations and therefore bears little resemblance to the two-place multiplication problems. It would then be more advisable to select the alternative task, which bears a closer resemblance to the goal. The ideal method for determining the starting point in this particular situation is to have Igor engage in a set of graded tasks in arithmetic. When he reaches a point at which he begins to perform poorly and fails to complete a problem, he has undoubtedly passed the ideal starting point. At that point, the level should be dropped back to the highest one at which he had achieved success; the starting point has then been determined.

Arithmetic is a subject that is generally taught in sequences of steps of increasing difficulty. Many behaviors, however, are not arranged in so logical a sequence. Again, let us consider Violet, who fails to speak aloud in the presence of adults. We have already suggested one starting point, clearly audible speech in the presence of peers. But suppose that Violet has not been observed speaking aloud so that others can clearly hear her. Some other starting point must be identified. Violet can be seated close to an adult who will reinforce any approximations to speech: facial expressions, gestures, sighs, grunts, whispered words, and other rudimentary behaviors resembling attempts to communicate. By reinforcing the entire range of such behaviors over many trials, it should be possible to increase their frequency. Whispering, for example, is one such behavior. Should Violet's whispering be fairly consistently heard, only *it* would be selectively reinforced, and reinforcement for other behaviors would be withheld. Whispering would therefore continue to increase in frequency, and a starting point for shaping audible speech would have been established. Van Der Kooy and Webster (1975) taught an "electively mute" six-year-old child who did not speak outside the home at all by starting with an avoidance response. After trying various positive ways to help him talk, they occasioned an early approximation by splashing him during swimming period. The splashing was terminated when the child said "No" or "Go away." Once this approximation to conversational speech was being uttered regularly and negatively reinforced, it was possible to prompt and positively reinforce others.

Carrying out shaping.   We have already discussed the stepped progression of shaping. The behaviors that intervene between the starting point and the terminal goal are broken down into a set of steps, or successive approximations. A few very important factors must be considered at this point. How *large* should each step be? How *long* should one remain at each step before proceeding to the next? What should be done in the event that the behavior begins to disintegrate? Unfortunately, there are no simple answers to these questions. It is necessary to observe the behavior of the individual client closely. If they are making consistent and satisfactory progress, it can be assumed that the size of each step and the amount of practice at each level have been appropriately selected. If, on the other hand, progress begins to level off, to falter, or to deteriorate, the selections should be reexamined. Let us refer again to Igor, who was having trouble with arithmetic. Suppose that the teacher has decided to increase the number of problems required for completion each day by one. On the first day Igor is given and completes one problem and is reinforced. On the second day he is given two problems. He finishes the first and starts the second, but he fails to complete it. Reinforcement is not delivered. On the third day Igor fails even to complete the first problem for that day. Quite possibly the teacher has set the requirements too high. A more successful sequence might be completing one problem each day for five days, then completing one problem and starting a second each day for five days, then completing two problems on each of five days and so on. The situation should be arranged so that the client will be able to succeed much more often than he fails, for when he fails reinforcement is not forthcoming, and the behavior can begin to disintegrate. It is entirely possible that at some later time the step size can be increased. Perhaps after the student is consistently completing five problems a day correctly the next requirement can be completion of six problems for only three, rather than five, days. This interval can continue until the terminal goal of ten completed problems is reached.

Let us consider now the selection of step size and the number of trials at a particular level for the client who fails to speak aloud. The starting point has been selected: Violet's whispering in the proximity of an adult. Next, the sequences of steps to be followed is planned. First, Violet remains next to the adult until she whispers loudly enough to be clearly understood for five consecutive statements. Naturally she will be reinforced for each of these utterances. The adult may say, "Violet, you've made an interesting point" and repeat it to others, or she may agree, smile, allow Violet access to a favorite activity, or use any of the other reinforcers that have been determined to be effective for Violet. Once the criteria for success in the first step have been met, the second step can be taken: Violet's chair is moved back about a foot. The same criteria and procedures as in step 1 can be employed again. The procedure continues little by little until Violet is seated across the room from the adult. Again, her behavior must be carefully observed. If the new behavior progresses consistently, then it can be safely assumed that appropriate criteria for practice and success at each level have been selected. To repeat, any disintegration of the behavior suggests the need for smaller steps and more repetitive practice.

Sometimes the step sizes originally selected are too small or the client is required to remain at one particular level for too long a time. Steps that are too small become apparent when the client begins to be inattentive and to show other signs of boredom. This problem can also be put to an empirical test. The size of the steps can be increased to determine whether or not the client's performance will begin to improve. If it does, then it is apparent that the altered conditions should remain in effect. This type of situation probably occurs often in the shaping of new behavior in large group settings. Because there are many members in the group, steps appropriate to the majority are selected. The few who are capable of acquiring the new behavior in larger units and with less practice may become inattentive or engage in other than the assigned activity. There are some alternatives: Different materials can be substituted for those individuals, or perhaps some of the steps or practice items can be eliminated.

Occasionally, progress seems to be smooth, and then the client suddenly seems to reach a "plateau"—and does not seem to make further progress. In such a situation, it is possible that too much practice has been given at one step and that the behavioral approximation has become too firmly established at that level. In order to reinstate progress, it may be necessary to make the next approximation very easy and to give a few trials of several small steps. The whispering client, for example, may have been given too many reinforced opportunities to whisper at one particular distance from the adult. Whispering, rather than speaking aloud, may thus have become more firmly established than desirable. An appropriate alteration in the plan might be to move the client a couple of inches back every few days, rather than a foot at a time. Under such circumstances, she might be forced to whisper more and more loudly and ultimately begin to combine more audible sounds with the whispers.

Combining discriminative stimuli with shaping.   If a complex behavior, or its components, is not present in the repertoire of the individual, it will not be possible to occasion that behavior through the presentation of discriminative stimuli (S^Ds) like instructions or prompts. Such stimuli, however, may be used to help occasion *approximations* to that response. Returning to Violet, who failed to speak aloud, let us consider this procedure: Assuming that Violet has begun to whisper to the adult next to her, we could use S^Ds to occasion more frequent emissions of that response, saying, for instance, "Good; I like the point you made" (reinforcement) and then, "Would you please say it again?" (S^D). Other whispering responses could be occasioned by asking Violet other questions, nodding expectantly toward her, or gesturing. Similar prompts were used by Van Der Kooy and Webster (1975) to teach their "electively mute" client to speak.

Combining imitative prompting with shaping.   An imitative prompt is a specific type of discriminative stimulus. It may occasion an imitative response, especially if in the past the client has been reinforced for responses resembling in topography the model's response. Just as other S^Ds may tend to occasion approximations, an approximation to a behavior that is too complex for direct imitation may be modeled. Rather than simply waiting for the approximation to the desired behavior to be emitted, the change agent can demonstrate the approximation to the client. This procedure is often used by speech therapists attempting to shape the proper enunciation of a word. A client may be able to enunciate only one or two components of a complex word. When presented with a picture of a ball of string, he may pronounce "fing," the "str" combination being absent from his repertoire. The components of "str" are presented as models for the client to imitate. The s sound is modeled, and the client is asked to repeat it a number of times; then the t is presented several times and then st. The procedure is continued until the response is shaped; the client combines and properly enunciates first the single sound, the two-letter and three-letter blends, and, finally, the whole word. Teachers use a similar procedure to shape the various components of many academic tasks, including handwriting, computation, and reading, as do parents teaching their youngsters self-help skills like dressing, washing, and eating. Such an approach was used to teach conversational skills to four adjudicated delinquent girls. First, conversational gestures were demonstrated and, when imitated, were reinforced. Next, conversational feedback was demonstrated and, when imitated, reinforced. After training, the girls' skills were rated higher than those of non-delinquent girls and high-school peers (Minkin et al., 1976).

Combining physical guidance with shaping.   Physical guidance is often used to occasion approximations toward motor skills. Hardiman and colleagues (1975) guided Penny's successive approximations as she learned to climb. They have described how limited guidance was given; when the approximation was emitted, it was reinforced: "Good Penny, you put a different foot in each step" (1975, p. 405). Thomas and colleagues (1976) helped several community-bound young retarded women to acquire housekeeping skills—clothes folding, floor mopping, and table washing—by guiding and reinforcing approximations of the skills. Skidgell and Bryant (1975) have recommended the same approach to teaching various dining skills to people deficient in those skills.

Combining fading with shaping.   We have discussed how the shaping procedure can be facilitated by occasioning approximations through the presentation of appropriate S^Ds. It is also usually desirable to remove those S^Ds before a new step in the shaping procedure is initiated. This precaution is particularly important if acquisition of approximations to the terminal goal is to be firmly incorporated into the learner's repertoire. A musician developing virtuosity in the performance of a particular musical selection must become less and less dependent upon the coaching of his teacher and the notations in the score. Similarly, graduated guidance has been used to reduce retarded clients' dependence upon physical guidance while learning approximations to walking (O'Brien, Azrin & Bugle, 1972). In each instance, cues and prompts to approximations were faded.

Fading and shaping procedures are frequently combined in the development of programmed instructional materials. Programmers often find that, when fading is used, individuals make fewer errors than they would were they required to progress without assistance. As errors are less likely to be emitted in the first place, they are less likely to be recalled or to recur.

Skinner and Krakower's "Write and See" instructional handwriting program (1968) illustrates how fading can be a useful tool in the hands of the educator. Reese has described the program lucidly in the following passage:

> The handwriting program shapes successively closer approximations of writing by immediate differential reinforcement of the correct response and by gradual attenuation of the controlling stimulus. The controlling stimulus is a letter which the child traces. Portions of the letter are gradually faded out, and the child composes increasingly more of the letter freehand until he is writing the whole letter himself. Immediate differential reinforcement is provided by a special ink and a chemical treatment of the paper. The child writes with a pen which makes a black mark when the letter is properly formed, but which turns the paper orange when the pen moves from the prescribed pattern. The child thus *knows as he is writing* whether or not he is drawing the letter correctly, and he can immediately correct a response by moving the pen so that it makes a black mark. Under these conditions, the children learn quickly; they learn to write well; and they love it. (1966, p. 57)

Taber and Glaser (1962) used a similar approach to teach young children to read color names. When the children saw a color, they could say its name, but they were unable to read the name of the color. Taber and Glaser then presented each color name printed in its respective color. The colored letters were gradually replaced by black letters until all were black. Reinforcement was contingent upon correct responses. What began as color naming ended as reading names of colors.

Strengthening the newly acquired behavior. Once a new behavior has been shaped, it resembles any other behavior that is present in the repertoire of the individual *at low strength*. It is therefore very important to take the newly achieved goal behavior and submit it to the same type of strengthening procedures that were described in Units 8–10. Reaching the terminal goal is not sufficient. The client who has begun to speak aloud will revert quickly to whispering if her audible talking is not immediately and consistently reinforced for a great many trials. Applying the principles that relate to strengthening a behavior should increase the likelihood that the new behavior will persist. Then, once firmly established, procedures can be designed to maintain it. These procedures are discussed in Units 24–26.

PERSONALIZED SYSTEM OF INSTRUCTION AND SHAPING

Consider how a **personalized system of instruction (PSI)** incorporates the various principles of effective shaping:

Flora enters a room in her school containing several file and storage cabinets. A young woman, Gwen, about her own age is seated at a table. "Hi, Gwen. I'm ready for the study questions for Unit 16 on shaping." The young woman rummages through the files and locates a set of mimeographed sheets stapled together. The pages, entitled "Unit 16. Shaping," contain the reading assignment, a few paragraphs introducing the topic, and approximately forty "study questions," each followed by sufficient empty space to accommodate a written response. "Thanks, Gwen. See you on Tuesday when I should be ready to take the Unit Mastery Quiz."

Flora returns to her room and reads the assigned pages through once. Then she takes the study questions and, rereading the material, completes each with the response that appears appropriate. After a few hours of reading, answering, checking, and studying, she feels that she has mastered the unit. On Tuesday she goes to a separate study area near the quiz room to review her material briefly one more time.

Then, returning to Gwen, she announces, "I'm ready for the quiz on Unit 16."

"Here you are, Unit 16, form B."

Flora signs for the quiz form and sits down to write the answers on a separate answer sheet. The quiz contains a series of questions, of the short-essay type and others, requiring brief responses. Based upon the study questions, all essential points of the unit are probed, with some questions requiring integration of several parts. When Flora completes the quiz to her satisfaction, she returns the quiz form and takes her answer sheet into another room, the *proctor* room. There her proctor, Virgil, a more advanced student, takes her answer sheet and checks it against his key. "Questions 1–7 and 9–12 are fine, but number 8 is unclear. Could you explain why you think this illustrates the concept of reinforcing successive approximations?" Flora responds, apparently to Virgil's satisfaction. He asks her to write down her clarification. "Fine. You've mastered this unit." Virgil records Flora's "pass" on her folder, and Flora returns to Gwen for the next set of study questions.

This episode illustrates a PSI course in operation. In 1968 Keller described the system, using a similar illustration, in his now classic article "Goodbye Teacher" (Keller, 1968). In the article, Keller described a system of procedures based upon principles of behavior, similar in many ways to programmed instruction. Let us take a look at some of the distinguishing characteristics of PSI and see how they mesh with procedures based upon principles of teaching new behaviors that we have been discussing.

Goals Clearly Defined

In PSI, the goals of an instructional unit are precisely defined, for they are incorporated within the painstakingly prepared study questions. In preparing study questions, the instructor is faced with the reality of the goals selected. Each study question can be evaluated for its instructional and educational importance: "Does the question occasion a response that will serve as a foundation for other material?" "Is the question picky or important?" Consider "Define successive approximations" in contrast to "Describe the role played by successive approximations in teaching new behaviors, and illustrate with an original motor behavioral example." In the first instance, the instructor will probably realize that memorizing a simple verbal sequence without any understanding of the applicability of the concept would suffice. In the latter instance, however, a far more sophisticated response, involving comprehension and application, is called for. It is possible, also, to design study questions that call for other than cognitive responses: "Take the wire and solder it to the metal. Then show it to your proctor." (See Sulzer-Azaroff, McKinley & Ford, 1977, for practice in setting significant instructional goals.)

Reinforced Student Responding

In a PSI course the instructor does the preliminary work of designing study questions, quizzes, and answer keys. The student actively participates by reading, completing study questions, and responding to quiz questions. In this manner the student emits responses that function as approximations to various instructional or behavioral goals. Each approximation is reinforced with what are usually *appropriate* reinforcers for many students: being correct, progress toward completion of requirements, peer approval, and so on. Those reinforcers are delivered for *each* appropriate response with *minimal delay*. If the quality or quantity of reinforcers is inappropriate, they may easily be supported with supplemental systems, like reinforcing lectures, discussions, field activities, films, other interesting educational experiences, or even token systems (see Unit 28).

Appropriate Step Size

As with programmed instruction, PSI materials are readily adjusted to the performance levels of individual students. Through empirical assessments, in which materials are tried, evaluated, and revised, instruction can be adapted to the requirements of groups of individuals. For advanced students, higher unit levels, enrichment units, rapid fading of prompts, or larger study assignments may well meet their requirements. Simpler or shorter study assignments, easier questions, more cues and prompts faded gradually, and other such adjustments may be made for the student performing at the less sophisticated level.

Effectiveness

When PSI is used appropriately,[3] it can be an impressively effective instructional tool. An ever-increasing number of research reports indicates that precisely engi-

---

[3] Designing an effective PSI course involves a technology the training in which is beyond the scope of this book. For additional information see Keller and Sherman (1974), Johnson and Ruskin (1977), and issues of the *Journal of Personalized Instruction*.

neered PSI courses result in higher performance levels, both for students (Born, Gledhill & Davis, 1972) and for proctors (Johnson, Sulzer-Azaroff & Maass, 1975). Although used primarily at higher educational levels, it is beginning to be applied more broadly to younger students. McLaughlin and Malaby (1975) reported their use of PSI with sixth graders. Students performed much better under the system and expressed their preference for it. Apparently PSI holds considerable promise for instruction of children, youth, and the adults being trained to serve those populations.[4]

Summary

Shaping is a procedure used to form behaviors that do not exist in the behavioral repertoires of individuals and groups. Shaping works by reinforcing successively closer approximations to the desired terminal behavior. It requires clear specification of the terminal behavior and its dimensions, as well as effective use of the principles for strengthening a behavior. In addition, the shaping procedure requires careful observation to determine how large each step size should be and how long the client should remain at a particular step or successive approximation.

Shaping can often be accomplished more rapidly when combined with the use of discriminative stimuli (S^Ds). This combination is the integral feature of programmed and personalized instructional programs.

References

Barlow, D., Agras, W. S., Leitenberg, H. and Wincze, J. P. Experimental analysis of the effectiveness of "shaping" in reducing maladaptive avoidance behavior: An analogue study. *Behavior Research and Therapy,* 1970, **8**, 165–173.

Bloomfield, H. H. Assertive training in an outpatient group of chronic schizophrenics: A preliminary report. *Behavior Therapy,* 1973, **4**, 277–281.

Born, D. G., Gledhill, S. N. & Davis, M. L. Examination performance in lecture discussion and personalized instruction courses. *Journal of Applied Behavior Analysis,* 1972, **5**, 33–44.

Cooke, T. P. & Apolloni, T. Developing positive social-emotional behaviors: A study of training and generalization effects. *Journal of Applied Behavior Analysis,* 1976, **9**, 65–78.

Hardiman, S. A., Goetz, E. M., Reuter, K. E. & LeBlanc, J. M. Primis, contingent attention and training: Effects on a child's motor behavior. *Journal of Applied Behavior Analysis,* 1975, **8**, 399–409.

Harris, F. R., Wolf, M. M. & Baer, D. M. Effects of adult social reinforcement on child behavior. In S. W. Bijou & D. M. Baer (Eds.), *Child development: Readings in experimental analysis.* New York: Appleton, 1967.

Johnson, K. R., & Ruskin, R. S. *Behavior instruction: An instructive review.* Washington, D.C.: American Psychological Association, 1977.

Johnson, K., Sulzer-Azaroff, B. & Maass, C. A. The effects of internal proctoring upon examination performance in a personalized instruction course. *Journal of Personalized Instruction,* 1976, Vol. 1, Issue 2, 113–117.

---

[4] A PSI manual accompanies this book.

Keller, F. Goodbye Teacher. *Journal of Applied Behavior Analysis*, 1968, **1**, 79–89.

Keller, F. S. & Sherman, J. G. *The Keller plan handbook: Essays on a personalized system of instruction*. Menlo Park, Calif.: Benjamin, 1974.

Kirsch, I., Wolpin, M. & Knutson, L. N. A comparison of *in vivo* methods for rapid reduction of "stage fright" in the college classroom: A field experiment. *Behavior Therapy*, 1975, **6**, 165–171.

Krumboltz, J. D. & Krumboltz, H. B. *Changing children's behavior*. Englewood Cliffs, N.J.: Prentice-Hall, 1972.

McLaughlin, T. F. & Malaby, J. E. Elementary school children as behavioral engineers. In E. Ramp & G. Semb (Eds.), *Behavior analysis areas of research and application*, Englewood Cliffs, N.J.: Prentice-Hall, 1975. Pp. 319–328.

Minkin, N., Braukmann, C. J., Minkin, B. L., Timbers, G. D., Timbers, B. J., Fixsen, D. L., Phillips, E. L. & Wolf, M. M. The social validation and training of conversational skills. *Journal of Applied Behavior Analysis*, 1976, **9**, 127–139.

O'Brien, F., Azrin, N. H. & Bugle, C. Training profoundly retarded children to stop crawling. *Journal of Applied Behavior Analysis*, 1972, **2**, 131–137.

Reese, E. P. *The analysis of human operant behavior*. Dubuque, Iowa: William C. Brown, 1966.

Reynolds, G. S. *A primer of operant conditioning*. Glenview, Ill.: Scott, Foresman, 1968.

Skidgell, A. & Bryant, R. *The Mansfield training program in dining skills*. Mansfield Depot, Conn.: Mansfield Training School, Psychology Department, 1975.

Skinner, B. F. Teaching machines. *Science*, 1958, **128**, 969–977.

Skinner, B. F. & Krakower, S. A. *Handwriting with write and see*. Chicago: Lyons & Carnahan, 1968.

Sullivan Associates Program, *Programmed reading book*. ed. by C. D. Buchanan. New York: McGraw-Hill, 1965.

Sulzer, B., Hunt, S., Ashby, E., Koniarski, C. & Krams, M. Increasing rate and percentage correct in reading and spelling in a class of slow readers by means of a token system. In Ramp, E. A. & Hopkins, B. L. (Eds.), *New directions in education: Behavior analysis*. Lawrence: University of Kansas, Dept. of Human Development, 1971. Pp. 5–28.

Sulzer-Azaroff, B., McKinley, J. & Ford, L. *Field activities for educational psychology: Carrying concepts into action*. Santa Monica, Ca.: Goodyear, 1977.

Taber, J. I. & Glaser, R. An exploratory evaluation of a discriminative transfer learning program using literal prompts. *Journal of Educational Research*, 1962, **55**, 508–512.

Taber, J. K., Glaser, R. & Schaefer, H. *Learning and programmed instruction*. Reading, Mass.: Addison-Wesley, 1965.

Thomas, C. B., Sulzer-Azaroff, B., Lukeris, S. E. & Palmer, M. Teaching daily self-help skills for long term maintenance. In B. Etzel, J. LeBlanc & D. Baer (Eds.), *New developments in behavioral research: Theory, method, and application*. Hillsdale, N.J.: Erlbaum, 1976.

Van Der Kooy, D. & Webster, C. D. A rapidly effective behavior modification program for an electively mute child. *Journal of Behavior Therapy and Experimental Psychiatry*, 1975, **6**, 149–152.

TEACHING NEW BEHAVIOR: CHAINING

After mastering the material in this unit, you should be able to
1. Define and illustrate each of the following terms:
   a. Links
   b. Chain
   c. Chaining (forward *and* backward)

2. Describe and illustrate the dual-stimulus function played by each behavior in a chain.

3. Discuss and illustrate how chaining incorporates task analysis.

4. List and illustrate the major variables that facilitate chaining.

5. Describe how reinforcement is delivered during the development of a chain.

6. Give an example of combining chaining with shaping, S^Ds, and fading.

7. Describe how to strengten a chain once it occurs.

Flossie was learning to play tennis. Her instructor showed her the steps in serving:

1. Place your feet so they are at a 45-degree angle from the net.
2. Hold the racket down over your shoulder.
3. Grasp the ball toward the tips of your fingers.
4. Position your hand over the foot closest to the net.
5. Toss the ball up gently.
6. Strike the ball with the racket.

The tennis serve had to be analyzed and broken down into its component tasks, because it was too difficult for Flossie to learn the serve as a single, unitary behavior. Once it was broken down, it was then possible for Flossie to perform each of the subtasks in sequence, and the ball was properly served. When the ball landed in the proper place, that was reinforcing to Flossie. In the language of behaviorism, the component tasks, or subskills, are called **links**. The links are joined together in a sequence called a **chain**. The procedure that teaches the individual ultimately to perform the sequence as a unitary behavior is a **chaining procedure**. A distinction may be made between **forward** and **backward chaining**, depending upon which of the chain links are connected first. The tennis serve exemplifies a forward chain, for training starts with the link that occurs first in the sequence: positioning the feet. This link is then joined with holding the racket over the shoulder (the second link) and so on. Backward chaining progresses in the opposite direction, starting with the last link. Backward chaining would be difficult in the tennis serve, but, as we shall see, it is particularly appropriate for some difficult behavioral sequences.

CHAINING DEFINED

The formal definition of the chaining procedure is *the reinforcement of combinations of simple behaviors already in the repertoire of the individual to form more complex behaviors*. Charlie's mother, who wishes to teach him to brush his teeth, may be able simply to combine several behaviors that Charlie has already emitted into a more complex chain. Charlie may already know how to place paste on a brush, place the brush against his teeth, move the brush up and down, and so forth. When these separate behaviors are combined in proper sequence, the complex behavior of tooth brushing will have been established.

ESTABLISHING BEHAVIORAL CHAINS

How can a series of previously learned responses be combined and strengthened when reinforcement appears to occur only at the end of the behavioral chain? "You brushed your teeth; now I'll read you a story." Flossie is reinforced when her serve is good. Students going to lunch are reinforced with food only after engaging in a long series of behaviors. The whole sequence of tasks that Fern engages in when she washes her hair is reinforced only by clean, neat hair at the end of the sequence. Solving a complex arithmetic problem will be reinforced only after a solution has been obtained. Greater relief from asthma symptoms (negative reinforcement) was obtained only after the children learned how to use a complex device that delivered brochodilator medication to the lungs (Renne & Creer, 1976). Such delays may introduce a complication, considering our previous discussion of the need for immediate reinforcement in strengthening behavior. How is it possible that chains do become established, often without considerable difficulty? The answer presumably lies in conditioned reinforcement.

We learned earlier that, when a stimulus or event is paired with or directly precedes reinforcement, it will tend to acquire reinforcing properties itself over time. The stimuli that acquire such reinforcing properties serve to forge the links in the chain into a complex response that can be strengthened or maintained by a single reinforcing event. The skillfully placed final serve in a game of tennis and the last expert throw of a bowling ball each signals to the player that a victory or a good score is at hand. The feel of the racket as it makes perfect contact with the ball may become reinforcing in itself. Such stimuli reinforce the immediately preceding responses, for example, the stance, or position, of the player. Over time that stance will begin to signal that a skillful response will follow. It will occasion the swing or throw. It is in this manner that the stimulus components of a complex behavioral chain operate in dual fashion, both as discriminative stimuli, which occasion the subsequent component responses, and as reinforcing stimuli, which reinforce the links that occur immediately before them.

For an illustration of the same phenomenon, consider the complex behavior of brushing one's teeth, as it is broken down into its subtasks, or links: taking the brush, applying paste, turning on the water, wetting the brush, applying it to the teeth, moving it up and down in various positions, rinsing the mouth and the brush, putting away the brush, and putting away the paste. If putting the brush and paste away has in the past been consistently paired with a reinforcing stimulus (S^r) in the form of approval from Mother and a story, the brush and paste in their proper place become a signal that reinforcement is imminent; therefore it should become a discriminative stimulus (S^D). Through further pairings with reinforcement (S^r), the discriminative stimulus (S^D) itself (putting the brush and paste away) will begin to reinforce (S^r) the *prior* link in the chain (rinsing the brush). Through a similar process, rinsing the brush will become both an S^D that sets the occasion for putting the brush and paste away *and* a conditioned reinforcer (S^r) for the prior link in the chain, rinsing the mouth, and so on. This process is illustrated in Figure 17.1.

Each behavior in a chain, then, has a dual-stimulus function. Each reinforces the behavior that it follows, and each serves as an S^D to occasion the behavior that it precedes.

A chaining procedure is frequently selected to teach a new complex behavior when chains other than the desired ones are occurring. For example, if Charlie had rinsed his mouth without moving the brush up and down, the appropriate chain, as shown in Figure 17.1, would not have occurred. If, after rinsing his brush he threw it at another person before putting it away, the desired chain would also not have occurred. Each link must occur in succession without any

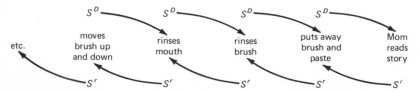

Figure 17.1 Example of stimulus components of a complex behavioral chain operating in a dual fashion.

omissions or intervening occurrences in order to form the target chain. A different chain or complex behavior occurs when links are omitted or interpolated.

Figure 17.2 diagrams a task analysis of the chain "washing hair at the sink," one of several target behaviors that were selected for a group of community-bound institutionally retarded women (Gustafson, Hotte & Carsky, 1976). As in the tooth-brushing illustration the sequence of behaviors must follow the specified order for hair washing to be considered correct. What if step 8 (rinsing hair thoroughly) were omitted? The client would hardly have clean hair.

USING CHAINING EFFECTIVELY

As contingency managers and behavior analysts obviously expend so much of their time and energy in attempting to establish behavioral chains, it might prove helpful if we gave some consideration to a few procedures designed to facilitate

Name:_____

Washing Hair at Sink

Date:							
1. Collect shampoo, towel, comb							
2. Remove blouse or shirt							
3. Place shampoo, towel, comb near sink							
4. Adjust water to lukewarm							
5. Wet hair thoroughly							
6. Apply shampoo to hair							
7. Rub into hair and scalp to form suds							
8. Rinse hair thoroughly							
9. Towel dry hair							
10. Place cap on shampoo							
11. Comb out hair							
12. Put clothing back on							
13. Return shampoo, towel, comb to respective places							

Figure 17.2 Task analysis of the chain "washing hair at the sink." (Gustafson, Hotte & Carsky, 1976)

the development of such chains. We shall first emphasize the importance of a precise task analysis, then discuss the wisdom of forging complex behaviors, when possible, from behavioral links already in the repertoire. Then we shall consider backward chaining, or starting with the final link. This technique has been used with impressive success in many animal-training experiments (Holland & Skinner, 1961) and has been found to be a particularly fruitful teaching technique. We shall, finally, discuss other methods involving two procedures used in combination, like chaining combined with the presentation of various types of discriminative stimuli (S^Ds), fading, and shaping. They can also be valuable aids to teaching complex behaviors.

Analyzing the Task Precisely

As with shaping, it is very important to have a clear description of the steps to be followed in a chaining procedure. Because the sequence of component behaviors is so crucial to the development of the appropriate target behavior, each component and its place in the sequence must be precisely specified. Analyzing a task is not always as simple as it seems. (Nor are all task analyses performed on simple tasks. For instance, the last two units in this textbook are based upon a task analysis of an applied behavior-analysis report.) We have found that we have omitted or insufficiently described crucial links in a chain from time to time—and you know what happens when a chain has a weak link! In a bow-tying task analysis, we neglected to include tightening the bow after it was formed, and naturally the bow came apart. As a demonstration, try to do an "arm chair" analysis of a task that is very familiar to you, like washing dishes, putting on an article of clothing (perhaps a necktie or panty hose), or boarding a public bus. Then try it out on yourself or a cooperative friend to see whether or not you have actually included all the links in the chain.

Using Links Already in the Response Repertoire

A fairly basic principle for establishing chains efficiently, one that should be obvious by now, is to try to form the chain from behaviors that are already part of the individual's repertoire. It is easier to teach children to write their names if they can already write each of the component letters than it is to shape the writing of each letter as part of the instructional procedure. It is easier to teach children to dress themselves if they already know how to button, zip, tie, and snap than it is to teach them those component behaviors simultaneously. It is probably easier for someone to stand up and speak before a large audience for the first time if she already has the behaviors of looking at people when speaking to them, organizing materials, speaking loudly enough to be heard at a distance, speaking distinctly, and using appropriate gestures than if she has failed to acquire some of those components.

Frequently, it is possible to achieve terminal behaviors that are almost identical but are actually composed of different response components. Teaching community-bound institutionalized women to wash their hair in the shower, rather than at the sink, is an example. For some people, giving an effective speech before a large audience may include some behaviors different from those just specified: using an informal, conversational style rather than a more formal and tightly organized approach; showing slides, rather than focusing attention on the speaker by using gestures; and so on.

When there is a close resemblance between two acceptable complex terminal behaviors, the behavior with more components that are fairly well established in the person's repertoire is probably the one that will be acquired more easily. Fern can snap but not tie. In teaching her to dress herself, her contingency manager should provide clothing with snaps and not strings, if possible. That would be the instructional route to take.

Starting with the Final Link

In Unit 8 we discussed the development of stimuli as conditioned reinforcers. We learned that stimuli may take on conditioned-reinforcing properties as a function of being paired with either unconditioned or conditioned reinforcers. The discussion emphasized that it takes many pairings of a stimulus with a reinforcer before the stimulus will itself assume reinforcing properties. In the tooth-brushing example discussed above, which link in the chain is paired most frequently with Mother's reading a story—that is, the reinforcer? The behavior of putting the brush and paste away, because it is the one that is emitted with the greatest proximity to, the shortest delay before, the reinforcing story. Putting the brush and paste away under these circumstances should, in time, come to operate as a reinforcing event in itself. It will be a stronger reinforcer than the previous link in the chain, rinsing the brush. We have learned that the shorter the delay between the response and the reinforcement, the more effective the reinforcement is. From the point of view of immediate reinforcement, it therefore seems logical in training chains of responses that they be started, whenever feasible, with the final links in the chain and not at the beginnings. That is, a good way to teach a complex behavior is to use backward chaining. In the tooth-brushing illustration, first Mother could read the story after the brush and paste were put away. Next, the reinforcement would be made contingent on rinsing the brush and putting it and the paste away. Once this chain had occurred fairly frequently, the reinforcement could be made contingent on rinsing the mouth and so on, until the entire chain had solidified into a complex behavior.

A backward-chaining procedure was designed by one of the authors to teach a six-year-old child in a special-education class to assemble a four-piece wooden jigsaw puzzle. First, one piece was removed and replaced in the correct position but only partially inside its space. When the child pushed the piece the rest of the way, he was congratulated for completing the puzzle and given some food. After several successful trials at that very simple level, the piece was removed to the side of the space. The child was then required to pick it up and put it in its place before earning reinforcement; this step was repeated several times. The next step involved moving the piece off the board. When replacing that one piece was mastered and had been practiced, a second piece was added to the requirement for the chain, and the child had to replace two pieces. The same procedure was followed as with the first piece. Ultimately all four pieces were removed, and the child had to complete the entire puzzle before he could be reinforced. Although this procedure was fairly time consuming, the child rarely missed a reinforcer. Learning to complete that puzzle made it easier for him to work others. Probably the most significant aspect of the training project was that "playing" with the puzzle was the first play activity that this particular child had engaged in for three years. For most of his waking hours he had previously sat and rocked in a chair, twiddled his fingers, and made incomprehensible sounds. To have been able to perform this task appropriately, just as other children of his age could do, was quite a milestone.

To illustrate backward chaining further, here is a computation example (Benoit, 1972). A sixth-grade teacher wanted to help a student, Igor, switch from working multiplication problems by the method illustrated in Figure 17.3A to solving them by that illustrated in part B, as a preliminary to learning to multiply two-digit numbers, as in part C.

	A		B	C
478	8 × 8 =	64	478	23
× 8	8 × 70 =	560	× 8	× 43
	8 × 400 =	3,200	3,824	69
		3,824		92
				989

Figure 17.3 Three steps in learning to multiply.

The teacher had been using forward chaining for months without success and so decided to try backward chaining. The major steps for multiplying two-digit numbers by two-digit numbers were outlined: (1) multiply the ones times the ones; (2) multiply the ones times the tens; (3) leave a place for the zero; (4) multiply the tens times the ones; (5) multiply the tens times the tens; and (6) add partial products. The last step resulted in the correct answer and social reinforcement from the teacher. Figure 17.4 illustrates the actual steps taken.

Printing = steps by teacher
Handwriting = steps by Igor

1.　94
　　× 57
　　658
　　4700
　　5358 (step 6)

2.　73
　　× 67
　　511
　　4380
　　4891 (steps 4–6)

3.　40
　　× 19
　　360
　　400
　　760 (steps 3–6)

4.　23
　　× 43
　　69
　　920
　　989 (steps 1–6)

Figure 17.4 Backward chaining in teaching multiplication.

Several practice trials were given at each step. Within thirty minutes, Igor was multiplying appropriately.

The hair-washing chain could be taught to Fern by means of backward chaining; she could be allowed to start by returning the materials to their proper places, with the attendant performing the rest of the chain as usual. Next, she could put her clothing on and return the materials several times until those two behaviors were linked together smoothly. Next, she could comb out her hair and so on until the entire task was learned.

We have tried backward chaining to train staff supervisors to use behavioral procedures. The reinforcer, evidence of effective client training, was achieved first by implementing "prepackaged" training programs. Then, little by little, the supervisor-trainees assumed more and more of the responsibility for formulating programs, always terminating the sequence with effective procedural outcomes.

There are several questions that may be asked about the advisability or necessity of teaching a complex behavior by means of a backward chaining procedure: Is there sufficient evidence to support using this approach in all situations? Can people not learn just as well by adding behavioral components from the beginning? The answers to both questions are unclear at this time. Not much research has been conducted on this topic with human subjects. But where the procedure has been used, especially in teaching a behavior that has been very difficult for an individual to learn and in teaching clients with delayed language, it has demonstrated its success. The fact is that most conventional instruction is organized in a "logical" sequence, beginning at the beginning and ending with the completed behavior. For example, a student is asked to write his name, "Charles." He writes "C," and the teacher says "Good." As he writes each succeeding letter, he is praised by the teacher. In contrast, in the backward-chaining approach "Charle___" is supplied. Charles must first fill in the last letter, then the last two letters, the last three, and so on. It is the guess of the authors, pending adequate empirical evidence, that both approaches probably are effective in teaching. After all, children do manage to learn quite effectively in school, perhaps because of the discriminative role played by language. Probably the backward-chaining procedure can make its greatest contribution either when a client has a language deficit or experiences difficulty in acquiring a complex behavior through traditional methods.

Using Verbal and Guiding Discriminative Stimuli

In addition to the discriminative stimuli (S^Ds) that are an integral part of the response chain, supplementary S^Ds may be used to facilitate forging of specific links in the chain. Verbal directions, gestures, written instructions, and similar S^Ds may effectively shorten the time needed to establish a fairly simple behavioral chain. For example, Renne and Creer (1976) taught asthmatic children to use the intermittent positive-pressure breathing device (IPPB) by prompting the links of eye fixation, facial posturing (keeping the mouth firmly around the mouthpiece while not puffing the cheeks and while breathing through the nose), and diaphragmatic breathing. Prompting of the last link consisted of "pushing in on the abdomen of the subjects while, at the same time, instructing them to breathe out as fully as possible from their mouths. They were then told to use their stomachs to push the experimenter's hand away while breathing in as deeply as possible through their mouths" (1976, p. 4). Proper responding was rewarded with tickets (accompanied by social praise) that could later be exchanged for surprise gifts. Similarly, in our tooth-brushing illustration, if Charlie's mother had said, "Remember to rinse your brush and to put the toothbrush and toothpaste away" and had consistently reinforced the emission of those links, they might have been acquired more rapidly than if she had simply waited for them to be emitted spontaneously.

Combining Imitative Prompting with Chaining

Children and youths frequently do imitate behaviors that are novel for them— printing letters, repeating lines of poetry, doing homework and crafts projects, and so forth—as long as the behavior modeled is not too complex and most of the behavioral components are already in their repertoires. Complex behavior can thus often be occasioned by simply providing a model. Much complex language is probably learned in this manner, as demonstrated in a series of studies with language-deficient normal children (Guess et al., 1968; Wheeler & Sulzer, 1970; Whitehurst, 1971; Lutzker & Sherman, 1974; Clark & Sherman, 1975). With more complex behavioral models, however, direct imitation may be difficult to accomplish. Acquiring the proper sequence of behaviors in a more complex chain may prove too difficult if the entire sequence is presented all at once. For example, in the tooth-brushing illustration, allowing an older sibling to act as a model emitting the entire sequence might have been sufficient to occasion the chain for some children. With longer or more complex chains, like organizing and conducting a debate, however, one might have more success if the chain were broken down into shorter sequences and each sequence presented as an imitative prompt. The clients could then first imitate each link in the chain. Then the chain could be gradually unified in the manner previously described, and the segment prompts could be phased out. That is exactly how hair washing and other everyday living skills were taught to the community-bound clients described by Gustafson, Hotte, and Carsky (1976). When necessary, each link in the chain was occasioned by some form of prompt, either a tell, a show, or a guide prompt.

At this point the reader may ask, "Why not simply provide discriminative stimuli, such as directions or models, to teach all complex behavioral chains?" The answer lies partially in the fact that directions or imitative prompts may not be adequate S^Ds for all clients. They may not reliably occasion the desired response. Similarly, it is often the same client for whom directions are ineffective for whom it is also difficult to find an effective model. In addition, many instructional and behavioral goals are much more complex than those we have illustrated, and the components of the particular chain may not be in the individual's response repertoire.

Combining Fading with Chaining

The S^Ds that have been added to occasion the emission of each of the links of the chain must be removed before one can assert that the behavioral goal has been achieved. In the solution of long division problems, for instance, the ultimate goal would probably be for the students to carry out the entire process without any external prompts. If the teacher said, "First compare the divisor and the dividend to see which is larger," and waited for the students to do so; then said, "Now place a decimal point to the right of the dividend," and waited for them to do so, and so on, few would agree that the terminal behavior (being able to solve long division problems) had been acquired. The criterion for acceptable acquisition of the response chain would probably be the correct solution of a number of long division problems completed without the assistance of the teacher.

As with shaping, it is obvious that a gradual fading of the intermediate prompts in a complex chain of behaviors is necessary if the goal behavior is to be emitted smoothly and with precision. Too abrupt a removal of these S^Ds would probably result in the breakdown of the behavioral chain. The prompting described for the asthmatic clients was faded by first gradually eliminating the "hand-against-the-abdomen," followed by verbal instructions as appropriate responding increased. Similarly, those links in the hair washing chain that were occasioned by either a guided, modeled, or verbal prompt were faded gradually, moving from the most intrusive to the most natural, as in Units 13 to 15.

As each prompted link in a behavioral chain occupies a sequential position, there is the question "At which link should we begin to fade S^Ds?" As the link of the chain that probably has the greatest strength is the last one, it seems logical that the prompt occasioning that final link is the first one that should be removed. In the example of long division, the instruction to reduce the fraction to the smallest common denominator should be removed first. As that final link and the one immediately before it become fairly well joined, the S^D for the preceding link (the instruction to place the remainder over the divisor) may then be eliminated and so on until the entire chain is performed with perhaps only a single S^D at the beginning, like the instruction to divide 987 by 31.

Combining Shaping with Chaining

Certainly chaining will take place more rapidly if all the behavioral links of the chain have already been developed. Occasionally, however, one or two of the links are weak or not developed in the individual's repertoire. For instance, Fern may have a difficult time rinsing the shampoo out of her hair, or Flora, the student in the college PSI course, may be unable to fill out her study guide in sufficient detail. Each missing or weak link can be shaped and then strengthened through reinforcement. Once that has been accomplished, the chain can be developed. If most links in a chain are absent from the repertoire, however, we should give serious consideration to the selected target behavior. In all likelihood it is over-ambitious for the individual client, and an alternative, probably a more basic behavioral objective, should be sought.

STRENGTHENING RESPONSE CHAINS

The first time that Charlie brushes his teeth, that Fern dresses herself correctly, or that Flora fills in her study guide in sufficient detail the response is still rather weak, for the chain, unless strengthened, can easily be disrupted. Components may still be omitted, their order confused, or inappropriate components added. Charlie may take his brush, wet it, and replace it. Fern can leave some of her snaps open, and Flora may again answer her questions too sketchily. It is crucial, if a complex behavioral chain is to persist intact, that *the full chain, emitted in proper order, be effectively reinforced* as often as possible, with minimal delay, with adequate amounts of reinforcers known to be effective for the individual. Mother would therefore have to observe Charlie's tooth brushing to be sure that it was correctly carried out and would have to follow immediately with a favorite story. Fern's supervisor should take the time to see that she has properly dressed herself and should compliment her on the accomplishment. Flora's instructor should check her study guide several times and should comment positively, when it has been completed in sufficient detail. (In this instance, a slightly more delayed reinforcer, demonstrating mastery of the material by passing the unit quiz, will support the behavior in a more natural fashion once it becomes better established.) As in all instances in which behaviors are at low strength, these optimal conditions must be continued. Eventually, it will be advisable to shift to the sorts of procedures described in Units 24–26 for maintaining well-established behaviors.

Summary

Chaining forms new behaviors by combining existing simple behaviors into more complex ones. It probably works best when the separate behavioral components are already present in the individual's repertoire. Backward chaining, starting with the final link, can be fruitful. Discriminative stimuli like instructions, gestures, imitative prompts, and their gradual removal, fading, can serve to facilitate the acquisition of a complex chain; or, if a few links are weak or absent, they can be shaped. Once the chain is fully developed, it should be strengthened through effective reinforcement procedures.

References

Benoit, B. Backward chaining. *The Learning Analyst Newsletter.* 1972, **1**, 6–7. (California State University, Department of Counselor Education, Los Angeles).

Clark, H. B. & Sherman, J. A. Teaching generative use of sentence answers to three forms of questions. *Journal of Applied Behavior Analysis,* 1975, **8**, 321–330.

Guess, D., Sailor, W., Rutherford, G. & Baer, D. M. An experimental analysis of linguistic development: The productive use of the plural morpheme. *Journal of Applied Behavior Analysis,* 1968, **1**, 297–306.

Gustafson, C., Hotte, E. & Carsky, M. Everyday living skills. Unpublished manuscript, Mansfield Training School, Mansfield Depot, Conn., 1976.

Holland, J. G. & Skinner, B. F. *The analysis of behavior.* New York: McGraw-Hill, 1961.

Lutzker, J. R. & Sherman, J. A. Producing generative sentence usage by imitation and reinforcement procedures. *Journal of Applied Behavior Analysis,* 1974, **7**, 447–460.

Renne, C. M. & Creer, T. L. Training children with asthma to use inhalation therapy equipment. *Journal of Applied Behavior Analysis,* 1976, **9**, 1–11.

Wheeler, A. J. & Sulzer, B. Operant training and generalization of a verbal response form in
a speech-deficient child. *Journal of Applied Behavior Analysis,* 1970, **3**, 139–147.

Whitehurst, G. J. Generalized labeling on the basis of structural response classes by two
young children. *Journal of Experimental Child Psychology,* 1971, **12**, 59–71.

Reducing Behavior: Positive Approaches

After mastering the material in this unit, you should be able to

1. Define and offer illustrations for each of the following terms:
   a. Differential reinforcement of low rates (DRL)
   b. Differential reinforcement of other behavior (DRO) (omission training)
   c. Behavioral contrast
   d. Reinforcement of alternative behavior (Alt-*R*)

2. List and discuss two major advantages and two disadvantages of the DRL schedule.

3. List, discuss, and illustrate the factors that influence the effectiveness of a DRL procedure.

4. Carry out an effective DRL procedure.

5. List and discuss two major advantages and disadvantages of the DRO procedure.

6. List, discuss, and illustrate the factors that influence the effectiveness of a DRO procedure.

7. List, discuss, and offer illustrations of the four major advantages of using the Alt-*R* procedure.

8. List three guidelines for selecting the alternative behavior.

9. List, discuss, and illustrate the factors that influence the effectiveness of the Alt-*R* procedure.

10. Carry out an effective Alt-*R* procedure.

11. List the chief disadvantage of reinforcing alternative behavior.

Remember Lucretia, who used her sand spade as a weapon against her playmates; Fern, who disturbed the other members of the workshop by wandering around and talking with them instead of working; Pearl, who followed no instructions at all and spent so much time engaging in repetitive hand movements that there was no time for much else; Dexter, who spent too much time off task; Mr. Grump, who was so critical and sarcastic; and Ms. Kvetch, who complained so much? Such behavior plagues change agents, as well as parents, and often the individuals themselves. Children who aggress against others, who disturb or disrupt the functioning of the group, who fail to comply with any adult instruction (to their own detriment and that of others), and who "waste time" create a challenge that may appear insurmountable. Staff members who, perhaps inadvertently, behave in a manner that is counterproductive to achieving program goals often compound the problem. For that reason, those sorts of behavior are frequently targeted for change in behavior-analysis programs.

Should any behavior be targeted for reduction? We have tried to make a strong case for selecting constructive goals, rather than focusing on reduction of behavior. We continue to support that concept, on the basis of both ethics as well as pragmatics. Ethically, it is more to a client's advantage to develop new productive behaviors than simply to eliminate behaviors from the repertoire. Pragmatically, focusing on the development of new behavior tends to generate positive collateral behaviors, like more positive self-statements, and the client is much more apt to remain in the situation and to continue to progress. There are times, however, despite the best efforts of those concerned, when the focus must shift to behavioral reduction. In our opinion, those times are usually when a particular behavior is dangerous or destructive to the client or others or when it seriously impedes the client's or others' ability to function to their own and society's benefit (see Stolz, 1976, for an extensive discussion of this and related issues). In particular, when clients and society agree, without coercion, that a goal is to their mutual benefit, reductive procedures can be strongly defended. Let us consider a few examples. Lucretia's aggression toward the other children is dangerous to them and also interferes with their ability to play in peace. Fern's disturbing others in the workshop keeps her and them from earning their wages and improving to qualify for better positions. Pearl's repetitive hand motions demand her constant attention and interfere with her learning from the environment. (Lovaas, Litrownik, and Mann, 1971, found that autistic children engaging in self-stimulatory behavior were less responsive to environmental stimuli than were others.) Mr. Grump's sarcasm interferes with his students' progress by reducing their performance rates. Dexter's low rate of task completion, however, seems to be a different story. The major event with which his low task completion interferes is higher task completion. He has not disrupted the class and is harming only himself by realizing less of his potential than he might. In his case, we could make a strong argument for limiting behavioral objectives only to those to be strengthened, unless, of course, Dexter himself argues in behalf of a combined program to increase on-task and reduce off-task behavior. He might elect such a program if he were concerned about achieving rapid results.

Once an ethically responsible decision to target a behavior for reduction has been made, first consideration should be given to those procedures that are least intrusive (most natural) and to those that are most positive, or "benign." Only if such procedures are found to be unsatisfactory should we consider in turn some of the more negative or intrusive methods like withholding reinforcers (extinction), removing reinforcers (response cost), removing the opportunity to earn reinforcers (timeout), requiring that behavior be corrected (overcorrection), and presenting aversive stimuli contingent upon the behavior (punishment). We begin with the most positive methods for reducing unwanted behavior: positive approaches to behavioral reduction. All use reinforcement.

The first approach, **differential reinforcement of low rates (DRL)**, involves reinforcing lower rates of a behavior. The second, **differential reinforcement of other behavior (DRO)**, provides for the regular delivery of reinforcement, contingent upon the absence of the unwanted behavior. The third, **reinforcing alternative behavior**, allows reinforcement to perform the function of reducing unwanted behavior by strengthening desirable alternatives.

All three procedures have one major advantage in common: Because all depend upon the application of reinforcement, all serve to emphasize how even a goal as distasteful as trying to eliminate problem behaviors can be approached constructively. As reinforcement is involved, all three require that the rules for effective reinforcement (Units 8, 9, and 10) be followed. Also, in each instance, reinforcement should be withheld completely following the unwanted response.

DIFFERENTIAL REINFORCEMENT OF LOW RATES

On occasion, certain responses must be reduced but not necessarily eliminated. Consuming small amounts of sugar may be appropriate for a diabetic child, whereas too much can be dangerous. The student who writes too quickly and ends up handing in a sloppy paper, the swimmer who needs to work to perfect a stroke, the ballet dancer who performs more rapidly than called for by the score—all must be slowed down. Tim's tendency to dominate group discussions to the extent that others can hardly "get a word in edgewise," Fern's interacting with other workshop members, and Ms. Kvetch's complaining are examples of behavior that perhaps should be reduced but not necessarily eliminated. It is okay for Tim to participate and Fern to interact—but not as often. The procedure best suited for this change is the differential reinforcement of low rates schedule.

DRL Defined and Illustrated

The laboratory definition of a DRL procedure states that reinforcement is contingent upon responses that are being emitted at low rates—upon responses that are spaced relatively far apart. A monkey will receive a banana pellet for pulling a chain only if he has not pulled that particular chain for t moments previously. If he should pull the chain too soon a new interval of t moments is initiated. In other words, *t* moments must elapse before chain pulling will produce reinforcement. The variation on this theme that is also to be discussed here changes the contingency slightly. In the present instance reinforcement is delivered at the end of the interval, "when the number of responses (*n*) in a specified period of time is less than, or equal to, a prescribed limit" (Deitz & Repp, 1973). It is clear that, if this contingency were applied in the laboratory, the monkey would automatically receive a banana pellet at the end of the interval (whether he pulled the chain or not), as long as he had pulled the chain fewer than *n* times during the interval. The delivery of the pellet would not have to be contingent upon a chain pull. For contingency managers who have many demands upon their attention, this variation seems to make it easier to conduct a DRL program with groups of clients. All that is required is that responses up to *n* number within an interval be counted. If the number *n* is reached before termination of the interval, reinforcement is withheld at the end of the interval. If *n* responses have not been emitted by the end of the interval, reinforcement is delivered, whether the particular target behavior is being emitted at the moment or not. Several examples should help to clarify the use of this procedure.

Tim's excessive talking during group counseling is becoming a pain in the ear. The counselor decides that it is only fair to allow other clients a chance to participate too, but Tim dominates the discussion. A DRL procedure is selected because the counselor does not want to use a procedure that might eliminate Tim's participation altogether. The goal is reduction, not elimination. Tim is thus reinforced for a reduced number (below baseline) of verbal contributions during a specified period of time.

A high-school ceramics teacher, Mr. Bisk, is discouraged by the "unimaginative" productions of his students; the only objects that they mold are ashtrays, cups, and vases. He discusses this concern with the students. Some express discomfort at the suggestion that they produce original things. They would like to be allowed to continue making some of the conventional objects. The teacher concurs, realizing that some students may experience failure in attempting to be original. A set of assignments is mutually agreed upon: For each of three methods— the coil method, the wheel method, and simple modeling—each student is to produce between three and five objects. To qualify for an "A" at the end of the semester, each student must make no more than one cup, ashtray, or vase in each category.

Advantages of DRL

Positive approach. DRL provides a program for the regular delivery of reinforcement and therefore offers the same advantages as other positive procedures: Good things still continue to happen! Certainly it would be possible to slow response rates in other ways: to yell at clients when they hurry, to ignore them altogether, to keep reminding them to slow down, to feed them tranquillizing drugs, and all kinds of other possibilities. But here is a situation in which behaving individuals do not lose out. They can still earn their reinforcers and go merrily on their way.

When a nonaversive procedure is sought to reduce the rate of a behavior, the DRL procedure should be given careful consideration.

Tolerant approach. The DRL procedure reflects built-in tolerance for the targeted undesirable behavior. It communicates the message, "What you're doing is okay, as long as it's not done to excess." The procedure promotes moderation. Although too much clowning is a nuisance, an occasional antic indicates desirable assertiveness. Dominating the conversation is boorish, but contributing to it from time to time is socially desirable. Everyone complains once in a while. That is okay. Ms. Kvetch just should not complain all the time. DRL is the procedure of choice when an individual wishes to moderate but not to eliminate a habit like eating sweets, drinking alcoholic beverages, or smoking. It is particularly amenable to self-management techniques.

Convenient and effective. The DRL procedure has been shown to be effective with a variety of clients. For example, Deitz and Repp (1973) reported its successful use with a group of ten trainable mentally retarded (TMR) children who engaged in frequent "talk out" behavior (talking, singing, humming without teachers' permission) and with an office-procedure class of fifteen "normal" high-school senior girls who frequently engaged in social discussions inappropriate to the class setting. The TMR children had had a baseline of 32.7 "talk outs" per fifty-minute session. The contingency was set so that, when the group made five or fewer talkouts in fifty minutes, each member would receive two pieces of candy of their selection. Talking out among the TMR children immediately declined to an average of 3.13 instances per session. The senior girls averaged 6.6 social discussions per fifty-minute session. For them the DRL procedure was instituted in four phases. The first phase stipulated that, when fewer than six such discussions occurred during the period for each of the first four days of the week, the Friday class would be a "free" period, to be used as the students pleased. During the second phase, the criterion was changed to fewer than three discussions. This figure was reduced to zero during the final phase. In addition to finding the DRL procedure very easy to use, the high-school teacher reported that the reinforcer "free time" worked well. "She found it more useful to have four days in which the students are not disruptive and are working than to have five relatively disruptive days" (Dietz & Repp, 1973, p. 462). DRL was also used effectively to reduce the "talk outs" of an eleven-year-old fifth-grade male and the out-of-seat behavior of a twelve-year-old sixth-grade female (Dietz & Repp, 1974). In each instance the behavior was reduced when nonexchangeable gold stars were made contingent on two or fewer responses per period.

Allowance for progressive reduction in response rate. The time-based DRL system readily lends itself to a progressive reduction in response rate. As mentioned previously, there are two alternative methods of accomplishing such reduction: the laboratory method, in which the response limit is kept stable and the time interval increased (for example, glancing at speech notes no more than once every ten seconds, then no more than once every fifteen seconds, and so on), or the maintenance of a stable time interval but with a reduced response criterion, as in Deitz and Repp's study (1973) of high-school seniors. Because the approach is so readily amenable to progressive rate reductions, it may be preferable to the "cold turkey" requirements of differential reinforcement of other behaviors (to be described later in this unit) and punishment (see Unit 22), both of which require that the behavior not occur at all—in DRO so that reinforcement will be forthcoming, in punishment so that aversive consequences can be avoided.

In a sense, a progressive DRL procedure is analogous to the shaping procedure, for it reinforces closer and closer approximations to the goal. In this instance, however, the goal is behavioral reduction, rather than behavioral increase, as in shaping. Nevertheless, both procedures have the advantage that very difficult-to-achieve goals can eventually be reached with maximum success. Here is an example: A resident of one institution for retarded children had been excluded from classes designed to teach preacademic skills. A clinician was seeking a method that would enable her to return to class. Whenever she was brought to the classroom, however, she screamed, threw objects around the room, ran around, shouted, and was generally disruptive most of the time. In fact, baseline data revealed that the longest interval that she would sit without disrupting was seventy seconds. Punishment was rejected, for no one wanted the predictable negative side effects, and intense punishment was not deemed ethically acceptable. There were no isolation facilities, and the child had no experiences with tokens; nor had she personal possessions to which she appeared to be attached, so fines could not be used. Extinction was tried, but, as can be imagined, it drove the teacher to desperation as the already high rate of disruption rose even higher. A DRL procedure was therefore selected. Because the mean rate of acceptable behavior (sitting and not disturbing) was about forty-seven seconds, a fifty-second DRL interval was selected. The number of "acting out" responses that could occur during the interval was placed initially at two, then at one, then at zero. This schedule made it possible for the child to receive frequent reinforcement; it was hoped that eventually the duration of acceptable behavior would increase, allowing for an increase in the DRL interval. Then perhaps a new procedure (for example, token reinforcement for intervals of specified "good" or on-task behavior, followed by skill achievement) could be substituted.

Disadvantages of DRL

Time.   Compared to the more efficient reductive procedures to be discussed later (punishment and response cost), DRL procedures take time. One would not select a DRL procedure to reduce violently assaultive behavior by a very strong person, for tolerating even a very low rate of such a behavior is not feasible. Some more rapidly effective procedure would be more appropriate.

Focus on undesirable behavior.   By its nature, a DRL procedure focuses the contingency manager's attention upon the undesirable behavior, which may occur at no higher a rate than n times per $t_2 - t_1$. When attention is directed to the undesirable behavior, emission of desirable behaviors may be overlooked. Here is an example: Two clients apparently "had it in for each other." They were verbally abusive and would tease each other and occasionally get into physical altercations. The boys, normal adolescents, were working with a guidance counselor. She decided that it would be a good idea to transfer control of the program to the boys, so that they could manage their own behaviors. First, she thought that she would ask the boys to record the number of times per class period, lunch, and study hall that they teased, made negative remarks, or hit each other. But fortunately the counselor thought before she made the recommendation. She realized that it would make much more sense for the boys to record and notice any increases in cooperative and mutually reinforcing behaviors. Following a conference with each, plus some role playing, or positive practice, she asked the boys to record the times they helped each other and the times that they reinforced each other (saying "thanks," "it really makes me feel good when you thank me," "right on," "nice going," and so on). The boys selected their own reinforcing contingencies as well, and the program was very successful. In addition, the guidance counselor and several teachers who had been informed about the plan began to pay much more attention to cooperative acts between the two boys, probably further enhancing the effects of the program.

In a large-group program, however, it is often easier for the contingency manager to use the DRL procedure, removing access to reinforcement with the first infraction, then forgetting about or not implementing the procedure for the duration of the interval. Contingency managers may then find themselves focusing on the undesirable behavior and may actually inadvertently reinforce it with this increased attention. This possibility is a danger in using DRL and should be guarded against. Some sort of device, like making a minimum of three positive comments for desirable behaviors during a given hour, may help to counteract this potential hazard.

Using DRL Effectively

Effective reinforcement procedures.   To use DRL effectively, it is necessary also to use reinforcement procedures effectively. The reinforcers must be appropriate for the individual or group, and they should be delivered as soon as possible after the completion of the interval. Reinforcement should be combined with S^Ds; for example, the arrangement that reinforcement will be contingent upon less than a given number of infractions within a specific time period can be posted. The contingency manager and client can agree on rules to serve as S^Ds. A clock visible to both the contingency manager and the client would be another appropriate S^D, and the clients' attention to the clock might be initially prompted by pointing to it. As the lower frequency of behavior becomes well established, reinforcement should be delivered less frequently (see Units 24–26). Naturally, reinforcement is completely withheld following any occurrence of the unwanted behavior.

Using Baseline Data to Determine Duration of DRL Interval

It might be tempting for contingency managers to select some arbitrary DRL interval, because of convenience: a half-hour, a day, a class period, and so on. In some instances, an arbitrary selection may turn out to reflect a lucky guess, and behavioral improvement may be demonstrated. But, to maximize the likelihood of success, it is a good idea to proceed systematically from where the client is to where he should be. A base-rate assessment, taken over several days until a pattern of stability emerges, is the most appropriate method. That is, it is best to assess the rate at which the target behavior is being emitted and to select an interval that will guarantee reinforcement more often than not. In the example of the disruptive retarded girl, the initial mean duration of sitting attentively was forty-seven seconds, so a fifty-second duration was selected. This choice permitted her to receive reinforcement fairly frequently. As always, the client's behavior provides the guidelines for appropriate procedural design.

Increasing Interval Gradually

Too gross a change in the duration of the interval will produce the same disruption as the selection of too large a step in a shaping procedure. It is far preferable to proceed gradually, increasing the length of the interval very slowly. The clients' behavior will provide information about the appropriateness of the change; persisting major disruptions mandate a rapid retreat to a shorter interval. We planned to lengthen the interval for our retarded student from fifty seconds to ten minutes, so that the teacher could assume full management of the program. We had to wait, however, until 80–90 percent of the fifty-second intervals were nondisruptive before extending the interval to one minute, then two, and so on.

Combining DRL with Other Procedures

In addition to using S^Ds like models, rules, and explanations of the program and its contingencies, some investigators have successfully combined DRL with other reductive procedures to accomplish more rapid reduction in unwanted behavior. For instance, more than n unwanted behaviors in an interval results in a token loss. The Good Behavior Game (Barrish, Saunders & Wolf, 1969; Harris & Sherman, 1973) is an example of such a combination, which may bring more rapid results. It will be described in Unit 27. Then the approach is no longer totally positive, however.

DIFFERENTIAL REINFORCEMENT OF OTHER BEHAVIORS (DRO)

We shall now discuss how differential reinforcement of other behaviors, DRO, can be planned as part of a program to reduce an undesirable behavior. Like DRL, the DRO procedure also approaches the goal of behavioral reduction positively.

DRO Defined and Illustrated

Differential reinforcement of other behaviors is a variant of the differential-reinforcement procedure discussed in Unit 12, but it is directed specifically at *reduction* of a particular behavior. "The DRO schedule refers to a procedure in which a reinforcer follows any performance the [individual] emits except a particular one" (Ferster & Perrott, 1968, p. 524). In the laboratory, a DRO procedure usually includes the programming of reinforcement delivered according to some specific schedule, *except* when the individual engages in a particular response. For instance, food may be regularly delivered when the subject engages in any behavior other than pressing one particular bar. In applied situations, reinforcement also follows some prescribed pattern. The client receives reinforcement *except* when he engages in a particular behavior. Because reinforcement is contingent upon the *omission*, rather than the *commission*, of a behavior, the DRO procedure may also be labeled **omission training**.

DRL involves recording or looking for the target responses during a specific period of time; in DRO we record or look for the target response at a specific moment. If the target behavior is not occurring at that moment, the reinforcer is delivered. If the target response is occurring, then the reinforcer is not delivered. For example, a music student can be told that he is doing fine and can receive a nod or smile every ten seconds, *unless* he is playing an incorrect note at that moment. Or perhaps the teacher is called to the office and puts a monitor in charge of the class. The monitor is asked to watch the clock and every thirty seconds to place a mark on the blackboard (which represents an extra minute of recess) *unless* any student is out of her seat *at that time*. Eric frequently sucks his thumb. The contingency manager sets a timer at irregular intervals; it rings on the *average* once every five minutes. Each time that the timer rings Eric is observed. If his thumb is not in his mouth, he receives a token. (How could this system be applied to Pearl's hand ritual?) Frank has a habit that annoys his teacher: He embellishes many of his school papers with doodles. The teacher uses a system of giving him a star for every paper that does *not* contain those embellishments. Differential reinforcement of other behaviors is the procedure being used in each of the examples.

A common variation of the procedure is to set the contingency so that, if *no* response occurs *during* an interval, then any *other* behavior emitted at the end of the interval is eligible for reinforcement. Technically this contingency combines a DRO with a DRL of zero, for reinforcement is contingent upon a zero rate of responding throughout the whole interval. (This variation has also been referred to simply as a "DRO procedure"; see Repp & Deitz, 1974; Reynolds, 1961.) For example, this contingency was used to reduce a youngster's rate of fighting during recesses. At the end of each recess without a fight he earned a check. These checks were exchanged later in the day for free time in the classroom or in a special activity center with a friend of his choice.

Advantages of DRO

Rapidly reducing behavior.   Beside being a positive approach, DRO reduces behavior fairly rapidly. It permits reinforcement of the individual for engaging in an infinite variety of behaviors other than the one specified exception. It is usually a very powerful procedure. While occasionally there is an individual who engages in problem behavior at such a high rate that "other" behavior is not apt to occur (for example, the rocking of an autistic child), most individuals have all sorts of options available, and usually they take one of them. As a result, the one nonreinforceable behavior begins to drop out quite rapidly (Reynolds, 1961). If there is a behavior that has been reduced quickly and at all costs, like self-destructive or aggressive behavior, and if fast-acting procedures like presenting S^Ds and punishment are rejected, DRO may accomplish the aim effectively.

Because of its very powerful reductive effect, DRO is frequently used during the second A, or reversal, phase of an ABAB design, to demonstrate the effectiveness of a reinforcer in an experimental situation (see Units 7 and 32). DRO tends to show a stronger effect than simple extinction or noncontingent reinforcement (Goetz, Holmberg & Le Blanc, 1975). Baer, Peterson, and Sherman (1967), for instance, performed a study in which they taught profoundly retarded children to imitate. First, the children were reinforced with food and praise for engaging in imitative behaviors; such behaviors increased substantially. In order to demonstrate that the reinforcing contingencies were responsible for the change, a DRO schedule was instituted. Reinforcement was then delivered after the passage of a period of time in which imitative behavior was not emitted. Imitative behavior plunged rapidly under DRO. When imitation-contingent reinforcement was reinstituted, the children again began to imitate at a high rate.

Using DRO Effectively

Careful scheduling of reinforcement.   DRO is a differential-reinforcement procedure. The techniques for increasing the effectiveness of differential reinforcement apply to DRO as well. In addition, because the DRO procedure makes reinforcement contingent upon the omission of the target behavior, careful reinforcement scheduling is very important. The schedule for reinforcing omission of the undesirable behavior should be specified in advance. In order to ensure the greatest likelihood of success for the individual, the time interval should be kept short at first, allowing the client to earn frequent reinforcement. After the undesirable behavior has begun to diminish in rate, the intervals can be gradually extended. For example, when Eric sucks his thumb, his peers tease him. Eric, his parents, and the dentist all wish to eliminate the behavior. A DRO procedure is put into effect. An observer watches Eric. Following every one-minute interval, Eric is given a token that he can exchange for some selected back-up reinforcer, provided that his thumb is not in his mouth at that moment. The delivery of the token is paired with smiles, praise, and other conditioned reinforcers. When the frequency of thumb sucking has diminished by perhaps 50 percent, the interval is lengthened to two minutes. This pattern can continue until the terminal goal is reached.

If it is practical, the DRO schedule that requires omission of the behavior throughout the interval should be selected. For, when reinforcement is contingent only upon the omission of the response at the moment when the interval terminates, the unwanted behavior still can continue during the interval. Eric can suck his thumb during the interval and still receive reinforcement at the end, as long as his thumb is not in his mouth at that precise moment. The suggested DRO schedule does not permit *any* thumb sucking during the interval. Consequently, the behavior would be reduced more rapidly. As we think about it, however, we realize that this contingency is much harsher; therefore intervals should be kept very short initially, in order for the individual to experience reinforcement. Also, this apparently more powerful arrangement requires constant monitoring. If the target behavior is subtle or occurs at a high rate, the person administering the program must watch closely to catch any instance of it. For a self-recording client, such a program might interfere with other activities. Even when the observer is another individual, the DRO procedure may require that observer's full attention. It is necessary to balance the presumably more effective schedule against the less effective, but also less demanding one. Even if it requires additional staff, surely in instances of dangerous or destructive behavior a strong argument could be made for the DRO combined with a DRL of zero.

Combining DRO with other procedures.   Effective reinforcement of other behaviors, combined with extinction of the unwanted behavior, is obviously essential. In addition, Repp and Deitz (1974) have reported the successful combining of whole-interval DRO with other procedures to reduce aggressive and self-injurious behaviors of institutionalized retarded children. In one study, this DRO was combined successfully with timeout: denying the child access to reinforcement for a period of time (see Unit 20). A timer was initially set for a five-second interval. During the program the interval was gradually increased to thirty minutes. If the child made no aggressive responses during the interval, he was given an M & M when the bell rang. If he made an aggressive response, the timer was stopped, and he was restrained for thirty seconds of timeout. In a second study, the DRO was combined with punishment. When various aggressive classroom behaviors occurred the child was told "no." Otherwise, reinforcement was delivered following periods of time during which aggressive behaviors did not occur. A third study combined DRO with fines (see Unit 19 on response cost). Tokens were earned for five minutes of response omission; each inappropriate response resulted in loss of tokens. "In each case, the DRO procedure combined with other techniques proved to be manageable for the teacher and successful in reducing the inappropriate behavior" (Repp & Dietz, 1974, p. 313). When DRO is combined with aversive stimuli, like fines and loss of reinforcement opportunity, it loses the advantage of being a completely positive approach. Combining DRO with the reinforcement of alternative behaviors, to be discussed later, maintains the advantage of an all-positive program.

Disadvantages of DRO

Other behavior possibly worse.   All behaviors other than the one to be eliminated are equally eligible for reinforcement under DRO conditions. This arrangement could conceivably mean that one would find oneself in the position of reinforcing a behavior that was just as bad as or perhaps even worse than the behavior to be eliminated. Pearl is given a small piece of fruit or a raisin every five minutes, provided that she has not engaged in her hand routine. It just so happens that she is rocking at the end of five minutes when the fruit is given to her. Rocking may increase as a result. This sort of problem is more apt to manifest itself among clients who have many undesirable behaviors in their repertoires. It seems best, when working with clients who frequently emit various problem behaviors, to turn to one of two alternatives: either to put *several* of the most serious of the undesirable behaviors on DRO simultaneously (provided that a sufficient number of reinforceable intervals will be available to allow the program a chance to work) or to elect another reductive procedure.

Behavioral contrast. If a DRO (or any other reductive procedure) is used for a specific behavior, it becomes very important to ensure that the behavior does not receive reinforcement at other times. If a particular behavior is placed on DRO under certain stimulus conditions, it is possible that the response rate, though decreasing under the condition paired with DRO, will increase under the other condition. Evidence for this possibility is derived from a study performed by Reynolds (1961). Pigeons that had been reinforced for key pecking continued to be reinforced for key pecking under one discriminative stimulus (S^D) and *were reinforced for not key pecking (DRO) under a different S^D*. Although the rate of key pecking under the DRO-correlated stimulus was practically eliminated, responding under the non-DRO stimulus conditions increased to a level higher than before. This phenomenon was labeled *behavioral contrast*. Although data on this phenomenon in human subjects are insufficient, it seems advisable to watch for the possible occurrence of a contrast effect during the use of DRO. For instance, whenever the contingency manager leaves the room it is a good idea to measure the rate of Pearl's hand routine. A substantial increase over base rate while the contingency manager is out of the room, coupled with elimination of the behavior while she is present, would suggest the presence of a contrast effect.

REINFORCING ALTERNATIVE BEHAVIORS (ALT-R[1])

The last reductive procedure that we shall discuss in this unit will receive the greatest emphasis. The technique of reinforcing a behavior that offers an alternative to an undesirable behavior has been mentioned several times elsewhere in this book: in the discussions of reinforcement, differential reinforcement, stimulus control, extinction, and DRO. But, because the procedure is constructive and has much to offer practitioners, it is being treated separately here.

Alt-R Defined and Illustrated

The technique of reinforcing alternative behaviors is almost self-explanatory. It consists simply of strengthening a specific behavior or behaviors that offer alterna-

[1] *R* stands for "response." We prefer to use the term "behavior."

tives to unwanted behavior. When this procedure is adopted, the unwanted behavior is first identified and operationalized. Then potential alternative responses (abbreviated Alt-*R*s by Reese, Howard, and Rosenberger, 1976) that would reduce the probability of emission of the undesirable behavior are considered. After careful consideration, one or several of the alternative behaviors are selected to be strengthened. For example, Fern frequently wanders about the workshop distracting other participants. If she were doing her assigned work, she would not be distracting the others. Task-completion behavior is thus chosen for strengthening, and her distracting behavior decreases. Violet spends her recess and lunch time quietly isolated in a corner. Turning one end of a jump rope, engaging in conversation, sitting with peers, and participating in a game are activities that are incompatible with social isolation. Strengthening those behaviors should reduce the frequency of Violet's moments alone. Vernon is frequently in trouble with the police. He breaks windows, pilfers from stores, sprays paint on walls, and shoots BBs at passers-by. All this behavior occurs during school hours while Vernon is playing truant. Attending school is incompatible with those behaviors. If Vernon's school attendance is strengthened (an alternative behavior), his lawless behavior should decrease.

Many behavior analysts who have been consulted about classroom behavioral problems have elected to use the Alt-*R* procedure. Allen and colleagues (1964) worked with a preschooler who seldom played with other children. Rather than punishing or using only extinction on the isolate behavior, they decided to reinforce her with attention whenever she interacted with other children (an alternative to isolate behavior). Her isolate behavior diminished substantially. A similar approach was used to diminish hyperactivity in a preschooler (Allen *et al.*, 1967). Flitting from one activity to another brought the child no reinforcement, but engaging in one activity for predetermined periods of time was socially reinforced. Hyperactivity was reduced as a result.

A similar procedure is used to achieve specific terminal goals in clinical treatment programs. One of the authors was working with a client who, like Pearl, constantly moved her hands in front of her face in ritualistic fashion. This and several other **autistic-like** (repetitive, nonfunctional) behaviors were selected as responses that should be reduced. They interfered with the client's attending to relevant environmental stimuli and were very distracting in social settings, especially the classroom. The approach selected was Alt-*R*. A large group of hand-involved instructional and play behaviors was shaped and strengthened: playing with sand, putting pieces of puzzles together, piling up blocks, painting, and so on. None of those behaviors had been emitted with much frequency in the past. Once they had been sufficiently reinforced, they began to be emitted much more often. The child was spending most of each session in more normal play and instructional activities. Ritualistic hand movements were never attended to, either positively or aversively, yet they gradually diminished, for they could not coexist with the more constructive behaviors. A similar approach by the teacher yielded parallel results in the classroom.

Advantages of Alt-R

Lasting reduction of behavior.   Once the alternative behavior occurs at a rate high and steady enough to prevent emission of the undesirable behavior, the latter has been, at least temporarily, eliminated. As long as the alternative behavior is *maintained* at a high and steady rate, the undesirable behavior is not apt to return. Therefore, by following the rules for maintaining high rates of behavior, we can achieve an enduring reduction of the undesirable behavior. (See Unit 26 for methods of promoting and maintaining high response rates.) Vernon's school attendance should maintain, along with the reduction of stealing and destruction of property. Something like this result was actually accomplished by a graduate student as a project for a class. A habitually truant teenager whose only apparent interest was sports cars was allowed to earn sports-car magazines by working on academic assignments, the completion of which would earn him points. A specific number of points could be used to purchase the magazines. The student's school attendance increased substantially.

Positive approach.   We have seen that extinction has some negative consequences for clients. The same is true of response cost, timeout and punishment (see Units 19, 20, and 22 respectively). Either reinforcers are withheld or withdrawn, or aversive consequences are presented. With Alt-*R* clients continue to receive reinforcement. A carefully planned program will yield regular reinforcement and all the good things that go along with it. If there is any generalized responding to stimuli in the setting, it should be positive. Clients are also more likely to remain in situations that yield reinforcement. In our clinical illustration, the child with autistic-like behaviors always attended sessions willingly and never made an attempt to leave. Had we scolded, slapped, or withheld attention whenever the undesired hand movements occurred, the situation might have been very aversive to her. She might have tried to leave or, at least, refused to cooperate in the program.

Constructive approach.   In selecting alternative behaviors, it is usually possible to find one or more desirable alternatives that will be beneficial to the client. In the illustrations cited, increased social interactions, completing tasks, and learning to engage in normal play activities undoubtedly served to help the clients progress personally, educationally, and socially. Again, this advantage is in contrast to other reductive procedures (extinction, punishment, response cost, and timeout) that focus on eliminating behavior. Eliminating behavior does not enhance learning, nor does it enhance development.

Comfortable approach.   Many practitioners are unwilling to use aversive contingencies. They view their jobs as helping children and youths to develop to their fullest possible potentials. They do not want to spend their time scolding, punishing, threatening, or intentionally ignoring clients. They do want to help clients to learn, to acquire behaviors that are beneficial to them. Reinforcing a productive, desirable alternative to an unwanted behavior is well suited to those ideals.

Selecting the Alternative Behavior

Striving for behavioral incompatibility.   When selecting the alternative behavior or array of behaviors, the practitioner should be careful to emphasize desirable alternative behaviors that are not apt to be emitted simultaneously with the behavior targeted for reduction. For, if such compatibility is accidentally present, both behaviors may be strengthened. Let us suppose that Vernon not only gets into trouble during school hours while truant but also manages to steal and destroy property while in school. Simply reinforcing school attendance, then, will not assist in reducing those behaviors. It may even accidentally strengthen them in the school setting. It is therefore necessary to be much more specific in selecting alternative reinforceable behaviors. Doing school work at his desk, participating in group activities, or engaging in wood working and art projects may not be compatible with stealing and destruction. The practitioner must be careful to avoid strengthening such other activities as allowing Vernon to go on errands, to remain alone without supervision, or to have access to free and unstructured time, for the behaviors are in no way incompatible with the undesirable behaviors. He could conceivably write on walls while on an errand, go through and remove objects from students' desks while alone in the room, and so on.

Selecting behavior already in the response repertoire.   Given a set of alternative responses among which to choose, if all other factors are equal, it is a good idea to select one that is already present in the repertoire of the client. The goal should be accomplished more quickly if the alternative behavior is already being emitted at some rate above zero. The time that it takes to shape a behavior may involve considerable delay. Let us suppose that Humphrey, a shy adolescent, wishes to reduce his tendency to isolate himself socially. Any of the following alternative behaviors may be selected: playing chess, conversing, working on committees, participating in debates, and many others. If he has been occasionally observed playing chess and working on committees with other youths but never engaging in unstructured conversation with others, the former behaviors will probably be much easier to strengthen than the latter ones. (Later it would be possible to begin shaping the latter behaviors also.)

Selecting behavior likely to be maintained by the environment.   Even though contingency managers often spend considerable time with their clients, they usually cannot remain with them constantly. Again, all things being equal, the alternative behavior should be one that others in the client's environment will tend to support. Many behaviors, for instance, are incompatible with verbal aggression: polite, well-modulated speech; no speech; minimal speech; whispered words; incomprehensible words; and so on. But some of the behaviors would yield the client little reinforcement in the outside world. Not speaking, whispering, and utterance of incomprehensible words would probably undergo extinction. On the other hand, polite, well-modulated speech is more likely to receive reinforcement from some sources. The point is that incompatible behavior should be *practical*; practical behaviors have social import and are apt to be maintained through "natural" consequences.

Using Alt-R Effectively

In addition to the factors to be considered in selecting incompatible behaviors, the optimal use of reinforcement and other behavioral procedures in the program will enhance the effectiveness of the Alt-*R* procedure.

Combining Alt-*R* with other procedures. Beside reinforcement, the most obvious procedure to combine with Alt-*R* is extinction. If at all possible, reinforcement for the undesirable behavior should be eliminated. For instance, let us assume that adult attention serves as a reinforcer for the shy adolescent, Humphrey. Beside attending to Humphrey while playing chess, adults should minimize attention to him when he remains alone. Sometimes this approach is not consonant with the "intuitive" one. It seems that what comes naturally to a parent, teacher, or counselor is not *always* the most effective technique. In this illustration, for instance, the natural tendency might be to cajole, urge, or otherwise try to encourage Humphrey to interact with the group. Such attention might, however, despite all good intentions, actually serve to strengthen isolate behavior. Again, this example underscores the importance of an empirical approach: *Measured* observations tell what effects a given procedure is having.

It is also possible to use a punishment procedure in conjunction with Alt-*R*. Punishment should reduce the undesirable behavior quickly, but, as we shall see, it has many disadvantages. Its combination with other procedures should therefore be limited as much as possible to dangerous, destructive, or severely disruptive behavior.

If a promising alternative behavior is not present in the client's repertoire, differential reinforcement, shaping, or chaining can be used to assist in its development, as we saw in the example of the child with the ritualistic hand movements. If the behavior is under stimulus control, the practitioner may present imitative prompts, verbal directions, and other S^Ds to occasion the response, so that it can be strengthened. If, for instance, a hyperactive client responds correctly to the direction "Please, do your work," it would make sense to give that instruction and thus begin a program of reinforcing increasingly longer periods of on-task behavior. As always, the contingency manager must be very sensitive to the effects of such instructions. Do they simply occasion on-task behavior, or do they reinforce "disruptive" behavior by providing contingent attention? In order to find out, the contingency manager can try instructions for a few days and observe their effects upon frequency or duration of disruptive behavior. If the attention is reinforcing, there will be an increase in the behavior. It would then be preferable to wait for on-task behavior to be emitted by itself or to prompt and reinforce a peer located nearby to occasion it, rather than to give the instruction. Once the target subject's rate has increased, a program of reinforcing on-task behavior can be started.

Modeling is a very useful supplementary procedure in group situations. The appropriate behavior of a model doing an assigned task, for instance, while others are engaged in a nontask or disruptive activity provides an imitative prompt. "Igor, I sure am pleased to see you working quietly"; "Wow, Clyde is really getting down to work now, too." Such comments often serve to occasion similar peer behavior so that they too can be reinforced. Kazdin, Silverman, and Sittler (1975) delivered a verbal prompt—"Dave, look at Ted [the target subject]"—and immediately delivered nonverbal approval to Ted, the target subject, who was used as the model because he was behaving attentively. Under those conditions both children's attentive behavior improved. A similar effect was shown by Christy (1975), who used tangible rewards. Modeling, then, is an effective means of reducing undesired group behavior without requiring the use of aversive consequences or focusing on the "disruptive" behavior.

Disadvantages of Alt-R

Delayed effect. Just as any reinforcement procedure takes time to achieve its results, Alt-R accomplishes its aims relatively slowly. Until the alternative behavior is being emitted at a fairly high rate, time is still available for the undesirable behavior to be emitted. Until Humphrey interacts with others frequently, he still has the opportunity of remaining alone. Until on-task behavior is emitted sufficiently often, disruptive behavior can remain at disturbingly high levels. By combining Alt-R with other procedures, it may be possible to speed up the process to some extent. Using punishment or stimulus change in order to reduce rapidly the undesirable behavior, while the alternative behavior is being reinforced simultaneously, may reduce the time lag. But again, once punishment is introduced, some of the major advantages of reinforcing incompatible behaviors (that it is a positive and comfortable approach) are lost.

Mixed evidence of effectiveness. A given Alt-R procedure does not guarantee that the target behavior will decrease in occurrence. For example, in one study (Ferritor et al., 1972) with third-grade students and in a second (Eggleston & Mayer, 1976) with ninth- and tenth-grade students attempts were made to increase academic performance while indirectly reducing student inattention. Math-performance contingencies increased the percentage of correct problems completed, but student attending declined. Others, however (Sulzer et al., 1971; Ayllon & Roberts, 1974), found that, when reading performance was reinforced, disruptive behavior decreased. In Ayllon and Roberts' study (1974), when students were reinforced with tokens for reading achievement, their rates of disruption fell dramatically. Similarly, in the study by Sulzer and colleagues (1971), as disruption decreased the students doubled or tripled their rates of progress in reading and spelling over those of the previous year, their attendance improved, and they were often overheard to say positive things about school—all with practically no negative consequences.

Similarly, Ferritor and colleagues (1972) found that contingencies designed to improve attending and to reduce disruptions did not indirectly improve academic performance. When Eggleston and Mayer (1976) reinforced attending behavior, however, not only did attending behavior increase but also the number and percentage of math problems completed also increased.

Various interpretations may explain these mixed findings. Subject matter and grade level may differentially influence the effects of the procedure. But the reinforcement of on-task behavior, like math or reading, without concurrently achieving a decrease in disruption or inattention may be explained by other factors. Clients may engage in a variety of undesirable behaviors. For example, Igor spends about 10 percent of his time during math period disrupting and 70 percent "doing nothing" (drawing, looking out the window, helping peers with projects, and so on). The teacher is most concerned with reducing the disruptive behavior because it interferes with classroom learning. It is decided to reinforce Igor's math productivity as a positive means of reducing his disruptions. But when math productivity increases from 10 percent to 65 percent, disruptive behavior remains at about 10 percent. Why? The nontargeted "doing nothing" behaviors, rather than the disruptive behavior, have decreased. Not only should the alternative desirable behavior be incompatible with the undesirable behavior, but other behaviors that are also incompatible with it should be identified, monitored, and, if appropriate, modified.

Fortunately, these studies do agree in one respect: All found that when both attending *and* math performances were reinforced, both increased *maximally*. Rather than reinforcing only the incompatible behavior, it is necessary to reinforce other behaviors targeted for improvement as well. If the goal is to increase attention and the number of tasks correctly completed, then attending behavior, as well as task completion, should be reinforced. This combined approach will enhance the attainment of multiple goals.

Summary

Reinforcing low rates of a behavior differentially (DRL) is an excellent method of decelerating behavior that occurs too frequently. DRL is easily adapted to use with groups of young people and can be combined with other procedures to reduce unwanted behavior rapidly.

Differential reinforcement of other behaviors (DRO) can be a rapid and effective method of reducing undesirable behaviors, provided that reinforcement is withheld under all conditions following each occurrence of the undesirable behavior and that it is possible, at least initially, to program very frequent reinforcement for other behaviors. Although requiring close monitoring, DRO combined with a DRL of zero is a particularly powerful reductive procedure. DRO is probably best reserved for use with individuals who emit other undesirable behaviors infrequently.

When carefully selected alternatives to an undesirable behavior are reinforced, the undesirable behavior should diminish in rate. The Alt-R procedure therefore brings about behavioral reduction indirectly. A constructive behavior interferes with the emission of an undesirable one. If the desirable behavioral alternatives are properly strengthened and maintained, the Alt-R procedure can produce long-lasting results. Because the approach is positive, practitioners can use it with comfort. Appropriate reinforcement techniques, a guarantee of incompatibility, and combined use with other procedures, particularly extinction of the undesirable behavior, should accomplish behavioral reduction with maximum effectiveness. Although slower than some reductive procedures, Alt-R has many advantages that make it worthy of selection as a regular applied behavior-analysis procedure.

References

Allen, K. E., Hart, B. M., Buell, J. S., Harris, F. R. & Wolf, M. M. Effects of social reinforcement on isolate behavior of a nursery school child. *Child Development,* 1964, **35,** 511–518.

Allen, K. E., Henke, L. B., Harris, F. R., Baer, D. M. & Reynolds, N. J. Control of hyperactivity by social reinforcement of attending behavior. *Journal of Educational Psychology,* 1967, **58,** 231–237.

Ayllon, R. & Roberts, M. D. Eliminating discipline problems by strengthening academic performance. *Journal of Applied Behavior Analysis,* 1974, **7,** 71–76.

Baer, D. M., Peterson, R. F. & Sherman, J. A. The development of imitation by reinforcing behavior of similarity to a model. *Journal of the Experimental Analysis of Behavior,* 1967, **10,** 405–416.

Barrish, H. H., Saunders, M. & Wolf, M. M. Good Behavior Game: Effects of individual contingencies for group consequences on disruptive behavior in a classroom. *Journal of Applied Behavior Analysis,* 1969, **2,** 119–124.

Christy, P. R. Does use of tangible rewards with individual children affect peer observers? *Journal of Applied Behavior Analysis,* 1975, **8,** 187–196.

Deitz, S. M., & Repp, A. C. Decreasing classroom misbehavior through the use of DRL schedules of reinforcement. *Journal of Applied Behavior Analysis,* 1973, **6,** 457–463.

Deitz, S. M., & Repp, A. C. Differentially reinforcing low rates of misbehavior with normal elementary school children. *Journal of Applied Behavior Analysis,* 1974, **7,** 622.

Eggelston, D. & Mayer, G. R. The effects of reinforcement contingencies upon attending behavior and academic achievement of high school students. Unpublished manuscript. California State University, Los Angeles, 1976.

Ferritor, D. E., Buckholdt, D., Hamblin, R. L. & Smith, L. The noneffects of contingent reinforcement for attending behavior on work accomplished. *Journal of Applied Behavior Analysis,* 1972, **5,** 7–17.

Ferster, C. B. & Perrott, M. C. *Behavior principles.* New York: Appleton, 1968.

Goetz, E. M., Holmberg, M. C. & Le Blanc, J. M. Differential reinforcement of other behavior and noncontingent reinforcement as control procedures during the modification of a preschooler's compliance. *Journal of Applied Behavior Analysis,* 1975, **8,** 77–82.

Harris, V. W. & Sherman, J. A. Use and analysis of the "good behavior game" to reduce disruptive classroom behavior. *Journal of Applied Behavior Analysis,* 1973, **6,** 405–417.

Holland, J. G. & Skinner, B. F. *The analysis of behavior.* New York: McGraw-Hill, 1961.

Kazdin, A. E., Silverman, N. A. & Sittler, J. L. The use of prompts to enhance vicarious effects of nonverbal approval. *Journal of Applied Behavior Analysis,* 1975, **8,** 279–286.

Lovaas, O. I., Litrownik, A. & Mann, R. Response latencies to auditory stimuli in autistic children engaged in self-stimulatory behavior. *Journal of Abnormal Psychology,* 1971, **7,** 39–49.

Reese, E. P., Howard, J. S. & Rosenberger, P. B. Behavioral procedures for assessing visual capacities in non-verbal subjects. In B. C. Etzel, J. M. Le Blanc & D. M. Baer (Eds.), *New developments in behavioral research: Theory, methods and applications.* New York: Erlbaum, 1976.

Repp, A. C. & Dietz, S. M. Reducing aggressive and self-injurious behavior of institutionalized retarded children through reinforcement of other behaviors. *Journal of Applied Behavior Analysis,* 1974, **7**, 313–325.

Reynolds, G. S. Behavioral contrast. *Journal of the Experimental Analysis of Behavior,* 1961, **4**, 57–71.

Stolz, S. B. Ethics of social and educational interventions: Historical context and a behavior analysis. In T. A. Brigham & A. C. Catania (Eds.), *Analysis of Behavior: Social and educational processes.* New York: Irvington-Neiburg Wiley, (in press).

Sulzer, B., Hunt, S., Ashby, E., Koniarski, C., & Krams, M. Increasing rate and percentage correct in reading and spelling in a fifth grade public school class of slow readers by means of a token system. In E. A. Ramp & B. L. Hopkins (Eds.), *A new direction for education: Behavior analysis 1971.* Vol. 1. Lawrence: University of Kansas: Follow Through, 1971. Pp. 5–28.

Reducing Behavior: Response Cost

After mastering the material in this unit, you should be able to

1. Define and offer illustrations of
   a. Response cost
   b. Bonus response cost
   c. S^{D-}

2. Define and illustrate the differences among extinction, punishment, and response cost.

3. List and discuss the advantages and disadvantages of response cost.

4. Tell how to use response cost effectively.

5. Describe specific situations in which response cost would and would not be the best behavioral procedure; justify your positions.

6. Describe and illustrate how stimuli can be developed to "inhibit" behavior by means of extinction, punishment, and response cost.

7. Summarize the advantages and disadvantages of different inhibiting stimuli.

Increased knowledge of current national and world events was selected as a goal for residents of Achievement Place, a community home for "predelinquent" boys (Phillips et al., 1971). It was selected because of its relevance to academic performance in school and because it is suitable to promoting conversational skills. The boys watched an evening news broadcast on television. Afterward, they were asked questions about the content of the broadcast. Initially, few questions were answered correctly. Then points exchangeable for various back-up reinforcers were awarded for correct answers. There was a slight increase in the number of questions correctly answered. Only when the award of points for correct answers was limited to occasions when 40 percent or more of the answers were correct and when a *point penalty* for failing to meet the 40 percent criterion was added, however, did correctness substantially increase. Point loss provided a powerful contingency for reducing errors.

Technically, the point-penalty system is a **response-cost system**, for it consists of the *removal or withdrawal of a quantity of reinforcers, contingent upon a response*. Response cost has been incorporated into many behavioral programs with impressive results.

Response cost is an aversive procedure, and as such it may evoke countercontrol behaviors among clients and those representing their interests. As with other aversive procedures, ethical and legal issues may be involved. Consequently, before implementing formal response-cost procedures, institutional review, contracting, and a review of governmental policy and law should be undertaken. Of the aversive procedures to be presented in this book (others are timeout, overcorrection, and punishment), however, response cost is relatively benign and minimally intrusive. Its use for reducing individually or socially dangerous destructive behaviors should not be too difficult to justify.

Another relatively benign aversive procedure is the presentation of discriminative stimuli for aversive consequences (S^D-s). They are discriminative stimuli that develop their stimulus-control properties by being present when a given behavior is followed by response cost or one of the other aversive consequences to be discussed later. Let us consider how these procedures can be designed to operate effectively as components of behavioral programs for children and youth.

RESPONSE COST DEFINED

Response cost is the *response-contingent withdrawal of specified amounts of reinforcers*. Removal of a certain number of tokens, the imposition of a fine, and a cut in salary contingent upon a specific behavior are illustrations of response cost. A familiar response cost (a fine equal to $25) contingent upon a response (speeding) would be diagrammed this way:

$$\text{Response cost:} \quad \underset{\text{(speeding)}}{R} \longrightarrow \underset{\text{($25 fine)}}{S^{rc}}$$

A *quantity* of reinforcers is withdrawn. Technically, response cost differs from punishment in that punishment involves *presentation* of an aversive stimulus to reduce the rate at which a behavior is emitted, rather than the *withdrawal* of a certain amount of reinforcers. Fining a client ten points for fighting is a response-cost procedure. Slapping him is "punishment" for the fighting if its contingent application reduces the rate of that behavior (see Unit 22). The operations of response cost and punishment are diagramed thus:

Response Cost	Punishment

$$R \longrightarrow S^{rc}$$
(fighting)   (10-point fine)

$$R \longrightarrow S^{P}$$
(clowning, fighting)   (slap)

A quantity of reinforcers is withdrawn.   An aversive stimulus is presented.

It is possible to apply response cost to tangible reinforcers. For instance, a parent may take away a child's dessert contingent upon some misbehavior. Because of the nature of the response-cost procedure, its use in applied settings is usually limited to the withdrawal of exchangeable or other conditioned reinforcers like grades, points, and tokens. In order to remove specified amounts of a reinforcer, the individual must have "some level of positive reinforcement . . . available in order to provide the opportunity for . . . withdrawing that reinforcement" (Azrin & Holz, 1966, p. 392). Little would be accomplished by imposing a fine on someone who had no money, and it would be impossible to remove a primary reinforcer that had already been consumed.

RESPONSE COST ILLUSTRATED

A yardage penalty in football is also a response cost, as are breakage costs for college-dormitory residents. In schools, a typical informal use of response cost is removing points toward a grade or lowering a student's letter grade, contingent upon some unacceptable performance. As token systems are being used with greater frequency in various settings, response cost is illustrated by the removal of tokens contingent upon specific behaviors (see Unit 28 for an extended discussion of token economies with children and youth). In a classroom economy conducted by Sulzer and her colleagues (1971), as in other backups, there were fixed charges for certain disruptive behaviors. Whenever a student disturbed others at their work by throwing objects, tokens were charged.

ADVANTAGES OF RESPONSE COST

Strong and Rapid Behavioral Reduction

Several laboratory studies have been conducted (Weiner, 1964; 1969; Reese, 1966) on human performance under response-cost contingencies. Weiner found that, for many subjects, response cost rapidly reduced simple instrumental responses. Response cost has been used increasingly in applied settings because it suppresses problem behaviors rapidly. The procedure has rapidly and effectively suppressed violent behaviors of psychiatric patients (Winkler, 1970), aggressive statements and tardiness by predelinquent boys (Phillips, 1968; Phillips et al., 1971) off-task behavior and rule violations in classrooms (Iwata & Bailey, 1974), and many other mal-adaptive behaviors (see Kazdin, 1972, for an excellent integrated review of the procedure).

There does seem to be some variability in the effectiveness of response cost, probably resulting from individual histories (Weiner, 1969). Burchard and Barrera (1972) used a response-cost system designed to suppress such maladaptive behaviors as personal assaults, swearing, and property destruction in institutional-ized retarded adolescents. They found that even fairly steep fines reduced those behaviors for only five of the six youths; for the sixth youth, the results were in the opposite direction. This finding suggests the necessity of determining empiri-cally whether or not a particular cost technique can indeed reduce a given indi-vidual's performance.

Possible Long-Lasting Effects

In several studies it has been reported that response cost has produced persistent suppression of speech disfluencies (Kazdin, 1973; Siegel, Lenske & Broen, 1969) and weight gain (Harmatz & Lapuc, 1968). Other studies, however, have shown recovery of the target responses when the response-cost contingency has been removed (Birnbrauer et al., 1965; Iwata & Bailey, 1974). Although the reasons why are not known at the present time, it is the authors' guess that reinforcement and response-cost history, magnitude of the fine, length of time that contingencies remain in effect, and the schedule for removing contingencies are critical variables in determining the persistence of behavioral suppression.

Convenient Approach

Response cost can be a very convenient system, especially when used in conjunc-tion with point and token systems. The unwanted behavior is emitted; a token or point is removed immediately, quietly, and with little physical effort. In fact, it is suspected that, because response cost can be used so conveniently, it probably is used more often than it should be. For instance, George insults Jennifer, and the contingency manager says: "O.K. George. You're teasing. That will cost you 100 points!" Used with discretion, however, response cost could become a very effi-cient technique for eliminating behaviors with minimal disruption of other activi-ties. It would be easier to take a few points away from George when he was so disruptive that others were unable to do their jobs than to remove him from the room (timeout), scold him (punishment), or change his seat (changing S^Ds).

USING RESPONSE COST EFFECTIVELY

Allowing for Buildup of Reinforcement Reserve

For a response-cost system to function, it is necessary to allow the individual to build up a reinforcer reserve. If we assume that a token system has been instituted, then the clients must first be given the opportunity to accumulate lots of tokens—which usually occurs as a matter of course when a token system is introduced because such systems tend to be employed when weak behaviors are not sufficiently strengthened by the more usual reinforcers. Also, as we know, the best way to strengthen weak behaviors is to present reinforcement often. After the reserve has been accumulated it is possible to penalize certain performances by means of the contingent removal of specific numbers of tokens. Response cost probably has its strongest effect after a client has had an opportunity to cash in some of the tokens for the backup reinforcers. The client then works to avoid loss of the tokens. Such penalties, contingent upon specific behaviors, serve to reduce further occurrences of those behaviors. Whatever the response-cost system employed, this principle should hold. If, for instance, points toward a grade are used as reinforcers, the student should have the opportunity to earn a sufficient number of points before any of them is withdrawn.

Empirical Determination of Response-Cost Magnitude

Response cost, as suggested by Azrin and Holz (1966), has much in common with punishment. Both are aversive contingencies—one because positive reinforcers are removed, the other because aversive consequences are delivered. Both produce rapid and often permanent response suppression. Another similarity is in the intensity of the aversive consequences. Azrin and Holz (1966) found that, the more intense the aversive stimulus (for example, electric shock), the more effective the response suppression. The intensity of response cost is represented by the size of the fine. Indeed, Burchard and Barrera (1972) found that more severe costs, a thirty-as opposed to a five-token fine, suppressed maladaptive behaviors much more effectively. Such findings suggest that, if we are going to fine, we should impose a whopping fine! But there is a rub to this logic, for numerous studies have also reported success with minimal fines. Siegel and colleagues (1969) levied one-cent fines, and in some of our own work we have kept fine magnitudes to a minimum, yet the undesirable responses have been effectively suppressed. History probably plays a crucial role. If the individual has experienced a history of heavy fines, a small fine will have little effect. Otherwise, perhaps even a small fine will work well. In fact, in Burchard and Barrera's study (1972), the clients had had histories with contingencies that combined five tokens and five minutes of isolation (time-out) for serious infractions. Yet, when results of *either* five minutes of timeout *or* a five-token response cost were compared to those of either thirty minutes of time-out or a thirty-token response cost, the separate and smaller contingencies had weaker effects. Because the clients had already experienced the stronger combined contingency, the five-token fine seemed weaker by contrast. It is not surprising that the five-token fine had little effect in comparison with the much heavier thirty-token fine.

The way to select the appropriate cost to levy is again empirical. The maladaptive behavior must be monitored and various cost magnitudes attempted until the desired response suppression is reliably achieved. One word of caution, though: We should not increase the cost gradually, for then the client may adapt to the gradual increase (just as individuals have been noted to adapt to gradually increasing intensities of punishment). It is preferable either to return to baseline conditions for a fairly protracted period of time and then to implement the selected response-cost magnitude or to implement a much stronger cost suddenly and for several days and to monitor the effects.

Here is an example: Kent loves to shock his peers and group leaders by shouting out obscenities. His behavior disrupts the group regularly. Extinction and other positive procedures are rejected because too much of the group's time has already been wasted. Because the group has been operating on a point system, in which individually earned points are redeemable for optional activities, the contingency manager tries a response cost of one point for each episode. A one-point fine seems, however, to do no good. Ten points in this instance seem too harsh. So the cost contingency is dropped for a while, and a three-point fine is then instituted. Here is an instance of avoiding adaptation to aversive consequences by making the contrast sharper; rather than one point directly followed by three points, the sequence is one point, no points, three points. The three-point fine thus has a reasonable chance of suppressing the behavior.

Gregory has developed a charming habit: As other youths walk past his seat, he sticks out his foot and trips them. The tripped youth frequently falls, and the rest of the class laughs. Probably it is this laughter plus the consequences to the victim that maintain this obnoxious behavior. Each of the first few times that Greg pulls his stunt, the teacher fines him a point. Nevertheless, the behavior persists. The teacher then has the option of increasing the fine to two points or to some other level. Returning to a no-fine contingency is too risky, for the victims are in danger of being seriously hurt. The decision is made to implement a ten-point fine for tripping. Greg halts the behavior.

There are several other arguments for minimizing the magnitude of response cost, and they should be taken into account in the decision-making process. Very heavy costs may suppress not only the behavior of concern but other behaviors as well. If Kent is charged ten points every time he utters an epithet, he will soon be bankrupt with no chance of being able to earn an optional activity. He may then give up performing altogether, for what is the use? Then, of course, there is the humane desire not to be too harsh. Finally, as Doty, McInnis, and Paul (1974) have found, there may be problems in collecting fines that have been levied. Some fairly elaborate accounting procedures had to be developed in order to reduce refusals to pay fines.

Communicating the Rules of the Game

When individuals are informed of the specific contingencies operating upon their performance, they become more involved in determining the outcome of the situation. If clients are told that certain accomplishments will lead to specific gains and that other performances will lead to specific losses, they themselves participate in the contingency system. Sometimes it is helpful to have the clients role-play or to give them practice sessions to help them understand "the rules of the game." It is even possible for a group of clients to share in setting the response-cost penalties. Individuals can also impose contingencies upon themselves in order to achieve the goals that they seek. A client desiring acceptance at college can impose response-cost contingencies upon herself in order to achieve the necessary grade level. For instance, for every hour of television watching beyond the first two, $1 is donated to charity. As with any self-administered contingency, however, there is always the temptation not to apply it or to cheat. To overcome this problem, some contingency managers have found it helpful to return half the fine for correctly administering self-fines. Overall, this type of self-management is a step in the direction of self-control.[1]

Cost rules that are consistently implemented provide clients with a set of discriminative stimuli. Such and such behaviors will be penalized (S^D-s); others will be rewarded (S^Ds). The clients can learn to make discrimination more rapidly when the rules are available to them. The rules function as do other cues in the development of differential responses. Cost and earning rules are usually posted publicly for all participants to review. They serve as reminders that certain behaviors will lead to losses, others to gains, of specific quantities of reinforcers. Used in this manner, S^D-s function to inhibit (occasion low rates of) undesirable behaviors.

Combining Response Cost with Other Procedures

Response cost, like other reductive procedures, is not used in isolation but is combined with reinforcement of desired alternative behaviors. Because it frequently serves as a device for conveniently and rapidly reducing specific behaviors, response cost can be used *temporarily* to reduce interfering behaviors while alternatives are being strengthened. If a set of undesirable behaviors is suppressed, it is likely that the individual will begin to engage in approximations of more desirable behaviors. It will then be possible to shape or strengthen those behaviors. Ultimately, with increasingly frequent emission of the desirable behaviors, it should be possible to drop the cost contingency. A very high frequency of desirable behaviors will not allow the individual the opportunity to engage in frequent undesirable behaviors. An example is provided by a student whose noisy behavior disrupted the class. Initially the decision had been to give the student a point following each five minutes of quiet in-seat behavior. This system accomplished very little because the student almost never remained seated for five minutes. Two alternatives were then considered: to lower the time requirement for token reinforcement or to place a response-cost contingency upon the behavior. Because the first alternative would have required too much investment of time from the teacher, response cost was chosen. Each time the student threw an object in class, he was charged a specific number of points. He could earn the same number of points for five minutes of on-task behavior. On-task behavior increased sufficiently under those circumstances, and eventually it was rarely necessary to invoke the

[1] Skinner, in Part I of *Cumulative Record* (1961), and in *Beyond Freedom and Dignity* (1971), deals with such philosophical issues as freedom and self-control.

penalty. It would ultimately have been possible to dispense with the cost contingency altogether.

DISADVANTAGES OF RESPONSE COST

Several disadvantages of the response-cost procedure have already been suggested in the foregoing discussion. The fact that the procedure does not have a universally reductive effect, probably because of differences in reinforcement history, and the need for a reserve of conditioned reinforcers have already been mentioned. The danger of using penalties that are too large has also been mentioned. In addition, response cost, like other aversive contingencies, may generate escape and aggressive behaviors. When dessert is taken away, the child may throw a tantrum. Boren and Colman (1970) found that a group of delinquent soldiers with whom they used a fine system rebelled and stayed away from meetings. Other investigators (Doty, McInnis & Paul, 1974) have observed similar emotional reactions when extremely aggressive residents have refused to pay their fines, whereas some others have not found such results (Bucher & Hawkins, 1971). In our own work, we have found that, when fines are kept at reasonable levels and imposed without fanfare, while emotional reactions are ignored or, if serious, themselves fined, such reactions are not a major problem. One way that we have found particularly successful is to add the violations to the price chart of purchasable items. Clients can purchase time with a game for say twenty points and the opportunity to throw objects in the room for 100 points. We simply remark, when an object is thrown: "Oh, I see you just purchased the opportunity to throw something. I'll collect the 100 points." The semidazed client surrenders the points but is not eager to repeat such an expensive purchase in the future. Another method that we have found to work well is to return part of the fine if the client responds in a "responsibly adult manner," for example, paying the fine immediately and going right to work. This procedure has the added advantage of reinforcing responses incompatible with overt escape or aggressive reactions.

Some contingency managers have reported to us that they have been able to reduce the likelihood of aggressive reactions by using a modified response-cost system. We have chosen to call this procedure **bonus response cost**. Rather than taking away points or tokens that a client has earned, they have taken reinforcers away from a pool of potential bonus reinforcers. For example, Mrs. Ledger has set up a system for clients, who can earn tokens for engaging in various appropriate social and task behaviors. The clients and Mrs. Ledger have determined that each day will be started with ten bonus tokens. When a client misbehaves, a number of bonus tokens is lost. If no misbehaviors are emitted, all ten bonus tokens are received at the end of the day. Such a bonus response-cost system is worth trying in association with a regular reinforcement system, particularly to help control misbehaviors when regular response cost is considered inappropriate. It is important not to substitute bonus response cost for a regular reinforcement program, however. The reinforcement in this modified system is much too delayed for many clients.

REDUCING BEHAVIOR THROUGH STIMULUS CONTROL

Occasionally a situation arises in which it is important not only to reduce but also actually to inhibit or suppress a behavior that appears imminent. We shall use the term "inhibit"[2] when the presence of a particular antecedent stimulus (S^{D-}) results in a very low probability of occurrence for a particular behavior. This S^{D-} has acquired discriminative properties: The emission of the behavior *under those circumstances* is likely to be punished (or consequated by timeout or response cost). As tiny Tina approaches the hot stove, touching the stove must be inhibited. Let us discuss how these discriminative stimuli are developed and some of their advantages and disadvantages.

Stimuli Discriminative for Aversive Consequences

We have discussed how stimuli that precede, or are presented simultaneously with, response cost and other aversive consequences often acquire discriminative properties (S^{D-}s). They do so in a manner similar to that of development of stimuli discriminative for reinforcement (S^Ds). In the aversive situation, however, the discriminative stimulus serves not to occasion but in a sense to *inhibit* responding. Let us consider this illustration: Penelope has been goofing off in school for a few weeks. She now brings a report card with several failing grades. When her parents see the report card, they scold her and reduce her allowance. Henceforth, failing grades become discriminative for aversive consequences. When Penelope's next report card has failing grades, the probability that she will hand it to her parents is diminished: She conveniently misplaces the card.

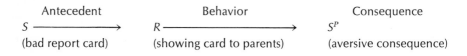

Antecedent	Behavior	Consequence
$S \longrightarrow$	$R \longrightarrow$	S^P
(bad report card)	(showing card to parents)	(aversive consequence)

When this sequence occurs repeatedly over time, the following pattern results:

$S^{D-} \longrightarrow$	R
(bad report card)	(inhibits showing to parents)

Advantages of Developing S^{D-}[3]

Although it is not our intention in this book to emphasize negative contingencies, there are some very clear advantages to developing stimuli that inhibit responding. Such signals may protect young children and dependent persons from danger, as when a parent shakes his head "no" as a youngster approaches an electrical outlet

---

[2] Other learning theorists (for example, Hull) use this term differently, to denote an internal state. The definition offered here is intended simply to describe a discriminative event.

[3] The symbol S^{D-} is sometimes used in place of S^Δ.

with a metal tool in hand. The S^{D-} may help the child to avoid the far more punishing contingency of electric shock. For behavior analysts who are charged with responsibility for a client's safety, it is important to know how to develop S^{D-}s effectively.

Developing Effective S^{D-}s

The S^{D-} is developed in the same manner as is the S^D (see Units 12–15), except that the consequence is aversive. Target responses emitted in the presence of potential S^{D-}s are consistently followed by aversive consequences demonstrated to be effective with the particular client. (We recommend the use of strong conditioned aversive stimuli, timeout, or response cost, rather than unconditioned aversive stimuli, whenever possible. Physical danger and ethical concerns contraindicate the latter.) Clear identification of the relevant stimulus properties is also important: "Any time you see a skull and crossbones—hands off." The client's attention should be focused on those properties. A study by Moser and Reese (1976) includes description of an instructional program designed to focus young retarded children's attention upon the letter forms found in such safety words as "poison" and "danger."

Disadvantages of S^{D-}s

The S^{D-} requires pairing responding with the presentation of negative consequences. As we frequently caution, such stimuli may generate aggressive, avoidance, and escape responses, so the procedure should be reserved for very serious cases. Because S^Δs, the stimuli that signal nonreinforcement, also serve to *inhibit* behaviors, they should be used whenever there is a choice (see Unit 12 for review of the means by which S^Δs are developed through pairing with nonreinforcement). A frown will develop inhibiting S^Δ properties if consistently paired with nonreinforcement, just as a frown paired with punishment acquires S^{D-} inhibiting properties. Although developing S^Δs through differential reinforcement may take longer (because extinction is involved) than developing S^{D-}s, the procedure is less aversive and generally preferable.

Summary

Although the effects of response cost may differ from individual to individual, it has often been found to reduce undesirable behaviors quickly and conveniently. In order to make effective use of this procedure, the client should have accumulated a reinforcement reserve, as illustrated in Figure 19.1, before being penalized with response cost. When *rapid* behavioral reduction is necessary and a reinforcement reserve has not been accumulated, the use of this procedure is of questionable value. The bonus response-cost procedure may, however, be applicable. Once a decision has been made to implement the procedure, the rules of the game should be communicated to the client before they are adopted, costs should be kept to a minimum, and the continued possibility of earning reinforcers like

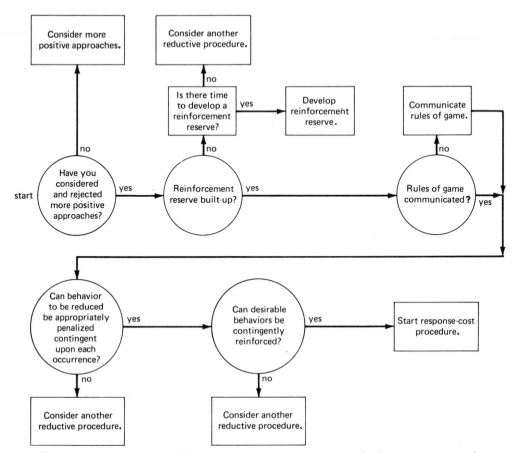

Figure 19.1   Response-cost flow chart. (We thank R. B. Benoit for his assistance in the development of this flow chart.)

points contingent upon desirable behaviors should *always* be part of the program. Response cost, because it is a negative approach, may promote aggressive and escape behavior. For that reason, it should be used sparingly and usually as a *temporary* expedient.

Antecedent stimuli paired with response costs or other aversive consequences, like timeout and punishment, acquire discriminative properties (S^{D-}), which serve to inhibit the occurrence of a behavior. Their advantages and disadvantages should be carefully reviewed before developing or implementing S^{D}-s.

References

Azrin, N. H. & Holz, W. C. Punishment. In W. R. Honig (Ed.), *Operant behavior: Areas of research and application.* New York: Appleton, 1966. Pp. 380–447.

Birnbrauer, J. S., Wolf, M. M., Kidder, J. D. & Tague, C. Classroom behavior of retarded pupils with token reinforcement. *Journal of Experimental Child Psychology,* 1965, **2,** 219–235.

Boren, J. J. & Colman, A. D. Some experiments on reinforcement principles within a psychiatric ward for delinquent soldiers. *Journal of Applied Behavior Analysis*, 1970, **3**, 223–233.

Bucher, B. & Hawkins, J. Comparison of response cost and token reinforcement systems in a class for academic underachievers. Paper presented at the meeting of the Association for the Advancement of Behavior Therapy, Washington, D.C., September 1971.

Burchard, J. D. & Barrera, F. An analysis of timeout and response cost in a programmed environment. *Journal of Applied Behavior Analysis*, 1972, **5**, 271–282.

Doty, D. W., McInnis, T. & Paul, G. L. Remediation of negative side effects of an on-going response-cost system with chronic mental patients. *Journal of Applied Behavior Analysis*, 1974, **7**, 191–198.

Harmatz, M. G. & Lapuc, P. Behavior modification of overeating in a psychiatric population. *Journal of Consulting and Clinical Psychology*, 1968, **32**, 583–587.

Iwata, B. A. & Bailey, J. S. Reward versus cost token systems: An analysis of the effects on students and teachers. *Journal of Applied Behavior Analysis*, 1974, **7**, 567–576.

Kazdin, A. E. Response cost: The removal of conditioned reinforcers for therapeutic change. *Behavior Therapy*, 1972, **3**, 533–546.

Kazdin, A. E. The effect of response cost and aversion stimulation in suppressing punished and non-punished speech disfluencies. *Behavior Therapy*, 1973, **4**, 73–82.

Moser, P. & Reese, E. P. Task difficulty as a variable in teaching word-recognition by fading and non-fading procedures. Paper presented at the meeting of the Eastern Psychological Association, New York, April 1976.

Phillips, E. L. Achievement Place: Token reinforcement procedures in a home-style rehabilitation setting for "pre-delinquent" boys. *Journal of Applied Behavior Analysis*, 1968, **1**, 213–223.

Phillips, E. L., Phillips, E. A., Fixsen, D. L. & Wolf, M. M. Achievement Place: Modification of the behaviors of pre-delinquent boys within a token economy. *Journal of Applied Behavior Analysis*, 1971, **4**, 45–59.

Reese, E. P. *The analysis of human operant behavior*. Dubuque: Brown, 1966.

Siegel, G. M., Lenske, J. & Broen, P. Suppression of normal speech disfluencies through response cost. *Journal of Applied Behavior Analysis*, 1969, **2**, 265–276.

Skinner, B. F. *Cumulative record*. (Enl. ed.) New York: Appleton, 1961.

Skinner, B. F. *Beyond freedom and dignity*. New York: Knopf, 1971.

Sulzer, B., Hunt, S., Ashby, E., Koniarski, C. & Krams, M. Increasing rate and percentage correct in reading and spelling in fifth grade public school class of slow readers by means of token systems. In E. Ramp & B. L. Hopkins (Eds.), *A new direction for education: Behavior analysis*. Vol. 1. Lawrence: University of Kansas.: Follow Through, 1971, pp. 5–28.

Weiner, H. Response cost effects during extinction following fixed interval reinforcement with humans. *Journal of the Experimental Analysis of Behavior*, 1964, **7**, 333–335.

Weiner, H. Controlling human fixed-interval's performance. *Journal of the Experimental Analysis of Behavior*, 1969, **12**, 349–373.

Winkler, R. C. Management of chronic psychiatric patients by a token reinforcement system. *Journal of Applied Behavior Analysis*, 1970, **3**, 47–55.

Reducing Behavior: Timeout

After mastering the material in this unit, you should be able to

1. Define and offer illustrations of
   a. Timeout
   b. Contingent observation
   c. Required relaxation

2. Define and illustrate the differences among extinction, timeout, response cost, and punishment.

3. List and discuss the advantages and disadvantages of timeout.

4. List and offer illustrations of the factors that influence the effectiveness of using timeout.

5. Describe specific situations in which timeout used by itself and combined with other behavioral procedures would and would not be the best behavioral procedure; justify your positions.

6. List and describe the safeguards that are helpful to include in a timeout program.

Seymour, Jacqueline, Esmerelda, and Fred form the "hard-core four" of a group of academic losers. They are assembled with others into a group of students with special needs, but their behavior is the basis for serious concern. Despite his extensive armamentarium of excellent instructional materials, their new teacher, Mr. F. R. Vescent, is rapidly becoming discouraged. Although the other students in the group staunchly attempt to complete their assignments, the hard-core four continually interfere. Egged on by the others, at least one seems always to be disrupting the larger group. All four steal pencils, hide work, tell jokes, clown, gang up during recess on peers who have "ratted" to the teacher, and in general impede efforts to provide a productive learning atmosphere. Mr. Vescent, well aware of the long histories of punishment and failure shared by these students, is reluctant to use punishment himself. But he finally realizes that, if any learning is to take place in the group, some reductive procedures will have to be implemented. Beside response cost, timeout is a procedure worthy of his consideration. Like response cost and punishment timeout is effective in reducing maladaptive behavior, and it may be appropriate to such a group.

After studying timeout fully discussed in this unit, the reader should be able to recommend a program for Mr. Vescent to follow.

TIMEOUT DEFINED

Timeout is a procedure by which *access to the sources of reinforcement is removed for a particular time period, contingent upon the emission of a response.*[1] It is similar to response cost in that both procedures involve the contingent withdrawal of reinforcement. But timeout does not involve the withdrawal of specific *amounts* of reinforcers as does the response cost procedure; rather, there is a contingent withdrawal of reinforcement for a specified period of *time.* Timeout is similar to extinction, for it too involves nonreinforcement. In extinction, however, the reinforcing stimuli are simply withheld; they are no longer delivered, contingent upon a response. Clarissa's suitor stops calling her because she never comes to the telephone when he calls. Cookies are withheld from the crying, demanding child, and crying and demanding lead to no change in the environment (no cookies are delivered). Extinction can be diagramed:

Extinction

$$R \xrightarrow{\hspace{3cm} /\!\!\rightarrow}$$

(telephoning Clarissa)

Telephoning Clarissa leads to no change in the environment

$$R \xrightarrow{\hspace{3cm} /\!\!\rightarrow}$$

(crying and demanding)

Crying and demanding leads to no change in the environment.

In timeout, however, something does occur in the environment, contingent upon the response. What occurs is *removal* of the opportunity to receive reinforcement. Either the individual is removed from the reinforcing environment, or the

---

[1] This definition is a variation of one offered by Reese (1966) combined with Ferster and Skinner's laboratory-derived definition (1957).

reinforcing environment is removed from the individual for some stipulated duration. Timeout can be illustrated by the crying child's being removed from the kitchen for a specific time (*t*)—in this instance for ten minutes—contingent upon crying for cookies. The opportunity to cry for cookies, therefore, no longer exists for that ten-minute period. (Another possibility is that the mother can contingently remove herself and the box of cookies from the kitchen, leaving the child in a nonreinforcing environment.) Timeout can be diagrammed thus:

Timeout

$$R \longrightarrow S^{to}$$
(crying, demanding)   (removal from room for ten minutes)

The individual is removed from the reinforcing environment for an amount of time.

Timeout differs from punishment in that the latter includes *presentation* of an aversive stimulus to reduce the rate of emission of a behavior, rather than the *withdrawal* of the reinforcing contingencies. Removing a client from a pleasurable group activity for five minutes because of clowning is a timeout procedure. The presentation of a verbal reprimand ("no") or even a smile can be called "punishment" for a particular client if its contingent application to the client's behavior results in *reduction* of that behavior. The operations that identify timeout and punishment are diagrammed this way:

Timeout	Punishment
$R \longrightarrow S^{to}$	$R \longrightarrow S^{p}$
(clowning) (five minutes out of room)	(clowning) ("No")
The client is removed from the room; the reinforcing environment is withdrawn.	An aversive stimulus is presented.

TIMEOUT ILLUSTRATED

Kevin pushes another youth into the pool; he is then ordered to sit on a bench for ten minutes. Mary sasses her mother; she is sent to her room. Robert throws a paper clip; the teacher sends him to stand in the cloakroom for a while. An entire class becomes rowdy; the children are all instructed to put their heads down for a brief period of time. A group of students in the senior class paint the statue of the school's namesake in psychedelic colors; they are suspended from school for a week. Vernon is caught in the act of taking money from another boy's coat pocket; he is required to stay at home for the weekend.

These episodes illustrate informal timeout contingencies in the natural environment. The reader can probably provide further illustrations, for timeout is commonly used.

ADVANTAGES OF TIMEOUT

Effective Reduction of Behavior

When a behavior-management procedure is frequently used, there is a good chance that it reinforces the users sufficiently often. Contingency managers are behaving individuals too. Procedures that reinforce them are maintained, and those that are reinforced intermittently are probably maintained even longer. Because of its widespread use, one can therefore assume that timeout works, at least temporarily or intermittently, in many settings.

Support for the assumption that timeout can be an effective reductive procedure is derived from many studies reported in the literature. Among them are some related to the reduction of undesirable client behaviors. Unable to control the disruptive behavior of delinquent boys around a pool table by means of other techniques, Tyler and Brown (1967) reported that brief confinement in a "timeout" room was useful in reducing misbehavior. Another study (Wolf, Risley & Mees, 1964) reported the use of a timeout procedure with an autistic boy. Each time that a temper tantrum occurred, they isolated the child from his peers and aides by placing him in a room for a few moments longer than the duration of the tantrum. His temper tantrums were virtually eliminated. A similar procedure was effectively used with the same child to reduce tantrums and pinching in school (Wolf et al., 1967). After trying another procedure (satiation) unsuccessfully, Lahey, McNees, and McNees (1973) were effectively able to control an obscene "verbal tic" (vocalizations accompanied by facial twitches) of a ten-year-old student through the use of timeout. After each occurrence of the "verbal tic" the student was removed from the classroom for a short period of time by his teacher. He was placed in an adjacent well-lighted 4×10-foot room that had originally been used for typing instruction. It was stripped of all objects and closed during the timeout period. Timeout "was quickly effective in this case" (1973, p. 104). Zeilberger, Sampen, and Sloane (1968) reported using a timeout procedure with Rorey, a four-and-a-half-year-old nursery-school child. Rorey's objectionable behaviors were screaming, fighting, disobeying, and bossing at home. The parents requested assistance from a behavior analyst. They were subsequently instructed to follow, under the behavior analyst's supervision, the following treatment:

1. Immediately after Rorey acts aggressively or disobediently, take him to the **timeout (TO) room**. [One of the family bedrooms was modified for this use by having toys and other items of interest to a child removed.] (boldface added)
2. As Rorey is taken to the TO room for aggressive behavior, say "you cannot stay here if you fight." As Rorey is taken to the TO room for disobedient behavior, say "you cannot stay here if you do not do what you are told." Make no other comments.
3. Place Rorey in the TO room swiftly and without conversation other than the above. Place him inside and shut and hook the door.

4. Leave Rorey in the TO room for two minutes. If he tantrums or cries, time the two minutes from the end of the last tantrum or cry.

5. When the time is up take Rorey out of the TO room and back to his regular activities without further comment on the episode, i.e., in a matter-of-fact manner.

6. Do not give Rorey explanations of the program, of what you do, of his behavior, or engage in discussions of these topics with him. If you desire to do this, have such discussions at times when the undesired behaviors have not occurred, such as later in the evening. Keep these brief and at a minimum.

7. Ignore undesirable behavior which does not merit going to the TO room. "Ignore" means you should not comment upon such behavior, not attend to it by suddenly looking around when it occurs.

8. Ignore aggressive or disobedient behavior which you find out about in retrospect. If you are present, treat disobedient behavior to other adults the same as disobedient behavior to you.

9. Reinforce desirable cooperative play frequently (at least once every five minutes) without interrupting it. Comments, such as "my, you're all having a good time" are sufficient, although direct praise which does not interrupt the play is acceptable.

10. Always reward Rorey when he obeys.

11. Special treats, such as cold drinks, cookies, or new toys or activities, should be brought out after periods of desirable play. It is always tempting to introduce such activities at times when they will interrupt undesirable play, but in the long run this strengthens the undesired behavior.

12. Follow the program 24 hours a day. (Zeilberger, Sampen & Sloane, 1968, p. 49)[2]

The employment of this timeout procedure, which was combined with the use of prompts (step 2), extinction (steps 7 and 8), and reinforcement (steps 9–11), decreased Rorey's objectionable behaviors.

USING TIMEOUT EFFECTIVELY

Removing Reinforcers that Support Undesirable Behavior

A teacher decided that she would try a timeout procedure with one of her students. Each time the child pushed or hit another child, he was told simply but firmly: "You cannot push. You must leave." Nothing more was said. (Further conversation might be reinforcing.) He was then immediately placed on a chair in the hall outside the classroom for five minutes. Things went along fine for a while.

[2] Reprinted by permission from J. Zeilberger, S. E. Sampen, and H. N. Sloane, Modification of a child's problem behaviors in the home with the mother as a therapist. *Journal of Applied Behavior Analysis*, 1968, **1**, 49. Copyright 1968 by the Society for the Experimental Analysis of Behavior, Inc.

His pushing and hitting behavior began to subside. But then the improvement seemed to stop. When the teacher investigated, she found that, several times when the child had been seated out in the hall, the principal had come by. Each time she had stopped, had asked the youngster why he was out in the hall, and had given him a sympathetic pep talk on the importance of getting along well with other children. Having never in the past received any attention from the principal, the child was probably being reinforced in his undesirable behavior by the well-intended, kindly lectures. A conference between the teacher and the principal cleared up the situation. The principal no longer stopped to chat when the child was on timeout in the hall. The undesirable behavior began to subside again, and timeout was again in effect and performing its function.

One of the authors had a similar experience while teaching in an inner-city school. Children who misbehaved while preparing for dismissal were told to return to their classroom and to remain after school for a while. Although this procedure was effective with some of the children, with others the reverse seemed to be true. Some children actually appeared to solicit the timeout. An informal analysis of the situation suggested that perhaps remaining in the classroom, watching the teacher decorate the room and performing other of her duties, may actually have been reinforcing. A switch in procedure showed that it was probably so. For these students, the teacher used staying after school and helping the teacher as a reinforcer for desirable classroom performance. The approach proved to be a powerful incentive for several students.

It is often difficult to identify and remove all sources of reinforcement in a situation. Identifying powerful reinforcers that sustain the behavior and removing access to them contingent upon a maladaptive behavior can, however, effectively suppress the behavior. McReynolds (1969) used ice cream as a reinforcer to facilitate a child's speech development. When the child lapsed into meaningless jargon, a timeout was instituted; it consisted of the experimenter's taking the ice cream and turning her chair away from the child. This timeout signaled nonreinforcement and produced a reduction of the jargon. One of the authors has used a similar procedure—dropping her head and remaining motionless for a brief duration—as a timeout consequence for whining, self-stimulation, and other events that interfere with instruction of autistic children.

A procedure called **contingent observation** (Porterfield, Herbert-Jackson & Risley, 1976) also contains elements of timeout. When children are working together in a group and certain maladaptive behaviors are emitted by one of its members, that child is placed a few feet away from the table. There the child has an opportunity to observe the others but not to participate in reinforceable learning responses.

Sometimes a person is so out of control that he cannot remain in the situation, nor can the milder timeout conditions described be implemented. Arranging a "quiet area" in a separate location could help. As all parents know, one such place is the child's bed—a place to calm down and relax. *Required relaxation* in bed was successfully used as an alternative to a timeout room to reduce rates of seriously maladaptive behaviors in adult males (Webster & Azrin, 1973). Alternatively, an empty room, an area behind a screen, or an alcove may suit this purpose. For persons who have been violently destructive, rooms without furniture or breakable windows have been used. Such isolation areas are probably not appropriate for persons other than those who are dangerously out of control[3] (see "Legal Sanctions," discussed later in this unit).

Avoiding Timeout from an Aversive Situation

Timeout from positive reinforcement can effectively reduce a behavior only if the individual's *environment changes from one in which reinforcement is available to one in which it is not*. The procedure will not work effectively if the environment switches from one in which *aversive* stimuli abound to one from which aversive stimuli have been removed. Esmerelda, who violently dislikes social studies, soon found that causing a disturbance when the subject was being taught would result in her being asked to leave the classroom. The teacher thus inadvertently negatively reinforced Esmerelda's disruptive behavior.

Avoiding Opportunities for Self-Stimulation

It is not wise to place in timeout a client who frequently engages in such self-stimulatory behavior as rocking, masturbation, or daydreaming. The nonreinforcing environment required for timeout conditions cannot be readily achieved with such a client. If placed in a nonstimulating isolated area, this client will probably engage in self-reinforcing activity. Rather than timeout, an opportunity for self-reinforcement will be provided; the target behavior will increase, rather than decrease, in frequency.

Ability to Implement and Maintain Timeout

Timeout is not a logical choice when the clients are so resistant that they cannot be placed and maintained in the timeout area. For large children and youths, this factor must be considered before final selection of this reductive procedure. Usually, youngsters will obey an authority figure and remain in timeout for the required duration. Some, however, may resist. When it is believed that unmanageable resistance will occur, timeout should not be selected (Benoit & Mayer, 1975). Becoming involved in a physical encounter with an adult in the presence of one's peers may actually reinforce some clients by contributing to their social status. If the resistance can be overcome, however, (that is, if the client is guided to the

---

[3] An alternative is to restrain dangerous behavior by means of camisoles or other devices. From a behavior-analysis point of view, the attention connected with implementation of such procedures may provide lots of inadvertent reinforcement for maladaptive behaviors, and they are advisable *only* when no other alternatives are available. Various legal decisions on restraint have been handed down. At this writing, it is probably legally acceptable for a qualified professional to give written orders for the *brief* use (a few hours or less) of safe restraints, provided that there is a written check each half-hour and that ten minutes of exercise are allowed each two hours. Behavior analysts should study current law, administration policies, and ethical standards when considering this procedure.

timeout area and, after attempting to leave it, is returned with five more minutes added on for the "attempted breakout"), timeout may prove effective.

Initial Use of Timeout as Consistently as Possible

Most people who have experience in working with children and youth know the importance of a consistent method of handling a particular situation. We have already discussed the need for consistently maintaining reinforcement and extinction conditions. With timeout, as well, consistency is a good idea (Zimmerman & Baydan, 1963). To reduce a behavior initially, the procedure should be applied as consistently as possible. Once it has been adequately reduced (to a predetermined criterion of no more than n responses per t time period), however, it may be possible to shift to an intermittent schedule. Such a shift was accomplished effectively in a study by Clark and colleagues (1973). An eight-year-old retarded child displayed behaviors that were considered disruptive and dangerous to other children: choking and attacking people, and materials. Consistent timeout was instituted following each category of behavior, one category at a time. Following substantial reductions in the behaviors, various timeout schedules were implemented. Low levels of the behaviors were maintained when the child was placed on timeout an average of each third response but not when the rate averaged only one in eight responses.

Keeping Duration Relatively Short

Logic may tell us that, if a little timeout works pretty well, a lot of timeout will work very well. But evidence suggests that this conclusion is correct only up to a point (Zimmerman & Baydan, 1963; Zimmerman & Ferster, 1963). It appears that, beyond a certain limit, longer timeouts provide no further reductive effect and sometimes even seem to disrupt behavior in other ways. In addition, there is some evidence to suggest that short timeouts are very effective (for example, Clark et al., 1973; Risley & Twardosz, 1974). In a study by Tyler (1965), outbursts by the youth resulted in a timeout period that lasted fifteen minutes; in two others (Wolf, Risley & Mees, 1964; Wolf et al., 1967) an autistic boy was isolated for brief periods of time, usually for a few minutes longer than the duration of any tantrum. In each instance, the undesirable behavior was reduced significantly. In another study (Bostow & Bailey, 1969), severe disruptive and aggressive behavior by two hospitalized retarded adults was reduced through use of a procedural package, one component of which was a two-minute timeout, the other differential reinforcement of desirable behaviors.

As with response cost, an individual's experience with timeout may influence the suppressive effects of various durations. White, Nielsen, and Johnson (1972) compared three different durations: one minute, fifteen minutes, and thirty minutes. They wished to determine whether or not the rate of suppression of severely disruptive behaviors in twenty institutionalized retarded persons was differentially affected by these various durations. On the average, both the fifteen-

and thirty-minute timeout periods produced greater suppression than the one-minute duration. But the one-minute duration did suppress behaviors effectively among five of six subjects for whom it was the first duration encountered. For those subjects who had already experienced longer durations, the one-minute duration had hardly any effect. In a study by Burchard and Barrera (1972) the maladaptive behavior of a group of mildly retarded adolescent boys was contingently treated with a five-minute timeout plus a five-token fine. The procedure was in effect for a two-year period. Then, when a comparison was made between a five-minute timeout *or* a five-token fine, maladaptive behavior increased. Apparently the weaker contingencies produced less suppression. Only a thirty-minute timeout or a thirty-token fine suppressed the behaviors appreciably by itself. The suggested moral is that, if we plan to use a brief timeout, we should not forget that the client is in timeout. Otherwise we build in a history of longer durations, and the brief one may lose its effectiveness. A signaling system, like a kitchen timer, can remind us that the time has expired; better still, a staff person, a friend, or another client can be assigned to monitor the timeout from a vantage point invisible to the client. The monitor can also ensure that the client is not in any danger.

Long timeouts can actually be risky, for the individual may adapt to the situation; then the procedure loses its effectiveness. Isolated for long periods of time, a client may find new means of obtaining reinforcement: self-stimulation, fantasizing, and so forth. Long timeout periods also present other problems. Some individuals may hesitate to enforce many lengthy timeouts for a particular behavior. A situation would then exist in which the timeout procedure would be inconsistently implemented, which would serve to defeat its effectiveness. Lengthy timeouts can also interfere with a client's learning. Let us suppose that every time a particular student engages in some specific behavioral category, he is sent to the principal's office for two hours. He thus misses the lessons given during that time. Because short timeout periods can be effective, there is no need to adopt long and potentially disruptive ones.

Clear Communication of Conditions for Timeout

A clear communication of the conditions under which timeout will be invoked will help clients to learn to discriminate acceptable from unacceptable behaviors, enhancing the reductive effects of the procedure. When Giselle and Griselda become embroiled in a fist fight, each is sent to a quiet place to calm down. When Dad hears the twins beginning to become upset with each other, he warns them, "Remember, if you can't play nicely with each other, you'll each have to go to a quiet place for a while." That warning, assuming that it has been regularly paired with the fighting ⟶ timeout contingency in the past, should inhibit the fighting.

Providing Desirable Alternative Behaviors

Provision of a desirable alternative behavior can substantially alter the effects of a timeout procedure. When such an alternative is made available, the behavioral reduction can occur more quickly and thoroughly. One study (Holz, Azrin & Ayllon, 1963) demonstrated this phenomenon with human subjects. When only one response was available to the subjects, timeout had only a minor reductive effect on the rates of performance. When a second response was made available to the subjects, the response treated with periodic contingent timeout was almost immediately eliminated. This idea can be transferred easily to applied situations. Let us assume that the painting of a symbolic object has become a traditional senior-class prank. If only one major symbol is available, perhaps the statue of the school's namesake, it will probably be painted. But let us suppose, on the other hand, that a large wall or billboard in the high school's main entry hall is made available to the senior class and that the students are allowed to decorate it to their hearts' content. Then the statue has a better chance of escaping unscathed. The chamber of commerce in one community does something similar around Halloween. Store windows are made available to children and youths to decorate. Contests are held for various artistic categories, and the children busily go to work decorating the windows. As a result, vandalism in the stores is minimal in that community on Halloween.

DISADVANTAGES OF TIMEOUT

Negative Contingency

The timeout procedure involves the withdrawal of the reinforcing environment. It is therefore a negative contingency. Stimuli paired with the timeout—like a frowning group leader pointing toward the timeout room—may acquire aversive properties. Ferster and Skinner (1957) have shown how a stimulus correlated with timeout can function as a punishing (that is, aversive) stimulus. An individual will usually work to avoid or escape from such stimuli and may even become aggressive in response to them (Oliver, West & Sloan, 1974). Most educators and clinicians prefer clients to be motivated *toward* achievement of positive goals (effective social behaviors, acquisition of scientific information, becoming more assertive, and other forms of "achievement"), rather than *away* from aversive circumstances (like a nonreinforcing environment). Timeout is ultimately a negative procedure.

Legal Sanctions

When timeout involves removing the client to an isolated room, the procedure can be labeled, from a legal perspective, *seclusion*. Case law related to seclusion then applies. Ennis and Friedman (1973) have cited court decisions establishing that adults, including those in seclusion, are entitled to adequate food, heat, light, ventilation, bedding, hygiene supplies, and clothing. Budd and Baer (1976) have reported several juvenile cases in which solitary confinement has been held unconstitutional. They have also singled out one case in particular, *Morales v. Turman* (1973), as applying to timeout procedures. They interpret specifications about dormitory confinement, placing a juvenile inmate alone in a locked room within his own dormitory, as relating to timeout. The *Morales* standard for the maximum duration of dormitory confinement is fifty minutes. The *Wyatt* decision (1972) has established judicial protections connected with seclusion of mentally handicapped institutional residents. Staff members are limited to isolating patients for no longer than one hour in emergencies in which they can harm themselves or others; a qualified mental-health professional must give the appropriate order in writing, and it must be put into effect within twenty-four hours or not at all. Each hour in seclusion the patient's physical and psychiatric condition is charted. Bathroom privileges are allowed.

For the mentally retarded seclusion is *prohibited* by the *Wyatt* decision, but "legitimate," professionally supervised "timeout" may be used in "behavior-shaping programs" (a term not defined in the decision). Another decision, *New York State Association for Retarded Children v. Rockefeller* (1973), prohibits seclusion of mentally retarded residents. In *Welsch v. Likins* (1974) it was decided that a baseline must be taken before timeout or seclusion and that it must be shown that the frequency of the objectionable behavior has decreased after the intervention. Otherwise timeout must be stopped.

The decisions in the *Wyatt, Carey,* and *Horacek* cases have direct implications for behavior modification. By outlawing or severely restricting seclusion as a treatment technique, the cases could well be interpreted as prohibiting a room-timeout procedure. This would seem to be a serious mistake, because timeout is one of the mildest aversive procedures available for handling undesirable behavior and has repeatedly been demonstrated to be a highly effective control technique (e.g., Bostow and Bailey, 1969; Clark, Rowbury, Baer, and Baer, 1973; Wolf, Risley, and Mees, 1964). When it is employed properly, timeout has three features which distinguish it from the usual seclusion, solitary confinement, or segregation practices. First, timeout is consistently administered contingent on occurrences of an undesirable behavior. Second, it is a brief procedure, often lasting between one and five minutes and rarely extending longer than 15 minutes (cf., Clark, Rowbury, Baer, and Baer, 1973; Risley and Twardosz, 1974). Third, the use of timeout is coupled with objective observation of whether or not it is fruitful in remediating the problem behavior. By contrast, traditional seclusion or solitary confinement procedures are usually employed on an unsystematic basis and, when used contingently, they are probably used for only extreme examples of the behavior. They are typically lengthy procedures, lasting hours or even several days, and with little or no monitoring of their effectiveness in modifying the undesirable behavior. Because of these important differences between the correct use of timeout and use of other seclusion practices, timeout would seem to be a humane and acceptable treatment procedure. It is to be hoped that future courts will recognize this distinction and, in so doing, specifically authorize room-timeout as a legitimate treatment procedure under the conditions outlined above. (Budd & Baer, 1976, pp. 214–215)

Public Reaction

An uninformed member of the public walks by a cubicle labeled "timeout booth" and recoils in horror. Some poor child is being kept in solitary confinement! A ruckus is raised, and the program is threatened—along with improvement in the client's behavior. Such episodes have been reported more than once. Perhaps, unaware that some act of serious destructiveness has been consequated by "timeout," we too might respond similarly. A number of *safeguards* will help to minimize the occurrence of such reactions:

1. Use the term "quiet place" rather than "timeout booth," a rather mechanistic sounding term. It does serve the purpose of quieting and relaxing an individual whose behavior is out of control.
2. Be sure that there is adequate lighting and at least a carpet on the floor. Placing a client in a room without furniture and nothing but a cold floor on which to sit is not very kind.
3. Remove all dangerous objects that the client is apt to use: items that can be torn from walls, objects with sharp corners, and anything that can be thrown or swallowed.
4. To prevent danger to the client, be sure that he can be observed. Set a timer to remind yourself when the timeout period has expired.
5. Use a quiet place only after more positive procedures, like reinforcing alternative responses, modeling, extinction, response cost, and such milder forms of timeout as *contingent observation* (Porterfield, Herbert-Jackson & Risley, 1976) have first been given reasonable consideration.
6. Obtain the informed consent of the client or the client's advocate, parent, or guardian, as well as permission of supervisors, before using the procedure. Check current policies and laws regulating the use of timeout and seclusion procedures.
7. Explain the procedure to visitors before they enter the setting. Mention all the safeguards that have been instituted, and show and interpret the baseline and intervention data that indicate effectiveness of the procedure.

Suppression of Other Behaviors

Timeout procedures may suppress other responses beside the target response. This result is more likely when the client has few S^Ds, or cues for discriminating the specific conditions under which the behavior is followed by timeout. In some instances, there may have been a failure to state rules clearly and consistently: "You may not bite—so you must go to the quiet room." In others, clients may be so disabled as to be incapable of making discriminations ("It's okay to talk here but not to bite people"). Such failure to discriminate was demonstrated in a study by Pendergrass (1972). Two severely retarded children were isolated for engaging in persistent high rates of misbehavior. Frequency records of the misbehaviors, as well as of some primitive social-interaction responses, were kept. While the timeout was in effect, the misbehavior diminished, but there was also a collateral reduction in social-interaction responses.

A Nonconstructive Contingency

In the absence of other procedures, like the reinforcement of alternative behaviors, timeout aims only to eliminate behaviors. Education and most therapies are devoted to the building of behavioral repertoires, rather than to their destruction. Such nonconstructive approaches can be justified only in certain situations. If the client's behavior interferes persistently with other activities or presents danger to others or to herself, a timeout procedure is justified. In less serious instances, a more positive approach is preferable.

Summary

Timeout from positive reinforcement is a procedure that has frequently demonstrated its effectiveness in reducing objectionable behavior. When the complete and consistent removal of opportunities to obtain reinforcement is made contingent upon a maladaptive

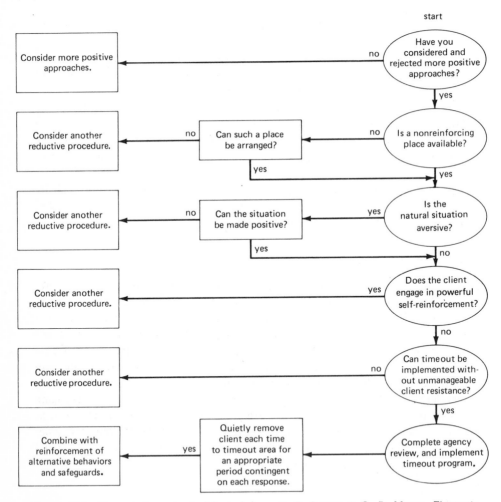

Figure 20.1 Timeout flow chart. Adapted from R. B. Benoit & G. R. Mayer. Timeout: Guidelines for its selection and use. *The Personnel and Guidance Journal*, 1975, **53**, 501–506.

behavior, while simultaneously alternative adaptive behaviors are reinforced, timeout reduces behavior effectively. By itself, however, it is neither positive nor constructive and should probably be limited to serious situations in which alternative reductive techniques would not do the job as expediently. The flow chart in Figure 20.1 summarizes the key points that should be considered *before* selecting and implementing timeout. Overlooking such factors reduces the likelihood of successful rate reduction.

References

Benoit, R. B. & Mayer, G. R. Timeout: Guidelines for its selection and use. *The Personnel and Guidance Journal,* 1975, **53**, 501–506.

Bostow, D. E. & Bailey, J. Modifications of severe disruptive and aggressive behavior using brief timeout and reinforcement procedures. *Journal of Applied Behavior Analysis,* 1969, **2**, 21–38.

Budd, K. & Baer, D. M. Behavior modification and the law: Implications of recent judicial decisions. *The Journal of Psychiatry and Law,* a special reprint, Summer 1976, 171–244.

Burchard, J. D. & Barrera, F. An analysis of timeout and response cost in a programmed environment. *Journal of Applied Behavior Analysis,* 1972, **5**, 271–282.

Clark, H. B., Rowbury, T., Baer, A. M. & Baer, D. M. Timeout as a punishing stimulus in continuous and intermittent schedules. *Journal of Applied Behavior Analysis,* 1973, **6**, 443–455.

Ennis, B. J. & Friedman, P. R. (Eds.). *Legal rights of the mentally handicapped.* Vols. 1–2. Practicing Law Institute, The Mental Health Law Project, Washington, D.C., 1973.

Ferster, C. B. & Skinner, B. F. *Schedules of reinforcement.* New York: Appleton, 1957.

Holz, W. C., Azrin, N. H. & Ayllon, T. Elimination of behavior of mental patients by response-produced extinction. *Journal of the Experimental Analysis of Behavior,* 1963, **6**, 407–412.

Lahey, B. B., McNees, M. P. & McNees, M. C. Control of an obscene "verbal tic" through timeout in an elementary school classroom. *Journal of Applied Behavior Analysis,* 1973, **6**, 101–104.

McReynolds, L. V. Application of timeout from positive reinforcement for increasing the efficiency of speech training. *Journal of Applied Behavior Analysis,* 1969, **2**, 199–205.

Morales v. *Turman,* 364 F. Supp. 166 (E.D. Tex. 1973).

New York State Association for Retarded Children v. *Rockefeller,* 357 F. Supp. (E.D. N.Y. 1973).

Oliver, S. D., West, R. C. & Sloane, H. N., Jr. Some effects on human behavior of aversive events. *Behavior Therapy,* 1974, **5**, 481–493.

Pendergrass, V. E. Timeout from positive reinforcement following persistent, high-rate behavior in retardates. *Journal of Applied Behavior Analysis,* 1972, **5**, 85–91.

Porterfield, J. K., Herbert-Jackson, E. & Risley, T. R. Contingent observation: An effective and acceptable procedure for reducing disruptive behavior of young children in a group setting. *Journal of Applied Behavior Analysis,* 1976, **9**, 55–64.

Reese, E. P. *The analysis of human operant behavior.* Dubuque: Brown, 1966.

Risley, T. R. & Twardosz, S. Suggested guideline for the humane management of the behavior problems of the retarded. Unpublished paper, State of Florida, Department of Health and Rehabilitative Services, Division of Retardation, 1974.

Tyler, V. O., Jr. Exploring the use of operant techniques in the rehabilitation of delinquent boys. Paper presented at the meeting of the American Psychological Association, Chicago, September 1965.

Tyler, V. O. & Brown, G. D. The use of swift, brief isolation as a group control device for institutionalized delinquents. *Behavior Research and Therapy,* 1967, **5**, 1–9.

Webster, D. & Azrin, N. H. Required relaxation: A method of inhibiting agitative-disruptive behavior of retardates. *Behavior Research and Therapy,* 1973, **11**, 67–78.

Welsch v. *Likins,* 373F. Supp. 487 (D. Minn., 1974).

White, G. D., Nielsen, G. & Johnson, S. M. Timeout duration and the suppression of deviant behavior in children. *Journal of Applied Behavior Analysis,* 1972, **5**, 111–120.

Wolf, M. M., Risley, T. R., Johnson, M., Harris, F. & Allen, E. Application of operant conditioning procedures to the behavior problems of an autistic child, a follow-up extension. *Behavior Research and Therapy,* 1967, **5**, 103–112.

Wolf, M. M., Risley, T. R. & Mees, H. L. Application of operant conditioning procedures to the behavior problems of an autistic child. *Behavior Research and Therapy,* 1964, **1**, 303–312.

Wyatt v. *Stickney,* 344 F. Supp. 373 (M.D. Ala. 1972 N.D.)

Zeilberger, J., Sampen, S. E. & Sloane, H. N. Modification of a child's problem behaviors in the home with the mother as a therapist. *Journal of Applied Behavior Analysis,* 1968, **1**, 47–54.

Zimmerman, J. & Baydan, N. T. Punishment of S responding of humans in conditional matching-to-sample by timeout. *Journal of the Experimental Analysis of Behavior,* 1963, **6**, 589–597.

Zimmerman, J. & Ferster, C. B. Intermittent punishment of S^Δ responding in matching-to-sample. *Journal of the Experimental Analysis of Behavior,* 1963, **6**, 349–356.

Reducing Behavior: Overcorrection

After mastering the material in this unit, you should be able to
1. Define:
   a. Overcorrection
   b. Restitutional overcorrection
   c. Positive-practice overcorrection
   d. Generality effect of overcorrection

2. List and discuss the advantages and disadvantages of overcorrection.

3. List, discuss, and illustrate the factors that influence the effectiveness of overcorrection.

4. Describe specific situations in which overcorrection would and would not be the behavioral procedure of choice. Justify your position.

Let us suppose that Pearl, who spends so much of her day engaging in stereotyped hand rituals, has been treated with both Alt-R and DRO procedures as part of a program to help her learn more adaptive behaviors. But the hand rituals occur so often that a reinforceable adaptive alternative has rarely been emitted, and there have not been many reinforceable intervals of time during which the hand movements were absent. Response cost has done little good, for there were few effective reinforcers to remove, and timeout would make no sense, for the behavior could easily continue while Pearl was isolated. In this instance, overcorrection may prove to be temporarily expedient. If the rate of the hand ritual can be reduced enough to make it possible to teach Pearl a few adaptive behaviors, then Alt-R or DRO would have more opportunity to succeed.

OVERCORRECTION DEFINED AND ILLUSTRATED

Overcorrection is a reductive procedure that was developed by Foxx and Azrin (1972). It may prove particularly useful in situations in which extinction, positive reductive procedures, response cost and timeout have little chance of succeeding. Overcorrection is a specific type of mild punishment designed to minimize the negative reactions caused by intense punishment. It has two basic components: "1) To overcorrect the environmental effects of an inappropriate act, and 2) to require the disruptor intensively to practice overly correct forms of relevant behavior" (Foxx & Azrin, 1973, p. 2). The first component is called **restitutional overcorrection** and is used when environmental disruption results from an inappropriate act. It requires that the individual restore the environment to a state much better than before the act. For example, a student who has overturned his desk will be required not only to put it back in its correct upright position but also to dust and clean it. A youth who marks up a wall is required not only to erase the marks but also to clean the entire wall.

The second component is **positive-practice overcorrection**; it involves repeated practice of a positive behavior. For example, the student who has overturned the desk would also be required to straighten, dust, and clean other desks in the room in addition to his own. The youth who has marked the wall may also be required to copy a set of patterns or forms on a bulletin board or piece of paper. The latter component accounts for the reeducation aspect of the procedure. In our examples the clients are taught positive or correct ways of treating desks and where and how to use pencils, crayons, or markers. Let us suppose that Flossie, despite fines, timeouts, and reinforcement for cleaning up, still continues to leave objects all over the living room. She should not only have to straighten the living room but also be required to straighten and clean another room in the house as well. In one study individuals receiving toilet training cleaned up traces of their accidents, washed their soiled clothing, showered themselves, and redressed in fresh clothing (Azrin & Foxx, 1971). Institutionalized retarded adults were taught not to steal one another's food: Not only were they required to return the snacks that they stole but also they had to practice the positive action of giving their own snacks to their victims (Azrin & Wesolowski, 1974). Foxx and Azrin (1972) have described another example of overcorrection for individuals who frequently fought or annoyed others. They did not cause physical damage, but they did cause a psychological disturbance or annoyance. They were required to apologize not only to the person disturbed but also to everyone present.

When no environmental disruption is created by an inappropriate act, restitutional overcorrection is not applicable; only positive practice is then used. One example is self-stimulatory behavior. Foxx and Azrin have described a child who frequently engaged in self-stimulatory head weaving:

Randomly weaving one's head from side to side is nonfunctional behavior because the behavior is independent of external control. Since head-weaving creates no environmental disruption, a Restitutional Overcorrection procedure is not applicable as a treatment. The Positive Practice Overcorrection rationale, however, could be used to teach and motivate the head-weaver to hold her head in a sustained orientation (not moving) and to move only for functional reasons, i.e., when instructed to do so. This Overcorrective Functional Movement training procedure would thereby be educative because the individual would be learning specific movements to specific directions, such as up, down, left, or right.

Any time that Tricia began head-weavnig, she was immediately given Functional Movement Training for five minutes. In beginning the training, the teacher used her hands to restrain Tricia's head. The teacher then instructed Tricia to move her head in one of three positions, up, down, or straight by stating, for example: "Tricia, head up." If Tricia did not immediately move her head in the desired direction, the teacher manually guided Tricia's head. Eventually, Tricia should respond to the verbal instructions alone in order to avoid the trainer's guidance as in conditioned avoidance (Azrin, Holz, and Hake, 1962). Tricia was required to hold her head stationary for 15 seconds, at the end of which another instruction was given. If Tricia moved her head during the 15-second period, the trainer immediately restrained her head. As Tricia began following the directions, the teacher faded out the manual guidance, but continued to "shadow" Tricia's head with her hands. The instructions were given randomly to ensure that Tricia was learning each individual instruction and not a sequence of instructions. (1973, p. 7)

ADVANTAGES OF OVERCORRECTION

Minimizing Disadvantages of Punishment

Overcorrection appears less likely than intense punishment to produce excessive negative generalization, withdrawal, aggression, or negative self-comments. It is not a painful procedure, nor does it provide an aggressive model. In fact, the modeled behavior is positive and constructive: Engaging in the positive practice of polite behavior as a consequence of rudeness may well provide positive instruction to peer observers.

Rapid and Long-Lasting Reduction

Overcorrection brings very rapid and long-lasting effects. For example, Foxx and Azrin have reported that "Overcorrection procedures reduced self-stimulation substantially on the first day and to a near zero level by the end of ten days and sometimes sooner" (1973, p. 11). They also found the reduction more rapid, complete, and long-lasting than that achieved by other separately applied reductive procedures like timeout, punishment (disapproval or slaps), and reinforcement of competing behavior when used on aggressive-disruptive behaviors (1972) and self-stimulating behaviors (1973). This finding is probably a function of the fact that new adaptive behaviors, apt to be supported by the natural environment, were substituted for the maladaptive ones.

Educative

Overcorrection teaches the client appropriate behaviors. It is not a means of inflicting discomfort, but a means of educating the client in desired patterns of behavior. The client—and not the teacher, parent, clinician, or someone else—must expend considerable effort to correct his own offenses. Educative procedures tend to be much more palatable to school personnel, administrators, parents, and the public.

USING OVERCORRECTION EFFECTIVELY

Ensuring Relevance to Misbehavior

If restitution or positive practice activity is not directly related to the misbehavior, the procedure is likely to seem arbitrary and punitive. Furthermore, as Foxx and Azrin have noted, "This characteristic of relevance should also motivate the educator to apply the restitution procedure since the educator would otherwise be forced to correct the general disturbance himself" (1972, p. 16). It is important that the misbehaving client directly experience the effort normally required by others to undo the disruption created by his misbehavior. For example, the client who overturns the desk is asked to set it upright and to dust and clean it. Clients who frequently had their hands in their mouths (Foxx & Azrin, 1973) or bite their hands (which resulted in formation of calluses that were then irritated, reddened, and torn open; Barnard et al., 1974) were required to brush their gums and teeth with a toothbrush that had been partially immersed in a container of oral antiseptic (mouthwash) and to wipe their outer lips with a washcloth that had been dampened with the antiseptic. This restitutional activity was initially selected by Foxx and Azrin because "mouthing of objects or parts of one's body results in exposure to potentially harmful micro-organisms through unhygienic oral contact. The Restitutional Overcorrection rationale suggests that this possibility of self-infection be eliminated" (1973, p. 4). In addition to the two-minute oral-hygiene procedure, the clients in the study by Barnard and colleagues (1974) were required to engage in two minutes of washing the affected areas, using a cotton swab and mild soap; one minute of hand drying; and two minutes of rubbing hand cream into the affected area. (A kitchen timer was used to determine the time.) Mouthing or biting hands was substantially reduced among all children in both studies.

Because Pearl's repeated self-stimulating hand movements back and forth before her face do not disrupt the environment, restitution would not be necessary. Relevant positive practice activities would be appropriate, however. Practice of appropriate hand positions could, for example, be required: waving "hi" and "bye-bye" under appropriate circumstances, manipulating constructive play objects, and so on. Can you think of some other positive-practice behaviors that would be relevant in this instance?

Consistent and Immediate Application

As we shall emphasize later, punishment is more effective when it is applied consistently and immediately. Also, immediate application of overcorrection every time that the misbehavior occurs promotes extinction conditions because clients have little or no time to be reinforced by the product of their misbehavior (Azrin & Hutchinson, 1967; Foxx & Azrin, 1972). In the example of the retarded adults who stole snacks from one another (Azrin & Wesolowski, 1974), the reinforcement was rapidly eliminated by the requirement that the stolen food be returned immediately, which changed the annoyance of the victim (apparently reinforcing to some of the culprits) to pleasure, by providing the victim immediately with additional snacks.

Extending Duration Without Reinforcement

While clients are engaged in overcorrection activities, their access to reinforcement or other reinforcing activities is removed (that is, a timeout condition is in effect). Consequently, the time involved should be greater than that needed simply to correct a wrong (for example, setting a chair upright). The duration should extend beyond the time needed to restore the environment. As pointed out in Unit 20, on timeout, this period *should not* be excessively long. Depending upon the behavior, two to fifteen minutes beyond the time needed to restore the disrupted environment is usually plenty.

To ensure that timeout conditions are approached during the overcorrection procedure, reinforcement must be kept to a minimum. Attention, praise, and approval should be avoided. Foxx and Azrin, in working with brain-damaged individuals who demonstrated aggressive-disruptive behaviors, were confronted with the problem of how to occasion the performance of overcorrection behaviors without using reinforcement. They concluded:

If direct positive reinforcement must be minimized during the restitution period, some procedure must be used for assuring the restitutive performance. Verbal instructions, if sufficient, should be one such alternative. Another satisfactory alternative is physical guidance in which the educator manually guides the desired movements using as much bodily pressure as necessary but reducing such pressure immediately as the offender begins to perform the movement voluntarily. If the desired movement slows down or stops, just enough pressure should be immediately reapplied to restore the movement to the desired rate. The slight annoyance caused by having one's limbs moved should serve as a motivator to initiate voluntary actions. The two procedures of verbal instruction and graduated guidance in combination should constitute a conditioned avoidance situation and lead to the instructions alone being effective. (1972, pp. 16–17)

Keeping Performance Consistent During Overcorrection

As already implied, it is important (if possible) for clients actively to perform the overcorrection activity without pause. Furthermore, it should involve the aversive feature of additional work and effort. For, as Foxx and Azrin have indicated, "an increased work or effort requirement is known to be annoying and serves as an inhibitory event" (1972, p. 16). However, *excessive force* should be avoided as injuries could result. It is best to wait patiently until violent resistance subsides.

Combining Overcorrection with Reinforcement of Alternative Behaviors

Overcorrection, like all the other reductive procedures discussed in this textbook, will have more lasting and rapid effects when combined with reinforcement of alternative behaviors at times other than during the correction period. When the client is behaving appropriately, other than during overcorrection—for example tidying her desk or assisting others—reinforcement is delivered. Opportunities *must* be made available for the client to obtain reinforcement for engaging in constructive behaviors.

DISADVANTAGES OF OVERCORRECTION

Limited Research

Because overcorrection is new, its use has not yet been reported in a wide variety of settings or with a variety of subjects or behaviors. Recent evidence suggests that its effectiveness may vary among behaviors or subjects. For example, Barnard and colleagues (1974) tried an overcorrection procedure on the head-banging behavior of three children aged four years, three years, and eighteen months. The older children's head banging resulted in bruises, bumps, and lacerations. The oldest had even fractured his skull. The youngest, on the other hand, had never injured himself. An attempt was made to have each child engage in the following overcorrection procedure after each occurrence of head banging: application of an ice pack to the head for three minutes, washing the bumped area for two minutes, drying the head for one minute, and combing or brushing the hair for one minute. Head banging was rapidly reduced in the two older children but not in the youngest. Perhaps the eighteen-month-old child was too young to engage in the procedure. It seems that the parents would have had to give him a lot of physical guidance that may have resulted in reinforcement. In any event, as the authors noted, "this new treatment procedure for head-banging seems very effective for some children, but probably warrants further exploration" (1974, p. 7).

The conclusions drawn about overcorrection have been based on a small number of studies. We believe that the procedure holds promise for practitioners as a palatable and effective means for reducing destructive and nonfunctional behaviors. Overcorrection may be just the procedure to allow Pearl to begin to engage functionally with her environment. It should, however, be regarded as experimental until more demonstrations appear in the literature.

Difficulty in Selecting Restitution Activity

The restitution activity must be relevant to the misbehavior. Sometimes it may be difficult to figure out just what the activity should be. (What would be an appropriate restitution procedure for the behavior of peeking under a lady's skirts?) When immediate action is called for, identifying an appropriately relevant activity on the spot can pose a problem. Perhaps research and experience with this procedure will help to resolve such difficulties. An alternative potential solution to this problem has been suggested in a study by Epstein and colleagues (1974). Their results suggest that an overcorrection procedure found effective for one behavior can be used to weaken a topographically different problem behavior. After a "hand" overcorrection procedure involving arm and hand exercises had been used with Andy and Bob, who demonstrated inappropriate hand movements, the same procedure was applied to Andy's inappropriate foot movements and Bob's inappropriate vocalizations. "Results for both children indicated that the hand overcorrection procedure suppressed inappropriate hand movements and inappropriate behaviors that were topographically dissimilar" (Epstein et al., 1974, p. 385). Nevertheless, this possible solution is certainly no panacea. First, as the investigators themselves noted, "more research is needed before specific overcorrection procedures can be recommended for any and all misbehaviors" (1974, p. 389). Second, if this **generality effect of overcorrection** is used, the prime educational advantage of overcorrection is lost, and the consequences are no longer relevant to the misbehavior. In essence, the procedure ceases to be overcorrection and becomes punishment. We need carefully to weigh the advantages and disadvantages of capitalizing upon the possible generality effects of overcorrection. This point is particularly important in light of *Morales* v. *Turman* (1973), which declares that repetitive nonfunctional tasks lasting "many hours" constitute cruel and unusual punishment in violation of the Eighth Amendment to the Constitution. (It should be noted that standard overcorrection procedures *are* functional, in that they are educative and correct the disturbed situation. They also span durations of thirty minutes or *less*, rather than many hours.) Each of these factors must be considered before a practitioner uses or recommends procedures based upon the possible generality effect of overcorrection for the sake of expediency.

One-to-One Ratio between Personnel and Students

Overcorrection studies have reported rapid results. Yet, as we have mentioned before, there is a requirement that the overcorrection procedure be instituted immediately and for a preestablished duration. In order to ensure consistent implementation of the consequences, the undivided attention of a staff member is necessary. Although conceivably a contingency manager, perhaps a classroom teacher, could oversee such activities, such a solution may not always be feasible. If the restitution activity is that the student right all overturned desks, someone must watch to see that he does so. If difficulty is encountered in righting the desks, physical guidance will have to be used (see Unit 14). Whenever physical guidance is necessary, however, safeguards *must* exist to *ensure* that extreme force, which may harm or endanger the client, is not permitted.

Before electing to employ such a procedure, therefore, it is necessary to consider in detail both the client, on one hand, and restitution and overcorrection activities, on the other, and to decide whether or not staffing is adequate for the anticipated duration of the procedure.

An Aversive Procedure

Like punishment, overcorrection is an aversive procedure, and most of the same disadvantages exist as for punishment, though generally to a lesser extent because of its milder nature. It should be used with caution, and its potential side effects should be constantly monitored. Under optimal conditions, the educative value of overcorrection may overshadow the aversive aspect and serve to develop new behaviors whose *subsequent* repetition can be reinforced positively. To this end it is particularly important to select a closely relevant task and to withhold reinforcement until completion of the overcorrection procedure.

Summary

Overcorrection is a punishment procedure that contains an educational component. It requires the individual to restore the environment to an improved state and to practice a positive behavior repeatedly. Although its broad systematic application in varied settings remains to be studied, it appears to be potentially useful for specific situations.

The overcorrection procedure has been placed toward the end of the units on reducing behavior because it is often intrusive and aversive, though less so than intense punishment. The repeated acts of restitution and positive practice can become aversive and interfere with other activities. In addition, because the procedures have been studied only to a limited extent, because it is sometimes difficult to select an appropriate restitutional activity, and because it requires additional staff time, overcorrection should be selected only after all concerned persons capable of understanding the procedure have consented to its use. Informed consent by clients or their advocates and by their parents or guardians is essential. Continuous supervision of staff implementation of the procedure is also a must. Because it is sometimes necessary to guide the restitution and positive-practice behaviors initially, it may be tempting to use undue force to guide the behavior. *Forcible guidance, to the extent that it may cause physical injury, should not be used.* If the client is vigorously resisting, the instructor must wait patiently, maintaining contact if possible, until the client calms down sufficiently to allow his movements to be guided. During that interval it is important that reinforcement in the form of attention be withheld. The instructor should avoid making visual contact and becoming involved in a physical altercation. For many clients, the latter could be powerfully reinforcing, and either the instructor, the client, or both might be hurt.

In order to avoid abuse of the procedure, an adequate number of trained staff must be available, as well as patient instructors and responsible supervisors. Otherwise the procedure should not be used. Assuming that overcorrection does achieve results as rapidly as the literature reports, however, such staffing requirements could probably be readily justified. Even with all the safeguards operating, overcorrection is still best reserved for very resistant behaviors, those that are seriously disruptive or dangerous, or situations in which few adaptive alternative behaviors are available to be strengthened.

References

Azrin, N. H. & Foxx, R. M. A rapid method of toilet training the institutional retarded. *Journal of Applied Behavior Analysis*, 1971, **4**, 89–99.

Azrin, N. H., Holz, W. C. & Hake, D. F. Intermittent reinforcement by removal of a conditioned aversive stimulus. *Science*, 1962, **136**, 781–782.

Azrin, N. H. & Hutchinson, R. R. Conditions of the aggressive behavior of pigeons by a fixed-interval schedule of reinforcement. *Journal of Experimental Analysis of Behavior,* 1967, **10**, 195–204.

Azrin, N. H. & Wesolowski, M. D. Theft reversal: An overcorrection procedure for eliminating stealing by retarded persons. *Journal of Applied Behavior Analysis,* 1974, **7**, 577–581.

Barnard, J. D., Christophersen, E. R., Altman, K. & Wolf, M. M. Parent mediated treatment of self-injurious behavior using overcorrection. Paper presented at the meeting of the American Psychological Association, New Orleans, August 1974.

Epstein, L. H., Doke, L. A., Sajwaj, T. E., Sorrell, S. & Rimmer, B. Generality and side effects of overcorrection. *Journal of Applied Behavior Analysis,* 1974, **7**, 385–390.

Foxx, R. M. & Azrin, N. H. Restitution: A method of eliminating aggressive-disruptive behavior of retarded and brain damaged patients. *Behavior Research and Therapy,* 1972, **10**, 15–27.

Foxx, R. M. & Azrin, N. H. The elimination of autistic self-stimulatory behavior by overcorrection. *Journal of Applied Behavior Analysis,* 1973, **6**, 1–14.

Morales v. *Turman,* 364 F. Supp. 166 (E.D. Tex. 1973).

Reducing Behavior: Punishment

After mastering the material in this unit, you should be able to
1. Define and offer illustrations for each of the following terms:
   a. Punishment
   b. Aversive stimulus
   c. Punishing stimulus (S^P)
   d. Unconditioned aversive stimulus
   e. Conditioned aversive stimulus

2. Compare and contrast the various types of aversive stimuli described in this unit, and describe how each is developed.

3. List and discuss the advantages and disadvantages of punishment.

4. List, discuss, and illustrate the factors that influence the effectiveness of punishment.

5. Describe and illustrate how to develop an S^{D-} by means of punishment.

6. Discuss why punishment is used so frequently.

7. Describe specific situations in which punishment would and would not be the behavioral procedure of choice. Justify your positions.

One of the most sensitive issues in a great many communities in America is the subject of discipline[1] in community facilities, schools, and homes. What is usually meant by "discipline" is the application of punishment, frequently corporal pun-

---

[1] The punishment section of this unit is an extension of an article by Mayer, Sulzer, and Cody (1968).

ishment. Parents are divided into factions on this subject. Some favor the use of punishment as a means of teaching children respect for authority. Others object to letting "strangers" administer corporal punishment to their children.

Professionals in public facilities find themselves in equal perplexity about the use of punishment. Some authorities believe that "to spare the rod spoils the child." At the other extreme authorities preach the gospel of permissiveness and allowing for "self-expression." Even laws and judicial decisions provide no clear-cut guidelines. According to Budd and Baer (1976), the *Wyatt* decision limits the use of electric-shock devices with mentally retarded residents to "extraordinary circumstances, to prevent self-mutilation leading to repeated and possibly permanent physical damage to the resident and only after alternative techniques have failed." Shock treatments may be administered only after approval of the institution's human-rights committee; with the express and informed consent of the resident or, if he is incapacitated, the next of kin; and under the direct and specific order of the superintendent (Budd & Baer, 1976). The *Wyatt* decision prohibits nonvoluntary electric shock treatment of mentally ill institutional residents. The rights of public schools to use corporal punishment continue to be debated in state and Federal courts, however. Quite naturally, the adherents of these extreme positions insist that what they favor is best for the child. This conflict leaves professional practitioners, like school and agency personnel, in something of a dilemma. For behavior analysts, questions of morality and legality are difficult to resolve, for they involve subjective judgments of individual rights, as well as of relative risks and benefits of therapy (Stolz, 1975).

Our intention in this unit, however, is not to provide philosophical or emotional support for or against the use of punishment. Rather, the major thrust will be to present the empirical evidence that is available on this topic. We trust that behavior analysts will operate within the guidelines of their professional ethical codes; follow the U.S. Department of Health, Education and Welfare *Guidelines for Human Subjects Research*, particularly as they relate to the informed consent of clients capable of understanding the procedure or of advocates, parents, or guardians; obtain approval through institutional and consumer review; provide for continual supervision of the program to ensure that procedures are implemented as described; develop their own personal ethical frame of reference; stay fully informed of all legal developments affecting their practice; and incorporate in program reports statements of moral, ethical, and legal client safeguards[2] (see Units 3, 7, 34, 35).

In this unit, readers will not be told what is right and wrong about the use of punishment; instead they will be informed of the variables that appear to make punishment effective, as well as of the behavioral results and side effects that have been identified. Perhaps they will come to the same conclusion about the use of punishment that we have: Punishment is a procedure that generally should be reserved for serious maladaptive behaviors, like extreme destructiveness toward

---

[2] Many state agencies are developing policies on the use of aversive procedures with clients (see Connecticut Office of Mental Retardation Policy #9).

oneself or others and negative behaviors that persistently interfere with the adaptive functioning of clients and peers.

Even though the information to be presented has been empirically derived, it should be regarded as tentative, for there are relatively few published reports of punishment techniques experimentally analyzed in applied settings. This lack is probably owing to the serious ethical, moral, and legal issues connected with such studies. Those studies that do appear in the literature on applied behavior analysis, for example Lovaas and Simmons (1969) and Risley (1968), have been limited to the remediation of dangerous self-destructive behaviors or of seriously debilitating chronic behaviors. Consequently, many of the conclusions presented in this unit are based on extrapolations from laboratory studies. Once practitioners become familiar with these research findings and the possible implications for particular settings, however, their decisions on punishment practices should be based on ground firmer than simply feeling and "intuition."

PUNISHMENT DEFINED

The term "punishment" has many connotations. Some see it as a physical pain applied by one or more individuals to another individual or group. For example, a mother wishes to convince her son that it is naughty to pull the tablecloth off the table. She slaps his hands vigorously so that he really feels it. She apparently believes that it is the pain that enhances the probability of his learning that tablecloth snatching is bad.

Others view punishment as a psychological "hurt" administered to an individual or a group. An example of this notion is the teacher who holds a youth up to public ridicule before the class. Apparently, he believes that the best way to teach students that they have done something wrong and that they should not do it again is to shame or embarrass them, that is, to "hurt" them psychologically.

Furthermore, an event may be described as punishing by the person who administers it while the recipient does not actually feel punished. For example, adults are likely to identify spanking as a punishing activity. Yet a child or youth may solicit spankings because of the concurrent reinforcement in the form of attention. Spanking is then not necessarily punishing.

In other situations, different interpretations are attached to the term "punishment." Because of the ambiguity of the term, it must be clarified before we can conduct a meaningful discussion on the topic. We have therefore selected an operational definition paraphrasing one offered by Azrin and Holz (1966): *Punishment is a procedure in which the presentation of a stimulus contingent upon a behavior reduces the rate of emission of the behavior.* Punishment can be said to have occurred only if the individual's rate of emitting the dependent behavior has been demonstrably reduced. Punishment, like reinforcement, is defined solely by its effect upon behavior. Any procedure is therefore identified as punishing if it involves a stimulus event that contingently follows a given behavior and reduces its rate. If a father reprimands his child for interrupting him and the interruptions then cease, the reprimand has been punishing. If, however, interruption continues with the same or greater regularity, the event has not been punishing. In fact, if the interrupting behavior increases in rate, the reprimand has been reinforcing, rather than punishing.

AVERSIVE STIMULI

The stimulus that functions as a punisher may be labeled an **aversive**[3] **stimulus**. In most instances, when a given stimulus functions as a punisher it also functions as a stimulus that the individual will actively work to remove or avoid. Although there are some occasional exceptions to that rule (Church, 1963; Solomon, 1964), the term "aversive stimulus" is used in this book to apply to both classes of stimuli: punishing (S^P) and negatively reinforcing stimuli.

Unconditioned Aversive Stimuli

Some types of stimuli have universally punishing effects. Strong physical blows, electric shocks, very bright lights, and very loud sounds are examples. Any of those intense stimuli that are administered contingent upon a specific behavior will generally serve to reduce its rate of emission unless the individual has become adapted to the aversive stimulus. When a small child is severely spanked for dashing out into the street, she will be less likely to do so in the future. If a boy received a relatively strong shock by touching the frayed part of an electric cord, he would be less likely to touch a frayed cord again. The same would be true of a child who was burned by touching a hot stove. In general, stimuli that are aversive in the absence of any prior learning history are called **unconditioned aversive stimuli**, abbreviated S^P (punishing stimulus), in this textbook.

Using unconditioned aversive stimuli in public facilities, like schools, hospitals, clinics, or institutions, raises several legal, ethical, and practical issues. Certainly a child who returns home from a school with a set of bruises resulting from physical punishment may well have grounds for legal action against the school. At the very least, he would have grounds for questioning the ethics of such a violent procedure.

It will become apparent in the subsequent discussion that, the more intense the punishment, the more apt it is to be lastingly effective. Consequently, a client may well become bruised as a result of physical punishment. Yet many children are often paddled without receiving visible bruises. The following remarks by Skinner, calling into question the widespread use of punishment in schools, graphically illustrate the point:

The cane is still with us, and efforts to abolish it are vigorously opposed. In Great Britain a split leather strap for whipping students called a taws can be obtained from suppliers who advertise in educational journals, one of whom is said to sell three thousand annually. (The taws has the advantage, shared by the rubber truncheon, of leaving no incriminating marks.) (1968, p. 96)

[3] The spelling of "aversive" is frequently confused with that of the word "adverse." The reader is cautioned to note this distinction.

Conditioned Aversive Stimuli

Much in the same way that a formerly neutral stimulus acquires reinforcing properties (see Unit 8), some stimuli may be conditioned as a result of being presented just before or along with the unconditioned aversive stimulus. A good example of a conditioned aversive stimulus is the word "no," spoken in a loud, sharp tone. For most individuals this "no" has, in all likelihood, been paired with the delivery of an unconditioned aversive stimulus. A mother shouts "No!" as the child touches the hot stove. Both the loudness of the sound and the burning heat of the stove contribute to the child's being brought under the control of that stimulus. Behaviors followed by loud, sharp "no"s will probably be diminished, at least temporarily. As long as the "no" is at least occasionally followed by a strong aversive stimulus, it should continue to function in itself as a conditioned aversive stimulus. A teacher places a mark on the blackboard when a student fails to follow the rules of the Good Behavior Game (see Unit 27; Barrish, Saunders & Wolf, 1969). The mark functions as a conditioned aversive stimulus because it has been present when other aversive conditions have prevailed. Other examples of conditioned aversive stimuli include frowns; gestures, like shaking a finger; or motions, like clenching a fist or swinging a hand as if preparing delivery of a spanking or a blow.

Using Aversive Stimuli in Human Services

The informal use of aversive stimuli in human services is fairly common. Punishment is sometimes used because an adult is angry with a child and the child is a "safe" target. Frequently, punishment rapidly reduces behaviors, thus negatively reinforcing contingency managers. Teachers and personnel in community facilities often find that using conditioned aversive stimuli—saying "no," frowning, or gesturing threateningly—often accomplishes their purposes. Yet some clients, like Pearl, fail to respond to conditioned aversive stimuli. For Pearl, who exhibits "autistic-like" behaviors, a specific stimulus may not have been conditioned to become aversive. There may be other unidentified conditioned aversive stimuli that control her behavior, or she may respond only to unconditioned aversive stimuli. Possibilities might be contingent darkness, used by Hewitt (1965) in conjunction with a speech program for an autistic child, or aversive tickling, as used by Greene & Hoats (1971) to reduce the frequency of self-destructive head banging. The teacher, clinician, or other contingency manager could consider the desirability of teaching clients like Pearl to respond to a conditioned aversive stimulus. Such a goal probably could be accomplished in much the same way that a reinforcer is conditioned. But would the procedure be justifiable and worth the time and effort? There are many factors to be considered in making this judgment. The subsequent material on the subject of punishment suggests that, considering all the undesirable consequences of punishment, in most instances the effort would be hardly justified, though Pearl's case could be an exception. The contingency manager would, however, be better advised to concentrate on the development of some more constructive alternative techniques before conditioning aversive stimuli.

Stimuli That Signal Nondelivery of Reinforcement

Frequently, when a behavior is punished, the individual also fails to receive reinforcement. It is not necessarily true, however, that the punished behavior goes totally unreinforced. Esmerelda, who is fresh to her teacher, may indeed be punished by the teacher, yet she may simultaneously be reinforced by the smiles, giggles, and nods of some of her fellow students. Conversely, there may be some stimuli that, though not followed by aversive stimuli, may still be followed by extinction, response-cost, or timeout conditions. A mark in the Good Behavior Game signals that a reinforcing activity will be withheld. That is how marks acquire conditioned aversive properties. Here we are considering the situation in which a stimulus (whether by itself "punishing" or not) serves to cue a period of non-reinforcement. Discriminative stimuli that have been followed by the nondelivery of reinforcement (S^Δs) begin to acquire aversive properties (Azrin & Holz, 1966). Clyde's mom may order him to pick up his toys in the playroom, where receiving attention or other reinforcers from friends and family is unlikely. The verbal instruction becomes aversive under those circumstances. A more mildly stated "no" following an incorrect response to a question may also become aversive if reinforcement from teacher or parent has never accompanied the incorrect responses. The groan of the coach as the pitcher appears about to throw the ball incorrectly and the wail of the crowd as the pop fly glides toward the fielder's glove are other illustrations of such kinds of stimuli. The coach's groan cues the pitcher that his pitch will not be approved; the wail of the crowd cues the batter that he will not be cheered.

Stimuli thus need not necessarily be followed by only unconditioned or strongly conditioned aversive stimuli in order to become aversive. If they have been repeatedly followed by the nondelivery of reinforcement, they can also become aversive. A staff situation may be used to illustrate this phenomenon. Ms. Charming has repeatedly requested of her superior, Ms. Ann Thrope, funds for tokens, back-up reinforcers, and recording equipment for her workshop program. Ms. Thrope fails to deliver every time. After a while, Ms. Charming begins to dislike Ms. Thrope and avoids eating lunch at the same table with her. Ms. Thrope's presence has become aversive. Stimuli, like warnings and threats, presented repeatedly just before timeout, response cost, or overcorrection may also, as mentioned earlier, become conditioned aversive stimuli.

ADVANTAGES OF PUNISHMENT

Rapidly Stopping the Behavior

A five-year-old retarded client was inducing hundreds of epileptic seizures daily by moving his hands rapidly before his eyes and blinking. Aversive consequences rapidly reduced those behaviors (Wright, 1973). Punishment used with maximum effectiveness offers the advantage of a rapid halt in a behavior and long-term reduction of its future occurrence (Azrin, 1960). Persistent vomiting (Kohlenberg, 1970) and ruminating (Cunningham & Linscheid, 1976) by dangerously malnourished patients were rapidly reduced by means of electric shock. In many programs serving children and youth, the need for rapid modification of a client's behavior is apparent, as when an individual is endangered. For instance, immediate action must be taken to stop a child from running into a busy street or maneuvering to push another child over a guard rail. In addition to restraining the individual, an intense punishing stimulus, like a loud, sharp verbal reprimand or a slap, may be appropriate.

A potential dilemma, however, is raised by the *Wyatt* guidelines for the use of shock[4] with the retarded. Budd and Baer have commented that the dilemma

> . . . concerns the ruling that shock can be employed with the retarded "only after alternative techniques have failed." (344 F. Supp. at 401) It could be argued that this requirement conflicts with another *Wyatt* standard, which directs staff workers to employ the least restrictive alternative in providing treatment. More specifically, it could be considered more restrictive to delay the use of a powerful, but (presumably) effective technique—shock—while exhausting all milder but (presumably) less effective alternatives than to provide shock treatment at the outset. As Baer (1970) noted in his discussion of the choice of punishment techniques:
>
> > That question, *How long will it take?* is the morally critical question, in my opinion. For as time goes by while the therapist tries his hopefully more benevolent or more basic methods, the patient still undergoes punishment while he waits for a good outcome. In effect, the therapist has assigned the patient to a punishment condition from which he might have long since removed him (p. 246).
>
> Thus, for behavior problems as serious as mutilating one's body it would seem most humane for the courts to allow early use of shock treatment in special cases, rather than reserving this technique until all possible alternatives have been exhausted. In place of a general court ruling, the decision of if and when to prescribe shock treatment for particular cases might best be made by an institution's advocacy committee in consultation with staff personnel. In this way, residents with serious problems which require a very powerful therapy technique such as shock punishment would have an opportunity to receive more efficient treatment than is presently permitted by *Wyatt's* ruling (1976, pp. 219–220).

Facilitating Discrimination

Punishment of specific behaviors is informative to clients. Marshall (1965) has reviewed considerable evidence indicating that punishment of a response under specific circumstances is "informative" to individuals. When punishment is paired with clearly discriminative stimuli, like instructions and gestures, it assists youngsters to discriminate acceptable from unacceptable behaviors more rapidly. For example, pushing on the stairs may be dangerous, though it may be acceptable in specific playground games. A conditioned aversive stimulus like a frown, gesture, or "no," used to communicate to children that pushing is unacceptable on the stairs may thus help them to make such a discrimination. To promote the acquisition of the discrimination further, a direction may be presented: "Pushing is not

---

[4] In the rare instances in which brief low-level electric shock may be justifiably used —assuming that legal and ethical requirements have been met—great care must be exercised. Technical expertise and medical supervision are crucial. Keep in mind that *electric shock treatment can be dangerous!* (Butterfield, 1975) (italics added)

allowed on the steps." Every time that Lucretia pulls a toy from her playmate's hand she is sent to the periphery of the group for five minutes of contingent observation. The supervising adult says: "No, you may not grab toys. We ask for them politely." Lucretia learns to discriminate acceptable from unacceptable uses of her playmate's toys.

Instructive to Peers

Punishment of one individual's behavior may reduce the probability that others present will imitate that behavior. When such a "model" is punished for a misbehavior, others are less likely to imitate it in that situation. The behavior is more likely to be imitated in a situation in which it is followed either by no consequences or by reinforcement (Bandura, 1965b; 1965c). For example, if Lucretia is allowed to continue grabbing toys from others, her playmates may imitate her behavior. Seeing the behavior punished, the others are less apt to do the same thing. Through observing a model being punished for a particular behavior, others thus learn the conditions under which punishment is likely to be forthcoming. The conditions present when the behavior is emitted and punished develop aversive properties that reduce the likelihood that clients will emit the behavior in those conditions.

   Contingency managers can help clients to achieve better control by clearly specifying which behaviors are acceptable and which are not (Marshall, 1965). The clients gain greater behavioral control as they learn to discriminate those behaviors that are acceptable from those that are unacceptable. The following excerpt from a counseling interview with a fourth-grade girl, conducted by one of the authors, illustrates this point, showing how a student teacher mishandled her students when they were not in their seats as they were supposed to be.

STUDENT: Well, the thing is if the teacher lets them [the students] rile up the whole schoolroom and then makes them just slowly slow down, there will be just a mess. You know what I mean?

COUNSELOR: Kind of joke around with them, kind of edge them into their seats . . .

STUDENT: Yes, kid them, you know, kid them into getting into their seats and you will never get any place with them. But if you tell them, "Children, it's time to get to your seats" [in a firm, authoritative voice], they are all sitting in their seats, waiting for you to tell them what to do.

USING PUNISHMENT EFFECTIVELY

In this section we shall be concerned with a number of variables that have been identified as influencing the effectiveness of punishment. The specification of these variables has primarily been derived from an article by Azrin and Holz (1966). In general, the variables are related to the manner and situation in which the aversive stimuli are presented. They include escape opportunities, temporal and scheduling properties, intensity of the stimulus, and the effect of combining punishment with other procedures, like reinforcement and extinction.

Preventing Unauthorized Escape

Escape is one of the natural reactions to the presentation of aversive stimuli. If the client succeeds in leaving the situation, the opportunity to apply any procedure is, of course, lost. Punishment can therefore be effective in reducing the occurrence of misbehaviors only when the environment is so arranged that an *unauthorized escape does not occur* (Azrin et al., 1965; Dinsmoor & Campbell, 1956). If Pearl runs out of the room instead of participating in an overcorrection routine for self-stimulation, her rate of self-stimulation may not decrease.

There are, of course, escape behaviors that we would try to encourage. Those are appropriate behaviors that terminate aversive stimuli because they are acceptable alternatives. Lucretia might escape from contingent observation by indicating her readiness to play nicely and following through on that pledge. Pearl could escape overcorrection by cooperating in the positive-practice routine and returning to active participation in instructional tasks, rather than to self-stimulation. Such situations are actually episodes of negative reinforcement (engaging in a behavior leads to the removal of aversive stimuli). Naturally, when appropriate escape behaviors are emitted for a time, they should be positively reinforced.

Consistent and Immediate Application

Punishment is also more effective when the punishing stimulus is applied every time that the misbehavior occurs and as soon as possible following it (Azrin, 1956; Azrin, Holz & Hake, 1963; Zimmerman & Ferster, 1963). For example, if a client's misbehavior is hitting another child, the aversive stimulus should be applied immediately and every time he does so. Such a procedure should reduce the behavior quickly and should help the child to discriminate more rapidly that hitting others is not an acceptable behavior. Similarly,

suppose a toddler has first run out into the street. To teach him the danger associated with being in the street, the child's parent might give the child one sharp spank as he picks the child up out of the street. This spanking would teach the child to associate the middle of the street with danger, but a spanking after he is safely back in the curb is poor timing. The child should associate the street with danger; the curb, with safety. (Krumboltz & Krumboltz, 1972, p. 206)

Extended periods of punishment should be avoided, or the effectiveness of the punishment will be reduced (Azrin, 1958). For example, clients soon become adept at "tuning out" a parent or teacher who constantly nags. Similarly, frequent spankings tend to lose their effect. It would thus be best to use procedures other than punishment for any but the most serious infractions, or the client may adapt to the overused stimulus.

Presentation at Strong Intensity

Punishment is far less effective when the intensity of the aversive stimulus is increased gradually than when it is initially introduced at its full intensity (Azrin & Holz, 1966). The use of low-intensity punishment alone—unaccompanied by other procedures—may be followed by an initial reduction in the behavior, but often a recovery of the behavior follows. Individuals appear to adapt easily to very mild aversive stimuli that are presented repeatedly and to those that are gradually increased in intensity (as many teenagers adapt to loud music), whereas the effects of strong aversive stimuli appear to be more enduring. In a specific instance, a hard slap on the hand may therefore be more effective in stopping a particular behavior for a long period of time than would several weak slaps or several slaps of increasing vigor. A firmly stated "no" seems more effective than a shake of the head followed by increasingly stronger head shakes and louder and louder "no"s.

It is less necessary, however, to use intense punishment to eliminate behaviors that are not well established in the person's behavioral repertoire. As mentioned in previous units, a variable that determines the strength of a behavior is the frequency and schedule with which the behavior has been reinforced. A behavior that is not well established will obviously be easier to eliminate than one that is well established. We would therefore expect mild punishment to be sufficient to eliminate weak behaviors. Conversely, probably more intense punishment would be required to reduce the occurrence of well-established behaviors or override their intrinsically reinforcing effects. For example, little Bonnie reaches to grab her dog Tiger's tail for the first time. A mild punishment, like a simple "no" or head shake, would probably be effective in eliminating the behavior. If Bonnie habitually torments her reinforcingly responsive Tiger, however, mild punishment will probably be insufficient to override the effects of the reinforcer than will more intense or consistent punishment.

Combining with Extinction

Punishment combined with extinction results in a more rapid elimination of the behavior than when either punishment or extinction is used alone (Azrin & Holz, 1961; 1966). If rapid elimination of a behavior is sought, it is therefore a good idea to include, along with the delivery of a contingent aversive stimulus, the removal of the reinforcers maintaining that behavior and to make them contingent upon only desirable alternative behaviors. We have noted that a stimulus acquires conditioned aversive properties when it cues that no reinforcement is forthcoming. Such conditioning would be delayed if the individual had been simultaneously reinforced. Similarly, the effectiveness of a punishment procedure will be reduced if the emission of the behavior is followed by the delivery of both aversive and reinforcing stimuli. If little Bonnie persists in tormenting Tiger, we can posit that the dog's responsiveness is sufficiently reinforcing to override the effects of the aversive consequences. The client whose disruptive behavior yields him not only an aversive scolding but also the approval of his peers will more likely disrupt in the future than if peer approval were absent. In this instance, the task of the contingency manager is somehow to reduce the emission of peer approval, possibly by means of some of the procedures previously discussed. For instance, the few peers who do not demonstrate approval can be praised, which reinforces alternative behaviors and provides positive models. Stimulus conditions may be altered: For example, the offending client can be moved to a location where his actions are less observable and thus fail to occasion peer approval. Or other procedures can be tried.

Sometimes it is extremely difficult to remove reinforcement for engaging in a specific behavior, especially when the behavior provides its own source of immediate reinforcement, as Tiger's responsiveness reinforces Bonnie's tormenting. The behavior may then persist, even though it is punished. In our society, such a situation is probably the root cause of some extremely serious problems—for example, antisocial behaviors like theft, rape, child molesting, and drug abuse. Such behaviors often yield the individual very rapid and often very powerful reinforcement, whereas any punishment that is administered is usually delayed and intermittent—and, as a result, not too effective. This partially explains why systems of criminal justice are so often ineffective and why recidivism rates are so high. For behaviors in this category, it would be better to use alternative reductive methods and, if feasible, to provide opportunities for the individual to achieve equivalent or stronger reinforcement from more acceptable sources. In the example of stealing, this goal might be accomplished by offering alternative socially desirable behaviors through, say, training in a skill that is both intrinsically reinforcing and highly remunerative. As long as a successful thief has no socially acceptable way to earn coveted things in life, stealing will probably continue. Only if the client escapes from punishment *and* engages in heavily reinforced acceptable alternative behaviors will it be likely to cease. Other "intrinsically" reinforcing behaviors may be reduced also through reinforcement of incompatible responses. While Bonnie is playing an enjoyable game she is less likely to tease Tiger. If she were showered with positive attention for petting Tiger gently, she would be even more likely to acquire that behavior, which is incompatible with teasing. Journals in the behavior-therapy area (see, for example, *Behavior Therapy, Behavior Therapy and Experimental Psychiatry,* and *Behavior Research and Therapy*) have been publishing some very promising experimental and case reports of procedural combinations effective in changing antisocial sexual and drug-abuse behaviors. Many of the procedures promote alternative or incompatible behaviors or both—sometimes in conjunction with even more effective reductive procedures.

Occasionally we notice an individual continuing in a behavior, although apparently consistently and immediately punished for doing so. In fact, the same stimuli may function aversively for that individual under other circumstances. The situation is the apparently paradoxical one labeled *masochism*. What usually occurs is a chain of events that sometimes terminate in positive reinforcement. Some individuals fail to be reinforced in the more usual ways for accomplishments, work, and so forth. They may ultimately receive reinforcement only after engaging in a particular behavior and being punished for it. Let us take the example of the child Tim, whose mother is frequently occupied with other things and often fails to pay attention to him. But, when Tim hurts himself, pokes his younger brother, or accidentally breaks a lamp, she rushes over and yells at him or spanks him. Then, in a moment of remorse, she cuddles him and says that she is sorry for punishing him. Tim soon learns that one sure way to obtain affection from his mother is to hurt himself or to do something naughty. In school and institutional settings children and youth often engage in similar types of behavioral chains. The misbehaving child is given attention while the others are ignored. Misbehavior, though punished, will persist if it is the *primary* way in which reinforcement can be received.

These examples illustrate how difficult it may be to remove all sources of reinforcement for a punished behavior. As long as such sources of reinforcement remain, the behavior will be very difficult to eliminate by means of punishment alone. It will not be possible to combine it with extinction effectively.

Combining Punishment with Stimulus Control

As with other procedures, when the conditions under which punishment will be delivered are made explicitly clear, its effectiveness will be more powerful: "Do not smoke. Violators will be prosecuted" functions as an S^{D-}, informing people that smoking in that situation will probably be punished. Phrases like "Falling rock zone," "High voltage lines—danger"; symbols like

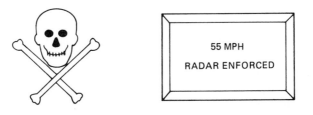

and the auditory stimulus so familiar to dwellers in tornado county—the tornado warning siren—have a similar function. As we described in Unit 19, the S^{D-} develops in almost exactly the same manner as the S^D, by being consistently present when certain consequences follow a behavior. Here a given response is consistently *punished* when those stimuli are present. (The reader may wish to review the procedures for effectively developing stimulus control.) In teaching a client, then, that under specific conditions a given act will be punished, *every time that act is emitted under those conditions it should be immediately punished by the strong delivery of a stimulus that is known to be aversive for that individual.* If Clyde steps out into traffic when the traffic light is red and the sign says "Wait," he is immediately scolded—a powerful aversive for Clyde. "Don't pull Tiger's tail" should function as an S^{D-} when Bonnie reaches for the tail. Should she proceed, she would be punished by Mother and perhaps by Tiger's snarling, growling, or taking a nip at her.

In the human services, the same sort of consistency should be followed. Children and youths should be clearly informed about the conditions under which acts will be punished: "Hurting others, destroying or taking other people's materials will be punished by . . ." In a group situation, especially with older children, it makes sense to involve the clients in the specification of rules. For, as we have mentioned (see Unit 7), they will then be more aware of those rules, and peer support of the rules will be more likely. Occasionally staff rules also have to be clarified. Again it is a good idea to involve staff members in setting and clarifying rules that affect their performance. Staff organizations frequently fulfill that function, for example, clarifying the conditions for dismissal: "In other than cases of imminent danger [specified in detail], hitting clients will be grounds for immediate dismissal." Such clear explication of rules will reduce the likelihood that specific acts will occur under given circumstances.

Combining Punishment with Reinforcement of Alternative Behaviors

We have already mentioned that very intense punishment will reduce well-established undesirable behaviors more effectively than milder intensities of punishment. Milder punishment will generally reduce well-established behavior only temporarily. It is possible, however, as we have discussed earlier, to use milder punishment in order to obtain a more lasting reduction of the behavior if the individual is simultaneously given access to an alternative reinforceable behavior (Azrin & Holz, 1966). The use of punishment intense enough to override very powerful reinforcement effects is frequently neither feasible nor ethical. This combined procedure should, however, prove attractive to practitioners, who seek the rapid and long-lasting effects of punishment but who are unwilling or unable to use strong aversive stimuli. Mild aversive stimuli, like a "no," a frown, or a head shake, may be sufficient to stop the occurrence of a behavior, *provided* that the individuals already have alternative desirable behaviors in their repertoires and the environment offers them access to, and reinforcement for, engaging in those behaviors. For example, Moore and Bailey (1973) have successfully combined punishment with reinforcement to reduce the "autistic-like" behaviors of a three-year-old girl. The mother was taught to apply negative verbalizations (for example, "No!" or "Don't do that") and physical interactions (withholding affection, spanking, and so on) contingently as punishers and positive verbalizations (for example, "That's good!" or "I'm proud of you") and physical interactions (like hugs and kisses) as reinforcers. An analysis of the mother's behavior suggested that her use of reinforcement combined with "her increased use of social punishment for inappropriate behavior was the key factor in the child's increasing responsiveness" (Moore & Bailey, 1973, p. 497). Similarly, a client may give the wrong answer to a question, handle some equipment carelessly, or start to hit someone. A simple "no" or a head shake will probably be sufficient to stop such behavior from recurring, provided that the client has been reinforced for engaging in desirable responses. To facilitate the effect, such alternatives should be made explicit to the client: "No, the answer is not sixty-five; eight times eight is one less, or _____"; "No, don't lift a microscope by the lens piece. Place your hand beneath the base"; "No, you may not hit the children when they tease you, but you may tell me, and I'll take care of it." The verbal directions alone will have an effect only if the contingency manager makes certain to reinforce the client for giving the right answer, handling the equipment properly, or informing him when being teased.

DISADVANTAGES OF PUNISHMENT

Although effectively administered punishment is a technique that serves to reduce behavior quickly for long periods of time and seems to decrease the probability that observers will imitate punished behavior, some undesirable reactions have been observed as a consequence of punishment.[5] Aside from the legal, moral, and safety issues already mentioned, they include withdrawal, aggression, generalization, imitation, peer reactions, and negative self-statements.

Causing Withdrawal

Clients may withdraw in response to punishment. The literature has indicated repeatedly that an organism will escape from a punishing situation if possible (Azrin et al., 1965). This phenomenon is often illustrated in cartoons depicting exaggerated instances of predictable behavioral phenomena: The husband, nagged by his wife, stomps out of the house; the severely scolded child packs a hobo pack and heads around the corner; the employee, after being chewed out by the boss, quits. In the real world, the staff member whose efforts are regularly punished by criticism or failure is often absent or late and may eventually resign. Similarly, the student who is repeatedly reprimanded may become "sick," cut class, or drop out of school altogether. Escape may be symbolic or indirect, rather than literal. For example, the student may doodle or hum while the teacher is criticizing. In either instance the social process is disrupted, and communication breaks down.

Causing Aggression

Clients often become aggressive in response to aversive stimuli. Azrin, Hutchinson, and Hake (1963) have shown that, upon delivery of shock, normally friendly monkeys will begin to fight vigorously. Azrin (1964) has shown similar responses to aversive stimulation by a wide variety of organisms, and Oliver, West and

---

[5] Skinner (1968) has discussed many of the pitfalls of punishment. For an amusing set of illustrations of punishment, see R. Mager's film *Who Did What to Whom?*, issued by Research Press, Champaign, Illinois.

Sloane (1974) demonstrated that, when human subjects were shocked, their rate of aggression increased ninefold over baseline. A film cliché illustrates the same principle: The Keystone Cops and Laurel and Hardy often dramatized the development of a simple, unintentional accident into a grand melée. Many instances of aggression related to punishment occur in normal daily life. The youth who is accidentally nudged responds by hitting. The berated spouse who does not actually leave the situation argues angrily in response. Small children, when spanked by parents, will try to hit back or will pummel smaller siblings, punching bags, or other handy items. In our highly socialized culture, many have learned to express aggression subtly, rather than overtly. The student who makes "wise" remarks and the teacher who is sarcastic have found means to express their aggression in more socially acceptable fashion. But aggression, whether overt or disguised, does interfere with normal social functioning (Azrin & Holz, 1966).

Causing Generalization

Generalization occurs with both reinforcement and punishment. As we saw in Unit 12, it occurs in this manner: The individual responds in similar ways to stimuli that resemble or contain properties of the stimulus that was present when the behavior was originally learned. Humans are generalizing when they decide to eat after seeing food on a plate, a menu, a colorful picture of food—or after sniffing the aroma of food being prepared.

Behaviors associated with a punishing stimulus may also be occasioned by other stimuli that have the same properties. In one classic study (Watson & Rayner, 1920) an eleven-month-old child's conditioned fear of a rat was generalized to all furry objects. Punishment for a specific behavior in school may also produce responses that temporarily generalize. For example, the student may respond to being scolded for speaking out of turn with aggression toward, or withdrawal from, the teacher, the principal, the subject he is studying, the school, and so forth. Or he may stop responding altogether, ceasing to speak, write, read, or work in school for a time because conditioned aversive properties are present in other environments. Ultimately, the fact that the punishment is delivered for a specific act may be discriminated. But achieving this discrimination takes time and careful planning by the teacher. *Clients have to be informed that they have been punished for specific acts. Presentation of clear antecedent stimuli before various desirable behaviors and considerable positive reinforcement following various desirable behaviors should help them to make the necessary distinctions.*

Modeling Punishment

In our discussion of the advantages of punishment, we mentioned that clients are less likely to imitate a punished behavior. What they may imitate, however, is the act of delivering punishment (Bandura & Walters, 1963; Bandura, 1965a). In Unit 14, we discussed how people tend to imitate the behaviors of persons who have prestige, especially when those behaviors are reinforced. Settings like schools and group residential facilities are particularly apt to provide opportunities for such unintentional teaching to take place. There the teacher or group leader uses punishment and is reinforced by the immediate cessation of aversive events—negative reinforcement! Mr. Rod, popular poetry instructor on campus, calls on Jeremy, who has been gazing out the window, and asks him to discuss the implications of the poem that has just been read. Jeremy, not having attended, launches into an extended discussion of irrelevant material. With a single sarcastic remark, Mr. Rod "cuts him down" and leaves him red-faced but silent. Although Jeremy's window gazing may be reduced at least temporarily, Mr. Rod's sarcasm has been reinforced by the termination of Jeremy's aversive discussion. In addition, the other students have witnessed this turn of events and are primed to use a similar response when people have been inattentive to them. Finally, we have only to observe young children engaged in fantasy play or residents of institutions in which control is largely aversive, to see emission of imitated punishment.

We live in a violent world, and we wonder why violence is so persistent. By now, we have seen a number of situations that produce violence: aggressive reactions to extinction, punishment, and other aversive contingencies. Here is one more major source to add to the list: People with prestige and power (those in control of contingencies) may actually be teaching aggression by modeling it! It is important to be sure that punishment is appropriate before responding with unplanned aversive consequences. When punishment is selected because a behavior is so dangerous or disruptive that it must be stopped quickly, we should try to set up an environment in which other students or clients will not observe the delivery of punishing stimuli.

Teaching the Punished Act

We have determined that clients who observe a behavior's being punished are not likely to imitate it under the same stimulus conditions. But another disadvantage of punishment is that, once attention has been drawn to the punished act, it may be imitated under different stimulus conditions (Bandura, 1965a). For example, peers may imitate previously unnoticed behaviors that they have seen punished—like swearing, cheating, or stealing—when the contingency manager is not around. Contingency managers may thus not wish publicly to punish behaviors that they believe have not been previously noticed by peers or have not been observed in their repertoires, for the undesirable behaviors may then be called to their attention and possibly imitated in other situations.

Producing Peer Reactions

When individuals are continually singled out for punishment, they may themselves become stimuli to be avoided or ridiculed. Peer reactions may thus pose a serious threat to the well-being of the punished client. Such negative effects may be reduced by giving the client a chance to make up for his misbehavior or by offering an acceptable alternative. Giving clients opportunities to receive praise is likely to reinstate them socially with their peers. For example, the client can be asked to help perform some prestigious task, like gathering or handing out materials, or, following particularly good behavior, he may even be placed in charge of a group activity or event.

Punishment may also occasion peer support or sympathy for the punished child, the "underdog" effect. Peer reinforcement would oppose the effects of the punishment, perhaps resulting in an eventual increase, rather than a decrease, of the undesired behavior. When such an effect is observed, it is well to change the approach. The situation can be discussed with the group, or a different punisher or reductive procedure can be selected.

Causing Negative Self-Statements

The use of punishment may negatively influence the clients' statements about themselves or their environment (school, home, and the like), like those measured by responses on paper-and-pencil tests of self-esteem. What people say about themselves or about their environment after they have been punished is more likely to be negative, particularly if the aversive stimuli are directed at the individual, rather than at the behavior ("You're a bad boy"; "Jim hasn't grown up yet. He still behaves like a two-year-old"). The importance of this point cannot be overlooked. Studies like one by Wattenberg and Clifford (1964) have indicated that what clients say about themselves is related to school achievement. Other studies (Flanders, 1965; Ludwig & Maehr, 1967; Staines, 1958) have also indicated that teachers' comments directed to the child, rather than to her behavior, modified students' self-reports or self-concepts in the direction of the comments. If aversive stimuli must be used, they should never be directed at the client ("You're a bad boy") but at the behavior ("No, don't hit Jane"). This approach helps clients to recognize that it is a specific behavior that is unacceptable and not all of their behaviors.

Again, it is desirable to encourage alternative behaviors that provide opportunities for positive reinforcement. This helps clients to discriminate which *specific* behaviors are tolerated and which are not. For example, the group leader punishes Desmond when he hits Violet; then she makes a point of reinforcing him when he does play cooperatively, cleans up his toys, distributes milk cartons, and so on, for as many other such activities as possible. Furthermore, reinforcement in the form of praise is likely not only to occasion and strengthen desired behaviors but also to increase positive, and reduce negative, statements made by clients about themselves and the setting (Bandura, Grusec & Menlove, 1967; Brehm & Cohen, 1962; Davidson & Lang, 1960; Flanders, 1965).

A FINAL CAUTION

Why do people continue to use punishment? Their behavior is maintained, as is most behavior, by reinforcement: When an individual experiences aversive conditions, the opportunity to aggress can be very reinforcing (Azrin et al., 1963). Perhaps more important, even mild punishment usually results in rapid (but not necessarily enduring) cessation of the undesirable behavior (Azrin & Holz, 1966). In Unit 10 we learned that terminating an aversive stimulus is reinforcing. Many of the behaviors that contingency managers wish to reduce are aversive to them. Punishment will briefly and quickly reduce that behavior. A study by Martin (1974) illustrates this effect. Several young children were sometimes praised for staying on task when requested to play with objects like beads or blocks. Sometimes they were reprimanded for being off task. When reprimanded, their rate of on-task behavior was higher than it was under praise for the on-task condition. This result would undoubtedly reinforce the contingency manager's use of reprimands. Negative side effects may not become manifest for quite a while, or they may never become apparent to the punisher. In the Martin study (1974), a generalization phase demonstrated that, despite their working faster when reprimanded, children later avoided using the objects with which they were playing when reprimanded. Such an example of negative generalization might not be observed by the punishing agent right away, if at all. People who are unaware of principles of behavior will in the absence of more desirable reductive techniques, continue periodically to paddle, spank, criticize, ridicule, or otherwise punish children and youth.

Monitoring Potential Negative Side Effects

Because punishment may generate various negative side effects, including overuse, whenever it *is* used, it is important that not only the target behavior but other behaviors as well be measured. Evidence of negative generalization, attempts to withdraw from the situation, aggressive reactions, peer reactions, and negative self-statements should all be measured. Data suggestive of marked increases in those side effects—or evidence of their absence—will be useful in making decisions about whether to continue using the procedure or to shift to another.

Summary

Punishment is one of several methods for reducing or eliminating undesirable behaviors. If used with maximum effectiveness, it serves to reduce the occurrence of a specific behavior quickly and for a long time. It can be "informative" and may decrease the probability that an observer will perform the punished behavior under similar conditions.

There are many disadvantages to the use of punishment. Unconditioned aversive stimuli and other forms of severe punishment are generally inappropriate, except perhaps in situations in which there is imminent danger to the client or to others. Conditioned aversive stimuli can be, and are being, used in most settings. Practitioners must be aware, however, that punishment can produce various negative side effects. Although it can be an effective management procedure, evidence suggests that using it with *maximum* effectiveness is difficult in many situations. Practical, legal, moral, and ethical considerations often countermand the use of intense punishment. Punishment, however, may be justified when a behavior presents a clear danger or seriously blocks an individual's progress, or when less aversive intrusive methods have failed. Alternative procedures for reducing client behaviors should always be considered first. The decision to use punishment or other procedures to reduce maladaptive behaviors depends upon a variety of considerations: the seriousness of the behavior, the frequency of its occurrence, time factors, whether or not the act is public, patience, ethics, practicality, and, as always, contingency control. Institutional and consumer review and informed consent by the client or his advocate should always be secured first.

When a punishment procedure is selected, it must be employed cautiously with careful monitoring of its effects. Desirable alternative behaviors must be reinforced, and reinforcement for the punished behavior should be completely withheld. Behavior analysts can, through observations, informal conferences, and in-service training programs, assist contingency managers to be constantly aware of the effects that their behavior has on clients' behavior and the reverse. Furthermore, such consultants should help prepare contingency managers to anticipate and to handle negative reactions to punishment.

References

Azrin, N. H. Effects of two intermittent schedules of immediate and non-immediate punishment. *Journal of Psychology,* 1956, **42**, 3–21.

Azrin, N. H. Some effects of noise on human behavior. *Journal of Experimental Analysis of Behavior,* 1958, **1**, 183–200.

Azrin, N. H. Effects of punishment intensity during variable-interval reinforcement. *Journal of the Experimental Analysis of Behavior,* 1960, **3**, 128–142.

Azrin, N. H. Aggressive responses of paired animals. Paper presented at the symposium on Medical Aspects of Stress, Walter Reed Institute of Research, Washington, D.C., April 1964.

Azrin, N. H., Hake, D. G., Holz, W. C. & Hutchinson, R. R. Motivational aspects of escape from punishment. *Journal of the Experimental Analysis of Behavior,* 1965, **8**, 31–44.

Azrin, N. H. & Holz, W. C. Punishment during fixed-interval reinforcement. *Journal of the Experimental Analysis of Behavior,* 1961, **4**, 343–347.

Azrin, N. H. & Holz, W. C. Punishment. In W. A. Honig (Ed.), *Operant behavior: Areas of research and application.* New York: Appleton, 1966. Pp. 380–447.

Azrin, N. H., Holz, W. C. & Hake, D. F. Fixed-ratio punishment. *Journal of the Experimental Analysis of Behavior,* 1963, **6**, 141–148.

Azrin, N. H., Hutchinson, R. R. & Hake, D. F. Pain-induced fighting in the squirrel monkey. *Journal of the Experimental Analysis of Behavior,* 1963, **6**, 620.

Baer, D. M. A case for the selective reinforcement of punishment. In C. Neuringer and J. L. Michael (Eds.), *Behavior modification in clinical psychology.* New York: Appleton, 1970.

Bandura, A. Behavioral modification through modeling procedures. In L. Krasner & L. P. Ullman, (Eds.), *Research in behavior modification.* New York: Holt, Rinehart and Winston, 1965a. Pp. 310–340.

Bandura, A. Influence of models' reinforcement contingencies on the acquisition of imitative rseponses. *Journal of Personality and Social Psychology,* 1965, **1**, 589–595.

Bandura, A. Vicarious processes: A case of no-trial learning. In L. Berkowitz (Ed.), *Advances in experimental social psychology.* Vol. 2. New York: Academic Press, 1965c. Pp. 1–55.

Bandura, A., Grusec, J. & Menlove, F. Some social determinants of self-monitoring reinforcement systems. *Journal of Personality and Social Psychology,* 1967, **5**, 449–455.

Bandura, A. & Walters, R. H. *Social learning and personality development.* New York: Holt, Rinehart and Winston, 1963. Pp. 223–236.

Barrish, H. H., Saunders, M. & Wolf, M. M. Effects of individual contingencies for group consequences on disruptive behavior in a classroom. *Journal of Applied Behavior Analysis,* 1969, **2**, 119–124.

Brehm, J. W. & Cohen, A. R. *Explorations in cognitive dissonance.* New York: Wiley, 1962.

Budd, K. & Baer, D. M. Behavior modification and the law: Implications of recent judicial decisions. *The Journal of Psychiatry and Law,* a special reprint, Summer 1976, 171–244.

Butterfield, W. H. Electric shock: Safety factors when used for the aversive conditioning of humans. *Behavior Therapy,* 1975, **6**, 98–110.

Church, R. M. The varied effects of punishment on behavior. *Psychological Review,* 1963, **70**, 369–402.

Cunningham, C. E. & Linscheid, T. R. Elimination of chronic infant ruminating by electric shock. *Behavior Therapy,* 1976, **7**, 231–234.

Davidson, H. R. & Lang, G. Children's perception of their teachers feelings toward them related to self-perception, school achievement, and behavior. *Journal of Experimental Education,* 1960, **29**, 107–188.

Dinsmoor, J. A. & Campbell, S. L. Escape-from-shock-training following exposure to inescapable shock. *Psychological Reports,* 1956, **2**, 43–49.

Flanders, N. A. Teacher influence, pupil attitudes, and achievement. *Cooperative Research Monograph,* 1965, No. 12.

Green, R. J. & Hoats, D. L. Aversive tickling: A simple conditioning technique. *Behavior Therapy,* 1971, **2**, 389–393.

Hewitt, F. M. Training speech to an autistic child through operant conditioning. *American Journal of Orthopsychiatry,* 1965, **35**, 927–936.

Kohlenberg, R. J. The punishment of persistent vomiting: A case study. *Journal of Applied Behavior Analysis,* 1970, **3**, 241–245.

Krumboltz, J. D. & Krumboltz, H. B. *Changing children's behavior.* Englewood Cliffs, N.J.: Prentice-Hall, 1972.

Lovaas, O. I. & Simmons, J. O. Manipulation of self destruction in three retarded children. *Journal of Applied Behavior Analysis,* 1969, **2**, 143–157.

Ludwig, J. O. & Maehr, N. M. Changes in self-concept and stated behavioral preferences. *Child Development,* 1967, **35**, 453–468.

Marshall, H. H. The effect of punishment on children: A review of the literature and a suggested hypothesis. *The Journal of Genetic Psychology,* 1965, **106**, 23–33.

Martin, J. A. Children's task preferences: Effects of reinforcement and punishment. Paper presented at the meeting of the American Psychological Association, New Orleans, August 1974.

Mayer, G. R., Sulzer, B. & Cody, J. J. The use of punishment in modifying students' behavior. *Journal of Special Education,* 1968, **2**, 323–328.

Moore, B. J. & Bailey, J. S. Social punishment in the modification of a pre-school child's "autistic-like" behavior with a mother as therapist. *Journal of Applied Behavior Analysis,* 1973, **6**, 497–507.

Oliver, S. D., West, R. C. & Sloane, H. N., Jr. Some effects on human behavior of aversive events. *Behavior Therapy,* 1974, **5**, 481–493.

Risley, T. The effects and side effects of punishing the autistic behaviors of a deviant child. *Journal of Applied Behavior Analysis,* 1968, **1**, 21–35.

Skinner, B. F. *Technology of Teaching.* New York: Appleton, 1968.

Solomon, R. L. Punishment. *American Psychologist,* 1964, **19**, 239–253.

Staines, J. W. The self-picture as a factor in the classroom. *British Journal of Educational Psychology,* 1958, **28**, 97–111.

Stolz, S. B. Ethical issues in research in behavior therapy. In W. S. Wood (Ed.), *Professional issues in evaluating behavior modification.* Champaign: Research Press, 1975, Pp. 239–256.

Watson, J. B. & Rayner, R. Conditioned emotional reactions. *Journal of Experimental Psychology,* 1920, **3**, 1–14.

Wattenberg, W. W. & Clifford, C. Relation of self-concepts to beginning achievement in reading. *Child Development,* 1964, **35**, 461–467.

Wright, L. Aversive conditioning of self induced seizures. *Behavior Therapy,* 1973, **4**, 712–713.

Wyatt v. Stickney, 344F. Supp. 400–401 (M.D. Ala., 1972 N.D.)

Zimmerman, J. & Ferster, C. B. Intermittent punishment of S responding in matching-to-sample. *Journal of the Experimental Analysis of Behavior,* 1963, **6**, 349–356.

Extending Behavior: Generalization Training

After mastering the material in this unit, you should be able to
1. Define and illustrate generalization training.

2. List and discuss the variables that promote generalization.

3. Discuss the relevance of generalization training to special programs and artificial settings.

4. Use generalization training to occasion a behavior in more than one setting.

Working in cooperation with a behavior analyst, Ms. Charming, the workshop supervisor, has assisted her client Fern to attend to tasks and to complete her work assignments at an acceptable level. Fern is now ready to seek employment in a community workshop. But will her recently acquired skills be extended and maintained in the new setting? Lucretia has learned to play cooperatively with a particular group of children. What will happen when she finds herself in a different group? Dexter completes his math and science work satisfactorily and is now concerned about social studies. What does applied behavior analysis have to offer to assist in extending a behavior into a new situation?

The various procedures that have been discussed in the preceding units are designed to increase, establish, and reduce specific behaviors. They serve, in essence, as the major focus of applied behavior-analysis programs. Let us recall, however, that the full behavior-analysis model includes a series of essential components: preliminary steps, goal selection, specification of objectives, selection of measures and contingencies, a series of procedural steps—plus evaluation, maintenance, generalization, and communication (see "summary," Unit 7 and Figure 7.2). Consequently, even though a behavioral procedure may have demonstrated its effectiveness, the job is not yet complete. Maintenance, generalization, evaluation, and communication remain. Evaluation is planned before implementation of procedures and is carried out during the program. But, because methods of evaluation are not behavior-change procedures and are also rather technical, they will not be fully treated until near the end of the book. We turn our attention in the next four units to behavioral principles and procedures that relate to generalization and maintenance.

Dexter and his teacher have negotiated and carried out a very effective contract. Contingent upon study behaviors, Dexter has been earning for himself and the class points that can be exchanged for special privileges. It is late in the semester, and the following year must be considered. Dexter does not want to depend upon the point system forever and would like to terminate it. Yet he, his teacher, and the school psychologist are all afraid that the recently acquired study behaviors may not persist in the new situation. What kind of programming will promote maintained responding under various environmental conditions? Generalization and intermittent reinforcement can assist in achieving such goals. Let us turn first to generalization.

GENERALIZATION DEFINED AND ILLUSTRATED

Generalization training focuses on antecedent stimuli. It extends stimulus control to conditions other than those in effect when the behavior was originally learned— for example, from therapy to home, from one task to another, from school to community. In Unit 12, generalization was described as the phenomenon by which a *behavior conditioned in one stimulus situation tends to be emitted in other stimulus situations*. Generalization implies the absence of control by a discrete set of discriminative stimuli. When a child stops what she is doing at the word "no" in a new situation, she may be generalizing a response learned at home. Baby Bonnie, who calls lions, elephants, and all other quadrupeds "doggies," is also generalizing. Similarly, adults may attempt to kill harmless or even beneficial spiders and snakes because they are generalizing from harmful species.

In Unit 12, the focus was upon techniques for enhancing discriminative stimulus control: teaching clients to discriminate among different stimulus conditions and to emit appropriate responses in the presence of each. Taught to discriminate appropriately, Baby Bonnie will no longer mislabel the lion at the zoo "doggie." In this unit our concern is quite different. Here the objective is to present methods for *promoting* generalization so that behaviors acquired or strengthened under one set of conditions are more likely to occur under other conditions. If taught to generalize appropriately, Dexter can transfer study habits acquired in one setting into other settings.

Effective behavior-change programs usually require that behaviors learned in an instructional setting be generalized to many situations in and out of that setting. The student is expected to apply the skills acquired in reading lessons to handling materials in social studies and science, as well as to reading menus, application forms, novels, and rest-room door signs. It is assumed that workshop trainees will carry their newly acquired skills into actual job situations. The assumption that generalization will occur spontaneously is frequently fallacious, however (O'Leary & Drabman, 1971).

Counselors and therapists often assume that behaviors learned in the counseling or therapy office will be generalized or transferred to the home, classroom, and other settings. In one study (Kennedy & Thompson, 1967), in fact, it was reported that a first-grade child's increased attending behavior, learned in counseling, did generalize to classroom subject matter. The time that he spent attending during arithmetic lessons increased by 14 percent, even though contingencies were not manipulated during arithmetic class.

EFFECTIVELY PROMOTING GENERALIZATION TRAINING

The spontaneous transfer of instructional or therapy gains across settings tends to be more the exception than the rule, however (Kazdin & Bootzin, 1972; Rincover & Koegel, 1975; Stokes, Baer & Jackson, 1974; Tracey, Briddell & Wilson, 1974). Training residential staff or teachers in a workshop does not necessarily mean that they will follow through in the living unit or classroom. A language-deficient child taught to speak in a one-to-one session may not speak elsewhere. If generalization is desired, training for generalization should be made an integral part of the instructional program and should be implemented either during the program or after the criterion for success in achieving the behavioral objective has been met. It should not be left to chance.

Emphasizing Common Elements

Emphasizing common elements may help clients to generalize a behavior learned in one situation to other situations. The situations must share common elements, and those elements should be emphasized. When it is possible to identify the discriminative stimuli under which a client has first emitted a specific behavior, as well as the reinforcing or other stimulus consequences, it is naturally easier to teach her to generalize. Once these stimuli have been identified, many of them can be introduced into the new situation. The two situations will then have many common elements, which will enable the client, in a sense, to form a conception of the occasions on which the response should occur.

Effective teachers make frequent use of methods for facilitating generalization training, though they may not be aware of doing so. They do so when teaching academic subjects, as well as social and other behaviors. Such teaching goes on all the time. For example, a teacher says:

You know the word *ball.*
Now we are going to learn the word *fall.*
Notice the *a-l-l* at the end of the word *ball.*

It says *all*.
The word *fall* also ends in *all*, and it is pronounced *f-all*.
Now, how do you pronounce *t-a-l-l*?

The teacher is selecting the common elements among the words "ball," "fall," and "tall." These elements are emphasized, which tends to facilitate learning.

A consultant helped a recreation leader who seldom used reinforcement to reinforce one of her clients, Humphrey, socially each time that he participated in a discussion. The goal was to increase his participation. The recreation leader successfully carried out the program with Humphrey, but her use of social reinforcement was not generalized to other clients: She seldom used social reinforcement with anyone else. The consultant pointed out similarities between Humphrey and Claude. Claude was another participant in the group, who also seldom talked, was about the same age, and had similar interests. After she had generalized her reinforcing response to Claude, the consultant began pointing out the common features between these two boys and others and suggested that reinforcement would probably work for them too: "After all, it worked in similar circumstances." Eventually, the reinforcing responses were generalized to the others.

Seymour's counselor is assisting him to learn to interact more positively with a new client, Mike: to talk to him and smile at him. She observes that Seymour is already friendly with Fred and notes several similar characteristics of Fred and Mike. Deciding to use generalization training in an attempt to achieve her goal, the counselor points out to Seymour the characteristics that Fred and Mike have in common. She hopes that he may then be more likely to respond to Mike as he does to Fred. Similarly, in the counseling illustration taken from Kennedy and Thompson (1967), the behavior analyst might have indicated to the first-grader that he was now "attending" better to the counselor and that he should be able to do the same with other adults in the classroom. It seems, however, that generalization to the classroom from a counseling setting is even more likely to occur when *group* counseling, rather than *individual* counseling, is used during transition. A group-counseling situation bears a greater resemblance to the child's classroom than the individual counseling setting does.

Behavior analysts have the responsibility to help other practitioners and the public to realize the importance of generalization to special and remedial programs. Unless generalization training is programmed to accompany procedures in special settings, behaviors learned in such programs are not likely to be generalized to natural settings (Walker & Buckley, 1972; Walker, Hops & Johnson, 1975). For example, special classrooms have been set up for "educationally handicapped" (EH) children and youths in many school districts. Frequently, these classes have small numbers of students and at least one teacher with trained aides for each. Much of the material used is different from that of the regular classroom. Often in such an environment many students learn appropriate academic and social behaviors. Then, upon being *mainstreamed* into regular classrooms—and to the dismay of those involved—the gains made in the EH classroom do not carry over to the regular classroom. A major reason is that conditions have not been arranged to facilitate generalization.

The EH and regular classroom situations are too dissimilar to promote generalization. There are differences in the numbers of students and teachers and in the types of materials and tasks requested of students. Also changes in the frequency of reinforcement encountered in moving from the EH classroom to the regular classroom may almost resemble extinction conditions. If generalization is to occur, discriminative stimuli—like similar rules, instructional materials, and schedules of activities—should be provided, and no abrupt change in reinforcement schedules should take place. A few school districts have set up "halfway" classes to help bridge the gap between the two very different types of classrooms. Others gradually introduce students into regular classroom settings or train "regular" classroom teachers in the procedures used by EH teachers. For example, Walker and colleagues (1975) developed an elaborate program for training regular classroom teachers in many of the behavioral strategies used in experimental classrooms. Sheltered workshops for developmentally delayed or disabled persons help to smooth the transition to regular vocational positions. Halfway houses perform similar functions for youths moving back to the community from correction facilities or for retarded citizens moving toward full community placement.

Too often, however, no provisions are made to promote generalization, and then people are dismayed when generalization does not occur. The behavior analyst must ensure that such provisions are made.

Switching to Intermittent Reinforcement

When a behavior is well established under specific stimulus conditions, a shift to intermittent reinforcement *before generalization training* may accomplish two purposes: first, promoting maintenance in that setting and, second, facilitating generalization. Intermittent reinforcement for response maintenance will be discussed in Unit 24. As for the facilitation of generalization, there is some suggestion that behaviors that are intermittently reinforced will generalize more effectively than those that are continuously reinforced. Koegel (1975) found that, when his autistic clients were not reinforced every time they emitted desired responses in the training sessions, they were more likely to generalize the responses to new settings.

Identifying and Using Discriminative Stimuli

The stimuli common to situations often function as discriminative stimuli (S^Ds) and thus serve to foster generalization. Not all the stimuli in a situation have controlling properties or function as S^Ds. Generalization is more likely to occur when the S^Ds are present across situations. When common antecedent-stimulus elements are introduced and generalization does not follow, the appropriate S^D has not been identified; others will have to be tried. That is what Rincover and Koegel (1975) found in their study with autistic children. For example, in individual therapy a client was taught to touch his nose upon request. It was assumed that the request was the S^D. In the classroom, however, the client did not touch his nose upon request by the teacher or therapist. The table and chairs from the therapy room were found to be the controlling S^Ds. They had to be present before the client would touch his nose upon request. The behavior would occur most anywhere (for example, outdoors) and at the request of anyone *only* if the table and chairs were present. Some children, then, do not respond to "appropriate" cues or are "micro selective," which results in restricted stimulus control. In the next section we address ourselves to methods for avoiding or ameliorating such situations.

Training the Response under a Variety of Stimulus Conditions

Generalization is more likely to occur when the behavior is instilled under a variety of stimulus conditions (Corte, Wolf & Locke, 1971; Garcia, 1974; Kale et al., 1968; Lovaas & Simmons, 1969; Stokes, Baer & Jackson, 1974). For example, in the previously mentioned study of autistic children by Rincover and Koegel, using several therapists in multiple settings would have helped "by making it difficult for idiosyncratic and unreliable stimuli to acquire control over appropriate responding" (1975, p. 245), which is, in essence, what Stokes, Baer, and Jackson (1974) did when teaching hand waving (a social response) to four institutionalized ten-to-thirteen-year-old retarded clients. For three of the subjects, this form of greeting was generalized to other staff members only after they received training in a variety of settings (playroom, corridor, and courtyard) from more than one experimenter. Generally, training by two or three contingency managers in several different settings seems necessary if generalization is to occur across settings (Corte, Wolf & Locke, 1971; Garcia, 1974; Lovaas & Simmons, 1969; Stokes, Baer & Jackson, 1974).

Adding S^Ds and Altering Reinforcement Conditions

Often it is helpful temporarily to combine natural and supplementary stimuli, like instructions or gestures that have been observed to have discriminative control over some of the client's other behaviors. Those can be used in the original training situation and shifted to the novel one along with the client, or they may be applied in the new situation. Parents, teachers, aides, or other staff members may cue the behavior with requests. Dexter could be reminded to chart his task completion in social studies. Jackson and Wallace (1974) found supplementary S^Ds helpful adjuncts in teaching a "disturbed" fifteen-year-old girl to generalize speaking more loudly from a laboratory cubicle to the classroom. For the transition to be complete, however, the supplementary S^Ds must eventually be faded.

Care must also be given to the selection and use of reinforcers if generalization is to be facilitated. Provision for moving away from artificial reinforcing contingencies should be made. For example, each of the prime variables that influence reinforcer effectiveness—quality, quantity, immediacy, schedules, and possibly others—should be examined to determine whether or not any departs substantially from the manner in which it is contingently arranged in the natural environment. If so, the program must include a plan for phasing back to natural consequences. In the previous units on reinforcement, we have discussed how this guideline is followed in moving from artificial to natural kinds of reinforcers. Exactly the same methods could be used in other programs in which the quality or kind of reinforcer is unnatural to the situation. Introducing delay of reinforcement has also been discussed. Again reinforcement should be progressively diminished until its frequency approximates that of the natural situation. Fern has been receiving tokens upon completion of each task. Delay is introduced; the tokens are saved for her and presented at the end of each session for a few weeks, then at the end of each week (the pay schedule that she will encounter in her new setting). The data should always inform the programmer of the adequacy of the program. A serious deterioration in behavior suggests that delay has been introduced too abruptly and that one should back up a step or two before reintroducing more gradual progressions in delay.

The quantity of reinforcers delivered during programs employing optimal reinforcing contingencies may often be quite rich in comparison with that present in the natural environment. Let us recall that an adequate amount of a reinforcement is necessary to support initially high rates of responding. It may have taken 100 points to persuade Flossie to eat her spinach the first few times, but after a while it should be possible and even advisable gradually to reduce the number of points and eventually to award no points, as at a normal mealtime.

Summary

Generalization training extends stimulus control to conditions or settings other than those under which the behavior has been acquired or strengthened. Often such a transfer is desirable, for the necessity to teach the same behavior repeatedly in each new situation is thus avoided. In order to facilitate generalization, it is helpful to stress common elements, to identify and use S^Ds, to teach the response initially under a variety of stimulus conditions, to combine temporarily such generalization training with supplementary S^Ds, and to alter reinforcement conditions.

References

Corte, H. E., Wolf, M. M. & Locke, B. J. A comparison of procedures for eliminating self injurious behavior of retarded adolescents. *Journal of Applied Behavior Analysis,* 1971, **4**, 201–213.

Garcia, E. The training and generalization of a conversational speech form in nonverbal retardates. *Journal of Applied Behavior Analysis,* 1974, **7**, 137–149.

Jackson, D. A. & Wallace, R. F. The modification and generalization of voice loudness in a fifteen-year-old retarded girl. *Journal of Applied Behavior Analysis,* 1974, **7**, 461–471.

Kale, R. J., Kaye, J. H., Whelan, P. A. & Hopkins, B. L. The effects of reinforcement on the modification, maintenance, and generalization of social responses of mental patients. *Journal of Applied Behavior Analysis,* 1968, **1**, 307–314.

Kazdin, A. E. & Bootzin, R. R. The token economy: An evaluative review. *Journal of Applied Behavior Analysis,* 1972, **5**, 343–372.

Kennedy, D. A. & Thompson, I. Use of reinforcement technique with a first grade boy. *The Personnel and Guidance Journal,* 1967, **46**, 366–370.

Koegel, R. L. The generalization and maintenance of treatment gains. Paper presented at the Association for Advancement of Behavior Therapy, San Francisco, December 1975.

Lovaas, O. I. & Simmons, J. A. Manipulation of self-destruction in three retarded children. *Journal of Applied Behavior Analysis*, 1969, **2**, 143–157.

O'Leary, K. D. & Drabman, R. Token reinforcement programs in the classroom: An overview. *Psychological Bulletin*, 1971, **75**, 379–398.

Rincover, A. & Koegel, R. L. Setting generality and stimulus control in autistic children. *Journal of Applied Behavior Analysis*, 1975, **8**, 235–246.

Stokes, T. F., Baer, D. M. & Jackson, R. L. Programming the generalization of a greeting response in four retarded children. *Journal of Applied Behavior Analysis*, 1974, **7**, 599–610.

Tracey, D. A., Briddell, D. W. & Wilson, G. T. Generalization of verbal conditioning to verbal and nonverbal behavior: Group therapy with chronic psychiatric patients. *Journal of Applied Behavior Analysis,* 1974, **7**, 391–402.

Walker, H. M. & Buckley, N. K. Programming generalization and maintenance of treatment effects across time and across settings. *Journal of Applied Behavior Analysis*, 1972, **5**, 209–224.

Walker, H. M., Hops, H. & Johnson, S. M. Generalization and maintenance of classroom treatment effects. *Behavior Therapy*, 1975, **6**, 188–200.

Maintaining Behavior: Intermittent Reinforcement

After mastering the material in this unit, you should be able to
1. Define and offer illustrations for each of the following terms:
   a. Schedule of reinforcement
   b. Intermittent reinforcement
   c. Continuous .einforcement (CRF)
   d. Intrinsic motivation
   e. Reinforcement density

2. List and give illustrations of the major advantages of intermittent reinforcement.

3. Describe with an example how one should proceed in switching from continuous reinforcement to intermittent reinforcement, first, without using supplementary reinforcers and, then, with supplementary reinforcers.

4. Along with fading, use generalization training and intermittent reinforcement to maintain the occurrence of a behavior under more than one set of conditions.

Fern has been receiving tokens for each task completed in the prevocational workshop that she attends. When she transfers into a full-fledged workshop job, she will not receive such frequent reinforcement. Rather, she will be paid on a weekly basis. To prepare her for the shift, token delivery could be abruptly terminated. But it is reasonably feared that her task completion would then be disrupted. Is there some way to avoid such disruption in the face of a reduction in reinforcement?

The issue of maintaining acquired behavior once the frequency of reinforcement has been reduced or eliminated is one that has been given considerable attention by behavioral psychologists in recent years. The publication *Schedules of Reinforcement* (Ferster & Skinner, 1957) demonstrated how experimental situations can be structured so that firmly acquired behaviors maintain in the animal laboratory for long periods of time. This goal was accomplished both with noncontinuous reinforcement and in the complete absence of any reinforcement. Further research has also repeatedly demonstrated that, given certain conditions, prolonged periods of maintained responding can be achieved.[1] The conditions that have resulted in such maintained performance involve the manner in which the environment delivers reinforcement. More specifically, they involve the *schedule* of reinforcement, ". . . the rule followed by the environment . . . in determining which among the many occurrences of a response will be reinforced" (Reynolds, 1968, p. 60).

Human performance under various schedules of reinforcement has also been investigated both in the laboratory and in field settings. Hutchinson and Azrin (1961) found that one form of schedule performance by mental-hospital patients, though not identical with, did resemble similar schedule performance by various animals. This resemblance was also observed among mental defectives (Ellis, Barnett & Pryer, 1960) and among chronic psychotics (Lindsley, 1960). Continuing research on schedule effects among human beings (Bijou & Orlando, 1961; Deitz & Repp, 1974; Holden & Sulzer-Azaroff, 1972; Long, 1962; 1963; and Weiner, 1969) is making it possible to extend conclusions reached about the behavior of animals under various reinforcement schedules to human behavior. Such research is also aimed at discovering those characteristics of schedule performance that are specific to human behavior. Because the resemblance of schedule performances in animals and human beings has been found to be close but not identical, much more experimental work will have to be performed with human subjects. Until then, only tentative statements can be made about the applicability of the principles of intermittent reinforcement to the performance of children and youth.

INTERMITTENT REINFORCEMENT DEFINED AND ILLUSTRATED

When we say that a behavior is being **intermittently reinforced**, we mean simply that *some, but not all, emissions of the response are being reinforced.* Many specific reinforcement schedules fall under the very general label of "intermittent reinforcement." Mother does not give Tina a drink of water each time that she asks for one, just sometimes. Asking for a drink is thus intermittently reinforced. Ernie is appointed captain of the team only after a certain interval has past since

[1] Many of the significant studies of maintenance of behavior through schedule control have been reported in various issues of the *Journal of the Experimental Analysis of Behavior.* For a thorough, programmed treatment of reinforcement schedules see Thompson & Grabowski (1972).

he was last allowed to be captain. In the meantime his requests to lead the team are denied. The requests are thus intermittently reinforced. Because different reinforcement schedules tend to generate performances that differ from one another, several of the more extensively investigated schedules will be discussed individually in Units 25 and 26. There are, however, some generalities that hold true for many different intermittent reinforcement schedules. They will be presented in this unit.

ADVANTAGES OF INTERMITTENT REINFORCEMENT

In Unit 10 we learned that the best way to strengthen a weak behavior is to reinforce it as often as possible, preferably continuously. Assuming that continuous reinforcement (CRF) has firmly established the behavior in the individual's repertoire, we can raise the question whether or not such a schedule should be maintained. Fortunately, it is not necessary: Continuous reinforcement is neither the most effective nor the most efficient way to maintain behavior. Furthermore, as mentioned previously, some evidence suggests that intermittently reinforced responding may generalize more effectively as well (Koegel, 1975). It may thus actually be preferable to stop reinforcing every emission of a response and to switch to an intermittent reinforcement schedule.

Delaying Satiation

One reason for shifting away from continuous reinforcement is that individuals may become sated if they receive too much reinforcement. Let us consider how long responding maintains under CRF. The response of lifting a fork to the mouth is continually reinforced by the consequence of food in the mouth. Although unlimited quantities of food may be available, the behavior of lifting the fork will eventually stop and will not be resumed for a prolonged interval. We can then assume that the individual has been sated. Under CRF scheduling, satiation occurs fairly rapidly, especially when the reinforcers are unconditioned: food, drink, or sex, for example (Holland & Skinner, 1961). With conditioned reinforcement, satiation effects are somewhat delayed; with generalized reinforcement, they are delayed even further. But satiation does eventually occur under very dense, or rich, reinforcement schedules. Although Clyde continues to scribble "pictures" for an approving parent or teacher, he will stop scribbling after a while. The approval may have been reinforcing, but its effect has become temporarily inadequate to support the behavior, especially as continued scribbling probably requires increasing amounts of effort from Clyde. If Fern has acquired an unusually large hoard of tokens, she may also tend to reduce her rate of working for token reinforcement.

If the goal is to keep well-established behaviors going, it then becomes important to avoid satiation. One way is to stop reinforcing each and every emission of the behavior and to reinforce intermittently instead. Fewer reinforcers will then be received for an equivalent number of responses, and the behavior will continue to be emitted longer before the satiation effect manifests itself. The hungry child, in the early stages of learning to use a fork, will usually drop a lot of the food. The behavior of lifting the fork to the mouth will thus result in reinforcement on an intermittent schedule. If enough food reaches the child's mouth to maintain the attempt, many fork-lifting responses will be emitted—more than an adult or a child adept in the use of the fork would emit. Natural consequences have provided an intermittent reinforcement schedule, and satiation effects have been delayed. The behavior (lifting the fork) maintains for a long time.

A shift from continuous to intermittent reinforcement should be incorporated into the planning of behavior-analysis programs. Let us consider how this goal might be accomplished in helping Fern to establish good-grooming skills. For several days or weeks the attendant has commented how nice Fern's hair looks each and every time she combs it. When data show that combing behavior is well established (perhaps over several weeks), the attendant begins to skip complimenting Fern occasionally. Reinforcement thus shifts from continuous to intermittent.

Maintaining Performance under Extinction

Intermittent reinforcement provides for longer periods of maintained responding while reinforcement is being delivered. What happens when reinforcement is ultimately discontinued, that is, under extinction conditions? Experimental data suggest that a history of intermittent reinforcement tends under extinction conditions to generate performance that maintains longer than that generated by a history of CRF. The way in which people perform with food-vending machines, in comparison with their performance on gambling slot machines, illustrates this phenomenon. Which performance persists longer when reinforcement is no longer forthcoming? Usually, when coins are inserted into a vending machine and the lever pressed, those responses are reinforced by the delivery of an item like candy. Individuals with such a CRF history at the vending machine give up quickly when the behavioral chain is no longer reinforced and the machine no longer dispenses the item. They may drop two or three more coins into the machine, but pretty soon that form of responding ceases. What of the slot-machine players? They insert coin after coin into the slot machine. Occasionally the jackpot is hit and a pile of coins drops. More often than not, the number of coins in the jackpot is less than the number already spent. Yet, even though the machine may break down and no further winnings may result, slot-machine performance tends to maintain for quite a while, at least longer than vending-machine performance. (If extinction conditions were maintained indefinitely, customers would give up. The slot machine would no longer be used, and the machine owner would lose business. Slot machines are therefore usually not intentionally programmed to withhold delivery of coins permanently. They are simply programmed to reinforce intermittently.)

Maintained performance under extinction conditions, following intermittent reinforcement, can be observed in all facets of life. Griselda continues shooting at the basket with a basketball for a pretty long time, for she has occasionally made a basket in the past. Helen will continue to take her medication daily for a while in the absence of reinforcement when she has had a history of being reinforced intermittently with prizes and approval from the nursing staff for her performance. Humphrey, who has won chess contests, will continue to enter competition many times in the absence of victory before his attempts cease. These illustrations contrast with the performance of individuals who have had histories of CRF schedules. Giselle, the basketball whiz who has sunk just about every basket she has shot in the past would probably give up quickly (and in a fit of frustration) if after many attempts she were unable to put the ball through the hoop. For the patient who has received inordinate attention from the staff each time he has decided to take his medication, a sudden withdrawal of attention contingent on that behavior might be devastating: He might stop taking his medication altogether. A similar reaction could beset the chess champion of the neighborhood. Having won every chess match in the past, he might, after defeat, cease entering chess competitions.

Undesirable, as well as desirable, behaviors show similar characteristics as a function of the scheduling history. Another familiar illustration is the "spoiled" child or youth who has been reinforced very heavily in the past by doting parents. But, if the day comes when reinforcement is no longer delivered, performance stops fairly abruptly. Henrietta has been consistently successful in obtaining attention by threatening to drop out of school. Advised by the family therapist to ignore such statements completely (but to attend to positive statements about school), the parents find that the threats increase briefly and then cease rapidly. Had they been attended to intermittently, they would have persisted much longer.

Maintaining Well-Established Behaviors

It is undoubtedly reassuring to practitioners that intermittent reinforcement maintains well-established behaviors more effectively than does continuous reinforcement. It is this fact that makes the whole notion of employing behavioral procedures in group settings feasible. Chaos could be the only result if teachers were to try to reinforce certain specific behaviors of each of twenty-five or forty students in each of their classes. First of all, they would be so busy concentrating on how to respond to whom that they would probably forget what they were trying to teach. Second, in many instances it would be patently ridiculous to use continuous reinforcement with all members of such a group. An example will illustrate the potential absurdity of such a situation: The teacher decides to reinforce Jimmy, Susie, Ralph, George, Tommy, and Ebenezer continuously for contributing to group discussions. "How did you spend your vacation?" he asks. All six children raise their hands! Then what? It is apparent that only one child can be called upon at a time. But actually that is fine. If all six former noncontributors do manage to raise their hands simultaneously, the behavior is probably becoming fairly well established in their repertoires. They are probably ready for the switch from continuous to intermittent reinforcement. Each child can be called on in turn. Assuming that intermittent reinforcement effectively maintains behavior, the teacher has found a practical and efficient means of employing behavioral procedures in the classroom.

Intermittent reinforcement is also very helpful to consultants who work with teachers and parents. For example, Cossairt, Hall, and Hopkins concluded in their study:

A notable aspect of the study was that teacher praise maintained and even increased when teachers were placed in an intermittent schedule of social praise. This would seem to indicate that the excuse that principals and supportive staff do not have time for the social reinforcement of teacher behavior is invalid. Operant principles of reinforcement systematically applied would therefore seem to be functional in helping principals and consultants accomplish their primary goal, which should be improving instruction. It would also seem that this could be done with a minimal amount of time and effort. (1973, p. 100)

Intermittent reinforcement, as in the study by Cossairt, Hall, and Hopkins, need not always be administered in person. This fact can save even more of the consultant's time. For example, Holden and Sulzer-Azaroff (1972) were able to maintain teachers' implementation of suggested behavioral procedures by means of frequent but intermittent phone calls. Intermittent reinforcement, then, can save the consultant time while supporting procedural effectiveness.

People must be careful not to use their knowledge of reinforcement principles as an excuse not to reinforce. MacDonald, Gallimore, and MacDonald (1970) noted that parents and relatives needed support (reinforcement) in the form of face-to-face meetings or telephone conversations at least *twice a week* in order to maintain behavioral contracts between them and their adolescent children for increasing school attendance. Similarly, Walker and colleagues (1975) reported having to consult with teachers once a week during program implementation. We strongly recommend that, if the consultant cannot contact the consultee or contingency manager at least once or twice a week during the early phase of the program to reinforce implementation, the program *not* be started. This point is particularly important for consultees who have not had many previous reinforcing experiences in using behavioral procedures. This point was emphasized in a study by Hunt and Sulzer-Azaroff (1974), who found that only approximately 25 percent of their clients' parents followed through with jointly determined programs in the absence of intermittent reinforcement. All were reported complying with the programs when frequent intermittent positive feedback was delivered.

DEVELOPING "INTRINSIC MOTIVATION"

Not only does intermittent reinforcement make the whole notion of using behavioral procedures systematically in group settings possible, but it is also necessary if individuals are to become **intrinsically motivated**. This fact was pointed out in the units on positive reinforcement. Intrinsic reinforcement implies an absence of extrinsic reinforcement. Extrinsic reinforcers therefore have to be phased out if a behavior is to be intrinsically reinforcing. This phasing out is accomplished through intermittent reinforcement. For example, two girls, Giselle and Griselda, are learning to play basketball. When Giselle first attempts to play, she is reinforced practically every time: "Great try! That's better; You're doing fine." These extrinsic social reinforcers are paired with smiles, hugs, and other reinforcers from her family and peers. As Giselle becomes more proficient in the game, the frequency of such comments gradually decreases (intermittent reinforcement). She then starts to play for longer and longer periods of time without extrinsic reinforcers. Eventually she spends long periods shooting baskets by herself. This activity has become a *high-frequency activity*. Others might say that Giselle is *intrinsically motivated* to play basketball. Basketball appears to be an intrinsically reinforcing activity because it occurs with few or no "extrinsic" reinforcing consequences. On the other hand, Griselda is ridiculed when she misses a few shots in her game. She thus avoids playing. When asked to play at school, something similar happens, magnified by her lack of experience. Does Griselda spend her free time playing basketball? No. She spends it in an activity in which she has experienced reinforcement: reading.

Both Giselle's parents and Griselda's parents believed that it was important to read to their children when they were young and they selected lots of interesting stories. When Griselda's parents read to her, they cuddled and played with her and asked and answered questions about the stories. Books and reading were paired with a variety of positive reinforcers. Soon Griselda actively sought out story time. When she started school she would pay close attention to the teacher whenever a story was read. This attention resulted in her receiving more positive reinforcement from the teacher. She would attend to anything associated with books. When she was taught how to read, again she applied herself and continued to receive reinforcement. As she became more proficient in reading, the extrinsic reinforcement was thinned out. Eventually she spent her free time reading and enjoying books. This activity, because it had been paired with reinforcement, had become a reinforcer: a high-frequency behavior. Or, as others would say, Griselda was intrinsically motivated to read.

On the other hand, Giselle experienced a very different reinforcement history. When her parents sat down to read to her, the activity was not made reinforcing. In fact, when her attention wandered, they would criticize her lack of attention. (Perhaps they thought that, because reading was "good" for her, she should *want* to do it.) In any event it came to the point that at reading time Giselle was not around or would have some excuse or another activity to occupy the time. When school started, she was very inattentive, or "hyperactive," during story time. As a result, her teacher punished her. By the time that the teacher attempted to teach her to read, Giselle wanted nothing to do with the activity. To her it was *very* aversive. The result was more punishment in the form of teacher disapproval and poor grades. Does Giselle spend her free time reading? No! Reading for her was not initially paired with extrinsic reinforcers, which were then gradually removed, as they were for Griselda. Intrinsic motivation, then, is developed as a function of an individual's environmental experiences, or reinforcement history. It does not occur in the absence of intermittent reinforcement.

We should not, however, conclude that intrinsic motivation must be the goal of all programs. In some client populations it may be necessary to continue extrinsic reinforcement indefinitely. Profoundly retarded, autistic, or other children with severely impaired or delayed behavioral repertoires may need to have their efforts supported by extrinsic reinforcers, at least intermittently. Furthermore, most of us receive intermittent support for our efforts from extrinsic sources. We probably have to have some extrinsic encouragement to keep writing books, working on an assembly line, doing household chores, teaching youngsters, and other arduous tasks.

SWITCHING TO INTERMITTENT REINFORCEMENT

The reduction of **reinforcement density** (the frequency with which a particular response is reinforced) is a touchy affair. If reinforcement is withheld abruptly after many emissions of a behavior that has been on CRF, the behavior may disintegrate. Under such extinction conditions, the individual is likely to stop emitting the behavior, and he may exhibit some unanticipated behaviors like crying and hitting. Let us suppose that Mr. Grump has failed to pay Harry for mowing his lawn four or five times in a row. How long will the boy continue to mow the lawn? If a school district stopped paying its personnel for five or six months, they would probably quit. For Fern, who has been complimented by her attendant each time that she has combed her hair for several consecutive days, a sudden withdrawal of recognition for eight or ten attempts would probably send her back to her former grooming habits. The way to avoid such disintegration is to make the change progressively. It is also helpful to ease the shock of reduction in reinforcement density by adding discriminative stimuli, like reminders, and occasional supplementary reinforcers as well. In the following sections we offer suggestions on how the change can be accomplished smoothly.

Progressively Reducing Reinforcement Density

Once a particular behavior is no longer receiving continuous reinforcement, it becomes possible to increase the number of responses or the amount of time required before reinforcement. In fact, some animals and human beings are known to continue to emit particular behaviors in incredibly large numbers and over extremely long intervals before a single reinforcement is received. College students may read thousands and thousands of pages before obtaining the credit for a course. They attend school for approximately seventeen years before being reinforced with college diplomas. Novelists have been known to write for years and years before selling their first books, and the avid fisherman or hunter keeps the vigil for lengths of time that confound the uninitiated. Training students in similar kinds of persistence is one of the major goals of formal education. To have developed students who continue, on completion of their formal schooling, to be productive, even though financial, social, and other rewards may be infrequent, testifies to the success of an educational program. In order to achieve this goal, the schools must require their students to do progressively more work for longer time periods before receiving formal consequences. It is fine to praise each sentence that students compose in the second grade. But, if a similarly high rate of reinforcement for their writing persists through their senior year in high school, they will be in trouble. Once the contingency is removed, it is likely that the behavior (writing) will disintegrate. All the efforts made by such students' teachers will have gone for naught. Yet students do, on the whole, tend to maintain many behaviors that they have acquired in school. In general, our educational system is doing well in that regard. Progressive reduction in reinforcement density is practiced, probably without awareness. (White, 1975, found that teachers used fewer social reinforcers with older than with younger students.) But perhaps by placing emphasis upon the crucial need for such progressive reductions, we can encourage even more persistent student behaviors. Instructional programming requires planning not only of content, teaching methods, and evaluation techniques but also of the periodic rate with which reinforcement will be delivered. For instance, when a new subject area is introduced in high school, assignments may first be evaluated daily (assuming that feedback on the assignments is reinforcing), then semiweekly, weekly, biweekly, and so on. Reinforcement can be scheduled so that, by the end of the term, long intervals in the absence of such feedback are being tolerated by the students.

Such progressive reduction can also help clients to persist in their use of self-control techniques (for example, self-monitoring and self-administered consequences). Richards, Perri, and Gortney (1976) found that volunteer underachieving college students persisted in self-control techniques longer and obtained better grades when their group-counseling sessions met at 2-, 10-, and 28-day intervals, rather than once every other week.

Such a schedule would probably also work effectively with staff when new responsibilities were being incorporated into a program. In the early phases of training young children to play independently, staff members could circulate continuously around the room, patting, nodding, and smiling at the children as they played appropriately. Then gradually they could begin to circulate a little less frequently, progressively lengthening the intervals before dispensing social reinforcement for the task of independent play. Such an approach would necessitate a formidable commitment of time by the staff members in the early phases of any new instructional task. Their efforts, however, would be adequately recompensed when the clients had progressed to the successful completion of longer or larger tasks. To bridge that delay in reinforcement, the staff members might implement their own self-management scheme.

Gradually Reducing Reinforcer Density

A smooth change from continuous or very dense reinforcement schedules can be accomplished by means of a reduction that is fairly gradual in the beginning. In a situation in which one of the authors participated, a client was being trained to name objects. For each correct response, he was reinforced with food. Eventually he was able to label correctly each object in a set. Clearly, the natural environment could not provide such dense reinforcement conditions. Wishing to avoid satiation effects, we decided to begin reinforcing correct responses with food on an intermittent schedule. As functional language was very new to this child, it was very important to proceed with care. Rather than reduce the reinforcement to delivery of food after every third or fourth correct response, we *skipped* reinforcement after about one correct response out of four. As time went by, more and more trials went unreinforced with food until eventually the child had to label the whole set before the first food reinforcer was delivered. This reduction was achieved very gradually; it took many weeks, but the behavior maintained at a high level. As training progressed, it was possible to reduce the density of reinforcement for newly acquired behaviors a little more rapidly. Ultimately the child could continue to function with more abrupt shifts from CRF to a schedule in which only each fifth correct response was reinforced with food. The behaviors were maintained.

Contingency managers frequently make such gradual shifts to intermittent schedules on intuitive bases, as they do with many other behavioral procedures. The athletic coach continues to praise the members of the team as they acquire a new style of responding. The first-grade teacher consistently praises students as they print their names for the first few times. But, after each performance reaches a certain level, the density of reinforcement is gradually diminished. No longer is every single response made by the athletes praised. The teacher no longer compliments each student every time his or her name is written correctly. By carefully attending to this particular aspect of teaching method, however, the instructor can handle such shifts with consistent precision. Sensitivity to signs of satiation and behavioral disruption can be heightened. If the behavior ceases abruptly, though dense reinforcement remains in effect, reinforcement has been too dense. A different reinforcer will have to be substituted and the density of the original reinforcer reduced the next time it is used. If the behavior ceases abruptly and the disruption is accompanied by apparently emotional responses at a time when a change from continuous to intermittent reinforcement is being made, the reduction in reinforcement density has probably been too rapid. A hasty retreat to denser reinforcement schedules is indicated if the behavior is to be reestablished.

Supplementary S^Ds and Reinforcers

Another technique for smoothing the transition from continuous to intermittent reinforcement is to supplement the procedure with additional discriminative stimuli and reinforcers. The part played by S^Ds in occasioning behaviors has been discussed in previous sections. To reiterate, S^Ds, antecedent stimuli that have been repeatedly paired with reinforcement, communicate that a particular behavior will probably be reinforced. Verbal S^Ds in particular can therefore temporarily assist in maintaining the emission of high frequencies of behaviors or continued responding over fairly long intervals. The most obvious examples are verbal instructions like "As soon as you complete fifty problems, you will be excused for lunch" and "After you've worked on our staff for twenty-five years, you can retire at half-pay."

Written instructions, gestures, signals, and so forth can also function in similar ways. Thumbs up and a broad grin from a person in the distance signal that good news will soon be forthcoming. The interval required to reach a particular floor at the top of a skyscraper is bridged by the changing numbers of the elevator sign. The clock on the classroom wall signals that the time for dismissal is approaching.

Institutional staff members can use such S^Ds with their clients. They can, for instance, facilitate maintained responding by communicating response requirements. Signs or instructions, like "All those who have completed the eight room-cleaning requirements will be allowed to go to the recreation center" and "A gift certificate for entrance to the movies will be given to all who arrive at the work-shop on time five days in a row," can help to avoid the behavioral disruption that may otherwise occur during the transition to longer and larger requirements. Later such S^Ds can be faded.

If we stop to think, it becomes fairly apparent that most reinforcers dispensed by human beings are accompanied by other, though perhaps weaker, reinforcers. Harry is handed money for an excellent job of yard work with a smile and a compliment. The winning touchdown is rewarded not only with another victory for the team but also with cheers, pats on the back, a parade atop the shoulders of teammates, newspaper headlines, and sometimes even scholarships or lucrative contracts to play on professional teams. Reinforcers dispensed in the normal course of the school day usually occur in clusters as well. Jeremy composes a lovely poem. Mr. Rod gives him an "A," smiles at him, asks him to post the poem on the bulletin board, suggests that he submit it to the school paper, and so forth. Let us suppose that for Jeremy the major reinforcer is the "A" because he needs a high average in order to enter college. Nevertheless, the teacher can use the less powerful reinforcers effectively. It might be possible, for example, to use them to bridge the gaps between graded assignments. Other examples of excellent, but ungraded, poetry could be maintained in the interim through praise, smiles, and other weaker reinforcers, as before. Such supplementary reinforcers could teach persistence in creative writing as the teacher initiated a progressively more intermittent schedule of reinforcement.

A transition from token to other forms of reinforcement can also serve to supplement intermittent reinforcement. Having found no other way to motivate Mervin to fulfill his responsibilities at home, his parents have instituted a token system. For each responsibility fulfilled, Mervin receives a token. The parents pair delivery of the tokens with praise, smiles, nods, and pats on the back. When Mervin completes a series of chores, the tokens are exchanged for a certain number of card games with his parents. Mervin begins to perform as desired. Tasks are completed in increasing numbers. The parents, however, have a number of other concerns. They want to stop the token system. Checking each activity or chore and delivering a token immediately upon its completion are time consuming and interrupt their other activities. Even Mervin seems to have become tired of playing cards, an activity that he has earlier embraced with enthusiasm. The time for shifting to less frequent reinforcement and ultimately to eliminating token reinforcement altogether is obviously at hand. Gradually the change is made. The parents deliver tokens after the completion of two, then three chores; ultimately Mervin receives tokens only when he has completed all his chores. The cost for a card game is also increased gradually so that Mervin has less and less opportunity to play cards for the amount of work completed. As often as possible, however, when the parents notice that Mervin is hard at work, they come by, compliment him for doing such a nice job, pat him on the back, and smile. Even when they are busily occupied with other activities, like cleaning or watching television, they stop periodically and compliment Mervin if he is hard at work but ignore him if he is not. Such events, though perhaps only weak conditioned reinforcers, can help to provide a smooth transition, first, to progressively longer ratios of reinforcement, then eventually from a token system to a program in which reinforcers more natural to the home setting can be used.

Summary

Behaviors maintain better if the density of the reinforcement is reduced. Reduction is accomplished by means of switching from continuous reinforcement (CRF) to intermittent reinforcement, which prevents the individual from becoming sated and provides a history that tends to maintain the behavior longer under extinction conditions. Intermittent reinforcement is usually more practical to administer and is necessary for the development of "intrinsic motivation." A smooth transition to intermittent reinforcement may be effectively accomplished by making the change gradual and progressive and by supplementing the procedure with additional S^Ds and reinforcers.

Intermittent reinforcement works hand in hand with generalization, as well as with fading. They all are essential for developing behaviors that are less dependent upon the contingent actions or reactions of specific others in their environment.

References

Bijou, S. W. & Orlando, R. Rapid development of multiple-schedule performances with retarded children. *Journal of the Experimental Analysis of Behavior*, 1961, **4**, 7–16.

Coissairt, A., Hall, R. V. & Hopkins, B. L. The effects of experimenter's instructions, feedback, and praise on teacher praise and student attending behavior. *Journal of Applied Behavior Analysis*, 1973, **6**, 89–100.

Deitz, S. M. & Repp, A. C. Differentially reinforcing low rates of misbehavior with normal elementary school children. *Journal of Applied Behavior Analysis*, 1974, **7**, 622.

Ellis, N. R., Barnett, C. D. & Pryer, M. W. Operant behavior in mental defectives: Exploratory studies. *Journal of the Experimental Analysis of Behavior*, 1960, **3**, 63–69.

Ferster, C. B. & Skinner, B. F. *Schedules of reinforcement.* New York: Appleton, 1957.

Holden, B. & Sulzer-Azaroff, B. Schedules of follow-up and their effect upon the maintenance of a prescriptive teaching program. In G. Semb, *Behavior analysis and education—1972.* Lawrence: University of Kansas, Follow Through, 1972. Pp. 262–277.

Holland, J. G. & Skinner, B. F. *The analysis of behavior.* New York: McGraw-Hill, 1961.

Hunt, S. & Sulzer-Azaroff, B. Motivating parent participation in home training sessions with pre-trainable retardants. Paper presented at the meeting of the American Psychological Association, New Orleans, September 1974.

Hutchinson, R. R. & Azrin, N. H. Conditioning of mental hospital patients to fixed-ratio schedules of reinforcement. *Journal of the Experimental Analysis of Behavior,* 1961, **4**, 87–95.

Koegel, R. L. The generalization and maintenance of treatment gains. Paper presented at the meeting of the Association for Advancement of Behavior Therapy, San Francisco, December 1975.

Lindsley, O. R. Characteristics of the behavior of chronic psychotics as revealed by free-operant conditioning methods. *Diseases of Nervous System Monograph Supplement,* 1960, **21**, 66–78.

Long, E. R. Additional techniques for producing multiple-schedule control in children. *Journal of the Experimental Analysis of Behavior,* 1962, **5**, 443–455.

Long, E. R. Chained and tandem scheduling with children. *Journal of the Experimental Analysis of Behavior,* 1963, **6**, 459–472.

MacDonald, W. S., Gallimore, R. & MacDonald, G. Contingency counseling by school personnel: An economical model of intervention. *Journal of Applied Behavior Analysis,* 1970, **3**, 175–182.

Reynolds, G. S. *A primer of operant conditioning.* Glenview, Ill.: Scott, Foresman, 1968.

Richards, C. S., Perri, M. G. & Gortney, C. Increasing the maintenance of self-control treatments through faded counselor contact and high information feedback. *Journal of Counseling Psychology,* 1976, **23**, 405–406.

Thompson, T., & Grabowski, J. G. *Reinforcement schedules and multioperant analysis.* New York: Appleton, 1972.

Walker, H. M., Hops, H., & Johnson, S. M. Generalization and maintenance of classroom treatment effects: *Behavior Therapy,* 1975, **6**, 188–200.

Weiner, H. Controlling human fixed-interval performance. *Journal of the Experimental Analysis of Behavior,* 1969, **12**, 349–373.

White, M. A. Natural rates of teacher approval and disapproval in the classroom. *Journal of Applied Behavior Analysis,* 1975, **8**, 367–372.

unit 25

Maintaining Behavior: Interval and Limited-Hold Schedules

After mastering the material in this unit, you should be able to
1. Define and offer illustrations for each of the following terms:
   a. Interval schedules of reinforcement
   b. Fixed-interval (FI) schedules
   c. Variable-interval (VI) schedules
   d. Limited-hold schedules
   e. Primed response

2. List and describe the characteristics of performance according to an interval schedule.

3. Discuss the advantages and disadvantages of interval schedules.

4. Compare and contrast response rates and consistency under fixed- and variable-interval schedules. State the reasons for the variations between them.

5. Describe what can be done to produce a rapid rate of responding under a variable-interval schedule.

The youths living in a community group home were working toward the goal of keeping their rooms tidy. In order to accomplish that goal, they elected a manager who was to inspect the room daily, as in the Achievement Place program (Phillips et al., 1973). The manager awarded set numbers of points to his peers, contingent upon their meeting specific criteria. The accuracy of the manager's evaluations was maintained through intermittent checks by the house parents, who awarded points contingent upon their agreement with the manager's judgment. The rates of acceptably tidied rooms had become high and steady. But the future had to be considered. Soon several of the youths would be returning home, where it was unlikely that daily room checks would be made. So a different system was tried. Instead of daily inspections, spot checks would be conducted at unpredictable times. The schedule of reinforcement was altered from continuous to intermittent.

In Unit 24 we considered the fact that intermittent reinforcement serves to maintain behavior in applied settings. We shall now examine the ways in which specific schedules of reinforcement affect performance, because different schedules can generate performance characteristics that differ subtly or even dramatically from one another. The rate and consistency of a behavior, as well as opportunities for competing behaviors, both while the schedule is in effect and after reinforcement has been discontinued, are characteristics of interest to practitioners: contingency managers and behavioral analysts. This unit will be directed toward these factors as they relate to the simpler interval and limited-hold schedules. In the next unit we shall introduce ratio schedules and schedules of differential reinforcement of high rates of behavior.

The area of reinforcement schedules is extremely broad, and many complex combinations and permutations have been investigated. The human environment, being as complex as it is, probably more closely approximates combinations of such complex schedules. Such combinations will not, however, be explored in this book, not because they are unimportant or irrelevant, but because they would take us beyond the basic and into the advanced realm of behavioral analysis.[1] Here the specific schedules that appear to have particular pertinence to practitioners, as well as the simpler combinations, will be emphasized.

INTERVAL SCHEDULES DEFINED AND ILLUSTRATED

Interval schedules are dependent upon the *passage of specific periods of time*. Ratio schedules, to be discussed in Unit 26, depend upon numbers of responses. When a particular response is scheduled for reinforcement following the passage of a specific amount of time, and that time requirement is held constant, the schedule is a **fixed-interval (FI) schedule**. For example, Chuck and his teacher have decided that it is desirable for him to spend more time working on his assignment during social-studies class and less time looking around the room and out the window. After behaviorally defining working as "writing correct answers to questions covering the material," the teacher sets a kitchen timer for five-minute intervals. If Chuck is working as specified just after the timer rings, he is reinforced with a token. Otherwise, as soon as the behavior occurs after the termina-

---

[1] Students wishing more complete discussions of specific simple and complex reinforcement schedules should see Thompson and Grabowski (1972) and Ferster and Skinner (1957).

tion of each five-minute interval, a token is delivered. Fixed-interval schedules are abbreviated "FI," and the schedule in this illustration would be called an "FI 5," a fixed-interval five-minute schedule. An FI schedule *specifies that reinforcers are to be delivered contingent upon the emission of a particular response that occurs following the passage of a specific amount of time.* Most pay schedules are FI schedules. As long as Mr. Smith is at the office, he is paid each Friday. Reinforcement is directly contingent upon the response of his coming to the pay window. If Mr. Smith is ill or out of town on Friday, his check remains available until such time as he does come to the pay window. In group programs for children and youths, many events are scheduled on regular bases: recreation and lunch periods, periodic evaluations, delivery of progress reports, classes in specific subjects, and many others. At home various events are also scheduled at fixed times: meals, chores, music practice, radio and television shows, and so on. If the group-home manager inspected rooms every other day, the schedule would be an FI-2 day schedule. When the recurring events have reinforcing properties and are delivered contingent upon a specific response, they are on FI schedules:

$$S \longrightarrow R \longrightarrow S^r$$

(every two days)   (tidy room)   (points)

Every other day the response of meeting criteria for a tidy room will be reinforced with points. In another instance,

$$S \longrightarrow R \longrightarrow \text{(activity period)}$$

(one week elapsed)   (completing assignments) S^r

following an interval of a week, completing assignments will be reinforced with an "activity period."

Variable-interval (VI) **schedules** operate in a similar manner, except that the time interval varies; that is, the time requirement is not held constant but is a *specified average.* Chuck's teacher could have set the kitchen timer differently. She could, for instance, have randomly varied the intervals between zero and ten minutes, so that over time, the length of the intervals would average about five minutes. Such a schedule would be called a "VI 5," or "variable-interval five-minute," schedule. On the average of every two weeks, the elected manager of the community group home makes a tour of inspection. Those residents who have met their responsibilities are invited to participate in a special reinforcing activity that evening—perhaps making popcorn or fudge, listening to favorite records, or the like. The inspections are on a VI schedule. Under VI scheduling it is possible for reinforcers to be delivered both very close together and very far apart. Inspections can take place as close together as two days in a row or as far apart as once in four weeks. This characteristic of VI schedules may generate performances different from those generated by FI schedules. In the following discussion such differences, along with some of the general properties of interval-schedule performance and how they may be related to the applied setting, will be examined.

CHARACTERISTICS OF INTERVAL-SCHEDULE PERFORMANCE

Laboratory animals and human beings tend to generate different response charac-teristics under interval schedules. Interval schedules, which promote very predict-able patterns among different animal subjects (Ferster & Skinner, 1957), appear to generate more variability among human subjects. Apparently such factors as instructions (Lippman & Meyer, 1967) and, more important, reinforcement history (Weiner, 1964) account for much of this variability. Within the broad range of varied performances under interval reinforcement schedules, however, some gen-eralizations can be drawn. Because it is possible to design a particular history of a particular response for an individual, we can obtain fairly tight control of interval-schedule performance (Weiner, 1969). It is possible, for instance, to generate either very rapid or very slow rates of responding under VI schedules, depending upon which prior schedules have been used with the same response. How this goal may be achieved will be discussed later. Here we shall make a general survey of such VI characteristics as rate, consistency of responding, error patterns, and maintenance of performance during extinction.

Relatively Low Rate of Responding

The rate of responding during maintenance phases of applied behavior-analysis programs is often an important issue. If a relatively low rate of responding is tolerable, an interval schedule may be the best solution. An interval schedule car-ries only one simple requirement: The specific response must occur at least one time following each specified time interval. A pigeon can peck a disk once at the end of a required interval and receive its grain. Chuck, who is on a fixed-interval five-minute schedule (FI 5), can technically receive his token as long as he spends just ten seconds looking at his page in each five minutes. (In contrast, a ratio schedule requires that a number of responses be omitted as a condition for rein-forcement.) It is not typical, however, for an individual on an FI schedule to respond with only one response per interval. What frequently happens among laboratory animals, for instance, is that they pause following reinforcement. Then, as the interval progresses, responding begins to accelerate. Under the temporally based FI schedule, individuals are not penalized by postponement of reinforce-ment if they fail to respond for a while, as they would be under a response-based schedule like a ratio schedule. Reinforcement is postponed under an FI schedule only when no response occurs immediately following the interval requirement. Chuck would begin to lose out on receiving tokens only if he were not looking at his book after the five-minute interval. The group-home resident would miss his reinforcer only if his room were untidy when it was time for inspection. It could conceivably remain a mess up until that time. So FI schedules tend to generate lower response rates than ratio schedules, though, over time, responding does usually maintain at least at a rate sufficient to allow individuals to earn reinforcers when they become accessible.

In general, responding is more rapid under VI than under FI schedules. The variable nature of the VI schedule allows the individual to be reinforced at unpredictable times. This unpredictability appears to keep the individual emitting responses at a fairly constant rate and thus has the effect of yielding more responses per time period. If Chuck had no way of predicting when he would receive a token for work, he would be more likely to keep working just on the chance that the timer might signal. The group-home resident would be more apt to maintain a tidy room under a system of spot checks, a variable-interval schedule. But still there is a limit, imposed by the scheduled interval, on the number of responses that can be reinforced under VI. Very high rates of responding contribute nothing to the amount of reinforcement received. Rates are therefore less likely to be greater than or equal to those based on response frequency. In general, interval-schedule performance rates tend to be equal to or lower than frequency-based performance rates.

Some factors have been identified as influencing the rate at which a response is emitted under interval schedules. They include the size of the intervals and the schedule history of the particular response. (Previous schedule history will be discussed in Unit 26.) Why the size of the required interval has an effect on the overall rate of performance should be fairly apparent. As the individual is required to make at least one response per designated time interval in order to receive maximum reinforcement, the shorter the required time interval, the higher the rate. Were Chuck on an FI 2 minute schedule, he would have to read at least once each two minutes in order to earn the maximum number of tokens. On an FI 9 minute schedule, he would have to read only once each nine minutes for maximum payoff. If room inspection were hourly, rather than on alternate days, much more tidying would be going on. An FI schedule, then, makes it possible to manipulate the response rate easily by either shortening or lengthening the time interval.

Consistency of Performance

Fixed-interval responding is often very slow following reinforcement, gradually accelerating as the interval progresses, yielding a *fixed-interval scallop*. Because of the nature of the FI schedule, persistent responding throughout the interval is not required. What frequently happens among laboratory animals is that, immediately following FI reinforcement, they tend to engage in other responses. As grain has never been delivered immediately following a previously reinforced peck, it does not "pay" for the pigeon to resume pecking right away. Instead it pauses: It struts, coos, preens, and flaps its wings before again accelerating disk pecking as the interval progresses to its end. Unlike animals, human subjects working in the laboratory tend to respond more consistently under FI schedules (Weiner, 1969). Yet, in the natural setting, instances of postreinforcement pauses can occasionally be identified. Figure 25.1 shows the FI scallop generated by the U.S. Congress as responding accelerates before adjournment. Students who are quizzed or graded at regular intervals often tend to study sporadically. As the interval progresses, studying behavior increases in an accelerating fashion. While study behavior is low, other response rates are higher: playing, working on other assignments, and

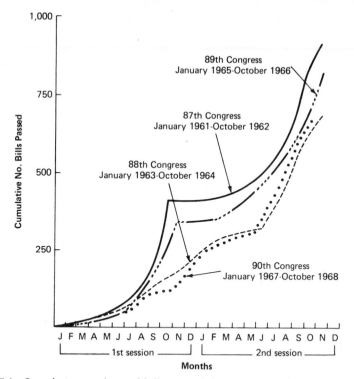

Figure 25.1 Cumulative numbers of bills passed during the legislative sessions of Congress from January 1961 to October 1968 (Weisberg & Waldrup, 1972, p. 95).

so on. Mawhinney and colleagues (1971) measured minutes of studying per day by college students under daily and three-weekly quiz conditions. (Quizzes probably consist of both reinforcing and aversive contingencies.) Figure 25.2 indicates that studying was relatively consistent under the daily schedule, though it accelerated during the three-week schedule. During social-studies class, Chuck could conceivably look out the window, disrupt, get a drink, doodle, or engage in other behaviors in the early phases of each five-minute interval. Yet he could still remain eligible for and receive maximum token reinforcement as long as he emitted at least one work response in each five minutes. How might the group-home resident's room look on the day between fixed alternate-day inspections?

Such inconsistency does not usually occur under variable-interval schedules. As reinforceable responses cannot be predicted—some occur close together, others farther apart—the individual tends to maintain a steady pace of responding (except when reinforcement occurs too often at the extremes of the interval). Two successive pecks sometimes yield grain to the pigeon, so pecking continues following reinforcement. Students whose instructors give "surprise" quizzes also tend to keep up better with their assignments. Whether the purpose is to avoid failure or to seek success, studying is maintained, and students are less likely to engage in competing activities. Following a spot inspection by the elected manager, residents would probably continue to meet their responsibilities at a pretty constant rate,

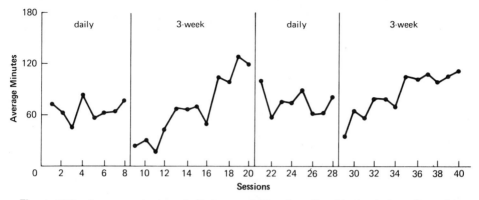

Figure 25.2 Average minutes studied per session by all subjects during alternating daily and three-week testing conditions (Mawhinney *et al.*, 1971, p. 262)

just in case an inspection were to be conducted the next day. Because variable-interval performance is typified by consistency, whereas fixed-interval performance may not be, it is probably a good idea ultimately to switch from FI to VI when consistency of performance is desired.

Error Patterns

Different patterns of error production may emerge under some interval schedules. Davidson and Osborne (1974) have noted that the children who served as subjects in their study of matching-to-sample performance produced the largest number of errors in the second quarter of each interval under fixed-interval matching. Children operating under variable-interval schedules distributed errors more evenly within the interval.

Continued Responding During Extinction

Practitioners can do an excellent job by making appropriate use of contingency-management procedures, that is, by presenting contingencies that strengthen, shape, or weaken specific performances. But the issue of maintaining behavior after the termination of contingency-management programs is just as crucial. Fortunately, experimentation in the behavioral area has revealed that intermittent reinforcement is the key to such behavioral persistence under extinction, or non-reinforcement, conditions.

Interval schedules tend to generate responding that maintains longer during extinction than does that generated by continuous reinforcement (CRF). In general, if a particular response has been maintained on a schedule with a very long interval requirement, the response will probably maintain longer than if the interval has been fairly short (Reynolds, 1968). This tendency again underscores the importance of using a program that progressively extends the interval before reinforcement. It would be insufficient to terminate the reinforcement program when Chuck was functioning on either an FI 5 or a VI 5 schedule just because the terminal goal—doing social-studies assignments—had been achieved. A sudden withdrawal of the reinforcing contingencies might result in disruption of the response before much time had passed. It would probably be preferable to lengthen the required interval gradually until token delivery was made contingent upon continuing to complete his assignments for days or perhaps even weeks. By that time, removal of the tokens would hardly be noticed.

If the intention of the practitioner is to design a program that will yield responses that continue to occur *consistently* once the reinforcing contingencies have been removed, a variable-interval schedule would probably be the training schedule of choice. The regular responding that is characteristic of performance under VI-reinforcement schedules appears to maintain itself under extinction. Laboratory animals that have been trained on VI schedules have continued to respond in similar fashion under extinction conditions. Responding maintains without pausing; though, of course, over extended periods of time the rate diminishes and ultimately ceases. On the other hand, performance under extinction following FI training tends to be interspersed with numerous periods of nonresponse before its ultimate cessation. In the event that a fixed-interval training schedule is selected, for practicality or convenience, it is usually possible eventually to switch to a variable schedule before removing all reinforcing contingencies. The group-home manager could switch from alternate days to a VI 3 day schedule, then continue progressively to alter the schedule in the direction of a sparse VI schedule.

In a program conducted by a special-education teacher, a switch was made from a schedule closely resembling an FI to one similar to a VI schedule. In order to reduce a student's thumbsucking, she gave him a token each time that the bell on a kitchen timer rang, provided that his thumb was not in his mouth. During the first phase, the timer was set at regular intervals. In the next phase, numbers from one to twenty were selected at random: Numbered paper slips were drawn from a bowl and replaced each time. The numbers were listed in the order in which they were drawn. The timer was then set for the intervals indicated by the sequence of numbers on the list. The random selection of intervals from one to twenty thus provided a schedule that operated on a variable interval averaging ten minutes (VI 10).

ADVANTAGES AND DISADVANTAGES OF
INTERVAL SCHEDULES

The primary advantage of interval schedules is ease of implementation. They are time-based, so that, rather than counting responses, one simply has periodically to check a clock, timer, or calendar or respond to a visual or auditory signal. When there are competing demands upon the time and attention of contingency managers, the interval schedule is particularly appealing.

The promotion of consistent responding during reinforcement can be accomplished through the use of a variable schedule. One must be cautious, however, about selecting a fixed-interval schedule if consistency during reinforcement and after its termination is desired.

Another disadvantage of an interval schedule is that it may promote a low or moderate response rate. This problem should be avoidable through programming of an initial phase during which schedules (for example, ratio schedules; see Unit 26) are selected to generate high response rates. If an inordinate number of errors during one particular part of an interval cause difficulty, then fixed-interval schedules should probably be avoided in favor of VI schedules.

USING INTERVAL SCHEDULES EFFECTIVELY

The available information on interval schedules serves as a guide to their effective application. In brief, if a low-to-moderate rate of responding is acceptable, one can schedule reinforcement following a moderate interval size. To increase the response rate, one should start with a shorter interval and gradually increase it. Alternatively, one can first implement a schedule that will promote high response rates, like those to be discussed in Unit 26, then switch to an interval schedule. While reducing the density of strong reinforcers, one should also intersperse less powerful reinforcers among the strong ones. One of the jobs of the group-home manager could be to compliment peers whose rooms were neat between formal inspections. For consistency of responding during and following reinforcement, a variable-interval schedule is preferable.

LIMITED-HOLD SCHEDULES

One way to increase the rate of performance under an interval schedule is to impose an additional restriction on performance. That restriction requires that a primed response (the first response following termination of the required interval) must occur within a specific time limit if reinforcement is to be made available (see Figure 25.3).

Under a limited-hold schedule individuals must hurry in order not to lose the opportunity to be reinforced, whereas under a simple interval schedule they can afford to delay responding. That is, under a limited-hold schedule reinforcement is available only for brief periods. This type of schedule is one that many of us have probably learned to use without awareness. Teachers give grades only when an assignment is completed within a certain time. The group is dismissed for recreation as soon as the members come to order; but, if they fail to come to order within a certain number of minutes, recreation time will be over, and the opportunity will be lost. Grungy George never combs his hair or cleans his fingernails. He and his dad agree that Dad will check his appearance before dinner each day. If George looks neat and clean he will receive his allowance. If not, there will be no allowance, and he will have to wait until the next day. The limited-hold con-

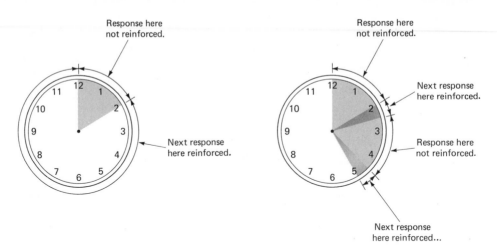

Fixed interval of 10 minutes; the first response following termination of the interval is reinforced.

The limit is 2 minutes following the 10-minute interval; if no response occurs during those 2 minutes, reinforcement will no longer be available.

Figure 25.3   The fixed-interval and limited-hold schedules compared.

tingency increases George's neatness. In a seventh-grade social-studies class, the teacher assigned a project: Each student was to bring in ten newspaper clippings. The students would present their current-events items to the class and would receive credit toward their grades. The teacher did not specify a time by which the clippings were due. Some students went for several weeks without doing the assignment and then, toward the end of the marking period, began to bring in sheaves of clippings. The last week before report cards were to be distributed, the class was overloaded with current-events presentations. The teacher was forced to postpone presentation of the next planned subject unit, and some of the students never did complete the assignment. In order to avoid such a situation in the next marking period, the teacher added a restriction: Credit would be given only once a week, on Friday. The students had only one week in which to collect and present the news clippings. They could receive no credit if they brought the clippings in on the following Monday. The opportunity for reinforcement was available for only a brief period. Laboratory studies demonstrate that the imposition of a short limited hold has the effect of increasing response rates (Reynolds, 1968). In the situation described here, we might expect the new policy to have a similar effect. In order to avoid losing out on the opportunity to earn credits, the students would probably bring in clippings regularly and more often. One way, therefore, to speed up responding under interval schedules is to restrict the time during which reinforcement is available to a brief period, to use a limited-hold contingency. Other ways will be discussed in Unit 26.

Summary

Interval schedules have been defined and discussed. When the terminal goal of the behavioral program is the maintained emission of a behavior at low to moderate rates, an interval schedule, in which intervals have been *gradually* increased is effective. VI schedules are apt to promote consistent responding while a scallop pattern may develop under VI schedules. The rate of responding under an interval schedule can often be increased by also employing a limited-hold schedule. Such a schedule requires that the primed response occur within specific time limits; otherwise reinforcement is withheld until the next interval ends.

References

Davidson, N. A. & Osborne, J. G. Fixed ratio and fixed interval schedule control of matching-to-sample errors by children. *Journal of the Experimental Analysis of Behavior,* 1974, **21**, 27–36.

Ferster, C. B. & Skinner, B. F. *Schedules of reinforcement.* New York: Appleton, 1957.

Lippman, L. G. & Meyer, M. E. Fixed-interval performance as related to instructions and to subject's verbalizations of the contingency. *Psychonomic Science,* 1967, **8**, 135–136.

Mawhinney, V. T., Bostow, D. E., Laws, O. R., Blumenfeld, G. T. & Hopkins, B. L. A comparison of students' studying behavior produced by daily, weekly, and three-week testing schedules. *Journal of Applied Behavior Analysis,* 1971, **4**, 257–264.

Phillips, E. L., Phillips, E. A., Wolf, M. M. & Fixsen, D. L. Achievement Place: Development of the elected manager system. *Journal of Applied Behavior Analysis,* 1973, **4**, 541–561.

Reynolds, G. S. *A primer of operant conditioning.* Glenview, Ill.: Scott, Foresman, 1968.

Thompson, T. & Grabowski, J. G. *Reinforcement schedules and multioperant analysis.* New York: Appleton, 1972.

Weiner, H. Conditioning history and human fixed-interval performance. *Journal of the Experimental Analysis of Behavior,* 1964, **7**, 383–385.

Weiner, H. Controlling human fixed-interval performance. *Journal of the Experimental Analysis of Behavior,* 1969, **12**, 349–373.

Weisberg, P. & Waldrop, P. B. Fixed interval work habits of Congress. *Journal of Applied Behavior Analysis,* 1972, **5**, 93–97.

Maintaining Behavior: Ratio and Differential-Reinforcement Schedules

After mastering the material in this unit, you should be able to

1. Define and offer illustrations for each of the following terms:
   a. Ratio schedules of reinforcement
   b. Fixed-ratio (FR) schedules
   c. Variable-ratio (VR) schedules
   d. Ratio strain
   e. Adjusting schedule
   f. Differential reinforcement of high rates (DRH)

2. List and describe the characteristics of ratio-schedule performance.

3. List and describe the factors that influence response-rate characteristics, for example, consistency under ratio-schedule performance.

4. Discuss the advantages and disadvantages of ratio schedules.

5. Describe and illustrate how ratio and DRH schedules can increase response rates under interval scheduling, and outline the steps to follow for accomplishing a smooth transition from a ratio to an interval schedule.

6. Maintain a selected target behavior at a high but consistent rate of performance.

In Unit 25 we learned that interval schedules tend to generate low or moderate response rates. Yet high rates are often desired. We now turn our attention to two schedules that produce high response rates: ratio and differential reinforcement of high-rates (DRH) schedules.

RATIO SCHEDULES

Ratio Schedules Defined and Illustrated

We have learned in Unit 25 that interval schedules are dependent upon the passage of specific periods of time. When reinforcement is made contingent upon *the emission of a given number of responses before one response is reinforced*, the schedule is called a **ratio schedule**. Sometimes there is a fixed number of responses required before the response is reinforced. Then the schedule is called a **fixed-ratio (FR) schedule**. The classical illustration of an FR schedule comes from industry and is called "piecework." When each twentieth piece of equipment is assembled the worker is credited with $5. In school, an FR schedule might involve giving a student a certain number of points upon completion of three pages in his workbook. (The term "fixed-ratio schedule" is often abbreviated for the sake of convenience. In the last illustration, for example, reinforcement would be delivered at the ratio of three page units to one reinforcer, and the schedule could be abbreviated FR 3.)

More typical of reinforcement schedules in applied settings, however, is the **variable-ratio (VR) schedule**. Although in the VR schedule reinforcement is also contingent upon a response following a number of responses, *the number of required responses varies*. Typically a VR schedule in the laboratory is programmed for an average number of required responses. For example, a pigeon is to be reinforced on the average of once for each fifty disk-pecking responses. Variable ratio schedules are also usually abbreviated, and in this instance the schedule would be abbreviated VR 50. Let us suppose that Fern is packing items in boxes with sections that vary from four to eight, with an average of six. If she were reinforced with points toward her paycheck after packing each box, she would be working on a VR 6 schedule.[1]

Characteristics of Ratio-Schedule Performance

Ratio schedules tend to generate specific performance characteristics while they are in effect and under extinction conditions, when reinforcement is no longer delivered. Among laboratory animals, performance characteristics under different ratio schedules are quite distinct and predictable (Ferster & Skinner, 1957), but among human beings such characteristics cannot be predicted with as much pre-

[1] In reality, any one individual is usually operating under many different complex schedules at one time. We have simplified the material here to make the discussion easier to follow.

cision. Nonetheless, general patterns of ratio performance have manifested themselves in studies in which simple (Hutchinson & Azrin, 1961), as well as complex (Bijou & Orlando, 1961; Long, 1962; 1963; Davidson & Osborne, 1974), schedules of reinforcement have been tested with human subjects. Among the predictable general performance characteristics of ratio responding are high and fairly consistent rates while the schedule is in effect and continued responding under at least the early phases of extinction conditions. These performance characteristics will be examined in a little more detail so that the factors that appear to influence each can be identified.

High rates of responding.   With ratio schedules, reinforcement is contingent upon the emission of a number of responses. The more rapidly individuals respond, therefore, the sooner they are reinforced. Rapid responding also allows the accumulation of more reinforcers within a given time period. Naturally, individuals tend to work more rapidly under ratio schedules than under interval schedules. Typists being paid by the page will be likely to work as quickly as possible: The faster they type, the more pages they can complete within a given period, and the more money they can consequently make. Similarly, a client who is allowed out to play upon completion of a number of assigned homework pages will probably make haste to finish.

Several specific factors have been found to affect rates of responding on a single task, however. Among those that are more relevant to human services are the ratio of nonreinforced to reinforced responses and the gradualness with which the reinforcement schedule is phased out.

Several investigators have studied the effects of the size of the ratio requirement upon the response rate. Hutchinson and Azrin (1961) demonstrated that human responding was comparable to animal responding under ratio schedules (Boren, 1956; Skinner, 1938). Their general finding was that, to some maximum level, the larger the response requirement, the more rapid the response rate. Beyond that level the rate of responding drops. This finding has been further supported by applied behavior analysis. Stephens and colleagues (1975) compared various schedules of reinforcement in order to determine the effects of ratio size upon the rate at which retarded children learned picture names. Each time a picture was correctly labeled, the verbal stimulus "good" was presented. Various schedules of contingent candy delivery, however, operated during different phases. It was found that both continuous candy delivery and very infrequent candy delivery (FR 25) generated low response rates. When the continual "goods" for correct responding were paired with candy on each fifth correct trial, response rates were considerably higher.

If Fern packs two boxes of uniform size under an FR reinforcement schedule within a specified time period, she can be expected to pack more boxes in *proportionally* less time. For instance, we would expect that a ten-box requirement (FR 10) would take five times as long as a two-box requirement, yet the experimental findings suggest that ten boxes would be packed in less than five times the time required for two boxes. All other factors being equal, the rate per box would be higher if reinforcement were made contingent upon a ten-box requirement than upon a two-box requirement.

It therefore seems logical to conclude that high ratio requirements are effective. But individuals and tasks vary, and it is therefore impossible to predict when this principle may break down. At some point the ratio requirement becomes too large, and the individual may begin to pause at unpredictable times. He is then said to be suffering from **ratio strain**. Abrupt increases in ratio requirements may also be accompanied by avoidance and aggression, as Hutchinson, Azrin, and Hunt (1968) have found. Ultimately, as we indicated previously, responding can disintegrate altogether. Of course, increasing the ratio gradually will delay such effects. Kirby and Shields (1972) programmed an adjusting FR schedule for a student who seldom completed his math assignments. Starting with praising and marks of "correct" for each two problems completed correctly, the FR schedule was gradually increased to four, then to eight, and so on until twenty problems had to be completed correctly before praise would be given. Achievement remained high throughout. Eventually, however, a point can be reached at which the steady high rate begins to slow down, as in Stephens and colleagues' picture-naming study (1975). At that point, the ratio can be reduced to the level at which rapid responding resumes. Then the requirement can be even more gradually increased.

Let us suppose that a clinic staff is trying to increase the rate at which it completes training assignments. The supervisor begins paying compliments and writing notes each time that staff members complete an assignment. This reinforcement has the effect of increasing the rate of completion. Eventually the notes are written less often, but compliments continue as staff members complete their assignments. As time goes by, reinforcement diminishes, but the response rate rises. Eventually, weeks go by without delivery of any contingent reinforcers. Then the rate of completing assignments begins to decline sporadically, so the reinforcers are reinstated occasionally. The rate of completion of assignments is then revived and remains at its high level.

A generalization can be extracted from this discussion: If the goal for a particular program is a high response rate, it is probably best to use an **adjusting schedule**, to increase the ratio requirement gradually until the behavior reaches its peak or the increase stops and the rate levels off and remains steady. If the rate of responding begins to disintegrate, a temporary reduction in the ratio requirement should solve the problem.

Consistency of performance.   Animal studies (Reynolds, 1968) have shown that a subject may tend to pause immediately after reinforcement under large FR (fixed ratio) requirements. This phenomenon is not, however, consistently observed in human FR performance. Generally, performance is less variable under fixed-ratio than under fixed-interval schedules. The individual assigned a fixed number of pages to complete before receiving bonus points may or may not stop working for a while after receiving the points. If the required number of pages is very large, pausing may be more likely after the points are received than when a few pages are required. At least the possibility of a pause before the next response exists, and the consistency of responding may thus be disrupted. During the pause the individual may engage in behaviors other than the one desired: doodling, leaving the room, daydreaming, and so on.

Variable-ratio (VR) performance, however, is almost never characterized by postreinforcement pauses. Let us look at an illustration of a VR reinforcement schedule. Fern is being reinforced on a VR 6 schedule. *Bonus* points are delivered on the average of every six boxes packed. The actual reinforcement program can be diagramed as follows:

$7R \longrightarrow S^r$ $4R \longrightarrow S^r$ $10R \longrightarrow S^r$ $2R \longrightarrow S^r$

$(RRRRRRR) \longrightarrow S^r$ $(RRRR) \longrightarrow S^r$ $(RRRRRRRRRR) \longrightarrow S^r$ $(RR) \longrightarrow S^r$

Each R represents the response of packing a box. By looking at the way that the responses are *distributed* just before reinforcement, we can see that in some instances reinforcement follows a fairly large number of responses ($10R$), whereas in other instances it follows just a few responses ($2R$). The client has no way of anticipating when the next reinforcer will be delivered. It can be after two boxes are packed or after ten boxes are packed. Because reinforcement may be imminent, work is quickly resumed. There is no postreinforcement pause. Analogous is the situation in which the teacher collects written assignments at random, spot checking on an average of every fifth page completed by each student. Some students could conceivably complete ten pages before the teacher checked and praised them for their performances. Others might have two pages in a row checked. Such a VR schedule would be likely to maintain performance at a steady rate, with hardly any pauses following reinforcement. Because VR schedules do not tend to generate pauses in performance, whereas FR schedules, particularly those with high ratio requirements may, VR appears to be the type of schedule that can best be employed when the objective is to maintain a consistent performance rate.

Continued responding in extinction.   Ratio schedules, like interval schedules, have been shown to provide reinforcement histories that tend to sustain performance once reinforcement has been terminated. There are differences in performance following the termination of different kinds of ratio schedules, and some of their important characteristics have been identified. It will probably be useful to become familiar with those characteristics.

Performance following the termination of an FR schedule is characterized by bursts of responding at the same high rates that were emitted when the schedule was in effect (Reynolds, 1968). The problem is that, between the bursts of high responding, the periods of nonresponding become longer and longer. Eventually, the frequency of the response bursts diminishes to almost zero, and the frequency of the periods of nonresponding increases. Ultimately the behavior may cease to be emitted at all.

Cindy's mother usually refused her daughter's initial requests for money, figuring that if Cindy really needed it she would ask again. Cindy had learned that money was usually forthcoming after her third request (an FR 3 schedule). On Cindy's thirteenth birthday her mother decided that Cindy should earn her own spending money. The next time Cindy came with a request for funds, her mother told her to find a baby-sitting job. Cindy continued to plead but to no avail. She went away for a while and then returned ("It always worked before"). The pleading resumed. But her mother was steadfast, and the requests for money stopped before long. (Had her mother relented, Cindy's requests for money would have returned to their former level almost immediately.) Another illustration of this phenomenon can be taken from a community setting. Every Friday the young residents from a group home were taken on an outing, provided that they had fulfilled their assigned weekly responsibilities. As the price of fuel increased, the outings were discontinued, and no alternative special privileges were substituted. Completion of assigned responsibilities continued at a high rate, but occasionally a few failed to complete their tasks. After a while several seemed to give up completely. The major point here is that, after an FR schedule has been discontinued, responding may maintain for a short while during extinction. But, assuming that no other contingencies have taken control, the overall rate of responding will eventually approach its prereinforcement level.

A VR schedule tends to generate behavior that will maintain much longer under extinction conditions. In fact, a history of a VR schedule with a very high ratio requirement (that is, very thin reinforcement density) for a particular response can yield an exceedingly high and persistent performance pattern under extinction conditions. For example, Professor Fogg gave a few spot quizzes during the first half of the semester, then stopped giving them. His students did their assignments religiously "just in case." Out of approximately twenty entries, Uncle Herman had the luck to win a trip to Florida in one contest, a $5 gift certificate in another, and a case of dog food in a third. And, although Uncle Herman has not won a thing for many years after his streak of luck, he still spends all his spare time entering contests. Once Helen had taken her medication regularly for several weeks, her doctor and her nurse occasionally complimented her "for being such a good, responsible patient." Although later in the year such compliments were no longer delivered, Helen continued to take her medication regularly for a fairly long time.

The staff used to cuddle and comfort little Leroy only when he hurt himself. He began to hurt himself more and more often. The staff agreed to cuddle him when he was being pleasant but to limit attention to only essential care when he hurt himself. The plan was implemented. From time to time, however, a visitor would pick Leroy up and cuddle him when he seemed to have hurt himself. His self-injurious behavior persisted. Visitors were instructed, rather than cuddling him, to report incidents in which Leroy appeared to be hurt so that the staff could respond appropriately. Visitors were encouraged to cuddle Leroy only when he was behaving well. It took a long time before Leroy's self-injurious behavior was eliminated.

In most instances, no matter what the schedule history, a response will diminish and eventually return to its preintervention level when extinction conditions are maintained completely. Under VR histories it simply takes much longer. Typical performance following the termination of VR reinforcement consists of very long, sustained, and rapid bursts of responses, interspersed with gradually increasing periods of nonresponding similar to those following termination of an FR schedule. But in VR performance the periods of nonresponding usually begin later and occur less frequently than in FR performance. If Cindy's mother had given her money after an irregular number of requests, the requests would probably have persisted much longer. If the group outings had been scheduled irregularly, rather than regularly, the residents would probably have sustained the performance of their assignments for a longer period of time after the outings had been terminated.

Two important practical conclusions can be drawn from the fact that a well-established history of a thin VR schedule of reinforcement tends to generate very persistent performance under extinction conditions. First, if the terminal goal of a program of behavior change or of an instructional sequence is maintenance of the response once contingencies are removed, a variable-ratio schedule of reinforcement that has been gradually thinned should best suit the purpose. Second, conversely, an undesirable behavior should *never*, if possible, be maintained by such a schedule. As the schedule tends to make behavior very resistant to extinction, eliminating it will prove very difficult.

Advantages of Ratio Schedules

The main advantage of intermittent reinforcement in general is, of course, its promotion of maintained responding. The reinforcement schedule based on number of responses, the ratio schedule, offers a few specific advantages. The first and most obvious is that it tends to generate high response rates—a point that probably does not have to be reiterated at this time. A second advantage, related to the first, is that, when an initial phase of ratio reinforcement is programmed, high rates can also be achieved under interval schedules. Weiner (1964) found that the rate of key-pressing responses by humans on FI schedules was markedly affected by their previous experience on the apparatus. Those subjects who had histories of receiving FR reinforcement performed on an FI schedule at rates that were quite high—similar to their FR schedule performance. Other subjects who had histories of being reinforced only when they responded very slowly continued to respond very slowly when the schedule was switched to FI. Over a great many sessions, the rates among some of the subjects who responded at high FI rates began to diminish but never to the low levels of their more slowly responding counterparts. The significance of this point for practitioners is that there is a possibility of achieving a reasonably high rate of performance under interval scheduling. Let us say that Fern's supervisor prefers to use FI reinforcement for convenience's sake. In order to avoid the potentially low rates that are known sometimes to characterize FI performance, she plans an initial phase of FR reinforcement. After all, she does not want Fern to work only toward the end of each interval. An aide agrees to help. They start with a fairly low ratio requirement—FR 5; after every fifth item packed Fern is reinforced. The aide keeps track of the responses and arranges to have the tokens delivered at the appropriate times. The ratio of required responses is gradually increased to about FR 30. Then, when Fern is spending most of the time working on her assignment, a switch to an FI schedule is made. Ultimately, the supervisor can take over contingency control without assistance and remain fairly confident that the high rate of responding will maintain for quite a while. A periodic shift back to an FR schedule, with the assistance of the aide, could further ensure the maintenance of the high rate of response.

A third advantage of ratio schedules is that they are particularly easy to use when the target response results in a permanent product. Permanent products can simply be counted as they are produced, and reinforcers can be presented as scheduled: after so many boxes packed, problems solved, answers to questions written, buttons buttoned, tables cleaned, beds made, pages typed, complimentary notes sent, and so on. (Let us recall that determining the reliability of measurement is also simplified through the use of permanent-product data.)

Fourth, ratio schedules may be used to facilitate the transition from artificial to natural reinforcement. This goal is accomplished through scheduling of two sets of consequences for the target response: the weaker but more natural consequences more frequently and the more powerful artificial consequences less often. As long as a stronger reinforcer is continually paired with a weaker, the latter should begin to acquire its own reinforcing properties. Lucretia is observed to share a toy upon the request of a playmate. Her mother smiles, nods "Um-hum," and gives her daughter a hug, a powerful reinforcer for Lucretia. As the rate of sharing increases, her mother continues smiles and hugs, but the ratio of hugs begins to diminish to about every other sharing response, then to about every third one, and so on. The smiling and nodding contingent upon sharing seem to maintain the response successfully, and hugs have been reduced to a ratio that Lucretia's mother can easily manage. (Much later, when the rate of sharing is sufficiently high and stable, even the contingent smiles and nods may be presented intermittently; the rate is still likely to persist.)

Using Ratio Schedules Effectively

In our discussion of ratio schedules we have attempted to identify several response characteristics that should have direct bearing upon programming for maintained responding. Ratio schedules promote high response rates. If consistency of responding is an issue, however, the ratio schedule should have a variable base. Because of the disruption in responding that tends to accompany abrupt shifts to higher ratio requirements (ratio strain), it is best to adjust the ratio requirement gradually. Then, along the way, the schedule should be supplemented with other, perhaps less powerful reinforcers like praise and other social events. Then it should be possible to continue increasing the ratio requirement until an optimum limit (or **asymptote**) is reached and the rate no longer increases. It may be difficult to determine whether or not a "true" limit has been reached, however, for ratio strain, rather than some inherent limitation on rate, may be operating.

A temporary reduction in the ratio requirement, followed by perhaps an even more gradual increase, may provide the evidence by which to judge whether or not the absolute limit has been reached.

Dexter has made very satisfactory progress in his study behavior. He is managing his own contingencies, using a point system. He has designed a reinforcement menu for himself, with a number of preferred activities costing specific numbers of points. He can go to the science museum for 50 points, read a chapter in his science-fiction book for 25 points, call his friend for 10 points, and visit a pal in another community for 500 points. For the first week that the system is in operation he assigns himself one point for each paragraph that he reads, as long as he can summarize the paragraph to himself in one sentence. The next week he ups the requirement to two paragraphs per point, the next to a page. Eventually two pages, then five, then a chapter is required for a single point. But Dexter notes that his studying has begun to fall off precipitously. He is finding all sorts of excuses for not working. One day he has a headache. He accidently leaves his books at school a couple of times. His friends keep calling him, and he just cannot seem to terminate the conversations. Is it possible that the ratio requirement has something to do with the disruption? What he should try to do is to drop back a few steps, say to the requirement of two pages per point, and to reestablish his previous high rate. Then he can proceed more cautiously—from two pages to three, four, six, and so on. If the more gradual progression does not promote a breakdown in rate, fine. But, if disruption occurs again, perhaps he should just drop back a little bit and stay there.

Disadvantages of Ratio Schedules

The ratio-strain problem that may be encountered during too rapid an increase in ratio requirement has already been discussed, and some possible solutions have been offered. An additional problem in the implementation of ratio schedules is that the topography of the response may begin to disintegrate at very high rates. Davidson and Osborne (1974) found that children produced a high proportion of errors immediately after reinforcement in an FR matching-to-sample task. Using a ratio schedule to maintain adequate amounts of practicing scales on the piano, Bruno von Burn awards himself a point for every ten scales that he practices. The points can then be exchanged for minutes during which he allows himself to play current hit tunes. His rate of practicing scales increases, but his technique begins to deteriorate. This sort of problem appeared when McLaughlin and Malaby (1975) examined the effects of awarding points for completion, rather than for accuracy, of math assignments by fifth and sixth graders. Their rates increased, but accuracy deteriorated. Similarly, Sulzer and her colleagues (1971) investigated, as one phase of a study, the effects of rewarding on-task behavior but not accuracy. They found that fifth graders worked at a much higher rate when points were delivered for on-task performance but that their accuracy also deteriorated. In both studies, however, during phases when accuracy requirements were in operation, inaccurate responding was minimized. If Bruno wanted to be sure that his technique would not disintegrate, he would have to define the response more carefully. Just completing scales would not be adequate. Only scales meeting a predetermined standard of acceptability would count toward the ratio. Consequently, to avoid the deterioration in response topography that might accompany the high rates promoted by ratio schedules, it is particularly important that the standards for an acceptable topography be established beforehand. Then reinforcement is delivered only contingent upon the emission of the topographically correct number of responses required to complete the ratio. If topographical errors persist, the ratio requirement can be reduced until the appropriate topography is reliably emitted, or an additional rule can be appended to the contingency arrangement: All responses in the series must be topographically correct, or no more than x percent error will be allowed. The mastery requirement in personalized systems of instruction (PSI) illustrates one way that inaccuracy of responding can be minimized. The student must complete a predetermined number of units to earn a grade; quizzes must be passed at 90 percent level of correctness or better if the student is to be allowed to proceed. In this manner, he is prevented from committing too many errors while rushing through the material in the course.

As ratio schedules are based upon numbers of responses, it is necessary to keep count of the responses as they are being emitted. This requirement can present a problem if clients cannot reliably keep track of their own rates of responding or if there are no support staff or elaborate instruments to accomplish the task. Many alternatives may be considered in those circumstances: peers, volunteers, inexpensive instruments like shopping counters and others (see Unit 6). As maintained emission of a given response in the total absence of contingent reinforcement is very improbable, some provision must be made for intermittent reinforcement to occur either naturally or as part of the program. Interval schedules are usually much easier to implement, but, as previously indicated, they are not conducive to high rates. When it is difficult to keep count of a response *and* high rates are desired, it is usually most practical to start with a ratio schedule. Once responding has been established, one can switch to an interval schedule. The following material on differential reinforcement of high rates contains an illustration of how such a switch can be achieved smoothly.

DIFFERENTIAL REINFORCEMENT OF HIGH RATES

Another method for producing high rates of responding is a schedule of differential reinforcement of high rates (DRH). In establishing a DRH schedule, sequences of responses are observed very closely. *Reinforcement is delivered only when several responses occur in rapid succession over a previously established rate.* When pauses are interspersed, reinforcement is postponed. High rates are differentially reinforced in preference to low rates. This schedule is thus the opposite of the DRL schedule discussed in Unit 18. (The reader may wish to review that material.) When the mile runner completes his run in less than four minutes, the crowd cheers. Completion times greater than four minutes are not cheered. When Chuck correctly completes all the problems in his workbook within a week, he is given an "A." If he takes longer, the grade is a "B." Returning to the illustration of Grungy George, let us suppose that he combs his hair and cleans his nails only once a week. Then a friend visits, and George combs his hair and cleans his nails four days in a row. The sequence is reinforced, not only by his allowance but also by social reinforcers and perhaps some extra money to entertain his friend. Such powerful contingencies are repeated with George each time that he looks neat and clean for several days in a row. In this manner, the response rate is more likely to increase. Once the rate reaches an acceptable level, it will be possible to switch from the DRH to an interval schedule.

Sometimes the DRH schedule is combined with other schedules in order to achieve a rapid rate of responding, particularly when we seek to provide the kind of history that will promote a rapid rate of responding under a variable-interval schedule. For illustrative purposes let us consider Desmond, who has been participating in a prevocational workshop. The supervisor knows that Desmond can do the sorting work because, when he sits down with him on a one-to-one basis, he completes it correctly. In a group setting, however, the work is not completed. Desmond is labeled "lazy" and "obstinate." Rather than doing his work, he wanders around the room a lot and earns another label: "hyperactive." After careful observation, however, it is determined that Desmond has been functioning on a CRF schedule. His work is completed if, after completing each task, he receives reinforcement in the form of attention from the supervisor. The average assignment is about twenty-five sorting tasks (VR 25). The supervisor thinks that he would be able to attend to Desmond about once an hour under ordinary circumstances. Placing Desmond's responding on a VI of one hour at this time is, however, apparently like placing him under extinction conditions. It is thus decided to return to a CRF, to reinforce him with a brief interval of attention for each sorting task completed. To facilitate this plan, Desmond is asked to raise his hand on completion of each task. This requirement is soon changed to an FR 2: After the completion of every two tasks, he raises his hand for recognition and reinforcement. The schedule is then changed to a VR 3; the number of tasks Desmond is asked to complete before raising his hand varies among two, four, and three. This schedule is very soon changed to VR 5. During this phase of providing a history of ratio reinforcement, the amount of time taken to complete several tasks is also noted. If the specified number of tasks is completed correctly within less time than average, a bonus reinforcement (for example, an extra coffee break) is delivered. In this manner, the DRH is combined with the variable-ratio schedule. Soon it is decided to change over to a VI schedule of reinforcement. The supervisor tells Desmond that he wants to see how many tasks he can complete before he checks and that he will be back shortly. A VI schedule of five minutes is selected because that is the average time that it takes Desmond to complete five tasks under the VR 5 schedule. The change will thus go practically unnoticed by Desmond. After approximately five minutes, then, the supervisor checks back. If Desmond is working on his task, the supervisor reinforces him. If he has completed more problems than usual in the amount of time that has elapsed, the supervisor differentially reinforces this high rate of behavior (DRH) with extra praise, recognition, or some sort of bonus.

The VI 5 is then gradually adjusted to VI 8, VI 15, VI 30, and VI 60 (one hour). Throughout the variable-interval schedules a limited hold is also used. If a specific number of sorting tasks is not completed, no reinforcement is delivered for that interval. This combination of a ratio history, DRH, and limited hold helps Desmond to work quickly and for extended periods, thus enhancing his eligibility for actual competitive employment.

We have also used this same combination of schedules with clients who were having difficulty in math. They too were considered "lazy," "obstinate," and "hyperactive" and "needed constant attention" before they would complete their math assignments. The same type of program was developed for them as for Desmond. The reader should try to describe it.

Summary

Ratio and DRH schedules have been defined and discussed as procedures for maintaining behaviors at high rates. Ratio schedules generally produce higher rates of responding than do interval schedules. When the goal is to maintain a behavior at a high rate while avoiding the necessity of counting responses before the delivery of reinforcement, however, a subsequent interval schedule can be planned. Provision of a ratio- or DRH-schedule history and a limited-hold requirement should increase the rate of performance under interval scheduling.

The initial switch from continuous to ratio schedules should be so arranged that progressive increments in ratio requirements are implemented gradually. By supplementing the gradual progression of ratio requirements with less powerful reinforcers, we may avoid ratio strain.

References

Bijou, S. W. & Orlando, R. Rapid development of multiple-schedule performances with retarded children. *Journal of the Experimental Analysis of Behavior,* 1961, **4**, 7–16.

Boren, J. Response rate and resistance to extinction as functions of the fixed ratio. *Dissertation Abstracts,* 1956, **14**, 1261.

Davidson, N. A. & Osborne, J. G. Fixed ratio and fixed interval schedule control of matching-to-sample errors by children. *Journal of the Experimental Analysis of Behavior,* 1974, **21**, 27–36.

Ferster, C. B. & Skinner, B. F. *Schedules of reinforcement.* New York: Appleton, 1957.

Hutchinson, R. R. & Azrin, N. H. Conditioning of mental hospital patients to fixed-ratio schedules of reinforcement. *Journal of the Experimental Analysis of Behavior,* 1961, **4**, 87–95.

Hutchinson, R. R., Azrin, N. H. & Hunt, G. M. Attack produced by intermittent reinforcement of a concurrent operant response. *Journal of the Experimental Analysis of Behavior,* 1968, **11**, 489–495.

Kirby, F. & Shields, F. Modification of arithmetic response rate and attending behavior in a seventh grade student. *Journal of Applied Behavior Analysis,* 1972, **5**, 79–84.

Long, E. R. Additional techniques for producing multiple-schedule control in children. *Journal of the Experimental Analysis of Behavior,* 1962, **5**, 443–455.

Long, E. R. Chained and tandem scheduling with children. *Journal of the Experimental Analysis of Behavior,* 1963, **6,** 459–472.

McLaughlin, T. F. & Malaby, J. E. The effects of various token reinforcement contingencies on assignment completion and accuracy during variable and fixed token exchange schedules. *Canadian Journal of Behavioral Science,* 1975, **7,** 411–419.

Reynolds, G. S. *A primer of operant conditioning.* Glenview, Ill.: Scott, Foresman, 1968.

Skinner, B. F. *The behavior of organisms.* New York: Appleton, 1938.

Stephens, C., Pear, J. L., Wray, L. D. & Jackson, G. C. Some effects of reinforcement schedules in teaching picture names to retarded children. *Journal of Applied Behavior Analysis,* 1975, **8,** 435–447.

Sulzer, B., Hunt, S., Ashby, E., Koniarski, C. & Krams, M. Increasing rate and percentage correct in reading and spelling in a class of slow readers by means of a token system. In E. L. Ramp & B. L. Hopkins (Eds.), *New directions in education: Behavior analysis.* Lawrence: University of Kansas, Department of Human Development, 1971. Pp. 5–28.

Weiner, H. Conditioning history and human fixed-interval performance. *Journal of the Experimental Analysis of Behavior,* 1964, **7,** 383–385.

Contingency Packages
with Groups

After mastering the material in this unit, you should be able to
1. Describe and illustrate each of the following contingency packages:
   a. The Good Behavior Game
   b. Contingent recreation
   c. The contingency bank
   d. The activity table
   e. The treasure box
   f. The slot machine
   g. The grab bag
   h. Home reports
   i. Warm fuzzies and compliment meters
   j. Family contracting program

2. For each contingency package, identify the component procedure and the factors that will enhance the package's effectiveness.

3. Set up and conduct a program utilizing a contingency package.

Excitement, novelty, surprises, a reinforcing environment—they are what this unit is all about. Here we turn to a series of interventions that involve combinations of behavioral procedures. For instance, the Good Behavior Game uses reinforcement, punishment, DRL, and stimulus-control procedures. These procedures are combined into a "contingency package" that serves as a unitary treatment strategy. In a sense, many applied behavioral procedures are actually "packages" of procedures—a point to be developed further in Unit 31. The packages described in this unit are simply more elaborate than those previously discussed.

Many of them are designed to obtain rapid results, to facilitate learning,

CONDUCT PROGRAM

and to keep behavioral disruptions at a minimum. Many may be implemented easily with groups of children and youths by contingency managers (teachers, parents, and staff members) with little preparation and few artificial contrivances. Other packages, like token economies, to be discussed in Unit 28, require far more careful planning and implementation. The basis for selecting a package rests on a number of obvious and subtle considerations. When those considerations are not very obvious, we offer guidelines for making the selection and for effectively implementing the program.

We start with the Good Behavior Game, a management package that is simply conceived, as well as easy to implement. Next we shall consider a series of reinforcement-program packages, progressing from the more natural and less complex *contingent recreation, contingency bank, activity table, treasure box, slot machine, grab bag, home reports, warm fuzzies and compliment meters* to a more complex program package—the *family contracting program*. Most of these packages have been developed by professionals working directly with children and youth. It is hoped that readers will find them appropriate for direct application and as a basis for formulating their own innovative packages.

THE GOOD BEHAVIOR GAME

As mentioned previously, the Good Behavior Game is composed of several behavioral procedures: reinforcement (see Units 8–10), stimulus control (see Units 12–15), punishment (see Unit 22), and DRL (see Unit 18). It was formally conceived and first implemented by Barrish, Saunders, and Wolf (1969) to help teachers and seriously disruptive students. In their study the teacher divided her fourth-grade class into two groups and listed several rules: Students were not to be out of their seats or to talk with their classmates without permission during specific class times; if any member of a team violated the rules, that team received a mark next to its name; the team or teams that had fewer than a criterion number of marks or the team that had the fewest marks by the end of the day "won" the game. All members of the winning team(s) were allowed special privileges: first position in line for lunch, extra recess, special time for projects, victory tags, and so on. Later Harris and Sherman (1973) used the game in a fifth grade and in a sixth grade to reduce various disruptive behaviors: throwing objects, whistling, talking out, and so on. The rules were written on the chalkboard. As in the study by Barrish, Saunders, and Wolf (1969), the team with the fewest marks or the team or teams that obtained below a certain criterion number of marks would win the game. "Each member of the winning team(s) was allowed to leave school 10 minutes early at the end of the day. Members of the losing team were required to remain in the classroom working on assignments until the regular dismissal time for the school" (Harris & Sherman, 1973, p. 408). The Good Behavior Game significantly and reliably reduced disruptive student behaviors in both studies.

The game offers several advantages. Most children seem to enjoy it. It is easy to implement and does not require the contingency manager to attend differentially to each and every individual with reinforcement or punishment. The practitioner should, however, be prepared to deal with an individual or two who may decide not to play the game. In both studies such instances were reported. To solve that problem, the investigators placed the dissenters on teams of their own, rather than penalizing other teammates. The same consequences existed for all three teams as before but with one addition: Each check over criterion equaled five minutes after school. After a few days this procedure seemed effective. Harris and Sherman reported that "after the fifth day of this condition the students on the third team asked to be returned to their former teams; the teacher allowed them to do so" (1973, p. 416). Both teams involved went on to win the game on subsequent days. Similarly, Butterworth and Vogler (1975) placed any fifth-grade child who committed two violations (only the first would count against his team) in a timeout room. The child did not enjoy the special privileges if his team won and had to make up the lost time after school.

One successful adaptation of this game for school classes and other groups has been to divide each group into six or eight teams. The group designates five to seven positive behaviors for which points can be earned and five to seven negative behaviors for which points can be lost. Before the last half-hour of the day, negative team marks are subtracted from the positive points of each team. Any team that receives no negative marks receives bonus points. The other portions of the game remain the same.

The Good Behavior Game is strictly a group-management game. We would like to encourage those who plan to use the game to combine it with other procedures directed toward task accomplishment. Let us recall that a reduction in disruption is no guarantee that more task-relevant or adaptive behaviors will be acquired. Let us now turn therefore to some contingency packages that may be applied toward that purpose.

CONTINGENT RECREATION

Contingent recreation is a simple reinforcement program that capitalizes on the Premack principle. Activities in which clients frequently engage when given a free choice are made contingent upon the occurrence of desired behaviors. These high-frequency activities often include bike riding, extra recess, art, using a phonograph, writing on the blackboard, feeding the fish, talking with a friend in the back of the room, being first at lunch or recess, and so on (see Unit 9).

Such contingencies can be delivered to an individual, to a row, to a table, to the residents of a ward or building wing, or to an entire group. For example, let us suppose that a group of students and a teacher decide that they must improve rates of task completion. For reinforcers, they decide that individuals can elect to use their free time in either extra recess, art projects, or visiting with friends. Whenever the group improves its average rate of task completion over the previous baseline, an extra five minutes of free time is earned. Exceptional improvement earns ten minutes.

Hopkins, Schutte, and Garton (1971) used a variation of this procedure to improve the quality and speed of printing and writing in a first- and second-grade classroom. All the toys, games, and other materials with which the children were observed to play frequently were placed in an "enriched playroom" section of the classroom. These objects included a television set, Lincoln logs, a box, a set of wooden blocks, toys, an old typewriter, a fish tank, dolls, flash cards, checkers, and several picture and story books. In addition, children were allowed to bring objects from home as long as they kept them in the "playroom." As soon as each child's assigned tasks were finished and scored, she was allowed to spend the rest of the period in the playroom. But any child who became too noisy had to return to her seat for the remainder of the period. Similarly, Sanders and Hanson (1971), using the same contingent play-area concept with third-grade students, reported that all members of the class increased the numbers of their completed assignments while poorer students concomitantly received more of the teacher's available time than they previously had.

THE CONTINGENCY BANK

The contingency bank, described by McGookin (1976), is a positive-reinforcement procedure that can be used by one or more groups. It has many elements of the contingent-recreation package, but it is more flexible because it can be delivered immediately after any targeted behavior. Laminated bank checks are imprinted with the name of the contingency manager. The checks may be cashed for varying minutes of bank time. The contingency manager and the group plan the system together.

A client given a check for appropriate behavior goes to the designated area, the contingency bank, to redeem the time printed on the check. The contingency bank contains the pooled reinforcing activities of each participating group leader. Banks typically include chess sets, books, puzzles, and other games and activities found to be highly motivating.

When a client arrives at the bank, he deposits his check in a "vault" and sets a kitchen timer for the amount of time designated on the check. He then selects one activity and engages in it until the timer goes off, at which time he returns to his group. Later the checks are collected so that they can be reused.

Once clients have been introduced to the checks and the operation of the timers, little adult supervision is required. If need be, responsible peers can function as "bank guards." Clients who overstay their earned time may be denied the privilege of using the bank for the day or the week. A well-stocked bank can often handle from seven to ten children at a time without direct adult supervision.

THE ACTIVITY TABLE

The activity table may be used instead of a separate playroom when space or staff does not permit the latter. Materials for a wide assortment of reinforcing activities— interesting reading materials, checkers, chess, cards, a television with earphones, and so on—are arranged on a table. Participants are permitted to go to the table for x number of minutes, either individually or in groups, whenever the predetermined behavioral criterion has been met.

This program has several variations. It may be used as an immediate reinforcer: "John, you are working so well, why don't you take a ten-minute break at the activity table?" Or the system can be a little more structured. For example, 3×5 cards can be placed next to each client. Each time that one or more participants are noted engaging in a preselected behavior, they earn checks on their respective cards. Each check can be worth a given number of minutes at the activity table. At specified times throughout the day individuals or groups cash in their accumulated time at the time table. The selection of particular activities is based upon objective determination of which yields the most efficient and effective results for that group.

THE TREASURE BOX

The treasure box contains games and activities appropriate to the functional level of the children in a group. For example, for a group of ten- to twelve-year-olds it might contain such items as the game Battleship, checkers, chess, and Scrabble. It is used in the same way as the grab bag (see pp. 374–375). Children who are observed engaging in the predetermined behavior are permitted access to the treasure box for a stated period of time. Stansberry described how four primary core teachers used the treasure-box idea:

The primary core at Bushard School, Fountain Valley, Calif., has been using positive reinforcement to help increase classroom functioning for the past two years. This year each of the classrooms has a "treasure box" which is used to provide immediate reinforcement for appropriate academic and social behavior. Included in the "Treasure Boxes" are high interest items such as a Light Bright, Flower Pops, Spin Art, blocks, clay, Constructo Straws, Lincoln Logs, etc. Each of the four "Treasure Boxes" contain 3 or 4 games or activities.

Every two weeks the teachers exchange "Treasure Boxes." The effect of this has been to have a series of highly motivating activities constantly available in the classroom. In order to reinforce a particular behavior, we review the description of that behavior. When it is observed, the child is directed to one of the activities available in the "Treasure Box." Because of the effects of modeling, the other boys and girls in the classroom soon begin to work in a similar fashion. I then wait a short while and send another child who is doing what has been stated.

I continue to reinforce throughout the day, usually having at least one child at an activity at any given time, whenever possible.

It really helps to let children know what you expect of them and then reinforce it. (1973; p. 4).

THE SLOT MACHINE

The slot machine, described by McGookin (1976), is a positive-reinforcement game that can also be used with a group—for all the residents of a particular building wing, for example. A target behavior for the class period, day, or week is selected—perhaps working on assigned tasks or playing cooperatively. A kitchen timer is set to go off at random intervals. When the timer sounds, one or more participants who have been engaging in the desired behavior throughout the interval are selected to take chances at the slot machine.

The slot machine can be as simple as three, four, or five paper cups turned upside down on a table. Under each of the cups is a slip of paper that describes some reinforcing activity or event. One slip may have written on it "Ten minutes of free time with a buddy." Another may read "Worth one ice-cream bar at lunch." On some occasions no reinforcing activity will be found under one of the cups.

The participant may receive the reinforcer under the selected cup. If desired, the participant may also designate others who have been observed emitting the behavior to take chances on the slot machine. Sometimes an entire subgroup meets the criterion. Then a representative may be selected to "take a chance" at the slot machine on behalf of the group. Whatever is specified under the cup is gained by each group member.

This procedure is repeated at various times throughout the day. When the slot machine is first introduced, time intervals should be kept short. As the desired behavior begins to improve, the length of the intervals can be increased. This procedure is exciting and full of surprises as clients decide which cups to choose and find certificates for unexpected reinforcers concealed beneath them.

THE GRAB BAG

The grab bag is a positive-reinforcement program that also offers excitement, surprise, and novelty. As with the slot-machine game, desirable behaviors are jointly designated by the group and the contingency manager. The behavior may be an improvement in some personal, social, or academic area: maintaining a health practice, sportsmanship, math scores, housekeeping tasks, class participation, helping others, and so on. As in the slot-machine game, clients who exhibit one of the desired behaviors are selected to reach into the grab bag and to pick something out for themselves. Again, the program should be used more frequently at first and then gradually less often.

The grab bag can contain practically any object. It is usually best to obtain suggestions and contributions from the participants themselves. Often students and their parents are willing to donate various games, novelty items, or toys no longer being used. Notes can also be placed in the grab bag: "You may leave three minutes early for lunch"; "You and a friend may have an extra five minutes of recess." Jackson bought a ten-cent shopping bag and painted it with bright colors. "Into the bag went all sorts of goodies, ranging from penny bubble gum to a note which said 'you get to choose our P.E. game today,' to a sixty-cent jump rope" (1972, p. 5). (See Unit 9 for ideas for other reinforcers.)

HOME REPORTS

Behavior-analysis programs are more likely to yield successful results when effective coordination with the home is maintained. Occasionally, the contingencies provided in service facilities operate at cross purposes to those in the home. For instance, school personnel may have arranged reinforcement for Seymour's cooperative behavior. At home, however, his parents may be inadvertently reinforcing his uncooperative behavior by attending to it. The client, caught in the cross fire, may become confused, and development of the target behavior is then impaired. A procedure to bridge the gap between the home and the service facility would clearly be advantageous.

One method is to design a coordinated program in which the two settings function cooperatively. Such coordination would be especially effective for a youth for whom the available school-based reinforcers are not sufficiently effective, or for the clinic client whose major source of reinforcement is at home. Esmerelda is really "turned on" to current hit musical records. The school is in no financial position to present her with records when she demonstrates improvement in her academic performance, but her parents are willing to provide them from time to time. Seymour's favorite pastime may be going on camping trips with his parents. The clinic staff would not ordinarily be capable of supplying such a reinforcing activity when he demonstrated increases in cooperative group behavior, but his parents may be willing to arrange a camping trip. The **daily report card** is simply a contingency arrangement between the key individuals in two settings: the home and the school, the school and the residential cottage, and so on. In one place a consequence, like a rating or a mark on a check list or card, is delivered as soon as possible following the emission of the target behavior. A delayed consequence, like a reinforcing activity, is presented later. The residents of Achievement Place

(Bailey, Wolf & Phillips, 1970) brought home cards from their teachers indicating how well each had performed specified behaviors each day. This procedure, of course, allowed for much more frequent delivery of appropriate consequences. Delay was substantially minimized by this daily delivery, in comparison with the report cards that are typically delivered each six to eighteen weeks in public schools. At Achievement Place, when the youths brought home report cards showing that they had met the criteria for acceptable behavior, they were allowed such privileges as watching television and permission to go places. Another successful use of the daily report card was reported by Todd and colleagues (1976). In their study two boys from "normal" classes received daily report cards. For "acceptable" reports they were reinforced with privileges, like being able to stay up late, visit friends, choose new clothes, and other tangible and activity reinforcers. Three unacceptable reports in a row resulted in a one-day suspension from school. To determine whether or not behavior was "acceptable," the teacher was cued to observe and record the boys' behavior by a pocket timer set to buzz at predetermined variable intervals. The program was reliably and effectively implemented without assistance, and disruptive behavior was successfully reduced. A variation of this procedure was used by a guidance counselor participating in a workshop. A high-school student who had a low rate of completing assignments, was given a card to be signed by each of her several teachers; it indicated whether she had or had not completed the assignment for each period. At home privileges were provided according to the proportion of "acceptable" marks. Completion of assignments increased substantially.

In each of these examples, the home environment supported progress in another setting. In addition, through the mutual planning of the daily report-card system, there was effective coordination of programming between the two—increasing the likelihood that both would implement similar strategies.

Similar to the daily report card are special messages to parents, as illustrated in Figures 27.1 and 27.2 (McGookin et al., 1974). The certificate in Figure 27.1

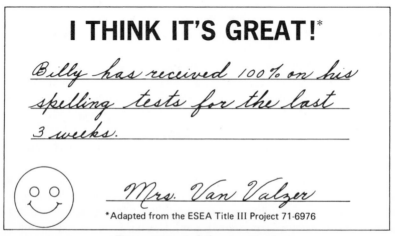

I THINK IT'S GREAT!*

Billy has received 100% on his spelling tests for the last 3 weeks.

Mrs. Van Valzer

*Adapted from the ESEA Title III Project 71-6976

Figure 27.1   A daily report card.
(Adapted from ESEA Title III Project 71-6976)

READING ASSIGNMENT NOTE

Date _____

Dear _____

I have been collecting my reading work for two weeks and am now

handing in _____ % more of all reading work assigned.

_____
Student Signature

_____
Parent Signature

Figure 27.2   A reading-assignment note.

was printed on parchment-like paper and was used to provide recognition for children and youths who excelled or improved in any specified behavior. The accomplishment was described in the blank lines, and the card was signed by the appropriate adult. The "reading-assignment note" in Figure 27.2 was more specific. It was used to inform parents of increases in the percentage of reading assignments completed. The parents' names and the student's signature were filled in by the student. After the parents received the note, they signed it and returned it to the teacher.

The daily report card and other positive messages sent home to parents serve a dual function. They frequently serve to reinforce the clients' behavior directly, beside functioning as S^Ds to prompt parents and occasionally the contingency manager to deliver reinforcement. Many teachers who have used such notes have reported that they appear to improve school-home relations. Parents begin to seek out school personnel to compliment them for their efforts and attempt to cooperate with them more when the opportunity arises.

WARM FUZZIES AND COMPLIMENT METERS

Because social reinforcement may not only increase the occurrence of a target behavior but also enhance the student's self-esteem, many individuals have sought ways of providing a socially reinforcing group environment. One way is to encourage peers to reinforce one another socially.

Jackson has described how several teachers in her school district provided a socially reinforcing environment. Some teachers used **fuzzy-grams**; others used **compliment meters**:

On the bulletin boards of several schools in the Fountain Valley School District are the words: "Send a fuzzy-gram to a friend." [A fuzzy-gram is shown in figure 27.3.] Fuzzy-grams are in a pocket on the board and members of the class may write a note on them to someone in the class. Only positive statements may be written on the fuzzy-grams and the message should make the recipient "feel warm and fuzzy inside." They may be delivered to the

person or put up on the board.

Another idea that helps children focus on the positive is the "compliment meter." The meter looks like a thermometer and can be drawn on the chalk board or be on a chart. Children write compliments to other members of the class and put them in a gaily decorated box: "I liked the way you helped Minerva," or, "Your book report was very good." At the end of each day, the number of compliments are counted and the notes passed out. The total is added to the meter. When the class reaches a pre-determined goal, they may go on a picnic, have a popcorn party, have an extra twenty minutes for games, or some such treat. If a class is difficult to motivate, the teacher may give small rewards at increments along the way to the final goal.

The "compliment meter" can be used for an individual as well as a total group. This can be a massive self-esteem builder when all the class members reinforce good behavior

Figure.27.3　A fuzzy-gram.

with their positive notes. In one class, a teacher made a "work-meter." When a target child completed an assignment, five points were put on his "work-meter." When he earned a certain number of points, the whole class got a treat. [An example of the compliment/work-meter is shown in figure 27.4.] (1974, p. 3).

Such activities can be used in almost any group setting. They appear to foster a pleasant, cooperative, caring, and cohesive group atmosphere.

The next contingency package consists of a combination of several reinforcement procedures adapted for use in the family setting. Notice that the system has some characteristics that are more formally incorporated in token programs.

THE FAMILY CONTRACTING PROGRAM

Interacting family members often find themselves in conflict with one another, causing much frustration and antagonism. Some members may think that they are being exploited by others. In such instances a behavioral contract (Sulzer, 1962), similar to that described in the unit on goal setting (see Unit 3), may contribute to a solution to the problem. What the family contract accomplishes is the establishment of reciprocity among family members: "Reciprocity implies that 'each party has rights and duties' [Gouldner, 1960, p. 169] and further that 'items of value in an interchange must be exchanged on an equity or *quid pro quo*' [Jackson, 1965, p. 591] basis." (Stuart, 1971, p. 3)

According to Stuart (1971), a good behavioral contract specifies five elements:

Figure 27.4 A compliment meter.

1. Privileges to be gained after fulfilling responsibilities
2. Responsibilities specified in monitorable form
3. A system of sanctions for failure to meet responsibilities
4. A bonus clause for extended periods of nearly flawless compliance with contractual responsibilities
5. A means of keeping track of positive reinforcements given and received.

Children's fulfillment of their domestic responsibilities, for example, completing chores without a lot of nagging, is a problem for many parents and for direct-care personnel in residential facilities. The following example of a family-contracting program was developed by the members of one of the author's families, including a five-year-old girl and an eight-and-a-half-year-old boy. The first step required the whole family to sit down and decide together who was to be responsible for which chores. The list in Table 27.1 was prepared. For each responsibility met by 5:00 P.M. a specified small amount of money could be earned. Performance of optional responsibilities was not required but could be used to earn additional money if so desired. If any required tasks were not completed or in progress by 5:00 P.M., the child could no longer play, watch television, read or do anything other than sit in his or her room or perform the required tasks until they were completed. Furthermore, no money would be given for completion of any tasks after 5:00 P.M. Initially, the money, paired with lots of praise and recognition, was distributed at the end of each day. Praise was also given at the completion of each chore. Then gradually reinforcement was rescheduled to every other day, then to once a week, then, upon request, to about once every two or three weeks.

During the summer, all responsibilities had to be completed before morning play. Also, as indicated in Table 27.2, the responsibilities were increased somewhat. This increase was partially owing to the addition of a new long-haired puppy named Mitzie to the family.

Records indicate that the program has been implemented according to plan

---

TABLE 27.1.   RESPONSIBILITIES UNDER A FAMILY CONTRACT

Debbie (age 5)	Kevin (age 8½)
Daily Responsibilities	
1. Make bed	1. Make bed
2. Pick up room	2. Pick up room
3. Pick up toys from rest of house	3. Pick up toys from rest of house
4. Put trash out	4. Feed dog
Weekly Responsibilities	
1. Dust room	1. Dust room
2. Help clean dog area	2. Help clean dog area
Optional Responsibilities	
1. Mow lawn	1. Mow lawn
2. Trim lawn	2. Trim lawn
3. Weed	3. Weed

TABLE 27.2.   SUMMER RESPONSIBILITIES UNDER A FAMILY CONTRACT

Debbie (age 6)	Kevin (age 9½)
Daily Responsibilities	
1. Make bed	1. Make bed
2. Pick up room	2. Pick up room
3. Pick up own things in and out of house	3. Pick up own things in and out of house
4. Put own dirty dishes away	4. Put own dirty dishes away
5. Put trash out	5. Feed dog
6. Clean dog area	6. Train dog
7. Sweep family room area	7. Comb dog
Weekly Responsibilities	
1. Dust room	1. Dust room
2. Help put trash cans away	2. Clean and sweep patio area
	3. Help put trash cans away
Optional Responsibilities	
1. Mow lawn	1. Mow lawn
2. Trim lawn	2. Trim lawn
3. Weed	3. Weed
4. Clean garage	4. Clean garage

and is progressing satisfactorily. (We are keeping our fingers crossed.) Half the money that each child earns goes into a savings bank. The rest is allowance and is available to spend as the child wishes.

In the event that some additional structure may seem advisable, Weathers and Liberman (1975) suggest a five-step exercise to lead family members step by step to

1. Identify rewards for others
2. Identify rewards for self
3. Set priorities on desired rewards
4. Build family "empathy" by putting oneself in the other's position (playing the roles of others)
5. Set costs of providing rewards.

Each of the exercises consists of game-like activities, in which all family members participate, primarily in a simulated situational format. For readers desiring further competence in this area, Weathers and Liberman's book (1975) may prove a valuable resource. School personnel may refer to Homme and colleagues (1969) for material on contingency contracting in classrooms.

Summary

In this unit on contingency packages with groups we have described a series of programs that contingency managers may use to achieve rapid increases in adaptive client behaviors.

The Good Behavior Game and a variety of simple reinforcement packages may all be used with only minor amounts of staff effort, yet they may produce some very positive outcomes. Family-contracting programs require a bit more planning and care in implementation and followup. Each package consists of a combination of behavioral procedures. Familiarity with each should serve a dual purpose for the reader: as a review of various procedures presented earlier and as a basis for readily transportable and usable programs to be used with groups of children and youth.

References

Bailey, J. A., Wolf, M. M. & Phillips, E. L. Home-based reinforcement and the modification of pre-delinquents' classroom behavior. *Journal of Applied Behavior Analysis*, 1970, **3**, 183–184.

Barrish, H. H., Saunders, M. & Wolf, M. M. Good behavior game: Effects of individual contingencies for group consequences on disruptive behavior in a classroom. *Journal of Applied Behavior Analysis*, 1969, **2**, 119–124.

Butterworth, T. W. & Vogler, J. D. The use of a good behavior game with multiple contingencies to improve the behavior of a total class of fifth-grade students. *Los Angeles County Division of Program Evaluation, Research and Pupil Services Newsletter*, 1975, **13**, 3–5.

Gouldner, A. W. The norm of reciprocity: A preliminary statement. *American Sociological Review*, 1960, **25**, 161–178.

Harris, V. W. & Sherman, J. A. Use and analysis of the "good behavior game" to reduce disruptive classroom behavior. *Journal of Applied Behavior Analysis*, 1973, **6**, 405–417.

Homme, L., Csanyi, A. P., Gonzales, M. A. & Rechs, J. R. *How to use contingency contracting in the classroom*. Champaign: Research Press, 1969.

Hopkins, B. L., Schutte, R. C. & Garton, K. L. The effects of access to a playroom on the rate and quality of printing and writing of first and second grade students. *Journal of Applied Behavior Analysis*, 1971, **4**, 77–87.

Jackson, A. The grab bag—A motivation gimmick. *The Learning Analyst Newsletter*, 1972, **1**, 5.

Jackson, A. Fostering a positive classroom atmosphere by teaching kids to reinforce kids. *The Learning Analyst Newsletter*, 1974, **2**, 3.

Jackson, D. D. Family rules. *Archives of General Psychiatry*, 1965, **12**, 589–594.

McGookin, R. Personal communication, July 27, 1976.

McGookin, R., Mayer, G. R., Bibelheimer, M., Byrne, M. J., Thompson, L. & Jackson, G. M. *A model for an objectives based elementary school guidance and counseling program—Project GOALS*. Fountain Valley, Calif.: Fountain Valley School District, 1974.

Sanders, R. M. & Hanson, P. J. A note on a simple procedure for redistributing a teacher's student contracts. *Journal of Applied Behavior Analysis*, 1971, **4**, 157–161.

Stansberry, P. The treasure box. *The Learning Analyst Newsletter*, 1973, **1**, 4.

Stuart, R. B. Behavioral contracting within the families of delinquents. *Behavioral Therapy and Experimental Psychiatry*, 1971, **801**, 1–11.

Sulzer, E. S. Research frontier: Reinforcement and the therapeutic contract. *Journal of Counseling Psychology*, 1962, **9**, 271–276.

Todd, D. D., Scott, R. B., Bostow, D. E. & Alexander, S. B. Modification of the excessive inappropriate classroom behavior of two elementary school students using home-based consequences and daily report card procedures. *Journal of Applied Behavior Analysis*, 1976, **9**, 106.

Weathers, L. & Liberman, R. P. Contingency contracting with families of delinquent adolescents. *Behavior Therapy*, 1975, **6**, 356–366.

TOKEN ECONOMIES

After mastering the material in this unit, you should be able to
1. Define and illustrate each of the following items:
   a. Token economies
   b. Token
   c. Back-up reinforcer
   d. Bonus tokens
   e. Violation ticket

2. Discuss when one should consider instituting a token economy.

3. List and describe the factors that can maximize the effectiveness of a token economy.

4. Identify and discuss the advantages and disadvantages of using a token economy.

5. Describe methods of marketing and merchandising back-up reinforcers.

6. Identify and discuss the purpose of pairing positive social feedback with token delivery.

7. List several fundamental privileges to which clients should have noncontingent access.

8. Identify and discuss the practical planning of token economy logistics.

9. Identify and discuss the factors to consider in selecting back-up reinforcers.

10. Identify and discuss the purposes of record keeping, staff training, and providing reinforcing consequences for staff participation.

11. Identify and describe two basic methods for reducing behaviors within a token economy.

12. Specify at least three reasons why token systems should be gradually phased out.

13. Describe how to move from artificial to more natural reinforcers within a token economy.

14. Describe two ways in which a delay of token delivery may be introduced into a token economy and the purpose that delay serves.

15. Describe how to build in delay between token accumulation and token exchange.

16. Describe how delay is built into the "tiered" or "level" token economy.

17. Develop a program for the gradual removal of a token-economy system. Be sure to include various methods of building in delay and intermittent reinforcement.

The last procedural package to be presented in this book is the token economy. It is fitting that it be treated at this point, for it incorporates many of the procedures for increasing, teaching, reducing, and maintaining behavior that we have described. Consequently, a token economy can be a particularly powerful program. Before launching into such a program, however, it is well to reconsider for a moment. A token economy is intrusive. In many situations, instituting it would be like trying to kill a fly with an elephant gun. A simpler procedure would better suit the purpose.

When should we think about instituting a token economy? When we have tried other, more natural methods and they have not worked; when we are not satisfied with the outcomes of the various positive teaching and training methods that can be brought to bear; when we have tried matching tasks and materials to the interests and abilities of the clients; when scheduling, group arrangements, interesting activities, and other simple contingency arrangements have still not achieved the specified goals when we wish to avoid using strong aversive contingencies, then a token economy should be considered.

In this unit we shall present numerous examples of token economies. We shall also attempt to provide the reader with various methods for effective implementation with groups of children and youth. Because token economies are intrusive in many situations, extra precautions should be taken before implementing them. These precautions will be discussed along with some legal and ethical issues. We shall also introduce methods for reducing behaviors through token economies and discuss how tokens are eventually phased out and supplanted by reinforcers natural to the environment.

TOKEN ECONOMIES DEFINED AND ILLUSTRATED

A **token economy** is a contingency package that incorporates many effective behavioral procedures, primarily powerful reinforcement contingencies (see Ayllon

& Azrin, 1968, for a full treatment of this topic). The aspect that sets it apart from other packages is the delivery of a token as soon as possible following emission of a target response; the token is exchangeable at a later time for a reinforcing object or event. The other defining properties of a token economy will become apparent as this unit progresses.

Many societies have developed systems that incorporate principles of reinforcement with greater or lesser effectiveness, in order to strengthen or maintain the productivity of their members. In our society, the system is called "wage earning." Productive responding is rewarded—with some delays but typically on a regular schedule—by means of reinforcers that may be exchanged for what are usually adequate amounts of various unconditioned or strongly conditioned reinforcers. The reinforcers are, of course, money. Money actually is a form of **token**, for it functions as a reinforcer that can be exchanged at a later time for other reinforcers. Our economic system uses money far less effectively than it might, however, whereas a well-planned token program can incorporate features for maximum effectiveness.

Reports of precisely and effectively planned token economies in human services exist in the literature. Token economies have been used to assist adults with serious problems-in-living to develop much more effective coping strategies (Ayllon & Azrin, 1968; Schaefer & Martin, 1969). They have also been used to aid people with serious developmental delays, educational handicaps, and maladaptive behaviors to develop more adaptive, functional and constructive responses (Cohen & Filipczak, 1971; Walker & Buckley, 1975; and others). In fact, so successful have token economies been in assisting people to develop more constructive and adaptive behavioral repertoires that the literature on the topic has burgeoned; there are far too many studies to be cited here (for example, Kazdin & Bootzin, 1972; O'Leary & Drabman, 1971; Staats, 1973).

In work with children and youth, some of the more dramatic token-economy programs involve improvement of retarded children's academic skills (Bijou et al., 1967), academic and social skills among convicted delinquent youth (Cohen & Filipczak, 1971), academic skills among students from economically or culturally restricted backgrounds (Wolf, Giles & Hall, 1968; Sulzer, Hunt, Ashby, Koniarski & Krams, 1971), social and personal skills among predelinquent youth (Phillips, Phillips, Fixsen & Wolf, 1972), and daily-living skills among institutionalized retarded young women (Thomas, Sulzer-Azaroff, Lukeris, & Palmer, 1977). Token systems have enabled youths in trouble with their societies to return to the mainstream, retarded children to care for themselves and their surroundings and to become participating members of their communities, academically retarded students to catch up with or even surpass their age mates, and "normal" children to function more positively as family members.

What constitutes a well-designed token economy? Why are token economies so successful, and under what circumstances is their use justified? How is a token economy planned for immediate and long-range effectiveness? What are some of the legal and practical limitations of token economies? What problems may be encountered in their use, and how may those problems be avoided? It is to these and related questions that the following material is directed.

TOKEN ECONOMIES AND EFFECTIVE REINFORCEMENT

A well-designed token economy incorporates all the essential aspects of an effective reinforcement program. Initially, a targeted behavior, or an approximation of that behavior, is immediately and consistently reinforced by delivery of an adequate number of tokens. The token is any object or symbol that can be exchanged for a **back-up reinforcer**: one of an array of tangible reinforcing objects of events. The conditions for token delivery are clearly described. Sampling and novelty can be easily incorporated into the program. After the behavioral objective has been achieved, token delivery becomes intermittent. A progressively longer delay and reduction in the delivery of the reinforcers are gradually introduced, consonant with the principles of effective behavioral maintenance as discussed in Units 24–26. Tokens may be used to purchase an almost infinite variety of reinforcing objects or events. Satiation is therefore not much of a problem.

Here is an illustration of an actual token program used to increase a family's enjoyment of its summer vacation. Nine-year-old Flossie, her parents, and her brother were going on a long trip. All looked forward to it, but Flossie feared that she might periodically become bored and tired. Her parents were also concerned that she might tend to become irritable from the excitement and the irregular schedule. So Flossie and her parents sat down together and discussed the kinds of behaviors that would be acceptable and would ensure a pleasurable experience for all: being pleasant (absence of whining and complaining, presence of smiling and positive comments), trying new foods without negative comments, reasonable table manners (operationalized in detail), and a few others. Flossie thought that her performance should be evaluated three times a day: at lunch for the morning, at dinner for the afternoon, and at bedtime for the evening. She elected a self-recording system. A score card was prepared with several boxes for each day of the vacation. If Flossie judged that the targets for that time segment had been met, she would award herself a point for each. A bonus was included for marking the card on time. A system of bonuses for accurate scoring was also planned. Flossie's father was to check the card from time to time, at random. If he agreed that the scoring was accurate, bonus points would be awarded. If there was a disagreement, Flossie's mother would be consulted, and, if both parents agreed that some points were undeserved, they would be removed. A simple rejoinder by Flossie would be acceptable, but a heated argument would be penalized by a point loss.

Flossie wanted a multibladed camping knife more than anything else. The system enabled her to earn a maximum of about fifteen points a day, and it was decided that for each fifty points she would earn a camping-knife "blade." Under optimal conditions, she could earn about eight blades during the trip. The system was instituted. Flossie worked hard to earn her points and marked them down faithfully. By the end of the trip she had earned her eight-bladed Swiss army knife. Needless to say, all the members of the family enjoyed themselves, and Flossie was the heroine of the neighborhood as she proudly displayed (after careful instruction) her knife, with its scissors, fish scaler, and tweezers.

This example illustrates many components of an effectively operated token economy. Let us take a look at each of them.

IMPLEMENTING TOKEN ECONOMIES EFFECTIVELY

As briefly mentioned in Unit 9, tokens *given after minimum delay* can be used to bridge the time gap until reinforcers are available. Flossie used a check mark at the end of each predetermined block of time, with minimum delay. The bonus-point system for recording on time increased the likelihood that she would award herself points with minimum delay. Had it been planned simply to provide a reward at the end of the long trip, the delay would have probably been too much for a child her age. Do you remember as a child being told that, if you did such and such you could have a bicycle for Christmas or some other long-delayed reward? Remember how difficult it was to keep to the requirements for such a long period of time? Similarly, when a behavioral requirement is very difficult for a young person, it makes a lot of sense to break it into a series of component parts, reinforcing the accomplishment of each with the delivery of a token.

The work done by Phillips and colleagues (1972) at Achievement Place also very nicely illustrates the procedure of building in reinforcement for desired behaviors with minimum delay. At Achievement Place, "predelinquent" youths engage in a variety of activities necessary to the effective functioning of a group home. For instance, the organization of a group home requires that each member perform self-care tasks like dressing, grooming, cleaning up one's own area and participating in household activities like cleaning bathrooms. Then there are activities that are necessary to reasonable social functioning—cooperation, leadership, and other positive social behaviors. Because the Achievement Place program is striving to develop leadership qualities in the youths that it serves, it also provides for a system in which program participants are involved in the actual delivery of points. When youths are initially involved in the program, they receive points very soon after completing their required jobs. (Delay in delivery of reinforcement is built into the program at a later phase.) As in Flossie's example, the system incorporates point delivery with minimal delay.

Many other examples of economies in which token delivery occurs with minimum delay are found in the literature. Let us briefly summarize a few of them.

1. In a study of institutionalized retarded women, who were being prepared for eventual community placement, Thomas and colleagues (1977) awarded tokens to the women while they performed portions of several tasks. For instance, they were learning to fold their clothing after it came from the dryer. Each fold was rewarded with a cardboard token. Later on, it was possible to combine series of folds before delivery of the tokens. Similarly, mopping under the beds was rewarded immediately with tokens.
2. In another study, of young institutionalized retarded men functioning at a

somewhat higher level, poker chips were delivered for items correctly sorted (Frankowsky & Sulzer-Azaroff, 1975).

3. A group of college students sharing a house were concerned about the accomplishment of housekeeping tasks and the fulfillment of other responsibilities that would facilitate more pleasant group living (Miller & Feallock, 1975). A system was designed to provide for the daily reinforcement of job completion with credit toward rent reduction. Jobs included sweeping floors, straightening the group living area, food preparation, and others.

It should be apparent that token systems are appropriate to situations in which other, simpler systems do not work, particularly when the requirements are sufficiently difficult so that they probably would not be met under simple reinforcement systems based on attention, social praise, and less formal contingency arrangements described earlier. What the token system accomplishes more readily than other systems is provision for immediate or minimally delayed delivery of conditioned reinforcers.

Consistent Delivery of Tokens

A second principle of effective reinforcement can be recognized in the illustration of Flossie's summer vacation: the principle of consistency. Every time that Flossie met the predetermined requirements, she was able to award herself the appropriate number of points. Certainly, it would not have been possible to deliver a knife blade to her each time that she had met a criterion. But the points that she awarded to herself served to reinforce the target behaviors consistently until the combination of blades in the camping knife had been earned. In each of the programs cited so far, it was possible to deliver tokens after each instance in which behavioral requirements were fulfilled. In the Achievement Place program, tokens are backed up with privileges that cannot easily be delivered every time. In a series of classroom studies conducted by Sulzer-Azaroff and her colleagues (Campbell & Sulzer-Azaroff, 1971; Sulzer et al., 1971; Sulzer-Azaroff, Hunt & Loving, 1972), tokens in the form of points were delivered to students on completion of small academic tasks. Such back-up reinforcing activities as privileges, educational games, and enjoyable group activities certainly could not be delivered every time that the students completed a daily assignment in arithmetic, spelling, or the like. It was easy, however, to deliver points every single time that a student completed an academic requirement.

Providing Appropriate Amount

A token economy is ideally suited to delivery of appropriate quantities of reinforcers. Careful planning should ensure that back-up reinforcers are delivered in sufficient quantity to maintain performance. Such planning makes it possible to generate sustained responding while avoiding satiation. If Flossie had received a ten-blade camping knife every single time that she engaged in a period of desirable behavior, she would have accumulated a closetful of camping knives; certainly they would have lost their reinforcing value early on. Similarly, in the Achievement Place and classroom programs described, students could have easily become sated by some of the activities earned by tokens. As in all other aspects of applied behavior analysis, data-based planning is crucial. If clients are responding at a consistently high rate, then it should be assumed that adequate reinforcement is being provided. If responding begins to slow down, then we should question whether or not the client has obtained lots of a given back-up reinforcer or accumulated a great many points. If so, then it is likely that satiation is responsible. Sometimes we observe an abrupt cessation, or "strain," in responding after the long-awaited delivery of a backup reinforcer. For instance, it had taken many weeks to earn the required 500 points for a group picnic. After the picnic, the next event on the agenda was a party that would require another 500 points. We can guess that in this instance a cessation in responding was a function of the very high response requirement. Again, clever planning can avoid such disruptions. In the school study by Wolf, Giles, and Hall (1968), a system was designed to avoid such problems as satiation and "strain." Wolf and colleagues organized a system in which points were recorded on one of several pages. Each page represented a separate account. One account allowed the participant to spend points frequently for small, tangible rewards; another served as a savings record for larger, tangible rewards; another was used for long-range group-activity reinforcers. Points were distributed among the various accounts as they were earned. Therefore, even when a large number of points was spent for a back-up reinforcer, many remained on deposit in the other accounts. The participant was, in a sense, never broke and therefore did not have to face the discouragement of having no points. Sulzer and her colleagues (1971) and Sulzer-Azaroff, Hunt, and Loving (1972) used a similar procedure in their classroom programs. Students deposited half their points on each of two of the four pages of their booklets. One page was for short-range back-up reinforcers, the other for long-range reinforcers. In this way, some accumulation of points always remained. Regardless of the savings system used, it is probably a good idea to design it to minimize the likelihood that participants will spend all their points at once. "Prices" should be adjusted so that most participants in the program will be able to afford their back-up reinforcers and still have some points left over. If participants do tend to spend all their tokens, then some sort of insured-savings system should be designed or an interest program provided so that bankruptcy and consequent cessation of responding may be avoided.

Specified Conditions

When the rules of the game are clearly specified, the participant is more likely to follow them. When clients are aware of the conditions under which tokens may be earned, they are more likely to meet those conditions. Because Flossie participated in defining the rules under which she could earn her tokens, she was well aware of the operating contingencies. When some minor interpretive misunderstanding occurred, the system allowed for clarification. Achievement Place also sees to it that rules are clearly specified by the youths and house parents, so that they can develop strong discriminative control. Daily meetings are arranged so that any problems in interpretation can be resolved as they occur. To help clients to remember the conditions prevailing in their token economy, rules can be publicly displayed on pictorial or written charts, or they can be reviewed orally. In Campbell and Sulzer's program (1971), the rules for earning points with the Sullivan reading workbooks were reviewed at the beginning of each reading period. A student would remind the class: "First we read; then we mark; then we check." To strengthen further the stimulus control exerted by the rules, bonus points were distributed intermittently when students were observed abiding by those rules for a reasonable length of time.

Matching Quality and Type of Reinforcers with Clients

Token systems are ideally suited to matching clients with the quality of reinforcers effective for them. The only limitation is the breadth of the imagination of those involved. Back-up reinforcers may include an infinite variety of objects and activities, both *natural* and *artificial* to the situation (see Unit 9 for some ideas). For reasons mentioned in Units 23 and 24 (on generalizing and maintaining responding), it is preferable to use back-up reinforcers that are natural to the situation. As in all other aspects of applied behavior analysis, the client is always right, however. If a selected back-up reinforcer is not working, the data will inform us. It will then be necessary to try other back-ups until eventually an array that produces the desired response is identified.

Academic subject matter may function as a natural reinforcer in school. Students frequently prefer one academic activity to another. Because Flossie prefers reading to arithmetic, she could earn points, or tokens, for achievements in arithmetic, exchangeable for extra reading time. This sort of system can easily be incorporated into schools at all levels. Preferred activities are examples of natural reinforcers in institutions. For instance, if one workshop activity appears more appealing to a resident than another workshop activity, points could be earned for engaging in the latter; they would be exchangeable for extra time in the former. Clearly this approach is an application of the Premack principle in order to increase positive and constructive activities. Many of the activity reinforcers listed in Table 9.2 are natural to group programs with children and youth.

If natural reinforcers fail, we can try artificial back-up reinforcers, those not ordinarily present in a particular program. Although schools often schedule field trips to places of educational importance, a trip to the local ice-cream parlor is not usual. Yet such a trip, an artificial back-up reinforcer, could serve as a very powerful incentive for students. Other types of artificial reinforcers include edible and tangible items described in Unit 9. For instance, magazines, special articles of clothing, and grooming aids are provided as back-ups in various institutional programs (see Cohen & Filipczak, 1971). Artificial reinforcers should be considered when naturally available reinforcers do not seem to be doing the job adequately.

Obtaining Free and Inexpensive Tangible Back-Ups

Although impressed by the logic of a token system backed up by tangible reinforcers, human-services personnel often balk at the cost of tangible reinforcers. Let us consider various ways to assemble an array of tangible objects for minimum or no cost:

1. We can ask stores and industries in the community for rejects, excess spare parts, and other materials that can be used for constructing objects. Some of our students have been successful in obtaining broken cookies or day-old baked goods from a wholesale bakery. We have obtained imperfect dolls from a factory. Spools from a thread company and lumber scraps have made useful construction materials. (Certainly the safety and cleanliness of such objects must be taken into account, particularly if they are to be used by young or retarded children.)
2. We can ask parents, staff, and members of the community for "white elephants"—magazines, old toys, and all sorts of objects that have outgrown their usefulness to their owners. Again, it is important to be sure that the objects are safe and sanitary. One clever young lady who was conducting a token program placed a box in the lobby of her building; she attached a poem informing fellow employees that, as soon as the box was full, she would bring in a batch of home-baked cookies for a treat. She was able to amass several boxfuls of reinforcing items.
3. We can take advantage of junk-mail giveaways and promotional items: calendars, sales brochures, catalogues, free samples. We can obtain a copy of Cardozo's *The Whole Kid's Catalogue* (1975) or Salisbury's *Catalog of Free Teaching Materials*.
4. Old Christmas cards, birthday cards, playing cards, and other colorful paper items are great for collections. Shells, leaves, stamps, foreign coins—so many items that children like to collect are of minimal cost. This is a perfect place to use reinforcer sampling. The youngsters can start off with a noncontingent small "free" sampler of collection items like a small album or display box.
5. We can try a rental system. If the institution is fortunate enough to be equipped with toys or games, it is possible to rent objects for particular periods of time, rather than allowing a permanent exchange. We have followed this system with educational games like math puzzles, jigsaw maps, and anagrams. In one program, moderately retarded children could rent stuffed animals at naptime—a very powerful reinforcer (Elam & Sulzer-Azaroff, 1972).
6. We can buy objects in bulk at very low prices from companies that supply low-cost vending machines. A small amount of money can be stretched quite far when this sort of purchase is made.
7. As it is usually politically wise to include people on the program's periphery in planning and conducting a program, here is one area of which they can feel a part and to which they can make a real contribution. Such people can be asked to suggest other ideas and sources of tangible reinforcers. The value of their suggestions may come as a pleasant surprise, and they will be pleased at playing a significant role in the success of the program.

When unsure about what items to select, ask the clients for suggestions, or let them help select some items.

Keeping records of items purchased can also provide valuable information for making future selections. Ruskin and Maley (1972) found that for schizophrenic patients, edible reinforcers were by far the most powerful of the array available in their token store. (The records also showed some valuable information about program effectiveness, as well as the rate of purchasing grooming items, reflecting an increasing interest in their appearance.)

Marketing and Mechandising Back-Up Reinforcers

Kagel and Winkler (1972) have compared the token economy with a "closed economic system." They argue that the fields of economics and of applied behavior analysis have much to learn from each other. Surely those who conduct token economies may learn from both business and economics to enhance the effectiveness of their systems. (Ayllon & Azrin, 1968, have incorporated many economic principles in their token systems.) One basic consideration, the law of supply and demand, is certainly important in designing a token system. Atthowe (1973) reported that patients' activity diminished when either savings or debts accumulated. Prices for items should reflect this law: High-demand items should cost more, and low-demand items should cost less. As demands change, as in Ruskin and Maley's study (1972), prices can be adjusted accordingly. In order to avoid the problems that may accrue from arbitrary price changes, two groups of investigators (Campbell & Sulzer, 1971; Sulzer et al., 1971) adjusted prices on a regular basis. Students knew that each few weeks prices would be adjusted according to supply and demand.

An effective token system requires that demand be kept high. One technique that we have used to accomplish this purpose is to make only a few items available at any one time. When the array of choices is narrow, any one item is in greater demand than it would be if many choices had been available. As marketing experts have long known, novelty and change play a great part in the desirability of a piece of goods. Window displays are changed frequently to capitalize on this effect. In our token economies, we shifted the back-up reinforcers each week or two, so that some novel items were always available. The value of any single back-up reinforcer can also be enhanced if students are allowed to sample it briefly. Or it can be displayed attractively or depicted on the price chart. For some of our nonreading consumers, price charts included a color picture of each object and outlines of the number of tokens required. To keep the object in view of their young subjects, Staats and colleagues (1962) taped it to the top of a clear cylinder, in which marble tokens were placed. When the cylinder was filled, the object had been earned. To advertise, we have kept objects on display shelves or have attached them to plastic containers.

As in a business situation, *bonus tokens* may enhance productivity (Rickard et al., 1973). Children in a summer-camp remedial program increased their academic productivity when bonus tokens were delivered contingent upon increases over their best previous three-day records (that is, a DRH schedule was adopted).

Bonuses of this sort may be particularly useful when clients appear to have reached a plateau.

PAIRING TOKEN DELIVERY WITH POSITIVE SOCIAL FEEDBACK

If positive feedback, like praise or approval, were sufficient reinforcement for a given target response, there would be little need for a token economy. It is only when such feedback is not sufficiently reinforcing that a token system makes sense. Nevertheless, in the natural environment a desired response is much more likely to be followed by social feedback than by contrived reinforcement like tokens. We can predict the occasional delivery of some form of positive feedback: a smile, a nod, an "okay," a "good job," or a comment like "Having that file available really came in handy during the conference." So it is to the advantage of clients in token economies for positive social feedback to become reinforcing for them.

Positive social feedback becomes reinforcing just as other formerly neutral objects or events do. Let us recall that an object or event develops its reinforcing properties when it is repeatedly paired with the delivery of an unconditioned or strong conditioned reinforcer effective for the individual. Token delivery is thus paired with positive social feedback. The tokens, which derive their powerful conditioned properties from their back-up reinforcers, are paired with the originally neutral positive social-feedback events: "How terrific. You've done a beautiful job of making your bed. Here's your token." Not wishing to interrupt a client working in a sheltered workshop, the supervisor places a token on his board, pats him on the shoulder, and smiles.

Actually, one collateral advantage of a token-economy program is that tokens frequently function as S^Ds to occasion the contingency manager's delivery of more frequent social feedback (Breyer & Allen, 1975; Mandelker, Brigham & Bushell, 1970; Trudel et al., 1974). Breyer and Allen (1975) adopted a token economy as a "last resort" to increase a first-grade teacher's positive responding. Institution of the token system resulted in an increase in verbal praise *and* a decrease in aversive comments. The presence of tokens appeared to remind the contingency manager (the teacher) to look for and to reinforce positive behavior.

When a client's rate of responding persists over time (and an experimental analysis has been completed; see Units 31–33), it should be possible, by watching the data closely, to reduce ever so gradually the frequency of token delivery while continuing to present positive social feedback. It is to be hoped that the conditioned social events will begin to support the target behaviors. Jones & Kazdin (1975) were able to program response maintenance by means of such a procedure. They also supplemented the shift of tokens with a phase that included a peer-support system. Peers were reinforced at the end of the day if the target students had met their goals. Consequently, peers assisted the target students to meet those goals.

Involving the Group

In Unit 9 we discussed various individual and group reinforcing activities. Group activities are particularly effective when incorporated into a token program, for tokens may be shared, divided, or exchanged. When a goal involves mutual cooperation in the group, all members can work toward the advantage of the whole group. Each member must earn a number of tokens, and, when all have done so, a special activity is provided. Trips, dances, games, and performances (musical programs, puppet shows, or plays) can be shared by an entire group. Participating in or listening to presentations on interesting topics like ecology, natural foods, transcendental meditation, and auto repairs can also be shared by the group. To earn access to such activities, group members tend to assist one another to earn the requisite number of tokens. If one or two members fail to earn the requisite number, it is possible to adopt a *collective* system, in which all tokens are pooled until the total required is earned. Or the noncooperating members may be scheduled to engage in a simultaneous activity elsewhere or formed into a separate group, as in the Good Behavior Game (Harris & Sherman, 1973).

BACK-UP REINFORCERS AND THE LAW

Recent legal decisions have delineated fundamental privileges to which clients should have noncontingent access (*Wyatt*, 1972, pp. 379–386, 395–407). They include *communication*, that is, mail and some telephone privileges; *meals*, including access to nutritionally adequate meals in the dining room; the privilege of *wearing their own clean clothing*; space in specified areas; *heating, air conditioning, ventilation*, and *hot water*; specified *furnishings* for the residence unit and day room; *bathrooms* with clean, safe equipment and supplies; housekeeping and maintenance by the staff; and various clearly specified privileges connected with *religion, exercise, medical care, grooming, education*, and *social interaction*. (This list is discussed in more detail in Budd & Baer, 1976.) If there is any question about the legality of withholding or using a particular privilege, recent judicial decisions should be consulted.

LOGISTICS OF TANGIBLE BACK-UPS

Here are a few suggestions, based on our experience, that may help us to avoid problems in using tangible back-up reinforcers. We have found that children tend to become excited and try to trade in their tokens as soon as possible. Noise, confusion, and pushing often result. Our solution: order blanks. Order blanks can be delivered to the potential customers and orders either written in or checked off. If order blanks are given only to customers whose behavior is under control, children will quickly learn not to become unruly. To minimize jealousy and stealing, place each item in a bag, staple the order form to the top, label the bag with the customer's name,. and deliver it at departure time, to be taken home. Collect tokens just before placing items in bags.

OBTAINING APPROVAL AND INFORMED CONSENT

A token economy is an intrusive program, for it introduces many novel and arti-ficial stimuli into the situation. Consequently, approval and informed consent should be obtained from those who will be directly and indirectly involved: admin-istrators, parents, and naturally the participating clients.

Administrative Approval

First and foremost, it is important to check the plan out with administrators and supervisors. Although usually there is no problem, sometimes token economies disturb some people. They may have emotional responses to token economies until they realize that working under a token economy is no different from working for a salary. It is a system for reinforcing productive activity. But we should make sure that it can be undertaken in the setting. It is wise to talk to administrators and supervisors and to bring in baseline data on the clients' previous perform-ances. It is possible thus to demonstrate that, despite all the methods tried, suc-cess has not been achieved. The details of the token program can then be de-scribed. It may be necessary to negotiate. For instance, we can talk about the kinds of reinforcers that would be mutually agreeable.

Parental Approval

Next, we should talk to all the parents or their surrogates and explain the pro-posal. It is important to be honest and to explain in simple language how the program can help their children. Most parents, when presented with this sort of program, are enthusiastic; usually those whose children have not been succeeding in school or in a group program are very aware of and unhappy about it. They do not want their children to fail. It is important to talk with the parents, guardians, or advocates of *every single young child* to be included. We have called parents on the telephone and asked when they would be home. We went to visit every parent, and we answered questions. In this way we obtained the parents' informed consent and cooperation. If it is not possible to arrange direct visits, telephone calls, notes, letters, and so on may suffice. Questions should be answered and expressed concerns taken into account; it should be emphasized that this pro-cedure will probably be very effective. Data on token economies are exciting. People do learn well under such conditions, and they enjoy the experience. Occasionally parents may be anxious about reinforcers like trips or candy. These questions can be discussed and if necessary the program can be modified a little bit, so that instead of M&M's, the children receive raisins or cereal bits.

Participant's Approval

It is equally important to talk to the participants and obtain their consent. The plan and the rationale for it should be explained. There is no substitute for openness and honesty with young people. They know that they can do better than they have been doing. We must explain how we can assist one another. Participants can help in selecting reinforcers just by being themselves. We see what they choose to do and what they like: how they spend their time and what they volunteer for with enthusiasm. Do they volunteer to be monitors, to go and get materials, to assist in other ways? Their reactions can guide the choice of tangible reinforcers. We adopted this approach with a fifth-grade class. The children nominated five of their number to go and shop for them. The shoppers picked out various items that cost less than 50 cents each: modeling clay, beads, little toys, pencils. Participants can also share in planning assignments, selecting materials, recording systems, and other aspects of the program.

SELECTING TOKENS

What kinds of tokens should be used? We have used plastic Peabody chips, poker chips, points, and computer cards. In a study by Whitley and Sulzer (1970), numbers were punched out on two duplicate cards. Those numbers told how many tokens each student had. The experimentors kept one card and the students kept the other to avoid inaccuracies in accounting. Staff members will have suggestions. One of the easiest systems that we have tried is a dittoed sheet of paper on which boxes are placed, each containing 100 squares. The sheet can be folded into quarters to make a little booklet with 100 boxes on each page. An "x" in a box, marked in an unusually colored felt-tipped pen, is worth ten points, a diagonal mark five points. One point is indicated by a hatch mark. As long as each client's booklet is identified with his name and marks are made in a way that he himself cannot duplicate, the system works fine. An expenditure is indicated by striking through the box with a horizontal line.

In general, tokens suited to the population with whom we are working should be selected. Small metal or plastic objects may be fine for normal children over six or seven years old but not for young or severely retarded clients, because they may put them in their mouths and swallow them. Paper or cardboard tokens may be appropriate for most youngsters but not for those who are very destructive. In an unpublished study by Elam & Sulzer-Azaroff (1972), the teacher used paper tokens shaped as flowers. Because the students were young retarded children, it was feared that they would tear the flowers. So the teacher decided to hang the flowers high on the wall. Each time that a "token" was earned, a happy face was stamped on one of the petals (see Figure 28.1). When all the petals contained happy faces, the flower could be used to obtain the back-up reinforcer—usually "rental" of a cuddly stuffed animal for nap time.

Another kind of paper token that we have found particularly useful is a

Figure 28.1   A paper token for a retarded child.

construction-paper coin. Developmental Learning Corporation[1] manufactures rubber-stamp impressions of 1-cent, 5-cent, and 10-cent coins. They can be stamped on squares cut from construction paper. Such tokens serve a dual function—as tokens and for teaching computational skills. One teacher of a combination second- and third-grade class set up a program in which students could earn "1 cent" by engaging in behaviors like getting their work cards, "5 cents" for following directions, and "10 cents" for choosing an activity. They could earn five minutes of free time for "$1.50," the opportunity to be cashier for "$1.00," the chance to be first out for recess for "$1.00," writing on the blackboard for "$1.85," or helping the teacher for "$1.75."

In the study by Thomas and colleagues (1977), many of the clients could neither write nor count. But they could figure out the price of an object from the "price tag." The tag was a sheet of cardboard on which the outlines of the requisite number of tokens were drawn. The client had then only to fill in the outlines with her tokens to pay the correct amount. For other young or retarded children, pictorial representations of the cost may be used (see Figure 28.2). In college classrooms, bonus points toward grades function much as tokens do. Our students in a self-paced Personalized System of Instruction (PSI) course (Keller, 1968) earn

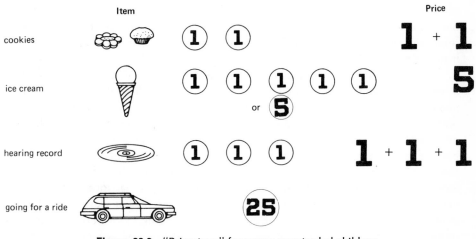

Figure 28.2   "Price tags" for young or retarded children.

[1] Developmental Learning Corporation, 3805 North Ashland Ave., Chicago, Ill. 60657.

bonus points for completing units earlier than the regular finishing date. Figure 28.3 is a sample progress chart. The quiz dates are noted on the horizontal line (the abscissa), and the units on the vertical (the ordinate). The bonus points are recorded on students' folders. The efficiency of this "token system" is supported by the fact that, when it is in operation, far more students complete the course early or on time.

Tokens may vary, from points in a grade book or on a chart or marks on a blackboard to much more elaborate objects, like play money or gift certificates. One should try simple systems first, using the more elaborate ones only if they are to serve additional purposes or efficiency requires them.

RECORD KEEPING

It has been repeatedly suggested that continuous records of program effectiveness be kept. In token economies, basic records consist of data on

1. Targeted responses, like rate of qualitatively adequate tasks completed, taken in both baseline and treatment conditions
2. Token exchanges, to determine high- and low-preference items in order to balance the economy
3. Token delivery, for example, numbers of tokens earned and conditions under which they have been delivered

These data contribute in two distinctive ways: First, they provide for accountability, allowing regular evaluation of the program; second, they provide useful information for staff members on how closely they are following the procedure and how effectively the system is working. The data also signal when to alter the price of a back-up, when to vary response requirements, when to begin to phase out the economy, and so forth. When the data indicate improvement in targeted responses, the staff is also reinforced; so are the clients if they are able to comprehend the results.

Another form of measurement that is particularly useful in token economies, as well as in other packaged programs, is assessment of collateral changes in other important behaviors. If, for instance, there is reason to believe that social behaviors will also change as an indirect function of the program, those, too, should be monitored. The data will provide information about whether or not the anticipated changes are occurring. If the changes are in the desired direction, then they also provide further reinforcement to the individuals involved. The study by Sulzer and her colleagues (1971) illustrates this point. In a classroom token economy, it was hoped that disruptive and aggressive social behavior would be reduced as students increased their rates of academic responding. Sure enough, when a powerful token-reinforcement system was implemented for academic performance, the data showed that the disruptive behaviors began to disappear. All participants found it reinforcing to see the data verifying these collateral effects. Un-

PROGRESS CHART

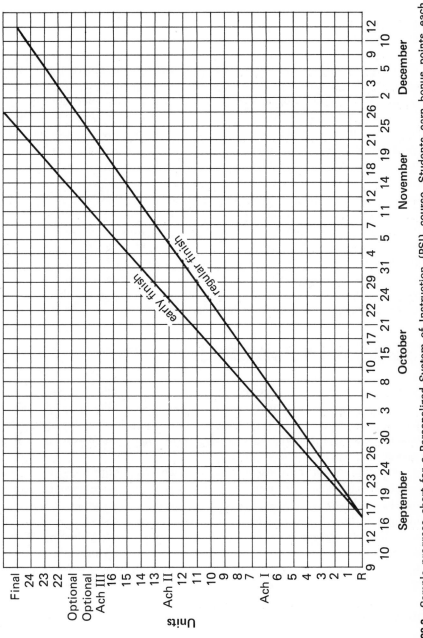

Figure 28.3 Sample progress chart for a Personalized System of Instruction (PSI) course. Students earn bonus points each time a unit is mastered on or above the early finish line.

399

programmed positive outcomes may also spread to the staff. Trudel and colleagues (1974) found that aides in a token-economy ward reinforced appropriate behaviors not selected for the token program more than did those in a control ward.

STAFF TRAINING

The success or failure of a token program rests upon the precision with which it is implemented. Precise monitoring and token-delivery methods must be followed. The delivery and other logistical systems must be implemented consistently. Appropriate records must be kept. To increase the likelihood that staff members do use the system appropriately, it is usually necessary to provide some staff training, a point emphasized by Atthowe (1973). This training may consist of lectures, discussions, reading assignments, modeling, and role playing. Recent evidence suggests that, the closer training is tied to the target performance, the more likely trainees are to comply with performance instructions (Gladstone & Sherman, 1975). If lectures, discussions, or other oral or written instructions are provided, they should therefore probably be supplemented with some direct practice. For instance, participants in a staff-training workshop may see a video tape of someone modeling delivery of a token. Then some of them can be assigned to play the roles of staff members and clients, while the others observe and offer feedback. We have tried this sort of system many times and have found that trainees and trainers both enjoy and learn from the experience.

CONTINGENCIES FOR STAFF PARTICIPATION

As we have repeatedly suggested in this book, instruction alone is often not enough. At least intermittent reinforcing consequences should follow the occurrence of a behavior if it is to persist over time. The principle also applies to staff implementation of contingency packages, particularly complex ones like token economies. As staff members function appropriately, some provision must be made for delivering reinforcing consequences for adequate performances. In a school or community facility, a supervisor may be the person to provide those consequences, perhaps in the form of written or oral feedback or some other reinforcing contingency. In homes, relatives may play that role. Or a system for self-monitoring and self-reinforcement could be adopted (see Thoresen & Mahoney, 1974). Even clients can be trained to reinforce staff, as was done in a program by Graubard, Rosenberg, and Miller (1971). Staff members, like all others, tend to persist in a response only as long as the contingencies support continued responding.

REDUCING BEHAVIOR WITHIN A TOKEN ECONOMY

Response Cost

Occasionally, undesirable behaviors may be emitted in a token economy. As long as individuals have accumulated tokens, response cost, described in Unit 19, is a relatively simple procedure to implement. Costs for engaging in various maladaptive or undesirable behaviors may be agreed upon by staff and clients. For instance, in the Achievement Place program there are specific penalties for such behaviors as fighting and unacceptable language, which interfere with the social organization of the facility. In one study a "violation ticket" system, detailing the offenses and the fines, was given to any patient who violates ward rules (Upper, 1973). Fines were subtracted from a fifteen-token reward that each patient received daily, resulting in a reduction in violations.

Time Out from Token Spending

A response-cost system requires the surrender of tokens after an infraction. Among most clients this surrender is relatively simple, particularly if a further penalty or fine is invoked when they fail to surrender the requisite tokens rapidly. With very young, retarded, or socially disturbed persons, however, attempting to recover penalty tokens may precipitate a crisis. Clients may become aggressive or resistant. An alternative approach is to invoke a penalty called "time out from token spending."[2] In this procedure, a specific time period during which the client may not exchange his tokens is invoked following an infraction. Of course, tokens may be earned during that time, but they may not be spent. It has been found that periods of "time out from token spending" from about half a day to a couple of days reduce disruptive or aggressive behavior effectively.

MAINTAINING BEHAVIOR CHANGED IN TOKEN ECONOMIES

Moving from Artificial to Natural Reinforcers

Although the effectiveness and feasibility of token systems backed by tangible and other artificial reinforcers readily justify their use, it is our belief that most such systems should be gradually phased out and replaced by more naturally available reinforcing contingencies, except perhaps with very deviant populations. There are several bases for this belief. First, such systems do take time and require additional resources; they also require careful planning and monitoring. If evidence of enduring performance is observed in their absence, then they are superfluous. Second, there is the argument, presented previously in Unit 8, that extrinsic reinforcement can interfere with intrinsic "motivation" (a mediating variable, attributed by theorists to individuals who continue responding in the absence of discernible extrinsic reinforcement). Theoretical arguments aside, if an individual is engaging in an adaptive or constructive behavior at a high rate over a long period of time, without any visible external reinforcement, the delivery of a tangible reinforcer is again superfluous. Third, people occasionally have strong emotional reactions to

---

[2] Christine Gustavson, Mansfield Training School, Mansfield Depot, Conn., personal communication.

the idea that children and youths will receive tangible rewards for behaving as they are "supposed" to behave. That argument has little justification from our point of view. Those persons should ask themselves how long they would remain at the repetitive, difficult, or demanding tasks that they are required to perform in the absence of tangible rewards. Why should mature adults expect young people who have experienced serious difficulties to accomplish what they themselves could not? Nevertheless, potential trouble from such sources can be avoided if a plan for shifting back to more natural contingencies is incorporated into the overall program. The last, and most compelling, reason from our point of view, is that schools and community human-services facilities do not normally dispense artificial reinforcers; being able to function when such reinforcers are absent enables the individual to move more freely within the larger system.

The scheme for moving from artificial to natural reinforcers was discussed in Units 23–26, along with various methods for extending and maintaining behavior. How is this return to natural reinforcement accomplished within a token economy? Here is the system that we have followed. Back-up reinforcers are replaced on a periodic basis. As responding reaches a high and stable level, we begin to introduce more activity and natural reinforcers. For instance, we begin to offer gift certificates for special activities and privileges: sitting at the teacher's desk, delivering messages, and so on. Then, later, gift certificates for time at high-interest educational activities, like playing word games, are offered as back-up reinforcers. Little by little, in this manner, it is possible to phase out the tangible and artificial activity reinforcers.

Introducing Delay for Long-Range Effectiveness

One of the prime advantages of token systems is that they allow the delivery of conditioned reinforcers *immediately* following emission of the target responses. Tokens are delivered following completion of an assigned task, or part of that task (for example, after each five problems of a larger group). As in all effective programming, the target response must be of a size and level of difficulty appropriate to the individual's repertoire. After the criteria for the accomplishment of the objective have been met, however, introduction of delay is desirable because immediate reinforcement is not characteristic of the "real world." In one instance (Thomas et al., 1977) retarded women learning to fold clothing were given tokens immediately following each correct fold, then following the folding of a few garments, and so on. In a sense, increasing the size or complexity of the response introduces a delay factor. Token delivery recedes farther and farther in time as the behavioral requirements are enlarged. Another example is provided by a classroom study (Sulzer et al., 1971). Students were initially assigned to complete a few pages in a workbook; when the pages had been completed, tokens were awarded. Later more pages were gradually added to the assignments, delaying the time when the tokens would be delivered.

Beside increasing the size of the response requirement, delay can be introduced into the program in another way—through addition of a time interval between the emission of the response and the delivery of the token. Delay of this sort occurs after the criterion for behavioral acquisition has been met: when the target behavior is being emitted at a high and consistent rate for several days or weeks. For instance, points can be delivered five minutes after problems have been completed or after the stack of clothes has been folded. Then again, while watching the data very carefully, the contingency manager may delay token delivery even longer, say, ten minutes—and so on.

Another important temporal aspect of a token economy is the time between token accumulation and token exchange. Again the rule is empirically based: The data tell us whether or not responding is continuing. For very young children or those with serious deficits, a frequent token exchange at the beginning of the program is crucial. In fact, the best way to teach a young or severely retarded child the "meaning" of a token is to assemble an array of powerful reinforcers, like ice cream and fruit juice, along with tokens like Peabody chips. The chips are kept in an apron pocket. The contingency manager seats herself next to the child and asks him to do something that is already part of his repertoire: "Look at me" or "Put your hand on your head." If the child does not follow instructions, she may guide a simple response. Following the emission of the response, she delivers small amounts of the reinforcer. When the rate of emitting the response appears to be high and steady, she smiles, praises the child, and hands him a token immediately following each response; then almost simultaneously she delivers the strong reinforcer and retrieves the token. Little by little, she introduces a few seconds' delay between delivery of the token and delivery of the back-up reinforcer. She retrieves the token just as the reinforcer is being offered. Later, or during another session, when the child appears to be accepting a delay of a minute or so, she delivers first one token for one response and then another for a second. Then she retrieves both tokens in exchange for the powerful reinforcer. Bit by bit, the token takes on its reinforcing value. Usually it is best to plan a few such sessions, over several days, always dropping back a few steps at the beginning of each session before progressing farther, for such clients do have difficulty retaining the newly acquired responses over long intervals.

In their evaluative review of the token economy, Kazdin and Bootzin (1972) mention that, though no supporting evidence is available, it is assumed that building delay into token systems increases resistance to extinction. Until such evidence is gathered, it seems reasonable to introduce delay between token receipt and exchange into the later phases of a token economy. Assuming that the criterion performance was achieved while the token exchange occurred at the end of the morning and at the end of the afternoon, we might shift token-exchange times first to once a day, then to every other day, then perhaps even to once a week.

The *tiered* and *level* systems used in some well-established token economies illustrate how delay can be incorporated. In the elegant and successful token economy used in the Achievement Place program (Phillips et al., 1972), when a youth begins the program, he enters a very highly structured "earn and lose" exchange system. Points are earned or lost almost moment by moment. Exchanges occur each couple of hours. As the youth progresses in developing target behaviors like acceptable social, academic, and maintenance behaviors, he moves into a daily, then a weekly, then a merit, then a homebound system. By the time when he is ready to return home, he has had a prolonged experience with self-managed delayed-reinforcement contingencies similar to those that he might well institute and maintain in his life outside Achievement Place.

Scheduling for Maintenance in the Absence of Tokens

Two important steps toward behavioral maintenance in the absence of tokens have already been discussed: moving from artificial to natural back-up reinforcers and building delay. The next step is gradually to reduce the frequency with which tokens are delivered, following the guidelines for maintaining behaviors set forth earlier (see Units 24–26). Intermittent reinforcement schedules must be adopted for behavioral maintenance. For example, Kazdin and Polster (1973) used tokens to reinforce conversation between two adult retardates. Conversation, clearly operationalized, was consequated by either continuous or intermittent token reinforcement. The subject who was intermittently reinforced for initiating conversation persisted in the behavior when tokens were removed, but the client whose behavior was continuously reinforced did not.

Rather than relying solely on gradual thinning out of tokens to achieve behavioral maintenance, however, we can adopt some short cuts. When tokens have been used with maximum effectiveness, they have been paired with other more natural stimuli, like praise. Praise, then, can gradually be substituted for tokens. We can also switch from tokens to the type of checks that were described in connection with the contingency bank in Unit 27. The next step after the switch to an intermittent schedule is gradually to switch from the checks (or directly from the tokens) to direct reinforcement by activities and other more natural reinforcers that have been used as back-up reinforcers: "Flossie, you are doing so well you have earned another blade to your knife"; "Dexter, you have really been working hard on your math; why don't you take a five minute break at the activity table?" Under such a system clients soon learn that they do not need tokens to obtain reinforcers. Once their behavior has been maintained in the absence of tokens, the direct use of back-up reinforcers can gradually be thinned out to enhance behavioral maintenance under extinction conditions.

Summary

Token economies are contingency packages that require considerable planning and care in their use and follow-up. The package consists of reinforcement, shaping, various reinforcement schedules, and often extinction and response cost. Generally a token economy is best reserved for instances in which less intrusive contingency arrangements have not been effective. Then, after proper clearance and planning, the token system can be implemented. Logistic, economic, legal, and other issues must be considered, and plans for the eventual phasing out of the system should be devised. The phasing out is accomplished by shifting from artificial to natural back-up reinforcers, by programming delay, and by gradually switching from tokens to natural contingencies in the environment.

References

Atthowe, J. M. Token economies come of age. *Behavior Therapy,* 1973, **4**, 646–654.

Ayllon, T. & Azrin, N. *The token economy: A motivational system for therapy and rehabilitation.* New York: Appleton, 1968.

Bijou, W. W., Birnbrauer, J. S., Kidder, J. D. & Tague, C. Programmed instruction as an approach to teaching of reading, writing, and arithmetic to retarded children. In S. W. Bijou & D. M. Baer (Eds.), *Child development: Readings in experimental analysis.* New York: Appleton, 1967.

Breyer, N. L. & Allen, C. Effects of implementing a token economy on teacher attending behavior. *Journal of Applied Behavior Analysis,* 1975, **8**, 373–380.

Budd, K. & Baer, D. M. Behavior modification and the law: Implications of recent judicial decisions. *The Journal of Psychiatry and Law,* a special reprint, Summer 1976, 171–244.

Campbell, A. & Sulzer, B. Motivating educable mentally handicapped students towards reading and spelling achievement using naturally available reinforcers in the classroom setting. Paper presented at the meeting of the American Educational Research Association, New York, February 1971.

Cardozo, P. *The whole kid's catalogue.* New York: Bantam, 1975.

Cohen, H. L. & Filipczak, J. *A new learning environment.* San Francisco: Josse-Bass, 1971.

Elam, D. & Sulzer-Azaroff, B. Group versus individual reinforcement in modifying problem behaviors in a trainable mentally handicapped classroom. Unpublished master's thesis, Southern Illinois University, 1972.

Fixsen, D. L., Phillips, E. L. & Wolf, M. M. Achievement Place: The reliability of self-reporting and peer-reporting and their effects on behavior. *Journal of Applied Behavior Analysis,* 1972, **5**, 19–32.

Frankowsky, R. & Sulzer-Azaroff, B. Individual and group contingencies and collateral social behaviors. Paper presented at the meeting of the Association for Advancement of Behavior Therapy, San Francisco, 1975.

Gladstone, B. W. & Sherman, J. A. Developing generalized behavior modification skills in high school students working with retarded children. *Journal of Applied Behavior Analysis,* 1975, **8**, 169–180.

Graubard, P. S., Rosenberg, H. & Miller, M. B. Student applications of behavior modification to teachers and environments on ecological approaches to social deviancy. In E. A. Ramp & B. L. Hopkins (Eds.), *A new direction for education: Behavior analysis, 1971.* The University of Kansas: Follow Through, 1971. Pp. 80–101.

Harris, V. W. & Sherman, J. A. Effects of peer tutoring and consequences on math performance of elementary classroom students. *Journal of Applied Behavior Analysis,* 1973, **6**, 587–598..

Jones, R. T. & Kazdin, A. E. Programming response maintenance after withdrawing token reinforcement. *Behavior Therapy,* 1975, **6**, 153–164.

Kagel, J. & Winkler, R. Behavioral economies: Areas of cooperative research between economies and applied behavior analysis. *Journal of Applied Behavior Analysis,* 1972, **5**, 335–342.

Kazdin, A. E. & Bootzin, R. R. The token economy: An evaluative review. *Journal of Applied Behavior Analysis,* 1972, **5**, 343–372.

Kazdin, A. E. & Polster, R. Intermittent token reinforcement and response maintenance in extinction. *Behavior Therapy,* 1973, **4**, 386–392.

Keller, F. S. "Goodbye, Teacher." *Journal of Applied Behavior Analysis,* 1968, **1**, 79–89.

Mandelker, A. V., Brigham, T. A., & Bushell, D. Jr. The effects of token procedures on a teacher's social contacts with her students. *Journal of Applied Behavior Analysis,* 1970, **3**, 169–174.

Miller, L. K. & Feallock, R. A behavior system for group living. In E. Ramp & G. Semb (Eds.),

Behavior analysis: Areas of research and application. Englewood Cliffs, N.J.: Prentice-Hall, 1975. Pp. 73–96.

O'Leary, K. D. & Drabman, R. Token reinforcement programs in the classroom: A review. *Psychological Bulletin,* 1971, **75**, 397–398.

Phillips, E. L., Phillips, E. M., Fixsen, D. & Wolf, M. M. The teaching family handbook. Lawrence: University of Kansas, Department of Human Devleopment, 1972.

Rickard, H. C., Melvin, K. B., Creel, J. & Creel, L. The effects of bonus tokens upon productivity in a remedial classroom for behaviorally disturbed children. *Behavior Therapy,* 1973, **4**, 378–385.

Ruskin, R. S. & Maley, R. F. Item preference in a token economy ward store. *Journal of Applied Behavior Analysis,* 1972, **5**, 373–378.

Salisbury catalog of free teaching materials. P.O. Box 1075, Ventura, Ca. 93001.

Schaefer, H. H. & Martin, P. L. *Behavior therapy.* New York: McGraw-Hill, 1969.

Staats, A. Behavior analysis and token reinforcement in educational behavior modification and curriculum research. In *Behavior modification in education: The 72nd year book of the National Society for The Study of Education.* Chicago: University of Chicago Press, 1973.

Staats, A., Staats, C. K., Schutz, R. E. & Wolf, M. M. The conditioning of reading responses utilizing "extrinsic" reinforcers. *Journal of the Experimental Analysis of Behavior,* 1962, **5**, 33–40.

Sulzer, B., Hunt, S., Ashby, E., Koniarski, C. & Krams, M. Increasing rate and percentage correct in reading and spelling in a class of slow readers by means of a token system. In E. A. Ramp & B. L. Hopkins (Eds.), *New directions in education: Behavior analysis.* Lawrence: University of Kansas, Department of Human Development, 1971. Pp. 5–28.

Sulzer-Azaroff, B., Hunt, S. & Loving, A. Increasing rate and accuracy of academic performance through the application of naturally available reinforcers. Paper presented at the meeting of the American Education Research Association, Chicago, April 1972.

Thomas, C. M., Sulzer-Azaroff, B., Lukeris, S. & Palmer, M. Teaching daily self-help skills for "long-term" maintenance. In B. Etzel, J. LeBlanc & D. Baer (Eds.), *New developments in behavioral research: Theory, method and application.* Hillsdale, N.J.: Erlbaum Associates, 1977.

Thoresen, C. E. & Mahoney, M. J. *Behavioral self-control.* New York: Holt, Rinehart and Winston, 1974.

Trudel, G., Boisvert, J., Maruca, T. & Loroux, P. Unprogrammed reinforcement of patients behaviors in wards with and without token economy. *Behavior Therapy and Experimental Psychiatry,* 1974, **5**, 147–149.

Upper, D. A "ticket" system for reducing ward rules violations in a token economy program. *Behavior Therapy and Experimental Psychiatry,* 1973, **4**, 137–140.

Walker, H. M. & Buckley, N. K. *Token reinforcement techniques: Classroom application for the hard to teach child.* Champaign: Research Press, 1975.

Whitley, A. D. & Sulzer, B. Reducing disruptive behavior through consultation. *The Personnel and Guidance Journal,* 1970, **38**, 836–841.

Wolf, M. M., Giles, D. K. & Hall, V. R. Experiments with token reinforcement in a remedial classroom. *Behavior Research and Therapy,* 1968, **6**, 305–312.

Wyatt v. *Stickney,* 344 F. Supp. 373; 344 F. Supp. 387 (M.D. Alabama, 1972).

A Comparative Summary for Procedural Selection: I

After mastering the material in this unit, you should be able to

1. For each behavior analysis procedure discussed,
   a. Describe and illustrate its operation
   b. List and give concrete examples of the variables that serve to maximize its efficiency
   c. Identify temporal characteristics, the durability of the effect, and other characteristics of the procedure
   d. Describe the relevance of each factor identified in 1.b and 1.c to the selection of a procedure

2. Given a specific problem, setting, and a choice of several behavioral procedures designed to achieve the same specific goal, select one or more and defend your selection. Implement the procedures with maximum effectiveness.

In Units 1–7 we outlined some of the factors that the behavior analyst should consider when initiating a program of behavior change. We emphasized the need to identify the problem and to select an objectively measurable goal behavior. Once the goal behavior has been identified and an objective specified, it becomes possible to select procedures to achieve it. To *increase* a behavior, for instance, positive or negative reinforcement can be used. To *occasion, inhibit, extend,* and *maintain* behaviors, various stimulus-control procedures can be used: verbal instructions, providing a model, physical guidance, generalization training, and fading. To *teach* new behaviors, shaping and chaining are appropriate. Extinction, punishment, overcorrection, response-contingent withdrawal of reinforcement, the Good Behavior Game, differential reinforcement, or methods using positive reinforcement can be used to *eliminate* or *reduce* undesirable behaviors. To *maintain* behaviors once they are being emitted at the desired level, several schedules of intermittent reinforcement are available.

As there are several alternative procedures designed to achieve the same goal, behavior analysts are free to consider other factors related to particular situations: How is the procedure used most effectively? Is it crucial to achieve the change quickly? What kinds of stimuli are necessary to the effective use of the procedure? How permanent is the effect of a given procedure? What additional factors must be taken into account? In this unit we shall review procedures for increasing behavior, stimulus-control procedures, and procedures for teaching new behaviors, in order to assist the behavior analyst to select appropriately for a variety of situations. The reader should be cautioned, however, that, although the following comparisons of behavioral procedures highlight *usual* characteristics, they should *not* be viewed as universal ones. Furthermore, these characteristics are defined on the basis of current limited knowledge. Our conclusions are likely to be refined, while some may be supplanted by the findings of future research.

We have offered many examples, hypothetical as well as actual, in which behavioral changes have been targeted. We have seen how staff members can improve their performance and how clients with various difficulties and deficiencies can increase health, academic, vocational, recreational, and other social and personal behaviors through behavioral procedures. Some of our illustrative characters should be familiar to the reader by now: Lucretia, whose parents sought to increase her rate of cooperative play; Dexter, who wanted to increase his academic performance; Fern, whose vocational productivity had to be increased; Ms. Charming, who wanted to increase the effectiveness of her procedures; and others. Suggestions have been offered to assist them toward those goals. Readers who have mastered the procedural portions of this book should by now have additional ideas about selecting procedures, not only for hypothetical cases but also for actual ones.

INCREASING BEHAVIOR

The rate at which a behavior is emitted increases as a function of either positive or negative reinforcement. The token economy, a contingency package that consists primarily of powerful reinforcement contingencies, is also particularly effective for increasing behavior. Table 29.1 summarizes these three alternatives and should prove useful to the practitioner concerned about selecting a procedure for increasing the rate of a behavior.

Behavior analysts must ask themselves several questions when selecting a procedure designed to increase the occurrence of a behavior:

1. Is it possible, given a specific behavioral problem in a specific setting, to use the procedure effectively? Although immediate continuous reinforcement of correct responding during swimming lessons would improve a given individual's performance, will an instructor who must also attend to thirty other individuals

be able to carry out the procedure successfully? Can the instructor use aides or peers to assist in the task?

2. How quickly does the behavior have to increase? Is the low rate of responding so serious that the behavior must be increased immediately, or is it possible to take more time and achieve a more lasting effect? For example, let us suppose that Henrietta is scheduled to take a standardized achievement test and that it is very important that she give her best performance. In earlier classroom testing situations, among students who fidgeted and talked out, she too has talked out and emitted other behaviors that interfered with her performance. Yet, when she has taken tests among on-task students in the class, Henrietta's performance has been superior. It would be justifiable to combine reinforcement with modeling and other stimulus-control procedures in order to achieve a more rapid increase in the target behavior.

3. How long should the change last? A parent may be happy to work in a relaxed atmosphere, allowing children to run about freely, to have friends over, to play records, and so on. This parent may be content if the children remain quiet only while guests are present, not seeking a permanent reduction in noisy activities.

Questions of this type must be answered every time that a procedure is to be selected, and they must be answered within the context of the situation. Behavior analysts have to be aware not only of the characteristics of each procedure and of the client's behavior but also of their own behavior characteristics. They must know, for instance, how effectively they themselves operate with given stimuli, among specific individuals, and within given situations. As they must also often operate within constraints imposed by an institutional structure, the community, and society as a whole, their decisions should be guided by practical, legal, and ethical considerations, as discussed throughout this book.

STIMULUS-CONTROL PROCEDURES

Stimulus-control procedures fulfill a variety of functions. They focus on the use of antecedent stimuli for occasioning, inhibiting, extending, and maintaining behaviors. They are also frequently combined with other behavioral procedures to speed or facilitate learning and to reduce errors. One thesis that has frequently been repeated in this book is that many behaviors change primarily as a function of contingent consequences. Yet, in our discussions of various procedures, the importance of antecedent stimuli—effectively designed instructional materials and other discriminative stimuli—has been emphasized.

Several stimulus-control procedures have been discussed: differential reinforcement for developing stimulus control, providing verbal instructions, providing a model, physical guidance, matching-to-sample, generalization training, and fading. The selection of a specific stimulus-control procedure will depend upon the function it is to perform. A given verbal direction or behavioral model can function as an S^D, S^Δ, or S^{D-} to occasion or inhibit a particular behavior, depending upon the previous consequences of the behavior in the presence of those stimuli. Physical guidance is used to occasion a behavior that does not occur spontaneously or when directions or imitative prompts fail. Matching-to-sample may teach clients to acquire difficult discriminations and concepts. Generalization training is used to extend the occurrence of a behavior to other stimulus situations, and fading reduces dependence upon supplementary or artificial S^Ds and facilitates behavioral maintenance under natural conditions. Stimulus-control procedures are often used to facilitate or supplement other procedures. In selecting such a procedure, each of the characteristics listed in Table 29.2 should be considered.

TEACHING NEW BEHAVIOR

The kinds of new behaviors that interest change agents working with groups of children and youths can be taught in several ways. For one client, the terminal behavior of clear speech may have to be shaped through reinforcement of approximations to appropriately articulated speech. For a staff member, the use of contingent attention and praise may have to be taught by means of reinforcing approximations to their use. Chaining, too, can be used when phrases of well-articulated words are grouped together in longer sequences or when the staff member learns the sequence: waiting for the response and immediately reinforcing it with praise.

Table 29.3 summarizes the various characteristics of shaping and chaining for training a new behavior. In selecting one of these procedures the behavior analyst should consider each of the characteristics listed in the table. Implied in the list are several important requirements: the necessity of deciding upon the direction that the change is to take through clear specification of the terminal goal; the necessity for "knowing" each individual through close, objective observation; the need to provide appropriate consequences; and availability of appropriate stimulus materials.

Summary

A comparative summation was provided to assist the behavior analyst in selecting and implementing procedures for increasing behavior, developing stimulus control, and teaching new behaviors. The operation of each procedure, the variables that serve to maximize its efficiency, the temporal characteristics, duration of effect, and other characteristics have been presented in comparative tables to facilitate selection and implementation of procedures. This comparative review will be extended to the reductive and maintenance procedures in Unit 30.

TABLE 29.1. PROCEDURES FOR INCREASING BEHAVIOR

Procedure	Operation	Maximizing Efficiency	Temporal Characteristics[a]	Duration of Effect[a]	Other Characteristics[a]
Positive Reinforcement	Positive reinforcer presented following response	1. Reinforce immediately 2. Specify conditions under which reinforcement will be delivered 3. Deliver sufficient quantity to maintain behavior without rapid satiation 4. Select reinforcer appropriate to individual 5. Use variety of reinforcers and reinforcing situations 6. Try to use high-frequency behaviors and other reinforcers found in natural environment 7. Provide opportunity for reinforcer sampling 8. Eliminate or reduce competing contingencies 9. Reinforce every response initially	Gradual 	Long-lasting	1. Positive (possible positive generalization) 2. Constructive 3. Occasions positive self-statements

[a] Assuming optimal use of the procedure.

TABLE 29.1 PROCEDURES FOR INCREASING BEHAVIOR (continued)

Procedure	Operation	Maximizing Efficiency	Temporal Characteristics	Duration of Effect	Other Characteristics
Positive Reinforcement (continued)		10. Combine with modeling and other S^Ds 11. Plan for intermittency, delay of reinforcement, and generalization once behavior has increased sufficiently			
Negative Reinforcement	Aversive stimulus removed following response	1. Remove aversive stimulus immediately 2. Ensure that stimulus is sufficiently aversive to individual 3. Apply every time 4. Specify conditions under which aversive stimuli will be removed	Gradual	Long-lasting	1. Negative (possible negative generalization) 2. Occasions avoidance, escape, and aggressive behaviors
Token Economy	Tokens, exchangeable for back-up reinforcers, delivered following target responses	1. Incorporate principles for maximizing efficiency of positive reinforcement 2. Clearly specify rules 3. Pair token delivery with social reinforcement 4. Select back-up reinforcers based upon effectiveness,	Moderately rapid results	Lasts only as long as token system is in effect, unless a maintenance program is implemented	1. Can be combined with reductive procedures 2. Requires time, effort, and previous planning 3. Should be used if other, more natural reinforcement programs have

TABLE 29.1 PROCEDURES FOR INCREASING BEHAVIOR (continued)

Procedure	Operation	Maximizing Efficiency	Temporal Characteristics	Duration of Effect	Other Characteristics
		availability, variety, and legality			not brought desired results
		5. Select tokens appropriate to population			
		6. Adjust costs of items regularly, according to supply and demand			
		7. Employ effective marketing systems			
		8. Maintain continual records			
		9. Train staff			
		10. Provide contingencies for staff participation			
		11. Shift from artificial to natural back-up reinforcers			
		12. Program delay and eventual maintenance without token delivery			

Procedure	Operation	Maximizing Efficiency	Temporal Characteristics[a]	Duration of Effect[a]	Other Characteristics[a]
Differential Reinforcement for stimulus control	Reinforcing response only in the presence of S^D; withholding reinforcement in the presence of S^Δ	1. Identify relevant stimulus properties 2. Use effective reinforcement and extinction procedures 3. Focus client's attention on relevant stimulus properties 4. Perhaps supplement temporarily with additional S^Ds 5. Initially introduce potential S^Δs very different from S^D 6. Initially introduce S^Δs only briefly and at weak intensities 7. Pause following an incorrect response 8. Provide correct practice trials following incorrect responses (after pause) 9. Shift control from irrelevant to relevant stimuli	Gradual	Long-lasting if behavior is intermittently reinforced in presence of S^D	1. Permits use of S^D and S^Δ presentation procedure for rapid behavior change 2. Minimizes and reduces errors, inappropriate behavior

[a] Assuming optimal use of the procedure.

Procedure	Definition	Guidelines	Speed of acquisition	Maintenance	Comments
		10. To inhibit response, present aversive consequences when response occurs in presence of potential S^{D-}			
Presenting verbal instructions	Presenting verbal prompts; reinforcing behavior	1. Analyze response components 2. Determine whether or not response is in repertoire 3. Determine whether or not response is under instructional control 4. Reinforce act of following instructions	Rapid when instructional stimuli control individual's behavior	Long-lasting when intermittently reinforced	1. Can be used to facilitate many other procedures 2. Verbal directions can also serve as S^Δs and S^D-s, depending upon consequences previously associated with behaviors in their presence
Providing a model	Exposing individual to model's behavior; reinforcing behavior	1. Select a model who is similar to observer, has prestige, is competent in the behavior to be imitated, and is cooperative with observer 2. Point out similarities, and use other S^Ds to occasion imitation 3. Model simple behaviors	Rapid when modeled stimuli control individual's behavior	Long-lasting when imitative acts are reinforced intermittently	1. Can be used to facilitate many other procedures 2. Model's behavior can also serve as an S^Δ or S^{D-}, depending upon consequences delivered 3. Can be used to provide S^D for client to engage in incompatible behavior

Procedure	Operation	Maximizing Efficiency	Temporal Characteristics	Duration of Effect	Other Characteristics
Providing a model (continued)		4. Provide rule governing or explaining behavior when teaching complex performance 5. Reinforce the model's behavior 6. Reinforce imitative behavior			4. Can be used to teach novel and complex performances
Physical guidance	Physically guiding behavior; reinforcing behavior	1. Secure client's cooperation 2. Use minimum pressure to guide movement 3. Help client to relax 4. Use graduated guidance to transfer control from guided responding to more natural S^Ds like models or instructions	Rapid, assuming cooperative client	Persists as long as guidance provided or until transferred to other S^Ds	1. Can be used to facilitate other procedures
Matching-to-sample	Presenting sample stimulus and one or more choice stimuli; reinforcing correct match	1. Identify relevant stimulus properties 2. Use effective reinforcement and extinction procedures	Gradual	Long-lasting	1. May be used for "errorless learning" 2. May be used to teach concepts

		3. Focus client's attention on relevant stimulus properties 4. Perhaps supplement temporarily with additional S^Ds 5. Initially introduce potential S^Δs very different from S^D 6. Initially introduce S^Δs only briefly and at weak intensities 7. Pause following incorrect response 8. Provide correct practice trials following incorrect responses (after pause) 9. Shift control from irrelevant to critical stimuli	Gradual	Long-lasting	1. Responding may be restricted to specific stimulus conditions via differential reinforcement
Generalization training	Presenting discriminative stimuli that were present during original training of response in presence of novel stimuli; reinforcing behavior	1. Emphasize common elements 2. Identify and use S^Ds 3. Train the response under a variety of stimulus conditions			

Procedure	Operation	Maximizing Efficiency	Temporal Characteristics	Duration of Effect	Other Characteristics
Generalization training (continued)		4. Combine with effective reinforcement and other stimulus-control procedures			2. Reduces necessity for "starting from scratch" under novel stimulus conditions 3. Risk of overgeneralization
Fading	Gradually removing S^Ds; reinforcing behavior	1. Identify prompts that reliably occasion desired response 2. Remove prompts gradually 3. Prompt just enough to occasion response reliably 4. Combine with effective reinforcement procedures	Gradual; prompted response emitted rapidly	Long-lasting	1. Minimizes errors 2. Can be used to facilitate control by critical stimuli, shaping, chaining and other procedures 3. Helps to overcome overdependence upon artificial prompts 4. Helps to facilitate maintenance 5. Can speed up effects of other procedures

TABLE 29.3. PROCEDURES FOR TEACHING NEW BEHAVIOR

Procedure	Operation	Maximizing Efficiency	Temporal Characteristics	Duration of Effect[a]	Other Characteristics[a]
Shaping	Reinforcing successive approximations to goal	1. Keep your eye on goal 2. Start with behaviors in individual's repertoire 3. Start with behaviors that most closely resemble goal behavior 4. Select step size that can be easily—but not too easily—achieved 5. Remain at a given step only long enough to incorporate it within individual's repertoire 6. Watch for behavioral disintegration; if it appears imminent, drop back a step or two 7. Combine temporarily with imitative and other stimulus-control procedures; then fade S^Ds 8. Use effective reinforcement procedures throughout 9. Strengthen newly acquired behavior	Gradual	Long-lasting	Positive, constructive approach; requires careful planning

[a] Assuming optimal use of the procedure.

419

TABLE 29.3. PROCEDURES FOR TEACHING NEW BEHAVIOR (continued)

Procedure	Operation	Maximizing Effectiveness	Temporal Characteristics	Duration of Effect	Other Characteristics
Chaining	Reinforcing combinations of more than one response link or behavioral component	1. Do careful task analysis 2. Select links in individual's repertoire 3. Start with final link 4. Occasion response combinations with imitative and other S^Ds; then fade S^Ds 5. Use effective reinforcement procedures throughout	Gradual; if links already in repertoire, may be faster than shaping	Long-lasting	Positive, constructive approach

A Comparative Summary for Procedural Selection: II

After mastering the material in this unit, you should be able to
1. For each behavior-analysis procedure discussed
   a. Describe and illustrate its operation
   b. List and illustrate the variables that serve to maximize its efficiency
   c. Identify the duration of the effect and other characteristics of the procedures
   d. Describe the relevance of the factors in 1.b and 1.c to the selection of a procedure.

2. Given a specific problem, setting, and several behavioral procedures designed to achieve the same specific goal, select one or more of the procedures and defend your selection over each of the alternatives. Implement the procedure(s) with maximal effectiveness.

A comparative summary of procedures for increasing behaviors, obtaining stimulus control, and teaching new behaviors was presented in Unit 29. In this unit we continue the comparative summary with procedures for reducing and maintaining behaviors. The reader should try to suggest some alternative procedures for reducing Harry's harrassment of his brothers; Reggie's swearing; classroom disruptions by Seymour, Jacqueline, Esmerelda, and Fred (the hard-core four); Mr. Grump's negativism; or Little Leroy's self-destructive behavior. Then the illustrative procedures offered in the text and those developed by the reader should be reviewed and some appropriate methods selected for maintaining them. In order to defend the procedural selection on legal, ethical, and practical grounds, the reader should refer to Unit 7. Assuming that first, the content of the procedural units are mastered; second, the procedural selection justified; and, third, appropriate clearance obtained, the reader should be ready to implement, under competent supervision, behavioral procedures with children and youth.

REDUCING BEHAVIORS

The selection of a reductive procedure can most responsibly be made when the behavior analyst refers back to the original behavioral objective. Careful prior planning should indicate which procedural characteristics best suit a particular objective. Beside essential ethical safeguards, several functional issues must be considered: How can the procedure be applied most effectively? How quickly is behavioral reduction to be achieved? How long should it be maintained? Will the behaviors be reduced under most environmental conditions, or will the reduction be limited to only some settings? Is the procedure positive and constructive, or does it require the use of aversive stimuli and aim only to remove but not to substitute behaviors? Are there some side effects that may be expected to accompany the use of the procedure?

Table 30.1 summarizes many characteristics of various procedures for reducing behavior. We have included extinction, DRL, DRO, Alt-R, response cost, timeout, overcorrection and one particularly useful package for groups of children and youth: the Good Behavior Game. The information in Table 30.1 may help behavior analysts to select procedures by allowing them to look at the total picture. They should consider not only how quickly the behavioral reduction can be predicted to occur but other factors also. A couple of cautions should be inserted here: First, prior to implementing procedures, especially those involving aversive stimuli or deprivation conditions (such as timeout, overcorrection, or punishment), informed consent should be obtained from the client, parents, advocates, and/or the agency human rights committee. Second, as little research has been conducted on many of these procedures in applied settings, *operating only on the strength of the characteristics as they are listed here is not enough.* As with all behavioral procedures, it is necessary to use systematic, objective observation to determine that the procedure is indeed operating in the anticipated direction and to watch for the eruption of undesirable side effects.

MAINTAINING BEHAVIORS

Once a behavioral objective has been achieved—behaviors have been reduced, acquired, or strengthened—the concern becomes one of maintaining the modification. This goal can be achieved only if the environment is supportive of the change. One of the best procedures for accomplishing it is intermittent reinforcement of the behaviors to be maintained. To assist the behavior analyst in selecting from among the various procedures, the general characteristics of intermittent reinforcement are reviewed in Table 30.2. Effectiveness, efficient use, resistance of the reinforced behavior to extinction, and other attributes are included. The table also includes some simple, specific intermittent schedules that share the same characteristics.

There are several points that the behavior analyst should consider in selecting a maintenance schedule: the optimum rate of responding to be maintained, the necessity for regularity or consistency of responding, the opportunity for the individual to engage in competing responses, and other practical issues. The objective for Violet, who learned to speak full sentences loudly enough to be heard across the room, carried a maintenance specification. Violet was to continue to speak in full, audible sentences for five days in a row during free play. It would not matter if Violet engaged in competing behavior part of the time. When the maintenance objectives are specified, the selection of a maintenance schedule is easier because the desired rate and consistency of responding are clear. In the example of Ms. Charming, who learned to use positive attention contingent upon desirable behavior, it would make sense for the workshop supervisor and behavior analyst to select a maintenance goal that would include a high degree of consistency. For example, when desirable behavior occurred during the workshop she would continue throughout the first half of the year to deliver contingent attention at least four times in each hour. To maintain delivery of attention to participants, contingent upon their engaging in desirable behaviors, the behavior analyst could select a variable-interval schedule. Daily visits to the workshop at varying times could be planned; during these visits Ms. Charming's continued use of the reinforcement procedure could be commented upon favorably or reinforced. (Or Ms. Charming could plan her own system, providing temporary cues to remind her to use social reinforcement.) Such a program would tend to assist her to maintain the newly acquired responses, at least until such time as the improved performances of workshop participants themselves began to take over their naturally reinforcing function.

One more important consideration in the selection of the maintenance schedule is assessment of the natural environment. As sooner or later, artificial reinforcement procedures are usually phased out, it is a good idea toward the end of the program to select a schedule that will begin to approximate the natural one. For instance, Mr. Rod continually reinforced Jeremy for attending in poetry class. The next term, when Jeremy was in Mr. Group's class, the improvements he had made disappeared. Why? Mr. Grump used a very sparse variable-interval schedule. Perhaps Mr. Rod should have programmed VI reinforcement into the final phase of his program.

Summary

The last two units have been included to assist the behavior analyst in selecting the most effective behavior-analysis procedures for given behavioral objectives. In order to make such a selection, they must consider several factors: First, the behavioral objective must be clearly specified; Second, the operation of each procedure, the variables that serve to maximize its efficiency, its temporal characteristics, the duration of its effects, and other issues and characteristics also have to be identified. A careful consideration of each before selection of a procedure will promote improved effectiveness and efficiency in behavior-analysis programs.

TABLE 30.1. PROCEDURES FOR REDUCING BEHAVIORS

Procedure	Operation	Maximizing Effectiveness	Temporal Characteristics[a]	Duration of Effect[a]	Other Characteristics[a]
Extinction	Withholding reinforcement following behavior	1. Identify all reinforcers for particular behavior, and withhold completely 2. Maintain procedure long enough to begin to show effect 3. Provide reinforcement for alternative behaviors 4. Specify conditions under which extinction conditions will be implemented, and follow through	Gradual	Long-lasting	Aversive stimuli not required; temporary increase in response rate; temporary spontaneous recovery; brief initial period of aggression; sometimes difficult to identify or withhold all reinforcers; aggressive behaviors may be imitated
Differential reinforcement of low rate (DRL)	Selective reinforcing of no more than a prespecified number of responses per specific period of time	1. Use effective reinforcement procedures 2. Use baseline data as guide for DRL-interval selection 3. Reduce rate requirement gradually and progressively 4. Combine with other procedures, like stimulus control	Gradual	Long-lasting	Positive (unless combined with aversives); convenient; tolerant; allows for progressive reduction; takes time; focuses attention on undesirable behavior
Differential reinforcement	Reinforcing on regular schedule	1. Schedule reinforcement carefully	Rapid	Long-lasting	Positive; "other" behavior could be

of other behaviors (DRO)	except following response	2. Increase ratio or interval requirements gradually and progressively 3. Ensure that response is not reinforced at other times 4. Combine with other procedures			worse; behavioral contrast possible if response allowed to occur at other times
Reinforcing alternative behaviors (Alt-R)	Reinforcing an alternative to behavior targeted for reduction	1. Ensure behavioral incompatibility 2. Select incompatible behavior from repertoire 3. Select behavior apt to be maintained by environment 4. Use effective reinforcement procedures 5. Combine with other procedures, particularly modeling	Gradual (more rapid when combined with aversive procedures)	Long-lasting	Positive, constructive, comfortable; if used with aversive procedures, no longer completely positive
Good behavior game	Two or more teams; team receives mark if member violates rule; team with fewest marks or below predetermined criterion levels win	1. Incorporate principles for maximizing efficiency of positive reinforcement 2. Clearly specify rules 3. Have program prepared for individuals who decide not to play.	Rapid	While system is in effect; more enduring if paired with reinforcement of desirable alternative behaviors	Helpful for reducing disruptive group behavior; enjoyable and easy to implement; may promote coercion among team members; some individuals may decide not to play; focuses attention on negative behavior;

TABLE 30.1.   PROCEDURES FOR REDUCING BEHAVIORS (continued)

Procedure	Operation	Maximizing Effectiveness	Temporal Characteristics	Duration of Effect	Other Characteristics
		4. Supplement with reinforcement of desirable alternative behavior			several variations can be used to focus more attention on positive behaviors
Response cost[b]	Withdrawing n amount of reinforcers contingent upon response	1. Allow for buildup of reinforcement reserve 2. Determine effective magnitude of response cost empirically 3. Communicate rules of game 4. Apply every time 5. Combine with reinforcement of alternative behaviors	Rapid	Long-lasting, particularly when combined with Alt-R	Negative; convenient; effect depends upon reinforcement history of individual; may occasion aggression and escape; associated stimuli may become aversive
Timeout[b]	Withdrawing reinforcement for t time, contingent upon response	1. Remove all reinforcers for all responses 2. Avoid timeout from aversive situations 3. Avoid providing opportunity for self-stimulation 4. Be able to remove and keep in timeout 5. Keep duration relatively short 6. Apply every time 7. Combine with reinforcement of alternative behaviors	Rapid	Long-lasting	Negative; stimuli paired with timeout become aversive; not constructive; may occasion aggression and escape

[b] Use only with informed consent of client, parent, advocate, and/or agency human rights committee.

Technique	Description	Guidelines			
Overcorrection[b]	Overcorrecting environmental effects and requiring positive practice of correct behavior	1. Make relevant to misbehavior 2. Apply consistently 3. Apply immediately 4. Arrange environment to inhibit escape 5. Combine with extinction and timeout conditions 6. Keep performance consistent during procedure 7. Combine with reinforcement of alternative behaviors 8. Avoid excessive force	Rapid	Long-lasting	Minimizes disadvantages of punishment but still aversive; educative
Punishment[b]	Presenting an aversive stimulus, contingent upon a response	1. Arrange environment to inhibit escape except via acceptable alternative behavior 2. Apply consistently 3. Apply immediately 4. Maximize intensity of aversive stimulus 5. Combine with extinction 6. Combine with reinforcement of alternative behaviors 7. Communicate the rules of the punishment contingency 8. Utilize safety precautions	Can stop behavior immediately	Long-lasting; may be permanent	Facilitates discrimination; may occasion negative generalization, avoidance, escape, and aggressive behavior; may occasion the punished response or the act of punishment by observers under other conditions; may occasion negative statements about self

[b] Use only with informed consent of client, parent, advocate, and/or agency human rights committee.

TABLE 30.2. PROCEDURES FOR MAINTAINING BEHAVIOR

Procedure or Schedule	Operation	Maximizing Efficiency	Response Characteristics		Other Characteristics
			Reinforcement in Effect	Reinforcement Removed	
Intermittent reinforcement (in general)	Reinforcing some but not all emissions of a specific behavior	1. Switch gradually and progressively from continuous to intermittent reinforcement 2. Supplement change with S^Ds 3. Supplement change with other reinforcers, especially those found in natural environment	Maintains performance; topography may be irregular at first	Performance maintains longer than under CRF	Delays satiation; efficient; convenient; facilitates development of "intrinsic motivation"
Fixed-interval schedule (FI)	Reinforcing the response after t amount of time	1. Start with short intervals; increase gradually and progressively 2. Temporarily shorten interval requirement if responding begins to disintegrate 3. For higher response rate, provide ratio, limited-hold, and/or DRH history	Lower response rates possible, accelerating toward end of interval ("FI Scallop"); postreinforcement pause in some instances	Scallop pattern: gradually accelerating rates, followed by gradually longer pauses; responding ultimately ceases	Much opportunity for competing responses; easy to implement
Variable-interval (VI)	Reinforce response following an average of t time	1. Start with short intervals; increase gradually and progressively	Moderate response rate; consistent responding	Consistent, moderate responding continues; slowly levels off	More closely approximates contingencies of natural environment

Schedule	Definition	Procedure	Response characteristics	Extinction	Comments
		2. Temporarily shorten interval requirement if responding begins to disintegrate 3. For higher response rate, provide ratio, limited-hold, and/or DRH history			
Limited-hold	Reinforcing responses emitted following t_1 time but no later than t_2 time	1. Select time unit on basis of observational records	Rate higher than interval performance	High for a while	
Fixed-ratio (FR)	Reinforcing every nth emission of the behavior	1. Start with low ratios; increase gradually and progressively 2. Temporarily reduce ratio requirement if responding begins to disintegrate	High response rates; postreinforcement pause following high-ratio requirements; otherwise generally consistent pattern of responding	Responding ceases over time, especially with low ratio histories; bursts of responding followed by pauses	Easy to program; requires continuous counting
Variable-ratio (VR)	Reinforcing the response following an average of n responses	1. Start with low ratios; increase gradually and progressively 2. Temporarily reduce ratio requirements if responding begins to disintegrate	High response rates; consistent responding	Longer responding than under FR but will ultimately cease; long bursts of responding followed by pauses	More closely approximates contingencies of natural environment; requires counting responses

TABLE 30.2. PROCEDURES FOR MAINTAINING BEHAVIOR (continued)

Procedure or Schedule	Operation	Maximizing Efficiency	Response Characteristics		Other Characteristics
			Reinforcement in Effect	Reinforcement Removed	
Differential reinforcement of high rates (DRH)	Reinforcing only bursts of responses emitted with less than t time between each response or with more than n responses within t time	1. Increase rate requirement gradually 2. Lower rate requirement temporarily if rate begins to disintegrate	Very high response rate	High for a while	

unit 31

Considerations in Evaluating Applied Behavior- Analysis Programs

After mastering the material in this unit, you should be able to
1. Define and offer illustrations for each of the following terms:
   a. Functional relation
   b. Behavior-analysis program
   c. Confounding variables
      (1) subject
      (2) task
      (3) environmental
   d. Applied research

2. Describe representative baselines, the purpose they serve, and how they can best be established.

3. Describe noncontingent baselines, the purpose they serve, and how they can best be established.

4. Discuss the purpose of single-subject experimental designs.

Violet, who several years ago was too shy to interact with other children, has become sufficiently assertive to function confidently as a newly elected member of the student council. Lucretia has developed the social skills to play cooperatively and contentedly with several children in the neighborhood. A couple of the kids even ring her doorbell, asking her to come out to play. Dexter has gotten down to work and is making progress toward his self-selected role as a professional in the ecology field. How significant, from a social, personal, or clinical point of view, are these changes? Were the outcomes achieved by chance, or did the applied behavioral programs have something to do with them? Are these modified behaviors apt to persist *independently* of formal programming? Although Violet, Lucretia, and Dexter may not particularly care how the changes were brought about, such information could be important for them at a later time or to others with similar histories and operating contingencies. From evaluation of the contribution of the behavioral program, it should be possible to repeat or **replicate** the procedures and thus to achieve similar results in the future. By probing or testing the current effectiveness of the behavioral program, we can evaluate the independence of the modified behavior. In this manner, applied behavior analysis contributes beyond the amelioration of a particular problem at a given time. It provides accountable procedures that people can apply at a later time either to prevent behavioral problems or to intervene effectively as such problems show signs of emerging. The role played by evaluation is an essential component of the applied behavior-analysis model. How that evaluation is conducted will be the focus of this and the next two units. In this unit we concentrate on three basic considerations: accountability, confounding variables, and identifying controlling variables.

ACCOUNTABILITY

In earlier sections of this book, we have considered methods for defining the problem; selecting goals and objectives; observing and measuring relevant behaviors; practical, ethical, and legal aspects of procedural selection; and the actual behavioral procedures designed to increase, occasion, inhibit, reduce, restrict, teach, extend, and maintain behaviors. Here we shall emphasize how applied behavior analysis qualifies as a data-based scientific approach, rather than as an approach founded on faith. The major advantage of such an approach is **accountability**. By recording data objectively and analyzing the function of procedural effects with scientific rigor, behavior analysts become accountable for their results; self-evaluation systems are an integral part of the programs' structure.

This feature has probably been one of the major reasons for the enthusiastic reception that behavior analysis has met among those serving children and youth. Many people are no longer content to accept methods simply because practitioners are trained to use them, because of a strong intuition that they will work, or because students, clients, and informal observers report that they work. Clients and consumers of human services want and deserve evidence that given methods are effective with the children and youths being served. Professionals also demand such evidence. It is to be hoped that the remaining material in this book will contribute to the current trend toward increased accountability in educational, as well as in other applied social and behavioral, services. The following comment on applied research in education should be valid for other human services as well:

An educational system based on expediency without a concomitant research program would be analogous to a medical treatment program based only on the use of currently available drugs and procedures, without research programs to develop new and better medical treatments. As an ongoing commitment to research is vital to progress in medicine, so a systematic and applied program of educational research is vital for extending our knowledge of teaching procedures and learning processes.

Traditionally, controlled educational research has been conducted in artificial laboratory situations or in contrived classroom settings by professional researchers. Applied educational research has usually been conducted in classrooms without adequate definition and control of classroom variables. We are convinced it is now possible for teachers and other educators to conduct precisely controlled curriculum and related educational research within the existing structure of the educational system. Although the classroom cannot, and perhaps should not, duplicate the rigidly controlled atmosphere of the experimental chamber, a reliable and stable situation can be provided in which meaningful research on teaching procedures and programs can be conducted. (Eaton *et al.*, 1972, pp. 1–2)

CONFOUNDING VARIABLES AFFECTING RESULTS

The variable that is presumed to produce the results of applied behavior-analysis programs is the program itself—the set of independent variables. Let us, however, examine what a behavior-analysis program actually consists of and then consider how some other variables may also account for the results.

What is an applied behavior-analysis program? This may seem a strange time to ask such a question, here near the end of the book. We have studied many specific procedures and should have an idea about what an applied behavior-analysis program is. But, in these last units, we are concerned about a crucial issue: demonstrating the existence of a **functional relation** between the intervention program and the accompanying evidence of behavioral change. A functional relation is demonstrated when changes in some event (the independent variable in a behavior-analysis program) alter the probability that other events (the dependent variables: behaviors in a behavior-analysis program) will occur. The identification of a functional relation should enable the practitioner and others to conclude unambiguously that it is the behavioral program and not some other set of events that has produced the change. So let us take a look at what actually goes on when a behavioral program is implemented, and then in the next two units we shall consider how to produce some order out of chaos.

Implementation of any behavioral procedure in applied settings is always accompanied by other events, as in the tightly controlled laboratory setting—though in the laboratory it is much simpler to identify exactly what is going on. As we argued in Unit 27, most applied programs involve combinations and permutations of procedures, or procedural "packages." The "treatment or intervention package," then, consists of a number of persons, objects, and events. The function of a treatment package must actually be analyzed in relation to the individual characteristics of the client (or group of clients), because individual (or group) characteristics and programs may interact. With their unique genetic and environmental histories, individual clients and groups respond differently to different programs.

In order to help clarify the situation, let us develop an illustration: Madame Truffle, French teacher at a northern New England high school, is in despair because her students have not been doing well. One junior-level class in particular includes apparently very capable students, who, since the beginning of the semester, have not done their homework regularly and consequently are not prepared for class. In previous years, students earning passing grades in the French class have traditionally taken a spring-weekend bus trip to Montreal. Madame Truffle has observed each year that, for the few weeks before the trip, the students have put in extra effort. But this year she would like to see the students make that kind of effort throughout the year. Following a conference with the behavior analyst, she decides to devote one class period to the problem. She discusses various alternatives with the students: They can skip the trip, the students who receive "A"s during each marking period may go, or each student can earn points for doing homework and trade them for eligibility to go on the trip. Madame Truffle also asks the students for their suggestions. Pelé Starr, popular soccer captain, offers a suggestion that meets with instant approval from the rest of the class. Four teams will be organized, with an even distribution of predictably conscientious students and "goof-offs." Each member of a team can earn points for the whole team, as long as all members have done their homework assignments. Good scores on quizzes and tests will earn bonus points for the team. This procedure will encourage the students to tutor or seek tutoring from one another. All teams can earn the trip as long as they earn the minimum required amount, but the winning team, the one with the highest number of points, will have first choice of seats on the bus and will be able to choose the itinerary to be followed in Montreal.

Now let us assume that the students have begun to complete assigned work more consistently and that their test scores have improved. What is responsible? The reinforcement procedure? The tutoring? The group variables of pressure and encouragement? The fact that the teacher has asked for and accepted suggestions from the class? The fact that any suggestion made by a soccer hero would have been heeded? The awareness that Madame Truffle cares so much about the students' performances that she had taken the time to design and implement a new method? That the system has prompted her to praise more and admonish less? We have no way of knowing. All that can be concluded is that the group-contingency "treatment package" may have worked. Any one or a combination of these variables or others could have been responsible. To sort out the individual contribution of each element, systematic component analysis would have to be made. Still, some components would actually have subcomponents. Would suggestions by any popular varsity player be heeded by the rest of the class, or is it essential that, as soccer is the most popular school sport, the suggestion come from a soccer player? We can see how easy it would be to become enmeshed in endless component analyses to determine just what the crucial variables are. Such component analyses are important for practical reasons, as when some components are costly or require inordinate effort. If any of them are contributing little to the success of the program, they should be eliminated. In many instances, however, there is probably no practical justification for conducting a component analysis: It is equally acceptable to evaluate the effects of the whole package in those instances.

To summarize, then, *a behavior-analysis program actually consists of a package or a combination of variables: procedures and other objects and events mediated by various persons in particular settings and interacting with the individuals who are directly and indirectly involved.* When the phrase "behavior-analysis program" is used, it should be understood that it is actually a conglomerate of variables. This point is important both for the evaluation of programs and for replication purposes.

How do we conclude that it is that combination of variables called the "behavior-analysis program" that is responsible for observed behavioral changes? It would be tempting to say, "Who cares, as long as things have improved?" But we may want to try the program again with the same or different clients or to recommend its use to others. Let us take a look at some variables in addition to the treatment package that may have affected, and perhaps even have been responsible for, the results. As such variables confuse or confound the results, we call them **confounding variables**. Then, in the next two units, we shall turn to methods for controlling confounding variables. For, if confounding variables are not screened out, we shall have no idea whether it is the program or something else that produces the outcome. Confounding variables are often divided into three classes: subject, task, and environmental (Underwood, 1957).

Subject Confounding Variables

Subject confounding variables include the entire domain of client characteristics: demographic background, previous learning history, and present behaviors. A partial list of potential subject confounding variables would include the specific behavioral problem, its frequency, its point of onset, and the client's stated expectations, reinforcement history, sex, age, and behavioral repertoire. The behavioral repertoire is dependent, of course, upon the client's previous learning experiences, physiology, and genetic endowment. A behavioral program might have been designed to increase completed French assignments. The increase actually might have been a function of the fact that the class was composed of many individuals so uniquely different from others in the past that they learned French more effectively than previous students. Or some subject-confounding variables other than the behavioral program could have been responsible for the increase over previous years.

Task Confounding Variables

Task confounding variables are derived from aspects of the experimental task: the materials, the apparatus, or other stimuli on which the experimenter is not focusing; aspects other than the arbitrarily defined variable (the selected behavioral approach; Kiesler, 1966). For example, a new edition of a text may provide superior instruction, or technicians recording behavior may score inaccurately. Sometimes, as we have seen in our earlier discussions, the order in which the independent variables are presented may produce sequence effects. A lean reinforcement schedule following a rich one may, for example, produce spuriously low levels of performance. Such events would confound the measured outcome, making erroneous the conclusion that the results are a function solely of the treatment. If different materials were associated with the delivery of points in a token economy for a physical-rehabilitation unit and were not identified as part of the program, the outcome of the specified reinforcement procedure would be confounded. Rather than the tokens, it may be the new equipment or some combination of other task-related variables that brings about an increase in the rate of completing exercises. Attributing the success to the program would thus be in error. Although it may appear that a functional relation has been demonstrated, the results may actually have been owing to any of the unrecognized task confounding variables. Any aspect of the behavior-analysis program, including even materials, supplies, and equipment that has not been clearly identified as part of that package (the independent variable) can thus confound attempts to evaluate unambiguously the effects of the independent variable. That is why it is crucial to report all task-related aspects of a program when communicating its outcomes to others, especially when replication of the treatment is under consideration—a point to be discussed in units 34 and 35.

Environmental Confounding Variables

Environmental confounding variables change concurrently with the experimental variable yet are different from subject or task variables. Examples include uncontrolled observer influence, the presence of additional personnel, and variations in time of day, season, weather, or location. Baseline data on a youth may have been consistently recorded just before lunch, when he was in location A. Treatment may have been instituted after lunch, when he was in location B. Any stimulus changes that occur concurrently with the experimental variable can confound the effects of the experimental variable, thus supporting ambiguous conclusions. The well-known Hawthorne effect, in which behavior changed solely due to experimental artifacts (Cook, 1962), illustrates an environmental confounding variable. Environmental confounding variables may also occur outside the experimental setting: for example, the death of a friend or relative of the client or a change in employment. In addition to subject and task variables, any of these environmental variables can influence treatment results.

IDENTIFYING CONTROLLING VARIABLES

What difference does the implementation of a given behavioral program make? What would behavior be like if the program had not been implemented? These questions provide the basis for the methodology used most in applied behavior-analysis studies. To answer them, we need considerable information about functioning before the intervention—sufficient to permit an educated guess about how the behavior would probably continue to be emitted in the absence of the intervention. This information, as we mentioned briefly in Unit 6, is provided by the baseline. The baseline may then be incorporated into an experimental-analysis design so that unambiguous conclusions about the contributions of the program may be drawn.

Establishing Baselines: Why and How

It is not difficult to understand why applied research in human behavior has only recently begun to be developed. So many confounding variables! So many problems to solve! Yet, if socially important problems of human behavior are to begin to be tackled, the "real world," or natural setting, must begin to function as the "laboratory." Behavior changes that can be accomplished only under artificially constructed laboratory conditions but never in the individual's own day-to-day environment are of only academic interest unless they can be generalized to treatment of social problems (Baer, Wolf & Risley, 1968). In this book we are concerned with **applied research** connected with assisting clients and practitioners toward the solution of social, educational, and personal problems. The laboratory must thus shift to the home, school, community, and related environments.

If the home, school, and community facilities—and the general environment—are to function as laboratories, behavior-change procedures will be implemented in those places, and the myriad confounding variables about which we have spoken will begin to insinuate themselves. The task seems formidable under such conditions. How do we begin to sort treatment effects from others? Start by establishing a baseline.

The baseline serves one primary purpose in applied behavior analysis: It provides a pretreatment standard against which treatment effects can be measured. This standard should closely resemble the typical pretreatment functioning of the individuals whose behavior is being measured. (Since the very act of observing behavior may alter its characteristics, one should not assume that baselines perfectly measure pretreatment functioning.)

Other treatment conditions may also be maintained, in order to generate baselines against which to measure different treatments. For example, reinforcement not contingent upon the targeted behavior, and variable-interval schedule conditions are often used to establish baselines against which other treatment effects can be measured. First, we shall look at methods for establishing a baseline that is as representative as possible of the client's functioning under natural conditions. Then we shall consider baselines assessed while other treatment conditions are in effect.

Establishing a representative baseline.   If a baseline is to serve as a standard of performance against which behavior changes can be measured, that baseline must be as reliable and valid as possible. Because reliability of measurement was discussed at length in Units 5 and 6, we shall not discuss it further in this unit. For a baseline that is presumed validly to represent typical functioning, the dependent variables should be measured *repeatedly* under the varied conditions that prevail in the normal lives of the clients. For home, classroom, or community-facility baselines, fluctuations that may be accounted for by weather, day of the week, periodic activities, and other cyclical events should be incorporated into the baseline. That is, the pretreatment phase should include enough measures to support a believable argument that the standard is as representative as possible of the day-to-day functioning of the client. Let us take a look at the percentage of homework completed by the juniors in Madame Truffle's class. The first thing that we notice about the data in Figure 31.1 is that percentage of homework completion by the class is not very high. Next we note the variability of the data: The percentage fluctuates from a low of about 9 percent to a high of about 53 percent. The repeated measures also show that Mondays are the poorest days for completion of homework and that there is general improvement during the week. The second Thursday is an exception: Wednesday night is Halloween. It is likely that a baseline of about two weeks will adequately represent student behavior. Unfortunately, no hard-and-fast rules about the length of a baseline can be made, for some responses are more variable or more sensitive to environmental events than others. The only suggestion that we can make is that it is better, from the point of view of experimental analysis, to have too many baseline measures than too few. Remember, the task is convincing ourselves and others of the effectiveness of the behavioral program. We do not want to suffer gnawing doubt that the baseline is atypical and that the changes under treatment conditions could have occurred without treatment.

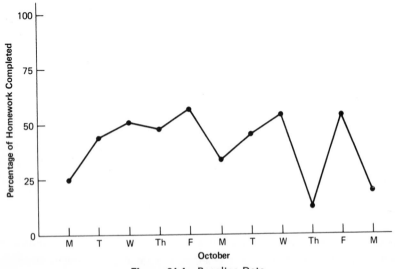

Figure 31.1   Baseline Data.
Percentage of Class Completing Homework Before Intervention.

How closely a baseline, taken by repeatedly measuring the dependent variable, resembles the "truly typical performance" depends upon how closely the environment during baseline data collection resembles the normal environment. When an experiment is about to be introduced, this resemblance may become strained. A study was conducted a few years ago (Sulzer et al., 1971) in a fifth-grade class. Various student behaviors were measured: numbers of reading and spelling items completed correctly, the ratio between items correct and items attempted (expressed as a percentage), and several social-response variables. The questions asked were "What direct effects would a token economy have on the academic performance measures?" and "What indirect effects would there be on the nontreated social behaviors?" In order to select measures that would be sensitive to the "motivational" effects, as well as for pedagogic reasons, it was decided to use programmed instructional materials, assessing the number of frames completed correctly on the first attempt. The students had not used programmed instructional materials in reading before and probably would not have used such materials in the fifth grade, had the experiment not been planned. Their performance with the programmed instruction during baseline could thus hardly have been labeled "typical." Furthermore, because social behavioral measures were also being taken concurrently, an observer sat in the back of the room, marking a sheet from time to time. Again the environment was altered and may have produced atypical behavior. To guard against strong reactivity to such changes, a fairly protracted **adaptation** period was provided, and the students did seem to settle into a routine, but we shall never know what were the distinct contributions of the experimental exigencies.

Despite not knowing about the effects of those research-related variables, we did obtain some very valuable information. When the token system was implemented (phase C), all the same variables remained in effect. The materials were the same. The same observer sat in the room. The teacher was asked to keep her excellent methods of classroom management constant throughout the year, and data were collected to ensure that she did. Crucial phases of the study were long enough so that the data convinced us that the performance had attained whatever stability it would. When student performance during the token program showed substantial increases over the baseline, it was therefore concluded with some confidence that the increase was not a function of the confounding research-related variables (see Figure 31.2).

Although it may be very difficult in some instances to establish a baseline that truly represents typical client functioning, adequate precautions should maximize the utility of the baseline, especially when all research-related environmental modifications are kept constant throughout all phases of the evaluative study. For an even more convincing case, data should be collected and presented to support the claim that these controls have been maintained.

Baseline taken under other treatment conditions. In most instances, a baseline includes all procedures except the *independent variable*—in applied behavior analysis, usually a treatment program. Once a baseline has been measured, the program

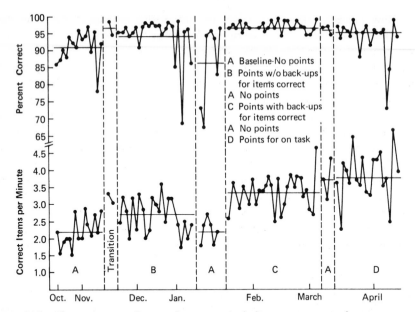

Figure 31.2 Class mean reading performance, including percentage of answers correct and numbers correct per minute.

is instituted, and later a functional relation is demonstrated through the use of one of the experimental analyses to be discussed in Units 32 and 33. There may be instances, however, when it is not feasible or desirable to withhold the independent variable completely during baseline conditions. Let us consider some illustrations of this point. A mother thinks that it may be her attention that is increasing a maladaptive social behavior in one of her children. Ideally, she could withhold attention and record the behavior for a representative time period to establish a baseline, then institute attention contingent upon a behavior incompatible with the maladaptive behavior. The mother, however, has doubts about the morality of withholding attention entirely from one of her children, not to speak of her lack of confidence that she can actually carry out such a control. *The solution for her lies in differential reinforcement of other behaviors during baseline.* Attention is given, but not contingent upon the alternative response. Then later, during the treatment phase, attention is provided, only then largely contingent upon the alternative response. (As it is most likely that the mother does ordinarily attend to her child at various times, this phase would resemble normal conditions.)

Sometimes a critic can argue: "Naturally the behavior is improving; the client is getting so many more rewards. His improvement has nothing to do with the behavioral program *per se.*" To counter such an argument, we may want to show that the amount of reinforcement is relatively constant during baseline and treatment; the only thing changed is the contingency relation between the response and the reinforcer. During baseline the reinforcer is not contingent upon the target behavior; during treatment, the reinforcer is delivered contingently. One way of accomplishing this goal is to deliver the reinforcer before the response. For a simple example, to compare contingent play time with noncontingent play time for its effects on task completion, let the children go out for extra play before the work time. Then during treatment they earn extra play time for task completion. The *amount* of reinforcement is thus held fairly constant. Changes can be attributed with more certainty to the contingency relation.

A baseline incorporating reinforcement that is not contingent upon the target behavior may have a pragmatic advantage also, for it allows us to continue delivering reinforcement during baseline. We have conducted a number of programs with severely handicapped youngsters. It has been necessary to make all sessions as reinforcing as possible, just to maintain the attentiveness of the client. If the treatment program includes the delivery of food, smiles, and praise, for example, the baseline incorporates these reinforcers—but on a basis other than contingent upon the target behavior. For instance, food, smiles, and praise—"You're working hard"—may be delivered once a minute, regardless of the response being emitted by the client, unless, of course, that response is maladaptive.

In this section we have presented a rationale and some guidelines for establishing baselines. We have also considered some problems encountered in establishing truly representative baselines; the value of modified baselines has been discussed. We have not considered some more sophisticated variations in establishing baselines, like those generated under particular schedules, yoked schedules, and others discussed by Sidman (1960), but we have considered the baseline that incorporates noncontingent reinforcement. Our rationale for inclusion or omission of these methodological discussions is our judgment of what is most relevant for the applied behavior analyst operating in educational and community facilities serving children and youth. Now we shall introduce methods used by applied behavior analysts to evaluate the effectiveness of specific behavioral programs.

Using Experimental Designs

The establishment of accurate baselines is a common first step in all single-subject experimental designs, reducing the contaminating influence of confounding variables. By itself, however, the baseline phase is insufficient for evaluation of the effectiveness of specific behavioral programs. It functions as a "pretest," or standard of performance, against which change can be measured.

How, then, does behavior analysis evaluate the effects of a behavioral treatment program unambiguously? How does it answer questions like "Does praising Dexter, contingent upon his completion of arithmetic problems, result in an increase in his arithmetic output?"; "Does the word 'no' from Flossie's parents result in an immediate and long-lasting cessation of her marking on the walls?" A valid conclusion about the effectiveness of such environmental changes could be made only if data were collected under controlled conditions. Single-subject (also referred to as *within-subject* and *single case*[1]) experimental designs provide

[1] See Hersen & Barlow (1976) for an extensive treatment of single case experimental designs.

one excellent structure for such data collection. They demonstrate the existence of functional relations between the dependent behaviors (completion of arithmetic problems or wall marking) and selected behavioral procedures, like praising or saying "no." They do so, first, by ensuring that not only the baseline but also each experimental phase is of a *sufficient length* so that the confounding effects of outside environmental variables are minimized. For instance, if a client is known to have started a paper route part way through a given experimental phase, it will be necessary to extend that phase long enough so that the effects of his having a paper route will become manifest and can be accounted for. Introducing an experimental change simultaneous with the client's new job would undoubtedly introduce ambiguity into interpretation of the data.

Second, single-subject designs, by allowing the possible influences of confounding variables to be screened out, provide for an experimental analysis. Such a screening process enables the experimenter to analyze the function of the treatment (the independent variable) less ambiguously and thus to draw certain conclusions about the lawfulness of the observed behavior. Various single-subject experimental designs are discussed in Units 32 and 33.

Summary

Applied behavior analyses must be accountable for the procedures they apply. Several categories of confounding variables emphasize the need for experimental controls in evaluation. To be unambiguously accountable, we have suggested, the behavior analyst should use scientific method and reliable standard measures to establish representative baselines to which changes in behavior under the independent variable can be compared. In addition, an experimental design is used to demonstrate convincingly that the effect of the independent variable is a function of the intervention and not of various confounding variables.

References

Baer, D. M., Wolf, M. M. & Risley, T. R. Some current dimensions of applied behavior analysis. *Journal of Applied Behavior Analysis,* 1968, **1**, 91–97.

Cook, D. L. The Hawthorne effect in educational research. *Phi Delta Kappan,* 1962, **44**, 116–122.

Eaton, M. D., Gentry, N. D., Haring, N. B. & Lovitt, T. C. Applying experimental analysis of behavior to investigating curriculum and making instructional decisions. Paper presented at Southern California Fourth Annual Conference on Behavior Modification, Los Angeles, October 1972.

Hersen, M. & Barlow, D. H. *Single case experimental designs.* New York: Pergamon, 1976.

Kiesler, D. J. Some myths of psychotherapy research and the search for a paradigm. *Psychological Bulletin,* 1966, **65**, 110–136.

Sidman, M. *Tactics of scientific research.* New York: Basic Books, 1960.

Sulzer, B., Hunt, S., Ashby, E., Koniarski, C. & Krams, M. Increasing rate and percentage correct in reading and spelling in a fifth grade public school class of slow readers by means of a token system. In E. A. Ramp & B. L. Hopkins (Eds.), *A new direction for education: Behavior analysis, 1971.* Lawrence: University of Kansas, 1971.

Underwood, B. J. *Psychological research.* New York: Appleton, 1957.

Single-Subject Designs: Reversal and Multiple Baselines

After mastering the material in this unit, you should be able to
1. Define and offer illustrations for each of the following terms:
   a. Behavioral principle
   b. Probe
   c. Intensive or single-subject experimental designs
   d. Reversal and its variations
   e. Multiple baseline across behaviors
   f. Multiple baseline across subjects
   g. Multiple baseline across situations

2. Specify the common advantages of single-subject designs.

3. List and describe the advantages and possible limitations of each of the four different single-subject designs listed in 1.d—1.g.

4. Describe a situation for each of the four designs that would make that specific design the best possible one to use. Be sure to justify your selection clearly.

Helen had been home from the hospital for several weeks. When she returned for her follow-up appointment with Dr. Daring, she was found to be in excellent condition. Helen produced her record, showing that she had taken her diabetes-control medication regularly. Dr. Daring, duly impressed, inquired about the program that Helen and her nurse had developed. "I should try that with all my patients," exclaimed Dr. Daring. She was seized by a gnawing doubt, however:

"Perhaps Helen's improvement is just a happy coincidence, and the procedure had nothing to do with it?" How could she overcome her doubts? She would need a demonstration of a functional relation between the procedure and an appropriately maintained self-medication regimen, not only for Helen but for other patients also. Perhaps a group experimental design would do: using the procedure with half her patients and not with the other half.

Group experimental designs have been used a great deal as research tools in the social sciences. Such designs, when appropriately conceived, minimize the effects of confounding variables upon results (see any one of the many current textbooks on psychological, educational, or mathematical statistics). A typical assumption underlying group experimental designs is that group scores can be adequately represented by computing statistical measures of central tendency (averages, means, and so forth) and the variability with which the scores are distributed (that is, the standard deviation). Well-designed group studies allow us to infer from one group to another and may therefore prove especially practical when we are drawing conclusions and making predictions and recommendations for groups. A group design might assist an architect in designing a building to increase the group average of given behaviors. It is not appropriate, however, to draw conclusions about any specific individual member of a group on the basis of a group design. Such a design would therefore not be suitable to the identification of variables controlling Helen's behavior. As it is with the factors affecting the behavior of individual clients that the human services are most concerned, the applied behavior-analyst serving children and youth must turn to those designs that will meet his purpose: **single-subject**, or **intensive**, (Thoresen & Anton, 1974), **designs**. Such designs have a dual advantage: They yield **behavioral principles** appropriate for individuals like Helen, as well as for groups of individuals, like Dr. Daring's other patients, while simultaneously reducing the confounding effects of extra-program variables.

ADVANTAGES OF SINGLE-SUBJECT DESIGNS

Behavioral Principles

Single-subject research yields a principle of behavior applicable to a particular individual (Bijou & Baer, 1960). For example, Dexter's completion of arithmetic problems was demonstrated, under conditions experimentally controlled by a single-subject design, to have increased as a function of his own record keeping and being praised by his parents, teachers, the guidance counselor, and others. Praise was found to be a general reinforcer for him: A valuable principle of Dexter's behavior was thus discovered. A single-subject design demonstrated that a self-recording and self-administered reinforcement system was effective with Helen. This type of finding contrasts with those obtained through group designs.

Typically, client change during treatment is obscured in group designs, and the relationship between change and treatment for individual clients may vary in fundamentally different

ways compared to the average change of a group of subjects. . . . However, intensive designs (single organism designs) . . . offer several advantages such as immediate data on how
treatment influences clients. (Thoresen & Anton, 1974, p. 553)

Sometimes principles that relate to a single individual are found to be equally
applicable to a number of individuals: Perhaps the procedure used by Helen
would work for Dr. Daring's other patients. When the same results are found
to be lawful—to be repeated, or *replicated*, among many subjects—they are said
to constitute a general *principle*. This principle should then apply to various
groups of individuals with characteristics similar to those of the single individuals
in each of the original studies. We have to know, however, what the characteristics are before such generalizations can be made. When results fail to be replicated (perhaps when a variation of the reward system is devised for one of Dr.
Daring's other patients), "the changes in experimental technique that the experimenter must use in order to replicate [the results] in other children may often give
a meaningful clue to the nature of each child's past history" (Bijou & Baer, 1960,
p. 151). Such clues may also lead to the identification of confounding variables
that must eventually be controlled if outcomes are to be optimized.

Reduces Subject Confoundnig

A particularly significant advantage of the single-subject design is that it minimizes
the effects of one of the strongest confounding factors in behavioral research,
individual client differences. The single-subject design allows comparisons between an individual's behavior under one condition and under other conditions.
For example, a single-subject reversal design was used to help answer the question
"Does praising Dexter, contingent upon his completion of arithmetic problems,
result in an increase in his arithmetic output?" Dexter's own performances during
the baseline period (no praise), treatment period (praise), and reversal period (no
praise) were compared. They were not compared with those of Ernie, Humphrey,
or Seymour, only with his own. Differences among individual subjects could not
therefore affect the outcome of the analysis.

Although the single-subject design does substantially reduce the problem
of subject-confounding variables, additional provision must be made to ensure
that characteristics of subject and experimenter are reported and that other forms
of uncontrolled task and environmental variables do not enter the situation and
affect the outcome of the program. In the French-class point system, for example,
it would be necessary to maintain the following conditions before, during, and
after the procedural changes: the presence of observers, record-keeping methods,
classroom-management techniques, general instructional routine, and all other
possible environmental-confounding variables—plus the general length and levels
of difficulty of responses required of the students and all other task-confounding
variables. (Naturally, when classroom experiments require collection of data on
academic performance over prolonged periods of time, the lengths of assignments
will vary somewhat from day to day, and the levels of difficulty will gradually
increase. However, because none of the changes is abrupt and because they are

not introduced at the beginning of a new experimental phase but are distributed evenly throughout all phases, they are treated as if they were constants.) Therefore in every single-subject experimental design, it is required that *all conditions, other than the systematic changes in the independent variable, be kept constant throughout the entire program*. With confidence that other variables are being prevented from affecting the outcome, it then becomes possible to test for the effects of the procedure upon the behavior and thus to demonstrate experimental control. If it were possible to increase or decrease the number of correctly completed French assignments of similar length and difficulty by concomitantly presenting or withholding points, the effectiveness of the point system would be demonstrated. If some condition other than the point system were responsible for the improvement, no decline in performance would accompany its removal nor would a subsequent increase accompany its reintroduction. When experimental control exists, factors like passage of time and other environmental and task variables can no longer be credited with responsibility for behavioral changes.

Experimental analysis[1] is an essential component of the behavior-analysis method. Consequently, each time that a behavior-analysis program is conducted, in a sense, an applied research study is conducted. Like the basic laboratory researcher, the behavior analyst is concerned with discovering factors that affect behavior in lawful ways. But, rather than experimenting to discover some abstract findings, the primary concern is with improving the effectiveness of socially important client behaviors (Baer, Wolf & Risley, 1968).

As we have already seen, however, the average applied setting seldom provides an ideal setting for research. "The analysis of socially important behavior becomes experimental only with difficulty" (Baer, Wolf & Risley, 1968, p. 92). It therefore becomes very important to structure the situation carefully, that is, to use adequate controls. For this reason, we shall now discuss some single-subject experimental designs that have been found particularly useful in analyzing the influence that programs exert upon behavior in applied settings.

REVERSAL DESIGNS

The term functional relation suggests that a change in the independent variable will produce systematic changes in the dependent variable (Holland & Skinner, 1961). If a particular independent variable (for example, the presentation of praise) is functionally related to the behavior of a particular individual (for example, rate of answering questions), the contingent presentation of the independent variable should systematically affect that behavior. If praise is a reinforcer, the rate of answering questions, for example, should increase. If praise is an aversive stimulus, the rate should decrease. If praise is indeed a reinforcer withholding it following answers to questions should also have a systematic effect: Under such extinction conditions, the rate should begin to decrease. When systematic changes in the dependent variable (rate of answering questions) occur as a function of the

[1] Sometimes called "functional analysis."

contingent presentation and withdrawal of an independent variable, there is evidence for the existence of a lawful functional relation. One then becomes confident that it is indeed the procedure, rather than some uncontrolled confounding variables, that has accounted for the changes in behavior. It is upon this logic that reversal designs are based.

From our brief discussion of reversal designs in Unit 6, we recall their characteristic form. First, baseline performance is measured. Next, the independent variable is introduced. Then the independent variable is removed. Usually the independent variable is introduced again. The first baseline is identified as the A phase; the experimental condition, in which the independent variable is introduced, is the B phase. The return to baseline conditions is the **reversal**, or **probe**; conditions are then identical with baseline conditions, and the "A" label is again appropriate. Reintroduction of the independent variable is labeled "B." A reversal design is thus often called an "ABAB design."

Figure 32.1 illustrates these phases in a classroom program designed to reduce a student's disruptive behavior. This particular study (Whitley & Sulzer, 1970) also included a follow-up phase after termination of the formal program.

Variations of Reversal Designs

There are some variations in the basic ABAB design that can be used when particular problems are present. In one variation, the reinforcer is presented in all phases of the study, but not contingent upon the target response during the repeated baseline conditions, as indicated in Unit 31. For instance, one study (Sulzer-Azaroff, Hunt & Loving, 1972) involved a tutoring program with a group of nine- and ten-year-old volunteers. The reinforcers were points, backed up by access to preferred activities like games, crafts projects, films, and trips. The dependent variable was each student's performance on academic assignments (number completed and percentage correct) in reading and arithmetic workbooks. It was reasoned that, if the baseline conditions included the task and *no* reinforcement, the students would not attend the voluntary sessions. Reinforcing activities were therefore made available to the students "noncontingently" during baseline. The students were allowed to participate in the activities, regardless of their performance on academic tasks. Then, once the experimental phase was in effect, they were required to *earn* access to the activities. Although the difference in performance between the A condition and the B condition was not as dramatic as it probably would have been had there been a total absence of reinforcement in the former, an increase in performance did occur. Of more practical importance is the fact that all but one of the students continued voluntarily to attend the sessions regularly.

A second variation of the ABAB design involves only a very brief baseline phase. This variation is used most frequently when many repeated baseline measurements would be patently absurd: Either the individual has never emitted the dependent behavior, or such emissions are so rare that repeated measurement makes no sense. Examples would include measuring the number of words to which a first-grader responds when he has never shown any evidence of reading

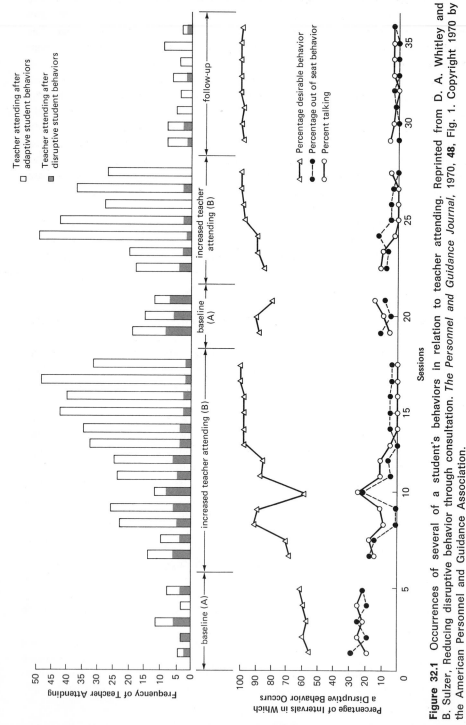

Figure 32.1 Occurrences of several of a student's behaviors in relation to teacher attending. Reprinted from D. A. Whitley and B. Sulzer, Reducing disruptive behavior through consultation. *The Personnel and Guidance Journal*, 1970, **48**, Fig. 1. Copyright 1970 by the American Personnel and Guidance Association.

448

in the past or counting the number of minutes a person spends on a particular task when she has never had an opportunity to perform the task before. The latter example occurred in one study (Ayllon & Azrin, 1968) in which the effects of a token system on the job performance of patients in a psychiatric ward were assessed. The jobs had not been available to the patients before, so it made little sense to take many repeated measurements of their typical performance. A baseline *is* available, however, and should be used. In this illustration, it would be zero. As it is usually difficult to anticipate exactly what will happen under reversal conditions, it does make sense to record at least a few initial baseline measures.

A third variation of the ABAB design involves addition of a DRO or an Alt-*R* phase (see Unit 18). When the dependent behavior, perhaps reading behavior, is not reversible—that is, when it is not affected by a return to baseline conditions—the independent variable (for example, contingent praise) can be applied to all *but* the dependent behavior or only to specific alternative behaviors during the second baseline phase. A sharp drop in reading behavior is evidence of the effectiveness of the independent variable.

Brigham and Sherman (1968) were able to teach preschool children to imitate English and Russian words accurately by reinforcing the imitation of the English words alone. When DRO procedures were used to reinforce differentially behaviors other than imitation of English or Russian words, accurate imitations by all subjects decreased, demonstrating the effectiveness of the reinforcement.

A similar approach was used by Wheeler and Sulzer (1970) in a language-training program. The percentage of sentences correctly used by a speech-deficient child has been plotted in Figure 32.2. The label "training form 1" repre-

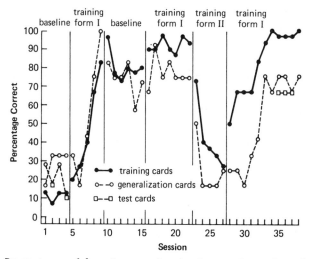

Figure 32.2 Percentages of form-1 responding in six experimental conditions. Adapted by permission from A. J. Wheeler and B. Sulzer, Operant training and generalization of a verbal response form in a speech deficient child. *Journal of Applied Behavior Analysis*, 1970, **3**, Fig. 1. Copyright 1970 by the Society of the Experimental Analysis of Behavior, Inc.

sents an experimental phase in which the child's approximations to full sentences were reinforced. The return to baseline conditions yielded only a minor effect. When Alt-R was instituted (training form II) and the child's incomplete sentence productions were also reinforced, the percentage of his correct responses dropped substantially. After a return to the first experimental condition, he quickly returned to a high rate of correct responding. The functional relation between the behavior and the reinforcing contingencies was demonstrated.

Goetz, Holmberg, and Le Blanc (1975) compared the effectiveness of a reversal in which social reinforcement was given independent of compliance with a reversal in which noncompliance was reinforced, in order to demonstrate the experimental control of the independent variable, contingent social reinforcement: "Thank you for picking up the blocks." During the first reversal condition attention was given in the form of irrelevant positive comments like "You're wearing a pretty dress." During the other reversal condition, comments like "I don't blame you for not picking up because it isn't any fun" were delivered contingent upon not picking up blocks. The latter procedure decreased compliance more rapidly, with less variability, and in fewer sessions, than did the former. The advantage, as the investigators noted, was that "this enabled the experimenter to demonstrate control quickly and return to shaping a desirable behavior" (1975, p. 82).

Advantages and Disadvantages of Reversal Designs

The major advantage of using a reversal procedure is, of course, that it demonstrates a functional relation between the dependent behavior and the intervention. It provides for accountability in the program. In addition, a reversal design can be used as a teaching tool, demonstrating to contingency managers just how effective their new procedures are. It also provides them with a basis for contrasting the effects of their typical (baseline) approach with those of another that has demonstrated its effectiveness. Because a reversal design can involve alternating reinforcement and extinction conditions, it may also facilitate the client's transfer from continuous to intermittent schedules.

There are a few disadvantages in using a reversal design. First, establishing and measuring baseline conditions take time, and the conditions themselves do not contribute to the actual behavioral change. We have discussed many more important aspects of baseline conditions that justify their use, however. In addition to the time problem, practitioners often fear that the modified behavior may not recover after the return to baseline conditions. The only reply to that argument is evidence that, once a behavior has been acquired, it can be reacquired more rapidly (Keller & Schoenfeld, 1950). In our experience, the desirable modified behavior has never failed to recover. Sometimes contingency managers like parents and teachers are unwilling to institute a reversal. They are generally quite pleased when a youth's behavior changes, and they may find it very difficult to accept the reversal requirement, regardless of how instructive it may be. Informing them that it is not necessary for behavior to be completely returned to its baseline level may be helpful. Usually a measured reversal over several sessions of one third to two thirds of the level measured during intervention is sufficiently convincing. There is, nevertheless, a temporary disruption in the program when a reversal design is used.

Whether they [reversal designs] are in fact detrimental is likely to remain an unexamined question so long as the social setting in which the behavior is studied dictates against using them repeatedly. Indeed, it may be that repeated reversals in some applications have a positive effect on the subject, possibly contributing to the discrimination of relevant stimuli involved in the problem. (Baer, Wolf & Risley, 1968, p. 94)

We might question the *ethics* of implementing probes, on the basis that it may be unethical to undo even briefly the positive effects of a successful behavioral program. Baer (personal communication) has argued that reversals may be justified on ethical grounds because they "test for independence." What the probe does is to provide information about the client's functioning in the absence of the behavioral program. If the behavioral program is not to become a permanent aspect of the client's environment, then responsible professionalism demands that the potential for independence from the program be determined through removal of the program from time to time. The probe fulfills this requirement nicely. It is probably appropriate, however, to agree with clients and consumers ahead of time on the strategy of using the probe. Intermittent "tests" can be arranged in advance to determine whether or not the changes are persistent. In fact, the second reversal in Figure 31.2 (the A between March and April) and the second A (sessions 19–21) in Figure 32.1 suggest that the target behavior was beginning to manifest its independence from the program. This suggestion is further supported during the follow-up phase in Figure 32.1, when the total frequency of teachers' attending responses was reduced approximately to its baseline level. Although the distribution of attending to adaptive behavior was greater than to disruptive behavior in comparison with baseline conditions, the students' adaptive behavior continued without disproportionate amounts of teacher attention.

MULTIPLE-BASELINE DESIGNS

Multiple-baseline designs offer viable alternatives to reversal designs. We have often found them useful, and they are more readily accepted by practitioners than are traditional reversal designs. There are several frequently used variations of the multiple-baseline design: across behaviors, across individuals, and across situations.

Across Behaviors

Baer, Wolf, and Risley (1968) have described the across-behaviors variation in the following passage:

In the multiple-baseline technique, a number of responses are identified and measured over time to provide baselines against which changes can be evaluated. With these baselines established, the experimenter then applies an experimental variable to one of the behaviors, produces a change in it, and perhaps notes little or no change in the other baselines. If so, rather than reversing the just produced change, he instead applies the experimental variable to one of the other, as yet unchanged, responses. If it changes at that point, evidence is accruing that the experimental variable is indeed effective, and that the prior change was not simply a matter of coincidence. The variable then may be applied to still another response, and so on. The experimenter is attempting to show that he has a reliable experimental variable, in that each behavior changes maximally only when the experimental variable is applied to it. (1968, p. 94)

McAllister and colleagues (1969) used this variation of the multiple-baseline research design to demonstrate the effect of the teacher's praise and disapproval upon target behaviors in two-high-school classrooms. Following baseline assessments, contingencies were placed first upon inappropriate talking, while baseline conditions were maintained for inappropriate turning around. Inappropriate talking diminished during that phase, and turning around remained relatively stable. Next the same contingencies were applied to turning around. A rapid decrease in that behavior was achieved. The effectiveness of the contingencies was thus demonstrated.

Schmidt (1974) also used this design to evaluate his effectiveness in counseling a client. An eighteen-year-old woman wished to increase her verbal skills. After a week of collecting baselines on her speaking at work, speaking loudly, and initiating conversations, he told her "that for each time she spoke to someone at work during any given day she could have two minutes that same day with her counselor, talking about anything she wished." Speaking at work increased from an average baseline of 1.0 to 8.2 times a day. Speaking loudly and initiating conversations remained near baseline levels of 1.6 and 0.6 times a day respectively. At the beginning of the third week the client was told "that she could now have only one minute of counselor time per day for each time she engaged in desirable verbal behavior but that she could now combine categories one and two—speaking at work and speaking loudly." The mean frequency for speaking at work increased to 15.8 times a day, and the count for speaking loudly increased to 5.2 times a day while initiating conversation remained near baseline level (.08). Finally, at the beginning of the fourth week one minute of counselor time was made contingent upon each occurrence of any of the three target behaviors. By the end of that week speaking at work had increased to 14.6 times a day, speaking loudly had increased to 12.2 times a day, and the mean count of initiating conversations had increased to 7.4 times a day. This design offered two major advantages for Schmidt: "First, working on one behavior at a time insured that the number of tasks would not be overwhelming to the client. Second, the multiple baseline design sorted out the importance of counselor time as a contingency" (1974, p. 204).

Moore and Bailey (1973) also used this design, as illustrated in Figure 32.3, with a three-year-old girl who showed "autistic-like" behavior. Baselines were taken on two of the child's behaviors: preacademic behavior, consisting of fifteen

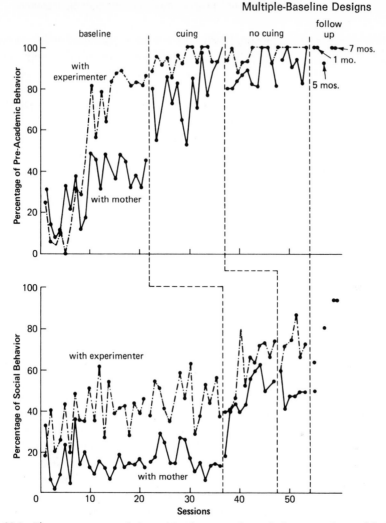

Figure 32.3 The percentages of the subject's preacademic behavior and social behavior with her mother and the experimenter during each training session. Solid line indicates mother; broken line indicates experimenter. In the cuing condition, the mother was given precise instructions. That is, she was cued when to give the subject a task, when to praise her, and when to punish her. In the follow-up sessions at one and seven months, the mother and the experimenter worked with the subject, but only the mother worked with the subject at the five-month follow-up. Note that the subject's performance of tasks with the mother and experimenter was the same for preacademic behavior in the one-month follow-up and for preacademic and social behavior at the seven-month follow-up session. (Moore, & Bailey, 1973, p. 502)

requests to interact with her mother or experimenter in specific ways. The results are presented in Figure 32.3.

A major consideration in using this design to demonstrate experimental control is that one must be reasonably assured beforehand that the dependent variables or target behaviors are not interdependent or highly interrelated. If they are, then a change in one target behavior can also be expected to change the others. For example, if smiles are associated with eye contact and answering questions, then an increase in any one of these target behaviors will probably be associated with similar increases in the others. Sometimes careful observation can help the practitioner to anticipate such an interrelation. The behavior analyst should ask: Was the client's smile associated with eye contact or answering questions? If each appears to occur separately, then there is some evidence that a multiple-baseline design across these behaviors may be appropriate. If the behaviors tend to occur together, it would be better to select an alternative design. Also, the greater the topographical differences among behaviors, the less likely they are to covary. This design, then, is particularly suitable when behaviors are as dissimilar as possible. (Multiple baselines may also be used to demonstrate generalization. Then, however, an alternative design, perhaps a reversal design, will be necessary for the experimental analysis.)

Across Individuals

The multiple-baseline design across individuals is practical for consultants. It is particularly useful for those who work with clients, patients, parents, teachers, or community personnel in more than one setting. Basically, the behavior analyst collects baselines on the same behavior by several persons. The effects of the intervention are tested first with one client while baseline conditions are continued with the other clients; then later the intervention is introduced with another client. The object is to show that, regardless of time, specific subject, and environmental factors, the behavior of each client changes substantially when—and only when—the intervention is introduced. For example, to demonstrate the functional relation between the intervention used with Helen and its effects upon maintenance of appropriate self-medication, several patients with low baselines of self-medication could be identified and treatment started for each at a different time. Similarly, Cossairt, Hall, and Hopkins (1973) investigated the effects of an experimenter's instructions, feedback, and feedback combined with social praise on the use by three elementary-school teachers of praise for students' attending behavior during math-instructional activity. Figures 32.4 and 32.5 are graphs of the results. The broken lines represent students' attending behavior (heads and eyes oriented toward teacher), and the solid lines represent teachers' praise. Note how the combination of feedback *and* social praise following instructions (the "package") appears more effective than either instructions or instructions followed by feedback alone.

The major difficulty in using such a multiple-baseline design is that the alterations in the behavior of one subject may influence or change other subjects' behaviors before intervention with those subjects. If such a result is likely (for example, if Helen's sister is also a patient who needs to improve her self-medication regimen), it would be best to select another design. This concern is paramount when attempting to change the behavior of several clients in the same classroom, residence, or other setting. That is why it is best used with clients from different

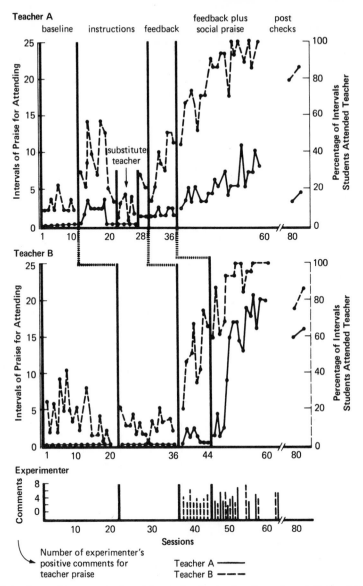

Figure 32.4 A graphic record of praising behavior by teachers A and B, the percentage of students attending each teacher, and the number of experimenter's positive comments for teacher-praise. (Cossairt, Hall & Hopkins, 1973, p. 94).

settings. By using this design with subjects who do not interact with one another, we can avoid unplanned carryover through modeling, instructions, vicarious reinforcement, and other events. We should also realize that this design is best for behaviors that do *not* require immediate action. The design calls for some subjects to receive treatment later than others. Delays in treatment must be tolerable, then, if this design is to be used.

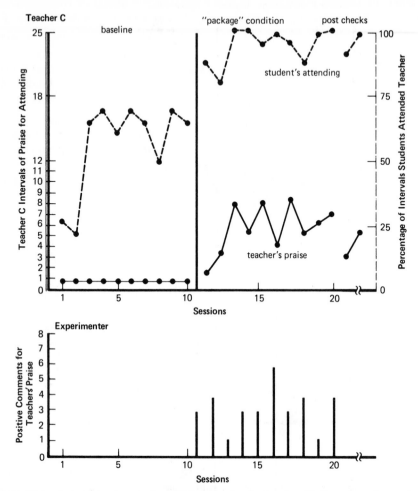

Figure 32.5 A graphic record of praising behavior by teacher C, the percentage of students attending her, and the number of experimenter's positive comments for teacher praise. (Cossairt, Hall & Hopkins, 1973, p. 95).

Across Situations

The third variation of the multiple-baseline design is that of across situations. In this design "data are collected for a target behavior for one or more subjects across different circumstances or situations" (Kazdin, 1973, p. 521). For example, baseline data on the behavior of one or more youths (perhaps a particular on-task behavior) could be collected in several situations—doing homework, yard work, and so on, for example—until it could be shown that the behavior changed substantially only when treatment was applied to it. In situations in which the treatment was not applied, on-task behavior would change little if at all.

Long and Williams (1973) used this design, in combination with others, with an inner-city seventh-grade class, in order to assess the effects of contingent free time on student behaviors. Baselines were taken in both the students' math and geography. Appropriate behavior improved maximally in each class only when contingent free time was used.

The major drawback of designs across situations is that, when there is much unprogrammed generalization of selected target behaviors across situations, the design will not perform as intended. If it is suspected that, when a client's behavior is changed in one situation, it will change correspondingly in others, it is best to select another design. The authors have found that some clients quickly generalize their behavior to other situations, whereas others do not. Such generalization appears to depend upon past experiences (that is, on the extent to which generalization has been reinforced in the past) and upon the similarities among the situations. Before using this design it would therefore be best to determine how readily the client generalizes a given behavior and to ensure that the situations are sufficiently dissimilar so that such unprogrammed generalization is unlikely to take place.

Summary

We have introduced the single-subject, or intensive, design in this unit. The focus has been on several reversal and multiple-baseline experimental designs for evaluating the effects of behavioral procedures. Each of these designs has been described, illustrated, and discussed. Each has its unique advantages and limitations, which must be considered in determining its appropriateness for evaluating a particular situation. These advantages and limitations, along with those of designs to be presented in Unit 33, are summarized in Table 33.1.

References

Ayllon, T. & Azrin, N. H. *The token economy: A motivational system for therapy and rehabilitation.* New York: Appleton, 1968.

Baer, D. M., Wolf, M. M. & Risley, T. R. Some current dimensions of applied behavior analysis. *Journal of Applied Behavior Analysis,* 1968, **1**, 91–97.

Bijou, S. W. & Baer, D. M. The laboratory-experimental study of child behavior. In P. H. Mussen (Ed.), *Handbook of research methods in child development.* New York: Wiley, 1960. Pp. 140–197.

Brigham, T. A. & Sherman, J. A. An experimental analysis of verbal limitation in preschool children. *Journal of Applied Behavior Analysis,* 1968, **1**, 151–158.

Cossairt, A., Hall, R. V. & Hopkins, B. L. The effects of experimenter's instructions, feedback, and praise on teacher praise and student attending behavior. *Journal of Applied Behavior Analysis,* 1973, **6**, 89–100.

Goetz, E. M., Holmberg, M. C. & Le Blanc, J. M. Differential reinforcement of other behavior and noncontingent reinforcement as control procedures during the modification of a preschooler's compliance. *Journal of Applied Behavior Analysis,* 1975, **8**, 77–82.

Holland, J. G. & Skinner, B. F. *The analysis of behavior.* New York: McGraw-Hill, 1961.

Kazdin, A. E. Methodological and assessment considerations in evaluating reinforcement programs in applied settings. *Journal of Applied Behavior Analysis,* 1973, **6**, 517–531.

Keller, F. S. & Schoenfeld, W. N. *Principles of psychology.* New York: Appleton, 1950.

Long, J. D. & Williams, R. L. The comparative effectiveness of group and individually contingent free time with inner-city junior high school students. *Journal of Applied Behavior Analysis,* 1973, **6**, 465–474.

McAllister, L. W., Stachowiak, J. G., Baer, D. M. & Conderman, L. The application of operant conditioning techniques in a secondary school classroom. *Journal of Applied Behavior Analysis,* 1969, **2**, 277–285.

Moore, B. L. & Bailey, H. Social punishment in the modification of a preschool child's "autistic-like" behavior with a mother as therapist. *Journal of Applied Behavior Analysis,* 1973, **6**, 497–507.

Schmidt, J. A. Research techniques for counselors: The multiple baseline. *The Personnel and Guidance Journal,* 1974, **53**, 200–206.

Sulzer-Azaroff, B., Hunt, S. & Loving, A. The contingent use of reinforcers usually available in the classroom. Paper presented at the meeting of the American Educational Research Association. Chicago, April 1972.

Thoresen, C. E. & Anton, J. L. Intensive experimental research in counseling. *Journal of Counseling Psychology,* 1974, **21**, 553–559.

Wheeler, A. J. & Sulzer, B. Operant training and generalization of a verbal response form in a speech deficient child. *Journal of Applied Behavior Analysis,* 1970, **3**, 139–147.

Whitley, D. A. & Sulzer, B. Assisting a fourth grade teacher to reduce a student's disruptive classroom behaviors through behavioral consulting. *The Personnel and Guidance Journal,* 1970, **48**, 836–841.

unit 33

Single-Subject Designs: Changing-Criterion and Multielement Designs and Further Issues in Accountability

After mastering the material in Units 31–33, you should be able to
1. Define and offer illustrations for each of the following:
   a. Changing-criterion design
   b. Multielement design
   c. Behavioral law

2. List and describe the advantages and possible limitations of the changing-criterion and multielement designs

3. Describe a situation for each of the designs compared in Table 33.3 that would make that specific design the most appropriate. Be sure to justify your selection clearly. (Use your response to number 4 in Unit 32 for part of your answer.)

4. Summarize the common advantages, strengths, and weaknesses of single-subject designs. (Use your response to number 2 in Unit 32 as part of your answer.)

5. Discuss how to determine the significance of a demonstrated functional relation. Include a list of criteria.

6. Describe what follow-up entails, and give two reasons why it is necessary.

7. Conduct a single-subject research experiment.

Ms. Charming had decided to evaluate the behavioral procedures that she planned to use, in order to demonstrate their effectiveness. One procedural plan for Fern was to reinforce increasing rates of completion of her assigned tasks. How could that be accomplished without using a reversal or multiple-baseline design? Flossie's teacher was interested in comparing two different procedures for "motivating" Flossie to initiate more creative writing. She was hoping to obtain the information relatively quickly. Let us turn our attention to two more recently developed designs: changing-criterion and multielement designs. Then we shall consider how to determine the significance of behavioral changes that occur.

CHANGING-CRITERION DESIGN

The changing-criterion design is a third type of applied behavior-analysis research design. Hall has described it:

In using the changing criterion design, the experimenter successively changes the criterion for consequation, usually in graduated steps, from baseline levels to a desired terminal level. If the behavior changes successively at or close to the set criterion levels, experimental control can be demonstrated. (1971a, p. 24)

This design is ideally suited for use in association with shaping or DRL reductive procedures. Both these procedures involve successively changing criterion levels. We do not mean to imply, however, that it is not an appropriate design for any other procedure. If other procedures are used, changing criterion levels must also be used if this design is to be applicable (i.e., progressive or adjusting schedule changes). Hall (1971b) illustrated the changing-criterion design with a response-cost procedure to reduce the smoking behavior of a twenty-three-year-old male graduate student. He had smoked twenty to thirty cigarettes a day for several years. The program was first set up so that, if he smoked more than fifteen cigarettes in a day, he would tear a dollar bill into tiny pieces and throw it away. This criterion of fifteen cigarettes remained in effect for five days; then it was changed to thirteen cigarettes for five days and so on. In discussing the study, Hall noted that "the systematic stairstep ceiling was never exceeded and in most cases was closely approximated. . . . Each 5-day phase acted as a baseline for the next 5-day phase and demonstrated that the self-imposition of the consequence of having to tear up a dollar bill was effective in keeping smoking below the criterion level" (1971b, p. 55).

   The next illustration should further clarify this type of design. Fern was not completing her workshop assignment of packing ten items in each box. Ms. Charming observed that she would do her assignments only with continuous reinforcement. But, when a continuous-reinforcement schedule was not in effect, the work would not be completed. There was also a baseline of zero unless individualized reinforcement was used. It was hypothesized that Fern's performance was under the control of a continuous-reinforcement schedule, rather than on a fixed-ratio schedule of 10 to 1. It was decided to change the criterion levels gradually, to thin the reinforcement until a fixed ratio of 10 to 1 demonstrated its control. A changing-criterion design was thus applicable.

Similarly, Hall (1971a) presented the data in Figure 33.1. Here, the changing-criterion design was used to demonstrate the control of reinforcement over the number of correct answers in math. Note that for criterion 8 the number of days was greater. *It is usually best to vary the number of sessions among criterion levels, in order to illustrate more clearly that the behavior remains at, or close to, the criterion level until it is changed. A replication across subjects, again varying lengths of time for criterion levels, would provide still further supportive evidence.*

Because the changing-criterion design depends upon the match between the value of the dependent variable and the preestablished criterion level, we must be cautious in setting such levels. If they are too close together, the behavior may "run away with itself," and the demonstration of control be lost. If too far apart, they may never be reached. Aunt Minerva decides to use a point system to help her to lose weight. The points will be exchangeable for a bikini and a trip to the south of France. She sets the criterion for receipt of points at a reduction of intake twenty calories below the level permitted during the previous week; this reduced level is to remain in effect for a week. The following week, the criterion is twenty calories fewer and so on. Thanks to a colorful photograph of Nice pasted to her refrigerator, a picture of a bikini from her favorite department-store brochure pasted to the cookie cupboard, and a number of other effective cues, her intake is reduced far more substantially than an average of twenty calories each week. Weight is lost, but so is experimental control. Because the calorie-intake level does not match the preestablished criteria, the controlling function of the variables is obscured. There is no demonstration that the independent variable, the point system, is responsible. Aunt Minerva should have set the criteria differently, at a level that would be challenging to meet yet could be met only with the "motivation" afforded by the points.

Similarly, any applied researcher who is considering a changing-criterion

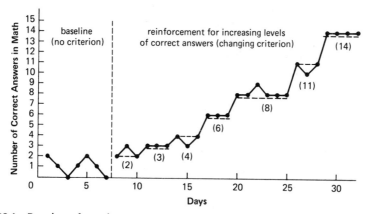

Figure.33.1 Results of a changing-criterion design for placing numbers of correct answers in math under control of reinforcement.

design should select the criterion level with care, so that the measures of the dependent variable are likely to match it. In the event that the behavior appears to run away from the criterion level, the latter can be made more stringent, thus allowing control to be reestablished.

MULTIELEMENT DESIGN

The multielement design also does not require a protracted baseline phase. Instead, baseline conditions and alternating independent variables are interspersed throughout the program. The design involves measurement of a behavior under alternating *discriminable* conditions of the independent variables. For example, we might wish to analyze the effects of three contingencies on task completion: no extra recess (treatment A), extra recess time with planned activities (treatment B), and extra recess time with free play (treatment C). The treatments could be alternated from day to day. Assuming that students knew the condition (A, B, or C) to be in effect on any given day, the effects of all three on task completion could then be compared and evaluated after several weeks.

In contrast to multiple-baseline and reversal designs,

the multielement baseline design does not consist of experimental phases where one behavior modification procedure is applied during several consecutive sessions until stability is achieved within that condition. Rather, experimental and baseline conditions are presented in alternation—on either a consistent or an unpredictable schedule—within sessions and/or from one session to the next . . . the experimental conditions of a multielement baseline procedure are alternated independent of changes in the behavior. A distinctive (potentially discriminative) stimulus is correlated with each condition and the effects of the treatment procedure(s) can be observed by comparing differential performances. Thus, if different patterns of responding develop, and each pattern is observed to be unique to a particular experimental condition—that is, if "the subject's behavior is fractionated by stimulus control over each separate element" (Sidman, 1960)—then experimental control has been demonstrated. (Ulman & Sulzer-Azaroff, 1975, p. 379)

The multielement design is being used more and more to analyze complex behaviors in educational settings. Harris and Sherman (1973) assessed math performance, in order to determine the effects of peer tutoring. To permit comparison between tutoring and nontutoring conditions, math assignments were separated into two daily sessions; problem type and difficulty were equalized. Peer tutoring occurred before only one of the two early sessions during any one phase: during some phases before the morning session, during others before the afternoon sessions. Such pairing of a contingency with a particular session yielded two different elements, allowing for a better-controlled comparison of the two conditions.

Investigating the effects of study questions, Semb, Hopkins, and Hursh (1973) compared three different conditions: study questions to which the student was instructed to supply the answers, study questions with answers furnished by the instructor, and no study questions. Each study guide was divided between the first two conditions. Quiz-performance data were analyzed by means of calculated mean percentages correct under each of the three conditions. The experimental design controlled for content differences, potential sequence effects, and passage of time, for every unit quiz incorporated the three conditions.

Three different adults were paired with three different contingency conditions in an attempt to determine whether or not such pairing would produce stimulus control of the cooperative play behavior of two severely retarded boys (Redd, 1969). Each session was divided among four different conditions, each with a specific stimulus. The first condition was baseline, in which no adult, and consequently no programmed contingencies, were present. Second, adult I was paired with a mixed schedule of contingent and noncontingent reinforcement. Third, adult II was paired with contingent reinforcement only. And, finally, adult III was paired with noncontingent reinforcement. As all four conditions occurred in random order during each session, it was possible to control for sequence effects and to monitor the evolution of stimulus control over time, thus demonstrating the thesis that different adults can acquire discriminable stimulus properties.

Lloyd and colleagues (1972) used a multielement design to investigate the reinforcing properties of university lectures. When different days of the week were paired with different contingency arrangements, each day developed discriminative properties for class attendance.

Advantages of the Multielement Design

The multielement design is especially appropriate when one is attempting to analyze complex behaviors. It permits comparison of the effects of one or more independent variables, for example no treatment versus one or two different treatments, the differential effects of three types of study questions (Semb, Hopkins & Hursh, 1973), or the effects of different contingencies on cooperative play (Redd, 1969). The design also possesses other distinct advantages (Ulman & Sulzer-Azaroff, 1975), including its appropriateness for studying dependent variables whose rates are less likely to be reversed following protracted presentations of the independent variable; the likelihood that differential effects will emerge relatively rapidly, thus allowing early termination of the evaluation if necessary; its appropriateness when unstable baselines are likely; its more ready acceptance by human-services personnel; and the technical advantages of minimizing confounding when one treatment is preceded by another, as well as behavioral-contrast effects (see Unit 18).

Let us hypothesize a classroom behavior-change problem and note the advantages of the multielement design. Let us suppose that an applied behavior analyst is called upon to assist a teacher with Flossie, a quick, highly verbal nine-year-old, who does only the schoolwork required of her but no more. Because Flossie is so verbally facile, her teacher would like to encourage her to write down more of her ideas as stories, critiques, poems, and so on. In conference, Flossie expresses a desire to write more on her own initiative, but she "just doesn't seem to be able to find the time." When asked if she thinks that she might produce more if she could earn time either by doing her own individual research in the library to prepare for a class play (something she apparently loves to do) or by doing research with a committee of peers, she shrugs her shoulders. It is decided that both individual and group contingencies can be tried, as well as no contingent research time (baseline condition). The dependent variable will be her self-initiated thematic products. According to a preselected random schedule, certain days are designated as "group," "individual," or "no contingency" days. Each morning a simple announcement is made: "Today we'll do group research"; "Today we'll do individual research"; "Today there won't be any library research." Flossie and the teacher agree to count the number of words in any self-initiated written work that meets a preestablished criterion for acceptability. (It must be in Flossie's own words; it should have no more than a certain percentage of spelling and grammatical errors; it should have a theme that Flossie has not used before; and so on.) For each x number of words, Flossie will earn points that can be exchanged for minutes of either group or individual research time—whatever is in effect on that particular day. In the event that it is a no-research day, the points will have no exchange value.

A multielement design is selected for the following reasons:

1. The comparison is complex. The design makes it possible to study the effects of the individual, of the group, and of no specifically manipulated contingency.
2. Writing themes is a skill that, once developed, is less likely to be reversed, in contrast to a simple operant response like staying seated. Probably the written theme will promote other forms of feedback (praise from others, self-satisfaction, and so on) and will thus became more "intrinsically" rewarding. Reversing conditions after a protracted treatment period may fail to produce a concomitant drop in performance. The multielement design, with its presentation of each independent variable for a brief period, should demonstrate the initial effects of the manipulations before they come under the control of "intrinsic" reinforcement.
3. There are many other demands upon the analyst's time. She would like to be able to terminate the intensive part of the study as soon as some stable outcomes manifest themselves and to follow up by sampling productivity randomly to assess the maintenance of the response over time. If there are strong differences in the effects of the two contingencies—if Flossie actually initiates more writing on days when she will be able to work in committee, rather than alone—those effects should become manifest quite early (between day 15 and day 20 on our hypothetical plot in Figure 33.2).
4. The preintervention assessment (days 1–4) yields an irregular baseline. On day 2 Flossie had received two ducklings and had composed a poem about them on the bus, writing it down at school. Although the data ascend over time, the design makes it possible to see the differential effects.
5. Flossie's teacher and the behavior analyst have been happy with the design. Let us assume that an ABAB design had been chosen instead. During the first B condition, perhaps under the group contingency, Flossie would have shown really dramatic increases in her rate of self-initiated writing. The teacher and analyst would both probably be distressed at the idea of reversing that effect for

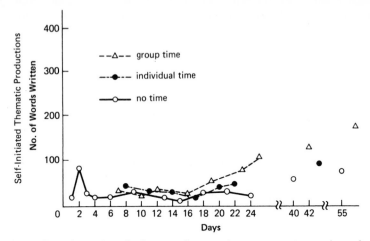

Figure 33.2 A hypothetical multielement design; the measure is number of words in thematic material "self-initiated" by Flossie under no contengencies, as well as under individual and group contingencies.

a long enough time to provide a believable demonstration. In the multielement design, there would be only a brief (in this instance, one-day) "reversal."

6. Let us consider an alternative method for comparing the two treatments. First, we can determine the baseline performance, then institute the individual contingency, then return to the nontreatment condition, then implement the group contingency, then return to the baseline condition, and so on. A problem might arise in analysis of the data: Let us suppose that both treatment conditions yielded measures substantially higher than those yielded during baseline conditions. If the group data were higher than the individual data, it might be because the group contingency was more powerful, or it might simply be that there was a positively accelerating trend toward more productivity concomitant with the passage of time. The multielement design protects us from the necessity for this interpretation, for all conditions are scattered over time. Or the group effect might reflect a contrast with previously individual conditions; it might not have emerged so strongly had prolonged exposure to the individual conditions not already occurred. Conversely, let us suppose that the group treatment had produced a lower rate than the individual treatment. Would it mean that the individual condition was more powerful or that the effect was more pronounced because of the *sequence* of conditions, so that protracted exposure to individual conditions had controlled later performance (that is, Flossie had begun to be sated with library research)? Again, the multielement design varies the sequence of conditions frequently, so that all treatments have very similar histories. We notice that by day 20 Flossie has experienced five group contingencies, five individual contingencies, and five sessions during which no contingencies have been administered. Yet the differential effects are manifest.

The multielement design is not one to be used for analysis of simple operant behaviors, for it must be planned and implemented with care. It should, however, open an avenue to more sophisticated analyses of complex behaviors in applied settings.

SELECTING APPROPRIATE SINGLE-SUBJECT DESIGNS

We should note that our discussion of functional designs in applied behavior-analysis research has by no means been exhaustive. In addition to several other designs that are used in complex research (see Hersen and Barlow, 1976), all the designs discussed in Units 32 and 33 can be combined in various ways. Figure 32.3 illustrates the use of a combined multiple-baseline-and-reversal design. Let us examine the figure closely to determine the rationale for using such a combination. Such an examination reveals a very important point: Experimental designs should be used to facilitate functional analyses of experimental questions. Experimental questions should not be altered to "fit" existing designs. The question always comes first!

To increase further the probability that we shall select the most appropriate general type of design to answer our experimental questions functionally, we have included a comparative table of design operations, conditions for selecting and avoiding them, and other advantages (see Table 33.1).

OTHER CONSIDERATIONS WITH SINGLE-SUBJECT DESIGNS

A few other issues related to single-subject designs are worthy of consideration. First, there are no hard-and-fast rules about the number of reversals, multiple baselines, criteria, or alternating conditions that are necessary to show the unquestionable effects of the experimental variable. When, however, a statistical analysis is employed, as in group designs, the suitability of the chosen inferential statistic must also be judged. In either single-subject or group designs, "the judgments required are highly qualitative, and rules cannot always be stated profitably" (Baer, Wolf & Risley, 1968, p. 95). The question remains open.

Another consideration has been implied previously: The single-subject design is *not* necessarily the most practical way to arrive at normative group decisions. Group experimental-research designs are more expedient. For example, let us suppose that a decision about whether or not to adopt a new set of programmed materials developed for an entire state system must be made. A group design that would compare the average scores before and after intervention with a sample of clients who had been selected at random to use the materials with the scores of a control group, a sample of clients who did not use the materials, could provide information valuable in making such an administrative decision. If, however, the behavior analyst, clinician, nurse, counselor, psychologist, teacher, or parent wants to know whether or not the new materials will help particular clients, a single-subject design is in order.

TABLE 33.1. FUNCTIONAL-ANALYSIS DESIGNS

Design	Operation	Select When	Avoid When	Other Advantages
Reversal (ABAB)	Measure baseline (A); apply procedure (B); return to baseline conditions (A); repeat procedure (B)	Extended baseline conditions can be tolerated before and during intervention	Behaviors not reversable; rapid results required; reversal of specific target behavior ethically irresponsible	Alternating A and B conditions may facilitate client's discrimination of relevant stimuli in the situation and transfer from CRF to intermittent schedules
Reversal with reinforcement not contingent upon target behavior during A condition	Same as ABAB, except reinforcers not contingent upon the targeted behavior during A and contingent upon the targeted behavior during B	Comparing effects of noncontingent with contingent reinforcement; target behaviors not emitted at all or at very low frequencies in the absence of reinforcement	Same as ABAB; independent variable expected to produce only slight effect	Same as ABAB; reinforcers available throughout
Reversal with DRO or Alt-R	Following intervention (B), apply contingencies when other than target behaviors occur; apply to alternatives to target behavior during reversal phase (A)	Target behavior resistent to reversal; rapid demonstration of control desirable	Same as ABAB; "other" behaviors may be dangerous or otherwise undesirable	Same as ABAB; reinforcers available during reversal
Multiple-baseline (General)	Measure baselines of several behaviors; apply procedure to one behavior, continuing baseline measures of other behaviors; apply procedure to second	Target behavior is nonreversible or reversal is undesirable	All behaviors require rapid change	Intervention not interrupted once instituted; consequently more acceptable than reversals to clients and staff

TABLE 33.1. FUNCTIONAL-ANALYSIS DESIGNS (continued)

Design	Operation	Select When	Avoid When	Other Advantages
	behavior; continue measuring treated and untreated behaviors; and so on			
Multiple-baseline across behaviors	Apply procedure to different behaviors one at a time with the same individual	Same as multiple-baseline; several behaviors of one individual targeted for change and independent of one another; demonstrating control of procedure across behaviors	Same as multiple-baseline; procedure may affect more than one behavior simultaneously	Same as multiple-baseline
Multiple-baseline across situations	Apply procedure to behaviors of one or more subjects across situations and at different times	Same as multiple-baseline; same behaviors of one or more individuals are targeted for change in more than one setting; demonstrating control of procedures across situations	Same as multiple-baseline; behavior change in one situation correspondingly apt to occur in other situations	Same as multiple-baseline
Multiple-baseline across individuals	Apply procedure to same behavior of different individuals at different times	Same as multiple-baseline; same behavior targeted for change among several individuals; demonstrating control of procedure across individuals	Same as multiple-baseline; changes in target behavior of one member may affect target behaviors of other members of group	Same as multiple-baseline

468

TABLE 33.1. FUNCTIONAL-ANALYSIS DESIGNS (continued)

Design	Operation	Select When	Avoid When	Other Advantages
Changing criterion	Apply intervention when behavior meets criterion level; change value of criterion at irregular intervals	Teaching new behaviors; intervention consists of graduated steps (as with DRL and *progressive* or *adjusting* schedule changes)	Responding is likely to exceed the criterion	May ideally serve programming needs when criteria are changed gradually and progressively
Multielement	Apply different interventions, each correlated with a specific stimulus, successively to the same behavior	Evaluating one or more different procedures; showing rapid effects over a limited time; targeting behaviors unlikely to be reversed; there is a problem achieving stable baseline; sequence and contrast effects should be minimized	Unwilling or unable to continue alternating conditions until clear differences are manifest	More acceptable than reversals in applied settings

Certain interventions may promote the development of irreversible behaviors. Once Chuck has been reinforced for correctly reading certain words, those responses will not usually "reverse" when reinforcement is withdrawn. When circumstances require comparison of the effects of two or more intervention conditions upon irreversible responses and when multiple-baseline and multielement designs are not possible because of generality across responses, a group statistical design may be most suitable. Similarly, an intervention condition may provide a history the effects of which cannot be eradicated. In the discussion of fixed-interval responding, we saw how the client's historical rate of response affected her response rate under FI reinforcement schedules. Theobald & Paul (1976) have demonstrated that a history of experiencing tangible reinforcers paired with praise affected the subsequent responses of patients to praise alone. Such historical variables are impossible to eliminate. When one intervention precedes another, subsequent behavior is affected—and possibly the reverse; sequence effects are very difficult to control. A group design with two treatment groups, each exposed to different treatment, and a control group may be the better analytic method in such instances.

DRAWING CONCLUSIONS FROM EXPERIMENTAL ANALYSES

The experimental-analysis designs presented here, reasonably free from confounding variables, demonstrate differences in the measured values of the dependent behaviors under baseline and one or more intervention conditions. Figure 32.1 shows the percentage of intervals scored nondisruptive under baseline conditions and under the intervention condition when the teacher has distributed her attention more heavily following adaptive (nondisruptive) behavior. (Data on teacher behavior serve to validate the extent to which the intervention has been carried out.) We are certain that different subject characteristics did not affect the results (for only one subject participated). Task-confounded variables were effectively controlled, as all aspects of the task were held constant during all phases of the program. Environmental factors were similarly controlled, and passage of time alone must be dismissed as accounting for the change because the change itself did not occur consistently as time passed. Rather, systematic changes occurred when, and only when, the teacher delivered the major proportion of her attention following adaptive behavior. The reversal, or second A condition, approximated baseline conditions in which a higher proportion of attention was delivered contingent upon disruptive behavior. Later, during follow-up, with a much smaller overall frequency of contingent teacher attention but still with a higher ratio of attention to adaptive than to disruptive behavior, the high level of adaptive behavior continued. Figure 32.1 presents a convincing demonstration that, for this student and this teacher under these particular conditions, there was a functional relation between the student's behavior and the contingency of teacher attention. When greater attention was delivered following adaptive behavior, disruption tended to decrease. When teacher attention followed disruptive behavior, it began to increase.

In a similar manner, we can study the results of experimental analyses and draw conclusions about the effects of the interventions.

DETERMINING THE SIGNIFICANCE OF A
DEMONSTRATED FUNCTIONAL RELATION

Inspection of the outcome of an intervention may reveal the existence of a functional relation: Behavior has changed as a function of the intervention. A further question must then be asked: "Of what significance is this demonstrated relation?" One traditional approach has been to base interpretations of significance upon probability theory, asking "What is the likelihood that these results could have been obtained by chance alone?" If it is concluded that chance was unlikely to have accounted for the outcome, then the data are more likely to be accepted as "statistically significant." In applied behavior analysis, however, the emphasis is more on *social, personal,* or *clinical* significance than on statistical significance. The applied behavior analyst asks the question "What importance does the demonstration of this functional relation have for particular individuals and their society?" Recall that in the early material on goal selection we discussed specification of behavioral objectives. An adequate behavioral objective is supposed to include a standard or criterion for determining its attainment. Should the intervention be functionally related to an improvement in the behavior to the preestablished criterion level, then we must certainly conclude that the outcome is "significant," for the achievement of the objective has been demonstrated.

Alternatively, the social, personal, or clinical significance of an outcome may be determined following intervention by noting changes in the targeted behavior and any accompanying collateral behaviors and asking "Does the altered behavior assist the individual to function more adequately in society?" (Risley, 1970). Questions about cost effectiveness and consumer satisfaction should yield additional evidence of social importance. (These two issues will be considered in detail in Unit 35.)

An experimental criterion may also be used to evaluate how significant the outcome of an intervention is. This point is determined by asking what the behavior is now and what the behavior would be if the experimental intervention had not occurred (Risley, 1970). According to Kazdin, there are a few ways in which results clearly meet the criterion for experimental significance.

First, performance during the intervention when plotted may not overlap with performance during baseline. The data points of baseline may not extend to the levels achieved by the data points during intervention. If this is replicated, either over time with a given subject (ABAB design) or across behaviors (multiple baseline design), there can be little question that the results are reliable. (1976, p. 268)

Figure 33.3, displaying the results of a token program designed to encourage asthmatic children to use inhalation equipment correctly, illustrates this point. Looking at the mean number of inappropriate behaviors during baseline and com-

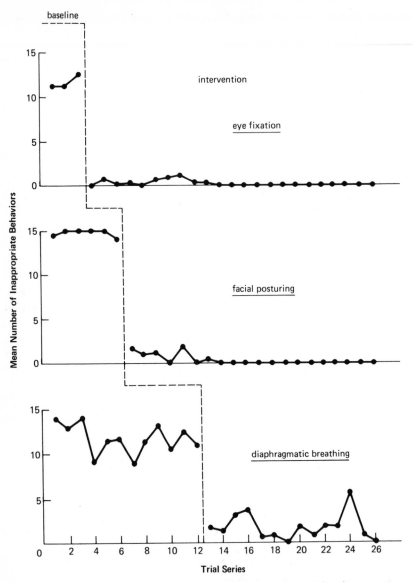

Figure 33.3 The mean number of inappropriate events recorded by the experimenters over a series of twenty-six trials with four subjects on three target responses: eye fixation, facial posturing, and diaphragmatic breathing. The maximum number of inappropriate responses per trial was fifteen for each behavior. (Renne & Creer, 1976, p. 6).

paring it with performance during intervention, we note that there is no overlap in the distribution of measures.

Kazdin offers a second criterion:

A more typical criterion for experimental evaluation is related to divergent slopes in baseline and treatment phases but is less stringent than completely nonoverlapping distributions. This criterion emphasizes the trends or slopes in each phase. . . . By alternating baseline and experimental phases, systematic changes in trend strongly argue for the experimental reliability of the effect. (1976, p. 268)

Figure 31.2 (taken from Sulzer *et al.,* 1971) illustrates this point. The trend toward reduced numbers and percentage correct in phase B was reversed in phase C, when points with back-ups were delivered for items correct.

A third form of experimental criterion for evaluating the significance of interventions has been suggested by Kazdin (1976): the use of statistics in intra-subject studies. This approach is justified in situations that do not allow convincing visual demonstrations. When the magnitude of an effect appears ambiguous, there is a danger that reliable results of theoretical importance may be rejected inadvertently because of the undramatic effects. Various single-subject inferential statistical tests have been designed to assess whether or not a given manipulation can be judged as having reliably produced a particular outcome (see Kazdin, 1976, and the series of articles in the *Journal of Applied Behavior Analysis,* 1974, **7**, 627–653).

Kazdin (1976) has suggested three occasions when the use of statistical analyses may be particularly helpful. First, such techniques may serve as a preliminary screening tool in new research programs, assisting the researcher to separate reliable but subtle effects from mere chance occurrences. Second, inferential statistics may be valuable in analyzing treatment effects when it is impossible first to establish a stable rate of baseline behavior. For example, it is usually recommended that in a reversal design (ABAB) the treatment (B) phase be introduced only after a stable baseline has been achieved. Either unstable data or a gradual trend in the data in the desired direction during the initial baseline phase would present a problem in assessing the treatment effect. Certain statistical analyses that permit examination of whether or not the introduction of the treatment has reliably accelerated the trend of the behavior change are, however, available. Third, the use of inferential statistics may be helpful in assessing therapeutic effects in less controlled environments, in which extraneous factors may serve to obfuscate important results. Of course, it would be most desirable to attempt to exert greater control over environmental factors, in order to control for other sources of variability. But, when such control is impossible, statistical analysis may be useful in determining the reliability of a particular treatment.

For those of us whose primary concern is the enhancement of personally, educationally, and socially important behaviors, however, another approach is available. For example, if the problem is lots of variability in the data, with many overlapping data points (lots of "high" days during baseline and lots of "low" days during treatment), then something should be done to modify the program, rather than trying to tease out the subtle effects of the data. In general, we concur with Michael's recommendation:

When a dependent variable is not under good control—when there is considerable unexplained variability even though the independent variable being studied is at a constant value —it is not usually necessary to go ahead with other planned manipulations. Further efforts can be made to obtain a more stable dependent variable or to discover and eliminate some of the sources of uncontrolled variation (1974, p. 651)

EVALUATING THE GENERALITY OF FINDINGS

Once a conclusion about the social and experimental significance of a finding can be defended, we may have to ask how generally applicable this finding is. Recall that earlier, when single-subject designs were discussed, we mentioned that those designs allow for generation of principles of behavior for particular individuals. When such a principle holds for more and more individuals *with similar characteristics*, we begin to see how generally it applies. In applied behavior analysis, replication of procedures with other subjects frequently has demonstrated their functional relation to similar outcomes. Examples have been presented repeatedly throughout this book. For instance, access to preferred activities contingent upon emission of a given response has repeatedly demonstrated its effectiveness in increasing the rate of emission of that response.

Procedural replications that produce similar findings among subjects with similar characteristics limit the generality of the findings to only that group. When replication also produces similar outcomes among subjects with different characteristics, with different responses, or in different settings, however, then the generality of the findings is broader. Usually principles of behavior that have very broad generality are called **behavioral laws**. The principles of immediacy, adequate amounts, and appropriate quality of reinforcement, as well as those of intensity of aversive stimuli are examples of principles that have been found repeatedly to demonstrate their controlling properties among many individuals over wide classes of behavior and under varied conditions. They can, therefore, be designated as laws of behavior. Remember, however, that laws have their limitations. Behavioral laws, too, may not apply in *all* instances. As investigation continues, we may well discover more limitations of many laws and principles that have been presented in this book.

EVALUATING LONG-TERM EFFECTS OF PROCEDURAL INTERVENTIONS

Experimental analysis demonstrates the effectiveness of the intervention program. Various factors allow us to conclude whether or not that outcome is socially and experimentally significant. *Evaluation is not complete, however, until follow-up assessments of behavior change have been conducted to demonstrate its maintenance and generality.* As has been emphasized in the units on maintenance, the mere occurrence of a behavior change does not, of course, mean that the change will persist or generalize to other responses or situations. The environment must be structured to maintain the behavior change or to cause it to generalize. An appropriate maintenance procedure is selected and used along with procedures designed to enhance generalization. If the environment is not structured to maintain the behavior change and if generality is not programmed, the behavior change will neither persist nor generalize. *It is thus of utmost importance that follow-up be planned in advance,* if the effectiveness of the procedure is to be demonstrated. The client's behavior is observed periodically so that we can *know* for certain whether or not his behavior is being maintained. Should the data indicate a deterioration, alterations in the program can be instituted in order to ensure continued maintenance of the behavior following the termination of the behavioral program.

Summary

The changing-criterion and multielement designs have been described, illustrated, and discussed. These designs, along with reversal and multiple-baseline designs have been compared in a table specifying the operation, conditions for selection and avoidance, and other advantages of each design. Questions of significance and generality have also been considered. In applied behavior analysis, significance is judged primarily on the basis of its social importance. Finally, the need for follow-up, to evaluate or provide for maintenance, and generalization have been reemphasized.

References

Baer, D. M., Wolf, M. M. & Risley, T. R. Some current dimensions of applied behavior analysis. *Journal of Applied Behavior Analysis,* 1968, **1**, 91–97.

Hall, R. V. *Managing behavior: Behavior modification: The measurement of behavior. No. 1.* Lawrence, Kans.: H & H Enterprises, 1971a.

Hall, R. V. *Managing behavior: Behavior modification: Applications in school and home. No. 3.* Lawrence, Kans.: H & H Enterprises, 1971b.

Harris, V. W. & Sherman, J. A. Use and analysis of the "Good Behavior Game" to reduce disruptive classroom behavior, *Journal of Applied Behavior Analysis,* 1973, **6**, 405–417.

Hersen, M. H. & Barlow, P. H. *Single case experimental designs.* New York: Pergamon, 1976.

Kazdin, A. Statistical analyses for single-case experimental designs. In M. Hersen & D. H. Barlow (Eds.), *Single case experimental designs: Strategies for studying behavior change.* New York: Pergamon, 1976. Pp. 265–316.

Lloyd, K. E., Garlington, W. K., Lowry, D., Burgess, H., Euler, H. A. & Knowlton, W. R. A note on some reinforcing properties of university lectures. *Journal of Applied Behavior Analysis,* 1972, **5**, 151–155.

Michael, J. Statistical inference for individual organism research: Mixed blessing or curse? *Journal of Applied Behavior Analysis,* 1974, **7**, 647–653.

Redd, W. H. Effects of mixed reinforcement contingencies on adults' control of children's behavior. *Journal of Applied Behavior Analysis,* 1969, **2**, 249–254.

Renne, C. M. & Creer, T. L. Training children with asthma to use inhalation therapy equipment. *Journal of Applied Behavior Analysis,* 1976, **9**, 1–11.

Risley, T. R. Behavior modification: An experimental-therapeutic endeavor. In L. A. Hamerlynck, P. O. Davidson & L. E. Acker (Eds.), *Behavior Modification and Ideal Mental Health Services.* Calgary: University of Calgary Press, 1970. Pp. 103–127.

Semb, G., Hopkins, B. L. & Hursh, D. E. The effects of study questions and grades on student test performance in a college course. *Journal of Applied Behavior Analysis,* 1973, **6**, 631–642.

Sidman, M. *Tactics of scientific research.* New York: Basic Books, 1960.

Sulzer, B., Hunt, S., Ashby, E., Koniarski, C. & Krams, M. Increasing rate and percentage correct in reading and spelling in a fifth grade public school class of slow readers by means of a token system. In E. A. Ramp & B. L. Hopkins (Eds.), *A new direction for education: Behavior analysis 1971*. Lawrence: University of Kansas, 1971.

Theobald, D. E. & Paul, G. L. Reinforcing value of praise for chronic mental patients as a function of historical pairing with tangible reinforcers. *Behavior therapy,* 1976, **7**, 192–197.

Ulman, J. D. & Sulzer-Azaroff, B. Multielement baseline design in educational research. In E. Ramp & G. Semb (Eds.), *Behavior analysis*. Englewood Cliffs, N.J.: Prentice-Hall, 1975. Pp. 377–391.

Communicating the Outcomes of an Applied Behavior-Analysis Program: I

After mastering the material in this unit, you should be able to

1. Discuss why and to whom the outcomes of a behavioral program should be communicated.

2. Discuss the behavior analyst's responsibility to report results in an ethical and comprehensible manner.

3. Describe what the "purpose" section of a report should include.

4. Describe the importance of including a clear description of
   a. Subject characteristics
   b. Others involved in project
   c. The setting
   d. Materials, supplies, and equipment

5. Describe what the procedural section contains.

In this era of shrinking resources, people are demanding evidence that the efforts that they support, yield, on balance, more benefit than cost to individuals and society. The methods just discussed are responsive to that demand by demonstrating benefits of applied behavior analysis. They go beyond a mere proclamation of effectiveness, as such proclamations are no longer sufficient. People want to be told *what* has transpired, *how* changes have been brought about, and *how* they satisfy humanistic concerns. The public is demanding to be informed. We see evidence of this trend in many facets of life. Manufacturers of food products, drugs, clothing, appliances, and other marketable items are being increasingly required to inform purchasers of the contents, anticipated benefits, and potential risks. Practitioners of medicine, dentistry, psychology, law, and other services are increasingly being required by law or by the fiats of professional organizations to inform clients about the effectiveness of their methods and how outcomes are being achieved. Similarly, behavior analysts have a responsibility, within ethical bounds, to inform clients and other consumers of their services about what and how any behavioral changes are accomplished. We urge that this responsibility be defined even more broadly: that outcomes of replications or novel procedures be communicated to fellow professionals and to the scientific community as well. In this unit and the next we shall discuss some specific aspects of oral and written communication, focusing in particular upon the ethics of communicating program results, the audience to be informed, and the selection of appropriate language and content.

Who has the right to be informed about the progress or ultimate outcome of a behavior-analysis program? What are some guidelines to consider in communicating to those persons? Certainly clients or their advocates must be kept informed continually. Parents and relevant others in each client's life also deserve nonprivileged information about progress and outcomes. Contingency managers usually want to be told how effective their efforts have been. Agencies and institutions wish to have their investments of human and material resources justified. The public at large and the scientific community stand to profit from information about procedural outcomes. It is only through such communication that the offerings of human behavioral services can be improved.

REPORTING TO CLIENTS AND ADVOCATES

Effective communication requires a careful selection of appropriate language. Children and youths have an infinite variety of behavioral repertoires. Some may have the receptive and expressive language of sophisticated adults, whereas others may comprehend but be limited in speech; still others may be unable to communicate even on the most rudimentary level. In the last instance, the client must be informed in the simplest manner possible about which responses indicate progress: "Wonderful, Pearl, you remembered how to hold the button correctly"; "Great, Sam, you're sharing your toys." Such informational feedback may actually, as we discussed in the units on stimulus control, teach the client some receptive language. With a client whose repertoire is severely limited, there is usually a parent or other individual to act as advocate. Again, the content and manner of communicating information depend upon the behavioral repertoire of the individual being informed. There is probably a happy medium for selecting language appropriate for clients or advocates, as well as for others. Oversimple language may be insulting, whereas oversophisticated or technical language may be confusing or cause resentment. An effective way to establish the appropriate level of detail for a report and the language to use is to ask the client or advocate himself to describe what has been happening. Graphs or other evidence of progress may be provided for reference. The behavior analyst can then use the client's vocabulary as a basis for extending or revising conclusions. Information is selected to fill in apparent gaps, and occasionally some technical language may be used. If, however, there are any obvious or subtle cues that the client does not understand the terms, the reports should be paraphrased, rather than formally defined: "Here when a free time was made contingent upon task completion—when you earned free time for completing your assignment—you can see that your work improved."

If a client can read or recognize written symbols, a written report may be supplied. The daily report card and task-analysis check lists discussed earlier may be used to inform clients, as well as parents. Similarly, notes, stars, pictures, wall charts, and other pictorial symbols can be used to keep clients informed of their progress. Graphs, of course, are kept current and provide an excellent source of regular information for clients. Needless to say, when clients manage their own contingencies and keep their own records, they are best informed about the program and their progress through it.

REPORTING TO CONSUMERS

Those individuals who are in daily contact with clients or who have a vested interest in their present and future functioning—parents, teachers, contingency managers, consumers who hire the services of the behavior analyst—should be informed about the program's continuing and ultimate effectiveness. As we have emphasized throughout this book, however, the application of behavior analysis must be ethically responsible. Consequently, reporting is bounded by ethical considerations and is conducted so that people to whom the report is directed comprehend the program and its results.

Ethically Responsible Reporting

Two major issues should be considered when a report on the results of a behavior-analysis program is in preparation: *privacy* and *confidentiality*. There may be circumstances in which an individual has sought assistance with a problem behavior about which he would prefer others not to become familiar. The behavior analyst may agree with the client on one of several precautions: Reports may be kept confidential, identification records may be disguised, identifying characteristics may be eliminated, or the like. In rare instances (as when danger to others is threatened), the behavior analyst may believe that disclosure is in the public interest. The client has the right to be warned ahead of time that the behavior analyst will not be able to keep such material confidential. Whatever decision is made, the terms should be clearly stipulated in advance so that misunderstanding will not be encountered later on. Even in a situation in which clients have little concern about communication of results, confidentiality should be maintained when results are made public: submitted for publication, used as illustrative instructional materials, and so on. Identifying characteristics, like names, should be omitted or changed. One can substitute numbers, initials, or fictional names for actual clients' names.

The right to privacy should also be maintained in informal settings. Those of us who are involved in and excited about our work are apt to want to share our sorrows and joys with others. Again, it is important that specific individuals not be identified unless permission has been expressly given by them, their advocates, or other appropriate persons or unless the material has historically been considered part of the usual domain of the agency or institution. Great care should be exerted to avoid identifying clients and those close to them in public places like restaurants, social gatherings, and other locations in which conversations may be overheard.

Remember also that local and national laws may affect clients' rights of access to records of which they are the subjects. Ethics suggests that clients who desire access to their records be shown such material, preferably with adequate professional explanations. Current United States law permits certain records to be made available to clients on request.

Comprehensible Reporting to Consumers

As in reporting to clients and their advocates, the behavior analyst must be careful to communicate with consumers as comprehensibly as possible. It is essential that consumers of the behavior analyst's services understand what has been accomplished, how it has been accomplished, and the significance of the outcome. Continued program support is most likely to depend upon such understanding. Again, the selection of appropriate language is critical. It is not enough simply to ask consumers from time to time whether or not they understand; one must not be misled by smiles and nods of agreement. When reporting orally to consumers, it is important to engage them in conversation so that they can communicate their understanding of what has transpired in their own words. One can ask them to offer suggestions for the future; in that way one is more likely to pick up misapprehensions. One may be cued about the appropriateness of the language being used, or may find that it is necessary to substitute more "popular" terms for technical ones. If one is at a loss for appropriate words, the glossary in this book can be consulted. We have attempted to use synonyms for various technical terms that are, it is hoped, comprehensible to the lay population. Beside nontechnical synonyms, illustrative examples of terms from varied contexts may also serve the purpose. We hope that the examples that we and our readers have supplied throughout the book and the accompanying study guide will provide a sufficient repertoire.

Some consumers prefer simple oral or written reports to more complex and thorough ones. Behavior analysts employed by schools, institutions, and community agencies have devised various systems for accomplishing this. Check lists and charts have been designed to reflect the accomplishment of tasks and subtasks (see the instruments described in Appendix 1). They are used to report periodically to parents, staff, or other consumers. Similarly, task-analysis check lists (see, for example, Figure 17.2) and forms resembling daily report cards have been used (see Figure 34.1). A section inviting a response from the recipient may also be included. It would serve as a basis for clarifying any concerns or misconceptions.

Client _____ Date _____

Behavioral goal_____

Procedure being used _____

_____

Progress to date _____

_____

Suggestions _____

_____

Subsequent plans _____

_____

Figure 34.1 Sample report form.

Naturally, graphs provide the most specific and succinct description of progress over time. Up-to-date graphs should be available and should be used to describe progress whenever consumers express an interest in viewing them. In the next section we shall begin to describe a system for writing a formal behavior-analysis report. Although professionals trained in the principles and procedures of applied behavior analysis are the most likely audience, other sophisticated consumers may also wish to read those reports. Within the ethical limits discussed, formal reports should be made available to them as well. Let us now turn to the system for preparing a formal behavior-analysis report.

FORMAL BEHAVIOR-ANALYSIS REPORTS

Formal behavior-analysis reports are written from the point of view of **replication**. To serve clients best, the report is prepared in sufficient detail so that others will be able to repeat the procedure in the future. If appropriate, the procedure may be adjusted for a new client, to include new behavioral objectives or implementation by different contingency managers. A carefully prepared report may even be read and followed by clients interested in further modifying, maintaining, or generalizing their own behavior. Writing a formal applied behavior-analysis report is similar to writing any complex set of instructions to be followed independently by others: a recipe for a gourmet dish, a theatrical script, an assemble-it-yourself tool shed or model airplane. The clearer the instructions, the more likely it is that the instruction followers will achieve success. The *Publication Manual* of the American Psychological Association (1974) suggests format and style for replicable psychological reports and serves as a foundation for the guidelines that we offer in this unit and the next. (An applied behavior-analysis task analysis [Ramey et. al., 1976] also served as a source for finer details.)

A second justification for a formal report is the discovery of new knowledge or procedural refinements that should, if ethically permissible, be communicated to the public. In this manner, programs that have demonstrated their effectiveness with individual clients may make a broader social contribution as well. The following sections are included in a formal behavior-analysis report to enhance clarity and replicability. The first is a statement of purpose.

The Purpose

At the beginning of the report a brief introductory section should state what the program is about and why it has been undertaken. This statement of purpose should include precise designation of the dependent variables, the behaviors targeted for modification, independent variables, the treatment program, and all procedural manipulations. To justify to the reader the selection of that particular program, one must summarize briefly the literature that suggested it. All behavior-analysis reports should also include introductory sections on relevant ethical issues and how they have been resolved. The long-term and short-term benefits to the client, the incorporation of principles of voluntariness and informed consent, and appropriate safeguards adopted with unusual or aversive procedures should all be reported. In a published research report it is common to begin with a review of the literature, a discussion of special considerations (practical, ethical, and administrative) relative to the particular program, and then a statement of purpose (the independent variables to be manipulated and the dependent variables to be measured). Often the purpose is stated as an *experimental question*: "If Dexter records his task completion and allows himself access to preferred activities as a consequence of improvement, *then* will his task completion increase?"

The Method

The description of method must be sufficiently precise to enable a reader to repeat the procedures exactly and to evaluate their appropriateness. An effectively written method section functions much as a theatrical script does. As we have found this analogy useful in helping students to prepare clear, complete program descriptions, we shall continue it throughout this discussion. In the method section the subjects, others involved, setting, materials, supplies, equipment, and procedures are described.

The subjects.   The clients, or subjects, in a behavioral-analysis program can be compared to the cast of characters in a play. Let us recall how a theatrical script describes each character: noting appearance, approximate age, some individual background, and so forth. By casting roles according to those descriptions, we can achieve a closer approximation to what was intended by the playwright. The importance of reporting clients' characteristics in detail in a behavior-analysis program report should be apparent, for individual differences may influence the outcome of the program, as we have discussed earlier. A clear specification of clients' characteristics is necessary if differences are to be kept from confounding accurate generalizations, normative conclusions, and the articulation of general principles or laws.

Some excellent guidelines for reporting subjects' characteristics for samples presumed to represent groups of children have been suggested by White and Duker (1973): A list of standards similar to those proposed in Table 34.1 could be used by journal editors to inform authors of what is required in describing the

TABLE 34.1. SUGGESTED STANDARD CHARACTERISTICS FOR REPORTING SAMPLES OF CHILDREN

Characteristic	Standard
Sample of children	
1. Number in sample	Required
2. Sex	Required
3. Age (or no. 5)	Required
4. Race	Required
5. Grade (or no. 3)	Required if in school
6. Family income	If available
7. Parental occupation	If available
8. Parental education	If available[a]
9. Social class	Never without no. 10
10. Social-class scale	Scale identified; data shown
11. Census-tract data	Required for school population
12. Neighborhood	Not if no. 11 is reported
13. Dialect	If special to sample
14. Ethnicity	Not if no. 11 is reported
Sample of pupils	
15. School (or institution)[b]	Never named; census-tract data described and used
16. Standardized group test score	Required, test named, and date given
17. Range of scores	Required
18. Standard deviation	Required
Sample as a sample	
19. Size of total pool	Required
20. How school was selected	Required
21. How class was selected	Required
22. How individual child was selected	Required

[a] Not necessary if no. 11 is reported.

[b] The institution should be described in terms of the population admitted, and items 16–18 should be required as the most appropriate measures.

SOURCE: White & Duker, 1973, p. 703.

individual clients in applied behavior-analysis programs. In addition, in a report of an applied behavior-analysis program, this section should include: description of the client's previous history with intervention programs and why they had been selected; specific physical, social, personal, and other behavioral characteristics like unusual deficits, strengths, excesses, important events in the client's life; ethical procedures followed in obtaining informed consent; and other safeguards. If a behavioral check list or other formal assessment instruments are used, the names of the instruments and the results of the assessment should be included. A common frame of reference for reporting subject characteristics should facilitate interpretability of results. Also perhaps some of the disparities in findings will be found to result from previously unrevealed differences among subjects.

Others involved.   To complete the listing of individuals involved in a stage production, the producer, director, stage manager, designer, and others are named. Certainly these people can make the difference between an outstanding performance and a flop. Similarly, the behavior analyst who conducts the experimental analysis; the parent, teacher, or therapist who acts as the contingency manager; the administrative staff; and the roles and expectations of others who affect the subject's environment should also be described in detail. For example, the degree to which the contingency manager is similar to the subject could influence his functioning as a model. We therefore suggest that the characteristics listed in Table 34.2 also be included in the report. Any instructions given to contingency managers, details about how their cooperation has been obtained, and other descriptive information may also prove of value.

The setting.   The stage set affects the action and mood of a play. The setting in which a behavior-analysis program is conducted also affects the progress of the program. We have discussed earlier the physical environment and environmental confounding variables and how they may be related to the behavior of clients and staff. The geographical location, the structure of the surroundings, topographical features, size, lighting and accoustical conditions, traffic patterns, and other physical properties that may have affected the program should be described in detail. In the event that structures have been modified, as with timeout facilities or learning cubicles, it is often useful to include a floor plan or diagram. Other special or unusual environmental events that have occurred during the program may be mentioned also.

Materials, supplies, and equipment.   Inclusion of a list of props and costumes is an essential accompaniment to the script of a play, just as the list of appropriate ingredients is essential to the successful preparation of a cheese soufflé. The report of a behavior-analysis program must also include lists of materials, supplies, and equipment in sufficient detail to facilitate exact replication. Otherwise, task-confounding variables may inadvertently affect the results. Instructional materials, instruments, data sheets, and such program devices as tokens and point charts are described in the report. If an object is a commercial product, its identification, price, and manufacturer should all be included. A picture, a diagram, or even the

TABLE 34.2. SUGGESTED STANDARD CHARACTERISTICS FOR DESCRIBING PERSONS INVOLVED WITH PROGRAM[a]

Characteristic	Standard			
	Behavior Analyst	Contingency Manager	Behavioral Technician	Others
1. Age—approximate	–	xx	–	xx
2. Sex	–	xx	x	xx
3. Race	–	xx	x	xx
4. Experience in using treatment approach	xx	xx	x	xx
5. Training in approach	xx	xx	x	xx
6. Demonstrated competence in using approach	xx	xx	xx	x
7. Experience in setting in which approach used—years	xx	xx	xx	x
8. Education	x	x	x	x
9. Social-class background, obtained from social-class scale	–	xx	–	xx
10. How selected	xx	xx	xx	xx
11. Language dialect	–	xx	–	xx
12. Physical description; distinguishing characteristics	–	xx	–	x
13. Relation with other key persons involved in program	xx	xx	xx	xx
14. Contingencies operating on individual fulfilling role in program	xx	xx	xx	xx

[a]xx—essential
  x—desirable
  – —nonessential

object itself may be included in the body of the report or as part of the appendix. **The procedures.**   Now the drama begins to unfold. The scene is set; the audience has been informed about the time and place and perhaps the season of the piece. The characters begin to speak their lines. Introducing the report of the behavior-analysis procedure is a statement about regular events, time of day, and other general procedural aspects. What is essentially the same as a set of stage directions follows. A description of the sequence of conditions and the function of each of those involved is included: how responses were defined; when and how often they were measured and with what instruments; how observers were trained; how and when reliability was assessed and experimental analyses conducted; how materials were used; how contingencies were managed; what each participant did during adaptation phases, baseline phases, treatment phases; the length of each phase; the basis for deciding to change conditions; and, if relevant, the degree to which procedures were implemented. A well-written procedural section precisely and objectively describes operations, citing references when appropriate and defining terms behaviorally. No subjective statements or interpretations are included (there is room for them later on). The section simply tells the reader how to duplicate the procedure in exact details. An ethical justification for any procedural selection that is not routinely used in that setting should be included, however.

Summary

In this unit we have introduced the reader to communication of the substance of applied behavior-analysis programs. Suggestions for communicating in a manner that is ethical and comprehensible to clients, advocates, and consumers have been provided. Guidelines for writing the purpose and method sections of formal reports designed for professional consumption have also been provided. Incorporation of such guidelines enables readers to replicate the methods used and to assess the appropriateness of procedures to their own settings and clients.

References

American Psychological Association. *Publication Manual.* (2nd ed.) Washington, D.C.: Author, 1974.

Ramey, G., Sovweine, J., Peters, J., Bernal, G., Sulzer-Azaroff, B., Johnson, K., & Hilpert, P. Development of guidelines for rating and preparing research articles in applied behavior analysis: A preliminary report. Paper presented at the meeting of the Association for Advancement of Behavior Therapy. New York, December, 1976.

White, M. A. & Duker, J. Suggested standards for children's samples. *American Psychologist,* 1973, **28**, 700–703.

COMMUNICATING THE OUTCOMES of AN Applied Behavior-Analysis Program: II

After mastering the material in this unit, you should be able to

1. Identify and illustrate the different conventions for displaying data clearly.

2. Discuss and illustrate several ways of transforming data, giving the rationale for each.

3. Describe how results can be reported through graphs and descriptive narratives.

4. Describe the contents of the conclusions and discussion sections and how they differ from those of the results section. Be sure to include in your discussion the factors that go into determination of a cost-benefit ratio.

FORMAL BEHAVIOR-ANALYSIS REPORTS: RESULTS AND CONCLUSIONS

Once the purpose and method sections have been presented, the data on the effectiveness of the program are communicated. They are what we turn our attention to in this final unit: the results and conclusions.

The Results

The measurements and other data resulting from a behavior-analysis program are usually reported in graphic form with accompanying discussion. Sometimes tables are also included. The graphs, or **figures**, are usually drawn according to a set of conventions that have been evolved in the field.

Conventions for displaying data.   The vertical axis of a graph, the ordinate, contains the scale for measuring the dependent variable, for example, the number of responses. The horizontal axis, the abscissa, contains the sequence of manipulations of the independent variable over time and is usually scaled in time units: days, sessions, trials, or the like. When numbers are plotted as functions of the passage of time, the resulting curve depicts the rate of responding over time, as in Figure 35.1. Of course, different studies may use different measures: latency, force, ratings (for example, a scale of 1–10), proportion, percentage, and so on. Nevertheless, the ordinate always contains the scale for that dependent variable (see Figure 35.2).
        For clarity of communication,

1. Vertical broken lines indicate changes in conditions or treatment phases.
2. Data points are discontinued between each phase.
3. Usually no more than one set of data is plotted on a graph; when more than one set is plotted, different symbols and connecting lines are used for each (for example,   ,   ,   ; see Figure 35.2.a).
4. "Dead space" is omitted to save space; such an omission is indicated by a break in the axis: (see Figure 35.2.a,d).
5. If there are many data points on the zero line, the ordinate extends beyond zero (see Figure 35.2.b).
6. If data are quite variable but *still experimentally or socially significant*, the ordinate should be contracted (see Figure 35.2c). (Logarithmic scales may also be appropriate here (see Koorland & Martin, 1975).
7. If data seem extremely stable, *obscuring a socially important change*, the ordinate should be expanded (see Figure 35.2.d).

A figure may present behaviors as *cumulative numbers* also. A change in the slope of the curve is the datum of interest. In Figure 35.3 the data from Figure 35.1 have been replotted as cumulative numbers of responses. Note the differences in

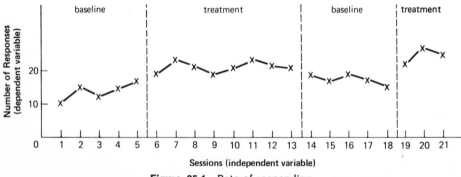

Figure 35.1 Rate of responding.

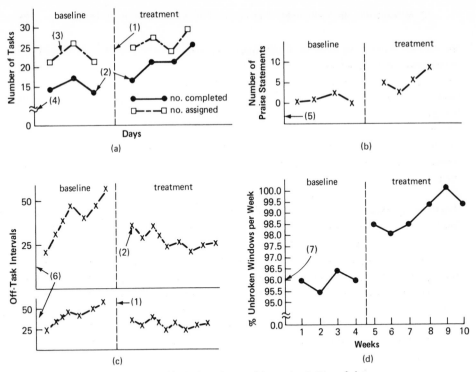

Figure 35.2 Variations in graphic presentation of data.

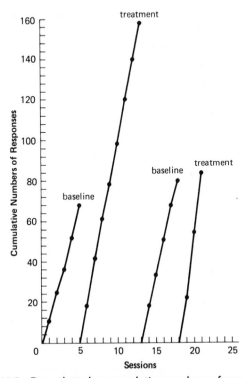

Figure 35.3 Data plotted as cumulative numbers of responses.

the slopes during baseline and treatment, with treatment showing behaviors accumulating at a higher rate.

Cumulative records are particularly useful for plotting acquisition data, like approximations achieved in a shaping program or links or subtasks in a chaining program. One major advantage of cumulative records is that they indicate at a glance the *total* number of responses under each condition. Figure 35.3 successively indicates sixty-eight responses during five baseline days, 159 during eight treatment days, eighty during five baseline days, and eighty-three during three treatment days.

Transforming data.   When the size of the measured dependent variable is the same both within and between sessions and within and between conditions, interpretations are simpler (see Unit 31 for discussion of task-confounding variables). Keeping the dependent variable constant in size is not a major problem for many behaviors encountered in applied behavior analysis, provided that a durable and reliable measure has been identified. The size of the responses measured—perhaps intervals scored for on-task behavior, number of praise statements delivered, points scored, and others—refined to a high degree of reliability, remains constant, so that variations observed in the data plots are more likely to be functions of other variables.

Let us consider, however, such dependent variables as tasks completed, pages read, successive approximations mastered, and number correct. Here there may be substantial variation between the size of one measured response and that of the next. Tasks or printed matter may vary in length and difficulty or complexity, as may the various steps that successively approximate a particular terminal behavior. The number correct may reflect all these problems plus an additional one: the difference between number attempted and number assigned, as well as the number incorrectly completed.

If the dependent variable is composed of nonuniform responses, like those just discussed, the data may be *transformed*, so that each point is uniformly related to the scale value—which means that, for a dependent variable like task completion, equivalent task sizes must be plotted. If difficulty is held constant, then a simple arithmetic transposition accomplishes the purpose, even though tasks may actually vary some from day to day. If the assignment is to complete all the problems on a page and there are different numbers of problems on the pages (perhaps twelve on one and eight on the other), it is necessary only to compute an average or mean percentage of problems completed. (If there is a very large variation in length of assignments from day to day, the problem will be compounded by such factors as fatigue, satiation, and adaptation.) For a comparison of numbers of correct responses completed under various treatment conditions, it is necessary not only to calculate the percentage correct but also to indicate the total number of items assigned or attempted and the number incorrect. Other transformations could include responses per minute, mean percentage correct, and so on.

Figures 35.4 and 35.5 suggest some alternative ways in which such informa-

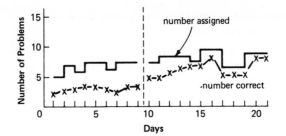

Figure 35.4   Proportion of correctly completed problems to number assigned.

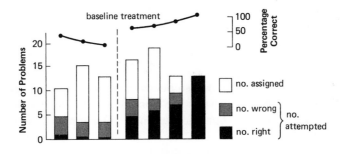

tion can be presented. The plot in Figure 35.4 enables the reader to see the number of correct responses in proportion to the number assigned. Figure 35.5 presents a second alternative, in which there are double axes, with number of problems on the left and percentages correct on the right. The percentage correct is usually calculated by dividing the number of correct items by number of items assigned times 100. Others, however, have divided the number of items correct by the number of items *attempted*. Changes in accuracy determined by the latter formula can be caused solely by changes in the number of items attempted. Klein (1975), for example, has recommended that in such an instance data be reported both for items attempted and for items assigned. Figure 35.5 permits reporting of both kinds of data.

Still another alternative recommended by Klein (1975) is to present the data in tabular form, as in Table 35.1, including each category in a separate column.

Any one of the formats presented here accommodates variability in response requirements. All furnish the opportunity to see results from several dimensions, but they may be confusing. If simplicity of communication is of primary importance, the response requirement should be kept as uniform as possible.

Occasionally data are reported for groups of individuals. To simplify communication, average performance per day may be plotted, as in Figure 31.2. If there is much variability in the performance of the various individuals, however, the extent of that variability should be reported. Then the reader will have an idea of just how representative of individual functioning the data are.

TABLE 35.1.   PRESENTATION OF DATA IN TABULAR FORM

Treatment Condition	Days	No. Assigned	No. Attempted	No. Correct	Percentage Correct Assigned	Percentage Correct Attempted
Baseline	1	10	4	2	20	50
	2	16	3	1	.06	33
	3	13	3	0	0	0
Average		13	3.3	1	6.68	27.6
Treatment	4	15	8	7	47	87.5
	5	17	8	7	41	87.5
	6	12	10	8	75	80
	7	17	13	12	70	92.3
Average		15.25	9.75	8.5	58.25	86.8

Figure legend.   The figure legend, written below the chart or graph, briefly describes in simple words the data displayed. The conditions and the measures are described, along with any other operation essential to interpretation of the graph.

Description of results.   When accompanied by clear, comprehensible figures or tables, the description of results is simple and straightforward. Essentially, it is limited to descriptions of data in relation to each phase of the program: the reader's attention is drawn to important aspects. For example, in connection with our hypothetical Figure 35.5 the following statement would suffice: "Figure 35.5 indicates that the number of problems assigned daily varied from ten to eighteen over the entire course of the program. During the baseline phase never more than two problems were solved correctly, whereas during treatment the number of correctly solved problems rose much higher."

   If unusual events have transpired during the program, events that may have been related to unusual data points, those too can be identified in this section. For instance, an unusually high number of problems may have been correctly solved on a day preceding a special activity, or an unusually low number of correctly completed problems may have occurred on a day when the student reported having a headache. It is acceptable to mention those events in the results section. Elaborate explanation and interpretation should, however, be left for the discussion section.

   If data transformations have been made or statistical analyses conducted, the method and results should naturally also be summarized in this section. Reliability and procedural data may also be reported here, along with data about any measured collateral changes. The descriptive aspect of the results section is like that part of a theatrical review in which external observable events are described: "The audience interrupted the play six times with applause. There were eight curtain calls. Of the people interviewed in the lobby, 60 percent indicated that it was the best of the season." The part of a theatrical review that expresses the critic's opinion is comparable to the discussion section in a behavior-analysis report, to which we now turn.

Conclusions and Discussion

The heart of a theatrical review is the critic's interpretation of the production. The performance is evaluated, comparisons made, and improvements suggested. The discussion section of a behavior-analysis report performs a similar function. The author draws conclusions about the effectiveness and significance of the program, considers problems that may have affected the outcome; suggests further applications, ideas for replication, or new methods; and relates the program to others attempted elsewhere.

Judging effectiveness. A behavior-analysis program is judged effective when previously identified terminal objectives have been achieved and when the relation between the independent and dependent variables has been demonstrated by means of experimental analysis. Then the writer can state with confidence, "We achieved what we set out to achieve, and the specified treatment was demonstrated to be responsible for the change." By considering the factors for determining social significance, discussed in Unit 33, conclusions can be drawn on that score: "If the application of behavioral techniques does not produce large enough effects for practical value, then application has failed" (Baer, Wolf & Risley, 1968, p. 96). Is the improvement in academic performance sufficient to affect subsequent learning? Is a nurse's increased use of praise substantial enough to affect the patient's behavior? Is a reduction in aggressive behavior great enough to keep other children from getting hurt? What is the practical significance of the modified behavior of the group? Are members too quiet and docile, or has the atmosphere improved sufficiently to support more academic productivity while maintaining active client involvement?

A question that should be asked before instituting a behavior-analysis program is "What *indirect* effects should the program accomplish, and how can they be monitored?"

Resulting data will provide evidence for drawing conclusions about side effects of the program. Follow-up and generalization data also serve as bases for drawing conclusions. Another way to evaluate the outcome is to judge it against a standard of comparison identified by others. One collects data on a group of students known to be learning enthusiastically and effectively and then compares the data with the behavior modified. The rates and intensities of aggressive behavior by a group of children judged "normal," "healthy," "active," "well-adjusted," and so on by respected judges can be checked. Clients and important people in their environment can be asked how satisfied they are with the changes. Braukmann and colleagues (1975) have used such data on *client satisfaction* as evidence of the effectiveness of their procedures with delinquent youths.

In schools consumer satisfaction may be determined by teachers, parents, supervisors, and other personnel rating changed behavior on various dimensions: adaptive function, attractiveness, and so on. Similar indicators of consumer satisfaction may be used in clinics, institutions, and other human-services facilities after clients and staff, community leaders, and others have been consulted.

Ready adoption of a treatment by persons faced with similar problem situations is probably another indicator of practical importance. The practical value of token systems in institutions, for instance, may be inferred from the frequency with which such systems are currently being adopted. (Widespread use alone is not, however, appropriate as the sole criterion of practical significance—witness the widespread use of punishment in schools!)

Considering confounding variables.   In the discussion section, the writer has the opportunity to muse about events that may have affected the outcome of the program. The possible effects of task, environmental, subject, and other uncontrolled variables may be mentioned. Consideration of such factors may lead to procedural refinements in replication of the program or possibly to development of new treatment methods.

Relation to other programs.   Usually a particular treatment program has been selected because its effectiveness has been communicated through the literature or in some other way. At the conclusion of a report it is useful to include a brief section comparing the treatment and its outcome with similar treatments reported by others. Such a comparison will assist the reader to interpret the program within a broader context and, if need be, to determine what the next step should be. Let us say that a client from a ghetto background has profited substantially from a program designed to enhance marketable skills. She later uses those skills to establish and operate a successful small business. Such an outcome is dramatic enough. But interpreting the results within a context of information about the effectiveness of similar procedures with clients having similar characteristics says a great deal more.

Cost-benefit ratio.   The ultimate basis for deciding the value of a particular behavior-analysis program is how much benefit has accrued in relation to its cost (Krumboltz, 1974). Both terms should be defined broadly. Benefits include improvement in the target behavior, as well as immediate and long-term advantage to the client, important others in her environment, and society as a whole. As we have seen earlier, these considerations are not necessarily lawfully related to one another. What may be beneficial to one person at one time may be detrimental to others. A program that is beneficial to clients should broaden their repertoires of adaptive behaviors while making available new sources of reinforcement and reductions in aversive consequences. Examples include broadened cognitive, affective, motor, and other repertoires that will increase positive opportunities for individuals in the near and distant future; meet their material needs and those of their families; promote enriched social relationships, positive personal attitudes, and feelings ("I'm a good person, and I feel content"); and make available many satisfying activities and interests. Simultaneously, similar opportunities should accrue to important people in their lives and to society as a whole. To the extent that such outcomes can be substantiated, the net benefit of a program is demonstrated.

Krumboltz (1974) has presented one way of estimating investments of staff time in evaluating cost efficiency. Two of his illustrations are presented in Tables 35.2 and 35.3.

TABLE 35.2. ACCOUNTABILITY RECORD FOR JOHN DOE, COUNSELOR[a]

| Accomplishment[b] | | | | Cost | |
Problem Identification	Method	Outcome	Activity	Hours	Dollars
Olive's mother telephoned; Olive is depressed, talking vaguely of suicide, no friends	Analysis of social reinforcers for Olive; training in social skills; Olive assigned to help new transfer student	Increased frequency of initiating social contacts from 0/month to 4/month; reports having 1 good friend vs. 0; mother reports Olive's depression gone—suicide talk from 1/month before referral to 0/month for 3 consecutive months	Conferences with Olive; Conferences with mother; Conferences with teachers	38 3 2	532 42 28 602

[a] Annual salary $14,000, contract 40 weeks at 40 hours per week, overhead factor 50 percent, effective rate $14 an hour.
[b] General goal A, adaptive behavior: to help students develop more adaptive and constructive behavior patterns.
SOURCE: Krumboltz, 1974, p. 642.

495

TABLE 35.3. ACCOUNTABILITY RECORD FOR JANE DOE, TEACHER

Problem Identification	Accomplishment[a]		Cost	
	Method	Outcome	Activity	Hours	Dollars

Problem Identification	Method	Outcome	Activity	Hours	Dollars
Over coffee in the teachers' lounge, teacher raised problem of discipline and readily agreed to experiment with alternative plan	Class observation; monitoring of behaviors to which teacher attended; teaching self-monitoring and attending to positive behaviors only	Teacher increased frequency of positive remarks to students from 2/hour to 15/hour, decreased negative remarks from 26/hour to 3/hour; class disruptions reduced from 8/week to 1/week; teacher reports greatly increased teaching satisfaction	Individual conferences with teachers; Class observations	3 3	42 42 ‾ 84

[a] General goal C, prevention: to devise developmental programs to prevent or ameliorate student problems.
SOURCE: Krumboltz, 1974, p. 644.

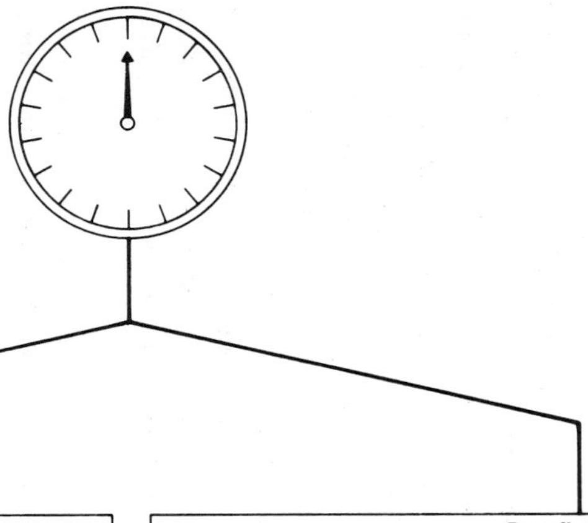

Cost Factors

	risks		time		effort		money		other	
	Sh	Lo	Sh	Lo	Sh	Lo	Sh	Lo	Sh	Lo
Client										
important persons in client's life										
service provided										
society										

Benefit Factors

	cognitive		affective		social		motor skills		time money		other	
	Sh	Lo	Sh	Lo	Sh	Lo	Sh	Lo	Sh	Lo	Sh	Lo

Sh—short term
Lo—long term

Figure 35.6 Graphic matrix for estimate of cost-benefit ratio.

497

Krumboltz suggested that each activity be grouped under one of three general goals: adaptive behavior, decision making, and prevention. Another heading, like "miscellaneous," might be used for such elements as the accountability report, faculty meetings, sick leave, and professional meetings. Krumboltz also suggested a section on ideas for changes, to be written by the contingency manager or behavior analyst. For example, "I'm sure I helped Olive overcome her depression, but the most effective technique, I think, was assigning her to help a new transfer student. The new transfer student became her best friend. Many other hours spent with her seem wasted" (1974 p. 645).

Once the hours and dollars have been calculated according to Krumboltz's formula, the information can be transferred into the matrix in Figure 35.6 for a more refined cost-benefit estimate. For cost also implies factors beside time, effort, and money expended by the staff; it includes expenditures by the client, other people, and society as well. It also includes a client-risk factor (Stolz, 1975).

The cost of continually scolding children in terms of fatigue and strained vocal chords, the monetary cost of providing a staff person for remedial instruction or to reduce maladaptive personal behaviors, and the ultimate cost of repairing vandalized schools resulting from a punitive school atmosphere are all illustration of the kinds of short-term, long-term, and societal factors that should be considered. In drawing a conclusion about the ratio between costs and benefits, the reporter should consider all these factors and their interrelation. The matrix presented in Figure 35.6 is designed to help the report writer to estimate the total cost-benefit ratio. Practioners should find such a form helpful in determining differential costs and benefits.

Such activities are helpful in constant evaluation and improvement of a program. Although perhaps initially time consuming, in the long run they appear to reduce time and effort invested and program costs.

Summary

It is not enough to demonstrate effectiveness through an experimental analysis. To be totally accountable, one must also communicate results in a manner that is ethical and comprehensible to clients, advocates, and consumers. A written report designed for professional consumption should include a clear and objective description of the program's purpose, methods, and results. Conclusions about the relative effectiveness of the interventions are then drawn, the significance of the findings is discussed. It is through such communications that we remain accountable and continue to contribute to advancement of knowledge, understanding, and above all humanitarian services.

References

Baer, D. M., Wolf, M. M. & Risley, R. R. Some current dimensions of applied behavior analysis. *Journal of Applied Behavior Analysis,* 1968, **1**, 91–97.

Braukmann, C. J., Fixsen, D. L., Kirigin, K. A., Phillips, E. A., Phillips, E. L. & Wolf, M. M. Achievement Place: The training and certification of teaching parents. In W. S. Wood

(Ed.), *Issues in evaluating behavior modification.* Champaign: Research Press, 1975. Pp. 131–152.

Klein, R. D. A brief research report on accuracy and academic performance. *Journal of Applied Behavior Analysis,* 1975, **8**, 121–122.

Koorland, M. A. & Martin, M. B. *Principles and procedures of the standard behavior chart.* Gainesville, Fla.: Learning Environments, 1975.

Krumboltz, J. D. An accountability model for counselors. *The Personnel and Guidance Journal,* 1974, **52**, 639–646.

Stolz, S. B. Ethical issues in research in behavior therapy. In W. S. Wood (Ed.), *Issues in evaluating behavior modification.* Champaign: Research Press, 1975. Pp. 239–256.

Epilogue:
Applied Behavior Analysis
and Moral
Responsibility

Behavior, like all other natural phenomena, is lawful. The actions of particular individuals are functions of various factors in their internal and external environments: genetic endowment, physical condition, physiology, and the series of external events that have impinged upon them. Regardless of their intentions or those of society, certain natural events will promote particular behavioral rates, others will reduce them, and still others may maintain, extend, or restrict the range in which a given behavior is apt to occur. These natural functions are neither moral nor immoral—they are amoral. When society acts to *arrange* events in order to promote, reduce, maintain, extend, or restrict behaviors, morality does become an issue, however. When the arrangements and the behavior they promote are consonant with the values of society, they are considered "moral"; when they oppose the values of that society, they are considered "immoral."

Humanism is a value frequently proclaimed by change agents serving children and youths in Western society. According to Gage and Berliner (1975), several values underlie the student's role in humanistic education:

1. Self-direction, with the instructor functioning in the role of guide or facilitator
2. Learning to learn, rather than rote acquisition of verbal material
3. Self-evaluation
4. The importance of feelings: trust, kindness, and so on
5. Freedom from threat

We too subscribe to the humanistic value system for children and youths. We hope that the reader has seen evidence of this underlying philosophy throughout this book.

The concept of self-direction has been emphasized in our discussions of the importance of involving students and clients in selection of goals and procedures, self-monitoring, self-administration of contingencies, and self-evaluation. We have not been so overpowered by that concept, however, that we believe that youngsters who have not yet developed repertoires sufficient to allow them to direct their own activities should be allowed to flounder and fail. Rather, we have suggested strategies aimed at the eventual dissolution of external control as individuals become more and more competent to arrange their own affairs.

Certainly instruction for rote learning may be derived from principles of operant behavior. We have illustrated how language, appropriate responses to instructions, simple discriminations, and various other behaviors may be effectively taught through the application of behavior principles. Those responses can be considered "rote" responses. But we have also indicated how those very same principles of operant behavior may be applied to far more complex behaviors: concept formation, application of skills, problem solving and evaluation strategies. It is such sophisticated repertoires that enable individuals to learn how to learn by arranging their own environments. We have tried to present several strategies for encouraging them to do so. But, before children can walk, they must crawl. Similarly, before children can learn to manage their own environments for learning, they must have the essential prerequisites: the ability to make effective use of stimuli in the environment. As long as Pearl lacked language and social skills, she could not profit from instruction mediated by books or teachers. Until Dexter developed the skill to plan his own time, identify the tasks that he should record, and evaluate his progress, he was not learning to learn optimally. Once he had learned these skills, he could apply them to enhancing his performance, not only in various school subjects but also in his extracurricular activities.

We have seen how children can be taught to evaluate their own progress and ultimate accomplishments through self-recording, matching-to-sample, and even using experimental designs. By learning how to apply shaping and stimulus-control procedures and to evaluate his own responses, Claude the Clod may be able to teach himself to perform more competently in sports. By applying the skills acquired in her personalized system of instruction, Flora should be able to teach herself the contents of other courses more effectively. Despite our distaste for rote learning as an ultimate goal, we have been careful not to cast it aside altogether. Rather, we have encouraged its use as a means to the end of enabling youngsters to earn the self-confidence that comes only with accomplishments and thus eventually enabling them to teach themselves what they want to learn.

If young people are guided or their learning is enhanced by those who follow the precepts of effective applied behavior analysis, they will find that people follow through with promised consequences. Communication with them will be honest and direct, fostering trust and other positive feelings. The contingencies to be managed will not be obscured by a pretense of nonstructure. Rather they will be openly identified, so that clients may clearly discern what they are and support them, negotiate about them, or defend themselves against them.

Clients will be freer from threat with contingency managers who possess repertoires of effective positive strategies and who do not have to resort frequently to negative ones. Aware of the undsirable side effects that tend to accompany aversive control, contingency managers will be much less apt to select such contingencies in the first place. When clients and advocates give their informed consent to behavioral goals and procedures, threat also should be minimized. But freedom from threat also implies freedom from danger and from self-inflicted harm. It involves the right to learn and to function socially without interference. Consequently, from a pragmatic and philosophical point of view, although we caution against the use of aversive procedures, we are nevertheless not so naive as to assert that aversive procedures should never be used. Rather, we urge that they be implemented only as temporary expedients until more positive procedures can sufficiently maintain nonthreatening behaviors.

It is probably in the area of accountability that applied behavior analysis can demonstrate its greatest potential for moral responsibility. For applied behavior analysis, as an accountable intervention strategy, embodies evaluation of its procedural effectiveness, thus constantly improving its offerings to the consumers that it serves. Unlike results of intervention strategies that are implemented with less precision, data on the success and failure of behavior-analysis interventions are readily accessible to scrutiny by clients, other consumers, and society at large. An informed society can then inspect its current and ideal values and judge the effectiveness with which those values are supported in behavior-analysis programs applied with children and youth.

References

Gage, N. L. & Berliner, D. C. *Educational psychology.* Chicago: Rand McNally, 1975.

appendix

Behavioral Assessment Systems[1]

Teaching requires a rather careful assessment of entering behaviors so as to evaluate the efficacy of any intervention program. The assessment of children with special needs presents some unique problems, insofar as global profiles of abilities are seldom educationally useful, or theoretically sound.

As an alternative to traditional assessment systems, attention has recently been directed at developing behavioral checklists to more clearly specify skill levels. Such checklists vary in sophistication, reliability, and validity. Some are quite specific in providing detailed task analyses that divide a particular skill into its component parts (e.g., Read Project Assessment Manual). Other are still rather global, but cover a wider range of behavior (e.g., Progress Assessment Chart). Still others provide the opportunity not only for assessing the level of a particular skill, but also some important parameters of performance (e.g., Educational Evaluation and Planning Package).

The following are but a sample of the available assessment packages. One recent annotated bibliography[2] reviewed 157 different behavioral checklists. It is anticipated that the recognition of the need for criterion based performance standards will foster the development of such assessment techniques.

Name.   Educational Evaluation and Planning Package, Vols. I and II

Available from.   Mass Center for Program Development and Evaluation
10 Hall Avenue
Medford, Ma. 02155

Cost. $4.20

Characteristics.   This assessment package covers the areas of activities of daily living, motor development, early language development, mathematics, later language

[1] Compiled by Gregory Ramey, University of Massachusetts at Amherst.

[2] Walls, R. T. Werner, T. J. & Bacon, A. Behavior checklists. In J. D. Cone & R. P. Hawkins (Eds.), *Behavioral assessment: New directions in clinical psychology*. New York: Brunner-Mazel, in press.

development, and social development. One rather unique feature of this comprehensive volume is the inclusion of not only a breakdown of specific skill areas, but also a specification of the level of assistance needed to perform the skill (e.g., verbal prompt, physical prompt, etc.). In addition, other educationally useful parameters of performance (e.g., duration, setting, frequency) are included.

Example

Skill: Activities of Daily Living   Sub-Skill: Grooming (3.0)

Skill Statement	Performs appropriately without assistance	Performs in the following manners — type/level of assistance				Performs in the following manners — parameters			Type of intervention required			Unobserved/not applicable	Cluster: Toilet Skills (3.3) — Comment: Special equipment, elaboration of categories checked
		verbal	physical	individual	small group	duration	setting	frequency	motor	cognitive	social		
eliminates (e.g., in clothing)													
eliminates occasionally when on toilet													
eliminates at regular times													
has no accidents if taken to toilet on schedule													
indicates when wet													
indicates when soiled													
indicates need to urinate													

Name.   The Santa Cruz Behavioral Characteristics Progression Observation Booklet

Available from.   VORT Corporation
P.O. Box 11132
Palo Alto, Ca. 94306

Cost. $6.95

Characteristics.   This 2400 item checklist is divided into 59 areas, including activities of daily living (e.g., toilet habits, dressing, nasal hygiene), auditory and visual perception, language, behavior control, academic behaviors (math, spelling, reasoning), advanced self-help skills (e.g., homemaking skills, pre-vocational skills), speech-reading, swimming, and wheelchair use. To complete the assessment, each child is assigned a column in the booklet. The children are then rated on a six point scale, indicating one of the following: behavior not displayed due to lack of opportunity, behavior not displayed, behavior displayed less than required frequency, behavior displayed appropriate frequency, physical handicap prevents demonstration of behavior, lack of availability of materials prevents demonstration of behavior.

Example

	1	2	3	4	5	6
13.0 Hits another, making excuses to teacher when confronted with deed						
14.0 Exchanges items for play						
15.0 Watches others play and may join in for a few minutes						
16.0 Plays individually with adult						
17.0 Hits another, voluntarily making excuses to third party (e.g., goes to teacher)						
18.0 Plays with one or two others						
19.0 Responds to and makes verbal greetings						
20.0 Plays cooperatively with another child (e.g., plays games requiring peer interaction)						
21.0 Shows affection for familiar person (e.g., hugs, pats, kisses, etc.)						
22.0 Accepts and shows affection appropriate to home, school, street						
23.0 Hits another, afterwards verbalizing reasons to the one hit						

Name.   Lexington Developmental Scale

Available from.   United Cerebral Palsy of the Bluegrass
P.O. Box 8003
465 Spring Hill Dr.
Lexington, Kentucky 40503

Cost. $5.60

Characteristics. This 452 item scale, standardized on children between the ages of 3 years to 7 years 4 months, evaluates five major areas: motor, language, personal and social, cognitive, and emotional. The first four areas are assessed on the basis of developmental age, whereas the fifth area, emotional, is scored on a five-point scale. It is intended for children "who have been diagnosed as having normal learning potential but who have one or more learning disabilities, show developmental lag, and/or have multiple handicaps" (p. 1). To facilitate educational planning, the results of this assessment can be summarized for a group of children. The children's names are noted in the vertical column, while their performance on particular subtasks (e.g., knowledge of big-little) is noted in the appropriate box.

Example

2–3 Years	Over-Under									
	Crooked-Straight									
	Big-Little									
	High-Low									
	Same-Different									
3–4 Years	Behind-In Front Of									
	Deep-Shallow									
	Next To									
	Over There									
	Go There									
	Come Here									
4–5 Years	Foreward-Backward									
	Tiny-Large									
	Smooth-Rough									
	Another Town									
	Our State									
	Another State									
5–6 Years	Neighbor									
	Part of Town: N, E, S, W									

Name.   Trainer's Guide (Performance Inventory)

Available from.   Research Press Co.
Box 3177
Champaign, IL. 61820

Cost. $1.95

Characteristics.   The purpose of the Trainer's Guide is to provide a specific checklist of the child's development in toilet training, behavior problems, dressing skills, grooming skills, mealtime skills, basic skills (e.g., hold head up, pick up an object), helping skills, and understanding and speaking skills. It is not based on any normative group, and does not yield any numerical score of a person's functioning ability. It is very useful in that it contains a very specific breakdown of the component skills involved in each task.

Example

Table Setting

---

0. Cannot do any part of setting the table.
1. Can put the glasses on the table with direction once the rest of the table is set.
2. Can put the glasses on the table on his own once the rest of the table is set.
3. Can put the spoons on the table with direction once the rest of the table is set, and put the glasses on himself.
4. Can put the spoons and glasses on the table himself.
5. Can put the knives on the table with direction, and the spoons and glasses himself.
6. Can put the knives, spoons and glasses on the table himself.
7. Can put the forks on the table with direction, and the knives, spoons, and glasses on himself.
8. Can put the forks, knives, spoons, and glasses on himself.
9. Can put the napkins next to the plates you have put out with directions; and put the forks, knives, spoons, and glasses on himself.
10. Can put the plate on the table with direction and set the rest of the table himself.
11. Can set the entire table completely on his own.

Name.   Progress Assessment Chart

Available from.   USA Distribution Center
Aux Chandelles
PAC Department
Post Office Box 398
Bristol, Indiana 46507

Cost.   Varies

Forms.   Three basic developmental forms are available
(Primary, I, II); three supplemental forms (Severe, 1-A, Downs Syndrome).

Characteristics.   The PAC provides for a measurement of skills in four basic areas: self-help, communication, occupation, and socialization. Children are first rated on their performance in specific subtasks of the four general areas (e.g., table habits). The results are recorded by filling in the area with the corresponding number on the circular diagram to allow a visual inspection of the child's skill level.

Example

SELF-HELP

Table Habits

1.	Uses spoon when eating without requiring help	....	....	....	....	A
2.	Drinks without spilling, holding glass in one hand	....	....	....	....	A
18.	Uses fork without difficulty (food may be cut and prepared)			....	....	B
19.	Capable of helping himself to a drink	....	....	....	....	B
34.	Serves himself and eats without requiring much help		....	....	....	C
51.	Uses table knife for spreading butter, jam, etc.	....	....	....	....	D
69.	Uses table knife for cutting without much difficulty	....	....	....	....	E
92.	Uses knife and fork correctly and without difficulty	....	....	....	....	F
93.	Pours liquids (e.g. coffee, milk)	....	....	....	....	F
109.	Uses knife for peeling fruit or slicing bread	....	....	....	....	G

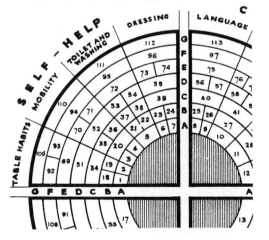

Name. Learning Accomplishment Profile

Available from. Kaplan School Supply Corp.
600 Jonestown Road
Winston-Salem, N.C. 27103

Cost. $3.00

Characteristics. The Learning Accomplishment Profile provides for the assessment of the young, handicapped child by recording the presence or absence of developmentally relevant skills. It is particularly useful in that it delineates criteria of performance, as well as notes the age range for the normal development of such skills.

Example

Behavior	Age (Dev.)	Assessment[a]	Date	Date of Achievement	Comments (criteria, materials, problems, etc.)
Manipulates egg beater	27 mos.	+	9/18/73		*WHIPPED SOAP SUDS. TEACHER HELD HANDLE.*
Enjoys finger painting	30–35 mos.	+	9/20/73		*FINGER PAINTED ON FORMICA TABLE — 10 MIN.*
Makes mud and sand pies	30–35 mos.	+	9/24/73		*MADE SAND PIES USING TEA.*
Paints strokes, dots, and circular shapes on easel	30–35 mos.	+	9/27/73		*IMITATED TEACHER WITH ½" BRUSH*
Cuts with scissors	35 mos.	+	10/2/73		*CUT ½" PARTIALLY CUT STRING*
Picks up pins, thread, etc., with each eye separately covered	36–48 mos.	—	10/3/73		
Drives nails and pegs	36–48 mos.	—	10/4/73		*THESE WILL*
Builds tower of nine cubes	36–48 mos.	—	10/5/73		*BECOME*
Holds crayon with fingers	36–48 mos.	+	10/8/73		*OBJECTIVES FOR THE*
Strings 4 beads	36–48 mos.	—	10/8/73		*CHILD*
Can close fist and wiggle thumb in imitation, R & L	36–48 mos.				
Puts 6 round pegs in round holes on pegboard	36–48 mos.				

[a] Mark + for positive demonstration of skill.
Mark − for negative demonstration of skill.

Abscissa The horizontal or x-axis on a graph. In applied behavior analysis the abscissa usually depicts successive trials or the passage of time.

Accountability Objective demonstration and communication of the effectiveness of a given program: behavioral outcomes, cost-benefit, consumer satisfaction, and so on.

Across-behavior multiple-baseline design A within-subject experimental design that involves: (1) Obtaining pre-treatment measures (baseline) of several *different behaviors;* (2) applying the intervention or experimental procedure to *one* of the behaviors until it is substantially changed while continuing to record the baseline measures of the other behaviors; (3) applying the intervention to a second behavior as in 2 above, and so on. This procedure is continued until it is determined whether or not each class of behavior changes systematically with the intervention.

Across-individuals multiple-baseline design A single-subject experimental design that involves: (1) Collecting baselines on the same behavior of several *different individuals;* (2) applying the intervention first with one individual while the baseline conditions are continued with the other individuals; (3) applying the intervention to the second individual's behavior as in 2 above. This procedure is continued until it is determined whether or not each individual's behavior changes systematically with the intervention.

Across-situations multiple-baseline design A single-subject experimental design that involves: (1) Collecting baselines on a behavior of one or more individuals across *different situations;* (2) testing the effects of the intervention *(independent variable)* first in one situation while the baseline conditions are continued throughout the other situations; (3) applying the intervention to the second situation as in 2 above. This procedure is continued until it is determined whether or not each individual's behavior changes systematically only in the situation in which the intervention is applied.

Adaptation The gradual change in behavior that often occurs after an individual is placed in a new environment or when novel stimuli are introduced into a familiar environment. When the rate of the behavior has stabilized, adaptation has taken place.

Adaptation period The phase in a behavior-analysis program during which *adaptation* (q.v.) takes place.

Adjusting schedule A schedule that changes according to some feature of the subject's performance. For example, a ratio requirement might be raised gradually as long as the ratio was completed within a given period of time. However, if pausing exceeded a given duration the ratio would be reduced. This procedure is continued until the behavior reaches some predetermined criterion.

Advocate An advocate is the client's agent and not a person who is employed to serve as an agent of other individuals, an organization, or institution. Advocates, who may be community representatives such as clergymen, law students, a panel of interested citizens, and so on, consider the program goals and procedures in terms of what is best for the *individual* client and argue on the client's behalf.

Alt-R See Reinforcement of alternative behaviors; Reinforcement of incompatible behaviors.

Anecdotal recording See Narrative recording.

Antecedent stimulus A stimulus preceding a behavior that may or may not exert discriminative control over that behavior.

Applied behavior analysis An intervention derived from the principles of behavior analysis, designed to change behavior in a precisely measurable and accountable manner; restricted to those interventions that include an experimental design to assess treatment effects. See also Behavior modification.

Applied behavior-analysis program A program that includes the full behavior analysis model (see Table 7.1). It includes the behavioral objectives; the selection and application

This glossary was prepared in collaboration with Ellen P. Reese.

of valid and reliable measures; regular recording; the consistent application of selected procedures based upon principles of behavior; plus an experimental evaluation of results. An applied behavior-analysis is sometimes referred to as a *behavior-analysis program, behavioral program, behavior modification program,* or an *application of behavior analysis.*

Applied behavior analyst An individual who has demonstrated the professional competencies of designing, implementing, evaluating and communicating the results of an applied behavior-analysis program.

Applied research Research that is directed toward an analysis of the variables that can be effective in improving the behavior under study [1]. It is confined to the examination of behaviors that are socially important. Applied research is usually conducted in a natural setting rather than in the laboratory.

Artificial prompt A discriminative stimulus that is not usually present in the environment. Since artificial prompts are intrusive, they should be faded or gradually eliminated before the goal is judged to be achieved (e.g., verbal instructions as a student learns a new motor behavior).

Artificial reinforcer A reinforcer that is not usually present in the natural setting, or is not a natural consequence of the behavior. For example, trinket rewards would be artificial reinforcers in many school programs.

Autistic-like behavior Nonfunctional, destructive, or otherwise maladaptive ritualized behaviors that some children persistently emit, often to the exclusion of adaptive behaviors (i.e., rocking, head banging, stereotyped hand movements). Youngsters who have severely delayed social repertoires but age-appropriate or superior motor skills, who have no identifiable physical or central nervous system impairment, and who emit high rates of autistic-like behavior are often labeled *autistic.*

Aversive stimulus A stimulus, also called a *punisher,* that has the effect of decreasing the strength (e.g., rate) of a behavior when it is presented as a consequence of (contingent upon) that behavior; a stimulus that the individual will actively work to avoid. A stimulus, the contingent removal of which results in an increase in the rate of the dependent variable. Nontechnically: an unpleasant object, or event. *See also* Negative reinforcer; Punishing stimulus.

Avoidance behavior A behavior that increases in rate when it postpones or avoids completely an aversive stimulus. Nontechnically: staying away from or doing something to keep from getting punished.

Back-up reinforcer An object or event that has already demonstrated its reinforcing effect on an individual. It is received in exchange for a specific number of tokens, points, or other exchangeable reinforcers.

Backward chaining procedure Effecting the development of a behavioral chain of responses by training the last response, element, or link in the chain first; the next to last, next; and so on until the entire chain is emitted as a single complex behavior.

Baseline The strength or level (e.g., rate, duration, latency) of behavior before an experimental variable or procedure is introduced. Baseline measures are continued until performance has stabilized and can be used as a basis of comparison to assess the effects of the experimental variable.

Basic research Research that is directed toward the discovery of the relation between any variables, usually by conducting experiments in the laboratory setting rather than in the field. The solution of practical problems is generally not the purpose of basic research.

Behavior Any observable and measurable external or internal act of an organism. A response. *See also* Response.

Behavior-analysis procedures Interventions that are used to bring about behavioral change through the application of behavioral principles. Behavioral procedures are used to increase, teach, maintain, extend, restrict, inhibit, occasion, or reduce behaviors. They serve as the core of most applied behavior-analysis programs.

Behavioral contract The goals and procedures of a behavior-analysis program, mutually agreed upon by the client and other involved persons, and modifiable by joint agreement. Also called a *contingency contract.*

Behavioral contrast   If behavior has been maintained in two (or more) situations, and a procedure that decreases behavior is introduced into one of these situations, the behavior may increase in the other situation(s). This occurs even though there has been no other change in the contingencies. This increase in one situation that accompanies a decrease in another is called (positive) behavior contrast.

Behavioral dimensions   Measurable descriptive characteristics of a behavior such as number of occurrences, intensity, duration, topography, and accuracy.

Behavioral law   An empirically derived statement of the relation between some behavior and the one or more variables that control it. To be considered a law the relation must have generality. The principle of immediacy of reinforcement has been demonstrated repeatedly with many individuals performing many classes of behavior under many conditions. It can therefore be considered a law of behavior.

Behavioral measurement   *See* Precise behavioral measurement.

Behavioral objective   A precise specification of the goal, including three essential elements: (1) behavior; (2) the situation or conditions under which it is to occur; and (3) the standard of acceptability or *criterion* level.

Behavioral principles   *See* Principles of behavior.

Behavioral technicians   Auxiliary workers such as observers and data recorders, whose services may be required to conduct some of the technical aspects of a behavior-analysis program.

Behavior modification   Interventions derived from the principles of behavior analysis. Designed to change behavior in a precisely measurable manner; often used interchangeably with the terms *applied behavior analysis* and *behavior therapy.* However, applied behavior analysis is restricted to those interventions that include an experimental design to assess treatment effects. Behavior modification and behavior therapy are often comprised of only three phases: (1) baseline; (2) treatment; (3) follow-up. When respondent procedures are emphasized, one tends to use the term *behavior therapy.*

Bonus response cost   *See* Response cost.

Bonus time   A group contingency package that capitalizes on the Premack principle. Time to engage in reinforcing activities is made available contingent on the occurrence of desired behavior(s).

Chain   Two or more behaviors that occur in a definite order within a behavioral sequence.

Chaining procedure   A procedure in which simple responses already in the repertoire of the individual are reinforced in sequence to form more complex behaviors.

Changing criterion design   An applied behavior-analysis design that involves successively changing the criterion for consequation, usually in graduated steps from baseline levels to a desired terminal goal. Experimental control is demonstrated if the behavior changes to meet or approximate each successively set criterion level. It is usually best to vary the number of sessions among criterion levels to more clearly demonstrate that the behavior remains at, or close to, the criterion level. A replication across subjects, again varying the duration of criterion levels, would provide further evidence of a functional relation between the intervention and the dependent variable.

Clients   Individuals whose behavior is the subject of the behavior-analysis program. In this text the term client often is used in place of *subject* and *patient.*

Coded interval recording sheet   An observation form, with letter codes for each behavior of concern designated upon it, allowing for the simultaneous recording of several behaviors. The presence or absence of each behavior is scored by making a slash mark through the letter that stands for that behavior. This form can be used with one or more subjects.

Coercion   The use of threats, oppressive contingencies, or disproportionately powerful incentives. Coersion emerges as incentives and threats gain strength, and the client becomes progressively less involved with goal selection.

Complete stimulus control   *See* Stimulus control, complete.

Complex behavior   Behavior consisting of two or more subsets of responses. (Almost all the behaviors with which human service practitioners are concerned are complex behaviors.)

Compliment meter   *See* Warm fuzzies.

Conditioned aversive stimulus (S^p)   A stimulus initially having no aversive properties, but that acquires aversive properties as a result of repeatedly accompanying or being presented just prior to or accompanying (1) the absence or withdrawal of reinforcers or (2) the delivery of unconditioned or other conditioned aversive stimuli.

Conditioned reinforcer (S^r)   A stimulus that initially has no reinforcing properties but, through frequent pairings with unconditioned or strong conditioned reinforcers, has acquired reinforcing properties.

Confounding variables   Variables that introduce ambiguity into an experimental study. Such variables make it impossible to evaluate precisely the effects of the independent variable. *See also* Environmental confounding variables; Subject confounding variables; Task confounding variables.

Contingencies   The specified dependencies between behavior and its antecedents and consequences. Contingencies can occur naturally or can be arranged as stimuli are presented, withdrawn, or withheld by people to affect either their own behavior or the behavior of others.

Contingency analysis   *See* Sequence analysis.

Contingency bank   A reinforcement system. Clients are given plastic laminated checks for appropriate behavior. The checks can be cashed at the appropriate time for varying minutes of bank time. The contingency bank contains the pooled reinforcing activities of the participating groups.

Contingency control   The ability to manipulate the environmental antecedents and consequences of a given behavior in order to achieve a specific behavioral goal.

Contingency managers   Individuals—parents, nurses, teachers, counselors, therapists, the clients themselves—who conduct the day to day operation of a behavioral program by systematically applying behavioral strategies or procedures to influence the client's behavior.

Contingency (game) table   A reinforcing contingency package. The contingency table contains a wide assortment of reinforcing activities. Clients are permitted to go to the table, either individually or in groups, whenever a predetermined criterion is met.

Contingent observation   A reductive procedure that contains elements of timeout. The individual is placed a few feet away from the reinforcing activity so that observation is possible but participation is not. (Used as a mild form of timeout.) *See also* Timeout.

Contingent reinforcement   A reinforcing event that occurs only as a consequence of the specified behavior.

Continuous reinforcement (CRF)   A schedule of reinforcement in which each occurrence of a response is reinforced.

Continuous response   A response that does not have a clearly discriminable beginning or end. Pouting, smiling, oriented toward, and other behaviors are often treated as continuous responses because it is difficult to determine when the behavior begins and terminates.

Control   The condition that exists when there is a *functional relation* between a performance and a particular event or independent variable. For example, if a child usually or consistently asks for ice cream while driving past the local ice cream stand, the response, requesting ice cream, is "controlled" by the antecedent event, passing the ice cream stand.

Countercontrol   The action taken by an individual in response to powerful or perhaps troublesome control by others. When both individuals are able to arrange contingencies that strongly effect each other's behavior, reciprocity may develop. However, when contingency control is primarily available to only one member of the pair, countercontrol will be weak and coercion or exploitation may occur. In such instances social regulations may be necessary to protect the rights of clients.

Criterion level   The standard used to indicate when the behavioral goal has been reached. A specification of an acceptable level of performance that the client is to achieve. Criteria are used to evaluate the success of a given behavior-analysis program.

Daily report card   A contingency arrangement between the key individuals in two settings: the home and the school, the school and the residential cottage, and so on. It is designed to coordinate the contingencies provided in the two settings. In one setting a consequence, such as a mark on a card, is delivered contingent upon the target behavior. The report is sent each day to the second setting, where a delayed consequence is presented.

Dependent behavior   The behavior being modified. In this text the term is used interchangeably with *Dependent variable.*

Dependent variable   A variable that is measured while another variable (the independent variable) is changed in a systematic way. When changes in the independent variable are accompanied by changes in the dependent variable, we say that the two are functionally related—that the level or value of the dependent variable is in fact dependent upon the level or value of the independent variable. In behavior analysis the dependent variable is usually behavior, and the independent variable is some condition that may affect the level of that behavior. *See also* Independent variable; Dependent behavior.

Deprivation   The withholding of a reinforcer for a period of time or the reduction of its availability, designed to increase the effectiveness of the reinforcer.

Differential reinforcement   (1) the reinforcement of one class (or form or topography) of behavior and not another; (2) the reinforcement of a response under one stimulus condition but not under another stimulus condition. Also, the reinforcement of one response under one stimulus condition while *other* responses are reinforced under different stimulus conditions.

Differential reinforcement of high rates (DRH)   A schedule that involves the selective contingent reinforcement of a grouping of responses that occur in rapid succession. High rates are differentially reinforced while low rates are not.

Differential reinforcement of low rates (DRL)   A schedule that involves the selected reinforcement of responses that occur at or below some predetermined rate. Low rates are differentially reinforced while high rates are not. "The rates upon which the decision as to reinforce or not is made may be 'averaged rates' taken as the average rate of responding over a specific interval, or 'operant-to-operant' rates, in which each interval between the initiation of one response and the next is measured and analyzed for the low-rate property." (5) The latter of these two methods selectively reinforces responses that are relatively far apart in time. While it is considerably harder to measure and analyze, it is the more effective means of the two for rapidly obtaining low rates of responding.

Differential reinforcement of other behaviors (DRO)   A procedure in which the occurrence of a particular class of behavior postpones delivery of reinforcement. Thus, the individual receives scheduled reinforcement *except* when engaging in the specified behavior. This procedure, which is also called *omission training*, usually results in a decrease of the specified behavior.

Direct observational recording   A method, sometimes called *observational recording*, in which a human observer records behavioral data as it occurs. Event and time sampling are both observational recording systems.

Discrete response   A behavior that has a clearly discriminable beginning and end. Lever presses, sneezes, and written answers to addition problems are examples of discrete responses.

Discrimination   The restriction of responding to certain stimulus situations and not others.

Discrimination may be established by the differential reinforcement (q.v.) of responding in one stimulus situation and the extinction or punishment of that response in other situations, or by the reinforcement of other behavior in the other situations.

Discriminative stimuli S^D—A stimulus in the presence of which a given response is likely to be reinforced. An S^D operates to "occasion" a particular response in that it signals the likelihood of reinforcement. S^Δ—A stimulus in the presence of which a given response is not reinforced. An S^Δ signals nonreinforcement and functions to "inhibit" or "suppress" the response. S^{D-}—A stimulus in the presence of which a given response is likely to be consequated with punishment, timeout, or response cost. An S^{D-} signals the likelihood of an aversive consequence and functions to "inhibit" or "suppress" the response. Stimuli are said to be discriminative when, after several pairings with consequential stimuli, their presentation or removal is accompanied by reliable changes in the rate of response.

Duration recording Recording the elapsed time during which an event occurs. For example, an observer could record the amount of time a youth spends on a task or talks on the phone.

Elicit In respondent or classical conditioning of reflexes, a verb that denotes the effect of a conditioned or unconditioned stimulus upon a conditioned or unconditioned response. In describing the salivary reflex of a dog, we would say that meat *elicits* salivation. Following conditioning, another stimulus, such as a tone, might also elicit salivation.

Emit In operant conditioning, a verb that describes the occurrence of behavior in the absence of any known eliciting stimulus.

Environmental confounding variables Environmental confounding variables do not include subject characteristics, apparatus, or other treatment variables. They are uncontrolled environmental variables that change concurrently with the independent variable. An example might be a change in seating during each phase of a reversal experimental design. Under such conditions, it is difficult to unambiguously evaluate the effects of the independent variable.

Errorless discrimination training Teaching the acquisition of a discrimination by carefully arranging a sequence of discriminative stimuli so that only correct responses are occasioned.

Ethical responsibility Operating according to ethical precepts: providing for voluntariness, informed consent, least intrusive and least restrictive, and most benign, effective procedures; obtaining, maintaining, and continuing development of competence, and so on.

Event recording An observational recording procedure in which one records the number of occurrences of a specified discrete behavior, such as times tardy, answers correct, or bites received by sibling, over a specified period of time. The interval may be, for instance, a classroom period, a day, or the duration of a meal or of a TV program.

Experimental analysis of behavior A scientific analysis designed to discover the functional relation between behavior and the variables that control it.

Experimental design An aspect of an experiment that is directed toward the control of confounding variables (experimental control). Several single-subject (within-subject) designs may be employed to demonstrate the existence of a functional relation between the dependent variable (the *dependent behavior*) and the independent variable (the *intervention* or *procedure*).

Extinction A procedure in which the reinforcement of a previously reinforced behavior is discontinued. In nontechnical language, extinction is often referred to as the appropriate withholding of rewards or attention or as the nonrecognition of behaviors that interfere with learning or development.

Extinction-induced aggression The aggressive behavior that often accompanies the early phases of an extinction program in the absence of any other identifiable precipitating events.

Fading The gradual removal of (usually artificial or intrusive) discriminative stimuli such as directions, imitative prompts, physical guidance, and other cues and prompts. In nontechnical terms, fading is used to foster independence from auxiliary stimulus control that may be necessary during the early stages of learning. It facilitates the "assumption of responsibility." Constant reminders and suggestions are no longer required.

Fixed-interval (FI) schedule *See* Interval schedules of reinforcement.

Fixed-ratio (FR) schedule *See* Ratio schedules of reinforcement.

Forward chaining Effecting the development of a behavioral chain of responses by training the first response or link in the chain first, the second next, and so on until the entire chain is emitted as a unitary complex behavior.

FR *See* Ratio schedules of reinforcement.

Frequency The number of times a behavior occurs. Usually expressed in relation to a given period of time.

Functional relation A lawful relation between values of two variables. In behavior analysis, a dependent variable (behavior) and a given independent variable (intervention or procedure) are *functionally related* if the dependent variable changes systematically with changes in the value of the independent variable. For example the greater the intensity of the aversive stimulus, the greater the response suppression.

Fuzzy-grams *See* Warm Fuzzies.

Generality effect of overcorrection When an overcorrection procedure reduces not only the behavior for which it was developed, but also topographically dissimilar behaviors.

Generalization, response (Induction) The spread of effects to other classes of behavior when one class of behavior is modified by reinforcement, extinction, and so on. For instance, reinforcement of a particular writing response may be accompanied by other writing responses that are similar but not identical to the reinforced response.

Generalization, stimulus The spread of effects to other stimulus situations when behavior is modified, reinforced, punished, and so on, in the presence of one stimulus situation. Generalization occurs when stimulus control is absent or incomplete (the child who calls all quadrupeds "doggie" is generalizing).

Generalization training A procedure designed to occasion in another stimulus situation a behavior emitted in one stimulus situation. Teaching the application of skills learned in one setting (i.e., clinic, school) in other settings (i.e. home, community). Programming for stimulus generalization.

Generalized reinforcer A conditioned reinforcer that is effective for a wide range of behaviors as a result of having been paired with a variety of previously established reinforcers. Due to this history, its effectiveness does not depend upon any one state of deprivation. Money is a generalized reinforcer. It has been paired with (and can purchase) a variety of other reinforcers.

Goal The goal tells you how the target behavior is to be changed: increased, decreased, maintained, developed, expanded, or restricted. It should be translated into a set of behavioral objectives prior to designing a program.

Good Behavior Game A group contingency package. The group is divided into two or more teams. Rules are specified. Originally, teams received a check against them if a members violated one of the rules. Reinforcers were provided for teams with less than the criterion number of marks or the team with the fewest marks at the end of a preset period. However, the Good Behavior Game can involve reinforcing consequences as well as response cost, providing points exchangeable for reinforcers for a team when members act according to the rules.

Graduated guidance The combined use of physical guidance and fading. A systematic, gradual reduction of physical guidance.

Home reports A contingency package designed to coordinate the contingencies provided in service facilities with those in the home, or to inform parents of the individual's positive progress. Daily reports, such as the daily report card, can be sent from those in one setting to the key individuals in another. Or, positive messages can be sent informing the key individuals of the client's progress. *See also* Daily report card.

Imitation   Matching the behavior of a model, or engaging in a behavior similar to that observed.

Imitative prompt   A discriminative stimulus. Behavior by a model designed to occasion an imitative response.

Incompatible behavior   A specific alternative response (Alt-R) or behavior that cannot be emitted simultaneously with another behavior. Behavior that interferes with the emission of specified other behavior.

Independent variable   The variable that is manipulated. In behavior analysis, the independent variable is often a behavioral procedure or package or other intervention or treatment program.

Indirect observation   A method of obtaining behavioral data that relies on self reports or on "memory" of what occurred, such as interviews or questionnaires. The behavior is not objectively recorded as it occurs.

Informed consent   In human services such as applied behavior analysis, clients (or their advocates) and/or parents and caretakers have the right to be informed about proposed outcomes and procedures and their advantages and disadvantages, and to participate in the selection or rejection of specific goals and procedures. This information must be communicated at a level that will be understood by the client if consent or rejection is to be considered "informed."

Inhibiting stimuli   Antecedent stimuli that signal nonreinforcement or an aversive consequence for a particular behavior. In this book these are the S^Δ and S^{D-} discriminative stimuli (suppressing stimuli).

Intensive designs   *See* Within-subject experimental designs.

Intermittent reinforcement   A schedule of reinforcement in which some, but not all, of the occurrences of a response are reinforced.

Inter-observer agreement assessment   A method for estimating the reliability of a behavioral observational system. Two or more independent observers compare the number of times they agreed in proportion to the number of observations they scored.

Interval schedules of reinforcement   A schedule in which reinforcement is made contingent upon the passage of *time* before the response is reinforced. (a) *Fixed interval (FI) schedule* —When a particular response following the passage of a specific constant amount of time is scheduled for reinforcement. For example, an FI 3 indicates that reinforcement follows the first occurrence of the *response* after three minutes have passed. (b) *Variable interval (VI) schedule*—When a variable time interval must occur prior to the reinforced response. The time interval has a specific average and usually varies within a specified range. For example, a VI 6 indicates that an average of six minutes passes before the *response* receives contingent reinforcement.

Intrinsic motivation   A term that is used to describe the phenomenon that some behavior is emitted at high rates in the absence of observable or extrinsic reinforcing consequences; presumably emitting the behavior is itself reinforcing.

Latency   The interval between the onset or presentation of the discriminative stimulus and the emission of the behavior it controls.

Learning   Any enduring change in behavior produced as a function of the interaction between the behavior and the environment. Often used to describe physical or cognitive skills, but also may refer to social, personal, and other behavioral categories.

Learning history   The sum of an individual's behaviors that have been conditioned or modified as a function of environmental events.

Limited hold   A restriction placed on a schedule requiring that the response eligible for reinforcement be emitted within a particular time limit or reinforcement will not be made available.

Link The response, or performance, that is combined with others in the development of a behavioral chain.

Maintenance procedures Applying schedules of reinforcement, altering reinforcers, and fading artificial prompts to promote the persistence of behaviors under natural environmental conditions.

Matching-to-sample A task in which the client selects from two or more alternatives the stimulus that matches or corresponds to a standard or sample.

Model The person whose behavior is imitated.

Modeling procedure A stimulus control procedure that uses demonstrations or modeling to prompt an imitative response (the *"show" procedure*).

Momentary time sampling A time sampling procedure that records a response only if it is occurring at the moment the interval terminates. For example, a timer goes off at the end of a ten-minute interval. The observer checks to see if Josh has his thumb in his mouth *at that moment.*

Multielement design A within-subject experimental design that involves presenting experimental and baseline conditions in alternation independent of changes in the dependent behavior. Different procedures, each correlated with a specific stimulus, are successively applied to the behavior. The effects of the treatment procedure(s) are then observed by comparing differential performances. For example, one might wish to analyze the function of three contingencies on a task completion: Treatment A=no extra recess; Treatment B= extra recess time with planned activities; Treatment C=extra recess time with free play. The treatments could be alternated from day to day. Assuming that the students had information available about the conditions to be in effect (A, B, or C) on any given day, the effects of each on task completion could be compared and evaluated after several weeks of implementing the experimental comparison.

Multiple-baseline designs A within-subject experimental design that attempts to replicate the effects of a procedure (treatment or intervention) across (1) different subjects, (2) different settings, or (3) different classes of behavior. The intervention is introduced independently to each subject (or setting or class of behavior) in succession. *See also* Across-behaviors multiple-baseline; Across-subjects multiple-baseline; Across-situations multiple-baseline; Within-subject experimental design.

Narrative recording A written running account of behavior in progress. The events are then ordered into a *sequence analysis* that specifies the behavior and its antecedents and consequences.

Natural reinforcer A nonintrusive reinforcer that is not artificially introduced. It is present in the natural environment. A smile or a good mark is usually a natural reinforcer in a school setting.

Negative reinforcement A procedure that involves the removal of an aversive stimulus as a consequence of a response and results in the maintenance or an increased rate of the behavior. A behavior has been negatively reinforced if it *increases* or is *maintained* due to the contingent *removal* or reduction of a stimulus. This procedure is sometimes referred to as *escape conditioning.* For example, when the child does as asked, the adult stops nagging. The child's behavior, doing as requested, has been negatively reinforced by the removal of the nagging.

Negative reinforcer A stimulus that, when removed or reduced as a consequence of a response, results in an *increase* or *maintenance* of that response. *See also* Aversive stimulus, which is used in this text in place of the term *negative reinforcer.*

Neutral stimulus An object or event that is neutral with respect to some property that it may later acquire. It does not reliably affect behavior in a particular context until it has been paired sufficiently often with some event that does have controlling properties (i.e., it has not yet developed into an S^D, reinforcer, etc.).

Objective measurement   Recording behavioral data unbiased by the observer's feelings or interpretations.

Occasion   To increase the likelihood of the emission of a response by arranging prior stimulus conditions. It is also used as an action verb in reference to operant behavior, where the response bears a probabilistic relationship (not a one-to-one relationship, as with *elicit*) to the occurrence of the S^D.

Omission training   *See* Differential reinforcement of other behaviors (DRO).

Operant behavior   Behavior whose rate or probability of occurrence is controlled (at least in part) by its consequences.

Operant level   The strength (e.g., rate, duration of behavior) prior to any known conditioning. (Baseline, which subsumes operant level, refers to the strength of behavior before the introduction of an experimental variable, but does not preclude earlier conditioning.)

Operational definition   The product of breaking down a broad concept, such as "aggressive," into its *observable* and *measurable* component behaviors (frequency of hitting or biting others, duration of scream, and so on).

Ordinate   The vertical axis on a graph. In behavior analysis, the response measure (e.g., frequency) usually is plotted on the ordinate.

Overcorrection   A reductive procedure consisting of two basic components.   (1) *Restitutional overcorrection* (or Restitutional procedure) requires the individual to restore the environment to a state vastly improved from that which existed prior to the act. (2) *Positive-practice overcorrection* (or Positive-practice procedure) requires the individual to repeatedly practice a positive behavior. When no environmental disruption occurs only the positive-practice procedure is used.

Partial-interval time sampling   A time sampling procedure (often labelled *interval recording* alone) that records the presence of the response when the response occurs even momentarily during the interval. The response need not occur throughout the entire interval as in *whole-interval* time sampling. Sometimes called *interval spoilage*, since any instance of the behavior "spoils" the interval.

Personalized system of instruction (PSI)   A method of teaching that is usually characterized by:

"(1) The go-at-your-own-pace feature, *which permits a student to move through the course at a speed commensurate with his ability and other demands upon his time.*

"(2) The unit-perfection requirement for advance, *which lets the student go ahead to new material only after demonstrating mastery of that which preceded.*

"(3) The use of lectures and demonstrations as vehicles of motivation, *rather than sources of critical information.*

"(4) The *related* stress upon the written word *in teacher-student communication;* and, finally:

"(5) The use of proctors, *which permits repeated testing, immediate scoring, almost unavoidable tutoring, and a marked enhancement of the personal-social aspect of the educational process."* [3]

Physical guidance   A form of response priming in which the appropriate body part or parts are "put through" or physically guided through the proper motion. For example, a swimming coach guiding the movement of a youth's arm to demonstrate the proper stroke is using the physical guidance procedure.

Positive practice (overcorrection)   *See* Overcorrection.

Positive reinforcement   A procedure that maintains or increases the rate of a response by contingently presenting a stimulus (a positive reinforcer) following the response.

Positive reinforcer   When a *stimulus*, such as an object or event, follows or is presented as a consequence of a response, and the rate of that response increases or maintains as a result, the stimulus is called a *positive reinforcer*. Praise, attention, recognition of achievement and effort, special events, and activities are positive reinforcers for many people. Nontechnical terms for a positive reinforcer include incentives, rewards, or "strokes."

Praise   *See* Specific praise; Positive reinforcer.

Precise behavioral measurement   The selection and implementation of accurate, clearly defined operations for recording and quantifying behavior. Precise measurement allows change to be measured and evaluated unambiguously.

Premack principle   A principle which states that contingent access to high frequency behaviors ("preferred" activities) serves as a reinforcer for the performance of low frequency behaviors.

Principles of behavior   Lawful relations between behavior and the variables that control it, discovered through experimental studies or analyses of behavior. They are used to predict future behavioral occurrences because the relations have been found to apply under many conditions and among many individuals and groups with different characteristics.

Probe   A phase in a behavior analysis experiment designed to test the effect of a given intervention. A *reversal* is a probe since it removes the intervention for a period of time to test behavior in the absence of the intervention.

Programmed instruction   The selection and arrangement of educational content based on principles of human learning. (4)

Prompt   An auxiliary discriminative stimulus presented in order to occasion a given response. Prompts are usually faded before the terminal goal is judged to have been achieved. (For example, "2+2 are ff—." The ff sound must be fade to judge that the student has achieved the goal of knowing how to add 2+2.)

Punishing stimulus   A stimulus, when presented immediately following a response, results in a *reduction* in the rate of the response. It this text the term *aversive stimulus* is used interchangeably with *punisher* or *punishing stimulus*.

Punishment   A procedure in which an aversive stimulus is presented immediately following a response, resulting in a reduction in the rate of the response.

Qualitative praise   The delivery of praise paired with the rationale or reason for its delivery. For example, rather than just saying "I like that" one would say "I like that because. . . ." This technique both reinforces a given behavior *and* assists the learner to form complex discriminations about the conditions under which the response is to be emitted. Often called *labeled* or *behavior-specific* praise.

Rate   The average frequency of behavior emitted during a standard unit of time. Formula: Number of responses divided by the number of time units. For example, if 20 responses occur in 5 minutes, the rate is 4 responses per minute.

Ratio schedules of reinforcement   A schedule in which reinforcement is made contingent upon the emission of a *number* of responses before one response is reinforced. (a) *Fixed ratio (FR) schedule*—When a constant number of responses must occur prior to the reinforced response. For example, an FR 3 schedule indicates that each third response is reinforced. (b) *Variable ratio (VR) schedule*—When a variable number of responses must occur prior to the reinforced response. The number of responses usually varies around a specified average. For example, a VR 6 means that an average of one of six performances is reinforced.

Ratio strain   A disruption in performance when ratio requirements are very high or are raised abruptly. An individual is said to be suffering from "ratio strain" when previously high rates of responding disintegrate. Ratio strain is avoided by increasing ratio requirements very gradually. It is treated by a temporary reduction in the ratio requirement.

Reactivity   The effect produced by experimental activities other than the independent variable. For example, just the presence of observers in the classroom may influence the dependent variable(s) or distort the validity of the data, as when a teacher uses more verbal praise than usual in the observer's presence. Reactivity is a *task confounding variable*.

Reinforcement   Arranging for the presentation of the reinforcing event or the removal of an aversive event to follow as a consequence of a behavior, resulting in an increase or maintenance of the behavior. Reinforcement is defined solely by the increasing or maintaining effect upon behavior. This book discusses two basic reinforcement procedures: *positive reinforcement* and *negative reinforcement*. Both increase or maintain behavior.

Reinforcement density   Frequency or rate with which responses are reinforced. The lower the ratio or shorter the interval required by a given reinforcement schedule, the denser the reinforcement.

Reinforcement history   *See* Learning history.

Reinforcement of alternative behavior or response (Alt-*R*)   A reinforcement procedure usually designed to reduce a given behavior by increasing specific behaviors that are alternatives to the behavior to be reduced.

Reinforcement of incompatible behaviors   A specific Alt-*R* procedure designed to increase the rate of a behavior or behaviors that cannot coexist with a behavior that has been targeted for reduction. For example, reinforcing the completion of work reduces those forms of disruption that are incompatible with working.

Reinforcement reserve   The unconsumed quantity of reinforcers in the possession of an individual or group. Frequently refers to a number of tokens or other exchangeable reinforcers.

Reinforcer   A stimulus contingent upon a behavior that increases or maintains the strength (rate, duration, etc.) of the behavior. A reinforcer is defined solely by the fact that it increases or maintains the behavior upon which it is contingent. *See also* Unconditioned; Conditioned; Edible; Tangible; and other classes of reinforcers.

Reinforcer sampling   A procedure that enables the client to come in contact with a reinforcer in order that the positive characteristics of the stimulus may be experienced. The procedure is useful in developing new reinforcing consequences for a given individual.

Reliable measurement   This occurs when the measuring device remains standard regardless of who uses it and under any conditions. It refers to the consistency of measurement. *See also* Reliability.

Reliability (inter-observer agreement)   A term used to refer to consistency of measurement. In applied behavior analysis it is often estimated by assessing the agreement between two or more independent data records. The agreement coefficient is often calculated as a percentage by dividing the number of agreements by the number of agreements plus disagreements, and then multiplying the fraction by one hundred. Agreement measures should be reported for each phase of a within-subject design when feasible. When estimating reliability of interval recording systems, only *scored* intervals should be included in the calculation.

Repertoire, behavioral   "The behavior that a particular organism, at a particular time, is capable of emitting, in the sense that the behavior exists at a nonzero operant level, has been shaped, or, if it has been extinguished, may be rapidly reconditioned." [2]

Replicate   To repeat an experimental procedure or finding.

Respondent behavior   A response that is elicited by antecedent stimuli; reflex behavior; an autonomic response that requires no previous learning, though such responses may be conditioned, as in Pavlov's famous experiments with the conditioning of dog's salivation responses. *See also* Elicit.

Response   A directly measurable behavior. Used interchangeably in this book with *behavior*.

Response chain   *See* Chain.

Response cost   A reductive procedure in which a specified amount of available reinforcers are contingently withdrawn following the response. Usually these reinforcers are withdrawn from the client's reserve, as with loss of points, yardage, or fines. However, in a modification of this procedure, *bonus response cost*, the reinforcers are taken away from a pool of potential bonus reinforcers that the client will receive if all are not withdrawn.

Restitutional overcorrection   *See* Overcorrection.

Reversal designs   An experimental design that involves the removal of the intervention in order to test its effect. For example, one frequently utilized reversal design involves: (1) obtaining a base rate of the target behavior; (2) applying the intervention or procedure;

(3) the reversal, a discontinuation of the intervention, and a reintroduction of the conditions in effect during the baseline period; and (4) a reapplication of the intervention. This design is used to determine whether or not the effect of the intervention can be replicated. (Often abbreviated, ABAB design.)

Satiation   The reduction in performance or reinforcer effectiveness that occurs after a large amount of that type of reinforcer has been delivered (usually within a short time period) following the emission of the behavior.

Schedule of reinforcement   The response requirements that determine when reinforcement will be delivered. See also Interval and Ratio schedules of reinforcement; Differentiation reinforcement of rates.

S^D, S^{D-}   See Discriminative stimuli.

S-delta   (S^Δ)   See Discriminative stimuli.

Self control   A self-management procedure in which individuals change some aspect of their own behavior. It generally involves four major components: (1) self-selection of goals; (2) monitoring own behavior; (3) selection of procedures; and (4) implementation of procedures.

Sequence analysis   A description of an individual's behaviors, and the events that appear to precede and follow those behaviors. Used to provide clues about the possible functional properties of various stimulus conditions.

Shaping   A procedure through which new behaviors are developed; the systematic reinforcement of *successive approximations* toward the behavioral objective. Sometimes PSI or individualized instruction is referred to as shaping.

"Show" procedure   See Modeling procedure.

Single-subject designs   See Within-subject experimental designs.

Social reinforcer   A reinforcing stimulus mediated by another individual within a social context. Praise (e.g., "That's a good job.") usually functions as a social reinforcer.

Specific praise   See Qualitative praise.

Spontaneous recovery   The reappearance, following an extinction procedure, of a response that had not been emitted for an extended time interval.

S^r   See Conditioned reinforcer; Reinforcement; Positive reinforcer.

S^R   See Unconditioned reinforcer.

Step size   The number of new responses in the subset, or the extensiveness of the change in topography that constitutes a *successive approximation* in a specific shaping procedure.

Stimulus   A physical object or event that does or *may* have an effect upon the behavior of an individual. Stimuli may be internal or external to the individual. Stimuli frequently arranged in behavior analysis programs include *reinforcing stimuli, aversive stimuli*, and *discriminative stimuli*.

Stimulus control   Stimulus control is said to occur when the antecedent stimulus systematically affects the probability of occurrence of the response. Thus, the response form or frequency is different under one "controlling" stimulus, or set of stimuli, then another. These controlling stimuli are referred to as *discriminative stimuli*. See also Discriminative stimuli.

Stimulus control, complete   An object or event is said to have complete stimulus control over a behavior when the emission of the behavior is very highly probable in its presence and very highly improbable in its absence.

Stimulus generalization   See Generalization, stimulus.

Stimulus presentation procedure   Presenting a discriminative stimulus to influence the probability of occurrence of the response.

Stimulus property   An attribute of the stimulus such as topography, texture, volume, size, intensity, and so on.

Subject confounding variables   Subject characteristics (demographic, learning history, present behaviors, etc.) that have not been controlled in an experiment but may affect changes in the dependent variable. Within-subject designs control for subject confounding variables by comparing the subject's performance under one condition with that under other conditions.

Subset of behavior   The group of simpler response components that form a more complex behavior.

Successive approximations   Behavioral elements or subsets, each of which more and more closely resembles the specified terminal behavior.

Supplementary reinforcers   Reinforcers used in addition to the major contingent reinforcer.

Target behavior   The behavior to be changed. In this book the term often is used interchangeably with "dependent variable or behavior."

Task analysis   Breaking down a complex skill or behavioral chain into its component behaviors, sub-skills, or sub-tasks. Each component is stated in its order of occurrence and sets the occasion for the occurrence of the next behavior. Task analyses are particularly useful in planning specific stimulus control and chaining procedures.

Task confounding variables   Stimuli associated with the behavioral procedure or treatment which, because they have not been controlled, may affect changes in the dependent variable. For example, tokens delivered by a teacher may result in *confounding* teacher attention with the token delivery.

"Tell" procedure   A stimulus control procedure that uses verbal or written instructions to prompt a response under appropriate conditions so that reinforcement may be delivered.

Terminal behavior   The behavior that is achieved at the end of a behavior-analysis program. The terminal behavior is described according to all its relevant behavioral dimensions and is usually assigned a criterion by which an acceptable level of performance is to be judged. Often used interchangeably with *behavioral* or *instructional objective, goal* and *target behavior.*

Timeout (TO)   A procedure in which the means of access to the sources of various forms of reinforcement are removed for a particular time period contingent upon the emission of a response. The opportunity to receive reinforcement is contingently removed for a specified time. Either the behaving individual is contingently removed from the reinforcing environment or the reinforcing environment is contingently removed for some stipulated duration.

Timeout room; timeout booth; quiet place   A facility that is arranged to minimize the reinforcement that an individual is apt to receive during a fixed time period. Procedures for using such facilities must conform to ethical and legal requirements.

Time sampling   A direct observational procedure in which the presence or absence of specific behaviors, within short uniform time intervals, are recorded. For example, an observer may observe for 10 seconds and record during the following 5 seconds the occurrence or nonoccurrence of the behavior. This procedure may continue for a specific 30-minute period each day. There are several time sampling variations: (1) *whole-interval time sampling,* (2) *partial-interval time sampling,* and (3) *momentary time sampling.*

Token economy   A contingency package. Tokens (exchangeable reinforcers) are given as soon as possible following the emission of a target response. The tokens are later exchangeable for a reinforcing object or event.

Token reinforcer   A symbol or object (check marks, poker chips) that can be exchanged at a later time for a "back-up reinforcer"—an item or activity. For example, money is a token. The extent to which tokens are reinforcing depends on the individual's experience and on the back-up items available. An *exchangeable reinforcer.*

Topography of response   The configuration or form of a response. (To determine the correct topography of a behavior, photograph an expert performing the behavior.)

Treatment   The behavioral procedures, intervention, or independent variable(s) being applied.

Treatment phase   The period of time during which the intervention is in effect.

Unconditioned aversive stimulus (S^p)   A stimulus object or event, such as a painful electric shock, a bee sting, or a sudden loud noise, that functions aversively in the absence of any prior learning history (i.e., its contigent occurrence is punishing).

Unconditioned reinforcer (S^R)   A stimulus, such as food, water, or sex, that is usually reinforcing in the absence of any prior learning history.

Valid measures   Measures that actually do measure what they are presumed to measure, without distortion.

Variable   Any behavior or condition in the individual's internal or external environment that may assume any one of a set of values. *See also* Independent variable; Dependent variable.

Variable-interval (VI) schedules   *See* Interval schedules of reinforcement.

Variable-ratio (VR) schedules   *See* Ratio schedules of reinforcement.

Voluntariness   The degree to which an individual agrees with a behavioral goal or program in the absence of coercion. Voluntariness is presumed to be present when the individual chooses and/or initiates action towards a goal in the absence of strong threats or unusually powerful incentives.

Warm fuzzies and compliment meters   A group contingency package that encourages peers to reinforce one another. Individuals write compliments to one another on a piece of paper called a fuzzy-gram. The number of compliments are counted and the total is added to a figure that looks like a large thermometer, called a compliment meter. When the group reaches a predetermined goal on the compliment meter the members receive a reinforcer.

Whole-interval time sampling   A time sampling procedure, often referred to simply as interval recording, that requires the response to be emitted throughout the entire interval for its presence to be scored. *See also* Time sampling.

Within-subject experimental designs   Research designs, sometimes referred to as *intensive designs,* developed to unambiguously evaluate the effects of the independent variable on the behavior of a single organism. *See also* Experimental design; Reversal design; Multiple baseline design; Changing criterion design; Multielement design.

X-axis   *See* Abscissa.

Y-axis   *See* Ordinate.

GLOSSARY FOOTNOTES

[1] Baer, D. M., Wolf, M. M., and Risley, T. R. Some current dimensions of applied behavior analysis. *Journal of Applied Behavior Analysis,* 1968, **1,** 91–97.

[2] Catania, A. C. *Contemporary research in operant behavior.* Glenview, Ill.: Scott, Foresman, 1968.

[3] Keller, F. S. Good-bye teacher. *Journal of Applied Behavior Analysis,* 1968, **1,** 79–89.

[4] Taber, J. K., Glaser, R., and Shaefer, H. *Learning and programmed instruction.* Reading, Mass.: Addison-Wesley, 1965.

[5] White, O. R. *A glossary of behavioral terminology,* Champaign, Ill.: Research Press, 1971.

Acker, L. E., 475
Agras, W. S., 234
Aikins, D. A., 208, 217
Alexander, S. B., 382
Allen, G., 393, 405
Allen, E., 294
Allen, K. E., 125, 129, 160, 257, 266
Altman, K., 303
American Psychological Association, 33, 38, 482, 483, 486
Anderson, R. C., 45, 46, 47, 183, 187, 212, 217
Anton, J. L., 444, 445, 458
Appolini, T., 222, 234
Armstrong, P. M., 113, 129, 148
Arnold, C. R., 160
Arrington, R. E., 62, 76
Ashby, E., 39, 58, 235, 267, 279, 368, 385, 406, 442, 475
Atthowe, J. M., 392, 400, 405
Axelrod, S., 127, 129, 160
Ayllon, T., 4, 10, 28, 85, 96, 99, 106, 116, 117, 118, 129, 138, 145, 264, 266, 289, 293, 385, 392, 405, 449, 457
Azrin, N. H., 4, 10, 85, 98, 109, 113, 116, 117, 125, 138, 142, 145, 151, 160, 206, 217, 222, 231, 235, 270, 272, 278, 285, 289, 293, 294, 296, 297, 298, 299, 302, 303, 306, 309, 311, 312, 313, 316, 317, 318, 320, 321, 333, 344, 358, 359, 367, 385, 392, 405, 449, 457
Bachrach, A. J., 49, 58
Bacon, A., 503
Baer, A.M., 290, 293, 405
Baer, D. M., 4, 10, 20, 24, 28, 38, 44, 47, 52, 58, 84, 88, 95, 97, 98, 126, 129, 130, 131, 160, 191, 200, 218, 222, 234, 235, 246, 257, 266, 289, 290, 293, 305, 310, 322, 323, 326, 329, 330, 394, 405, 406, 437, 442, 444, 445, 446, 450, 457, 458, 466, 475, 493, 498
Bailey, H., 452, 453, 458
Bailey, J. S., 271, 279, 287, 290, 293, 316, 323, 376, 382
Ballard, K. D., 67, 68, 76
Bandura, A., 156, 160, 191, 192, 193, 200, 311, 318, 319, 320, 322
Barlow, D., 222, 234, 441, 442, 466, 475
Barnard, J. D., 298, 300, 303
Barnett, C. D., 333, 343
Baroff, G. S., 86, 97
Barrera, F., 271, 272, 279, 288, 293
Barrish, H. H., 255, 266, 308, 322, 370, 371, 382
Baskin, A., 119, 128, 130
Baydan, N.T., 287, 294
Becker, W. C., 4, 10, 148, 160, 161, 163, 165, 175, 185, 187, 204, 217
Bellack, B., 66, 72, 76
Benoit, R. B., 159, 160, 242, 246, 286, 292, 293
Berberich, J. P., 201
Berkowitz, L., 200, 201, 322
Berliner, D. C., 502

Bernal, G., 46, 47, 486
Bernal, M. E., 69, 70, 76
Bernhardt, A. J., 125, 129
Bernstein, D. A., 196, 200
Bibelheimer, M., 97, 382
Bijou, S. W., 131, 160, 234, 343, 358, 367, 385, 405, 444, 445, 457
Birnbrauer, J. S., 160, 278, 279, 405
Blackham, G. J., 119, 120
Block, B. L., 194, 201
Bloomfield, H. H., 222, 234
Blumenfeld, G. T., 355
Boisvert, J., 406
Bolstad, O. D., 70, 76
Bootzin, R. R., 326, 330, 385, 403, 405
Boozer, H., 85, 97, 126, 131
Boren, J. J., 275, 278, 358, 367
Borkovec, T. D., 196, 200
Born, D. G., 234
Bornstein, P. H., 4, 10, 99, 106
Bostow, D. E., 287, 290, 293, 355, 382
Bowly, L., 69
Braukman, C. J., 51, 58, 107, 235, 493, 498
Brechner, K. C., 70, 76
Brehm, J., 320, 322
Breyer, N. L., 393, 405
Briddell, D. W., 326, 331
Brigham, T. A., 118, 129, 267, 393, 405, 449, 457
Broden, M., 67, 68, 76, 91, 98, 119, 125, 129, 160
Broen, P., 271, 279
Brook, F. S., 118, 129
Brooks, B. D., 32, 38, 90, 98
Brown, B. S., 93, 96, 98, 128, 129
Brown, G. D., 283, 293
Brown, P., 148, 160
Brown, W. C., 235
Bruce, C., 129
Brush, M. E., 77
Bryan, K. S., 208, 217
Bryant, R., 46, 47, 71, 230, 235
Buchanan, C. D., 235
Bucher, B., 86, 98
Buckholdt, D., 38, 266
Buckley, N. K., 118, 128, 131, 327, 331, 406
Budd, K., 28, 38, 84, 88, 98, 289, 290, 293, 305, 310, 322, 394, 405
Buell, J. S., 129, 160, 266
Bugle, C., 222, 231, 235
Burchard, J. D., 271, 272, 279, 288, 293
Burgess, H., 475
Burgess, R. L., 4, 10
Burnett, J., 187
Burton, R. V., 148, 161
Bushell, D., 4, 10, 99, 106, 118, 119, 120, 129, 393, 405
Butcher, B., 275, 279
Butterfield, W. H., 310, 322
Butterworth, T. W., 371, 382
Byrne, B., 191, 201, 382
Byrne, M. J., 97
Campbell, A., 57, 58, 109, 120,

129, 388, 390, 405
Campbell, S. L., 312, 323
Cantrell, M. L., 83, 98
Cantrell, R. P., 98
Cardozo, P., 391, 405
Carlson, C. S., 148, 160
Carlson, J. D., 204, 205, 217
Carsky, M., 54, 58, 239, 244, 246
Carter, V., 129
Catania, A. C., 100, 106, 267
Chadwick, B. A., 118, 129
Chalmers, D. K., 194, 201
Christopherson, E. R., 303
Christy, P. R., 114, 130, 257, 264, 266
Church, R. M., 307, 323
Clark, H. B., 129, 244, 246, 287, 290, 293
Clark, R. N., 4, 10
Clifford, C., 320, 323
Cody, J. J., 136, 145, 304, 323
Cohen, A. R., 320, 322
Cohen, H. L., 385, 390, 405
Coleman, A. D., 275, 278
Coleman, R. A., 111, 130
Cooke, T. P., 222, 234, 436, 442
Cooper, M. L., 126, 130
Conderman, L., 458
Cone, J. D., 503
Connecticut Civil Liberties Newsletter, 33, 38
Corey, J., 206, 217
Cormier, W. H., 128, 131
Corte, H. E., 329, 330
Cossairt, A., 85, 97, 126, 130, 337, 343, 454, 455, 456, 457
Craig, H. B., 111, 130
Craighead, W. E., 66, 70, 72, 76, 77
Creel, J., 406
Creel, L., 406
Creer, T. L., 99, 100, 107, 116, 131, 237, 243, 247, 472, 475
Croner, M. D., 194, 201
Csanyi, A. P., 32, 38, 382
Cunningham, C. E., 309, 323
Curtiss, K., 89, 97
Davidson, H. R., 320, 323
Davidson, N. A., 351, 355, 358, 364, 367
Davidson, P. O., 475
Davis, M. L., 234
Day, R. C., 118, 129
Dean, M., 58, 76
Debaca, P. C., 130
Deitz, S. M., 251, 252, 253, 256, 258, 266, 333, 343
DeReus, D. M., 99, 100, 107, 116, 131, 135, 145
Devine, J. V., 130
Diament, C., 77
Dinsmoor, J. A., 312, 323
Dockens, W. S., 10
Doke, L. A., 14, 24, 303
Dotson, V. A., 64, 76
Doty, D. W., 273, 275, 279
Drabman, R. S., 15, 25, 99, 100, 107, 116, 118, 119, 130, 131, 135, 145, 326, 331, 385, 405

Duker, J., 483, 486
Dunlap, A., 129
Eaton, M. D., 433, 442
Eggelston, D., 264, 265, 266
Elam, D., 127, 130, 391, 396, 405
Elliott, R., 148, 160
Ellis, N. R., 333, 343
Elmers, R. C., 99, 107
Engelmann, S., 163, 164, 175, 185, 187, 204, 217
Ennis, B. J., 289, 293
Epstein, L. H., 77, 301, 303
Erickson, L. M., 169, 170, 175, 185, 187
Etzel, B., 58, 218, 235, 266, 406
Euler, H. A., 475
Evans, M. B., 160
Farber, H., 9, 10, 68, 76
Fauke, J., 181, 187
Faust, G. W., 45, 46, 47, 183, 187
Feallock, R., 388, 405
Feingold, B. D., 105, 106
Ferri, H. J., 118, 130
Ferritor, D. E., 27, 38, 264, 266
Ferster, C. B., 256, 266, 281, 287, 289, 293, 294, 312, 323, 333, 343, 346, 348, 355, 357, 367
Filipczak, J., 385, 390, 405
Fixsen, D. L., 4, 10, 54, 58, 67, 68, 71, 76, 89, 91, 97, 107, 116, 131, 235, 279, 355, 385, 405, 406, 498
Fjellstedt, N., 185, 187
Flanders, N. A., 320, 323
Ford, L., 46, 47, 233, 235
Forehand, R., 125, 129
Foxx, R. M., 69, 76, 207, 217, 296, 297, 298, 299, 302, 303
Frankowsky, R. J., 127, 130, 388
Freitag, G., 86, 97
Freyman, D., 58, 76
Friedman, P. R., 289, 293
Gage, N., 502
Gallimore, R., 337, 344
Garcia, E., 329, 330
Garlinton, W. K., 475
Garton, K. L., 117, 130, 372, 382
Gary, A. L., 178, 187
Gelfand, D. M., 194, 201
Gentry, N. D., 442
Gibson, D. M., 76
Giles, D. K., 385, 388, 406
Ginsburg, R., 214, 218
Gladstone, B. W., 13, 24, 400, 405
Glaser, R., 197, 202, 224, 231, 235
Glass, D. C., 200
Gledhill, S. N., 234
Glover, J., 178, 187
Glynn, E. L., 67, 76, 91, 97
Glynn, T., 67, 68, 76
Goetz, E. M., 4, 10, 234, 257, 266, 450, 457
Gold, V. J., 86, 97
Goldiamond, I., 214, 217
Gonzales, M. A., 32, 38, 382
Goodenough, Florence, 21
Goodwin, D. L., 97
Gortney, C., 340, 344
Goslin, D. A., 200
Gouldner, A. W., 379, 382
Grabowski, J., 4, 10, 333, 344, 346, 355

Graubard, P. S., 118, 128, 129, 130, 400, 405
Green, D., 105, 108, 115, 130
Greene, R. J., 308, 323
Greenwood, C. R., 119, 128, 130
Grief, L., 160
Griffitt, W., 191, 201
Grusec, J., 320, 322
Guess, D., 244, 246
Guilford, J. P., 8, 10
Gullian, M. E., 94, 97
Gustavson, C., 54, 58, 239, 244, 246, 401
Hagen, R. L., 70, 76
Hake, D. J., 151, 160, 297, 302, 312, 317, 322
Hall, R. V., 67, 68, 76, 85, 91, 97, 98, 126, 129, 130, 148, 149, 160, 337, 343, 385, 388, 406, 454, 455, 456, 457, 460, 461, 475
Hamblin, R. L., 38, 127, 130, 266
Hamerlynck, L. A., 76, 475
Handy, J., 76
Hanson, P. J., 372, 382
Hardiman, S. A., 222, 230, 234
Haring, N. B., 442
Harmatz, M. G., 271, 279
Harris, F. R., 125, 129, 130, 160, 222, 234, 255, 266, 294
Harris, V. W., 99, 106, 266, 371, 382, 394, 405, 462, 475
Hart, B. M., 129, 148, 160, 266
Haskett, G. J., 189, 201
Hathaway, C., 127, 130
Haupt, E. J., 206, 217
Hawkins, J., 275, 279
Hawkins, R. P., 64, 76, 503
Hays, V. L., 76
Hendex, S. C., 4, 10
Henke, L. B., 129, 266
Herbert, E. W., 95, 97
Herbert-Jackson, E., 285, 291, 293
Hersen, M., 441, 442, 466, 475
Herson, J. L., 74, 77
Hewitt, F. M., 308, 323
Hillmer, M. L., 191, 201
Hilpert, P., 47, 486
Hoats, D. L., 308, 323
Holden, B., 333, 337, 343
Holland, A. L., 111, 130
Holland, J. G., 150, 160, 214, 217, 240, 246, 266, 334, 343, 446, 457
Holmberg, M. C., 257, 266, 450, 457
Holz, W. C., 138, 142, 145, 270, 272, 278, 289, 293, 297, 302, 306, 309, 311, 312, 313, 316, 318, 321
Homme, L., 32, 38, 117, 130, 380, 382
Honig, W. K., 145, 175, 278, 322
Hopkins, B. L.,77, 85, 97, 117, 119, 126, 130, 132, 148, 149, 161, 235, 267, 279, 330, 337, 343, 355, 368, 372, 382, 406, 442, 450, 454, 455, 456, 457, 462, 463, 475, 476
Hops, H., 327, 331, 344
Horne, W. C., 194, 201
Hosford, R. E., 67, 77, 149, 160
Hotte, E., 54, 58, 239, 244, 246
Howard, J. S., 21, 25, 142, 145,

150, 160, 211, 217, 257, 266
Huddleston, C. M., 98
Hull, C. L., 276
Hunt, G., 151, 160, 359, 367
Hunt, S., 39, 58, 138, 145, 235, 267, 279, 337, 343, 368, 385, 388, 389, 406, 442, 447, 458, 475
Hursh, D. E., 462, 463, 475
Hutchinson, R. R., 151, 160, 161, 299, 303, 317, 322, 333, 344, 358, 359, 367
Iwata, B. A., 271, 279
Jackson, A., 375, 378, 382
Jackson, D., 148, 160
Jackson, D. A., 326, 329, 330
Jackson, D. D., 379, 382
Jackson, G. C., 368
Jackson, G. M., 97
Jacobs, J., 118, 130
Johnson, C. A., 81, 97
Johnson, J. A., 67, 77
Johnson, K. R., 47, 58, 72, 76, 205, 217, 234, 486
Johnson, M., 294
Johnson, R. G., 193, 201
Johnson, S. M., 70, 76, 287, 294, 327, 331, 344
Johnston, M. K., 125, 130
Jones, F. C., 160
Jones, F. H., 99, 107
Jones, R. T., 119, 120, 130, 393, 405
Kagan, N., 67, 77
Kagel, J., 392, 405
Kahn, J., 192, 201
Kale, R. J., 329, 330
Kanareff, V., 194, 201
Kandel, H. J., 99, 106
Kane, J. F., 99, 106
Karraker, R. J., 130
Kass, R. E., 15, 25
Kassorla, I. C., 86, 97
Katz, R. C., 56, 58, 81, 97
Kaufman, K. F., 15, 25
Kaye, J. H., 330
Kazdin, A. E., 67, 68, 77, 91, 97, 119, 120, 125, 130, 131, 169, 170, 175, 185, 187, 264, 266, 271, 279, 326, 330, 385, 393, 403, 404, 405, 456, 457, 471, 472, 473, 475
Keirsey, D.W., 32, 38
Keller, F. S., 52, 58, 169, 175, 232, 234, 235, 397, 405, 450, 457
Kelley, C. S., 125, 130
Kelly, J. F., 151, 160
Kennedy, D. A., 125, 131, 326, 327, 330
Kent, R. N., 77
Kerr, N., 109, 131
Kidder, J. D., 160, 278, 279, 405
Kiesler, D. J., 435, 442
Kirby, F., 359, 367
Kirigan, K., 58, 498
Kirsch, I., 222, 235
Klein, R. D., 491, 499
Klock, J., 125, 131
Knight, M. F., 99, 107
Knowlton, W. R., 475
Knutson, L. N., 222, 235
Koegel, R. L., 326, 328, 331, 334, 344

Kohlenberg, R. J., 309, 323
Koniarski, C., 39, 58, 235, 267, 279, 368, 385, 406, 442
Koorland, M. A., 488, 499
Krakower, 222, 231, 235
Krams, M., 39, 58, 235, 267, 279, 368, 385, 406, 442, 475
Krasner, L., 322
Krumboltz, H. B., 115, 131, 198, 201, 215, 217, 226, 235, 312, 323
Krumboltz, J. D., 32, 38, 97, 115, 131, 149, 160, 193, 198, 201, 202, 215, 217, 226, 235, 312, 323, 494, 495, 496, 498, 499
Kubany, E. S., 68, 69, 77
Kulp, S., 61, 63, 77
Kupers, C. J., 193, 200
Lafleur, N. K., 193, 201
Lahey, B. B., 283, 293
Lande, A., 131
Lang, G., 320, 323
Lanzetta, J. T., 194, 201
LaPuc, P., 271, 279
Laws, O. R., 355
Layman, D., 99, 106
LeBlanc, J., 58, 218, 234, 235, 257, 266, 406, 450, 457
Leitenberg, H., 234
LeLaurin, K., 15, 24
Lenfestey, W., 189, 201
Lenske, J., 271, 279
Lepper, M. R., 105, 106, 115, 130
Levy, E. A., 193, 201
Liberman, R. P., 381, 382
Likins, 290, 294
Linder, D. E., 76
Lindsley, O. R., 54, 58, 109, 129, 333, 344
Linscheid, T. R., 309, 323
Lippman, L. G., 348, 355
Lipsett, L. P., 109, 131
Litrownik, A., 249, 266
Lloyd, K. E., 463, 475
Locke, B. J., 329, 330
London, P., 96, 97
Long, E. R., 333, 344, 358, 367
Long, J. D., 456, 458
Loroux, P., 406
Lovaas, O. I., 86, 97, 98, 191, 201, 249, 266, 306, 323, 329, 331
Loving, A., 138, 145, 388, 389, 406, 447, 458
Lovitt, T. C., 89, 97, 442
Lowry, D., 475
Ludwig, J. O., 323
Ludwig, P. J., 126, 131, 320
Lukeris, S., 58, 218, 235, 385, 406
Lund, D., 148, 160
Lutzker, J. D., 244, 247
Maass, C. A., 234
MacDonald, G., 337, 344
MacDonald, W. S., 337, 344
Madsen, C. H., 99, 107, 148, 160
Madsen, C. K., 99, 107
Maehr, M. L., 126, 131, 320, 323
Mager, R. F., 41, 43, 47, 317
Mahoney, K., 54, 58
Mahoney, M. J., 67, 68, 77, 97, 105, 106, 400, 406
Malaby, J. E., 66, 77, 118, 131, 234, 235, 364, 368

Maley, R. F., 392, 406
Mandelker, A. V., 393, 405
Mann, P. H., 87, 97, 192, 201
Mann, R., 249, 266
Markle, S. M., 214, 217
Marshall, H. H., 310, 311, 323
Martin, J. A., 321, 323
Martin, M.B., 488, 499
Martin, P. L., 69, 76, 385, 406
Martin, R., 30, 31, 33, 38, 84, 97
Martindale, A., 61, 63, 77
Maruca, T., 406
Mash, D. A., 76
Mausner, B., 194, 201
Mawhinney, V. T., 350, 351, 355
Mayer, G. R., 9, 10, 68, 76, 97, 120, 131, 136, 145, 159, 160, 192, 201, 204, 205, 217, 264, 265, 266, 286, 292, 293, 304, 323, 382
McAllister, L. W., 452, 458
McCandless, B. R., 212, 217
McClinton, B. S., 201
McCoy, J. F., 67, 77
McCutcheon, D. A., 212, 217
McDowell, E. E., 212, 217
McGookin, R., 91, 97, 372, 374, 376, 382
McInnis, T., 273, 275, 279
McKenzie, H. S., 99, 107
McKenzie, T. L., 99, 107
McKinley, J., 46, 47, 233, 235
McLaughlin, T. F., 66, 77, 118, 131, 234, 235, 364, 368
McNees, M. C., 283, 293
McNees, M. P., 283, 293
McReynolds, L. V., 285, 293
McReynolds, W. T., 205, 217
Mees, H., 86, 97, 109, 132, 148, 161, 283, 287, 290, 294
Melvin, K. B., 406
Menlove, F., 320, 322
Mercatoris, M., 66, 70, 72, 76, 77
Meyer, M. E., 348, 355
Meyerson, L., 76, 109, 131
Michael, J. L., 109, 131, 323, 475
Millenson, J. R., 137, 145, 150, 151, 160, 205, 217
Miller, L. K., 98, 107
Miller, M. B., 128, 130, 388, 400, 405
Minken, B. L., 99, 107, 235
Minken, N., 107, 222, 230, 235
Mitchell, M. A., 129
Mitts, B., 67, 68, 76, 91, 98
Monet, C., 180
Moore, B. J., 316, 323
Moore, B. L., 452, 453, 458
Moore, R., 214, 217
Morales, 86, 97, 289, 290, 293, 301, 303
Morrell, G., 67, 77
Morris, N., 85, 97, 126, 131
Moser, C., 267, 279
Moss, R. E., 67, 77
Mussen, P. H., 77, 457
Neilson, L. J., 161
Neuringer, C., 323
New York State Association for Mentally Retarded Children, 290, 293
Nielson, G., 287, 294

Nunn, L. K., 212, 217
O'Brian, F., 222, 231, 235
O'Leary, D. O., 77
O'Leary, K. D., 15, 25, 148, 153, 160, 326, 331, 385, 405
Oliver, S. D., 289, 293, 317, 323
Orlando, R., 333, 343, 358, 367
Osborn, J. G., 351, 355, 358, 364, 367
Packard, R. G., 118, 131
Palmer, M., 58, 218, 235, 385, 406
Panyan, M., 85, 97, 126, 131, 160
Parker, F. C., 77
Patterson, G. R., 94, 97, 157, 160
Paul, G. L., 70, 76, 196, 201, 273, 275, 279, 470, 476
Payne, J. S., 74, 77
Pear, J. L., 368
Pendergrass, V. E., 291, 293
Perloff, B. F., 201
Perri, M. G., 340, 344
Perrott, M. C., 256, 266
Pesses, D. I., 76
Peters, J., 47, 486
Peterson, R. F., 191, 200, 257, 266
Phillips, E. A., 4, 10, 58, 119, 120, 270, 279, 355, 385, 406, 498
Phillips, E. L., 4, 10, 54, 58, 67, 68, 71, 89, 91, 97, 107, 116, 119, 120, 235, 268, 270, 279, 345, 355, 358, 376, 382, 385, 387, 403, 405, 406, 498
Piaget, J., 21
Picasso, P., 180
Pierce, C. H., 99, 107
Polster, R., 404, 405
Porter, D., 214, 217
Porter, J., 74, 77
Porterfield, J. K., 285, 291, 293
Powell, J., 61, 63, 77
Powers, M. A., 187
Premack, D., 117, 122, 131
Pryer, M. W., 333, 343
Quevillon, R. P., 4, 10, 99, 106
Quilitch, H. R., 85, 97
Rabinowitz, F. M., 201
Rabon, D., 160
Ramey, G., 47, 105, 107, 482, 486, 503
Ramp, E., 76, 77, 217, 235, 266, 279, 368, 405, 406, 442, 476
Rayner, R., 318, 323
Rechs, J. R., 32, 38, 382
Redd, W. H., 463, 475
Reese, E. P., 21, 25, 65, 109, 131, 142, 145, 150, 160, 209, 211, 217, 231, 235, 257, 266, 270, 277, 281, 293
Reese, T. W., 21, 25, 142, 145, 211, 217
Renne, C. M., 99, 100, 107, 116, 131, 237, 243, 247, 472, 475
Renzaglia, G. A., 70, 77
Repp, A. C., 251, 252, 253, 256, 258, 266, 333, 343
Reuter, K. E., 222, 234
Reynolds, G. S., 134, 140, 145, 170, 175, 221, 235, 256, 257, 259, 267, 333, 344, 351, 354, 355, 359, 360, 368
Reynolds, J., 31, 38

Reynolds, N. J., 129, 266
Richards, C. S., 340, 344
Rickard, H. C., 392, 406
Rickert, E. J., 130
Rimmer, B., 303
Rincover, A., 326, 328, 331
Risley, T. R., 10, 14, 15, 16, 17, 20,
  24, 25, 44, 47, 52, 58, 86, 97, 99,
  107, 109, 131, 132, 148, 161, 283,
  285, 287, 290, 291, 293, 294, 306,
  323, 437, 442, 446, 450, 457, 466,
  471, 475, 493, 498
Roberts, M. D., 28, 38, 118, 129,
  264, 266
Roberts, R. R., 70, 77
Robertson, R., 160
Robertson, S. J., 99, 100, 107, 116,
  131, 135, 145
Rohen, T. H., 192, 201
Romanczyk, R. G., 72, 77
Roos, P., 86, 97
Rosekrans, M. A., 191, 201
Rosenbaum, M. E., 194, 201
Rosenberg, H., 128, 130, 400, 405
Rosenberger, P., 150, 160, 257, 266
Rosenthal, T. L., 193, 202
Ross, D., 192, 193, 200
Ross, S. A., 192, 193, 200
Rowbury, T., 293
Rushall, B. S., 99, 107
Ruskin, R. S., 392, 406
Rutherford, G., 246
Sailor, W., 246
Sajwaj, T. E., 303
Salisbury, 391, 406
Sampen, S. E., 283, 284, 294
Sanders, R. M., 70, 77, 372, 382
Saudargas, R. A., 160
Saunders, M., 255, 266, 308, 322,
  370, 371, 382
Schaefer, H., 197, 202, 224, 235,
  385, 406
Schaeffer, B., 201
Schmidt, G. W., 118, 127, 131
Schmidt, J. A., 452, 458
Schoenfield, W. N., 169, 175, 450,
  457
Schutte, R. C., 117, 130, 372, 382
Schutz, R. E., 406
Schwitzgebel, R. K., 33, 38, 84, 97
Scott, P. M., 148, 161
Scott, R. B., 382
Semb, G., 76, 217, 235, 343, 405,
  462, 463, 475
Seymour, F. W., 68, 77
Shamow, J., 206, 217
Shee, S. M., 67, 76, 91, 97
Sherman, J. A., 13, 24, 99, 106,
  191, 200, 233, 235, 244, 246, 247,
  255, 257, 266, 371, 382, 394, 400,
  405, 449, 457, 462, 475
Sherman, T. M., 128, 131
Shields, F., 359, 367
Sidman, M., 214, 217, 441, 442,
  462, 475
Siedentop, D., 47
Siegel, G. M., 271, 272, 279
Silberman, A., 119, 120
Silverman, N. A., 264, 266
Simmons, J. O., 306, 323, 329, 331
Siqueland, E. R., 109, 131

Sittler, J. L., 264, 266
Skidgell, A., 46, 47, 71, 230, 235
Skinner, B. F., 36, 38, 134, 145, 149,
  150, 151, 160, 161, 197, 201, 222,
  224, 231, 235, 240, 246, 266, 274,
  279, 281, 289, 293, 306, 317, 323,
  333, 334, 343, 346, 348, 355, 357,
  358, 367, 368, 446, 457
Sloane, H. N., 119, 128, 130, 283,
  284, 289, 294, 318, 323
Sloggett, B. B., 68, 69, 77
Smith, L., 38, 266
Snow, D. L., 118, 129
Solomon, R. W., 128, 131, 158,
  161, 307, 323
Sorrell, S., 303
Souweine, J., 47, 486
Staats, A., 385, 392, 406
Staats, C. K., 406
Stachowiak, J. G., 458
Staines, J. W., 320, 323
Stans, A., 118, 129
Stansberry, P., 373, 382
Steinhorst, R., 130
Stephens, C., 358, 368
Stephens, R. M., 77
Stewart, N. R., 193, 201
Stickney, 28, 84, 85, 89, 97, 115,
  132, 294, 323, 406
Stoddard, L. T., 214, 217
Stokes, T. F., 68, 77, 326, 329, 331
Stolz, S. B., 93, 96, 98, 128, 129,
  239, 266, 305, 323, 498, 499
Stotland, E., 191, 201
Striefel, S., 195, 201, 208, 217
Stuart, R. B., 379, 382
Sullivan Associates Program, 224,
  225, 226, 235
Sulzer, E., 32, 39, 382
Sulzer-Azaroff, B., 17, 25, 28, 39,
  47, 52, 57, 58, 65, 76, 77, 109,
  120, 127, 129, 130, 132, 136, 138,
  145, 185, 187, 205, 217, 218, 226,
  233, 234, 235, 244, 247, 264, 267,
  270, 279, 304, 323, 333, 337, 343,
  364, 368, 385, 388, 389, 390, 391,
  392, 396, 398, 402, 405, 406, 439,
  442, 447, 448, 449, 458, 462, 463,
  473, 475, 486
Suppes, P., 214, 218
Swisher, J. D., 192, 202
Taber, J. K., 197, 202, 224, 231, 235
Tague, C., 160, 279, 405
Tate, B. G., 86, 97
Taylor, L. K., 127, 131
Terrace, H. S., 169, 175, 212, 214,
  215
Terraciano, T., 206, 217
Tharp, R. G., 81, 97, 115, 131
Thaw, J., 17, 25, 65, 77
Theobald, D. E., 470, 476
Thomas, C., 17, 25, 52, 58, 65, 77,
  208, 218, 230, 235, 385, 387, 397,
  402, 406
Thomas, D. R., 67, 77, 148, 161,
  163, 164, 175, 185, 187, 204, 217
Thomas, J. D., 67, 76, 77, 91, 97
Thompson, E., 99, 107
Thompson, I., 125, 126, 131, 326,
  327, 330
Thompson, L., 97, 382

Thompson, T., 4, 10, 333, 344,
  346, 355
Thomson, C. L., 130
Thoresen, C. E., 67, 68, 77, 97,
  193, 201, 202, 400, 406, 444, 445,
  458
Timbers, B. J., 107, 235
Timbers, G. D., 107, 235
Todd, D. D., 376, 382
Tosi, D. J., 125, 131
Tracy, D. A., 326, 330
Truax, C. B., 5, 10
Trudel, G., 393, 400, 406
Tucker, R. D., 118, 119, 130
Turman, 86, 97, 289, 293, 301, 303
Twardosz, S., 16, 25, 287, 290, 293
Tyler, L., 160
Tyler, V. O., 283, 293
Ullman, P., 160, 322
Ulman, J. D., 127, 131, 462, 463,
  476
Ulrich, K. E., 127, 131
Underwood, B. J., 435, 442
Upper, D. A., 401, 406
Upshaw, K., 131
U.S. Dept. of Health, Education
  and Welfare, 33, 39, 305
Van Der Kooy, D., 228, 230, 235
Van Kirk, M. J., 206, 217
Vogler, J. D., 371, 382
Wahler, R. G., 128, 131, 158, 161
Waldron, M. A., 131
Waldrop, P. B., 350, 355
Walker, H. M., 118, 128, 131, 328,
  331, 337, 344, 406
Walker, M. B., 70, 77
Wallace, R. F., 330
Walls, R. T., 503
Walter, R. H., 156, 160, 318, 322
Walz, G. R., 67, 77
Warner, R. W., 192, 202
Watson, J. B., 318, 323
Wattenberg, W. W., 320, 323
Weathers, L., 381, 382
Webster, C. D., 228, 230, 235
Webster, D. R., 285, 294
Webster's New Collegiate Dic-
  tionary, 35, 39
Weiner, H., 270, 271, 279, 333,
  344, 348, 355, 362, 368
Weisberg, P., 350, 355
Welsh, 290, 294
Werden, D. A., 209, 218
Werner, T. J., 503
Wesolowski, M. D., 296, 299, 303
West, R. C., 289, 293, 317, 323
Wetherby, B., 195, 201
Wetzel, R. J., 81, 97, 115, 131
Wexler, D. B., 33, 39, 84, 97
Wheeler, A., 109, 132, 244, 247,
  449, 458
Whelan, P. A., 330
White, G. D., 70, 77, 287, 294
White, M. A., 340, 344, 483, 486
White, O. R., 170, 175
Whitehurst, G. J., 244, 247
Whitley, A. D., 192, 201, 396, 406,
  447, 448, 458
Wienckowski, L. A., 93, 96, 98,
  128, 129
Wiggins, J. S., 70, 77

Williams, D. E., 76
Williams, R. L., 456, 458
Willis, R. H., 194, 201
Wilson, C. W., 119, 132, 148, 149, 161
Wilson, G. T., 326, 331
Winett, R. A., 27, 39
Winkler, R. C., 27, 39, 270, 279, 392, 405
Winze, J. P., 234
Wisocki, P. A., 126, 132
Wodarski, J., 127, 130
Wolf, M. M., 4, 10, 20, 24, 44, 47, 52, 54, 58, 67, 68, 71, 76, 86, 87, 91, 97, 107, 109, 116, 125, 129, 130, 131, 132, 148, 160, 161, 222, 234, 235, 255, 266, 278, 279, 283, 287, 290, 294, 303, 308, 322, 329, 330, 355, 370, 371, 376, 382, 385, 388, 405, 406, 437, 442, 446, 450, 457, 466, 475, 493, 498
Wolfensberger, W., 97
Wolkin, J. R., 201
Wolpin, M., 222, 235
Wood, S., 77, 323, 498, 499
Wooldridge, R. L., 98
Worthy, R. C., 69, 77
Wray, L. D., 368
Wright, H. F., 65, 77
Wright, L., 309, 323
Wyatt, 28, 84, 85, 86, 88, 89, 97, 115, 132, 290, 294, 305, 310, 323, 394, 406
Yarrow, M. R., 148, 161
Zeilberger, J., 283, 284, 294
Zimmerman, B. J., 193, 202
Zimmerman, E. H., 148, 161
Zimmerman, J., 148, 161, 287, 294, 312, 323

Abscissa, defined, 72; graphing time intervals, 94; illustrated, 488–9, *511**

Abstraction (technical usage), defined, 173

Academic skills, peer-reinforcement of, 127; positive v. negative reinforcement, 86; reinforcers for, 109, 110–11, 118–21, 123–4; self-determination of reinforcers, 89

Accountability, in applied behavior analysis, 9; data collection, 88; importance of, 17, 432–3, 502; records of, 495–6; reliable measurement as basis of, 49; in token economies, 398, *511*

Accuracy as behavioral dimension, 45

Achievement, lack of (*see* Maladaptive behaviors; Underachievement)

Achievement Place (group home program), activity reinforcers in, 116; community support for, 16; daily report cards, 375–6; delayed reinforcement in, 403–4; described, 4; room inspection in, 345–6; self-management, 387

Actions, overt and covert, 3

Activity reinforcers, 116, 118–21

Adaptation phase, 73, 74, 75, 167 439, *511*

Adaptive behaviors, cooperative play, 44–5, 49, 52, 71; on-task behavior, 9, 62, 64, 67, 73; *See also* Skills, social

Adjusting schedule, 359, *511*

Advocacy, 31, 89, *511*

Aggressive behavior, aversive stimuli for, 86, 142–3; DRO for, 258; extinction-induced, 151, 156; response cost for,

270–71; sample operational definitions of, 65; treatment plan for, 283–4

Alternative responses (*see* Reinforcing alternative behavior)

Alt-*R*, Alt*r* (*see* Reinforcing alternative behavior)

American Psychological Association, code of ethics, 33

Analytic evaluation (*see* Skills, cognitive)

Antecedent (to target behavior), defined, 81, 82; illustrated, 82–3

Antecedent stimuli, clarifying, 318; conditions for, 169; defined, 163, *511*; discrimination of, 177; priming behaviors via, 176–200

Applied behavior analysis, ABCs of, 82; alternative solutions to, 14–15, 17, application of, 308; approach of, 6, 8, 19, 88, 224, 432–3; defined, 101, *511*; distinguished from other therapies, 19; effectiveness documented, 15–16, 86; model, 75; public nature of, 35, 84, 290–1; responsible use of, 5

Applied behavior analysis program, abbreviations for, 7–8; application of, 5–6; communicating outcomes of, 488–98; decision to implement, 9, 12–18, 75; definition of, 6–7, 7–8, 435, *511*; environment for, 73, 85–6, 87; ethical considerations, 31–3; evaluating effectiveness, 433–41; goals of, 7; measuring progress of, 93–5; objections to, 34; personnel, 8–9, 13–14, 68–9, 158, 400; prior considerations for, 15–18; reasons for failures of, 95; scope and limitations, 7, 8–9, 84, 169n

Applied behavior analyst (*see* Behavior analyst)

Arithmetic (*see* Skills, numerical)

Art appreciation (*see* Complex behaviors)

Artificial stimuli, as back-up reinforcers, 390; defined, 196; generalization training, 329–30; hierarchy of prompts, 206–7; ratio schedules, 363; selecting, 197–8, 206–7; in token economies, 390; transition to natural, 105–6, 206–9, 211–12, 329–30, 363; usefulness of, 197, 390

Assertiveness (*see* Adaptive behaviors)

Assessment packages, 503–9

Asthmatic children, improvement in, 98–9; IPPB taught to, 243–4

Asymptote, 363

Attending behavior, in classrooms, 125; and extinction procedures, 148–9; generalized from counseling sessions to classroom, 326; as inadvertent reinforcement, 263, 286, 375; and language deficiencies, 215; in parents, 61, 152–3, 180; as reinforcer, 81; and relevant stimulus properties, 180; in teachers, 62, 448; teaching, via shaping, 221

Auditory, visual, and tactile stimuli, discrimination, 167, 179; in fading, 209–12, 214; and modeling, 193

Autistic behavior, *512*; DRO inappropriate for, 257, 259, 295; edible reinforcers for, 109; illustrated, 13, 19; in mentally retarded, 155, 189; microselectiveness in, 329; multiple baseline design for evaluating change in, 453–4; procedures for: aversive stimuli, 308; behavioral chaining and, 241–2; Functional Movement Training, 296–7; generalization training, 328–9; intermittent reinforcement, 328; modeling, 189, 191; punishment and reinforcement, 317; response cost, 295; reinforcing alternative behaviors, 260, 261, 295; timeout, 283, 285, 295

Aversive consequence (S^P), 270, 276; See also Punishment

Aversive procedures, contrasted with positive procedures, 261; humanism, 501–2; listed, 269; state policies on, 304n

Aversive stimuli, advantages, 86, 172, 276–7; behavior- v. client-directed, 320; conditioned, 86, 308; defined and illustrated, 141, 269, 274, 276, 307, 512; disadvantages of, 86, 142, 172; ethical-legal restrictions of, 85–6; and extinction, 149; in human services, 308; and negative reinforcement, 141; signaling nonreinforcement (S^Δs), 276n, 309; unconditioned (S^P), 307

Avoidance response, 512; appropriate, 312; conditioning, 140; consequence of behavioral procedures, 142, 172, 275, 289, 312, 321, 359, 412, 424–7 passim; minimized in overcorrection, 297; reducing via shaping, 222; used to occasion response, 228; See also Side effects of behavioral procedures

Back-up reinforcers, administering, 394–5; defined, 386, 512; inexpensive, 390–2; legal restrictions, 394; marketing and merchandising of, 392–3; natural and artificial, 390; pricing, 392, 396–8; See also Token economies

Backward chaining, defined, 237, 512; immediate reinforcement and, 241–3; rationale for, 245

Baseline, 512; differential reinforcement of low rates and, 254–5; erroneous, 73; establishment of,74,75; modified, 439–40; noncontingent reinforcement, 437–41; rationale for, 437; representative, 437–9, 440; examples of, 223, 438; function of, 437; interview and questionnaire for, 81–3; multiple baseline design, 75; place in applied behavior-analysis model, 74–5, 93; prerequisite to implementing procedures, 93

Behavior analysis (see Applied behavior analysis)

Behavior analysis procedures (see Procedures)

Behavior analysis program (see Applied behavior analysis program)

Behavior analyst, 512; as arbitrator, 31; competence of, 16, 17, 85; contact with contingency manager, 337; flexibility required in, 88–9; legal responsibility of, 84; role and examples, 14, 178

Behavior change, criterion for determining, 44; monitoring, 7, 19; role of communication in, 20; voluntary, 37

Behavior modification (see Applied behavior analysis)

Behavior - recording techniques (see Recording data)

Behavioral approach, accountable, 9, 17, 432–3, 502; empirical, 224; in goal selection, 19; performance-based, 6; treatment-oriented, 88

Behavioral chains, 237

Behavioral Characteristics Progression Observation Booklet, 504–5

Behavioral contract, 513; family contract, 379–81; goal selection, 32–3, 90–1; informed consent, 89–90; sample, 90–1, 92

Behavioral contrast, 259, 513

Behavioral dimensions of response, 513; components of, 45, 220; illustrated, 43

Behavioral goals (see Goal selection)

Behavioral laws, 474; 513

Behavioral modifications effected by applied behavior analysis, classes of: extending, 162–218, 324–31, 409–10, 411–18; increasing, 98–144, 408–9, 411–13; inhibiting, 409–11, 414–18; maintaining, 332–67, 422–3, 428–30; occasioning, 162–218, 409–10, 414–18; reducing, 146–61, 248–323, 422, 423–6; teaching, 219–47, 410, 418–20; summarized, 6–7, 407–8; 513

Behavioral objectives, 513; checking validity of, 75; components: criteria, 44; flow chart, 46; response, 41; situation, 43; defined, 41; Instructional Objectives Exchange, 47; and measurement, 50; programmed instruction for, 224; relation to behavioral principles, 80; resources for preparation of, 47; samples of, 44–5

Behavioral principles, application of, 3–4; defined, 3, 512; relation to behavioral procedures, 4; relation to contingencies, 80

Behavioral problems (see Maladaptive behaviors)

Behavioral processes, 164n

Behavioral program (see Applied behavior analysis program)

Behavioral repertoire (see Repertoire)

Behavioral technician, 14, 512

Behaviors (see Adaptive behaviors; Complex behaviors; Maladaptive behaviors)

Bias in measurement, 69, 72

Bonus, for accurate self-recording, 386; in Good Behavior Game, 371; in ratio schedules, 360; in response cost, 275, 513; in token economies, 392

Brain-damaged persons, 299

Branching (teaching technique), 215

Case materials, defined, 21; procedural selection, 84

Case study, 49

Catalog of Free Teaching Materials (Salisbury), 391

Cerebral palsy, Lexington Developmental Scale, 505–6; motor skills, 219–20

Chaining procedure, backward, 237, 241–3; combined with other procedures, 243–5; cumulative records, 490; defined, 237, 513; effective use of: final link as starting point, 241–3; repertoire analysis, 240–1; task analysis, 240; establishing, 237–9; forward, 236–7; maintaining effects of, 246

Change agents, 5, 8, 13–14

Changing criterion design, 460–2, 469, 513; See also single-subject experimental designs

Children and youth, reinforcers for, activity reinforcers, 118–19; novelty, 137–8; social reinforcers, 123–4; tangible and edible reinforcers, 110–11, 391; See also Elementary school children; High school students; Preschool children

Classify (technical usage), 173

Client, advocate for, 31, 89; approval of in token economy, 396; countercontrol, 93; defined 13–14, 513; goal behavior, 30, 92, 226; involvement in goal selection, 29–33, 42; as recorder of data, 54, 66, 67–70; rights of, 31–3, 84–9 passim; See also Legal restrictions; Self-management

Coded interval-recording sheet, 62; 513

Coefficient of agreement, 52–3, 64–5, 70

Coercion, 36, 37, 38; 513

Cognitive skills, assessment of, 503–9; critical stimuli, 185–6; and hierarchy of prompts, 198; identification of stimulus properties, 178; listed, 173, 178, 185–6; stimulus control to teach, 176

College students, 66, 388; See also Personalized System of Instruction

Communicating outcomes, 95, 477–99; to clients and advocates, 478–9; confidentiality, 479–80; to consumers, 479–80; report form, 481–5

Community, applied behavior analysis in, 2, 16–17, 142, 290–1
Complex behaviors, 514; chaining to teach, 236ff.; stimulus control to teach, 176–200 passim; types of, 4, 51, 173, 175, 178, 180–1, 185–6, 226–7, 342, 433–6; See also Skills
Compliment meters, 378–9, 514; See also Social reinforcers
Conditioned aversive stimuli, 86, 308, 514
Conditioned reinforcers, 102–4, 514; defined, 102; delayed reinforcement, 134–5; in response cost procedure, 270
Conditioning, 6n, 135–6
Confounding variables, 514; examples of, 433–5; identifying, 436–7; kinds of, 435–6; reporting results, 494
Consequences, control of, 156–9; identification of, 81, 156–7; illustrated, 82–3; ineffective, 168; self-determination of, 89; suggested, as activity reinforcers, 118–20
Consumer satisfaction, enhancement of, 115; use of data in measurement, 51
Contingencies, competing, 139–40; considered in selecting dependent variable, 50; defined, 80, 514; grade, 72; identification of, 81–2
Contingency analysis, 81, 101
Contingency manager, competence, 85; controller of stimuli, 80; counselors as, 62; countercontrol over, 93; defined and illustrated, 13–14, 514; parent as, 14; as recorders, 54, 64, 68; reinforcement of, 95
Contingency packages, activity table, 373, 514; contingency bank, 372, 514; contingent recreation, 372; family contract program, 379–81; Good Behavior Game, 369–71; grab bag, 374–5; home reports, 375; slot machine, 374; treasure box, 373–4; warm fuzzies and compliment meters 378–9
Contingent observation, 285, 311, 514
Contingent stimulus, 101, 222, 372
Continuous reinforcement schedule (CRF), 514; compared with intermittent reinforcement schedule, 136; disadvantages of, 140, 335, 339, 351; to increase behaviors, 140; inducing hyperactivity, 366; in token economies, 404; transition to intermittent schedule of reinforcement, 335, 339–42; transition to ratio schedules of reinforcement, 342–3, 366, 367
Contract (see Behavioral contract)
Control (technical usage), 514
Conversational skills (see Skills)
Cooperative play, interval time-

sample recording, 60–1; reinforcing, 284; sharing, 44–5; shaping to teach, 222; subjectivity in measuring, 71
Correction procedure, 214–15
Cost-benefit, 28, 42, 494–7
Counseling, and extinction, 148, 149; and generalization, 326–7; importance of fading in, 205; social reinforcement in, 125
Counselor, guidance, accountability record, 495; behavioral contracting, 90; as contingency manager, 62; as observer, 50
Countercontrol, 93, 128, 514
CRF (see Continuous reinforcement schedule)
Creativity, documented increases in, 4; multielement design to evaluate procedures for encouraging, 463–6; reliable assessments of, 51; stimulus control of, 178; supplemental reinforcement for, 342; See also Complex behaviors
Criterion, 515; predetermining, for assessing competence, 85; specifying for behavioral objectives, 50
Critical stimulus properties, contrasted with supplementary stimuli, 182, 186; defined, 185; magnification of, 196–7; naturalness of, 198
Cuing, 69, 81, 135, 164; See also Prompting strategies
Cumulative numbers, graphing of, 488–90
Daily report card, 375–7, 515
Data-recording (see Recording data)
Delayed reinforcement, aim of education, 339; disadvantages of, 134; introducing into schedule, 330, 339–40, 402–4
Delinquent and predelinquent youth, group home for, 4; punishment of, 314; response cost with, 270–1; self-determination of consequences, 89; shaping conversational skills in, 230; success documented, 2; timeout with, 283; token economies with, 385; See also Achievement Place
Demonstrational prompts (see Modeling)
Dependent variable, baseline data, 439; defined, 50, 515; graphing, 94; relation to independent variable, 79, 433; time-sampling, 62; See also Target behavior
Deprivation levels, 515; temporal aspects of extinction, 150; and various reinforcers, 136–7
Development Learning Corporation, 397
Differential reinforcement, basic to stimulus control, 178; defined, 169–71, 515; effective use of, 176; properties summarized,

414; with several stimuli, 171–4; timeout with, 287
Differential reinforcement of high rates (DRH) combined with other procedures, 353, 366–7, 392; defined, 365, 515; properties summarized, 430
Differential reinforcement of low rates (DRL), 515; advantages, 251–3; baseline data, 254–5; combined with other procedures, 255, 258; compared to shaping, 253; duration of interval, 254–5; effective use of, 254; examples, 252; mentally retarded, 252, 253; properties summarized, 424
Differential reinforcement of other behaviors (DRO), advantages of, 256–7; autistic behavior (inappropriate for) 257, 259, 295; in baseline establishment, 440–1; combined with other procedures, 258; defined and illustrated, 250, 255–6, 515; disadvantages, 258–9; mentally retarded, 258; as omission training, 256; properties summarized, 424; in reversal design 449; scheduling reinforcement in, 257–8
Dining skills, Mansfield Training Program in, The, 71; scoring manual for, 71; shaping to teach, 222; task analysis, 46, 55
Discipline, 303–4
Discrete response, 515; measurement of, 54
Discrimination, antidote to generalization, 318; defined, 135, 515; See also Differential reinforcement; Discriminative stimuli
Discriminative stimuli, (S^D, S^Δ, S^{D-}), 516; combined with other procedures, 230–1, 238, 245, 264, 273–4, 291, 315–16, 328–9, 393; comparison between S^D and S^{D-}, 277; defined, 135–6, 165, 170, 276; distinguished from respondent behavior, 166; fading related to, 215; intrusive, 167–8; magnifying critical features, 197; presentation of: multiple stimuli, 173–5; stimulus change, 165; two stimuli and one response, 171–2; two stimuli and two responses, 172–3; reinforcing stimuli, 238; relation to S^Δs, 172–3; S^{D-} illustrated, 315; See also Prompting strategies, S delta; Stimulus control
Disruptive behavior, reducing, 99; activity reinforcers for, 118; illustrative procedures for: differential reinforcement of low rates, 252, 253; Good Behavior Game, 88, 225, 308–9, 370–1, 425–6; timeout, 281, 283; token economies, 398; interval time sampling, 60, 63; program assessment, 449, 451; sample

recording sheet for, 56; segregation, and opposition to, 87

Distortion (see Error, sources of)

DRH (see Differential reinforcement of high rates)

DRL (see Differential reinforcement of low rates)

DRO (see Differential reinforcement of other behaviors)

Duration, recording, 57, 66, 516

Echolelic language, 41

Edible reinforcers, 105, 109–12, 392

Education, 328, 339, 500; See also Instruction; Schools; Teaching

Education Evaluation and Planning Package, 503–4

Educators, 80, 126; See also Personnel; Teachers

Electric shock therapy, 309–10

Elementary school children, Good Behavior Game for, 370–1; Premack principle in, 117; programmed reading text for, 224; self-management, 91; strengthening behaviors of, 99

Elicit, (technical usage), 166, 516

Eliminating behaviors (see Reducing behaviors)

Emission (technical usage), 100, 516

Enduring product (see Permanent product)

Environment, in applied behavior analysis, 73, 85–7 passim, 103; changing via timeout, 281–2; conditions for reinforcement, 135–6; social, 30; structuring to maintain behavior, 153; varying for generalization training, 329

Environmental confounding variables, 43–4, 167, 436, 516; See also Confounding variables

Epilepsy, self-induced, 309

Error, sources of in evaluation, bias, 69, 72; expectation, 52, 72; reactivity, 53; subjectivity, 82

Errorless discrimination procedure, 516; correction procedure, 214–15; fading, 206; introducing S deltas, 213–14

Errorless learning (see Errorless discrimination procedure)

Errors, commission and ommission in programming, 84, 212; interval schedules of reinforcement, 351; ratio schedules of reinforcement, 364–5; tolerance of (frustration), 215

Escape behavior, 142, 172, 297, 317; See also Avoidance response

Ethical considerations, 516; client's rights, 31–5, 89–93; goal conflicts, 31–3; HEW guidelines for protection of human subjects, 33, 304; humanism, 501–2; human rights committees, 33, 304; safeguards, 26–38, 75; voluntariness, 35, 86–7

Ethology, 21n

Evaluation of treatment program,

accountability, 432–3, 495–6; confounding variables, 433–7, 494; establishing baselines, 437–41; follow-up, 474–5; in reports, 493–6; self-management and, 91, 432

Event sampling, alternative to time sampling, 62; defined, 66, 516; instruments for, 54, 55, 66; to monitor treatment program, 95; persons conducting, 54

Examinations, grading reliably, 52; Personalized System of Instruction, 233; reinforcing and aversive contingencies, 350; study patterns for, 351

Exchangeable reinforcers, defined, 115–16; described, 105–6; in response cost, 270; See also Token economies

Expectation (see Error, sources of)

Experimental analysis of behavior, 7, 49, 516

Experimental designs, 440–75, 516; See also Single-subject designs

Extending behavior, 6–7; generalization training for, 324–31; procedures summarized, 414–18; stimulus control, 162–218 passim

Extinction conditions, behavior maintenance under, interval schedules of reinforcement, 351–2; overcorrection, 298; vs. peer reinforcement, 157; ratio schedules of reinforcement, 360–2; transition from token economies, 404

Extinction procedure, advantages, 148–9; combined with other procedures, 150, 153, 154, 258, 263, 281, 284, 298–9, 313–14, 335; defined, 99, 142, 147, 516; diagrammed, 159; disadvantages, 151, 156–7; distinction between punishment and, 147, 152–4; properties of: aggressive side effects, 151; gradual, 150–1; increased response rates, 151; spontaneous recovery, 151–2; selecting, 159; summarized, 424

Fading discriminative stimuli, 203–18; combined with other procedures, 230–1, 245; defined, 204–15, 516; disadvantages of, 215–16; effective use of: gradualness, 206; transferring control, 207–8; transition from artificial to natural, 206; transition from irrelevant to relevant, 208–12; errors, minimizing: correction procedure, 214–15; de-emphasis of S deltas, 213–14; dissimilar S deltas, 213; properties summarized (Fading discriminative stimuli cont.), 418

Family (see Behavioral contract; Home; Parents)

Feedback, 68, 93, 126, 214–15; See also Punishment; Reinforcement

FI (see Fixed-interval schedules)

Fines (see Response cost)

Fixed-interval (FI) schedules of reinforcement, compared to fixed-ratio schedules, 359; compared to limited hold, 354; consistency, 351, 359; defined, 346–7, 517; and DRO, properties summarized, 428; response rates, 348–9; scallop, 349–50

Fixed-ratio (FR) schedules of reinforcement, adjusting schedule, 359; defined, 357, 517; postreinforcement pause, 359, 360; properties summarized, 429

"Flooding" (contrasted with shaping), 222

Foreign language (see Language)

FR (see Fixed-ratio schedules)

Freedom, 501–2; See also Voluntary behavior)

Frequency of behavior, 517; behavioral dimension, 45, 220; failure to increase, 104; measuring, 50, 63, 81; objective verification of, 122; Premack principle, 117–22

Frustration tolerance, lack of, 215–16

Functional analysis designs (see Experimental designs)

Functional relation, defined, 7, 517; demonstration of, 433, 442; determining existence of, 152; determining significance of, 471–3; implications of, 446

Generalization of response, defined, 136, 517; illustrated, 100, 221; in multiple baseline design, 457; side effect of punishment, 318, 321

Generalization of stimulus, 164, 165, 517; procedures summarized 414–16; training for, 324–31; See also Stimulus control

Generalization training, defined, 325–6, 517; effective use of: artificial stimuli replaced by natural, 329–30; common denominators, 327–8; discriminative stimuli, 328–9; intermittent reinforcement, 328, 329–30; varying conditions, 329; properties summarized (Generalization training cont.), 416–17

Goal Analysis, Mager (1972), 43

Goal behavior, client awareness, 226; goal-completion card, 92; sample of (in sequence analysis), 82–3; specifying dimensions of, 81, 220

Goal conflicts, administrative involvement, 31–2; advocacy, 30–1; client's social environment, 30; client participation, 30; contract negotiation, 32; identification of benefits, 29–30; institutional review, 33–4; parent involvement, 31–2

Goal selection, 27–47; in applied behavior analysis model, 75; client participation, 30, 91; confidentiality, 32; cost-benefit ratios in, 32; countercontrol in,

93; ethical-legal consideration, 27, 31–3; initial considerations summarized, 24; parent participation, 31–2; philosophic consideration, 32; priorities for, 41, 42; PSI, 232–3; publicizing, 28; in shaping, 226; staff participation, 32; voluntariness, 35, 37

Good Behavior Game, combined with differential reinforcement of low rates (DRL), 255; conditioned aversive stimuli, 308–9; defined as a contingency package, 369, 370–1, 517; flexibility, 88; properties summarized, 425–6

"Goodbye Teacher" (Keller), 232

Grades (see Daily report card)

Graduated guidance, of autistic children, 88; described, 207–8, 517; of mentally retarded, 88, 169–70; overcorrection and, 299

Graphing, conventions for displaying data, 488–92; cumulative numbers, 488–90; described, 71; during treatment and baseline periods, 93; examples of, 73, 74, 488–9; transforming data, 490–1; working graph illustrated, 94

Group contingencies, 127, 374, 393, 394, 463–4; See also Peer reinforcement contingencies

Group counseling, generalization to classroom, 326–7; increasing verbal participation, 149; social reinforcement in, 125

Groups, applied behavior analysis for, extinction-induced aggression in, 156; imitative behavior in, 192; procedures for: contingency packages, 369–78; contingent observation, 235; generalization training, 326, 327; intermittent reinforcement, 336–7; modeling, 264; shaping, 223; reinforcement for (Groups cont.): activity reinforcers, 127; immediate reinforcement, 134–5; social reinforcement, 125

Guernica (Picasso), 180–1

Guidance counselor (see Counselor, guidance)

Halfway houses, generalization training, 328; mainstreaming, 87, 192, 385

Handicapped, assessment package for, 508–9 generalization training for, 328; See also specific classes of handicap

Handwriting (see Skills, motor)

HEW guidelines for experimentation with human subjects, 33, 304

Hierarchy of prompting strategies, described, 198; and fading, 203–16 passim; transition from imitative to verbal, 208

High frequency behavior, contingent recreation, 372; intrinsic motivation, 338; Premack Principle, 117–22; in token econo-

mies, 390

High school students, activity centers for, 222; differential reinforcement of low rates, 252; evaluating improvement in French, 434–49 passim

Hints (see Prompting strategies)

History (see Learning history)

Home, daily report card, 375–6, 517; family contract, 379–81; negative reinforcement, 142–3

Human rights committees, 86, 304

Human services personnel, as behavioral technicians, 65; communication of rules by, 316; and conditioned aversive stimuli, 308; as contingency managers, 80; legal responsibility, 84; See also specific occupational titles

Hyperactivity, differential reinforcement of high rates (DRH) combined with variable interval schedule, 366; due to learning history, 338; extinction procedures for, 157–8; reinforcing alternative behaviors, 260

Hypochondria, 148

Imitative behavior, 518; echolelic language, 41; inadvertent reinforcement of, 156, 318–19; peer reinforcement, 374; teaching, 190–1; 193, See also Modeling procedure

Imitative prompts (see Modeling procedure)

Immediate reinforcement, advantage, 134–5; backward chaining and, 241; as behavior principle, 3; in Personalized System of Instruction, 233; in self-recording, 68

Inadvertent reinfocement, attention as, 263, 286, 375; in extinction procedures, 152–3; of imitative behavior, 156; of punished act, 319; of punishment, 318–19

Incentives (see Reinforcers)

Incompatible behaviors, reinforcing, 518; Alt-R, 262, 264–5; extinction procedures, 155; See also Reinforcing alternative behaviors (Alt-R)

Increasing behavior, 98–145; via conditioned reinforcers, 101–6; effects of scheduling on, 140; procedures for: modeling, 190–1; negative reinforcement, 140–4; positive reinforcement, 101–2, 140–1; summarized, 79–80, 409–11; token economies, 383–404; sources of failure, (Increasing behavior cont.) 104–5; versus reducing behavior, 249

Independent variable, defined relative to procedures, 79, 518; exclusion of in baseline, 439; monitoring, 95; relation to dependent variable, 79, 433; synonymous with treatment programs, 95

Individual, contingency, vs. group

contingency, 463–6; counseling, vs. group counseling, 327; matching reinforcers to, 104–6, 390

Infants, fading with, 205

Inhibiting behavior, procedures for, stimulus control, 412–18; 518; summarized, 413–17

Inservice training (see Settings for applied behavior analysis; Training, staff)

Institutional personnel, 68, 125–6

Institutional review, 33–5

Instructional objectives, (see Behavioral objectives)

Instructional prompts, (the "tell" procedure), cognitive skills taught via, 185–6; combined with other procedures, 192–3, 195, 208, 243–4, 263–4, 299; described, 181–2; effective use of: analysis of response components, 182–3; assessment of instructional control, 184; assessment of repertoire, 183–4; transition from modeling (Instructional prompts cont.), 208

Instrumentation to record behavior, automated, 70; mechanical, 54–5

Integration of special needs children, 84–6 passim; See also Mainstreaming

Intensity of behavior, 45, 220; See also Behavioral dimensions

Intermittent reinforcement schedule, advantages of: delay of satiation, 136, 334; enduring, 335; maintenance, 336–7; autistic behavior (Intermittent reinforcement schedule cont.), 328; defined, 333–4, 518; effective use of: gradual reduction of density, 340–1; progressive reduction of density, 339–40; supplementary S^Ds and reinforcers, 341–2; extinction (Intermittent reinforcement schedule cont.), 153, 157; facilitated by reversal design, 450; and generalization, 328; intrinsic motivation developed via, 337–9; maintaining behaviors via, 140, 336–7; programmed instruction, use in, 340; properties summarized, 428; in token economies, 342–3; transition to (from other schedules), 136, 339–42, 335

Interval schedules of reinforcement, 518; advantages and disadvantages: ease of implementation, 352–3; enduring, 351–2; low response rates, 353; effective use of: gradual increase in interval size, 353; limited hold, 353–4; in extinction conditions (Interval schedules cont.), 351–2; fixed (FI) vs. variable (VI): consistency, 349–50; defined, 346–7; error patterns, 351; response rates,

348–9; limited hold compared with (Interval schedules cont.), 354; ratio schedules compared with, 348, 359, 362; reinforcement density, 353; reinforcement history, 349; scallop, 350–1; transition from FI to VI, 352; transition from ratio schedule, 366–7; See also Ratio schedules of reinforcement

Interval time-sample recording system, advantages and disadvantages, 62, 66; coded interval-recording sheet, 62; event sampling as alternative to, 62; validity and reliability, 63–4

Intervention, aim, 115; direct vs. indirect, 27; measuring effects of, 74–5; phase defined, 79; physiological, 6, 169n; planning, via sequence analysis, 81; See also specific procedures

Intrusive stimuli, and hierarchy of prompts, 206–12 passim; overcoming, 177–9, 179–81

Irrelevant stimuli, examples, 196–7; v. relevant, 177–9, 179–81; transition to relevant, 208–12; See also Artificial stimuli; Natural contingency; Relevant stimuli; Supplementary stimuli

Isolate behavior, illustrated, 71; intermittent reinforcement and, 157; reinforcing alternative behavior, 260, 262–3; social reinforcement and, 125

Job interviews, shaping for, 222

Journal of the Experimental Analysis of Behavior, on maintenance via schedule control, 333n

Journals, research reports, dealing with recidivism, 314; documenting success of applied behavior analysis, 15–16, 88; reporting procedural effectiveness, 85; See also specific references

Kindergarten children (see Preschool children)

Kinesthetic cues, defined, 195; and fading, 207

Labeled praise (see specific praise)

Language learning, error correction, 214–15; foreign, 434–5, 449; foreign letter recognition, 164, 196; modeling and, 244; See also Speech; Verbal skills

Learning, 518; humanism in, 500–1; laws of, 85; relevant stimulus properties, 179–81; scope, 8; skills prerequisite for, 8

Learning Accomplishment Profile, 508–9

Learning disabilities, 328; See also Maladaptive behaviors; Mentally retarded

Learning history, 518; conditioned reinforcers and, 104; factors in, 168; influence on fixed interval, 349; interval schedules, 349, 366; irreversibility of, 470; modeling effectiveness, 194;

ratio schedules, 360–2; sample questions for obtaining, 82; variable ratio schedules, 363–4

Legal decisions affecting applied behavior analysis, Morales v. Turman, 289–90, 301; procedural selection and, 84; timeout and, 290; token systems and, 394; Wyatt v. Stickney, 84–6, 89, 115, 290, 304, 394

Lexington Developmental Scale, 505–6

Limited hold, to maintain behavior, 518; combined with differential reinforcement of high rates, 367; compared to fixed interval schedule, 354; properties summarized, 429

Links (in behavioral chains), defined, 237, 519; cumulative records and, 490; response repertoire and, 240–1

Low frequency behavior, 117–22

"Mainstreaming", defined, 87, 192; facilitated by token economies, 385; See also Halfway houses; Integration

Maintaining behaviors, 519; in extinction conditions, 157, 298, 351–2, 360–2; procedures for: differential reinforcement of high rates, 365–7; intermittent reinforcement, 140, 332–44, 351; interval scheduling, 346–55; ratio scheduling, 356–65; schedule selection for (Maintaining behaviors cont.), 333n, 430

Maladaptive behaviors, 82, 222; aggressive, 12, 49, 50, 65, 86, 142–3, 151, 156, 258, 270–1, 283–4; autistic, 13, 19, 109, 155, 189, 191, 241–2, 257–61, 283–5, 295–6, 308, 328–9, 453–4; disobedient, 283–4; disruptive, 56, 60, 63, 88, 99, 118, 225, 252, 253, 281, 283, 308–9, 370–1, 398, 425–6, 449, 451; echolelic responses, 41; elective mutism, 229–30; hyperactivity, 157–8, 260, 338, 366; hypochondria, 148; isolate, 71, 125, 157, 260, 262–3; obscenity, 152–4; self-destructive, 86, 306, 358, 361, 502; self-stimulatory, 158–9, 189, 286, 296–7; sloppiness, 346–55; stagefright, 222; temper tantrums, anger, 141, 179, 283; thumbsucking, 205, 257, 352; truancy, 90–1, 260–1, 337; underachievement, 12, 34–5, 340; violence, 285–7, 319

Martin's list of "behavior modification" techniques, 84

Masochism and punishment procedure, 314–15

Matching-to-sample skills, described, 190, 519; and fading, 209, 210; properties summarized, 416–17; ratio schedules of reinforcement, 358

Math performance, adjusting FR schedule, 359; chaining, 242–3;

fading, 206, 209–11; peer tutoring and program assessment, 462; shaping, 227–8

Measurement (behavioral), of academic skills, 53; baseline, 74; of duration, 56–8; independent, 52, 71, 94; objective, 49; of permanent product, 53; reliable, 49, 51–2, 75; of socially relevant behavior, 71; subjective, 71; of transitory events, 54

Measurement of treatment (see Evaluation of treatment program)

Mentally ill, documented improvement, 4; edible reinforcers and, 392; inaudible speech, 329; Premack principle with, 117; program assessment and, 451; response cost to suppress violence in, 270; schedules of reinforcement with, 333

Mentally retarded behaviors, maladaptive treated, 155, 252–3, 296, 299, 309; Born to Succeed (film by Ellen Reese), 209; documented improvement, 4; ethical considerations with, 34, 84–5, 89, 115, 290, 304, 394; as observers, 66; procedures used with, 150, 155, 169, 170, 191, 209–11, 252–3, 257, 258, 269, 271, 287, 290–1, 299, 329, 385, 387–8, 396–7, 403; reinforcers for, 109, 120, 125; skills taught, 193, 207–8, 209–11, 277, 358, 385, 387–8, 403, 463

Microselectiveness, in autistic children, 329

Misbehavior (see Maladaptive behavior)

Modeling procedure, combined with other procedures, 192–3, 244, 264, 311; defined, 190, 519; effective use of, 191–5; imitative skills, 190–1; the model: competence of, 194–5; as discriminative stimulus, 190; reinforcement of, 193; selection of, 191–2; similar vs. dissimilar, 192; in self-recording (Modeling procedure cont.), simplifying behavior to be modeled, 193; transition to verb-instruction, 208; See also Prompting strategies

Momentary time-sampling system, defined, 61, 519; distortion in, 63; spontaneous recording, 63–4

Monitoring, of behavior change, 7, 19; of contingency managers, 95; of procedures, 93–5; of self, 91

Morales v. Turman, timeout in, 289–90; overcorrection and, 301

Motivation, extrinsic, 105, 115

Motivation, intrinsic, defined behaviorally, 203–4, 518; development of via intermittent reinforcement, 337–8; in programmed instruction, 439;

threatened by extrinsic reinforcement, 105; token economies and, 401

Motor skills, and cerebral palsy, 219–20; fading to teach, 204; graduated guidance for, 17; modeling to teach, 189–96 passim; shaping to teach, 222, 230; See also Skills

Multielement Design, 519; advantages, 463–6; function of, 462–3; illustrated, 465; properties summarized, 469; See also Single-subject design

Multiple baseline design, across behaviors, 451–4; 511; across individuals, 454–6, 511; across situations, 456–7; 511; described, 74–5, 519; properties summarized, 467–8; See also Single-subject design

Narrative recording, defined, 21, 519; sample use of, 49

Natural contingency, as back-up reinforcers, 390; factor in success of Alt-R, 262–3; generalization training, 329–30; in ratio schedules, 363; starting point for selecting reinforcers, 105–6; transition from artificial, 105–6, 141–2, 203, 208, 329–30, 363, 401–2, 430; transition from fixed-interval to variable-interval schedules, 351; transition from supplementary stimuli, 203

Negative contingencies, humanism and, 501–2; listed, 250; See also Aversive stimuli; Good Behavior Game; Overcorrection; Punishment; Response cost; Timeout

Negative reinforcement, compared with other procedures, 142; defined, 140–1, 142, 519; justification for use, 143–4; illustrated, 237; properties summarized, 412; punishment and, 319; synonymous with aversive stimulus, 141n

New York State Association for Retarded Children v. Rockefeller (1973), on timeout procedures, 290

Noncontingent reinforcement, illustrated, 440–1; purpose of, 437

Nonverbal behavior (see Verbal skills)

Norm (see Baseline)

Novel reinforcers, 137–8

Numerical skills, adjusting FR schedule, 359; chaining, 242–3; fading, 206, 209–11; peer tutoring and program assessment, 462; shaping, 227–8

Nursery school children (see Preschool children)

Objectives (see Behavioral objectives)

Objectivity, 520; assuring, 52; defined relative to validity, 49;

verification of frequency, 122

Obscenity, 152, 154

Observation, 48–77; in applied behavior analysis model, 75, implementing systems of, 65–6; importance of, 14; independent, simultaneous recording of, 52, 56; interview as supplement to, 81

Observers, criterion, 71; distortion caused by presence of, 72–3; independent, 52, 71, 94; live, 53; reinforcement of, 72; reliability, 71–2; role in behavioral program, 14; who may serve as, 66

Occasioning behavior, 520; procedures for summarized, 414–18; stimulus control for, 162–218 passim

Omission, error of, 84, 212

Omission training, 212, 520

On-task behavior, 9, 62, 64, 67, 73; See also Adaptive behaviors

Operant behavior, defined, 6n, 520; emission and, 100n

Operant conditioning (see specific behavioral procedures)

Operational definition, applied to target behavior, 52; in coefficient of agreement, 65; defined, 6, 20, 520; of problem 6, 19–20, 24

Ordinate, defined, 72, 520; graphing dependent variable, 94; illustrated, 488–9, 491

Orienting, 221

Outcomes, communicating (see Communicating outcomes)

Outcomes, evaluating (see Evaluation of treatment program)

Overcorrection, advantages, 297–8; combined with other procedures, 296, 298–9, 300; defined, 296–7, 520; disadvantages, 300–1, 302; effective use of, 298–9; generality effect, 301; positive practice, 296–7, 298; restitutional, 296, 298

Parents, approval of, for token economy, 395; attending behavior of, 49, 61, 152–3, 180; as contingency managers, 14, 453; in goal selection, 31–2; maintaining participation of, 93; messages to, 376; negative reinforcement of (by children), 141; as observers, 56, 66, 81; in procedural selection, 89

Partial interval time-sampling system, advantages and disadvantages, 63, 67; defined, 61, 67, 520; example of coded score sheet, 62; reducing behavior, appropriate for, 63; score sheet, 61

Pavlov's dog, example of respondent conditioning, 169

Peer-reinforcement, activity reinforcers, 127; in extinction procedures, 157–8; in a multi-element design, 463–4; pun-

ishment and, 319–20; token economy, 393

Penalties (see Response cost; Timeout)

Performance, in adolescents, 99; assessment packages for, 503–9; baseline, 50; as basis of applied behavior analysis, 6; in teachers, 126

Permanent product, recording, advantages, 66; defined, 53, 66; ratio schedules, 363; See also Recording data

Permissiveness v. punishment, 304

Personal behavior (see Social skills)

Personalized System of Instruction (PSI), accuracy requirement, 365; bonus point system, 397–8; defined, 234, 520; goals defined in, 232–3; grading examinations, 52; illustrated, 232; progress chart, 399; shaping and, 232–3

Personnel (nonbehavior-analysts), occupations: civil service, 65–6; clinical, 80; counseling, 50, 62, 81, 90, 148, 205, 495; educational, 80, 126, 337; human services, 65, 80, 84, 308, 316; institutional, 68, 125–6, 342; psychotherapist, 205; speech therapy, 167, 223–30 passim; as recorders (Personnel cont.), 65–6; reinforcers for, 400; training of, 65, 71, 81, 85, 126, 158, 400; See also specific client populations and treatment settings

Phobias, reducing via shaping, 222

Physical guidance, combined with other procedures, 207–8, 230, 299; described, 195–6, 520

Physical skills (see Motor skills)

Positive practice, 296–8, 520

Positive reinforcement procedure, compared with negative reinforcement, 86, 141; defined, 101–2, 140–1, 520; effective use of, 101–2; modeling and, 193–4; properties summarized, 409–13; selecting reinforcers, 102–6; combined with other procedures: modeling, 194; punishment, 316–17; stimulus control, 179; timeout, 284; token economies, 393; See also specific procedures, effective use of

Praise (see Specific praise)

Premack principle, 521; appeal of, 117; in contingent recreation, 372; natural reinforcers and, 390

Preschool children, peer-reinforcement of, 127; Premack principle with, 117; reading taught, 206; reinforcing alternative behaviors in, 260; timeout procedure with, 283; See also Children and youth

Primary reinforcement, 105, 109–12, 150, 270, 392; Primed response, example of, 113; limited hold and, 353

Priorities, setting, 15–18, 24, 41, 42

Problem populations, delinquent and predelinquent, 1–4 passim, 89, 230, 270–1, 283, 314, 385; medically disabled, 98–9, 219–20, 243–4, 505–6; mentally ill, 4, 117, 270, 329, 333, 392; mentally retarded (see Mentally retarded)

Problems, realistic identification of, 12–14; prevention of, 8, 12, 24

Procedural selection, 75, 78–97; basis in behavioral principles, 2; combinations, 150; comparative summary for, 407–8, 421–2: increasing behavior, 408–9; 411–13; maintaining behavior, 422–3, 428–30; reducing behavior, 422, 424–7; stimulus control, 409–10, 414–18; teaching, 410, 419–20; contracting for (Procedural selection cont.), 90; countercontrol, 93; defined, 79–80; duration of effect, 149; effects enumerated, 6–7; ethical-legal considerations, 84; evidence in research literature, 85; experimental, 33–4; flexibility, 88; guide to recording techniques, 66; implementation, 95; intrusive and nonintrusive, 84; monitoring, 93–5; negative, 33–4; recording techniques and, 66, 68; self-management and, 91; as step in applied behavior-analysis model, 96

Procrastination and limited hold, 354

Professional and paraprofessional users of behavior analysis (see Personnel)

Programmed instruction, 521; advantages, 224; artificial discriminative stimuli in, 197; baseline data in, 439; fading in, 231; illustrated, 225; intermittent reinforcement in, 340; shaping and, 224–6, 231

Progress Assessment Chart, 503, 507–8

Prompting strategies, to aid stimulus control, 164, 168; artificiality, 197–8, 206–9, 211–12; 512; combined with other procedures: chaining, 243–4; intermittent reinforcement, 341–2; overcorrection, 299; reinforcing alternative behaviors, 329–30; timeout, 284; defined (Prompting strategies cont.), 182, 521; diminishing series illustrated, 206; hierarchy of, 198; kinds of, 181–6, 189–99, 341–2; overuse of, 198–9; size-prompting, 209–11

PSI (see Personalized System of Instruction)

Psychiatric patients (see Mentally ill)

Public reaction (to timeout), 290–1

Punishment (S^P) procedure, advantages, 309–11; combined with other procedures, 258, 282, 313–17; compared to response cost, 269–70; defined, 142, 147, 306–7, 521; disadvantages, 142, 317–21; distinguished from extinction, 147; effective use of, 312–17, 321; masochism, 314–15; properties summarized, 427

Randomness, in measurements, 63, 68–9; See also Variable interval schedules of reinforcement; Variable ratio schedules of reinforcement

Ration schedules of reinforcement, advantages, 358–9, 362–3; compared to interval schedules of reinforcement, 348, 359, 362; defined, 357, 521; disadvantages, 364–5; effective use of, 361–2; ratio strain in, 359, 363, 521; See also Fixed ratio schedules of reinforcement; Variable ratio schedules of reinforcement

Reactivity, in automated recording, 70; and baseline establishment, 439; defined, 53, 521

Reading skills, evaluating class performance, 440; fading, 206; programmed instruction, 224–5; safety words, 277; transition from irrelevant to relevant stimuli, 209

Read Project Assessment Manual, 503, 506–7

Recorders of data, client as, 62; institutional personnel as, 68; reinforcement of, 72; staff of, 65–6, 71; See also Observers; Recording data; Self-recording

Recording data, automated, 70; discrete events, 54–7; duration, 57–8; error in, 52, 53, 69, 71, 72; graphing, 71, 74, 488–91 passim; guide to selection of systems, 66–7; independent, 52; instruments for, 54–5, 70; interval time sample systems, 60–5; permanent product, 53; self-recording, 67; See also Error, source of; Measurement; Reliability of behavioral measures

Recovery, 142

Reducing behavior, Units 11, 18, 19, 20, 21, 22; differential reinforcement for, 250–1; extinction, 99, 147; Good Behavior Game, 370–1; v. increasing behavior, 239; procedures summarized, 422, 423–6; reinforcing alternative behaviors, 150; shaping, 222; token economy, 400–1

Reflexive behavior (see Respondent behavior)

Reinforcement, amount of, 136–7, 441; of contingency managers, 95; defined, 140, 521; generalization training and, 330; of imitative behavior, 191–5; kinds of: delayed, 134, 330, 339–40,

402–4; differential, 169–76, 287, 414; immediate, 3, 68, 134–5, 233, 241; inadvertent, 152–3, 156, 263, 286, 318–19, 375; negative, 140–4, 237, 319, 412; noncontingent, 437, 440–1; positive, 102–6, 140–1, 179, 284, 393; of observers (Reinforcement cont.), 72; satiation and, 112; self-selected, 68; stimulus control, contrast with, 164; surprise, and intrinsic motivation, 105; withdrawal of, 151–3; See also Negative reinforcement; Positive reinforcement

Reinforcement of alternative behavior (see Reinforcing alternative behaviors)

Reinforcement density, defined, 339, 522; interval schedules, 353; maintaining stimulus control, 216; progressive reduction of, 339–41; ratio schedules, 362

Reinforcement schedules (see Schedules of reinforcement)

Reinforcers, attention, 81; defined, 101, 522; identification and control of, 156–9; kinds of: activity, 116–22; back-up, 386–95 passim; conditioned, 102–4; edible, 105, 109–12; exchangeable, 105–6, 115–16, 270; natural, 105–6, 519; novel, 137–8; social, 123–7; tangible, 110–15, 270, 388–91, 394–5; unconditioned, 102–3; matching to individuals (Reinforcers cont.), 104–6, 233; Personalized System of Instruction, 233; reserve, 271–2, 278; selection of, 102, 104; self-determination of, 89; and sequence analysis, 22, 81

Reinforcer sampling rule, 138, 522

Reinforcing alternative behaviors, advantages, 261; combined with other procedures, 263–4: differential reinforcement of other behaviors, 258; extinction, 150, 154; overcorrection, 300; punishment, 316–17; timeout, 288; 511; defined (Reinforcing alternative behaviors cont.), 250, 259–60, 522; disadvantages, 264–5; hyperactivity reduced, 260; isolate behavior reduced, 260; mixed evidence of effectiveness, 264–5; properties summarized, 425; selection of behaviors, 262–3

Reinforcing stimulus (S^r), 238

Relevant stimulus properties, artificial cues and, 197; focus on, 179–81; identification of, 177–9; magnification of, 197; transition from irrelevant, 208–12

Reliability of behavioral measures, assessments of, 69–72; assurance of, 51–2, 69; coefficient of agreement as estimate of, 64, 71; defined, 49, 522; event recording, 55–6; interval record-

ing, 63, 64; observational, 71; permanent products, 53; training for, 71
Reliability coefficient (see Coefficient of agreement)
Reliability data (see Coefficient of agreement)
Repertoire (behavioral), 522; chaining and, 240–1; control of, 163; discriminative stimuli, 167; reinforcing alternative behaviors and, 262; of responses, 100, 183–4; of skills, assessing, 166
Replication of procedures, 522; rationale for, 432; in report forms, 481
Report card (see Daily report card)
Reporting outcomes, Units 34, 35; client characteristics, 483; describing data, 492; displaying data, 488–90; method, 482–6; personnel characteristics, 485; purpose 482; sample format, 481; See also Communicating outcomes
Required relaxation, 285
Respondent behavior, defined, 147, 522; distinguished from behavior under stimulus control, 166
Respondent conditioning, defined, 6; physiological responding, 169n; related to extinction, 147
Response (R), 522; chain, defined, 182, 522; consistency in reinforcement schedules, 349–50, 353, 359–60; dimensions, frequency, accuracy and duration, 43; discrete, 54; failure, 167, 180; indirect, 127; interference with, 43–4, 167, 436; physiological, 143; rote, 501; spontaneous recovery of, 151–2; See also Behavior; Response rates
Response, contingent withdrawal of reinforcement, response cost, 268–79; timeout, 280–94
Response cost, advantages, 270–1; building reinforcer reserve, 271–2; combined with other procedures, 258, 270, 274–5; compared to punishment procedure, 269–70; compared to timeout, 281; defined, 142, 269–70, 522; diagrammed, 269–70; disadvantages of, 275; effective use of, 271–4; flow chart, 278; illustrated, 270; penalty, amount of, 272–3; properties summarized, 426
Response rates, extinction procedures, 150; human and animal compared, 358; increase in, 151; interval schedules, 353, 348–9; limited hold, 354; ratio schedules, 358–9; reduction of, 99
Restitutional overcorrection, 296, 298, 522
Restraint, legal restrictions on, 84–6, 286n; See also Seclusion

Results, communicating, Units 34, 35; significance of 471–4
Retardation (see Mentally retarded)
Reversal designs, 522; advantages and disadvantages, 450–1; function, 446–7; illustrated, 448; illustrated in model, 74; properties summarized, 467; variations of, 447–50
Rewards (see Reinforcement)
Role-playing, differential reinforcement of low rates, 254; in family contracting, 381; and implementing response cost, 274
Rote responses, 501
S^D (see Discriminative stimuli)
S^{D-} (see Discriminative stimuli)
S Delta (S^Δ), aversive properties of, 309; compared to S^{D-}, 277; defined, 170; introducing to minimize errors, 213–14
S^P (see Aversive consequences; Punishment procedure)
S^r (see Reinforcing stimulus)
S^{rc} (see Response cost)
S^{to} (see Timeout procedure)
Sampling, (see Time sampling)
Satiation, defined, 112–13, 523; failure to achieve, 283; and intermittent reinforcement, 136; and multielement designs, 465; token economies, 386, 389
Schedule history, fixed ratio, 360–1; interval, 349, 366; variable ratio, 361–2
Schedules of reinforcement, defined, 140, 523; Ferster and Skinner, 333; maintenance via, 333n; See also Continuous reinforcement schedule; Intermittent reinforcement schedule; Interval schedules of reinforcement; Ratio schedules of reinforcement
School, activity reinforcers for, 118–21; contingency packages for, 369–78 passim; evaluating treatment packages in, 434–49; negative reinforcement, 142–3; novelty reinforcers, 138–9; tardiness, 143–4; token economies in, 390; truancy, 90, 337
School psychologist, 3, 12; as therapist, 8, 13, 17, 205; See also Behavior analyst; Counselor, guidance
Science, ecology, operationally defined, 80; goals of, 49
Scoring, and automated recording systems, 70; independent, 56; manual, example of, 71; recording sheet, examples, 61, 62, 64; See also Examinations
Seclusion, legal restrictions, 84–6; timeout and, 289–90
Self-care skills (see Skills)
Self-control (see Self-management)
Self-destructive behavior, and aversive conditioning, 86, 502;

and differential reinforcement of other behaviors, 258; and punishment, 306; and ratio schedules of reinforcement, 361
Self-esteem (confidence), and applied behavior analysis, 501; the "compliment meter", 378; and punishment, 320; social reinforcement of, 126
Self-evaluation, educational aim, 500; goal awareness, 226
Self-management, 523; advantages and disadvantages, 89–90; assessment of skills, 166; components of, 91; differential reinforcement, 252; documented improvement, 4; education, aim of, 500; progressive reduction of reinforcement and, 340; response cost procedure, 274; self-recording integral to, 67; token economies, 387
Self-recording, 66–70; instruments for, 67; in token economies, 386
Self-stimulatory behavior, extinction, 158–9; modeling, 189; overcorrection, 296–7
Sequence analysis, 523; as basis of behavior analysis, 82; components described, 21; illustrated, 23, 82–3; sample use of, 49; selecting dependent variables, 50
Settings for applied behavior analysis, community clinics, 156–7; community homes, 4, 16, 116, 345–6, 375–6, 387, 403–4; family homes, 14, 31–2, 56, 66, 81, 93; hospitals, 98–9, 164–5, 243–4, 443–4; institutions, 68, 125–6, 385–8 passim; recreational, 327; schools, 118–20, 138–44 passim, 181–6, 224–6; vocational workshops, 193, 207
Shaping procedure, combined with other pocedures, 222, 229–31, 245; cumulative records, 490; defined, 99–100, 220–3, 523; effective use of, 220, 226–9; for groups, 223–4; maintaining effects of, 231; Personalized System of Instruction, 232–4; physical guidance, 230; programmed instruction, 224–6; properties summarized, 419; in reducing behaviors, 222; skills, 222, 230, 231; subsets, 221
Sharing (see Cooperative play)
Shyness (see Isolate behavior)
Showing (see Modeling procedure)
Side effects, of aversive contingencies, 172; delayed manifestation of following punishment, 321; extinction-induced aggression, 151, 156; of increases in ratio requirement, 359; minimized in overcorrection, 297; summarized, 412, 424–7
Single-subject experimental design, 523; advantages, 444–6;

drawing conclusions, 470–3; evaluating generality and duration, 474–5; functions of, 440–2; vs. group designs, 444; kinds of, 74–5, 446–57, 460–4, 466–9

Situational analysis, 20–4; narrative recording, 21–3; test scores, records, etc. 20–1

Situational conditions, in reinforcement, 135–6; See also Stimulus control

Skills, academic, 86, 89, 109, 118–20, 127, 385; assessment packages for, 503–9; cognitive, 173, 176, 178, 185–6, 198, 503–9; conversational, 222, 230; dining, 46, 55, 71, 222; driving, 207–8; handwriting, 222, 231; housekeeping, 207, 387–8; matching-to-sample, 209–11, 358; motor, 17, 189–96, 204, 219–20, 222–30; numerical, 206, 209–11, 227–8, 242–3, 359, 462; reading, 206, 209, 224–5, 440; self-care, 2, 52, 71, 205, 208; social 44–5, 49, 52, 71, 79, 125; verbal, 103–4, 109, 119, 125, 149, 198, 449, 452

Sloppiness, 346–55

Social reinforcers, 523; advantages of, 126–7; examples of, 123–4; for institutional personnel, 125–6; to maintain behavior, 141–2; in token economies, 393

Social skills, goal of applied behavior analysis, 7; isolate behavior reduced, 125, 157, 260, 262–3; procedure for increasing, 79 passim; social reinforcers for, 125; See also Maladaptive behaviors; Skills; Verbal skills

Specific praise, 523; behavioral emphasis of, 125; to reinforce stimulus control, 199–200

Speech development, program assessment for, 449–50; response cost procedure for, 271; shaping, 223, 449–50; timeout procedure for, 285

Speech therapy, electively mute, 229–30; interfering conditions, 167; shaping and, 223–30 passim

Spontaneous recovery, 151, 159, 523

Staff (see Personnel; Training of staff)

Stage-fright, 222

Standardized test scores, 13, 20–1

Stimulus, defined, 80, 523; developing as reinforcer, 102–3; irrelevant, 197; related to reinforcement, 101; relevant properties, 178–80

Stimulus change, 164–5

Stimulus control, assessing for, 166–8; by client, 80; complete, 166, 186, 523; by contingency managers, 80; criterion of achievement, 199; defined, 99, 163, 523; development of, 168–9; and discriminative stimulus, 165–6; distinguished from rein-

forcement, 164; illustrated, 163; maintaining, 216, 199–200; multielement design to assess multiple stimuli, 171–5; procedures summarized, 414–18; response aspects, 181–198; reversal and, 451; stimulus aspects, 177–81

Stimulus discrimination (see Discriminative stimuli; Stimulus control)

Stimulus generalization (see Generalization of stimulus)

Strengthening new behaviors, chaining, 246; fading, 216; reinforcement, 68; shaping, 231; stimulus control, 198–9, 216; token reinforcement, 401–2, 404

Students (see College students; High School students)

Subject confounding variables, 435, 523

Subset of behaviors, 221, 524

Subtasks, 45–6; performance of, 98–9, 490

Successive approximations, defined, 221, 524; cumulative records and, 490; See also Shaping

Sullivan Associates Program, 224–5

Supplementary stimuli, combined with natural, 329; distinguished from critical, 182, 185; fading and, 203; in generalization training, 329–30; and intermittent reinforcement, 341–2; selecting, 196–8

Tabular form for data, 491–2

Tangible reinforcers, avoiding satiation with, 113, 388–9; examples of, 110–11; inexpensive, 391; jealousy over, minimizing, 394–5; response cost procedure, use in, 270

Tantrums, 141, 179, 283

Target behavior, defined, 19, 524; illustrated in sequence analysis, 82; multiple interrelated, complications with, 453–4; operational definitions and, 52

Task analysis, of a behavioral chain, 239; check list, 55; defined, 45, 524; teaching 183

Task confounding variables, 435-6; defined, 435, 524

Teachers, accountability record for, 496; as contingency managers, 80, 82–3; modifying tardiness, 143–4; as recorders, 68–9; recording attentiveness of, 62; reinforcement by program assessment, 93; reinforcement by students, 128; social reinforcement, 126, 139–40, 337

Teaching behaviors, chaining, 420; procedures summarized, 410, 419–20; shaping, 220ff.; See also Instruction

"Tell" procedure, 181–5 passim, 524

Thumbsucking, DRO, 257; fading with, 205; interval schedules of reinforcement for, 352

Timeout procedure (S^{to}), advantages, 283–4; combined with other procedures, 258, 281, 284; defined and illustrated, 142, 281–2, 524; disadvantages, 289–92; effective use of, 285–9; flowchart, 292; properties summarized, 426; safeguards in using, 290–1

Time-sampling system of recording, 524; See also Interval time-sample recording

Token, bonus point in PSI as, 397–8, 399; defined, 114–15; delayed reinforcement, 135; examples of, 113; selecting 396–8

Token economy, arguments against, 113–16; back-up reinforcers, 390–5; combined with other procedures, 270, 342–3, 392–4, 400–1; defined and illustrated, 384–5, 524; effective use of, 387–9, 400; illustrated results, 440; informal, 115; maintaining behaviors, 401–4; marketing and merchandising, 392–3; obtaining approval, 395–6; problems, logistical, avoiding, 394–5; properties summarized, 412–13; recording effectiveness, 398, 439, 449; reducing behavior, 400–1; satiation, 386, 389; selection of tokens, 396–8; strain (ratio), 389

Token Economy, The (Ayllon and Azrin), 85, 138

Topography, behavioral dimension, 43, 45, 220; determination of in ratio schedule, 365; of discriminative stimuli, 176; of response, 43, 45, 524

Training staff, children, 158; parents, 81; reliability, 71; supervision, 85; teachers, 126; in token economy, 400; workshop for, 65

Transitory events, 54

Treatment, package, function of, 433–4; phase, 79, 524; plan, for misbehavior, 283–4; synonymous with independent variable, 95; See also Intervention; Procedures, (specific procedures)

Truancy, reduction of, parental role in, 337; reinforcing alternative behavior, 260, 261; successful behavioral contracting, 90–1

Unconditioned reinforcers, defined, 102, 525; pairing with conditioned reinforcers, 103

Unconditioned stimuli, aversive, 307; distinguished from stimulus control, 169

Underachievement, institutional review, 34–5; progressive reduction of reinforcement, 340

U.S. Department of HEW guidelines, for human subject research (see HEW Guidelines)

Valid measurement, defined, 49, 525; momentary time sampling,

63; permanent products, 53; selection of 50–1

Variable-interval (VI) schedules of reinforcement, consistency, 351; defined, 347, 525; to establish baselines, 437; properties summarized, 428; rate of response, 348–9; in a token economy, 386; *See also* Fixed-interval (FI) schedules of reinforcement; Interval schedules of reinforcement

Variable-ratio (VR) schedules of reinforcement, advantages of, 359–61; defined, 357, 525; properties summarized, 429; *See also* Fixed-ratio schedules of reinforcement; Ratio schedules of reinforcement

Variables (*see* Confounding variables)

Verbal instruction (*see* Instructional prompts)

Verbal skills, extinction, 149; hierarchy of prompts, 198; and instructional control, 184; multiple baseline design for, 452; reinforcers for, 103–4, 109, 119, 125; reversal design for, 449; *See also* Language learning; Reading skills; Shaping

Verbal stimuli (*see* Instructional prompts)

Violet behavior, modeling of, 319; timeout for, 285–7 passim

Voluntary behavior, conceptualized as balance between client and other selected threats and incentives, 37; defined, 35, 525; illustrated, 36; synonymous with operant behavior, 100

Water Lilies (Monet), 180–1

Welsch v. Likins, 290

Whole interval time-samplng system, advantages and disadvantages, 63; defined, 61, 67, 525

Whole Kid's Catalog, The (Cardozo), 391

Withdrawal (*see* Escape behavior)

Wrist abacus, illustrated, 55

Wyatt v. Stickney, consumer satisfaction, 115; electric shock, 304; fundamental privileges, 394; implications for applied behavior analysis, 85–6; informed consent, 89; summary, 84; timeout, 290

2200   2200
  25   25
  96   96
        329
 330   2660 x
    2651   1
        17350